RAN

GW00499040

RANGE ROVER

WORKSHOP MANUAL

Publication Number SRR660ENWM
(Includes Pub.No. LSM 180WM)

PART TWO

Published by the
Technical Publications Department of

Land Rover
Lode Lane
Solihull
West Midlands, B92 8NW
England

INTRODUCTION

This workshop manual covers all petrol and diesel Range Rover Models manufactured between 1986 and the end of the 1993 model year. It contains the basic manual LSM180WM and all supplements and bulletins issued up to the beginning of the 1994 model year. Owners of 1994 Range Rovers should refer to a later manual available from Land Rover Limited.

Supplements and bulletins appear in chronological order and each contain their own contents listing. The start of each section can be easily located by the high-lighted border. When dealing with vehicles from 1987 model year onwards, readers should refer to not only the main manual but also the relevant supplements and bulletins.

For ease of handling the manual has been printed in two parts:

Part One.   Part One covers all petrol (not diesel) Range Rovers from 1986 up to the start of the 1990 model year. It contains the basic workshop manual issued in 1986, which is itself divided into five books, plus all supplements and bulletins issued up to the end of the 1989 model year.

Part Two.   Part Two contains details of all diesel powered models manufactured between 1986 and the start of the 1994 model year plus all general supplements and bulletins issued between 1990 and the start of the 1994 model year. **Part Two should always be used in conjunction with Part One.**

Whilst every effort is made to ensure the accuracy of the particulars in this manual, neither the Manufacturer, nor Brooklands Books Limited, or the Distributor or Dealer, by whom this manual is supplied, shall under any circumstances be held liable for any inaccuracy or the consequences thereof.

© Copyright Rover Group Limited. 1986, 1987, 1988, 1989, 1990, 1991, 1992 and 1993.

This book is published by Brooklands Books Limited and is based upon text and illustrations protected by copyright and first published in 1986 by Land Rover Limited and may not be reproduced transmitted or copied by any means without the prior written permission of Rover Group Limited.

CONTENTS

LAND-ROVER RANGE ROVER

RANGE ROVER
1990 MODEL YEAR

WORKSHOP MANUAL SUPPLEMENT

Publication Number LSM180WS5 Ed 2

Published by the
Technical Publications Department of

CONTENTS

CONTENTS
(Continued)

CONTENTS
(Continued)

CONTENTS
(Continued)

INTRODUCTION

For 1990 model year, V8 Range Rovers are all fitted with a 3.9 litre engine. The engine is available with high and low compression ratios. Where required by territorial legislation low compression models are fitted with catalyst exhaust systems, and use unleaded fuel only.

High and low comperssion (non-catalyst) engines are designed to run on both unleaded and leaded fuel.

The vehicle specification is further improved by the inclusion of the following features:

Lucas 14CUX micro-electronic EFI system.
Wabco anti-lock brake system (ABS).
Revised cooling system.
Heated front windscreen.
Two point central locking, four door vehicles.
Improved heater distribution.

The Range Rover Turbo D is further improved by the fitting of a 2.5 litre engine. Details of this engine may be found in a revised edition of the Turbo Diesel Workshop Supplement, Publication Number LSM180WS4.

ACCESSORIES AND CONVERSIONS

DO NOT FIT unnapproved accessories or conversions, as they could affect the safety of the vehicle.
Land Rover Ltd will not accept liability for death, personal injury, or damage to property which may occur as a direct result of the fitment of non-approved conversions to the Range Rover.

WHEELS AND TYRES

WARNING: DO NOT replace the road wheels with any type other than genuine Range Rover wheels which are designed for multi-purpose on and off road use and have very important relationships with the proper operation of the suspension system and vehicle handling. Replacement tyres must be of the makes and sizes recommended for the vehicle, and all tyres must be the same make, ply rating and tread pattern.

STEAM CLEANING

To prevent consequential rusting, any steam cleaning within the engine bay **MUST** be followed by careful re-waxing of the metallic components affected. Particular attention must be given to the steering column, engine water pipes, hose clips and the ignition coil clamp.

ENGINE SERIAL NUMBER - V8 ENGINE

The V8 engine serial number and engine compression ratio is stamped on a cast pad on the cylinder block, between numbers 3 and 5 cylinders.

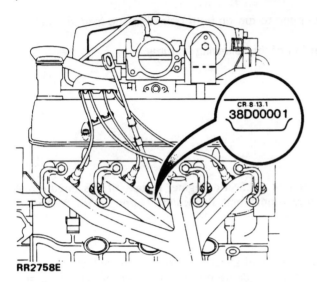

CR.8.13.1
38D00001

RR2758E

NOTE: The engines can be identified by the prefix, as follows:

35D - 9.35:1 compression, manual transmission
36D - 9.35:1 compression, automatic transmission
37D - 8.13:1 compression, manual transmission
38D - 8.13:1 compression, automatic transmission

ENGINE 3.9 V8

Type	V8
Number of cylinders	Eight, two banks of four
Bore	94.00 mm (3.700 in)
Stroke	71.12 mm (2.800 in)
Capacity	3950 cc (241 in ^{3})
Valve operation	Overhead by push-rod
Compression ratio	8.13:1
Maximum power	127 kW at 4550 rev/min
Compression ratio	9.35:1
Maximum power	134 kW at 4750 rev/min

Pistons

Clearance in bore, measure at bottom of skirt at right angles to piston pin	0.018-0.041 mm (0.0007-0.0016 in)

Piston rings

Number of compression rings	2
Number of control rings	1
No 1 compression ring	Molybdenum barrel faced
No 2 compression ring	Tapered and marked 'T' or 'TOP'
Width of compression rings	1.478-1.49 mm (0.058-0.059 in)
Compression ring gap	0.40-0.65 mm (0.016-0.026 in)
Oil control ring type	Hepworth and Grandage
Oil control ring width	3.0 mm (0.118 in)
Oil control ring rail gap	0.38-1.40 mm (0.015-0.055 in)

ELECTRICAL

Coil make/type	Bosch 0-221-122-392

FUEL SYSTEM

Fuel system type	Lucas hot wire system electronically controlled
Fuel pump - make/type	AC Delco high pressure (electrical) immersed in the fuel tank
Fuel pump delivery pressure	2,4 - 2,6 kgf/cm² (34 - 37 p.s.i.)
Fuel filter	Bosch in-line filter 'canister' type

Airflow sensor

Make and type	Lucas 'Hot Wire' 3AM

Injectors

Make and type	Lucas 8NJ

Electronic control unit

Make and type	Lucas 14CUX

Fuel pressure regulator

Make and type	Lucas 8RV

Fuel temperature sensor

Make and type .... Lucas 6TT

Coolant temperature sensor

Make and type .... Lucas 3TT

Bypass airvalve (Stepper motor)

Make and type .... Lucas 2ACM

Throttle potentiometer

Make and type .... Lucas 215SA

Lambda sensor

Make and type .... Lucas 3LS

SHIFT SPEED SPECIFICATION
Automatic ZF4HP22 Gearbox

OPERATION	SELECTOR POSITON	VEHICLE SPEED APPROX		ENGINE SPEED APPROX (RPM)
		KICKDOWN		
		MPH	**KPH**	
KD4 - 3	D	84 - 92	136 - 150	
KD3 - 2	3(D)	57 - 62	91 - 99	
KD2 - 1	2(D,3)	27 - 34	44 - 56	
KD3 - 4	D	N/A	N/A	
KD2 - 3	D(3)	60 - 63	96 - 104	4750 - 5200
KD1 - 2	D(3,2)	34 - 40	56 - 64	4600 - 5250
		FULL THROTTLE		
FT4 - 3	D	61 - 67	98 - 108	
FT3 - 2	3(D)	40 - 46	64 - 73	
FT3 - 4	D	74 - 80	119 - 129	3980 - 4330
FT2 - 3	D(3)	55 - 60	88 - 96	4350 - 4800
FT1 - 2	D(3,2)	29 - 34	48 - 56	3950 - 4650
		PART THROTTLE		
PT4 - 3	D	47 - 54	75 - 86	
PT3 - 2	D(3)	29 - 37	48 - 59	
PT2 - 1	D(3,2)	10 - 12	16 - 19	
		LIGHT THROTTLE		
LT3 - 4	D	26 - 30	43 - 49	1430 - 1650
LT2 - 3	D(3)	18 - 22	29 - 35	1420 - 1820
LT1 - 2	D(3,2)	9 - 10	14 - 16	1180 - 1220
		ZERO THROTTLE		
ZT4 - 3	D	19 - 25	31 - 41	
ZT3 - 2	D(3)	12 - 15	19 - 24	
ZT2 - 1	D(3,2)	6 - 7	10 - 11	
		TORQUE CONVERTER		
Lock up (IN)	D	51 - 54	81 - 86	1875 - 2000
Unlock (OUT)	D	49 - 52	78 - 83	1825 - 1930

NOTE: The speeds given in the above chart are approximate and only intended as a guide. Maximum shift changes should take place within these tolerance parameters.

ENGINE TUNING DATA

Type .... 3.9 Litre V8

Firing order 1-8-4-3-6-5-7-2

Cylinder Numbers
Left bank 1-3-5-7
Right bank 2-4-6-8

No 1 Cylinder location .... Pulley end of left bank

Timing marks .... On crankshaft vibration damper

Spark plugs
Make/type (8.13:1 Compression) .... Champion RN12YC
Gap .... 0,84 - 0,96 mm (0.033 - 0.038 in)
Make/type(9.35:1) Compression .... Champion RN9YC
Gap .... 0,84 - 0,96 mm (0.033 - 0.038 in)

Coil
Make/type .... Bosch 0-221-122-392

Compression ratio .... 8.13:1 or 9.35:1

Fuel injection system .... Lucas Hot-wire air flow sensor system
electronically controlled

Valve Timing	Inlet	Exhaust
Opens	32° BTDC	70° BBDC
Closes	73° ABDC	35° ATDC
Duration	285°	285°
Valve peak	104° ATDC	114° BTDC

Idle speed - controlled by EFI system .... 672 to 728 rev/min
- auto gearbox in gear, air con. operating .... 650 ± 28 rev/min
- auto gearbox in gear .... 600 ± 28 rev/min
- manual gearbox .... 700 ± 28 rev/min
- manual gearbox, air con. operating .... 750 ± 28 rev/min

Base idle speed
- idle speed control shut off .... 450-550 rev/min

**Ignition timing - dynamic at 800 rev/min
maximum**
8.13:1 compression, non catalyst .... 2° B.T.D.C. ± 1
8.13:1 compression, catalyst .... 6° B.T.D.C. ± 1
9.35:1 compression, non catalyst .... 4° B.T.D.C. ± 1

Exhaust gas CO content at idle .... 0.5 to 1.0% max.

Distributor
Make/type .... Lucas 35DLM8 electronic
Rotation .... Clockwise
Air gap .... 0.20-0.35mm (0.008-0.014 in)

Serial number, 8.13:1, non catalyst 42518A
- 8.13:1, catalyst 42648
- 9.35:1, non catalyst 45210A

Centrifugal advance

Decelerating check - vacuum hose disconnected

Distributor rev/min decelerating speeds	Distributor advance

8.13:1 non catalyst
2000	5° 30' to 8° 30'
1400	6° 18' to 8° 30'
800	2° to 4°

8.13:1 catalyst
2300	8° to 11°
1400	8° 36' to 10° 36'
600	1° 18' to 3° 18'

9.35:1 non catalyst
2200	7° to 10°
1400	7° 48' to 10°
650	1° to 3°

Fuel

8.13:1 compression, non catalyst	91 RON minimum unleaded
8.13:1 compression, catalyst	95 RON minimum unleaded
9.35:1 compression, non catalyst	95 RON minimum unleaded

TORQUE WRENCH SETTINGS

	Nm	ft lb	in lb
COOLING SYSTEM			
Oil cooler pipes	26 - 34	19 - 25	-
Radiator filler plug (plastic)	5 - 6	-	45 - 54
EMISSION CONTROL			
Lamda sensor	20	15	
ENGINE			
Oil cooler adaptor to oil pump cover	40 - 50	30 - 37	-
FUEL SYSTEM			
Air-Bypass valve (stepper motor)	17 - 22	13 - 16	-
All flexible hose securing clamps	1,1 - 1,3	-	10 - 12
Fuel feed pipe - hose to fuel rail	22	16	-
Plenum chamber to ram housing	22 - 28	16 - 21	
EVAPORATIVE LOSS CONTROL SYSTEM			
All flexible hose securing clamps	1,7	-	15
BRAKES			
Wabco ABS system			
Brake pipe connections to:			
- Hydraulic booster - M10	12 - 16	9 - 12	-
- M12	15 - 20	11 - 15	-
- Calipers	9 - 11	7 - 8	-
- Fourway connector rear axle	9 - 11	7 - 8	-
- Jump hose to brackets	11 - 13,5	8 - 10	-
- Jump hose female connectors	11 - 13,5	8 - 10	-
- Hydraulic pump and accumulator	12 - 16	9 - 12	-
- PCRV - M10	11 - 13,5	8 - 10	-
- PCRV - M12	12 - 14	9 - 10	-
Hydraulic booster to pedal box	22,5 - 27,5	17 - 20	-
Securing bolt, reservoir bracket	9 - 11	7 - 8	-
REAR AXLE ABS VEHICLES			
Hub driving member to hub	60 - 70	44 - 52*	-
Brake disc to hub	65 - 80	48 - 59*	-
Stub axle rear to axle case	60 - 70	44 - 52	-
Brake caliper to axle case	75 - 88	55 - 65	-
Disc shield to axle case	9 - 12	7 - 9	-
Sensor ring to brake disc	7 - 10	5 - 7	-
FRONT AXLE ABS VEHICLES			
Hub driving member to hub	60 - 70	44 - 52*	-
Brake disc to hub	65 - 80	48 - 59*	-
Stub axle to swivel pin housing	60 - 70	44 - 52*	-
Brake caliper to swivel pin housing	75 - 88	55 - 65	-
Upper swivel pin to swivel pin housing	60 - 70	44 - 52	-
Lower swivel pin to swivel pin housing	22 - 28	16 - 21*	-
Oil seal retainer to swivel pin housing	9 - 12	7 - 9	-
Swivel pin bearing housing to axle case	65 - 80	48 - 59*	-
Disc shield to bracket lower	7 - 10	5 - 7	-
AIR CONDITIONING			
Compressor hose	34 - 40	24 - 29	-
Receiver drier hose	14 - 21	10 - 15	-
Receiver drier switch	21 - 25	15 - 19	-
Compressor oil filler plug	8 - 12	6 - 9	-

NOTE: * These bolts to be coated with Loctite 270 prior to assembly.

COMPONENT	SPECIFICATION	AMBIENT TEMPERATURE								
		°C								
		-30	-20	-10	0	10	20	30	40	50
		°F								
		-22	-4	+14	+32	50	68	86	104	122
Brake reservoir	Brake fluid must have a minimum boiling point of 260°C (500° F) and comply with FMVSS/116/DOT4									

Approved fluids

Castrol/Girling 12624 DOT 4
Automotive Products 429S Super DOT 4

Approved grease

Rear ABS sensor bush

Staborags NBU - Wabco 830 502, 0634

Wacker chemie 704 - Wabco 830 502, 0164

Kluber GL301

ROLLING ROAD TESTING OF PERMANENT FOUR WHEEL DRIVE VEHICLES

WARNING: DO NOT ATTEMPT TO TEST ABS FUNCTION ON A ROLLING ROAD

Four wheel rolling roads

NOTE: Before testing the vehicle on a four wheel rolling road disconnect the valve relay - see Section 70 Brakes, page 11. The ABS function will not work, the ABS warning light will illuminate. Normal braking will be available.

Provided that the front and rear rollers are rotating at identical speeds and that normal workshop safety standards are applied, there is no speed restriction during testing except for any that may apply to the tyres.

Two wheel rolling roads

IMPORTANT: Use a four wheel rolling road for brake testing if possible.

NOTE: ABS will not function on a two wheel rolling road. The ABS light will illuminate during testing. Normal braking will be available.

If brake testing on a single rig is necessary it must be carried out with the drive shaft to the rear axle removed, AND neutral selected in BOTH main gearbox and transfer gearbox.

If checking engine performance, the transfer box must be in high range and the drive shaft to the stationary axle must be removed.

ABS BRAKE FLUID RESERVOIR

Check/top up fluid level

1. Park the vehicle on level ground.
2. Turn ignition ON, to activate hydraulic pump. If pump does not activate depress brake pedal several times until it is heard to operate.
3. When the pump stops, check that the level is between the 'MIN' and 'MAX' marks.
4. If the level is below MIN top up fluid level to the 'MAX' mark on reservoir, using the correct fluid, - see Section 09, Lubricants and fluids.

WARNING: Clean the reservoir body and filler cap before removing the cap. Use only fluid from a sealed container.
DO NOT OVERFILL THE RESERVOIR

FRONT AND REAR AXLE ABS VEHICLES

LST132

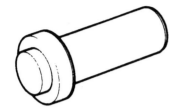

BEARING INSTALLER

LST133

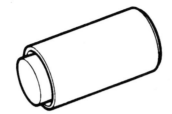

SEAL INSTALLER

LST137

SEAL INSTALLER

LST138

SEAL INSTALLER

18G 284AAH

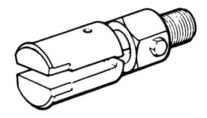

EXTRACTOR

EMISSION CONTROL

LST134

RR2873M

TORQUE ADAPTOR

FRONT AND REAR AXLE ABS VEHICLES

LST137

SEAL INSTALLER

LST133

SEAL INSTALLER

LST132

BEARING INSTALLER

18G 284AAH

EXTRACTOR

LST138

INSTALLER

EMISSION CONTROL

LST134

RR2870

TORQUE ADAPTOR

REMOVE ENGINE OIL COOLER ADAPTOR PLATE

Removing

1. Remove both oil cooler pipes.
2. Mark the position of the adaptor plate relative to the oil pump cover.
3. Remove the centre fixing and withdraw the adaptor plate.

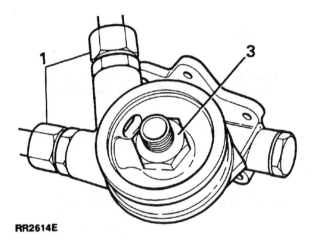

RR2614E

Refitting

4. Reverse the removal procedure, lining up the location marks to ensure pipe runs are correct. Ensure the pipes and centre fixing are tightened to the specified torque.

FIT ENGINE OIL FILTER

1. Clean the oil cooler adaptor mating face.
2. Coat the sealing ring of the new filter with clean engine oil.
3. Fill the filter with new oil as far as possible, noting the angle at which the filter is to be fitted.
4. Screw on the filter until the sealing ring touches the oil cooler adaptor mating face, then tighten it a further half turn by hand only. Do not overtighten.

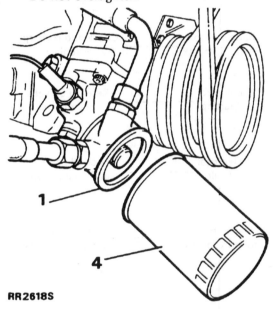

RR2618S

FAULT DIAGNOSIS

NOTE: The following fault diagnosis charts are intended as a guide only, having determined the possible fault refer to the appropriate section within the manual.
The charts have been updated to include the charcoal canister and purge valve fitted in certain markets. Refer to Emmission Control - Section 17 and Fuel Injection System - Section 19 for full details of charcoal canister/purge valve.

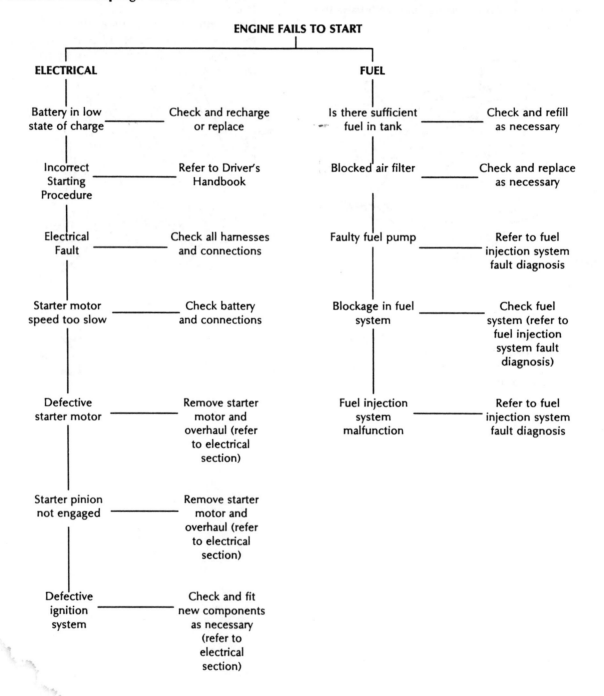

ENGINE FAILS TO START

ELECTRICAL

Battery in low state of charge	Check and recharge or replace
Incorrect Starting Procedure	Refer to Driver's Handbook
Electrical Fault	Check all harnesses and connections
Starter motor speed too slow	Check battery and connections
Defective starter motor	Remove starter motor and overhaul (refer to electrical section)
Starter pinion not engaged	Remove starter motor and overhaul (refer to electrical section)
Defective ignition system	Check and fit new components as necessary (refer to electrical section)

FUEL

Is there sufficient fuel in tank	Check and refill as necessary
Blocked air filter	Check and replace as necessary
Faulty fuel pump	Refer to fuel injection system fault diagnosis
Blockage in fuel system	Check fuel system (refer to fuel injection system fault diagnosis)
Fuel injection system malfunction	Refer to fuel injection system fault diagnosis

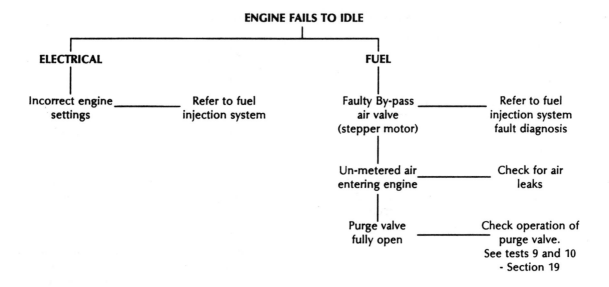

ENGINE FAILS TO IDLE

ELECTRICAL

Incorrect engine settings —— Refer to fuel injection system

FUEL

Faulty By-pass air valve (stepper motor) —— Refer to fuel injection system fault diagnosis

Un-metered air entering engine —— Check for air leaks

Purge valve fully open —— Check operation of purge valve. See tests 9 and 10 - Section 19

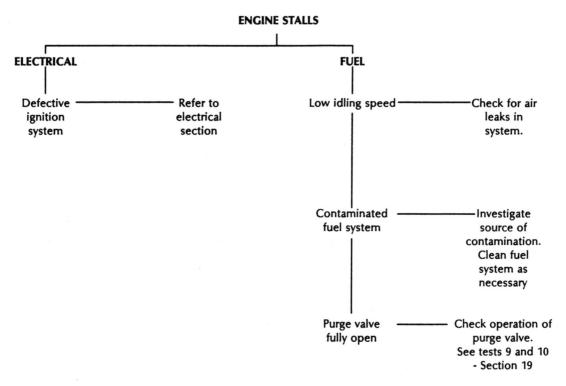

ENGINE STALLS

ELECTRICAL

Defective ignition system —— Refer to electrical section

FUEL

Low idling speed —— Check for air leaks in system.

Contaminated fuel system —— Investigate source of contamination. Clean fuel system as necessary

Purge valve fully open —— Check operation of purge valve. See tests 9 and 10 - Section 19

NOTE: SMELL OF PETROL IN ENGINE COMPARTMENT, POSSIBLE CAUSE: PURGE VALVE STUCK CLOSED (NO PURGE ON CHARCOAL CANISTER) See tests 9 and 10 - Section 19.

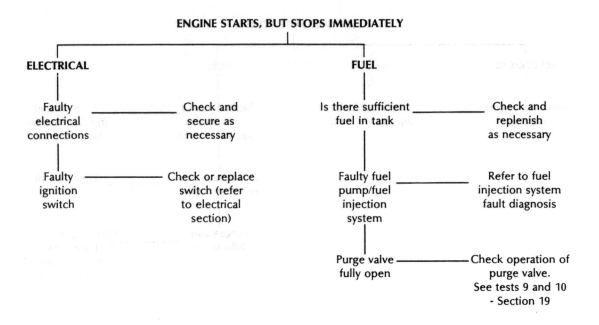

ENGINE STARTS, BUT STOPS IMMEDIATELY

ELECTRICAL

Faulty electrical connections —————— Check and secure as necessary

Faulty ignition switch —————— Check or replace switch (refer to electrical section)

FUEL

Is there sufficient fuel in tank —————— Check and replenish as necessary

Faulty fuel pump/fuel injection system —————— Refer to fuel injection system fault diagnosis

Purge valve fully open —————— Check operation of purge valve. See tests 9 and 10 - Section 19

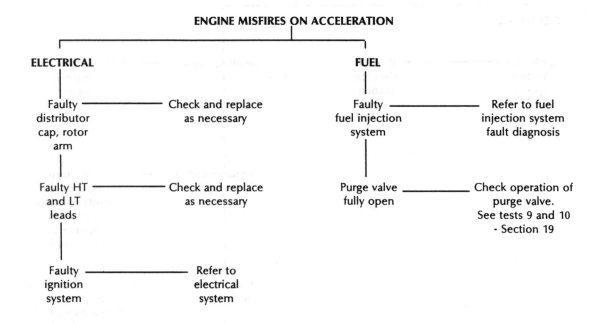

ENGINE MISFIRES ON ACCELERATION

ELECTRICAL

Faulty distributor cap, rotor arm —————— Check and replace as necessary

Faulty HT and LT leads —————— Check and replace as necessary

Faulty ignition system —————— Refer to electrical system

FUEL

Faulty fuel injection system —————— Refer to fuel injection system fault diagnosis

Purge valve fully open —————— Check operation of purge valve. See tests 9 and 10 - Section 19

ENGINE RUNS ERRATICALLY

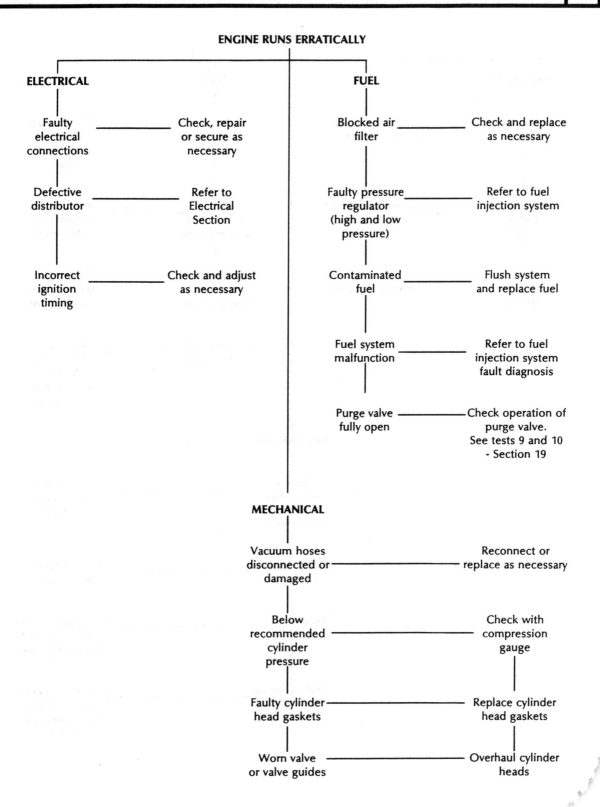

ELECTRICAL

Faulty electrical connections —————— Check, repair or secure as necessary

Defective distributor —————— Refer to Electrical Section

Incorrect ignition timing —————— Check and adjust as necessary

FUEL

Blocked air filter —————— Check and replace as necessary

Faulty pressure regulator (high and low pressure) —————— Refer to fuel injection system

Contaminated fuel —————— Flush system and replace fuel

Fuel system malfunction —————— Refer to fuel injection system fault diagnosis

Purge valve fully open —————— Check operation of purge valve. See tests 9 and 10 - Section 19

MECHANICAL

Vacuum hoses disconnected or damaged —————— Reconnect or replace as necessary

Below recommended cylinder pressure —————— Check with compression gauge

Faulty cylinder head gaskets —————— Replace cylinder head gaskets

Worn valve or valve guides —————— Overhaul cylinder heads

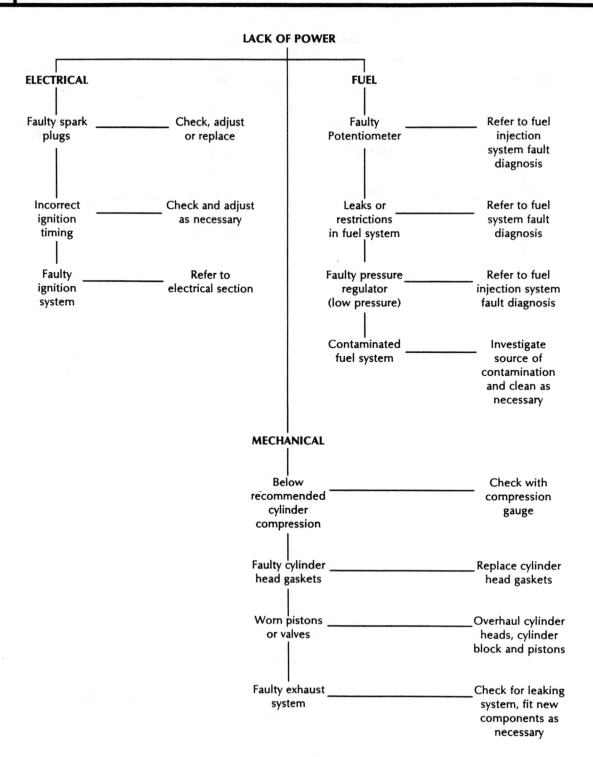

LACK OF POWER

ELECTRICAL

Faulty spark plugs ———————— Check, adjust or replace

Incorrect ignition timing ———————— Check and adjust as necessary

Faulty ignition system ———————— Refer to electrical section

FUEL

Faulty Potentiometer ———————— Refer to fuel injection system fault diagnosis

Leaks or restrictions in fuel system ———————— Refer to fuel system fault diagnosis

Faulty pressure regulator (low pressure) ———————— Refer to fuel injection system fault diagnosis

Contaminated fuel system ———————— Investigate source of contamination and clean as necessary

MECHANICAL

Below recommended cylinder compression ———————— Check with compression gauge

Faulty cylinder head gaskets ———————— Replace cylinder head gaskets

Worn pistons or valves ———————— Overhaul cylinder heads, cylinder block and pistons

Faulty exhaust system ———————— Check for leaking system, fit new components as necessary

EMISSION CONTROL

Charcoal canister and purge valve - where applicable

1990 model year vehicles incorporate evaporative emission control by means of a new charcoal canister with solenoid operated purge control valve.

The charcoal canister adsorbs and stores the fuel vapour that is emitted from the fuel tank when the engine is not running. The vapour is purged from the canister by outside air drawn through an orifice at the bottom of the canister by the application of manifold vacuum to the top.

A solenoid operated valve controls purging of the canister. The valve is controlled by the fuel injection ECU to ensure that purge normally takes place at engine speeds above idle and when the vehicle is in motion. The rate of purge will depend on engine speed, road speed and throttle position.

Purge valve fault diagnosis is included in Engine Fault Diagnosis - Section 12.

Testing purge valve operation is included in Fuel Injection Test Procedure - Section 19, Tests 9 and 10.

NOTE: If crimped hoses are removed it is essential that they are recrimped on reassembly to ensure a leak free joint.

Vacuum delay valve

The vacuum delay valve is not fitted to 3.9 litre models.

LAMBDA (OXYGEN) SENSOR

Remove and refit

The removal of the sensors from the exhaust system must only be carried out when the engine is cold.

Removing

1. Disconnect the battery negative lead.
2. Disconnect the electrical plugs from the sensors.
3. Unscrew and remove the sensors from the two exhaust downpipes.

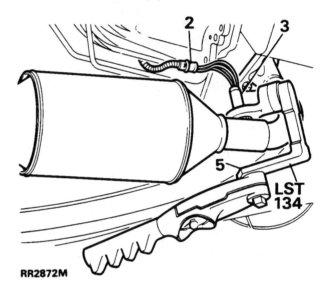

RR2872M

Refitting

4. Coat the threads of the sensors with anti-seize compound.

   CAUTION: To ensure that the efficiency of the sensor is not impaired. DO NOT allow anti-seize compound to come into contact with the sensor nose.

5. Screw in the sensor and tighten to the correct torque using special tool LST134.
6. Connect the electrical plugs and battery lead.

Charcoal canister

Remove and refit

Removing

1. Disconnect battery negative lead.
2. Disconnect both purge lines.
3. Release canister from its mounting brackets.

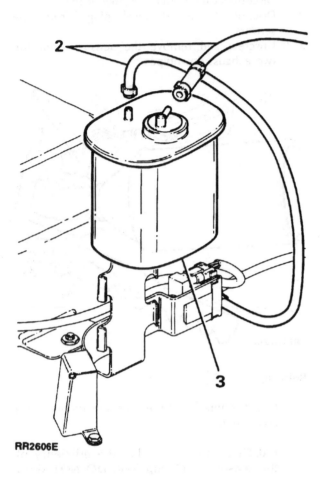

RR2606E

Refitting

4. Reverse the removal procedure, ensuring that the canister is securely located in its mounting bracket and both purge lines are fitted correctly to the canister.

Charcoal canister

Purge valve

Remove and refit

Removing

1. Disconnect the battery negative lead.
2. Remove the crimped connectors from the two purge valve pipes.
3. Disconnect the electrical connection.
4. Remove the edge clip retaining the purge valve and withdraw the purge valve.

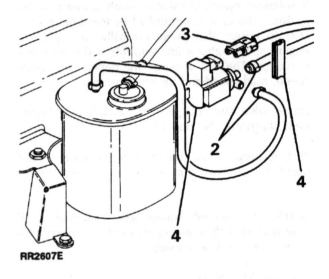

RR2607E

Refitting

5. Reverse the removal procedure ensuring the pipes are securely crimped.

FUEL INJECTION SYSTEM - Component location - RR2874

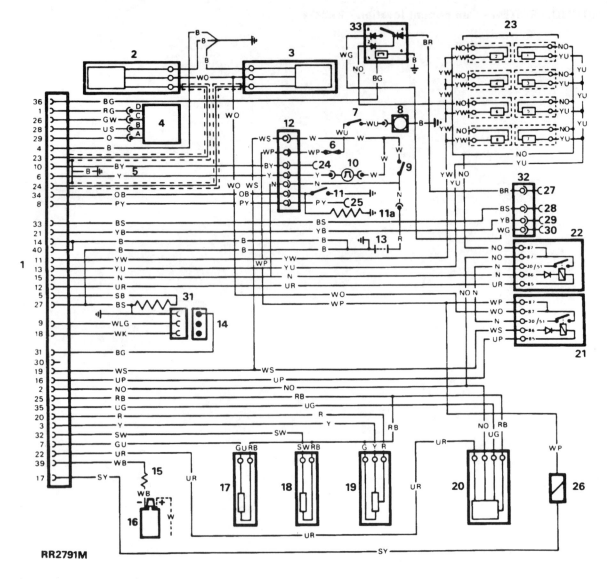

RR2791M

FUEL INJECTION - Circuit Diagram

1. 40 way connector to Electronic Control Unit (ECU).
2. Lambda sensor (left side - bank A).
3. Lambda sensor (right side - bank B).
4. By-pass air valve (stepper motor) (fast idle).
5. Lambda sensor screened ground.
6. Fuse 18 - main fuse panel.
7. Inertia switch.
8. Fuel pump.
9. Ignition switch.
10. Speed transducer (road speed input).
11. Neutral switch (automatic gearbox) (load input).
11a. Resistor manaul gearbox (510 ohms).
12. Main cable connector.
13. Battery.
14. Diagnostic plug.
15. In-line resistor.
16. Coil/-ve (engine RPM input).
17. Coolant temperature thermistor (sensor) (input).
18. Fuel temperature thermistor (sensor) (input).
19. Throttle potentiometer.
20. Air flow sensor.
21. Fuel pump relay.
22. Main relay.
23. Injectors-1 to 8.
24. Pick-up point E.F.I. warning symbol (instrument binnacle).
25. Heated front screen sense.
26. Purge control valve - if fitted.
27. 12V from fan relay.
28. Air conditioning output control.
29. Air conditioning load input.
30. Fan relay feed.
31. Tune resistor.
32. Heater/air con. cable connector.
33. Condenser fan timer control.

= = = Denotes screened ground.

NOTE: Lambda sensors fitted to catalyst vehicles only. Connections to pins 4, 23, 24, 30 and 31 are fitted on catalyst vehicles only.

INTRODUCTION

The 14 CUX Electronic Fuel Injection system provides a reliable and efficient microprocessor controlled fuel management system.

The function of the system is to supply the exact amount of fuel directly into the inlet manifold according to the prevailing engine operating conditions.

To monitor these conditions, various sensors are fitted to the engine to measure engine parameters. Data from the sensors is received by the Electronic Control Unit (E.C.U.), the E.C.U. will then determine the exact amount of fuel required at any condition.

The E.C.U. having received data from the sensors produces pulses, the length of which will determine the simultaneous open time of each bank of injectors in turn, which will govern the amount of fuel injected.

DESCRIPTION

ELECTRONIC CONTROL UNIT-ECU

The Electronic Fuel Injection system is controlled by the E.C.U. which is located under the front right hand seat. The control unit is a microprocessor with integrated circuits and components mounted on printed circuit boards. The E.C.U. is connected to the main harness by a 40 pin plug.

INJECTORS

The eight fuel injectors are fitted between the pressurized fuel rail and inlet manifold. Each injector comprises a solenoid operated needle valve with a movable plunger rigidly attached to the nozzle valve. When the solenoid is energized the plunger is attracted off its seat and allows pressurized fuel into the intake manifold.

TUNE RESISTOR

A 0.5 W tune resistor is located adjacent to the ECU, and plugged into the EFI cable assembly. The resistor value changes for different market applications as follows:
Red wire, 180 Ohms, Australia, Rest of the World.
Green wire, 470 Ohms, UK and Europe, non catalyst.
Yellow wire, 910 Ohms, Saudi non catalyst.
White wire, 3K9 Ohms, USA and Europe, catalyst.

ENGINE COOLANT TEMPERATURE THERMISTOR (SENSOR)

The coolant thermistor (sensor) is located by the front left hand branch of the intake manifold. The thermistor provides engine coolant information to the E.C.U. The E.C.U. on receiving the signal from the thermistor will lengthen slightly the time that the injectors are open, and reducing this time as the engine reaches normal operating temperature.

FUEL TEMPERATURE THERMISTOR (SENSOR)

The fuel temperature thermistor (sensor) is located in the fuel rail forward of the ram housing.The thermistor sends fuel temperature data to the E.C.U, the E.C.U on receiving the data will adjust the injector open time accordingly to produce good hot starting in highambient temperatures.

BYPASS AIR VALVE (STEPPER MOTOR)

The bypass valve is screwed into a housing attached to the rear of the plenum chamber, between the plenum chamber and bulkhead. The bypass valve has two windings which enable the motor to be energised in both directions thus opening or closing the air valve as required by the E.C.U.
The bypass valve will open and allow extra air into the plenum chamber to maintain engine idle speed when the engine is under increased (Electrical and Mechanical) loads.
The bypass valve will control engine idle speed when the vehicle is stationary.

LAMBDA SENSORS (O$_2$ SENSORS)

Catalyst vehicles only

The two Lambda sensors are located forward of the catalysts mounted in the exhaust downpipes.
The sensors monitor the oxygen content of the exhaust gases and provide feedback information of the air/fuel ratio to the E.C.U. Each sensor is heated by an electrical element to improve its response time when the ignition is switched on.

FUEL PRESSURE REGULATOR

The fuel pressure regulator is mounted in the fuel rail at the rear of the plenum chamber. The regulator is a mechanical device controlled by plenum chamber vacuum, it ensures that fuel rail pressure is maintained at a constant pressure difference of 2.5 bar above that of the manifold.

When pressure exceeds the regulator setting excess fuel is returned to the fuel tank.

FUEL PUMP

The electric fuel pump is located in the fuel tank, and is a self priming 'wet' pump, the motor is immersed in the fuel within the tank.

AIR FLOW SENSOR

The hot-wire air flow sensor is mounted on a bracket attached to the left hand valance, rigidly connected to the air cleaner and by hose to the plenum chamber inlet neck.

The air flow sensor consists of a cast alloy body through which air flows. A proportion of this air flows through a bypass in which two wire elements are situated: one is a sensing wire and the other is a compensating wire. Under the control of an electronic module which is mounted on the air flow sensor body, a small current is passed through the sensing wire to produce a heating effect. The compensating wire is also connected to the module but is not heated, but reacts to the temperature of the air taken in, as engine intake air passes over the wires a cooling effect takes place.

The electronic module monitors the reaction of the wires in proportion to the air stream and provides output signals in proportion to the air mass flow rate which are compatible with the requirements of the E.C.U.

THROTTLE POTENTIOMETER

The throttle potentiometer is mounted on the side of the plenum chamber inlet neck and is directly coupled to the throttle valve shaft.

The potentiometer is a resistive device supplied with a voltage from the E.C.U. Movement of the throttle pedal causes the throttle valve to open, thus rotating the wiper arm within the potentiometer which in turn varies the resistance in proportion to the valve position. The E.C.U. lengthens the injector open time when it detects a change in output voltage (rising) from the potentiometer.

In addition the E.C.U. will weaken the mixture when it detects the potentiometer output voltage is decreasing under deceleration and will shorten the length of time the injectors are open.

When the throttle is fully open, the E.C.U. will detect the corresponding throttle potentiometer voltage and will apply full load enrichment. This is a fixed percentage and is independent of temperature. Full load enrichment is also achieved by adjusting the length of the injector open time.

When the throttle is closed, overrun fuel cut off or idle speed control may be facilitated dependant on other inputs to the E.C.U.

The throttle potentiometer is 'self adaptive', which means that adjustment is not possible. It also means that the potentiometer setting is not lost, for example, when throttle stop wear occurs.

ROAD SPEED TRANSDUCER

The road speed transducer is mounted on a bracket located on the left hand chassis side member adjacent to the rear engine mounting. The transducer provides road speed data to the ECU. The ECU in turn detects vehicle movement from the road speed input and ensures that idle speed control mode is disengaged. Should the speed transducer fail in service the ECU idle speed control would become erratic.

The transducer also provides road speed data to the electric speedometer, the use of which deletes the need for the upper speedometer cable.

INERTIA SWITCH

The inertia switch is a mechanically operated switch located under the left hand front seat attached to the seat base rear cross-member.
The switch is normally closed and is in the ignition feed (fuse to fuel pump). In the event of a sudden impact the switch opens, and disconnects the electrical feed to the fuel pump. The switch is reset by pressing down the button.

RELAYS

The two electronic fuel injection relays are located under the front right hand seat. The main relay is energized via the E.C.U when the ignition is switched on and supplies current to the fuel injection system. The fuel pump relay is energized by the E.C.U. which in turn operates the fuel pump to pressurize the fuel system.

E.F.I. WARNING SYMBOL (Instrument binnacle)

An E.F.I. warning symbol incorporated into the instrument binnacle will illuminate when the E.C.U. detects that it cannot maintain correct air/fuel ratio due to a fault in one of the following fuel injection system components, or it associated wiring:

ECU (self check)
Air flow sensor.
Tune resistor.
Water temperature thermistor. (sensor)
Throttle potentiometer.
Stepper motor (incorrect base idle).
Speed transducer
Neutral switch/manual resistor
Fuel temperature sensor.

The symbol will illuminate on initial turn of the ignition key as part of the bulb check feature, and will go out after a few seconds.
If the symbol illuminates when the engine is idling or the vehicle is being driven it indicates a failure of one of the four functions, the vehicle should be driven with care, and the cause rectified, refer to test procedure for the particular functions. Should one of the functions fail, the vehicle can still be driven due to a limp home feature incorporated into the fuel injection system.

CONDENSER FANS

It should be noted that under high coolant temperatures, when the engine is switched off, the condenser fans will be activated and will run for approximately ten minutes.

PURGE VALVE

The operation of the charcoal canister purge valve is checked during the fuel injection system test. see TESTS 9 and 10 Section 19, page 12.

FUEL INJECTION SYSTEM

CAUTION: The fuel system incorporates fine metering components that would be affected by any dirt in the system; therefore it is essential that working conditions are scrupulously clean. If it is necessary to disconnect any part of the fuel injection system, the system MUST be depressurized. All openings left open after the removal of any component from the fuel system, MUST be sealed off to prevent ingress of dirt.

ENGINE SETTING PROCEDURE

If a major overhaul has been undertaken on the fuel injection/engine system, the following check and adjustments must be carried out before attempting to start the engine.
A. **Spark plug gaps** - see 'Section 05 Engine tuning data'.
B. **Throttle levers** - see 'Throttle lever setting procedure'.
C. **Ignition timing** - static - see 'Section 86 Electrical', of main Workshop Manual.

CAUTION: CATALYST VEHICLES - IF THE ENGINE IS MISFIRING, IT SHOULD BE IMMEDIATELY SHUT DOWN AND THE CAUSE RECTIFIED. FAILURE TO DO SO WILL RESULT IN IRREPARABLE DAMAGE TO THE CATALYSTS.

NOTE: If the previous checks and adjustments are satisfactory but the engine will not start, the ignition and fuel injection electrical circuitory must be checked using the appropriate recommended equipment.

Recommended Equipment -

Lucas 'Electronic Ignition Analyser'
Lucas Part Number - YWB 119.

Lucas Diagnostic Equipment - E.F.I.
Lucas Part Number - 60600965 (complete kit)

Individual part numbers for the E.F.I. kit are as follows:

Hand held test unit	- Model 2HHT
Lucas Part Number	- 84772
Interface unit	- Model 2IU
Lucas Part Number	- 84773
Serial link lead	
Lucas Part Number	- 54744753

Memory card
Lucas Part Number

UK	- 606 01 378
France	- 606 01 380
Germany	- 606 01 381
Italy	- 606 01 382
Spain	- 606 01 383
Holland	- 606 01 385
Denmark	- 606 01 384

Operating manual
Lucas Part Number

UK	- XXB 849
France	- XXB 852
Germany	- XXB 851
Italy	- XXB 853
Spain	- XXB 856
Holland	- XXB 854
Denmark	- XXB 855

Plastic case
Lucas Part Number   - 54744755

NOTE: The Lucas diagnostic equipment can be connected to the diagnostic plug located by the E.C.U.

Use in conjunction with the Lucas Operating Instruction Manuals.

If the above equipment is unavailable the tests can be carried out using a multi-meter, following the instructions given in the charts.

CAUTION: Ensure the multi-meter is correctly set to volts or ohms, dependent upon which test is being undertaken.

STATIC CHECKS

Carry out the following static checks before undertaking the continuity procedure:-

A. **Fuse C4** - in main fuse panel - is intact.
B. **Inertia switch** - not tripped.
C. **Fuel** - ample fuel in fuel tank.
D. **Battery Condition** - state of charge.
E. **Air Leaks** - no unmetered air entering engine system.
F. **Electrical Connections** - dry, clean and secure.

CONTINUITY TEST PROCEDURE

The continuity procedure and instructions on the following pages must be followed precisely to prevent damage occurring to any of the fuel system components.

To enable the tests to be carried out when the 40 way multi-plug is connected to the E.C.U., it is necessary to remove the two screws securing the shroud to the plug to enable the multi-meter probes to be inserted into the back of the appropriate pin.

CAUTION: Tests that require the plug to be removed from the E.C.U., must also have the meter probes inserted into the back of the plug. If the probes are inserted into the plug sockets, damage will occur to the sockets resulting in poor connections when the plug is reconnected.

TESTING

1. Remove the E.C.U., and harness plug from beneath the front right hand seat, access is gained through the rear opening of the seat base.
2. Remove the plug shroud and manoeuvre it along the harness until there is enough clearance enabling meter probes to be inserted into the back of the plug.
3. There are 6 pin numbers, 1, 13, 14, 27, 28, 40 moulded onto the rear of the plug for pin position identification as shown in the illustration number RR2800, (for clarity the electrical leads have been omitted).

CONTINUITY TEST PROCEDURE

PIN NOS.   CABLE COLOUR

1.	Red/green	26.	Green/white
2.	Brown/orange	27.	Black/grey
3.	Yellow	28.	Blue/grey
4.	Black	29.	Orange
5.	Grey/black	30.	Not used
6.	Yellow	31.	Black/green
7.	Green/blue	32.	Grey/white
8.	Purple/yellow	33.	Black/grey
9.	White/light green	34.	Orange/Black
10.	Black/yellow	35.	Blue/green
11.	Yellow/white	36.	Black/green
12.	Blue/red	37.	Not used
13.	Yellow/blue	38.	Not used
14.	Black	39.	White/black
15.	Brown	40.	Black
16.	Blue/purple		
17.	Grey/yellow		
18.	White/pink		
19.	White/grey		
20.	Red		
21.	Yellow/black		
22.	Blue/red		
23.	Blue		
24.	Blue		
25.	Red/black		

The last colour denotes the wire tracer colour.

NOTE: Connections to pins 4, 23, 24, 30 and 31 are fitted on catalyst vehicles only.

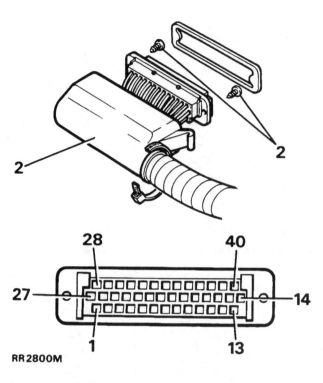

RR2800M

Pins 1 to 13 bottom row.
Pins 14 to 27 centre row
Pins 28 to 40 top row.

Tune select resistor test

It is recommended that this is carried out before Test 1, of Continuity Test Procedure.

TEST PROCEDURE	RESULTS - Check cables and units shown in bold
KEY 1. Tune select resistor	CORRECT READING AUSTRALIAN 171 - 189 Ohms - RED EUROPEAN (NON CAT.) 446 - 494 Ohms - GREEN EUROPEAN (CAT.)/USA 3700 - 4100 Ohms - WHITE SAUDI 864 - 956 Ohms - YELLOW **INCORRECT OHMETER READING CHECK:**
IGNITION OFF RR2812M	RR2813M

TESTS - Using a Multi-Meter - 14CUX system - Key to Symbols

The following continuity tests are intended as a guide to identifying where a fault may be within a circuit; reference should be made to the fuel injection circuit diagram for full circuit information.

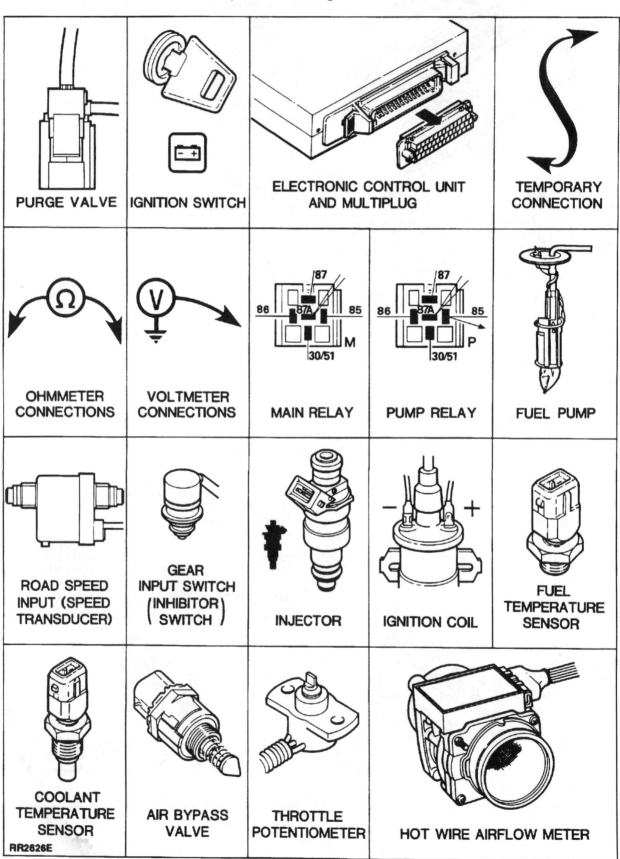

PURGE VALVE	IGNITION SWITCH	ELECTRONIC CONTROL UNIT AND MULTIPLUG	TEMPORARY CONNECTION
OHMMETER CONNECTIONS	VOLTMETER CONNECTIONS	MAIN RELAY	PUMP RELAY	FUEL PUMP
ROAD SPEED INPUT (SPEED TRANSDUCER)	GEAR INPUT SWITCH (INHIBITOR SWITCH)	INJECTOR	IGNITION COIL	FUEL TEMPERATURE SENSOR
COOLANT TEMPERATURE SENSOR	AIR BYPASS VALVE	THROTTLE POTENTIOMETER	HOT WIRE AIRFLOW METER

RR2626E

NOTE: All tests are carried out from the electronic control unit (ECU) harness multi-plug unless stated otherwise in the test procedure.

TEST PROCEDURE	RESULTS - Check cables and units shown in bold
1. Check battery supply to ECU	Voltmeter reading of battery volts - (mimimum battery voltage 10 volts) Proceed to Test 2 Voltmeter reading of zero volts Check:-

IGNITION OFF

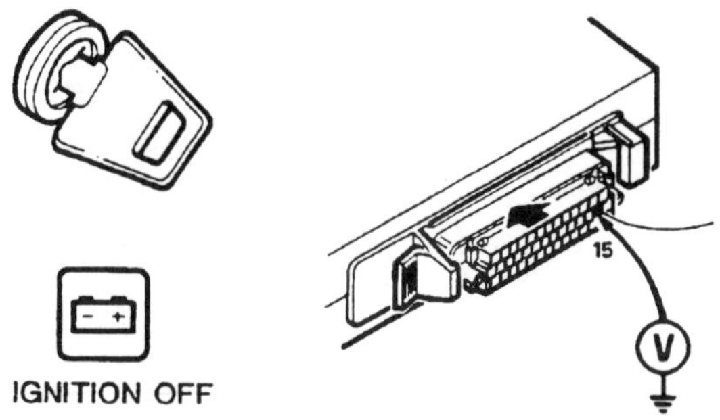

RR2627E

TEST PROCEDURE	RESULTS - Check cables and units shown in bold
2. Check ignition supply to ECU	Voltmeter reading of battery volts - (minimum battery voltage 10 volts) Proceed to Test 3 Incorrect reading check:-

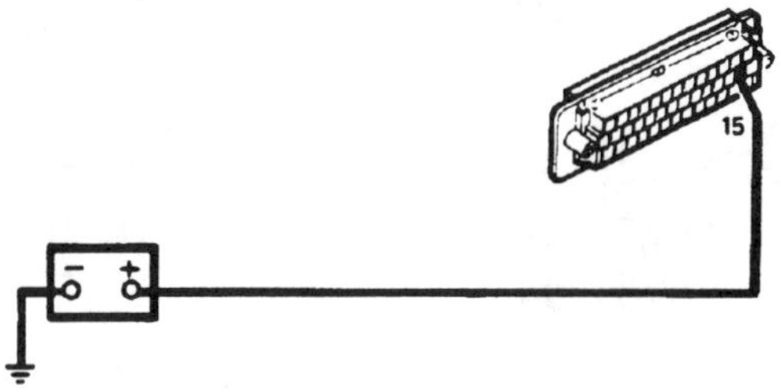

IGNITION ON

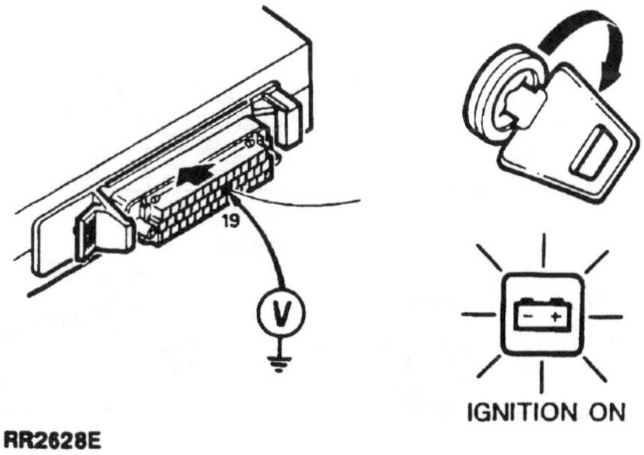

RR2628E

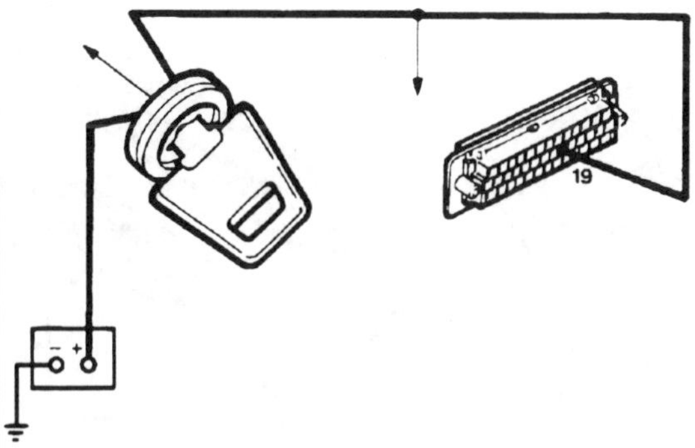

TEST PROCEDURE	RESULTS - Check cables and units shown in bold
3. **Check operation of Main relay**	Voltmeter reading of battery volts - Proceed to Test 5
	Voltmeter reading of zero volts - Proceed to Test 4

3

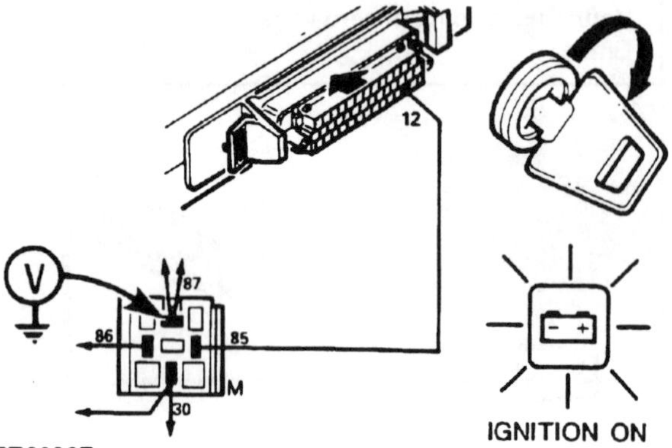

RR2629E

IGNITION ON

TEST PROCEDURE	RESULTS - Check cables and units shown in bold
4. **Fault Diagnosis Main relay circuits**	A. Voltmeter reading of battery volts - Check:- If OK Suspect ECU
	B. Voltmeter reading of zero volts Check:-

4

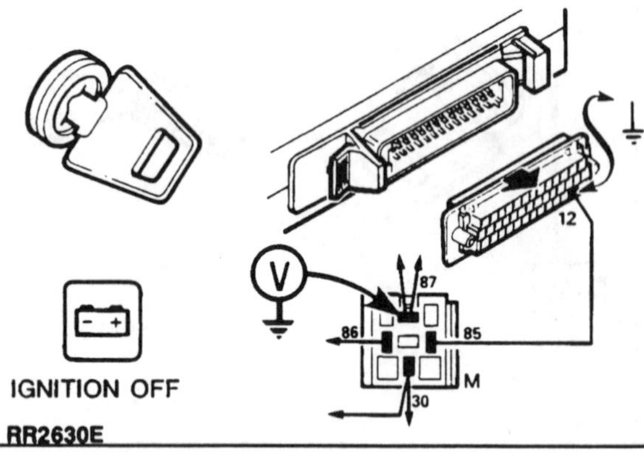

IGNITION OFF

RR2630E

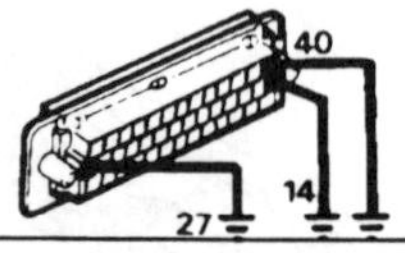

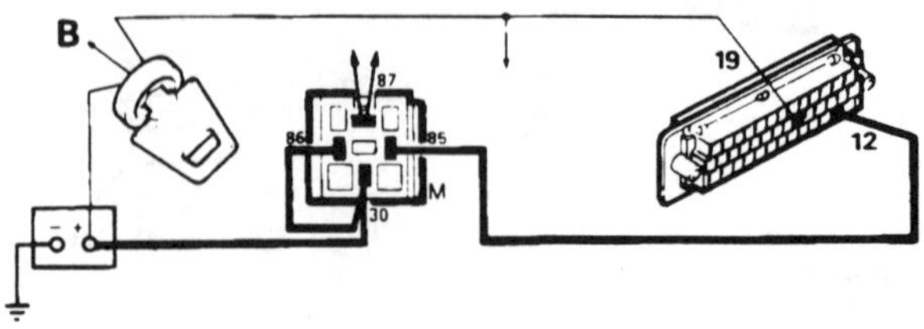

Continued

TEST PROCEDURE	RESULTS - Check cables and units shown in bold
5. **Check engine speed signal** **Cable and resistor**	Voltmeter reading of 9.5 volts ± 1 volt Proceed to Test 6
	Voltmeter reading of zero volts Check:-

5

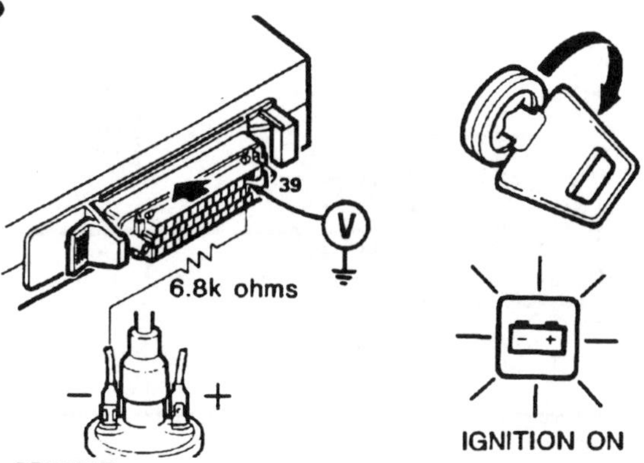

6.8k ohms

IGNITION ON

RR2631E

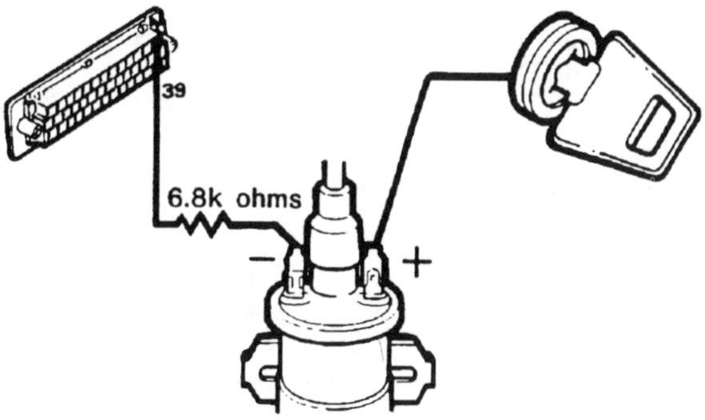

TEST PROCEDURE	RESULTS - Check cables and units shown in bold
6. **Check operation** **of pump relay**	Test lamp will illuminate for approximately 1 second when ignition is switched on If O.K - Proceed to Test 8
	Lamp does not illuminate Check:- If OK proceed to Test 8

6

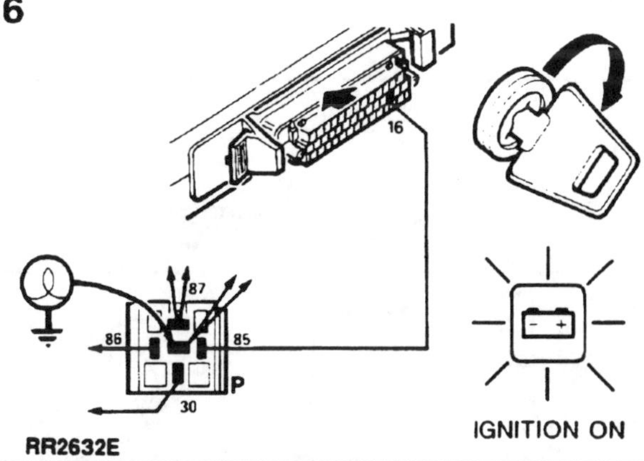

IGNITION ON

RR2632E

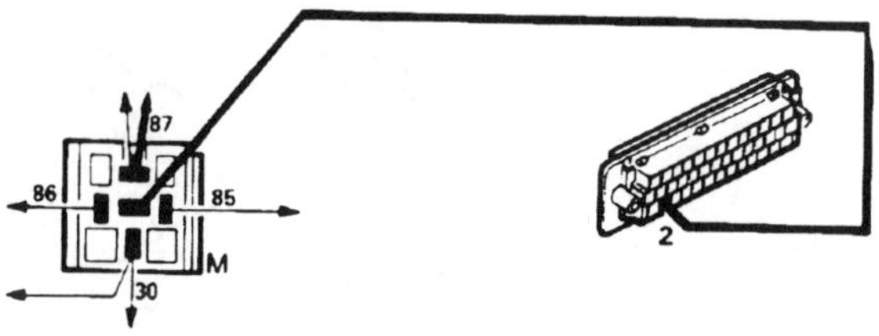

TEST PROCEDURE	RESULTS - Check cables and units shown in bold
7. **Fault diagnosis** **Pump relay circuits**	Voltmeter reading of battery volts - Suspect ECU
	Voltmeter reading of zero volts Check:-

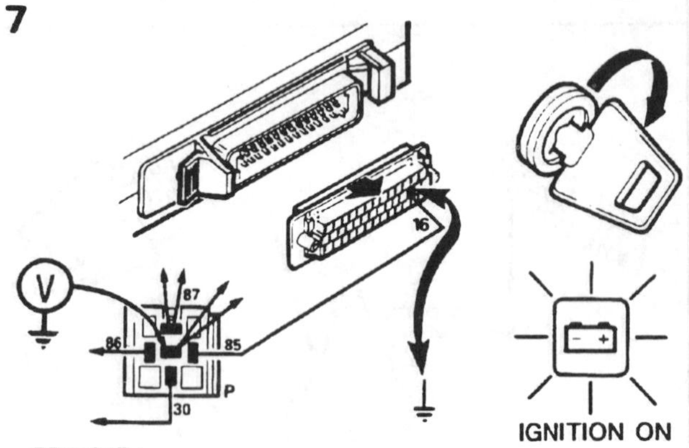

RR2633E

IGNITION ON

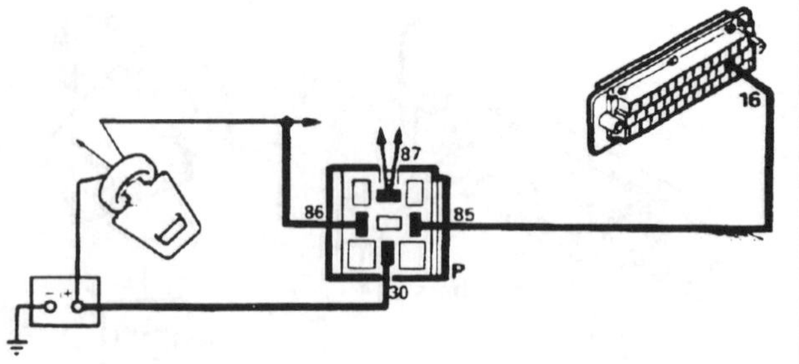

TEST PROCEDURE	RESULTS - Check cables and units shown in bold
8. **Check operation of Fuel pump** NOTE: It is not possible to place the multi-meter probes directly onto the pump terminals. A link lead attached to the pump is accessible behind the rear left hand wheel located between the chassis and stowage area floor panel. KEY: 1. Inertia switch 2. Fuse 18	Voltmeter reading of battery volts - Pump operating - Proceed to Test 10
	(A) Voltmeter reading of battery volts - Pump not operating Check:-
	(B) Voltmeter reading of zero volts Check:-

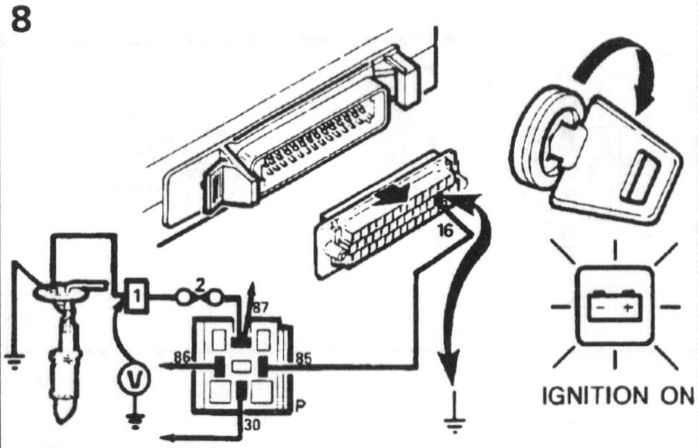

RR2634E

IGNITION ON

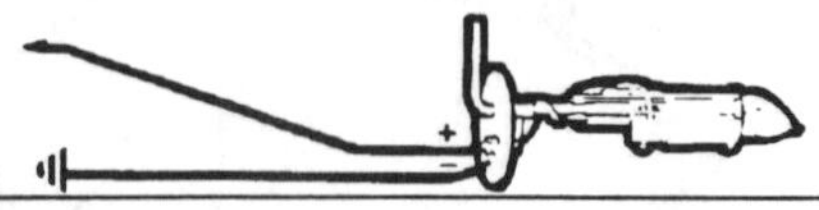

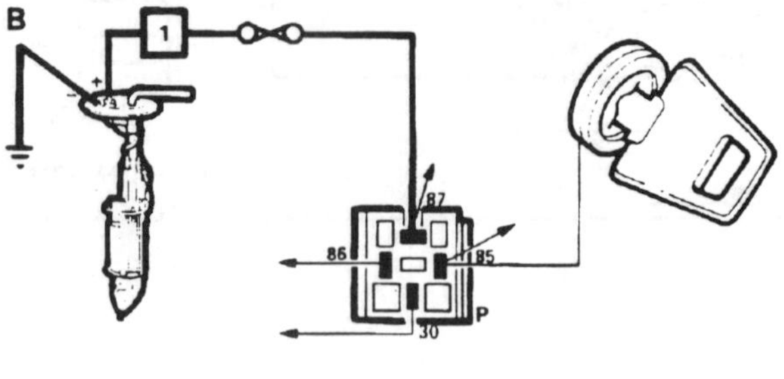

Continued

TEST PROCEDURE	RESULTS - Check cables and units shown in bold
9. **Check purge valve. Part 1 - seating - if fitted** 1. **Disconnect pipe from purge valve to plenum (at plenum)** 2. **Connect vacuum pump to pipe to purge valve** 3. **Apply vacuum of 2.5 in/Hg**	Vacuum should hold for 2.5 minutes If vacuum correct proceed to test 10
	If vacuum incorrect check:

9

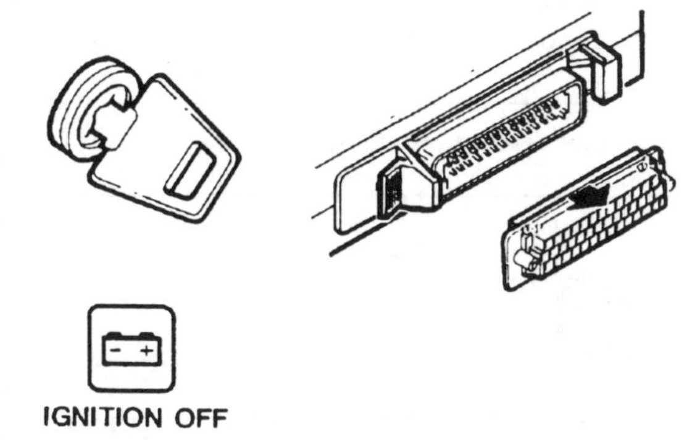

IGNITION OFF

RR2612E

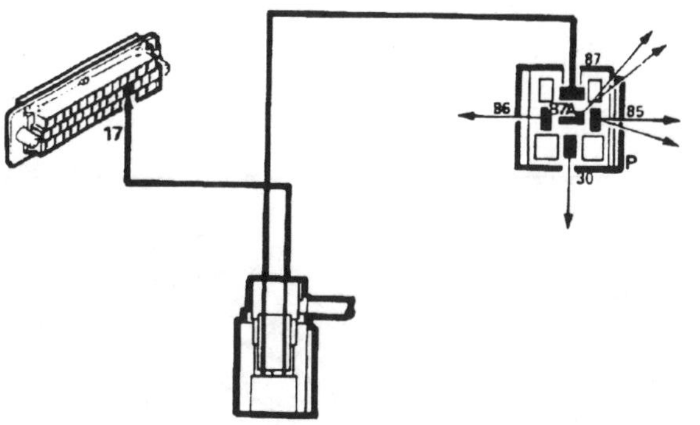

TEST PROCEDURE	RESULTS - Check cables and units shown in bold
10. **Check purge valve. Part 2 - operation - if fitted** 1. **Apply vacuum - 2.5 in/Hg, switch ignition on** 2. **Connect pins 16 and 17 to earth to energise pump relay.**	Vacuum should be released If OK proceed to test 11
	If vacuum not released check:

10

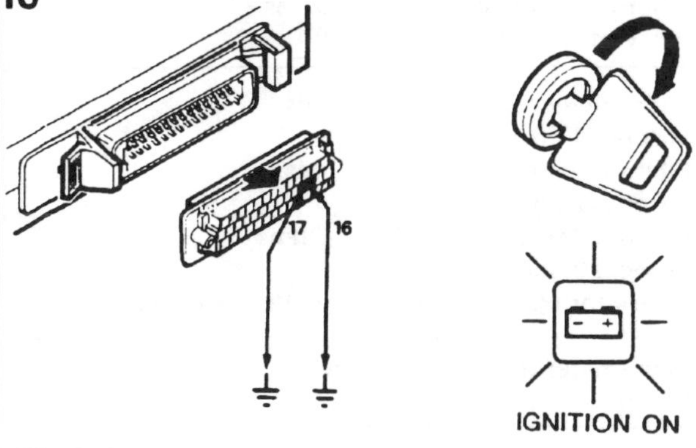

IGNITION ON

RR2613E

13

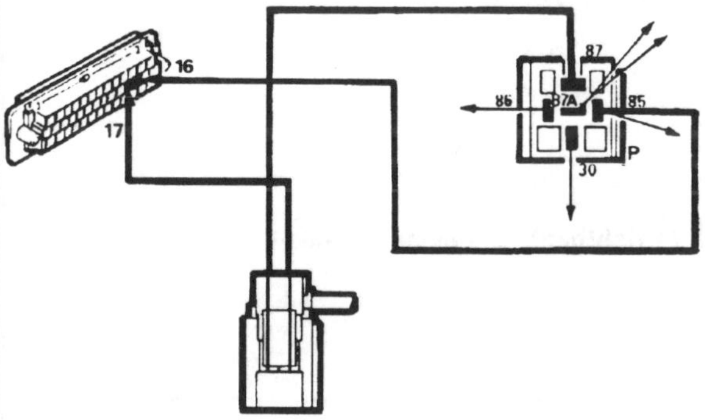

TEST PROCEDURE	RESULTS - Check cables and units shown in bold
11. Check injectors, Injector circuit	Ohm-meter reading of 4-4.5 Ohms - Proceed to Test 12
(Pin 13 left bank 'A' injectors 1,3,5,7).	Ohm-meter reading of 5-6 Ohms - Suspect 1 injector Ohm-meter reading of 8-9 Ohms - Suspect 2 injectors Ohm-meter reading of 16-17 Ohms - Suspect 3 injectors Check for open circuit injector(s) or wiring faults.
	Ohm-meter reading of Infinity Check:

11

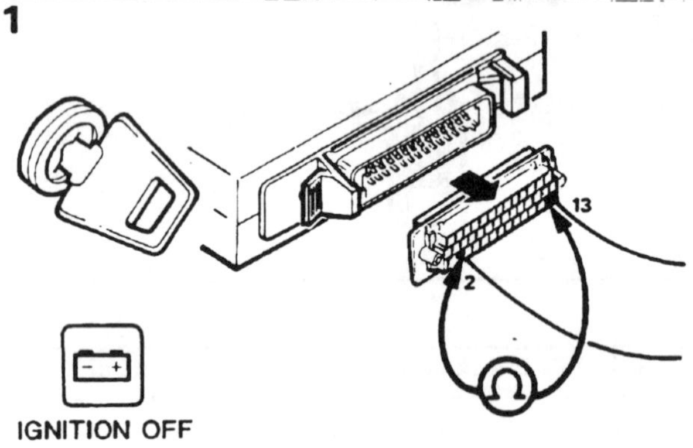
13
2
IGNITION OFF

RR2635E

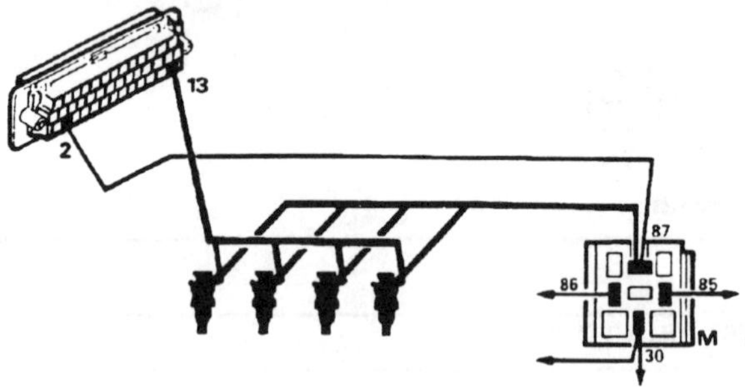
13
2
87
86
85
M
30

TEST PROCEDURE	RESULTS - Check cables and units shown in bold
12. Check injectors, Injector circuit	Ohm-meter reading of 4-4.5 Ohms - Proceed to Test 13
(Pin 11 rightbank 'B' injectors 2,4,6,8)	Ohm-meter reading of 5-6 Ohms - Suspect 1 injector Ohm-meter reading of 8-9 Ohms - Suspect 2 injectors Ohm-meter reading of 16-17 Ohms - Suspect 3 injectors Check for open circuit injector(s) or wiring faults.
	Ohm-meter reading of Infinity Check:

12

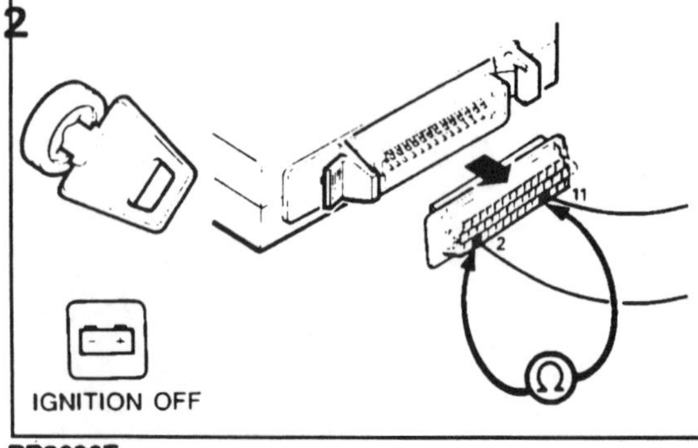
11
2
IGNITION OFF

RR2636E

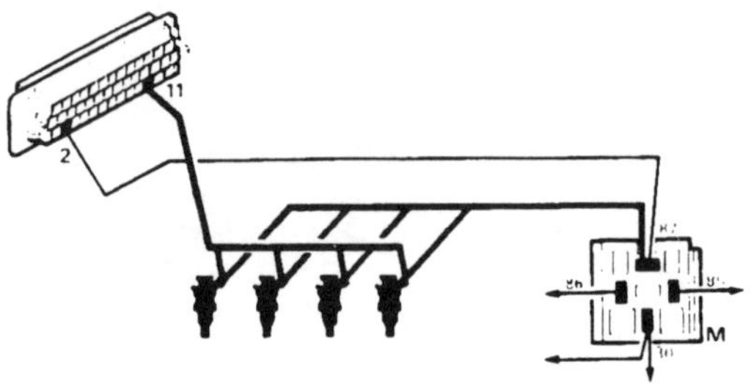
11
2
M

TEST PROCEDURE	RESULTS - Check cables and units shown in bold
13. **Check fuel temperature thermistor (sensor)**	Correct reading-temperature to resistance - Proceed to Test 14 (Refer to Temperature Conversion Charts in Test 14
	Incorrect Ohm-meter reading Check

13

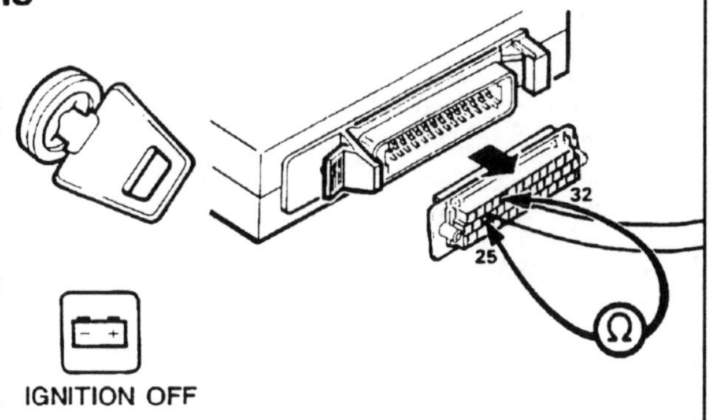

IGNITION OFF

RR2638E

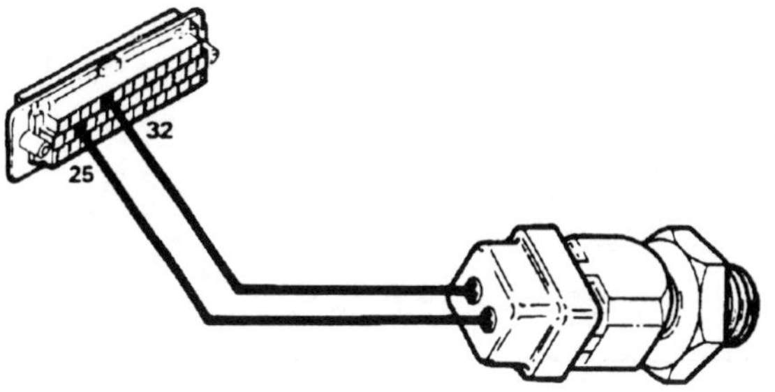

TEST PROCEDURE	RESULTS - Check cables and units shown in bold
14. **Check coolant temperature thermistor (sensor)**	Correct reading-Temperature to resistance - Proceed to Test 15 (Refer to Temperature Conversion Chart below.

Fuel and Coolant Temperature		Ohm-meter Reading Should be
°C	°F	Ohms
-10°	14°	9100 - 9300
0°	32°	5700 - 5900
20°	68°	2400 - 2600
40°	104°	1100 - 1300
60°	140°	500 - 700
80°	176°	300 - 400
100°	212°	150 - 200

Incorrect Ohm-meter reading
Check:-

14

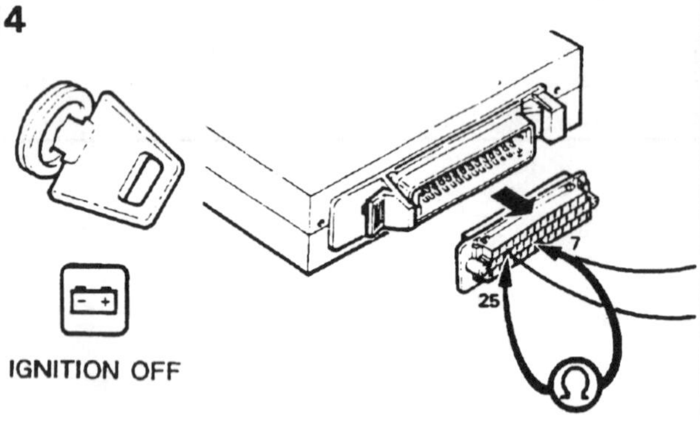

IGNITION OFF

RR2637E

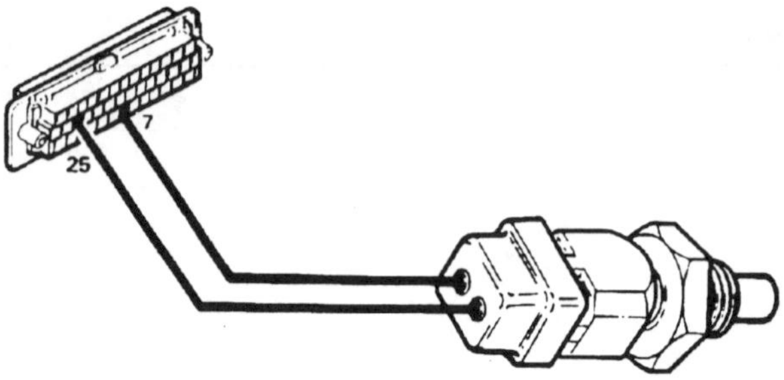

TEST PROCEDURE	RESULTS - Check cables and units shown in bold
15. **Check air bypass valve - Part 1**	Ohm-meter reading of 40-60 Ohms - Proceed to Test 16
	Incorrect reading Check:-

15

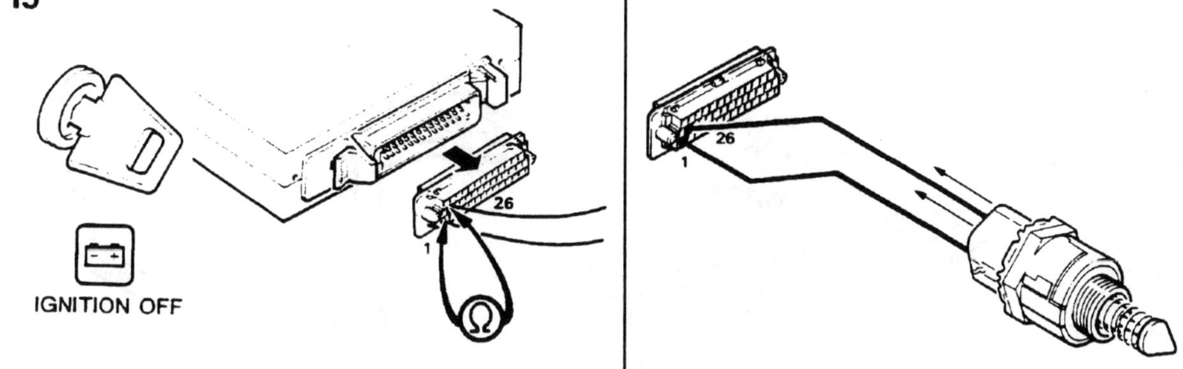

IGNITION OFF

RR2639E

TEST PROCEDURE	RESULTS - Check cables and units shown in bold
16. **Check air bypass valve - Part 2**	Ohm-meter reading of 40-60 Ohms - Proceed to Test 17
	Incorrect reading Check:-

16

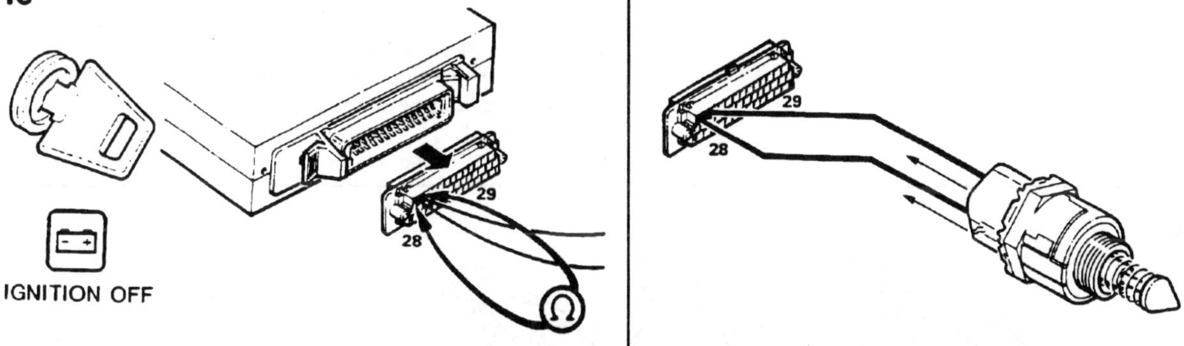

IGNITION OFF

RR2640E

TEST PROCEDURE	RESULTS - Check cables and units shown in bold
17. **Check throttle potentiometer - Part 1**	Ohm-meter reading of 4000-6000 Ohms - Proceed to Test 18
	Incorrect reading of Infinity Check:-

17

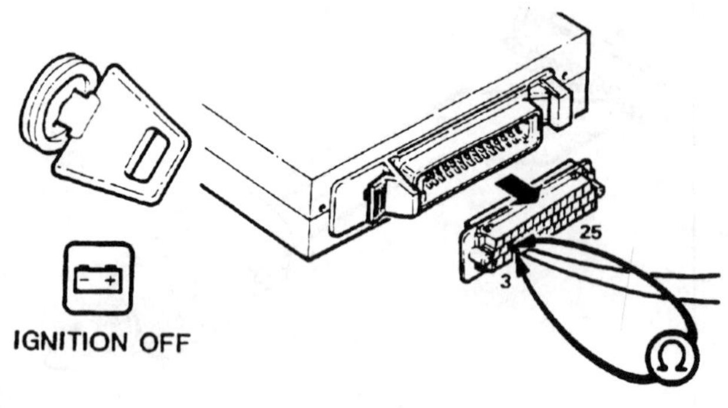

IGNITION OFF

RR2641E

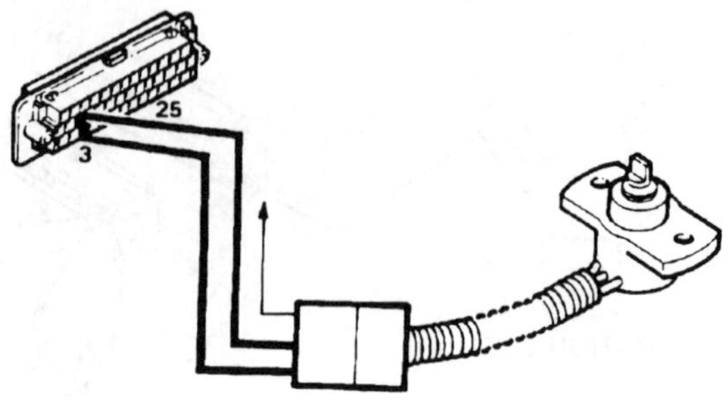

TEST PROCEDURE	RESULTS - Check cables and units shown in bold
18. **Check throttle potentiometer - Part 2**	Correct voltmeter readings- Proceed to Test 18
	Throttle closed: 0.085-0.545 volts) smooth) swing) between) closed) and
	Throttle open: 4.2-4.9 volts) open
	Incorrect voltmeter readings Check:-

18

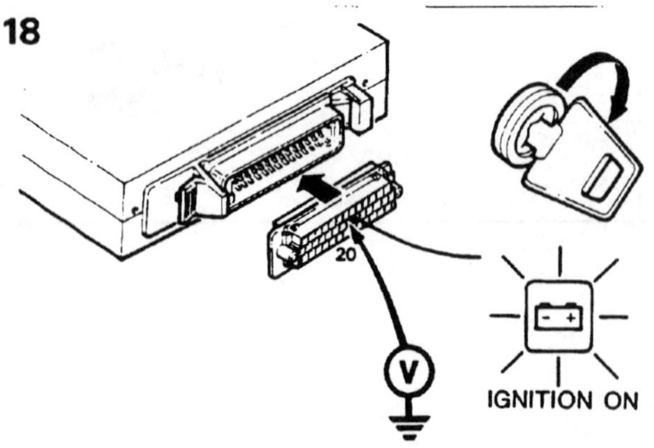

IGNITION ON

RR2642E

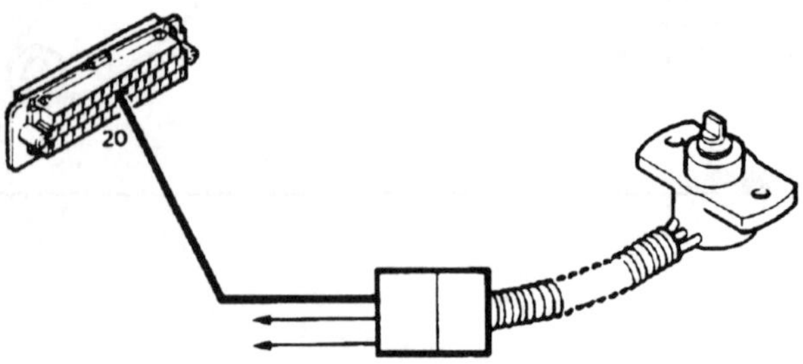

TEST PROCEDURE	RESULTS - Check cables and units shown in bold
19. **Check output of Airflow sensor**	Voltmeter reading of 0.2-0.7 volts- Proceed to Test 20
	Incorrect voltmeter reading Check:-

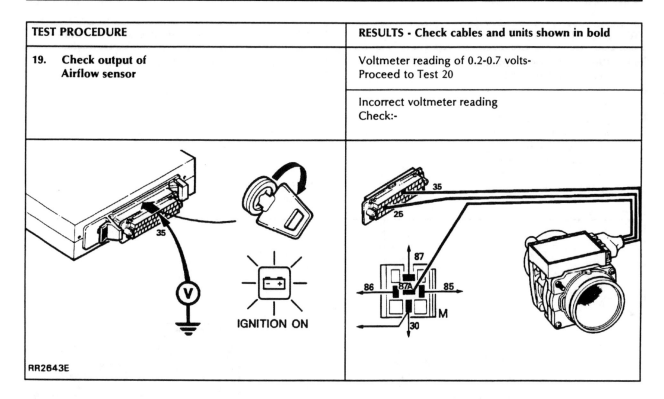

RR2643E

PRECAUTION:

Depressurize the fuel system when fitting the fuel pressure gauge or disconnecting/replacing fuel system components.

CAUTION: Thoroughly clean the immediate area around the fuel filter and hose connections before disconnecting the fuel feed line from the filter. Failure to do so could cause foreign matter to be present in the fuel system which would be detrimental to the fuel system components.

WARNING: The spillage of fuel from the fuel filter is unavoidable when disconnecting the fuel feed line, ensure that all necessary precautions are taken to prevent fire and explosion due to fuel vapour and fuel seepage.

DEPRESSURIZING PROCEDURE

a) Ignition off, pull pump relay off its terminal block.
b) Crank engine for a few seconds - engine may fire and run until fuel pressure is reduced.
c) Switch off the ignition.
d) Connect fuel pressure gauge in the fuel supply line between the fuel rail and the fuel filter, adjacent to the filter (see Test 20).
e) Reconnect the pump relay.

TEST PROCEDURE	RESULTS - Check cables and units shown in bold
20. Check fuel system pressure Service tool 18G 1500 **NOTE: Insert the pressure gauge in the fuel feed line immediately after the fuel line filter. The filter is located beneath the right hand rear wheel arch attached to the chassis**	(A) Expected reading 2,39-2,672 kgf/cm² (34.0-38.0 p.s.i.) (B) Pressure drop-max 0.7 kgf/cm² (10 p.s.i.) in one minute Proceed to Test 21

20

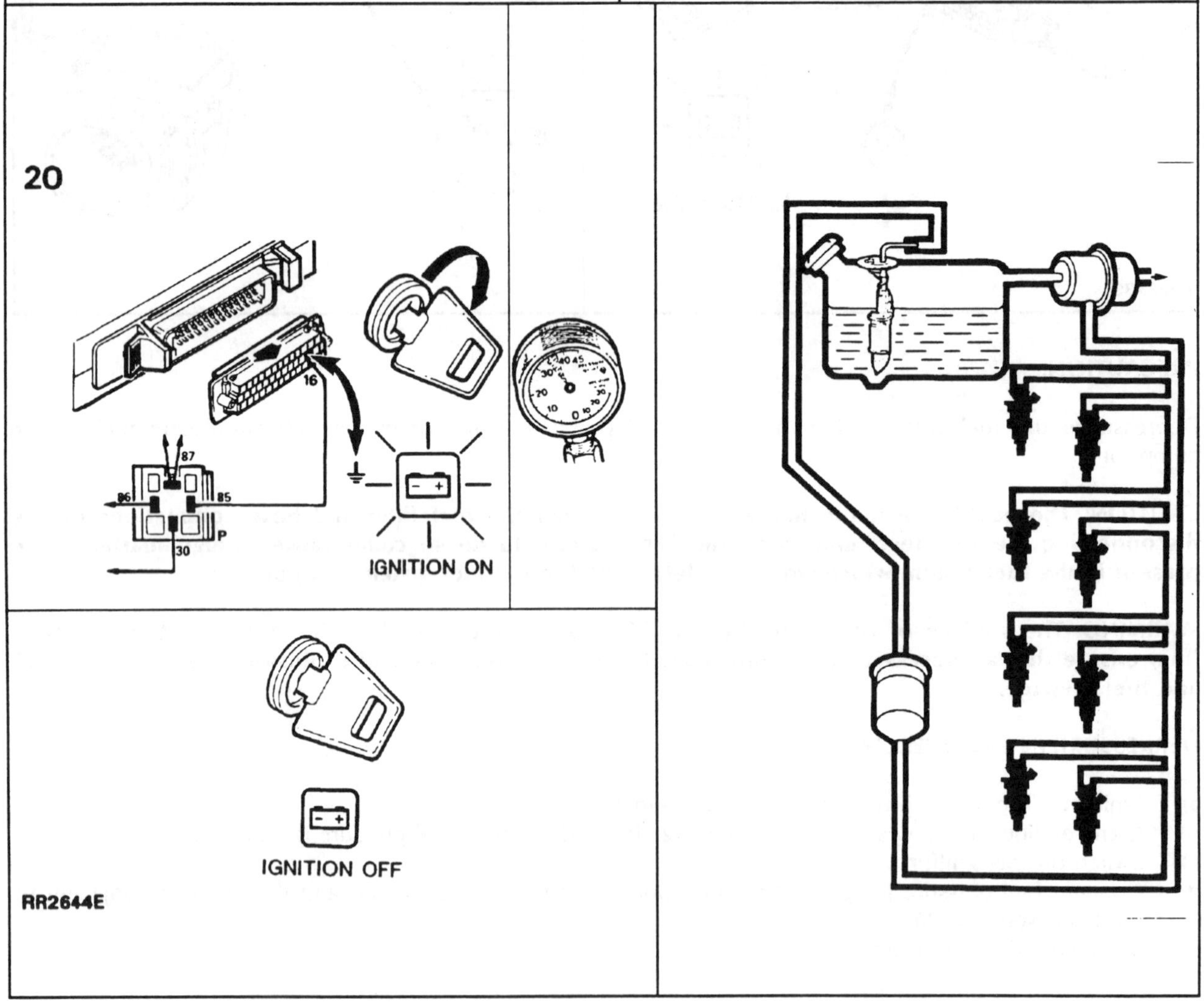
16
87
86
85
P
30
IGNITION ON
IGNITION OFF

RR2644E

TEST PROCEDURE	RESULTS - Check cables and units shown in bold
21. **Check for leaking injector** NOTE: Before removing any of the injectors, remove and examine the spark plugs, check for consistent colouration of plugs. A leaking injector will result in the appropriate spark plug being 'sooted up'. **Remove all injectors from manifold but do not disconnect from fuel rail**	**WARNING: Ensure that all necessary precautions are taken to prevent fire and explosion.** Replace any injector which leaks more than 2 drops of fuel per minute.

21

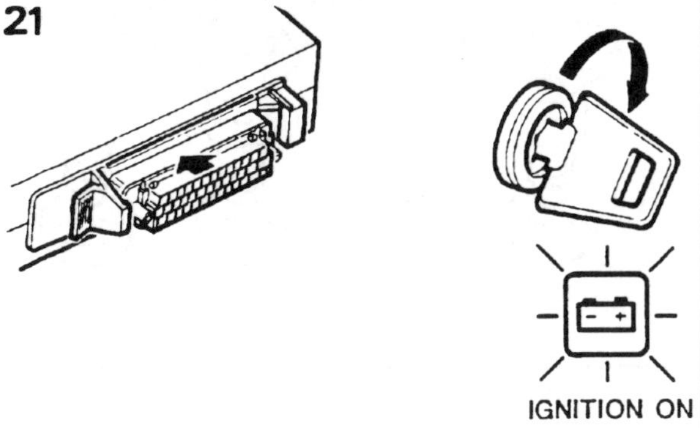

IGNITION ON

RR2645E

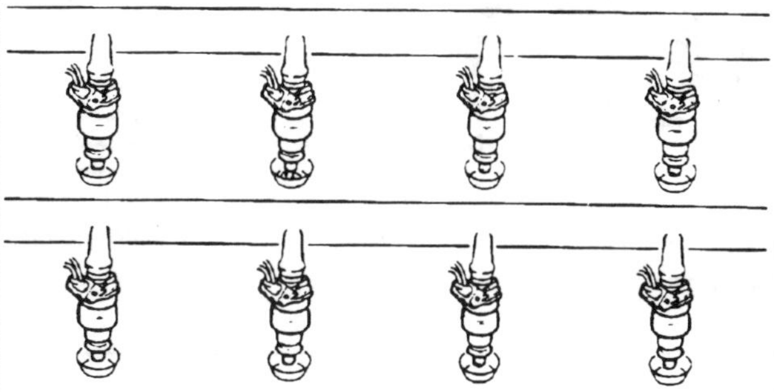

TEST PROCEDURE	RESULTS - Check cables and units shown in bold
22. **Check for injector operation** **Left bank 'A' injectors 1,3,5,7**	**WARNING: Ensure that all necessary precautions are taken to prevent fire and explosion.** Repeat test for other injectors Replace any injector which does not operate. **NOTE: Fuel flow is 160-175 cc (using white spirit) or 180-195 cc (using petrol) (minimum) per minute per injector, at 2.54 kgf/cm^2 (36.25 psi) system pressure at 20°C ± 2°C**

22

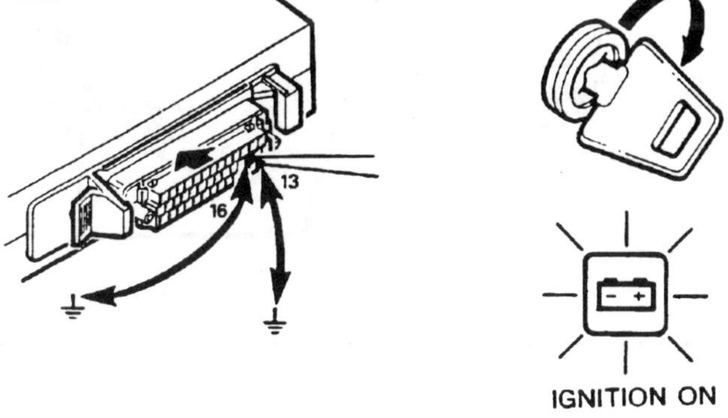

13

16

IGNITION ON

RR2646E

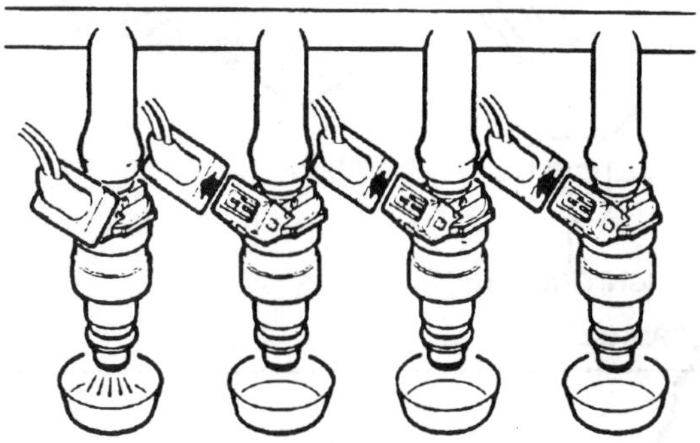

TEST PROCEDURE	RESULTS - Check cables and units shown in bold
23. Right bank 'B' injectors 2,4,6,8	**WARNING: Ensure that all necessary precautions are taken to prevent fire and explosion** Repeat test for other injectors Replace any injector which does not operate **NOTE: Fuel flow is 160-175 cc (using white spirit) or 180-195 cc (using petrol) (minimum) per minute per injector, at 2.54 kgf/cm² (36.25 psi) system pressure at 20°C ± 2°C**

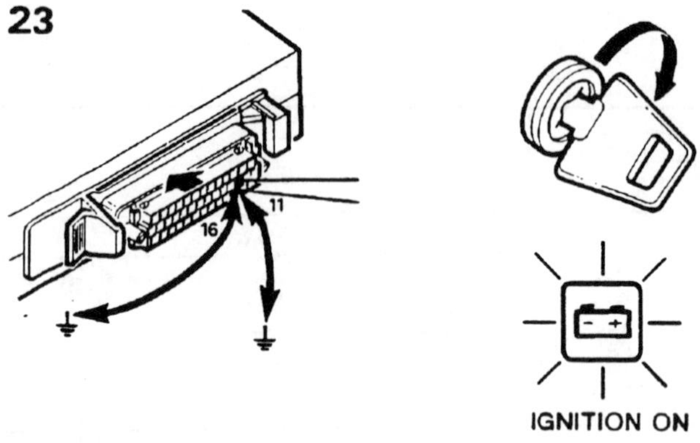

RR2647E

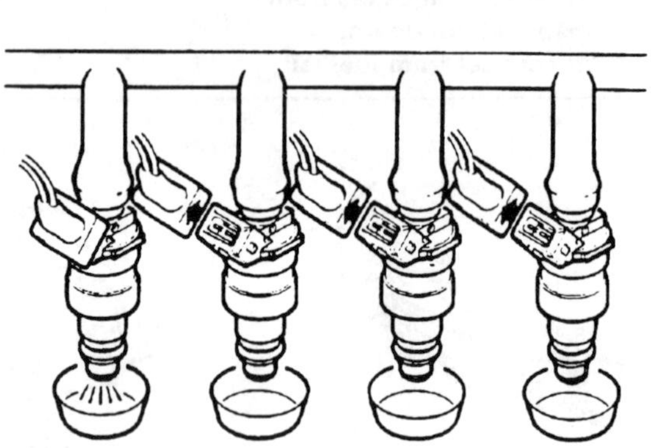

TEST PROCEDURE	RESULTS - Check cables and units shown in bold
24. Check gear switch input automatic	Voltmeter reading of zero volts- Neutral and park
	Voltmeter reading of 2.5-5.0 Volts -R.D.3.2.1 - Proceed to Test 26
	Incorrect reading Check:

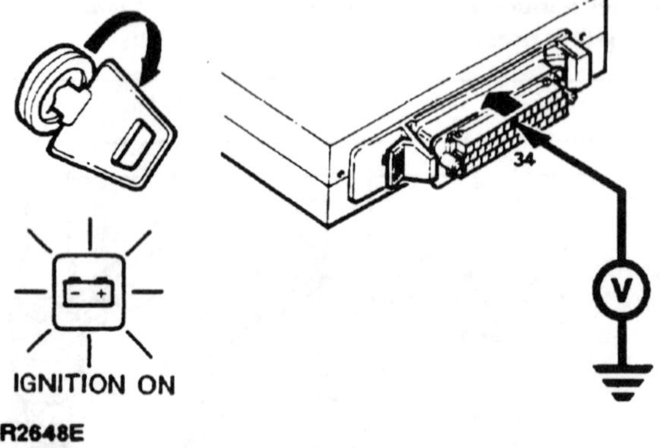

RR2648E

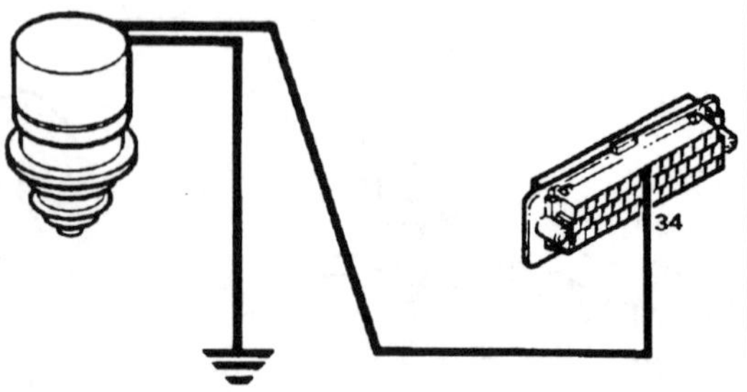

TEST PROCEDURE	RESULTS - Check cables and units shown in bold
25. **Check gear switch signal - manual vehicles** **KEY** 1) **Gear box resistor - 510 Ohms**	Voltmeter reading of 1.5 - 3.5V Proceed to Test 26
	Incorrect reading Check:

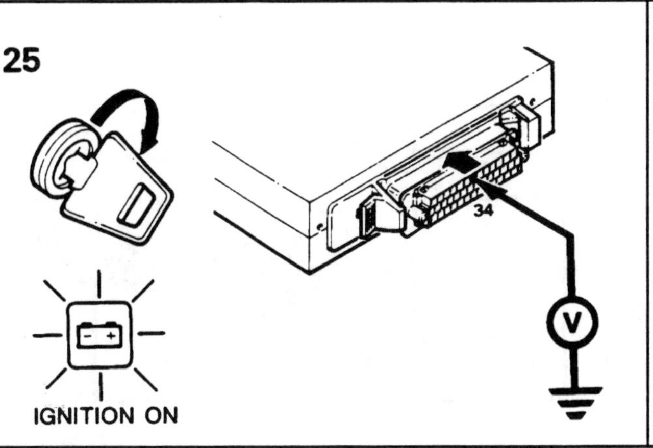

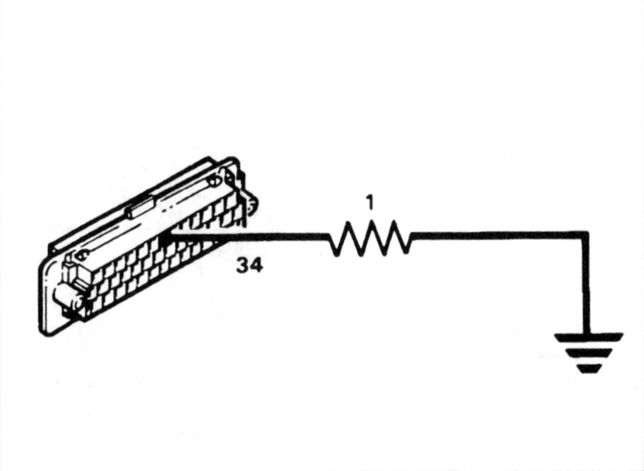

RR2890M

TEST PROCEDURE	RESULTS - Check cables and units shown in bold
26. **Check road speed input** **NOTE: Roll the vehicle forward slowly**	Voltmeter reading of 0 to 12V fluctuating 6 times per revolution - Proceed to Test 26
	Incorrect reading Check:

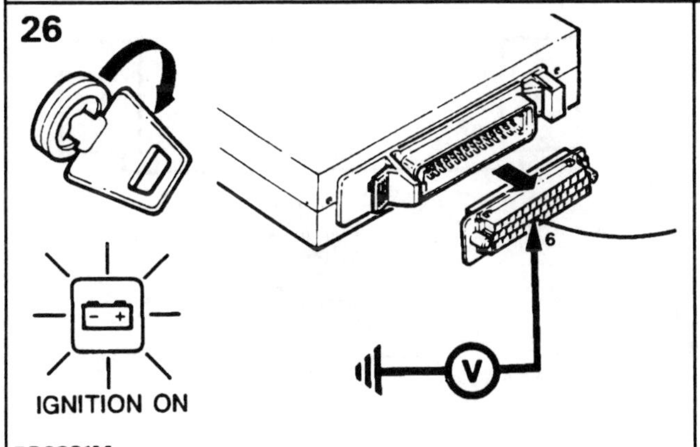

RR2891M

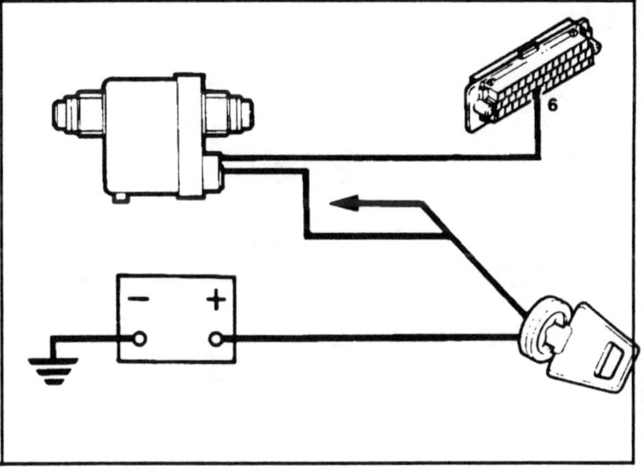

TEST PROCEDURE	RESULTS - Check cables and units shown in bold
27. **Check Lambda sensor heater coils** **- Catalyst vehicles** NOTE: **Remove pump relay from its connector**	Ohm-meter reading of 2.5-6.0 Ohms Proceed to Test 27a
	Incorrect reading Check:

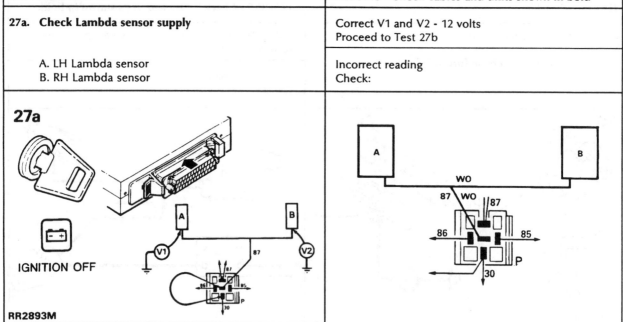

RR2892M

TEST PROCEDURE	RESULTS - Check cables and units shown in bold
27a. **Check Lambda sensor supply** A. LH Lambda sensor B. RH Lambda sensor	Correct V1 and V2 - 12 volts Proceed to Test 27b
	Incorrect reading Check:

RR2893M

TEST PROCEDURE	RESULTS - Check cables and units shown in bold
27b. Check Lambda sensor operation	Correct 0.50V - 1.00V fluctuating
Note: Select 'P' in main gearbox and run engine at 1000 rev/min, normal operating temperature **A. LH Lambda sensor** **B. RH Lambda sensor**	Incorrect 0.050 V - Check: Air leaks, faulty or contaminated injectors, low fuel pressure - if OK fit new Lambda sensor Incorrect 1.00V (not fluctuating) - Check: High fuel pressure, leaking injectors, saturated carbon canister - if OK fit new Lambda sensor. Incorrect approx. O.O.V - check:

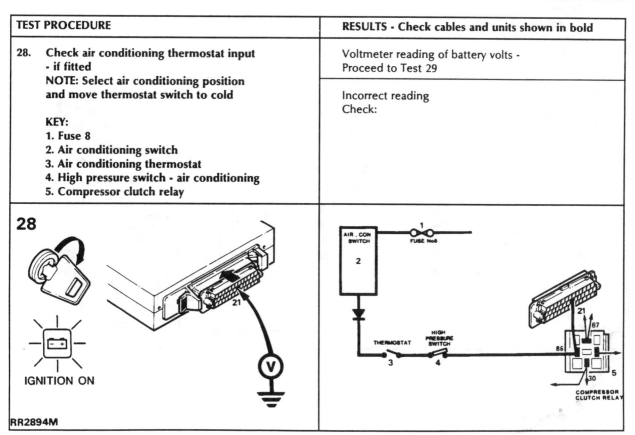

27b

A

B

RR2708E

TEST PROCEDURE	RESULTS - Check cables and units shown in bold
28. Check air conditioning thermostat input - if fitted **NOTE: Select air conditioning position and move thermostat switch to cold** **KEY:** **1. Fuse 8** **2. Air conditioning switch** **3. Air conditioning thermostat** **4. High pressure switch - air conditioning** **5. Compressor clutch relay**	Voltmeter reading of battery volts - Proceed to Test 29 Incorrect reading Check:

28

IGNITION ON

RR2894M

TEST PROCEDURE	RESULTS - Check cables and units shown in bold
29. **Check operation of compressor clutch relay - air con. vehicles** NOTE: Select air condition position, thermostat cold, and fan speed I, II or III	Voltmeter reading of 12 volts - Proceed to Test 31
	Incorrect reading of zero volts Proceed to Test 30

TEST PROCEDURE	RESULTS - Check cables and units shown in bold
30. **Fault diagnosis - compressor clutch relay - air con. vehicles** NOTE: Select air condition position, thermostat cold, and fan speed I, II or III KEY: 1. **Compressor clutch relay** 2. **Compressor clutch** 3. **High pressure switch** 4. **Thermostat** 5. **Air conditioning switch** 6. **Fan speed switch** 5. **Fuse A3**	Voltmeter reading of 12 volts - Check A
	Voltmeter reading of zero volts Check B

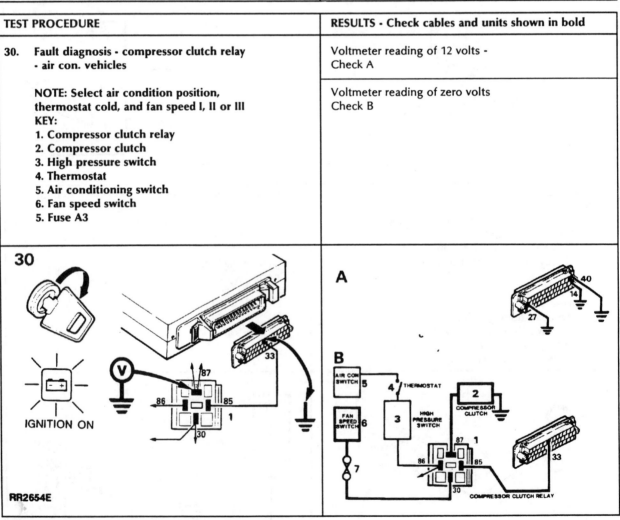

RR2653E

RR2654E

TEST PROCEDURE	RESULTS - Check cables and units shown in bold
31. **Check heated front screen input - if fitted** **NOTE: Engine running, heated front screen switched 'ON'** **KEY:** **1. Oil pressure switch** **2. Front screen timer unit** **3. Front screen switch**	Voltmeter reading of 12 volts - Proceed to Test 32
	Incorrect reading of zero volts Check:

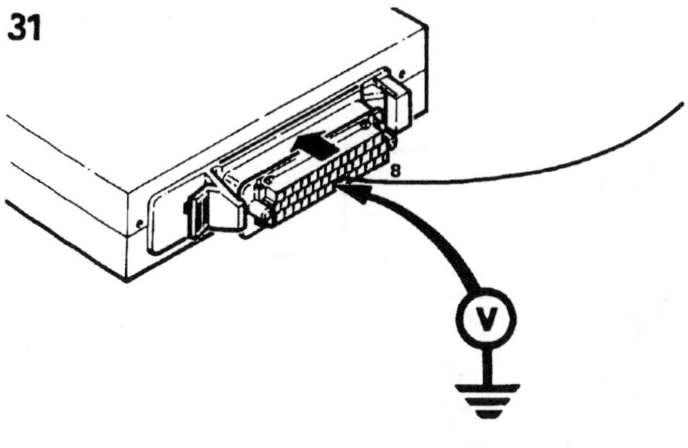

RR2655E

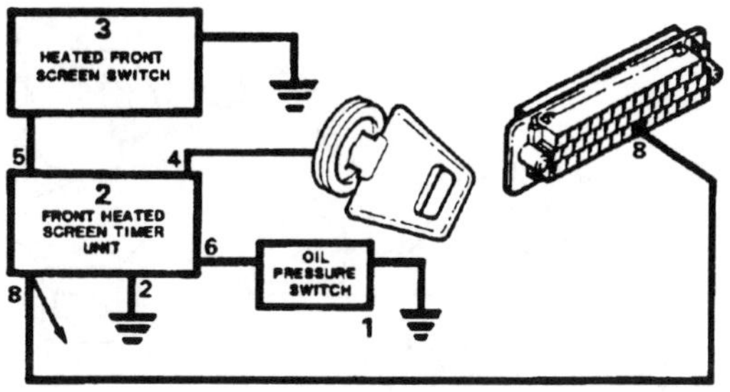

TEST PROCEDURE	RESULTS - Check cables and units shown in bold
32. **Check operation of condenser fan output - air con. vehicles** **Disconnect coolant temperature sensor and fuel temperature sensor and bridge plug connectors** **NOTE: Switch ignition 'ON' for 5 seconds, switch ignition 'OFF'** **The fan timer will operate the fans for 10 minutes approximately unless it is disconnected.** **KEY:** **1. Condenser fan timer** **2. Condenser fan relay**	Voltmeter reading of 12 volts - end of tests
	Voltmeter reading of zero volts Proceed to Test 33

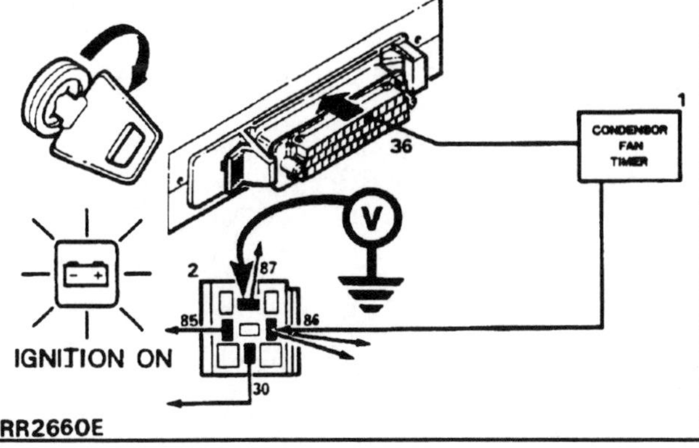

RR2660E

TEST PROCEDURE	RESULTS - Check cables and units shown in bold
33. **Fault diagnosis - condenser fan output - air con. vehicles** **KEY:** **1. Condenser fan timer** **2. Condenser fan relay** **3. Fuses A1 and A2** **4. Condenser fans**	Voltmeter reading of 12 volts - Suspect ECU Incorrect reading Check:

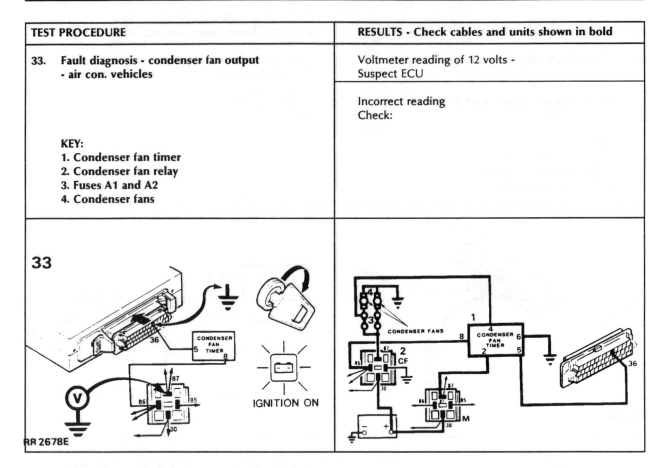

RR 2678E

After completing the tests with either the 'Diagnostic' equipment or multi-meter, re-test the vehicle to ensure the faults have been rectified. If faults still persist, recheck using the Lucas diagnostic equipment.

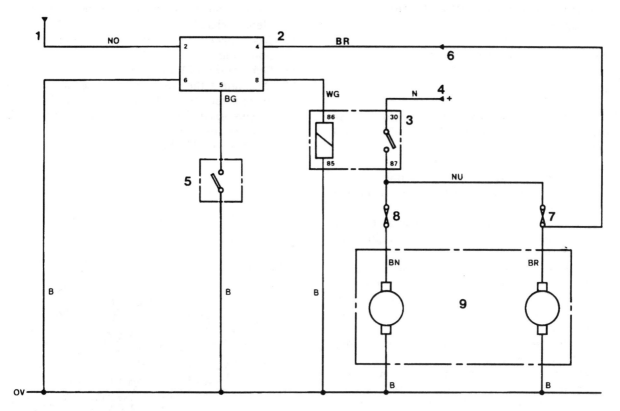

RR2610E

Condenser fan circuit diagram RR2610E

1. 12V from EFI main relay.
2. Condenser fan timer unit.
3. Fan relay.
4. 12V battery feed.
5. Trigger, from ECU.
6. 12V from fan relay.
7. Fuse A1-20 amp.
8. Fuse A2-20 amp.
9. Fan motors

Condenser fans/Condenser fan timer

Check operation

1. Start engine.
2. Move air con/heater control to air conditioning position.
3. Check condenser fans, if working the condenser fan relay and wiring to the fans is functioning.
4. If not working check fuses A1 and A2, and the voltage between connections 86 on fan relay and earth. If 12 volts is not present, check wiring back to air con switch.
5. If 12 volts is present, but fans NOT working, short out connections 30 and 87 on fan relay. If fans work fit new relay. If fans NOT working, check supply to fan relay from main harness.
6. Apply a 12 volt supply for at least two seconds to connection 5 on fan timer within **SIX SECONDS** of switching engine off. The condenser fans should run for 9.5 minutes ± 0.5 minutes, and switch off.
7. If the fans do not work after applying voltage to timer, short out connections 4 and 8 on fan timer, if fans work fit new fan timer. If fans do not work, check wiring.

OVERHAUL THROTTLE LEVERS AND THROTTLE VALVE - 3.9 V8 Model

Preparation, remove, overhaul and refit

Preparation

NOTE: Ignore instructions concerning cruise control components and kickdown cable if not applicable.

1. Disconnect the battery negative terminal.
2. Disconnect the electrical multi-plug from the bypass air valve (stepper motor).
3. Disconnect the small vacuum hose at the rear of the plenum chamber, located below the bypass air valve.
4. To assist re-assembly mark an identification line on the throttle cable outer covering directly behind the adjustment thumb wheel before disconnecting the throttle cable from the throttle lever.
5. Remove the cotter pin and clevis pin securing the throttle cable to the lever.
6. Carefully pry the adjustment thumb wheel from the throttle bracket. Lay the cable aside.
7. Release the retaining clip from the kick down cable and remove the clevis pin.
8. To assist re-assembly apply adhesive tape behind the rear adjustment nut on the kick down cable outer sleeve to prevent the nut moving out of position.
9. Release the front lock nut and remove it from the outer sleeve to enable the cable to be removed from the throttle bracket. Lay the cable aside.
10. Remove the vacuum hose from the cruise control actuator.

11. Remove the intake hose from the neck of the plenum chamber.
12. Disconnect the multi-plug to the throttle potentiometer.
13. Remove the PCV breather hose.
14. Disconnect the two coolant hoses in turn and immediately plug the end of each hose to prevent excessive loss of coolant. Identify each hose for re-assembly.
15. Remove the distributor vacuum hose.

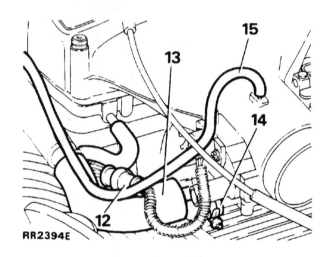

RR2394E

16. Release the two screws and remove the potentiometer.

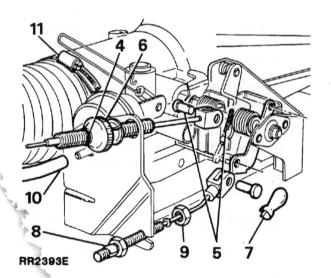

RR2393E

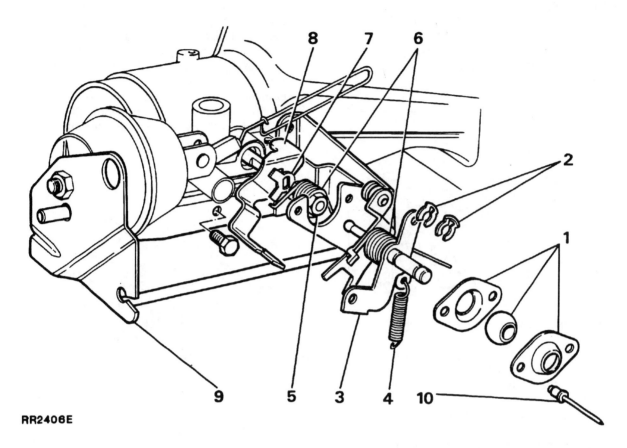

RR2406E

KEY

1. Spherical bearing
2. Retaining clips (2)
3. Countershaft assembly
4. Overtravel spring
5. Throttle spindle nut
6. Throttle return spring (2)
7. Tab washer
8. Throttle stop lever
9. Throttle bracket assembly
10. Pop rivets (2)

Remove throttle lever assembly

17. Remove the six screws securing the plenum chamber to the ram housing. Lift off the plenum chamber.
18. Remove the hose from the air bypass valve housing and plenum chamber air inlet pipe.
19. Unclip the cruise control actuator link. While holding the throttle fully open release the link from the countershaft assembly. Carefully return the lever assembly to the closed throttle position.
20. Release the tension on the inboard throttle return spring and slide the spring along the countershaft assembly to give access to the throttle shaft nut.

21. Bend back the the tabs of the lock washer.
22. While holding the throttle stop lever in the closed position, release the nut until it is free of the throttle valve shaft.
23. Release the tension on the outboard throttle return spring.
24. Unhook and remove the overtravel spring.

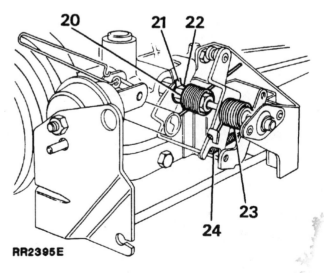

RR2395E

25. Remove the three bolts securing the throttle bracket to the plenum chamber and withdraw the bracket assembly.
26. Remove the tab washer and throttle stop lever from the throttle valve shaft.

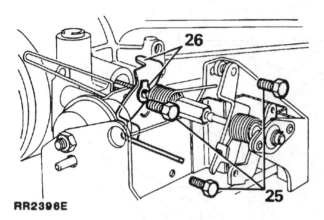

RR2396E

Inspect and overhaul throttle lever assembly

27. Remove the two retaining clips from either side of the spherical bearing.
28. Remove the countershaft assembly from the bearing.
29. If the spherical bush appears to be worn, dismantle as follows. Using a 4,7 mm (3/16 in) diameter drill, drill out the two pop rivets securing the spherical bearing to the throttle bracket assembly.
30. Split the bearing assembly and discard the bearing bush.

31. Pre-grease a new bush with Admax L3 or Energrease LS3 assemble the bush into the bearing retaining plates and pop-rivet the assembly to the throttle bracket with two 4.7 mm (3/16 in) diameter domed head rivets 9 mm (0.361 in)long.
32. Examine the bearing surface of the countershaft assembly. If worn fit a new assembly, otherwise wind the throttle return spring off the levers.

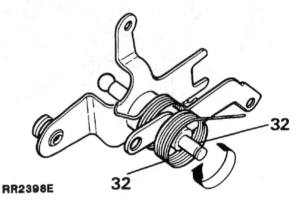

RR2398E

33. Wind a new spring onto the countershaft assembly noting that the small hooked end of the spring is wound on first.

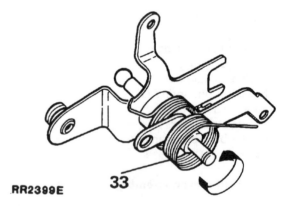

RR2399E

34. Pre-grease the shaft with Admax L3 or Energrease LS3 and fit the countershaft assembly to the spherical bearing and secure with the two clips.
35. Examine the throttle stop lever for wear, fit a new lever if necessary.

Inspect and overhaul throttle valve

36. Examine the throttle valve shaft for excessive wear between the bearing bushes in the plenum chamber and the shaft. A small amount of clearance is permissible. If excessive wear is evident fit new shaft and bushes as follows.
37. Remove the two split screws securing the throttle valve disc and withdraw the disc, taking care not to damage the shaft.

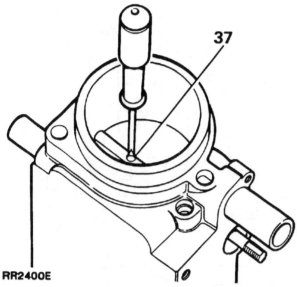

RR2400E

38. Remove the shaft and air seal from the plenum chamber.

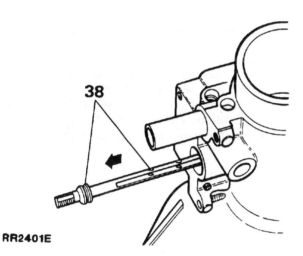

RR2401E

39. Using a suitable drift, drive out the bushes taking care not damage the bores in the plenum chamber.
40. Press in new bushes until they are flush with the throttle valve bore.

   CAUTION: Ensure that the bushes do not protrude into the bore as they will interfere with the movement of the throttle valve disc.

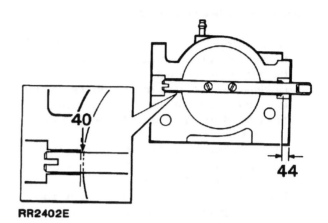

RR2402E

41. Fit the throttle valve shaft and disc, secure in position with the two split screws. Do not fully tighten the screws at this stage.
42. Rotate the throttle shaft 360° once or twice to centralise the disc in the bore. Tighten the two screws.
43. Rotate the shaft until the split end of the screws are accessible. Using the blade of a screw driver spread the split to secure the screws in the shaft.

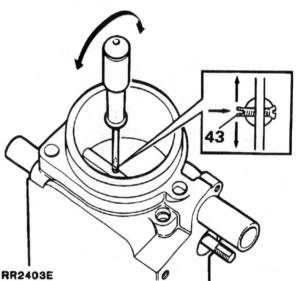

RR2403E

44. Pre-grease a new air seal with Admax L3 or Energrease LS3. Fit the seal pushing it down the shaft and into the counterbore until the seal is 6.0 mm (0.236 in) below the face of the plenum chamber.

Assemble throttle levers and bracket

45. Fit the stop lever to the throttle valve shaft followed by a new tab washer and secure with the interconnecting nut.
46. Holding the stop lever on its stop, tighten the interconnecting nut securely and bend over the tabs of the tab washer to lock the nut in position.
47. Fit the inboard throttle return spring noting that the small hooked end of the spring is nearest the plenum chamber.
48. Locate the hooked end of the inboard spring on the stop lever and wind up the straight end one full turn and anchor it in the appropriate slot.
49. Fit the countershaft to the interconnecting nut of the throttle valve shaft.
50. Fit the throttle bracket assembly and secure with the three retaining bolts.
51. Ensuring that the hooked end of the outboard spring is anchored by the lever, wind the spring up one full turn and locate the free end in its appropriate slot.
52. Fit the overtravel spring.
    Lightly grease the throttle return and overtravel springs with Admax L3 or Energrease LS3.

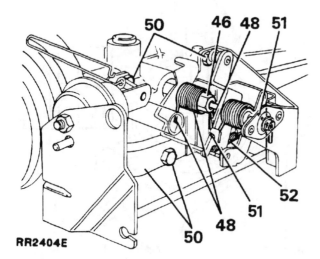

RR2404E

NOTE: If new throttle levers have been fitted the minimum throttle setting of the disc must be checked to ensure that it is 90° to the bore.

53. Using a depth vernier or depth micrometer from the mouth of the bore check the top and bottom of the valve disc. The disc must be within 0.5 mm (0.019 in) total indicator reading across the full diameter of the disc.
54. If the throttle disc is out of limits adjust the small set screw below the stop lever. Access to the screw is gained from the bottom of the plenum chamber neck adjacent to the throttle levers support bracket.

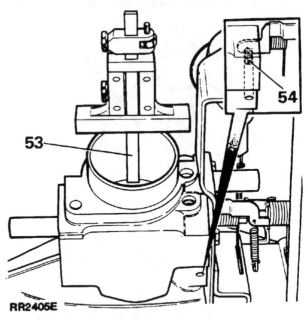

RR2405E

Refitting

55. Reconnect and adjust the cruise control actuator link. (See cruise control-actuator link setting)
56. Clean any previous sealant from the joint face of the plenum chamber and ram housing. Apply 'Hylomar' sealant to the faces and refit the plenum chamber. Tighten the bolts to the correct torque value-see section 06.
57. Reverse the remaining preparation instructions.

ELECTRONIC FUEL INJECTION-RELAYS

Incorporated in the fuel injection electrical system are two relays which are located beneath the front right hand seat. Access to the relays is gained through the opening at the bottom of the seat when the seat is in its fully forward position on the seat slides.

1. Fuel pump relay (mounted on a blue terminal block).

2. Main relay (mounted on a black terminal block).

3. Diagnostic plug.

4. Condenser fan timer unit.

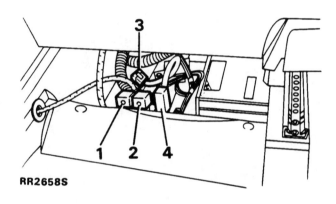

RR2658S

Remove and refit

Removing

1. Disconnect the battery negative terminal.
2. Pull the relay(s) from the terminal block(s).

Refitting

3. Reverse the removal procedure.

ELECTRONIC CONTROL UNIT (ECU)-14 CUX

NOTE: The ECU is not a serviceable item. In the event of a unit failure the ECU must be replaced.

Remove and refit

Removing

1. Remove the front and side seat base trim of the front right hand seat.
2. Adjust the seat to its most rearward position and raise the seat cushion height to allow access to the ECU fixings.
3. Disconnect the battery negative terminal.
4. Release the ECU plug retaining clip.
5. Maneouvre the front of the plug (in the direction of the bold arrow) and detach the other end of the plug from the retaining peg.
6. Release the two screws securing the ECU to the mounting bracket.
7. Withdraw the ECU from the spring clip and remove it from the vehicle.

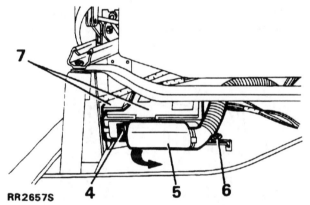

RR2657S

Refitting

8. Refit the ECU securely in the spring clip and fit the two screws.
9. Reconnect the ECU harness plug. Ensure that the plug is pushed firmly into its location and that the retaining clip secures the plug in position.
10. Reverse remaining removal procedure.

AIR CLEANER

Remove and Refit

Removing

1. Release the two clamps securing the air cleaner to the airflow sensor.
2. Release the two nuts and bolts securing the air cleaner to the left hand valance mounting bracket.
3. Detach the airflow sensor from the air cleaner, and lay carefully to one side.
4. Detach the air cleaner from the centre mounting bracket and withdraw from the engine compartment.
5. Remove the large 'O' ring from the outlet tube of the air cleaner, inspect for condition, fit a new 'O' ring if in poor condition.
6. Unclip the three catches securing the inlet tube to the air cleaner canister and remove the inlet tube.
7. Remove the nut and end plate securing the air cleaner element in position.
8. Withdraw the air cleaner element and discard.
9. Inspect the dump valve for condition and that it is clear of obstructions.

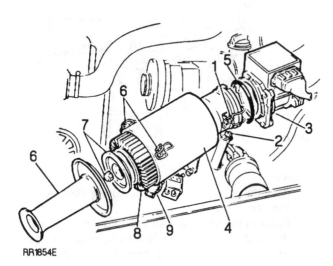

RR1854E

Refitting

10. Fit a new element and secure in position.
11. Refit the inlet tube to the air cleaner canister.
12. Refit the air cleaner to the mounting bracket and tighten the two nuts and bolts.
13. Clip the air flow sensor to the air cleaner.

AIR FLOW SENSOR

Remove and refit

Removing

NOTE: The air flow sensor is not a serviceable item. In the event of failure or damage the complete unit is to be replaced.

1. Disconnect the battery negative terminal.
2. Release the large hose clamp at the rear of the air flow meter and disconnect the hose from the sensor.
3. Disconnect the multi-plug.
4. Release the two clips securing the air flow sensor to the air cleaner case detach the sensor from the case and withdraw it from the engine compartment.

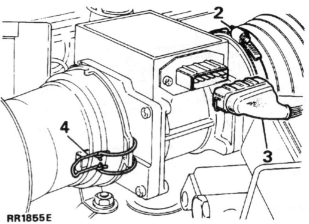

RR1855E

Refitting

5. Reverse the removal procedure ensuring that the multi-plug is firmly reconnected to the air flow sensor and that the hose clamp at the rear of the sensor is securely tightened, to prevent un-metered air entering the engine.

THROTTLE POTENTIOMETER

Remove and refit

Remove

1. Disconnect the battery negative terminal.
2. Disconnect the electrical three-pin plug.
3. Remove the two screws securing the switch to the plenum chamber and carefully pull the switch off the throttle valve shaft.

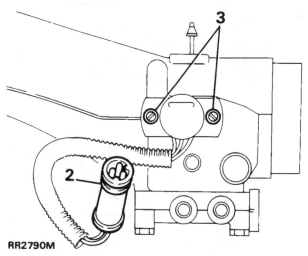

RR2790M

4. Remove the old gasket.

Refit

5. Fit a new gasket between the throttle switch and plenum chamber.
6. Align the switch and shaft flats; slide the switch on to the throttle shaft and secure the switch to the plenum chamber.

   CAUTION: The throttle mechanism must not be operated while the potentiometer is loosely fitted, otherwise damage may be caused to the potentiometer wiper track.

BY-PASS AIR VALVE (STEPPER MOTOR)

Remove and refit

Removing

1. Disconnect the battery negative terminal.
2. Remove the multi-plug from the unit.
3. Unscrew the valve from its location at the rear of the plenum chamber.
4. Remove the captive washer.

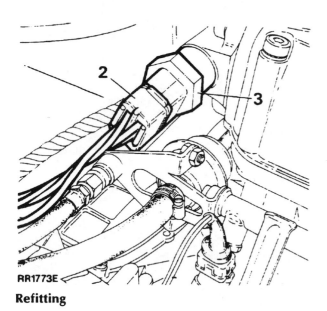

RR1773E

Refitting

5. Fit a **NEW** sealing washer.

   NOTE: If the same by-pass valve is being refitted clean any previous sealing compounds from the threads. Apply Loctite 241 to threads of the valve before reassembly.

6. Tighten the valve to the specified torque (see Torque values-section 06).
7. Reverse the remaining removal instructions.

SPEED TRANSDUCER - Electronic speedometer

Remove and refit

Removing

1. Place the vehicle on a hydraulic hoist and apply the parking brake.
2. Disconnect the battery negative terminal.
3. Raise the hoist and disconnect the speed transducer electrical plug.
4. Disconnect the speedometer cable from the transducer.
5. Do not remove the blanking cap.
6. Remove the single bolt securing the transducer to its mounting bracket and withdraw the unit from the vehicle.

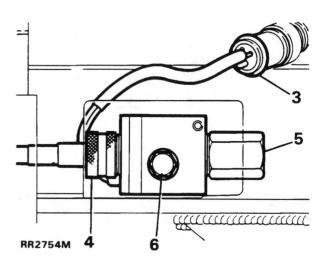

RR2754M

Refitting

7. Reverse the removal instructions.

INERTIA SWITCH

The inertia switch is located under the left hand front seat attached to the inner face of the rear front seat base. Access to the switch is gained through the opening at the rear of the seat base.

Remove and refit

Removing

1. Ensure the seat is in its fully forward position.
2. Disconnect the battery negative terminal.
3. Remove the two screws securing the switch to the cross member.
4. Withdraw the switch and disconnect the electrical multi-plug.
5. Remove the switch from the vehicle.

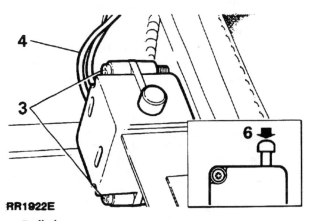

RR1922E

Refitting

6. Reverse the removal procedure ensuring that the multi-plug clips firmly into position, and that the plunger is reset (plunger is in its lowest position).

FUEL TEMPERATURE THERMISTOR (SENSOR)

Remove and refit

Removing

NOTE: No fuel leakage will occur when the thermistor is removed from the fuel rail therefore it is not necessary to depressurize the fuel system before removal.

1. Disconnect the battery negative terminal.
2. Remove the electrical multi - plug from the thermistor.
3. Release the thermistor from the fuel feed rail.

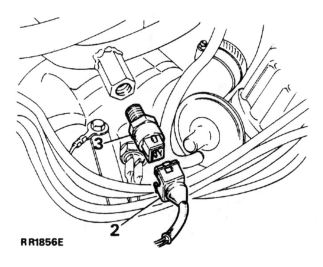

RR1856E

Refitting

4. Reverse the removal procedure, ensuring that the thermistor is tightened securely in the fuel rail.

COOLANT TEMPERATURE THERMISTOR (SENSOR)

Remove and refit

Removing

1. Remove the multi-plug from the thermistor.
2. Release the radiator bottom hose and partially drain the cooling system.
3. Refit the hose and tighten the clamp securely.
4. Remove the thermistor from the left hand front branch of the intake manifold.
5. Remove the copper washer.

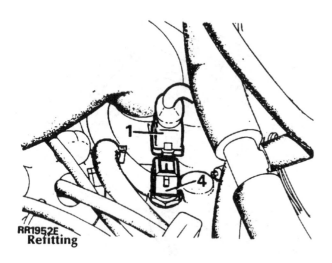

RR1952E

Refitting

6. Fit a NEW copper washer to the thermistor.
7. Fit the thermistor to the intake manifold and tighten securely.
8. Refill the cooling system.
9. Run the engine, check for water leaks around the coolant temperature thermistor.

RESETTING THROTTLE LEVERS

NOTE: The setting procedure outlined is applicable at minimum throttle condition only.

1. Ensure that the throttle valve is retained at its 90° vertical setting by holding down the stop lever and throttle/kick down lever denoted by the bold arrow while adjusting the throttle operating levers.

   NOTE: The stop lever seats on a factory-set adjustment screw which is located in the plenum chamber casting. The screw should not normally require adjustment. If new throttle bracketry and linkages are fitted it is advisable to check that the throttle valve is vertical before adjusting the screw.

2. Release the throttle operating lever securing screw and adjust the lever until contact is made with the top end of the slot in the throttle lever mounting bracket; retaining the lever in this position retighten the screw.
3. Lightly grease all throttle lever bearing surfaces and torsion spring with Admax 13 grease or a suitable equivalent.

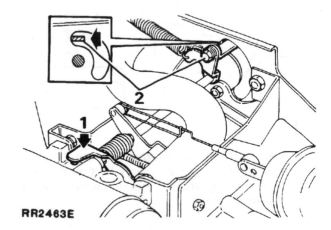

RR2463E

NOTE: Check the clearance between the cruise control actuator link and throttle lever (see Cruise Control Actuator Setting-Section 19, Page 47).

THROTTLE CABLE

Remove and refit

Removing

1. Remove the cotter pin and clevis pin securing the cable to the lever.
2. Carefully pry the throttle cable adjustment nut out of the linkage mounting bracket.
3. Withdraw the cable from the mounting bracket.

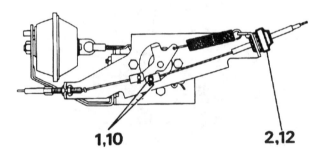

1,10   **2,12**

RR1954E

4. Release the outer cable from the retaining clips within the engine compartment.
5. Remove the lower dash panel from beneath the steering column.
6. Disconnect the cable from the throttle pedal and release the cable locknut.
7. Feed the cable through the bulkhead grommet and into the engine compartment.

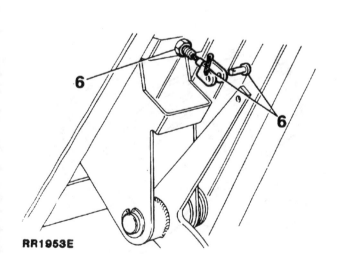

6

6

RR1953E

FIT NEW THROTTLE CABLE

8. Feed the new cable from the engine compartment through the bulkhead grommet.
9. Connect the cable to the throttle pedal.

10. Connect the cable to the throttle linkage, fit a new cotter pin and secure in position.
11. Clip the outer cable adjustment nut into the mounting bracket.
12. Adjust the outer cable to give 1.57 mm (0.062 in) free play in the throttle cable and check the throttle operation.

THROTTLE PEDAL

Remove and refit

Remove

1. Release the six screws securing the lower dash panel, lower the panel and disconnect the two electrical leads to the rheostat switch, detach the bulb check unit from the spring clip and remove the dash panel from the vehicle.
2. Remove the cotter pin and clevis pin securing the throttle cable to the throttle pedal.
3. Release the tension from the pedal return spring.
4. Remove the circlip from the pedal pivot pin.
5. Withdraw the pivot pin.

NOTE: It may be necessary to remove the steering column fixings enabling the column to be lowered to gain access to the pedal pivot pin circlip.

6. Withdraw the throttle pedal.

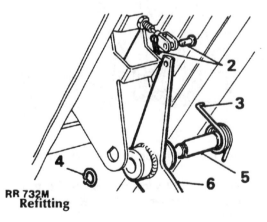

2

3

4

6   5

RR 732M

Refitting

7. Lightly grease the pivot pin and clevis pin before re-assembly.
8. Fit a **NEW** cotter pin to the clevis pin.
9. Reverse the remaining removal instructions.

PLENUM CHAMBER

Remove and refit

Removing

1. Disconnect the battery negative terminal.
2. Release the radiator bottom hose and partially drain the cooling system, reconnect the hose to the radiator.
3. Release the two large hose clamps from the neck of the plenum chamber and outlet bore of the airflow sensor and remove the hose from its location.
4. Release the clamps and remove the two coolant hoses from the bottom of the plenum chamber inlet neck. Identify each hose to aid re-assembly.
5. Remove the vacuum supply hose from the cruise control actuator.
6. Disconnect the actuating link at the cruise control actuator.
7. Remove the distributor vacuum hose, positive crankcase ventilation breather filter hose and servo hose.
8. Disconnect the throttle potentiometer multi-plug.

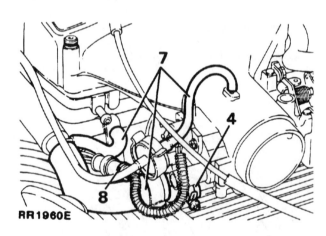

RR1960E

9. Disconnect the multi-plug from the air by-pass valve.
10. Disconnect the small vacuum hose at the rear of the plenum chamber, located below the air by-pass valve.
11. Remove the hose from the air by-pass valve to plenum chamber to enable the small return spring located below the throttle levers to be unhooked.

12. Release the two throttle return springs.
13. Remove the two bolts (with spring washers) securing the throttle cable and kick-down cable anchor bracket to the throttle lever support bracket, lay the assembly to one side.

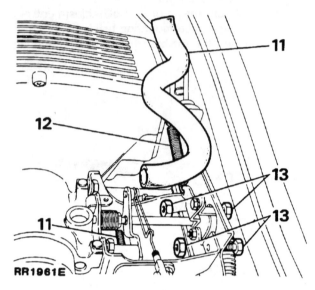

RR1961E

14. Remove the six socket head bolts (with plain washers) securing the plenum chamber to the ram housing.
15. Maneuver the plenum chamber and remove it from the ram housing.

NOTE: To prevent ingress of dirt into the ram tubes, place a protective cover over the ram tube openings.

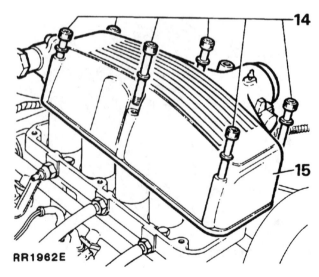

RR1962E

Refitting

16. Ensure that all mating faces are free from any previous sealing compounds.
17. Coat the mating faces of the plenum chamber and ram housing with 'Hylomar' sealant.
18. Refit the plenum chamber and tighten the six bolts to the specified torque (see torque values-section 06).
19. When refitting the small return spring, item 11 in the removal procedure, it must be noted that the 'hooked' open end of the spring **MUST** face the plenum chamber as shown in illustration RR2292E below.

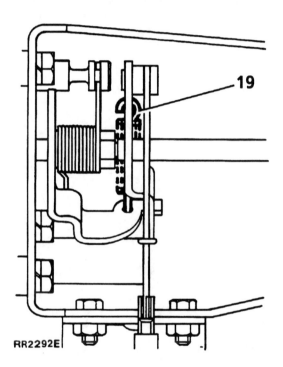

RR2292E

20. Reverse the remaining removal instructions.

    NOTE: Ensure that all hoses are connected securely to prevent un-metered air entering the engine.

RAM HOUSING

Remove and refit

Removing

1. Disconnect the battery negative terminal.
2. Remove the plenum chamber (see Plenum Chamber remove and refit).
3. Release the hoses from around the outer edges of the ram housing.
4. Remove the six through bolts (with plain washers) securing the ram housing to the intake manifold.

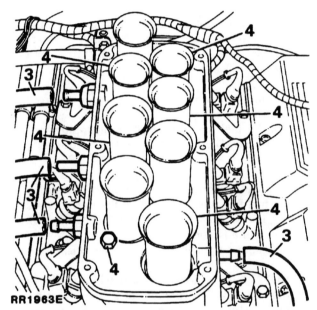

RR1963E

5. Lift the ram housing off the intake manifold and remove it from the engine compartment.
6. Place a protective cover over the top of the intake manifold inlet bores to prevent ingress of dirt.

Refitting

7. Ensure that all mating faces are clean and free from dirt and any previous sealing compounds.
8. Apply 'Hylomar' sealant to the intake manifold face before refitting the ram housing.
9. Fit the ram housing and retighten the bolts, working from the two centre bolts, diagonally towards the outer four bolts.
10. Tighten to the correct torque (See section 06-Torque values).

DEPRESSURIZING THE FUEL SYSTEM

WARNING: Under normal operating conditions the fuel injection system is pressurized by a high pressure fuel pump, operating at up to 2.4 to 2.6 kgf/cm² (34 to 37 p.s.i.). When the engine is stationary this pressure is maintained the system. To prevent pressurized fuel escaping and to avoid personal injury it is necessary to depressurize the fuel injection system before any service operations are carried out.

NOTE: If the vehicle has not been run there will still be a small amount of residual pressure in the fuel line. The depressurizing procedure must still be carried out before disconnecting the component within the fuel system.

WARNING: The spilling of fuel is unavoidable during this operation. Ensure that all necessary precautions are taken to prevent fire and explosion.

1. The fuel pump relay is located under the front right hand seat.
2. Pull the fuel pump relay off its multi-plug (see Electronic Fuel Injection Relays-Section 19, Page 28).
3. Start and run the engine.
4. When sufficient fuel has been used up causing the fuel line pressure to drop, the injectors will become inoperative, resulting in engine stall. Switch the ignition off.
5. Disconnect the battery negative terminal.

   NOTE: Fuel at low pressure will remain in the system. To remove this low pressure fuel, place an absorbent cloth around the fuel feed hose at the fuel rail and release the fuel feed hose compression nut.

Refitting

6. Refit the fuel feed hose.
7. Refit the fuel pump relay, reconnect the battery.
8. Crank the engine (engine will fire within approximately 6 to 8 seconds).

FUEL PRESSURE REGULATOR

Remove and refit

Removing

1. Depressurize the fuel system.
2. Disconnect the negative battery terminal.
3. Release the hose clamp securing the fuel return hose to the regulator and remove the hose.
4. Pull the vacuum hose from the rear of the regulator.
5. Remove the two nuts and bolts securing the regulator to the fuel rail, carefully ease the regulator fuel inlet pipe out of the fuel rail.
6. Withdraw the regulator from the engine compartment.

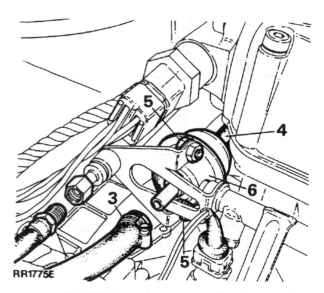

RR1775E

NOTE: If the original regulator is being refitted, fit a NEW 'O' ring to the fuel inlet pipe.

Refitting

7. Lightly coat the 'O' ring with silicon grease 300 before fitting the regulator to the fuel rail.
8. Reverse the removal procedure.
9. Reconnect the battery and pressurize the fuel system and check that there are no fuel leaks around the regulator connections.

FUEL RAIL-INJECTORS R/H AND L/H

Remove and refit

Removing

1. Depressurize the fuel system.
2. Disconnect the negative battery terminal.
3. Remove the plenum chamber. (See Plenum Chamber, remove and refit).
4. Remove the ram housing. (See Ram Housing remove and refit).

   NOTE: Place a cloth over the ram tube openings to prevent ingress of dirt into the engine.

5. Release the hose clamp and remove the fuel return hose from the pressure regulator.
6. Disconnect the multi-plug from the fuel temperature thermistor (sensor).
7. Disconnect the multi-plugs from the eight injectors.
8. Remove the five bolts securing the fuel rail support and heater pipe brackets to the intake manifold. Lay the heater pipes to one side.

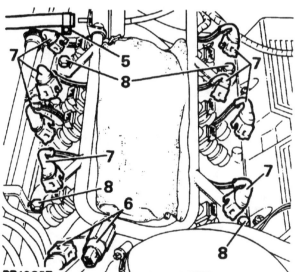

RR1965E

9. Remove the fuel rail, complete with injectors, from the intake manifold.
10. Remove the retaining clips securing the injectors to the fuel rail, ease the injectors from the rail.

11. If necessary, remove the two nuts and bolts securing the regulator to the fuel rail, and carefully pull the regulator away from the rail.

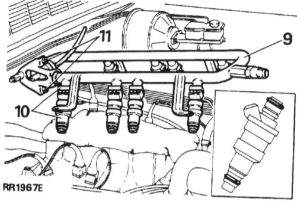

RR1967E

Refitting

12. Fit **NEW** 'O' rings, protective cap and supporting disc to the injectors, lightly coat the 'O' rings with silicon grease 300 and insert the injectors into the fuel rail, multi-plug connections facing outwards.
13. Refit the retaining clips.

    CAUTION: Care must be taken when refitting the fuel rail and injectors to the intake manifold to prevent damage occurring to the 'O' rings.

14. Fit a **NEW** 'O' ring to the pressure regulator lightly coat the 'O' ring with silicon grease 300 and secure the regulator to the fuel rail.
15. Fit the fuel rail and heater pipe assemblies to the intake manifold, secure the rail and pipes in position with the five bolts.
16. Reverse the remaining removal instructions.
17. Pressurize the fuel system and check for fuel leaks around the injectors and pressure regulator.

CRUISE CONTROL SYSTEM-HELLA GR66

-Option

CAUTION: DO NOT ENGAGE CRUISE CONTROL WHEN THE VEHICLE IS BEING USED IN LOW TRANSFER GEARS.

DESCRIPTION

The Cruise Control system consists of electro-mechanical devices, and comprises of the following components.

ELECTRONIC CONTROL UNIT (ECU)

The electronic control unit is located behind the lower dash panel attached to the underside of the instrument binnacle. The Microprocessor based E.C.U. evaluates the signals provided by the driver controls, brake pedal switch and the road speed transducer, and activates the vacuum pump in an appropriate manner. The E.C.U. also has a memory function for set speed storage.

DRIVER OPERATED SWITCHES

The main cruise control switch (1) is located in the auxiliary switch panel and activates the cruise control system. The steering wheel switches provide 'set/accelerate' and 'resume/decelerate' features. These switches provide the interface between driver and cruise control system.

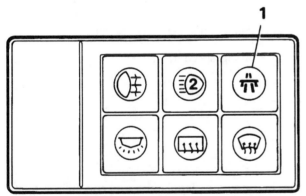

RR2680S

BRAKE PEDAL SWITCH

The Brake Pedal Switch is located under the lower dash attached to the brake pedal mounting bracket. The switch provides for fast disengagement of the cruise control system and rapid return of the throttle levers to the idle position when the brake pedal is applied.

ROAD SPEED TRANSDUCER

The Road Speed Transducer mounted on a bracket located on the left hand chassis side member adjacent to the rear engine mounting. The transducer provides road speed data to the E.C.U. The cruise control system cannot be engaged until the road speed exceeds 28 mph (45 km/h), the system will automatically disengage at a road speed of 26 mph (42 km/h).

VACUUM PUMP

The Vacuum Pump is located in the engine compartment attached to the left hand valance. The vacuum pump is energised when the main control panel is operated, and is actuated by the steering wheel and brake pedal switches. The pump provides a vacuum source to the cruise control actuator at the throttle levers. A control valve in the pump provides for steady increase of road speed or rapid purge of the system when the brake pedal is applied.

ACTUATOR

The Actuator is located in the engine compartment and is bolted to the throttle lever bracketry. The actuator provides the servo mechanism link between the cruise control system and throttle linkage and is operated by vacuum from the vacuum pump.

RELAY - NEUTRAL LOCKOUT

The neutral lockout relay is located under the rear of the right hand front seat. The relay will disengage the cruise control system if neutral, or park, is selected in the main gearbox, when the system is engaged.

FAULT DIAGNOSIS

If the system does not function the following checks must be carried out.

Fuse C5 - intact
Vacuum hoses - not split or disconnected
Actuator - diaphragm ruptured
Vacuum Pump - motor operational
Brake Switch - faulty or out of adjustment
Speed Transducer - faulty - check operation of unit
Electrical Leads - loose connections - faulty leads
Stop Lamp Bulbs - both bulbs faulty - replace: Fuse A5 intact.
Neutral relay - operational

PRELIMINARY CHECKS PRIOR TO TESTING

1. Ignition switch **"ON"**.
2. Fuse C-5 **"OK"**.
3. Cruise Control master switch **"ON"**.
4. Shift lever in 'D'.
5. Minimum 12.0V (Battery) available.

CRUISE CONTROL OPERATIONAL CHECKS

All system testing may be performed with a multi-meter and jumper wire at the ECU connector.

TEST PROCEDURE

Volt Meter Connections	Specified Result	Possible Problem if Results not as Specified
1. Terminal 1 and ground	Battery voltage	Fuse, wiring, master switch
2. Terminal 1 and 8	Battery voltage	Poor ground
3. Terminal 1 and 3	Battery voltage	Brake light ground, vent valve switch, wiring, brake light bulbs, neutral relay
4. Terminal 6 and 8 (press resume)	Battery voltage	Wiring, resume switch, spiral cassette
5. Terminal 2 and 8 (press set)	Battery voltage	Wiring, set switch, spiral cassette
6. Terminal 5 and 8 - Rotate left-rear wheel, right-rear wheel remains on ground	0-12V fluctuating 3 times per revolution	Wiring, speed transducer

VACUUM SYSTEM - VACUUM PUMP TESTS

Connect a jumper wire between: Terminal 4 and 8 & 7 and 8 - vacuum pump must run and fully retract activator diaphragm. Remove jumper from Terminal 4 (7 & 8 still connected). Pump stops, but diaphragm remains retracted. Remove jumper from Terminal 7 - diaphragm extends.

If results are not as specified check: vacuum hose/connections, vent valve/adjustment, wiring to vacuum pump, vacuum pump.

ROAD TEST

**CAUTION: DO NOT ENGAGE CRUISE CONTROL
WHEN THE VEHICLE IS BEING USED IN LOW
TRANSFER GEARS**

**WARNING: THE USE OF CRUISE CONTROL IS
NOT RECOMMENDED ON WINDING, SNOW
COVERED OR SLIPPERY ROADS OR IN HEAVY
TRAFFIC CONDITIONS WHERE A CONSTANT
SPEED CANNOT BE MAINTAINED.**

1. Start the engine and depress the main control
   switch to actuate the cruise control system.
   Accelerate to approximately 30 mph (50 km/h)
   and operate the 'set/acc' switch, immediately
   release the switch, remove the foot from the
   accelerator pedal, the vehicle should maintain
   the speed at which the 'set/acc' switch was
   operated.
2. Operate the 'set/acc' switch and hold at that
   position, the vehicle should accelerate
   smoothly until the switch is released. The
   vehicle should now maintain the new speed at
   which the 'set/acc' switch was released.
3. Apply the 'res/decel' switch while vehicle is in
   cruise control mode, the cruise control should
   disengage. Slow to approximately 35 mph (55
   km/h), operate the 'res/decel' switch,
   immediately release the switch and remove the
   foot from the accelerator, the vehicle should
   smoothly accelerate to the previously set
   speed. Increase the speed using the
   accelerator pedal and release the pedal, the
   vehicle should return to the previously set
   speed.
4. Operate the brake pedal, the cruise control
   system should **IMMEDIATELY** disengage
   returning the vehicle to driver control at the
   accelerator pedal. Operate 'res/decel' switch,
   vehicle should accelerate to previously
   memorised set speed without driver operation
   of the accelerator pedal.
5. Operate 'res/decel' switch and allow vehicle
   to decelerate to below 26 mph (42 km/h).
   Operate 'res/decel' switch, cruise control
   system should remain **DISENGAGED.**
6. Operate the 'set/acc' switch below 28 mph
   (45 km/h), the cruise control system should
   remain disengaged. Accelerate, using the
   accelerator pedal to above 28 mph (45 km/h),
   operate 'res/decel' switch, and remove the
   foot from the accelerator pedal, vehicle should
   smoothly adjust to the previously memorised
   speed.
7. Depress the main control switch in the
   auxiliary switch panel, cruise control system
   should **IMMEDIATELY** disengage and erase the
   previously set speed from the E.C.U. memory.

**STEERING WHEEL SWITCHES - Wiring
identification**

Illustration RR2258E shows the cruise control wiring
condition and colour coding from the steering
wheel switches to the cassette plug.

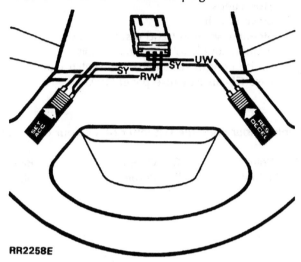

RR2258E

Cable colour code

RW -	Red/white
UW -	Blue/white
SY -	Grey/yellow

CRUISE CONTROL-Circuit diagram

1. Electronic cruise control unit
2. Vacuum pump
3. Brake switch/vent valve
4. Stop lamps
5. Brake switch
6. Steering wheel set and reset switches
7. Ignition supply to stop lamp circuit
8. Cruise control switch-auxiliary switch panel
9. Fuse C5-auxiliary fuse panel (10A)

10. 12V + supply to transducer
11. Speed transducer
12. Ignition load relay-item 1 main circuit diagram
13. Battery feed
14. Cruise control harness multi-plug identification
15. Ignition switch-item 8 main circuit diagram
16. Relay - neutral lockout
17. Start inhibit switch
18. Diode
--- Denotes exiting main cable circuit

Cable colour code-the last letter of a colour code denotes the tracer.

W	White	G	Green	U	Blue	R	Red	N	Brown
Y	Yellow	P	Purple	B	Black	S	Grey		

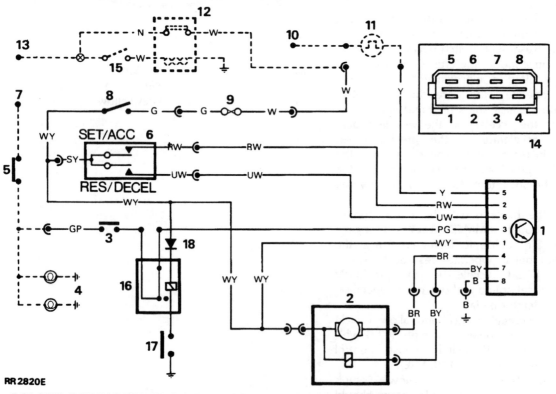

RR 2820E

COLOUR CODING/FUNCTION OF WIRING TO ECU MULTI-PLUG (ITEM 14)

TERMINAL NO.	COLOUR	FUNCTION
1.	White/Yellow	Main power from master switch
2.	Red/White	12V + from set switch (when pressed)
3.	Purple/Green	Ground via vent valve switch, brake light filaments, neutral relay
4.	Black/Red	To vacuum pump motor
5.	Yellow	To speed transducer
6.	Blue/White	12V + from resume switch (when pressed)
7.	Black/Yellow	To vacuum pump solenoid valve
8.	Black	ECU ground

BRAKE SWITCH-VENT VALVE

Remove and refit

Removing

1. Disconnect the battery negative terminal.
2. Remove the six screws securing the lower dash panel.
3. Lower the panel and disconnect the rheostat switch multi-plug and remove the warning lamp control unit from the retaining clip.
4. Withdraw the lower dash panel from the vehicle.
5. Disconnect the electrical multi-plug from the brake switch/vent valve.
6. Pull the hose from the switch.
7. Unscrew the adjusting nut and withdraw the switch.

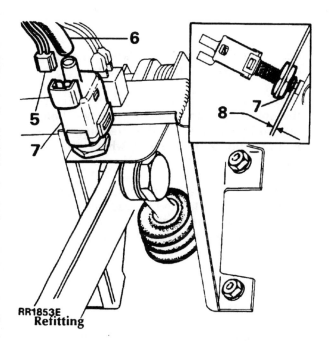

RR1853E
Refitting

8. Refit the switch and fit the adjusting nut. Adjust the valve to provide a clearance of 1.0 mm (0.039 in) between the valve body and inside shoulder of the contact button.
9. Fit the hose and multi-plug ensuring that they are secure.
10. Reverse the remaining removal instructions.

DRIVER OPERATED CRUISE CONTROL SWITCHES-STEERING WHEEL

NOTE: MAIN CONTROL SWITCH. The removal and refit of the main control switch and bulb replacement is included in the Electrical Section 86, of the main workshop manual, as part of the auxiliary switch panel removal.

Remove and refit

Removing

1. Disconnect the battery negative terminal.
2. Carefully prise the centre trim pad off the steering wheel.
3. Disconnect the electrical multi-plug located in the small opening below the steering wheel retaining nut.
4. Carefully prise the switch(es) out of the steering wheel spoke(s).
5. Release the small switch button from the opening within the spoke(s).
6. Carefully pull the switch and electrical leads through the spoke until access is gained to the electrical connections beneath the switch.
7. Disconnect the electrical leads from the switch and withdraw the switch(es).

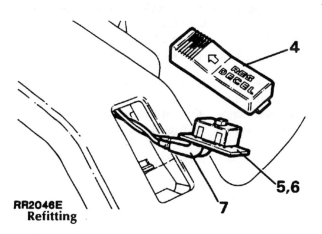

RR2046E
Refitting

8. Reverse the removal procedure ensuring that the electrical leads are fitted securely.

SPIRAL CASSETTE

The spiral cassette is located below the steering wheel encased in the steering column shroud. Access to the unit is gained by removing the aforementioned items.

NOTE: To enable the steering wheel to be refitted in its correct radial position, ensure the front road wheels are in the straight ahead position.

Remove and refit

Removing

Service Tools:
18G 1014 Steering wheel remover
18G 1014-2 Adaptor pins

1. Disconnect the battery negative terminal.
2. Remove the steering wheel centre trim panel.
3. Disconnect the electrical multi-plug located in the small opening in the centre of the steering wheel.
4. Remove the steering wheel securing nut and serrated washer, using service tool 18G 1014 and adaptor pins, withdraw the steering wheel.

   CAUTION: Apply adhesive tape to the upper and lower halves of the cassette to prevent the upper half of the spiral cassette rotating after the steering wheel is removed. Failure to do this will result in damage to the flexible tape inside the cassette.

5. Remove the six lower fixings securing the steering column shroud.
6. Release either the left hand or right hand fixing securing the top of the shroud.

7. Carefully ease the two halves of the shroud apart until access is gained to the electrical multi-plug on the bottom half of the cassette and disconnect the multi-plug.
8. Withdraw the cassette from the steering column.

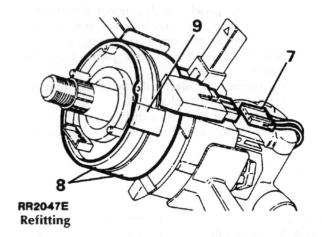

RR2047E
Refitting

9. Remove the adhesive tape retaining the upper and lower halves of the spiral cassette.

   NOTE: Ensure that the two driving pegs on the spiral cassette locate in the two holes on the underside of the steering wheel before refitting the steering wheel securing nut.

10. Reverse the removal instructions, ensuring that all electrical leads located beneath the steering column shroud are arranged so they do not become trapped between the shroud mating faces.

ACTUATOR

NOTE: The actuator itself is not a serviceable item, in the event of failure or damage fit a new unit.

Remove and refit

Removing

1. Disconnect the battery negative terminal.
2. Pull the short rubber elbow from the actuator.
3. Remove the nut securing the actuator to the throttle bracketry.
4. Detach the actuator from the bracket and maneuver the actuator operating link off the throttle lever.
5. Withdraw the actuator from the engine compartment.

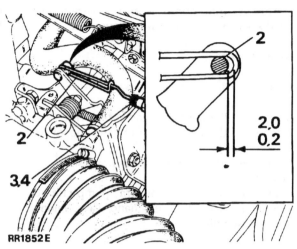

RR1852E

Adjust the Link

3. Remove the link from the actuator.
4. Rotate the socket joint on the actuator link clockwise or counter-clockwise to decrease or increase the operating length of the link.
5. Refit the link to the actuator and recheck the clearance between the link and lever.
6. With the trottle fully open, check that a gap of at least 3mm (1/8in) exists between the side of the actuator link ("A" in illustration) and the side of the small spring which connects the inner throttle lever to the outer throttle lever ("B" in illustration). Realign the actuator link by bending to achieve the correct gap if it is less than 3mm (1/8in). Recheck the clearance at closed throttle/open throttle and check that the actuator link slides smoothly in the groove of the throttle lever.

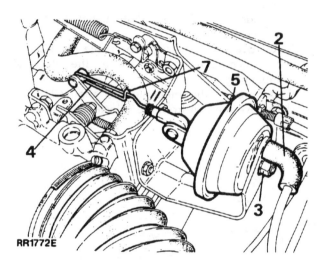

RR1772E

Refitting

6. Inspect the rubber diaphragm for condition. Fit a new Actuator assembly if the diaphragm is in poor condition.
7. Reverse the removal procedure, ensuring that the hook is fitted uppermost

ACTUATOR LINK-SETTING

NOTE: The setting procedure outlined is at minimum throttle condition only.

1. Ensure ignition is switched 'OFF'.
2. Check the clearance between the inside edge of the actuator link and recessed diameter of the throttle lever. Clearance should be 0.2 to 2.0 mm (0.008 to 0.080 in).

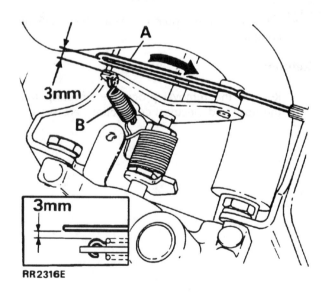

RR2316E

VACUUM PUMP

**NOTE: The vacuum pump is not a serviceable
item, in the event of failure fit a new unit.**

Remove and refit

Removing

1. Disconnect the battery negative terminal.
2. Disconnect the multi-plug from the top of the
   vacuum pump.
3. Disconnect the vacuum feed hose from the
   vacuum pump.
4. Withdraw the three vacuum pump rubber
   mountings from the left hand valance/inner
   fender assembly.

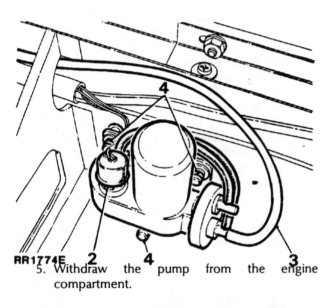

RR1774E

5. Withdraw the pump from the engine
   compartment.

Refitting

6. Reverse the removal procedure ensuring that
   the hose and electrical connections are secure.

ELECTRONIC CONTROL UNIT (ECU)
- CRUISE CONTROL

The cruise control electronic control unit (ECU) is
located behind the lower dash panel below the
steering column, and is attached to the underside
of the instrument binnacle, access to the ECU is
gained by removing the lower dash panel.

Remove and refit

Removing

1. Disconnect the battery negative terminal.
2. Remove the six screws retaining the lower
   dash panel.
3. Lower the panel and disconnect the electrical
   multi-plug from the rheostat switch and detach
   the warning lamp control unit from the
   retaining clip.
4. Withdraw the lower dash panel from the
   vehicle.
5. Remove the two fixings to enable the ECU to
   be lowered to give access to the electrical
   multi-plug.
6. Disconnect the multi-plug to the ECU, and
   remove the unit from the vehicle.

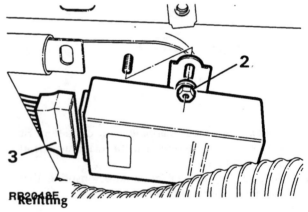

RR2048E

Refitting

7. Reverse the removal instructions ensuring that
   the electrical multi-plug is securely
   reconnected.

NEUTRAL LOCKOUT RELAY - CRUISE CONTROL

The neutral lockout relay is located under the rear of the front right hand seat Access to the unit is gained through the opening at the bottom of the seat when the seat is in its fully forward position.

Remove and refit

Removing

1. Ensure the seat is adjusted fully forward.
2. Disconnect the battery negative terminal.
3. Pull the relay from the terminal block.

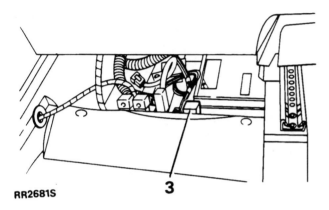

RR2681S   **3**

Refitting

4. Reverse the removal instructions.

COOLING SYSTEM

The 3.9 litre engine has a 'partial flow' type cooling system. A new radiator incorporates oil coolers in both end tanks - left hand side, automatic transmission oil cooler - right hand side, engine oil cooler.

A supplementary transmission oil cooler is still fitted in front of the radiator and condenser fans.

The automatic transmission oil high temperature warning light sensor is now fitted under the bonnet adjacent to the radiator end tank.

Note that manual gearboxes have oil cooling using the the cooler mounted in front of the radiator and condenser fans.

COOLANT

Drain and refill

Draining

WARNING: Do not remove the expansion tank filler cap when the engine is hot, because the cooling system is pressurised and personal scalding could result.

NOTE: The expansion tank is fitted with a screwed filler cap which incorporates a low coolant sensing unit.

1. Remove the expansion tank filler cap by slowly turning it anti-clockwise, pause to allow pressure to escape, continue turning it in the same direction and lift off.

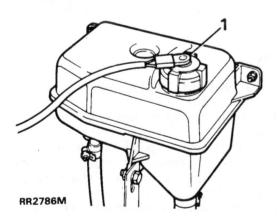

RR2786M

2. Remove the radiator filler plug and 'O' ring to assist drainage.

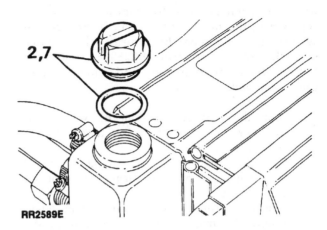

RR2589E

3. Disconnect the bottom hose at its junction with the radiator and allow the coolant to drain into a suitable container. Ensure that the container is clean if the coolant solution is to be re-used. Reconnect the bottom hose after draining and re-tighten the hose clamp.

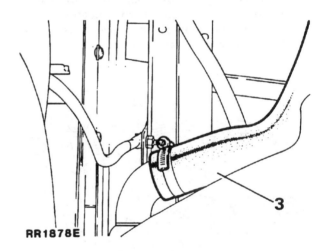

RR1878E

4. Remove the engine drain plugs, one each side of the cylinder block, beneath the exhaust manifolds. Allow the coolant to drain, refit and tighten the plugs.

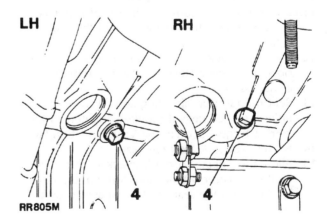

LH   RH

RR805M

NOTE: It is not possible to drain all the coolant retained in the heater system. Flush through the system, after draining, by pouring clean water into the fill tower, (see RR2659E), with the bottom hose disconnected and engine drain plugs removed.

5. Pour the correct solution of water and anti-freeze into the expansion tank until the radiator is full.
6. Start the engine and run it until normal operating temperature is attained, topping up as necessary.
7. Refit the radiator filler plug and 'O' ring, fitting a new 'O' ring if required. Tighten to the correct torque, see Torque Values, section 06.
8. Fit the expansion tank filler cap.
9. Allow the engine to cool, check coolant level and top up the expansion tank until the level reaches the seam of the expansion tank.

CAUTION: The following fill procedure MUST be followed if the heater pipes mounted on top of the rocker cover have been removed for any reason.

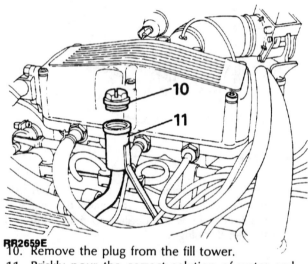

RR2659E

10. Remove the plug from the fill tower.
11. Briskly pour the correct solution of water and anti-freeze into the fill tower until the radiator is full.
12. Start the engine and run it until normal operating temperature is attained, topping up as necessary.
13. Refit the radiator filler plug and fill tower plug, fitting new 'O' rings if required. Tighten to the correct torque, See Torque Values, section 06.
14. Fit the expansion tank filler cap.
15. Allow the engine to cool, check coolant level in the expansion tank and top up until the level reaches the seam of the expansion tank.

RADIATOR/OIL COOLERS

Remove and refit

Removing

1. Drain the cooling system.
2. Remove the fan blade assembly.
3. Remove the fan cowl.
4. Disconnect the radiator top hoses.
5. Disconnect the four transmission (automatic only) and engine oil cooler connections to the radiator end tanks. Note that oil spillage will occur when connections are loosened. Blank off exposed oil connections.
6. Disconnect the transmission oil temperature sensor plug.
7. Remove the radiator securing brackets from each side.

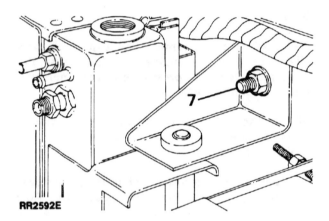

RR2592E

8. Remove the radiator unit by lifting from its location. Check the condition of the rubber mounting pads.

Refitting

9. Check that the radiator sealing strips are securely located.
10. Transfer the oil cooler adaptors if fitting a new radiator.
11. Reverse the removal procedure, ensuring that oil cooler connections are tightened to the specified torque values before fitting the fan blades and cowl.
11. Clean any coolant/oil spillage from the vehicle.
12. Check all connections for coolant/oil leaks.

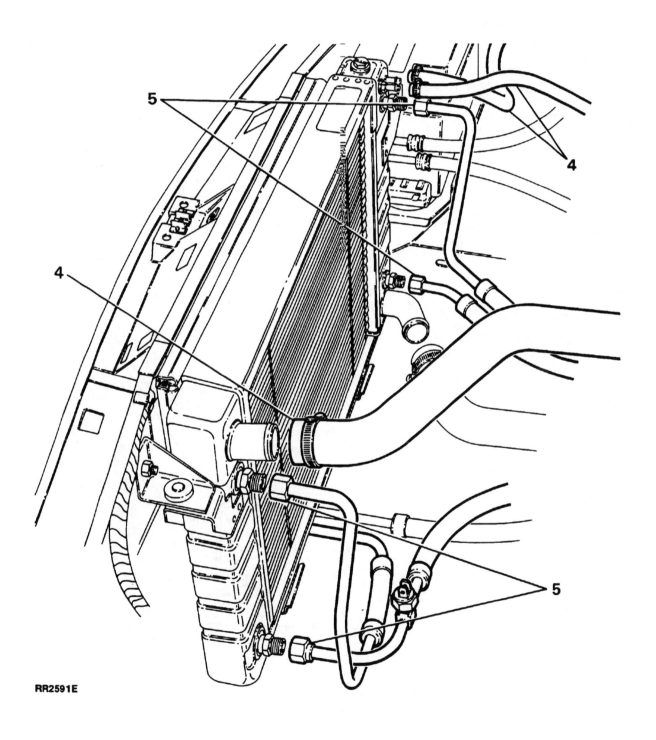

RR2591E

EXPANSION TANK

Remove and refit

Removing

WARNING: Do not remove the expansion tank filler cap when the engine is hot, because the cooling system is pressurised and personal scalding could result.

1. Remove the expansion tank filler cap by first turning it slowly anit-clockwise, pause to allow pressure to escape, continue turning it in the same direction and lift off.
2. Disconnect the two hoses from the bottom of the expansion tank, allowing the coolant to drain into a suitable container.
3. Remove three fixings bolts and remove the expansion tank from its mountings.

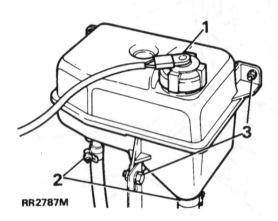

RR2787M

Refitting

4. Reverse removal instructions.
5. Replenish the cooling system.
6. Check for leaks around all hose connections.

COOLANT-DIESEL MODELS

Drain and refill

Draining

WARNING: Do not remove the expansion tank filler cap when the engine is hot. The cooling system is pressurised and personal scalding could result.

Note: The expansion tank is fitted with a screwed filler cap which incorporates a low coolant sensing unit.

1. Remove the expansion tank filler cap by slowly turning it anti-clockwise, pause to allow pressure to escape, continue turning and lift off.
2. Disconnect the bottom hose at its junction with the radiator and allow the coolant to drain into a suitable container. Ensure that the container is clean if the coolant solution is to be re-used. Reconnect the bottom hose after draining and tighten the hose clamp.

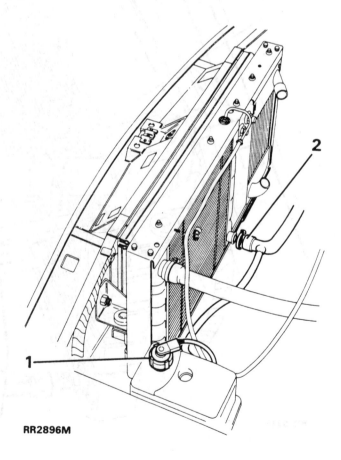

RR2896M

3.   Pour the correct solution of water and anti-freeze into the expansion tank upto the top of the level indicator post visible in the tank.

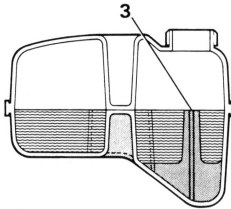

RR2897M

4.   Start the engine and run it until normal operating temperature is attained, topping up as necessary.
5.   Fit the expansion tank filler cap.
6.   Allow the engine to cool, check coolant level and top up the expansion tank to the top of the level indicator post, approximately half way up the expansion tank.

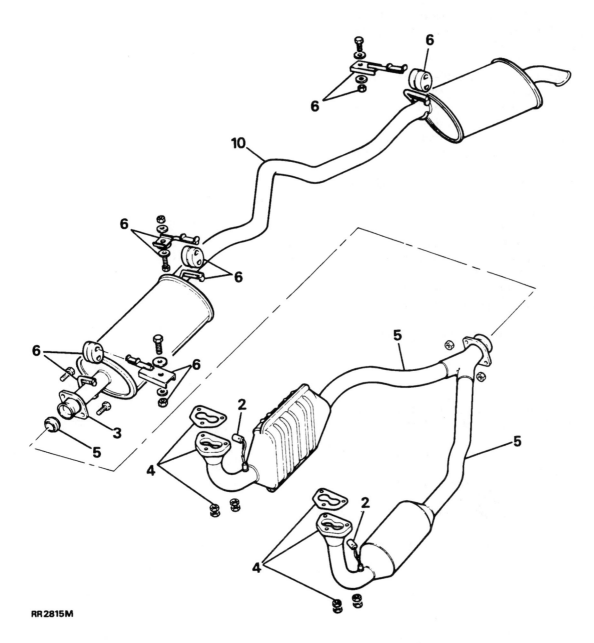

RR2815M

EXHAUST SYSTEM COMPLETE

NOTE: Ensure that no exhaust leaks are evident in either a new or old exhaust system, as this will affect vehicle performance.

WARNING: To prevent personal injury occurring from a hot exhaust system, DO NOT attempt to disconnect any of the components until ample time has elapsed to allow the exhaust system to cool.

Remove and refit

Removing

1. Raise the vehicle on a suitable ramp, apply the parking brake.
2. **Catalyst vehicles only:** Disconnect the two lambda sensor wiring connectors.
3. Remove the two bolts securing the rear exhaust assembly to the front exhaust assembly.
4. Remove the nuts and release the front downpipes fromt the manifolds. Discard the gaskets.

5. Lower the front exhaust assembly, retrieving the doughnut from the joint.

   NOTE: The assistance of a second mechanic is required for removing and refitting the rear exhaust assembly.

6. Remove the bolts securing the three hanger brackets to the chassis. Lower the exhaust assembly onto the rear axle. Detach the rubbers from the hanging brackets.
7. Place extended axle stands underneath the chassis, in front of the chassis mounted rear towing brackets.
8. Lower the hoist until the vehicle weight is supported securely on the stands.
9. Lower the hoist until the rear shock absorbers are almost fully extended.
10. Move the rear exhaust to a diagonal position with the centre silencer to the right of the vehicle.
11. Facing the rear of the vehicle, twist the assembly counter-clockwise until it clears the rear axle.
12. Remove the rear exhaust assembly from the vehicle.

Refitting

13. Position the rear exhaust assembly over the rear axle in a diagonal position, as for removing.
14. Twist the assembly clockwise until it is in the mounting position.
15. Reverse the removing instructions 1. to 9. using new manifold gaskets and applying exhaust sealer to the system joint.
16. Examine the system for leaks and ensure that the system does not foul any underbody components. Rectify as necessary.

REAR HUB ASSEMBLY ON VEHICLES FITTED WITH ANTI-LOCK BRAKES (ABS)

REMOVE, OVERHAUL AND REFIT

Service tools:
Hub oil seal replacer LST 137.
Drift 18G 134.
Dial gauge bracket RO 530106.

Remove

1. Slacken the rear wheel nuts, jack up the vehicle, lower onto axle stands and remove the road wheel.
2. Release the brake pipe from the axle, casing clips and remove the brake caliper retaining bolts then secure the assembly to one side.

    WARNING: Take care not to kink the brake pipe.

3. Lever off the dust cap.
4. Remove the circlip from the rear axle shaft.

KEY TO REAR HUB COMPONENTS

1. Dust cap.
2. Circlip.
3. Sensor ring retaining nut.
4. Drive member.
5. Drive member joint washer.
6. Drive member retaining bolt (five off).
7. Lock nut.
8. Lock washer.
9. Hub adjusting nut.
10. Keyed washer.
11. Outer bearing.
12. Hub.
13. Inner bearing.
14. Grease seal.
15. Brake disc.
16. Disc retaining bolt (five off).
17. Sensor ring.

5. Remove the five bolts and withdraw the driving member and joint washer.
6. Bend back the lock washer tab.
7. Remove the locknut and tab washer.
8. Remove the hub adjusting nut.
9. Remove the keyed washer.
10. Withdraw the hub and brake disc assembly complete with bearings.
11. Remove the outer bearing.
12. Remove the five nyloc nuts and withdraw the sensor ring.
13. Mark, for reassembly, the relationship between the hub and brake disc, if original hub is to be refitted.
14. Remove the five bolts and separate the hub from the brake disc.

    WARNING: A maximum of two road wheel retaining studs can be renewed. Should more studs be unserviceable a new hub with studs must be obtained.

15. Drift out the grease seal and inner bearing from the hub and discard the seal.
16. Drift out the inner and outer bearing tracks.

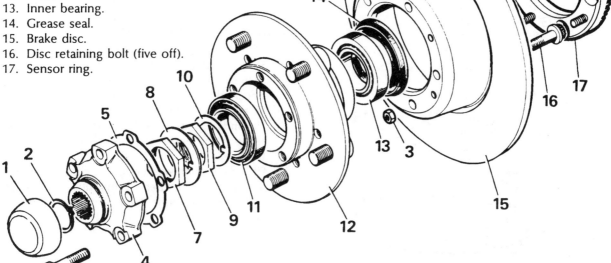

RR2766M

1

Refit

17. Clean and degrease the hub and drift in the inner and outer bearing tracks.

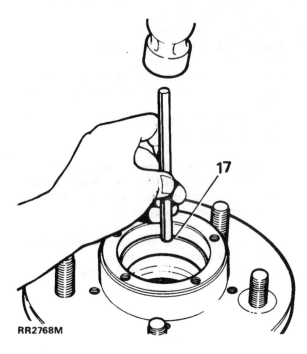

RR2768M

18. Pack the hub inner bearing with a recommended grease and fit to the hub.
19. With the lip side leading fit a new seal to the hub using special tool LST 137 seal replacer and drift 18G 134. Drive in the seal so that it is flush with the rear face of the hub. Apply grease between the seal lips.

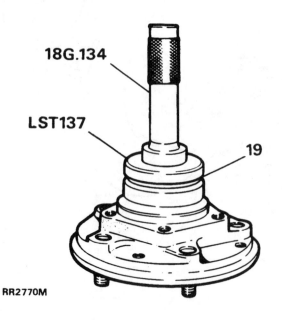

18G.134

LST137

19

RR2770M

20. Assemble the brake disc to the hub, lining up to the marks made during dismantling. Applying Loctite 270, fit and tighten the five retaining bolts to the correct torque.
21. If necessary renew any sensor ring studs applying Loctite 270 where the stud screws into the sensor ring. Fit the sensor ring using new nyloc nuts, ensuring it is correctly fitted to avoid tooth run out.
22. Grease as in instruction 18 and fit the outer bearing to the hub.
23. Clean the stub axle and rear axle shaft and retract the ABS sensor slightly from sensor sleeve.
24. Fit the hub assembly to the stub axle.
25. Fit the keyed washer.
26. Fit the hub adjusting nut and tighten by hand whilst rotating the hub until all end-play is taken up.
27. Mount a dial gauge using bracket RO 530106 and rest the stylus in a loaded condition on the adjusting nut.

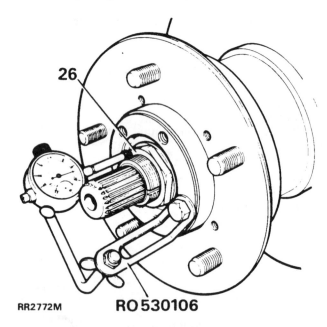

26

RR2772M   **RO 530106**

28. Slacken off the adjusting nut until a end-play of 0,013 to 0,05 mm (0.0005 to 0.002 in) is obtained.
29. Fit a new keyed lock tab washer.
30. Fit and tighten the hub adjusting nut and recheck the end-play before bending the lock tab over.
31. Fit a new joint washer to the driving member and fit the member to the hub and secure with the five bolts tightening evenly to the correct torque.

32. Fit the circlip to the rear axle shaft, ensuring that it locates in the groove.
33. Fit the dust cap.
34. Fit the brake caliper and tighten the two bolts to the correct torque. Secure the brake pipes to the axle casing.
35. Set the ABS brake sensor. Push the sensor through the bush until it touches the sensor ring. The sensor sets to its correct position when the hub is rotated.
36. Fit the road wheel, remove the axle stands and finally tighten the road wheel nuts.
37. Operate the footbrake several times to locate the brake pads before taking the vehicle on the road.

REAR STUB AXLE ON VEHICLES FITTED WITH ABS

Special tools:
Oil seal replacer LST 138.
Drift 18G 134.

KEY TO STUB AXLE COMPONENTS

1. Rear axle shaft.
2. Stub axle to axle casing bolt.
3. Mudshield.
4. Stub axle.
5. Stub axle joint washer.
6. Axle case.
7. Sensor bush sleeve.

REMOVE, OVERHAUL AND REFIT

Remove rear stub axle, axle shaft

1. Remove the hub complete as described in the operation to overhaul the hub assembly instructions 1 to 10.
2. Remove the six bolts retaining the stub axle to the axle casing.
3. Remove the mud shield.
4. Remove the stub axle and joint washer.
5. Pull-out the rear axle shaft from the axle casing.

Refit

6. Using a new joint washer fit, the stub axle and mudshield with the retaining bolts, to the axle casing tightening evenly to the correct torque.
7. Carefully fit the rear axle shaft to avoid damaging the stub axle seal.
8. Refit the hub assembly complete as described in the operation to refit the hub assembly instructions 23 to 37.

Renew rear stub axle oil seal

1. Remove and discard the oil seal. Lubricate the seal and lip with EP90 oil and using special tool LST 138 fit a new oil seal lipside trailing so that the seal is flush with the rear face of the stub axle.

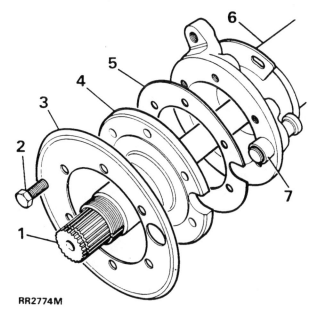

RR2774M

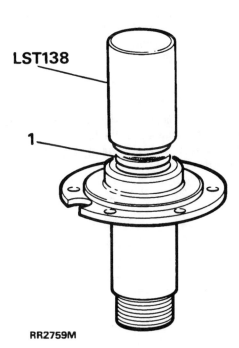

LST138

RR2759M

REAR DISCS ON VEHICLES FITTED WITH ABS

REMOVE, REFIT AND RECLAIM

Removing

1. Remove the rear hub assembly.
2. Remove the five nyloc nuts.
3. Remove the sensor ring.
4. Remove the five hub to disc retaining bolts.
5. Tap off the disc from the hub.

Refitting

6. Locate the disc onto the hub.
7. Apply loctite 270 and fit the hub to disc retaining bolts. Tighten to the correct torque.
8. Using new nyloc nuts fit the sensor ring.

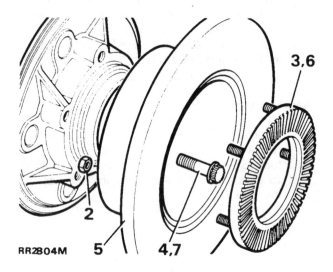

RR2804M

9. Using a dial indicator, check the total disc runout, this must not exceed 0,15 mm (0.006 in). If necessary reposition the disc.
10. Fit the hub assembly.

Disc Reclamation

Check the disc thickness. This dimension may be reduced to a minimum thickness of 12 mm (0.460 in). Equal amounts must be machined off both sides of the disc.

**FRONT HUB ASSEMBLY ON VEHICLES FITTED
WITH ANTI-LOCK BRAKES (ABS)**

Service tools:
Hub oil seal replacer LST 137.
Drift 18G 134.
Dial gauge bracket RO 530106.

REMOVE, OVERHAUL AND REFIT

Remove

1. Slacken the front wheel nuts, jack up the vehicle and lower onto axle stands and remove the road wheel.
2. Remove the brake caliper. See BRAKES section.
3. Lever off the dust cap.
4. Remove the circlip and drive shaft shim from the drive shaft.
5. Remove the five bolts and withdraw the driving member and joint washer.

KEY TO HUB ASSEMBLY

1. Dust cap.
2. Drive shaft circlip.
3. Drive shaft shim.
4. Drive member.
5. Drive member joint washer.
6. Drive member retaining bolt (five off)
7. Lock nut.
8. Lock washer.
9. Hub adjusting nut.
10. Keyed washer.
11. Outer bearing.
12. Hub.
13. Inner bearing.
14. Grease seal.
15. Brake disc (vented).
16. Disc retaining bolt (five off).

6. Bend back the lock washer tab.
7. Remove the locknut and tab washer.
8. Remove the hub adjusting nut.
9. Remove the keyed washer.
10. Withdraw the hub and brake disc assembly complete with bearings.
11. Remove the outer bearing.
12. Mark, for reassembly, the relationship between the hub and brake disc, if original hub is to be refitted.
13. Remove the five bolts and separate the hub from the brake disc.

WARNING: A maximum of two road wheel retaining studs can be renewed. Should more studs be unserviceable a new hub with studs must be obtained.

14. Drift out the grease seal and inner bearing from the hub and discard the seal.
15. Drift out the inner and outer bearing tracks.

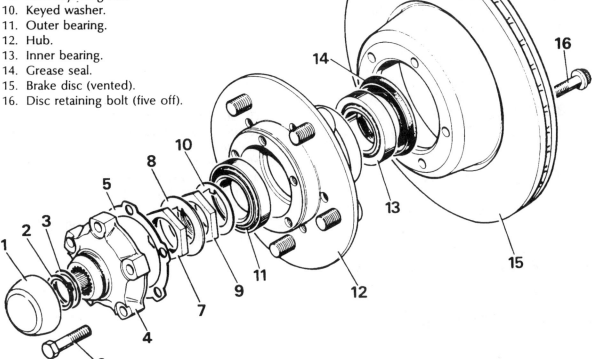

RR2747M

1

Refit

16. Clean and degrease the hub and drift in the inner and outer bearing tracks.

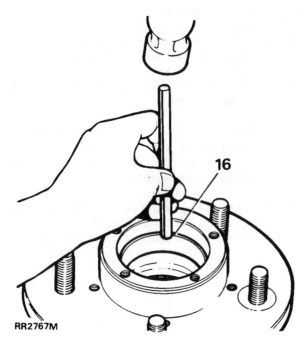

RR2767M

17. Pack the hub inner bearing with a recommended grease and fit to the hub.
18. With the lip side leading fit a new seal to the hub using special tool LST 137 seal replacer and drift 18G 134. Drive in the seal so that it is flush with the rear face of the hub. Apply grease between the seal lips.

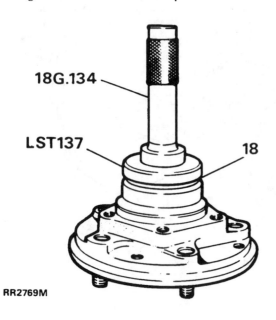

RR2769M

19. Assemble the brake disc to the hub, lining up to the marks made during dismantling. Applying Loctite 270, fit and tighten the five retaining bolts to the correct torque.
20. Grease as in instruction 17 and fit the outer bearing to the hub.
21. Clean the stub axle and drive shaft and fit the hub assembly to the axle.
22. Fit the keyed washer.
23. Fit the hub adjusting nut and tighten by hand whilst rotating the hub until all end-play is taken up.
24. Mount a dial gauge using bracket RO 530106 and rest the stylus in a loaded condition on the adjusting nut.

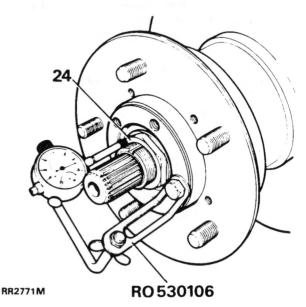

RR2771M   **RO 530106**

25. Slacken off the adjusting nut until a hub end-play of 0,013 to 0,05 mm (0.0005 to 0.002 in) is obtained.
26. Fit a new keyed lock tab washer.
27. Fit and tighten the hub adjusting nut and recheck the end-play before bending the lock tab over.
28. Fit a new joint washer to the driving member and fit the member to the hub and secure with the five bolts tightening evenly to the correct torque.
29. Fit the original drive shaft shim and secure with a circlip.

30. To check the drive shaft end-play mount a dial gauge using bracket RO 530106 and rest the stylus in a loaded condition on the end of the drive shaft.

31. Fit a suitable bolt to the threaded end of the drive shaft and using a pair of pliers move the drive shaft back and forth noting the dial gauge reading. The end-play should be between 0,08 to 0,25 mm (0.003 to 0.010 in).

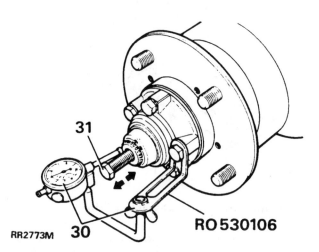

RR2773M **30**   **RO 530106**

32. If the end-play requires adjustment, remove the circlip, measure the shim thickness and fit an appropriate shim to give the required end-play.

33. Remove the bolt from the drive shaft, fit the circlip and dust cap.

34. Fit the brake caliper, see BRAKES section.

35. Bleed the brake system, see ABS brake bleed procedure.

36. Fit the road wheel, remove the axle stands and finally tighten the road wheel nuts.

37. Operate the footbrake several times to locate the brake pads before taking the vehicle on the road.

FRONT DISCS ON VEHICLES FITTED WITH ABS

REMOVE, REFIT AND RECLAIM

Removing

1. Remove the front hub assembly.
2. Remove the five hub to disc retaining bolts.
3. Tap off the disc from the hub.

Refitting

4. Locate the disc on to the hub.
5. Apply Loctite 270 and fit the hub to disc retaining bolts. Tighten to the correct torque.

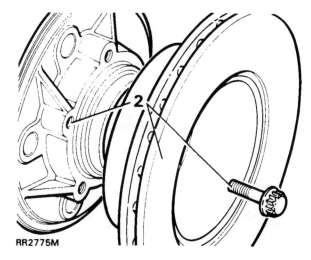

RR2775M

6. Using a dial indicator, check the total disc runout, this must not exceed 0,15 mm (0.006 in). If necessary reposition the disc.
7. Fit the hub assembly.

Disc reclamation

Check the vented disc thickness. This dimension may be reduced to a minimum thickness of 22 mm (0.866 in).
Material may be machined off the disc faces. On completion equal thicknesses of disc must remain each side of the vent.

OVERHAUL FRONT STUB AXLE, CONSTANT VELOCITY JOINT AND SWIVEL ASSEMBLY ON VEHICLES FITTED WITH ABS

Service tools:
18G 284AAH extractor.
LST 132 bearing installer.
LST 133 seal installer.

Remove stub axle, axle shaft and constant velocity joint.

1. Remove the hub complete as described in the operation to overhaul the hub assembly on ABS fitted vehicles.
2. Drain the swivel pin housing and refit plug.
3. Remove the six bolts retaining the stub axle to the swivel housing.
4. Remove the mud shield.
5. Remove the stub axle and joint washer.

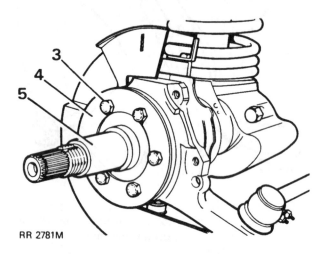

RR 2781M

6. Pull out the axle shaft and constant velocity joint from the axle casing.

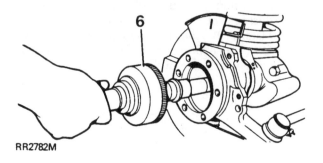

RR2782M

Remove constant velocity joint from axle shaft

7. Hold the axle shaft firmly in a soft jawed vice.
8. Using a soft mallet drive the constant velocity joint from the shaft.
9. Remove the circlip and collar from the axle shaft.

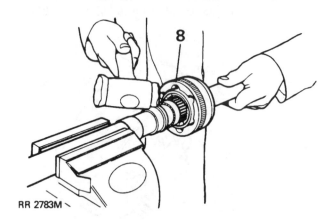

RR 2783M

Dismantle the constant velocity joint

10. Mark the relative positions of the constant velocity joint inner and outer race and the cage for correct reassembly.
11. Tilt and swivel the cage and inner race to remove the balls.

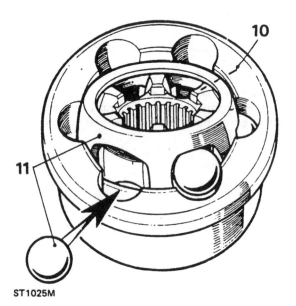

ST1025M

12. Swivel the cage into line with the axis of the joint and turn it until two opposite windows coincide with two lands of the joint housing.
13. Withdraw the cage.
14. Turn the inner track at right angles to the cage with two of the lands opposite the cage openings and withdraw the inner race.

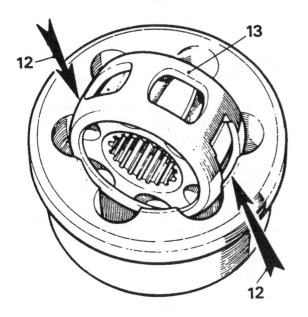

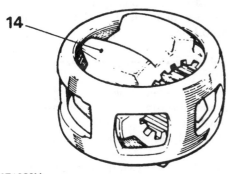

ST1026M

15. Degrease and examine all components for general wear and condition.
16. Examine the inner and outer track, cage balls and bearing surfaces of the constant velocity joint for damage and excessive wear.
17. To assemble the constant velocity joint, reverse the dismantling instructions and lubricate with a recommended oil.
18. Check that the end-float of the assembled joint does not exceed 0,64 mm (0.025 in).

Fit constant velocity joint to axle

19. Fit the collar and a new circlip.
20. Engage the constant velocity joint on the axle shaft splines and using a soft mallet, drive the joint home.

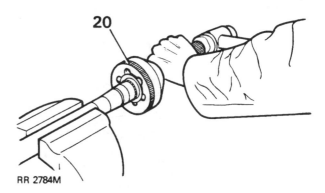

RR 2784M

Renew stub axle, thrust ring, oil seal and bearing

21. Drill and chisel off the thrust ring taking care to avoid damaging the stub axle.
22. Remove the bearing and oil seal using special tool 18G 284AAH and slide hammer. Ensure that the fingers of the tool locate behind the bearing to drive it out. Repeat for the oil seal.

18G 284 AAH

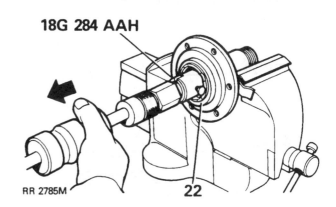

RR 2785M

Refit

23. Lubricate the seal and lip with EP90 oil and with the cavity side leading press in a new oil seal using special tool LST 133.

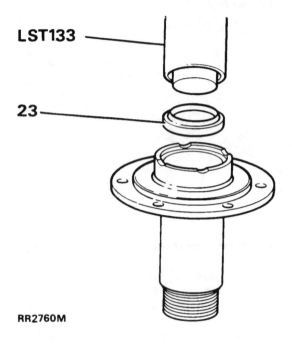

LST133

23

RR2760M

24. Using special tool LST 132, fit bearing with its part number visible when fitted, and flush with the end face of the stub axle.

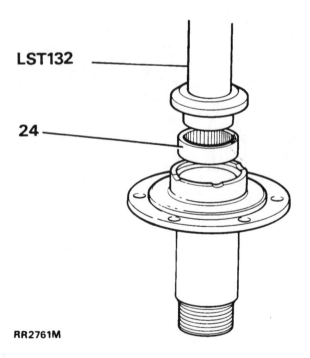

LST132

24

RR2761M

25. Press fit a new thrust ring onto the stub axle.

Remove swivel pin housing.

26. Remove the brake shield secured at the bottom by one nut and bolt, and midway by the lock stop nut.
27. Disconect the track-rod end ball joint from the housing.
28. Disconnect the drag-link ball joint.
29. Disconnect the jump hoses from the brake jump hose bracket.
30. Remove the ABS brake sensor.
31. Remove the six bolts securing the oil seal and retaining plate to the swivel pin housing. Prise the seal from the swivel pin housing.

   NOTE: The oil seal and retaining plate cannot be removed until the swivel pin bearing housing is removed.

32. Remove the two countersunk screws securing the brake damper/shield bracket, and the lower swivel pin to the housing.
33. Withdraw the lower swivel pin and joint washer by tapping the small protruding lug.
34. Remove the top swivel pin retaining bolts complete with the brake jump hose bracket.
35. Withdraw the top swivel pin and shims.
36. Remove the swivel pin housing while retrieving the lower taper bearing.
37. If the swivel pin housing is to be renewed, remove the drain, level and filler plugs and lock-stop bolt.

Remove and overhaul swivel pin bearing housing

38. Remove the seven bolts securing the swivel pin bearing housing to the axle case. Remove the swivel pin bearing housing.
39. Remove and discard the oil seal and joint washer.
40. Drift out the lower swivel pin bearing track.
41. Press out the top swivel pin bush housing assembly. Discard the thrust washer.
42. If worn, pitted or damaged, renew the swivel pin bearing housing.
43. Press in a new lower swivel pin bearing track.

44. Press in a new bush and bush housing. Ensure that the relieved lip of the bush housing faces towards the rear oil seal, as shown.

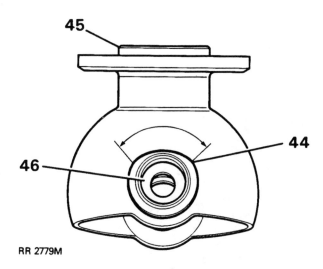

RR 2779M

45. With the seal lips trailing press the axle shaft oil seal flush into the rear of the housing. Grease the lips.
46. Fit a new thrust washer into the top swivel pin bush with the black P.T.F.E. coating uppermost. Check it is in position when fitting the top swivel pin.
47. Hang the swivel pin bearing housing oil seal and retainer plate over the back of the housing. Ensure they are in the correct assembly order.
48. Fit and secure the swivel pin bearing housing to the axle. Starting with the top fixing dowel bolt, tighten the bolts evenly to the correct torque.

Fit swivel pin housing

49. Grease and fit the lower swivel pin bearing to the bearing housing.
50. Place the swivel pin housing in position over the swivel pin bearing housing.
51. Using a new joint washer, fit the lower swivel pin with lip outboard. Do not secure with screws at this stage.
52. Fit a new sensor bush and new oil seal, lip side leading to the top swivel pin.
53. Lubricate with a recommended oil and fit the top swivel pin with existing shims.
54. Coat the threads of the top swivel pin bolts with Loctite 542. Fit the bolts and jump hose bracket (do not tighten).
55. Coat the threads of the lower swivel pin screws with Loctite 270 and fit, together with the damper and shield bracket. Tighten to the correct torque.

56. Tighten the top swivel pin and brake jump hose bracket securing bolts to the correct torque.

Check and adjust preload on bearings

57. The preload on bearings to be 0,18 - 0,23 mm (0.007" to 0.009") **without** the swivel housing oil seal and axle fitted, and reading from the centre of the swivel pin. The torque required to turn the swivel assembly from lock to lock to be 5.1 to 7.3 Nm (45 to 65 lbf ins). Adjust by removing or adding shims to the top swivel pin.
58. To take a reading construct item 58. Cut a metal plate to locate around the bolt heads. Weld a socket head to the plate, to locate over the centre of the swivel pin.

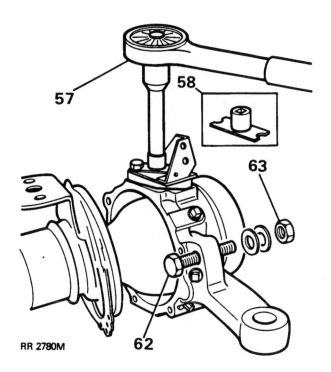

RR 2780M

Fit remaining components

59. Liberally apply (do not pack) a recommended grease between the lips of the swivel housing oil seal.
60. Secure the oil seal with the retaining plate and securing bolts tightening evenly to the correct torque.
61. Fit the track-rod and drag link and secure with new split pins.
62. Loosely fit the lock stop bolt for later adjustment.
63. Fit the brake disc shield. Leaving the middle fixing nut loose until the lock stop has been set.

KEY TO DRIVE SHAFT AND SWIVEL ASSEMBLY

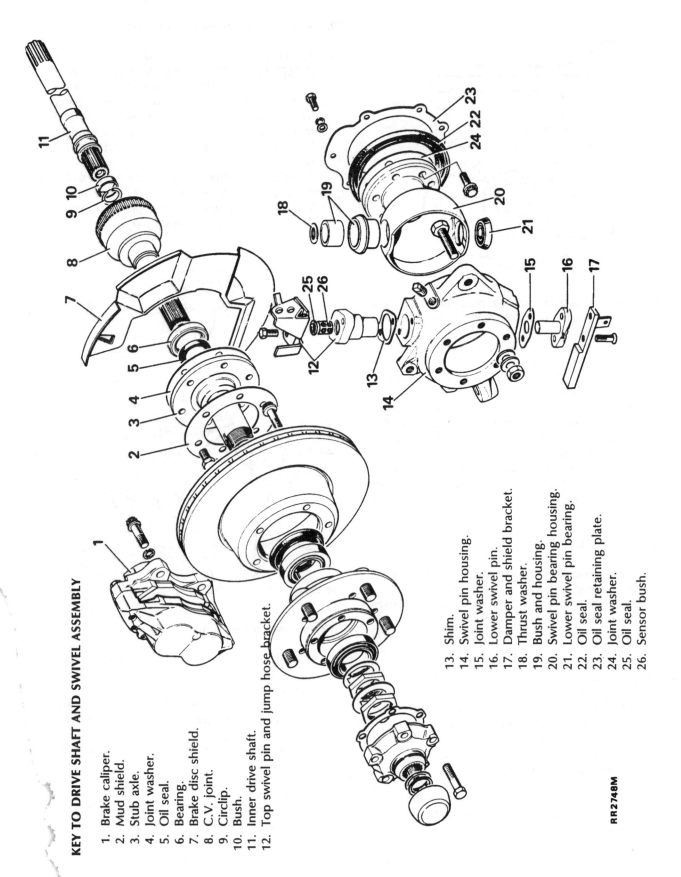

1. Brake caliper.
2. Mud shield.
3. Stub axle.
4. Joint washer.
5. Oil seal.
6. Bearing.
7. Brake disc shield.
8. C.V. joint.
9. Circlip.
10. Bush.
11. Inner drive shaft.
12. Top swivel pin and jump hose bracket.
13. Shim.
14. Swivel pin housing.
15. Joint washer.
16. Lower swivel pin.
17. Damper and shield bracket.
18. Thrust washer.
19. Bush and housing.
20. Swivel pin bearing housing.
21. Lower swivel pin bearing.
22. Oil seal.
23. Oil seal retaining plate.
24. Joint washer.
25. Oil seal.
26. Sensor bush.

RR2748M

Fit drive shaft and stub axle

64. Insert the axle shaft, and when the differential splines are engaged, push the assembly home.

   CAUTION: Take care not to damage the axle shaft oil seals.

65. Place a new joint washer in position on the swivel pin housing to stub axle mating face. Coat the threads of the stub axle bolts with Loctite 270.
66. Fit the stub axle with the keyway at the 12 o'clock position.

   CAUTION: Ensure that the constant velocity joint bearing journal is butted against the thrust ring on the stub axle. Before the stub axle is secured.

67. Place the mud shield in position and secure the stub axle to the swivel pin housing with the six bolts and tighten evenly to the correct torque.
68. Fit the brake jump hoses to the brake jump hose bracket.
69. To complete the assembly, follow instructions to fit front hub on ABS fitted vehicles.
70. Check that the swivel pin housing oil drain plug is tightly fitted and remove the filler and level plugs.
71. Inject approximately 0,35 litres (0.6 pints) of recommended oil until the oil reaches the level hole. Fit and tighten the filler and level plugs and wipe away any surplus oil.
72. Set the steering lock-stop bolt to provide a clearance of 20mm (0.787in) between the tyre wall and radius arm. Tighten the locknut which also secures the brake disc shield.
73. Fit the ABS brake sensor following the instructions in the brake section.

CLAYTON DEWANDRE - WABCO POWER ASSISTED HYDRAULIC BRAKE SYSTEM WITH INTEGRATED ANTI-LOCK BRAKE SYSTEM - ABS

INTRODUCTION

The purpose of ABS is to prevent the vehicle wheels locking during brake application, thus maintaining vehicle steerability and stability. This allows the vehicle to be steered whilst the brakes are applied, even under emergency conditions, and to avoid obstacles where there is sufficient space to redirect the vehicle.

WARNING: ABS IS AN AID TO RETAINING STEERING CONTROL AND STABILITY WHILE BRAKING.

- ABS CANNOT DEFY THE NATURAL LAWS OF PHYSICS ACTING ON THE VEHICLE.

- ABS WILL NOT PREVENT ACCIDENTS RESULTING FROM EXCESSIVE CORNERING SPEEDS, FOLLOWING ANOTHER VEHICLE TOO CLOSELY OR AQUAPLANING, I.E. WHERE A LAYER OF WATER PREVENTS ADEQUATE CONTACT BETWEEN THE TYRE AND ROAD SURFACE.

- THE ADDITIONAL CONTROL PROVIDED BY ABS MUST NEVER BE EXPLOITED IN A DANGEROUS OR RECKLESS MANNER WHICH COULD JEOPARDISE THE SAFETY OF THE DRIVER OR OTHER ROAD USERS.

SYSTEM DESCRIPTION

The brake system is hydraulically power assisted with an integrated, electronically controlled four channel anti-lock brake system (ABS).
The use of a power assisted brake system means that during brake application, additional hydraulic energy is provided by a hydraulic power unit.
This hydraulic power unit consists of an electrically driven pump and an accumulator which stores hydraulic energy in readiness for brake application. A pressure switch controls the hydraulic pump to maintain fluid pressure in the accumulator.

The hydraulic system comprises two completely independent circuits. The rear calipers and upper pistons of the front calipers form the POWER CIRCUIT . The lower pistons in the front calipers form the COMBINED POWER/HYDROSTATIC CIRCUIT .

CAUTION: THOROUGHLY CLEAN ALL BRAKE COMPONENTS, CALIPERS, PIPES AND FITTINGS BEFORE COMMENCING WORK ON THE BRAKE SYSTEM. FAILURE TO DO SO COULD CAUSE FOREIGN MATTER TO ENTER THE SYSTEM AND DAMAGE SEALS AND PISTONS, WHICH WILL SERIOUSLY IMPAIR BRAKE SYSTEM EFFICIENCY.

WARNING:

DO NOT use brake fluid previously bled from the system.

DO NOT use old or stored brake fluid.

ENSURE that only new fluid is used and that it is taken from a clean sealed container.

DO NOT flush the brake system with any fluid other than the recommended brake fluid.

The brake system must be drained and flushed at the recommended service intervals.

Fluid pressures of 170 bar (2466 psi) are produced by the hydraulic pump. It is essential that the procedure for depressurising the system is carried out where instructed.

COMPONENT DESCRIPTION

- Numbers refer to RR2705

Hydraulic booster unit (1)

Mounted in the same position as the conventional master cylinder/servo unit, the booster unit contains the following components: Fluid reservoir, power valve, master cylinder, isolating valve, ABS solenoid control valves, servo cylinder.

NOTE: The hydraulic booster unit is not a serviceable item, if internal failure occurs a new unit must be fitted. The fluid reservoir and its seals may be changed in the event of damage. Extreme care must be taken when changing seals to avoid ingress of debris.

Fluid reservoir (1.1)

Mounted on top of the booster unit, the plastic reservoir is subdivided internally to provide separate capacity for the brake fluid used in the hydrostatic and power circuits. A central tube incorporates a filter and a low fluid warning level switch.

1

HYDRAULIC COMPONENTS

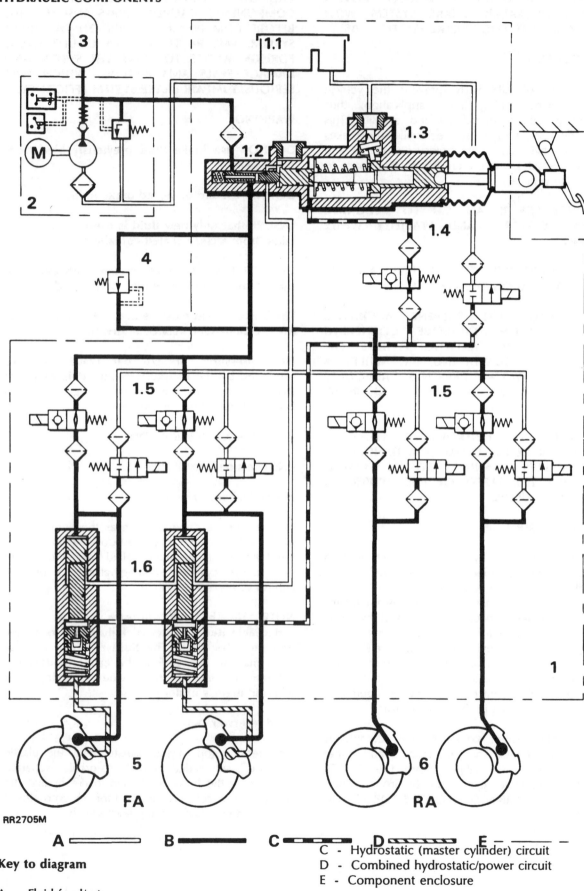

RR2705M

Key to diagram

A - Fluid feed/return
B - Power circuit
C - Hydrostatic (master cylinder) circuit
D - Combined hydrostatic/power circuit
E - Component enclosure

Power valve (1.2)

The power valve is an extension of the master cylinder, it controls fluid pressure in the power circuit in direct proportion to pressure in the master cylinder. The power valve is of spool valve design.

Master cylinder (1.3)

Operation of the master cylinder displaces a volume of brake fluid into the servo cylinders and increases fluid pressure. Piston movement inside the master cylinder will also activate the power valve. A tilt valve is incorporated to supply fluid to the master cylinder from the reservoir connection.

Isolating valve (1.4)

The isolating valve consists of two solenoid valves controlling fluid inlet and outlet. Their function is to disconnect the master cylinder from the servo cylinder and to connect the servo cylinder to the reservoir return during ABS function.

ABS solenoid control valves - 8 off (1.5)

Each pair, comprising inlet and outlet solenoid valves, controls ABS braking to each wheel. In response to signals from the ECU, the valves decrease, hold or increase brake pressure according to the need to retain wheel rotation and obtain optimum braking. The solenoid valves are designed to respond rapidly to ECU signals.

Servo cylinders - 2 off (1.6)

The servo cylinders have four functions.

1. To provide combined energy from both the hydrostatic and the power circuit to the brake calipers.
2. To provide 'brake feel' at the brake pedal.
3. To provide hydrostatic (master cylinder) braking through the servo cylinder to the calipers in the event of no power circuit pressure to the servo cylinder.
4. To provide braking from both the power circuit and from hydrostatic fluid remaining in the servo cylinder, in the event of no hydrostatic circuit pressure from the master cylinder.

Hydraulic power unit (2)

The hydraulic power unit comprises an electrically driven pump and a pressure switch. The pressure switch incorporates three electro-mechanical switches: one for the pump, another, at a different presure setting, to illuminate the pressure warning light. The latter switch plus the third switch inform the ECU of low pressure and that ABS function should cease whilst pressure remains low.
The pump also incorporates a non-return valve, a low pressure inlet filter, and a pressure relief valve to protect the system.

Accumulator (3)

The diaphragm accumulator is precharged with nitrogen, its function is to store hydraulic energy.

Pressure conscious reducing valve (PCRV) (4)

The PCRV valve is located between the power valve and the ABS solenoid valves for the rear axle. Its function is to limit the brake pressure to the rear axle.

Brake calipers - front - (5) rear - (6)

NOTE: To identify the separate hydraulic circuits, they are referred to as Hydrostatic and Power circuits.

Power circuit - The rear calipers and the upper pistons in. the front calipers form one circuit, supplied by direct hydraulic power from the power valve.

Hydrostatic circuit - The lower pistons in the front calipers form the other circuit, supplied with hydraulic energy from the servo cylinders comprising a combination of master cylinder pressure and direct hydraulic power.

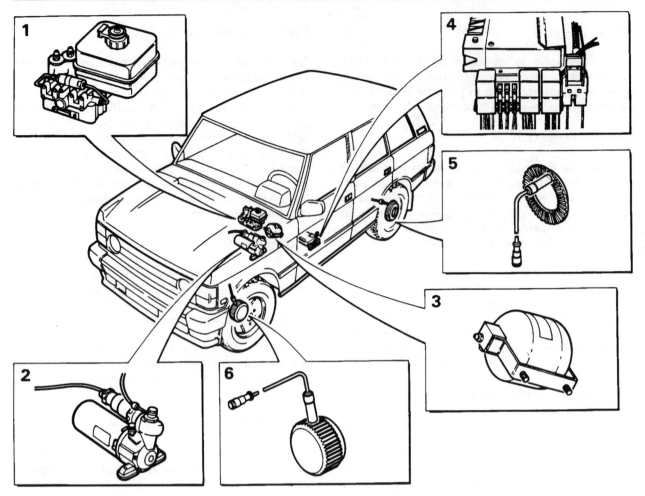

RR2706M

LOCATION OF COMPONENTS (RR2706M)

1. Hydraulic booster unit.
2. Power unit - hydraulic pump.
3. Accumulator.
4. Electronic control unit (ECU), relays and fuses.
5. Rear sensors/exciter rings.
6. Front sensors/exciter rings.

Electronic control unit - ECU

ABS operation is controlled by the ECU located under the left hand front seat, and earthed to the centre tunnel.

The ECU is connected to the ABS harness by a 35 way connector.

The ECU is a non-serviceable item, it must be replaced if failure occurs.

Sensors, exciter rings - 4 off

A sensor is mounted at each wheel, sensing a 60 tooth exciter ring. When the vehicle is in motion the inductive sensors send signals to the ECU. The front exciter ring is fitted to the outside diameter of the constant velocity joint in each front hub. The rear exciter ring is bolted to the rear

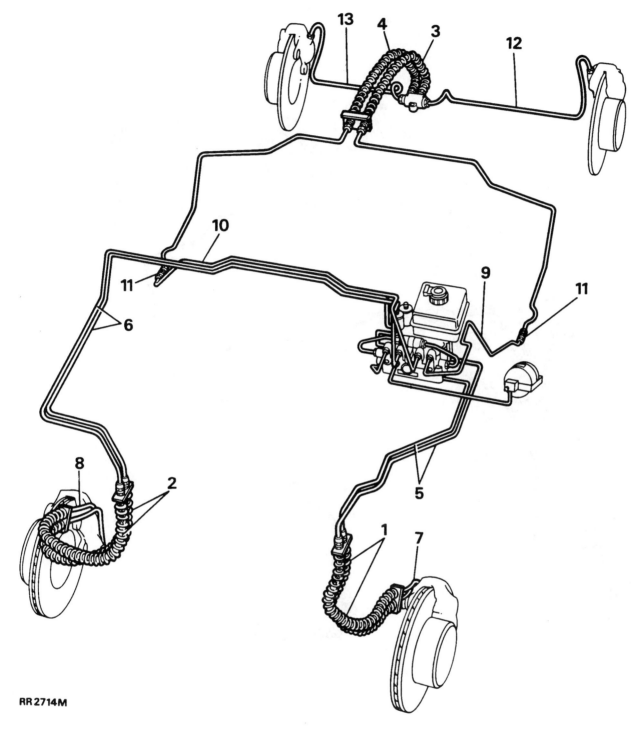

RR 2714M

Brake pipe layout - left hand drive

HOSES

1. Front left hand flexible hoses.
2. Front right hand flexible hoses.
3. Left hand intermediate hose
4. Right hand intermediate hose

PIPES

5. Feed to front left hand hose connector.
6. Feed to front right hand hose connector.
7. Feed to front left hand caliper.
8. Feed to front right hand caliper.
9. Feed to left hand intermediate hose.
10. Feed to right hand intermediate hose.
11. Two way connector.
12. Feed to rear left hand caliper.
13. Feed to rear right hand caliper.

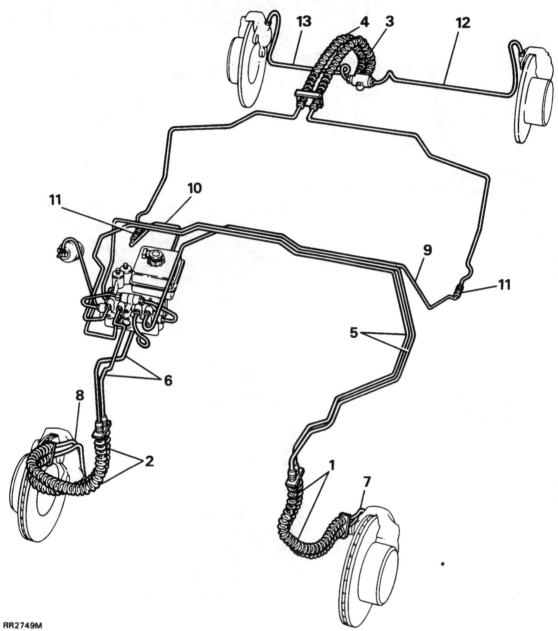

RR2749M

Brake pipe layout - right hand drive

HOSES

1. Front left hand flexible hoses.
2. Front right hand flexible hoses.
3. Left hand intermediate hose
4. Right hand intermediate hose

PIPES

5. Feed to front left hand hose connector.
6. Feed to front right hand hose connector.
7. Feed to front left hand caliper.
8. Feed to front right hand caliper.
9. Feed to left hand intermediate hose.
10. Feed to right hand intermediate hose.
11. Two way connector.
12. Feed to rear left hand caliper.
13. Feed to rear right hand caliper.

WARNING LIGHTS

Brake fluid pressure/level and handbrake warning light - (red) - 1

The warning light situated in the instrument binnacle indicates that there is insufficient pressure in the system and/or the fluid level is too low. The light will illuminate when ignition is switched ON and the engine is cranked as part of initial bulb check, and when the handbrake is applied.
If the pressure in the hydraulic system is lower than the cut-in pressure for the warning light, the light will illuminate. When the light is on the hydraulic pump will start. Therefore, if the light remains illuminated after bulb check and releasing handbrake, DO NOT drive the vehicle until the light extinguishes.

WARNING: IF THE LIGHT ILLUMINATES WHILE THE VEHICLE IS IN MOTION, THE FAULT MUST BE INVESTIGATED IMMEDIATELY. BRAKING WILL BE AVAILABLE AFTER A LOSS OF PRESSURE, BUT GREATER FORCE WILL BE REQUIRED AT THE PEDAL TO SLOW THE VEHICLE.

ABS warning light - (red) - 2

WARNING: Power assisted braking is not available if the ignition is switched off. An increase in effort at the pedal will be required to apply the brakes.

The ABS warning light situated in the instrument binnacle indicates that there is a failure in the ABS system. The light will illuminate when the ignition is switched ON , and will extinguish when the vehicle exceeds 7 km/h (5 mph) . This indicates that the system self monitoring check was successful, and the system performs correctly.
If the light remains on or subsequently illuminates with the ignition ON a fault in the ABS system is indicated. The self monitoring procedure is repeated frequently while the ignition is ON . If a fault is detected during self monitoring, the light will illuminate indicating that one or more wheels are not under ABS control.

WARNING: Reduced ABS control is possible with the ABS warning light illuminated depending on the severity and type of fault. If both ABS and brake failure warning lights are illuminated, loss of system pressure or hydraulic pump failure is indicated.
IT IS ESSENTIAL THAT THE DRIVER HAS THE FAULT INVESTIGATED IMMEDIATELY.

DRIVING THE VEHICLE

WARNING: On surfaces which are soft and deep, for example deep powdery snow, sand or gravel, braking distance may be greater than with non ABS braking. In these conditions wheel lock and the build up of snow or gravel under the wheels may be an aid to shorter stopping distance. However it is still an advantage to maintain the stability and manouevrability available with ABS control.

1. Switch on ignition, the system will automatically carry out its self test function. This will be felt as a slight movement in the brake pedal and a short, rapid series of clicks indicating that the solenoid valves have been checked.

2. Observe the warning lights, check that the handbrake/fluid pressure/level warning light extinguishes when the handbrake is released, indicating that power assistance is available. Note that the time taken to pressurise the system is approximately 20 seconds.

3. Start the vehicle and drive away, at 7 km/h (5 mph) the ABS warning light must be extinguished - see Warning Lights.

4. In road conditions where surface friction is sufficient to slow or stop the vehicle without wheel lock, the ABS does not operate.

5. In an emergency braking situation, if one or more wheels begin to slow rapidly in relation to vehicle speed, ABS will detect the wheel locking tendency and will regulate the brake pressure to maintain wheel rotation.

6. ABS operation will be felt as a vibration through the pedal, at the same time the solenoid cycling will be heard.

NOTE: Constant pressure on the foot pedal whilst ABS is operating is more effective than cadence braking. Do not pump the brake pedal as this may reduce ABS efficiency and increase stopping distance.

7. Downward travel of the pedal will also feel hard at the point at which ABS operates. little further pedal travel is possible at this point, BUT, force on the pedal can be varied to influence braking while ABS retains control.

BRAKE APPLICATION WITH PARTIAL FAILURE

WARNING: IF A FAULT DEVELOPS IN THE BRAKE SYSTEM IT IS ESSENTIAL THAT THE DRIVER HAS THE FAULT INVESTIGATED IMMEDIATELY.

NOTE: If, during braking, a drastically reduced resistance is detected at the pedal and braking effectiveness is very much reduced, failure of the non-powered (master cylinder) portion of the system is indicated. When this occurs DO NOT PUMP THE BRAKE PEDAL. Push the pedal through the free movement to obtain braking effort. For this reason it is essential that brake pedal travel is not obstructed by the addition of items such as extra footwell mats.

1. When power assistance is not available, ABS braking is not operative. Both warning lights are illuminated. Braking effort is available from the master cylinder only. This results in longer pedal travel and greater pedal effort required to decelerate the vehicle.

WARNING: FOOT PRESSURE ON THE PEDAL, USING MASTER CYLINDER ONLY, WILL NOT ACHIEVE THE SAME DEGREE OF BRAKING AS THAT AVAILABLE FROM POWER ASSISTANCE.

2. If the master cylinder fails, i.e. there is insufficient fluid in the master cylinder to create pressure, braking to all four wheels is retained and ABS remains operative. The red warning light will be illuminated if the cause of the master cylinder failure is a fluid leak and the level in the master cylinder is low enough to actuate the fluid level switch.

WARNING: LONGER PEDAL TRAVEL IS REQUIRED, BUT POWER ASSISTED BRAKING IS AVAILABLE AT A REDUCED EFFICIENCY.

3. If brake failure occurs due to a fractured brake pipe between a servo unit and a wheel, there will be no pressure in the master cylinder. The fluid warning light will be illuminated when the level in the reservoir is low enough to actuate the fluid level switch. The master cylinder and power valve will operate as for master cylinder failure. BUT, fluid from the power circuit will push all the moving parts in the servo cylinder associated with the failure to the limit of their travel. No pressurised fluid passes to those brake pistons served by the servo cylinder, but all other pistons in front and rear calipers will be supplied with direct pressure from the power valve. The pistons served by the other servo cylinder retain braking as fluid from the master cylinder is retained in the servo cylinder not associated with the leakage.

WARNING: BRAKE PEDAL TRAVEL WILL BE GREATER AND EXTRA PEDAL EFFORT WILL BE REQUIRED, ACCOMPANIED BY THE VEHICLE PULLING TO ONE SIDE.

Booster harness plug wiring details

(Right hand drive) - RR2691M

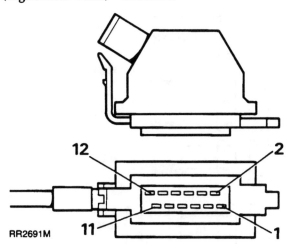

RR2691M

(Left hand drive) - RR2692M

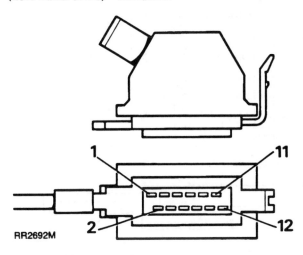

RR2692M

Pin Nos. Cable Colour

1. Slate/yellow.
2. Not used.
3. Slate/white.
4. Slate/green.
5. Slate/black.
6. Slate/purple.
7. Slate/orange.
8. Slate/brown.
9. Slate/blue.
10. Slate/pink.
11. Slate/red.
12. Not used.

ECU harness plug wiring details - RR2690M

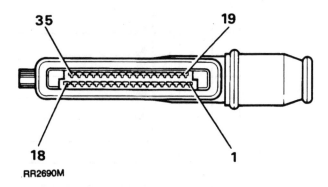

RR2690M

Pin nos. Cable Colours

1. Brown/pink.
2. Not used.
3. Not used.
4. Slate/yellow.
5. Slate/white.
6. Slate/red.
7. Slate/blue
8. Black/green
9. Green/pink
10. White/slate
11. Slate/orange
12. Slate/black
13. White/pink.
14. Black/pink.
15. Brown.
16. Black/green.
17. Black/brown.
18. Black/white.
19. Brown/pink.
20. Not used.
21. Slate/green.
22. Slate/purple.
23. Slate/pink.
24. Slate/brown.
25. Green/purple.
26. Black/slate.
27. Black.
28. Not used
29. Not used
30. White/black.
31. Black/yellow.
32. Black/orange.
33. Brown/black.
34. Brown/blue.
35. Brown/yellow.

**NOTE: The ABS harness plugs are sealed units and must not be dismantled.
The ABS harness is a non-serviceable item, in the event of failure a new harness MUST be fitted.**

ABS - Circuit diagram

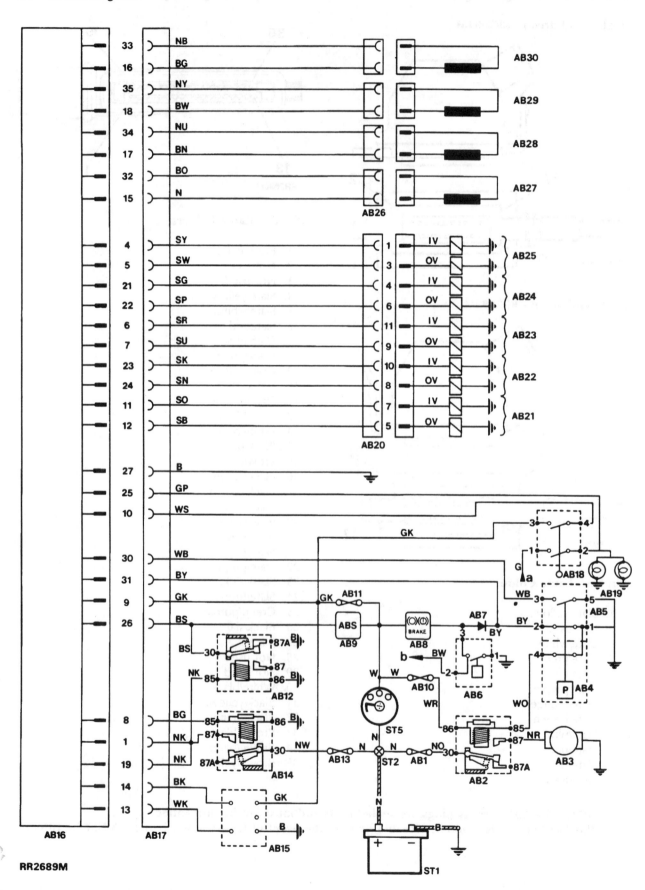

RR2689M

CIRCUIT DIAGRAM - RR2689M

ST1.	Battery
ST2.	Terminal post
ST5.	Ignition switch
AB1.	30 amp MAXI fuse - pump relay
AB2.	Pump relay - black
AB3.	Hydraulic pump
AB4.	Hydraulic pump pressure cut off switch
AB5.	Pump low pressure warning switch
AB6.	Reservoir fluid level switch
AB7.	Diode
AB8.	Brake fluid pressure/level warning light
AB9.	ABS warning light
AB10.	5 amp fuse, pump relay
AB11.	5 amp fuse, pin 9 ECU, diagnostic plug, brake light switch
AB12.	ABS warning light relay - green
AB13.	25 amp fuse, valve relay
AB14.	Valve relay - black
AB15.	Diagnostic plug
AB16.	Electronic control unit (ECU)
AB17.	35 way connector to ECU
AB18.	Brakelight switch
AB19.	Brakelights
AB20.	Multiplug to booster unit

Booster unit components AB21-25

IV   Inlet valve
OV   Outlet valve

AB21.	Isolating valve
AB22.	Front left solenoid valves
AB23.	Front right solenoid valves
AB24.	Rear left solenoid valves
AB25.	Rear right solenoid valves
AB26.	Sensor connectors (4)
AB27.	Front left sensor
AB28.	Front right sensor
AB29.	Rear left sensor
AB30.	Rear right sensor

a.	**12 volts from fuse A5**
b.	**To brake check unit**

CABLE COLOUR CODE

B	Black	G	Green	K	Pink	W	White
U	Blue	S	Grey	P	Purple	Y	Yellow
N	Brown	O	Orange	R	Red		

RELAYS AND FUSES

Incorporated in the ABS electrical system are three relays, located beneath the left hand front seat adjacent to the ABS ECU. Access to the relays is gained by removing the seat side trim.

Relay and fuse identification (RR2816M)

1. ABS warning light relay, green base - AB12
2. Valve relay, black base - AB14
3. Hydraulic pump relay, black base - AB2
4. Hydraulic pump relay fuse, 5amp tan - AB10
5. Stop light switch, diagnostic plug, ECU pin 9 fuse, 5 amp tan - AB11
6. Valve relay fuse, 25 amp white - AB13
7. Hydraulic pump relay fuse 30 amp green MAXI type fuse - AB1

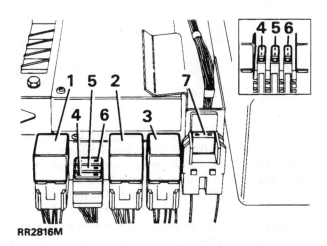

RR2816M

Inset shows fuse position on early 1990 vehicles.

GENERAL SERVICE INFORMATION

NOTE: ABS components ARE NOT serviceable.
Replace components that are found to be faulty.

Brake fluid precautions

WARNING: Do not allow brake fluid to come
into contact with eyes or skin.

CAUTION: Brake fluid can damage paintwork, if
spilled wash off immediately with plenty of clean
water.

CAUTION: Use only the correct brake fluid. If an
assembly fluid is required use brake fluid. Do
NOT use mineral oil, i.e. engine oil etc.

Check/top up fluid level

1. Park the vehicle on level ground.
2. Turn ignition ON, to activate hydraulic pump.
   If pump does not activate depress brake pedal
   several times until it is heard to operate.
3. When the pump stops, check that the level is
   between the MIN and MAX marks.
4. If the level is below MIN top up fluid level to
   the 'MAX' mark on reservoir, using the correct
   fluid, - see Section 09, Lubricants and Fluids.

   WARNING: Clean the reservoir body and
   filler cap before removing the cap. Use only
   fluid from a sealed container.
   DO NOT OVERFILL THE RESERVOIR

DEPRESSURISE

WARNING: Before bleeding the system or
working on any component in the brake system
the following procedure MUST be carried out to
depressurise the accumulator.

1. Switch off ignition.
2. Operate the brake pedal 30 times. Pedal travel
   will increase slightly and reduced resistance
   will be felt as pressure decreases.
3. Wait for 60 seconds, press the brake pedal
   four more times. This procedure will ensure
   that all pressure is evacuated from the system.

SYSTEM BLEED

EQUIPMENT: Bleed the system using a bleed
tube and a clean bottle containing a small
amount of clean fluid.

CAUTION: Clean all bleed screws, filler cap and
connections thoroughly using clean brake fluid
only. DO NOT USE MINERAL OIL I.E. ENGINE OIL
ETC.
MAINTAIN CLEANLINESS THROUGHOUT.

NOTE: During bleed procedure the reservoir
fluid level must not fall below the'MIN' level.
Regularly check level and keep topped up to
'MAX' level.

WARNING: Do not use previously used brake
fluid. Ensure that only new fluid is used and that
it is taken from a clean sealed container.
Carefully dispose of unwanted fluid in a sealed
container, marked USED BRAKE FLUID.

1. Switch off ignition and depressurise the
   system. Ensure that ignition remains OFF until
   instruction 7.
2. Fill the fluid reservoir with the specified fluid
   to the 'MAX' level.

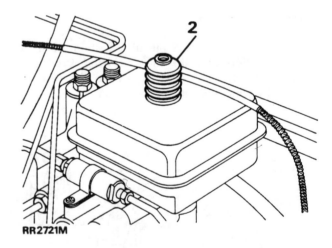

RR2721M

NOTE: Time consumed in filling the booster may
be reduced by fitting a rubber bellows unit to
the filler neck, and using hand pressure to
pressurise the booster. A spare bellows unit from
the booster push rod is suitable for this purpose.
Ensure the bellows unit is perfectly clean to
avoid foreign matter entering the system. Raising
the rear of the vehicle will assist the fill
procedure.

3. Depress brake pedal slowly and progressively
   five times, using full pedal stroke. Release the
   pedal for five to ten seconds, during this time
   air bubbles will rise into the reservoir.

4. Repeat instruction 3. until some resistance is felt. If no resistance is felt check that the clevis pin is connected to the correct (UPPER) hole in the brake pedal.

5. Bleed the four front caliper lower (hydrostatic) bleed screws in the conventional manner. Proceed in the order: outer bleed screw on the driver's side, opposite caliper outer bleed screw, inner bleed screw, inner bled screw driver's side. Depress the brake pedal slowly and progressively. Lock the bleed screw at the bottom of each stroke.

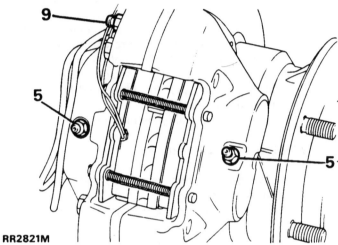

RR2821M

6. Bleed the hydraulic pump - open the bleed screw on the pump and allow fluid to flow until it is clear of air bubbles. Do not use the bleed bottle, use a clean absorbent cloth to prevent fluid spillage.

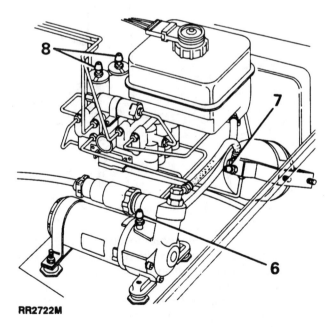

RR2722M

7. Bleed the accumulator - open the bleed screw. Switch on ignition, run pump for 3-4 secs, switch off and repeat procedure until no further air bubbles enter bleed bottle. Switch off ignition. Close the bleed screw.

8. Bleed the two hydraulic booster bleed screws. Open one bleed screw, depress the brake pedal, switch on ignition, run pump until no further air bubbles enter the bleed bottle. Close booster bleed screw, switch off ignition and release pedal. Repeat for other bleed screw.

9. Bleed power circuit at four calipers in turn. Depress pedal, open bleed screw, (upper bleed screw on front calipers). Switch on ignition, run pump for 3-4 secs, switch off and repeat procedure until no further air bubbles enter bleed bottle. Switch off ignition, close caliper bleed screw, release pedal.

10. Bleed master cylinder - switch ignition on. System pressure will increase until pump cuts out. If pump does not cut out after running for 45 secs, check system for leaks.

11. Bleed hydrostatic circuit calipers - open one front lower caliper bleed screw. Actuate brake pedal several times, using only the lower two thirds of pedal travel, until no further air bubbles enter the bleed bottle. Stop actuation if fluid warning light comes on and allow pressure to build up.

12. Close caliper bleed screw before releasing pedal, repeat for remaining three hydrostatic bleed screws.

13. Check/top up reservoir fluid level - see Check/top up fluid level.

14. Dry all connections, fully pressurise system and check for leaks. If two full brake applications switch on pump, from fully charged, rebleed system.

CALIPERS - Front and rear

Refer to main workshop manual for caliper remove and refit. Use a recognised hose clamp, using the approved procedure. If one caliper has been removed, and the use of a brake hose clamp has been effective in preventing fluid level falling below the minimum mark in the reservoir, bleed the brakes as follows:

Front caliper - bleed the front caliper at both power and hydrostatic circuits.

Rear caliper - bleed the rear caliper.

NOTE: If the excessive fluid loss has occured, bleed the complete brake system.

HYDRAULIC BOOSTER UNIT

Remove and refit

Removing

1. Disconnect battery negative lead, and depressurise the system.
2. Thoroughly clean the immediate area around the booster unit outlet ports and electrical connector.
3. Disconnect the electrical multiplug from the booster, and the connector to the low fluid switch located in the reservoir cap. Remove the booster earth strap.

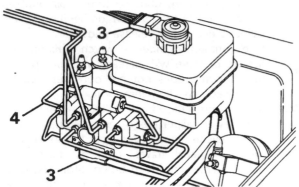

RR2723M

4. Remove brake pipes from booster unit including hydraulic pipes to the accumulator and hydraulic power unit. Note that each booster outlet port is numbered, and each brake pipe is marked with the corresponding number to aid reassembly. Seal each pipe and outlet port, as they are disconnected, with suitable plugs, to prevent ingress of foreign matter.
3. Working inside the vehicle remove the lower dash panel - see Body Section 76, main workshop manual.
4. Release the spring clip from the clevis pin securing the booster push rod to the brake pedal.

5. Remove the four nuts and plain washers securing the booster unit to the bulkhead.
6. Remove the booster unit.

Refitting

NOTE: New booster units are supplied in a sealed pack marked with a 'use by' date. DO NOT fit a booster if the date has elapsed, or if the pack is not sealed. DO NOT open the sealed pack until ready to fit the unit.

7. Reverse the removal procedure, ensuring correct fitment of pipes to booster unit. Finally tighten booster fixings and pipes to the correct torque value. Ensure that the clevis pin is fitted into the TOP hole of the brake pedal.
8. Adjust the brake light switch, pull out the black plunger, pull the brake pedal back fully to reset the switch.
9. Carry out the brake bleeding procedure.

RESERVOIR SEALS - Renew

With the booster unit removed, and brake fluid drained, is possible to fit new reservoir seals. Clean the unit thoroughly before removing the reservoir.

1. Remove the reservoir bracket securing bolt adjacent to the low pressure suction hose outlet.
2. Carefully ease the reservoir away from the booster unit.

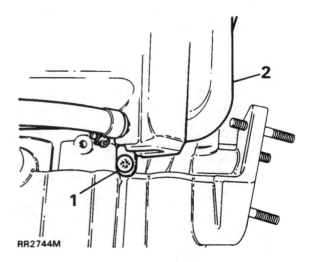

RR2744M

3. Remove the two seals located in the top of the booster unit. Avoid damage to the seals which could result in rubber particles entering the system.
4. Fit new seals and refit the reservoir, tightening the securing bolt to the correct torque.
5. Carry out the booster refitting procedure.

HYDRAULIC POWER UNIT (PUMP)

Remove and refit

Removing

1. Disconnect battery negative lead.
2. Depressurise the system.
3. Disconnect the braided hose to the accumulator.
4. Loosen the hose clip and disconnect the low pressure suction hose to the reservoir clamping hose to prevent fluid loss and ingress of debris.

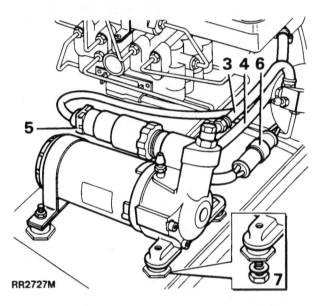

RR2727M

5. Disconnect the pressure switch multiplug.
6. Disconnect the power unit connector.
7. Working from below the unit remove four nuts and plain washers.
8. Remove the hydraulic power unit complete with mountings.

Refit

9. Reverse removal procedure. Check condition of sealing washers on high pressure hose. Fit new washers if necessary.
10. Bleed system, finally top up fluid reservoir.

ACCUMULATOR

WARNING: The accumulator is precharged with nitrogen. Handle with extreme caution. DO NOT puncture or burn if disposal is necessary.

Remove and refit

Removing

1. Disconnect battery negative lead.
2. Depressurise the system.
3. Remove the fluid inlet and outlet pipes from the accumulator.

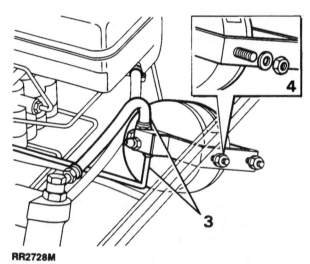

RR2728M

4. Remove the wheelarch inner liner and remove the two nuts and plain washers securing the accumulator.
5. Remove accumulator.

Refitting

6. Reverse removal procedure. Check condition of sealing washers on high pressure hose. Fit new washers if necessary.
7. Carry out brake bleed procedure.

ELECTRONIC CONTROL UNIT - ECU

Remove and refit

Removing

1. Remove the front and side trim from the left hand front seat.
2. Adjust the seat to its most rearward position and raise the seat cushion height to allow accesss to the ECU.
3. Disconnect the battery negative lead.
4. Release the ECU plug retaining clip.
5. Manoeuvre the plug in the direction of the arrow and detach the hooked end of the plug from the retaining post.
6. Remove the two screws securing the ECU to the mounting bracket.
7. Withdraw the ECU from the retaining clip and remove it from the vehicle.

SENSORS - front

CAUTION: If a sensor is removed for any reason, a NEW sensor bush and seal must be fitted.

Remove and refit

Removing

1. Disconnect the battery negative lead.
2. Disconnect the required sensor electrical connection, located on the inner wing panel adjacent to the decker panel.
3. Remove the sensor lead and pad wear harness plug from locating clips.
4. Thoroughly clean the area surrounding the sensor to prevent ingress of dirt. Using a suitable lever prise the sensor from its mounting bush.
5. Release the harness cable ties, remove the sensor lead from vehicle.
6. Remove the top swivel retaining bolts complete with brake jump hose bracket. Remove the sensor seal, and remove the sensor bush.

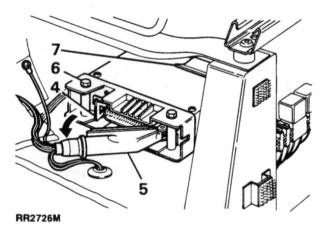

RR2726M

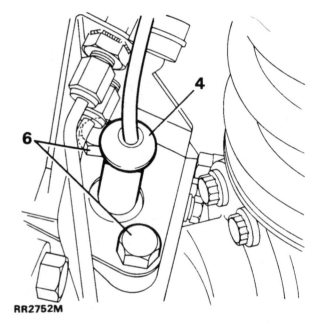

RR2752M

Refitting

8. Refit the ECU securely in the retaining bracket, fit and tighten the two screws.
9. Reconnect the ECU harness plug. Ensure that the plug is pushed firmly in to its location and that the retaining clip secures the plug in position.
10. Reverse the remaining removal procedure.

Refitting

7. Insert the new sensor bush and seal.
8. Refit the brake jump hose bracket, coating the bolts with Loctite 270.
9. Lightly coat the new sensor using EP 90 oil. Push the sensor through the bush until it contacts the exciter ring. Rotate the wheel, at the same time turn the steering from lock to lock to set the sensor air gap.

10. Ensure that the original routing is used for the sensor lead. Secure the lead in position.
11. Reconnect the sensor electrical connection.
12. Clear the error code - see FAULT DIAGNOSIS PROCEDURE. Drive the vehicle to ensure the ABS warning light is extinguished.

SENSORS - rear

CAUTION: If a sensor is removed for any reason, a NEW sensor bush must be fitted.

Remove and refit

Removing

1. Disconnect the battery negative lead.
2. Disconnect the required sensor electrical connection, located above the rear axle.
3. Remove the sensor from its locating clip.
4. Remove the bolts securing the mudshield.
5. Using a suitable lever prise the sensor from its mounting bush.
6. Release the harness cable ties, remove the sensor lead from vehicle.

NOTE: The two rear sensor leads are integral with the pad wear harness. In the case of sensor failure the complete harness must be changed.

7. Remove the sensor bush.

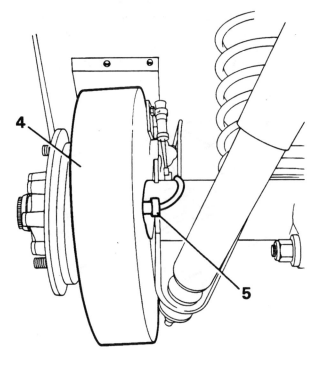

RR2753M

Refitting

8. Fit the new sensor bush.
9. Lightly grease the new sensor using silicone grease see - Section 09 for correct grease specification. Push the sensor through the bush until it touches the exciter ring. The sensor will be 'knocked back' to its correct position when the vehicle is driven.
10. Ensure that the original routing is used for the sensor lead. Secure the lead in position.
11. Reconnect the sensor electrical connection.
12. Clear the error code - see FAULT DIAGNOSIS PROCEDURE. Drive the vehicle to ensure the ABS warning light is extinguished.

STOP LIGHT SWITCH

Remove and refit

Removing

1. Turn ignition off and disconnect the battery negative lead.
2. Remove the lower fascia panel.
3. Disconnect the electrical connection to the switch.
4. Depressurise the system.
5. While depressing the brake pedal, pull the red sleeve and the black plunger of the switch FULLY forward.
6. Release the switch retaining clips.

NOTE: If clips are difficult to release, check that the red sleeve is FULLY forward.

7. Remove the switch.

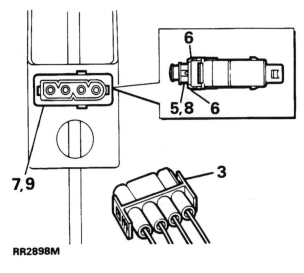

RR2898M

Refitting

8. Pull the red sleeve and the black plunger of the switch fully forward.
9. While depressing the brake pedal, fit the switch, ensuring the retaining clips are FULLY located.
10. While holding the switch firmly in place, pull the brake pedal back fully, to set the switch.
11. Check operation of the switch using the diagnostic box.
12. Reverse the remaining removal instructions.

EXCITER RINGS SEE AXLE SECTION OF MANUAL

ABS FAULT DIAGNOSIS

If a fault has occurred, or has been identified by the ECU self diagnostic function and the ABS warning light is illuminated, the system and components must be checked to locate and rectify the fault, enabling the faulty component or harness to be replaced.

NOTE: If the warning lamp has indicated a fault in the system, and no fault code has been stored in the memory, the cause of the fault is:

a) **Failure in electrical supply**
b) **Loss of hydraulic pressure**
c) **Faulty pressure switch**
d) **Bad ECU earth**
e) **Faulty warning light relay**
f) **System not fully charged before driving away**
g) **ECU not connected**

Before commencing the fault diagnosis procedure the following items must be checked:

1. Inspect all exposed cables for damage or abrasion.
2. Check earths on ABS system.
3. Battery - state of charge.
4. Fluid level in reservoir.
5. All ABS fuses and electrical connections.
6. Check hub end-float.

Fault rectification

1. The complete harness must be replaced if faults are found in the wiring harness.
2. DO NOT use unspecified cables or connectors, as this could jeopardise the safe function of the ABS.
3. DO NOT attempt to open the sealed 35 way connector to ECU.

Recommended equipment

**Wabco diagnostic controller
- 446 300 300 0**

FAULT DIAGNOSIS PROCEDURE

If diagnostic equipment is not available the following procedure can be carried out using the 'Blink Code' and a multi-meter. Faults are stored in the ECU memory in code form. The information can be retrieved by initiating and reading a series of flash and pause sequences on the ABS warning light.

Use of the blink code will determine the location of the fault prior to carrying out a multi-meter check, thus reducing multi-meter checking time.

Additionally the blink code can be used exclusively where a fault has occurred, and no other diagnostic equipment is available.

Recommended equipment

A female plug to fit the diagnostic plug, prewired to connect ECU pin 14 to earth by bridging the black/pink and black diagnostic plug wires.

To initiate the blink code carry out the following procedure:

1. Switch off ignition.
2. Remove the seat side trim to gain access to the ECU and relays, and on early vehicles the diagnostic plug. Unclip the access plate from the seat base front trim panel. Pull the blue diagnistic plug from its clip through the opening. Note that the diagnostic plug and fuse condition on early vehicles is shown in RR2742M.

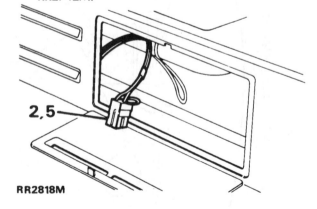

RR2818M

3. Remove the ABS warning light relay.

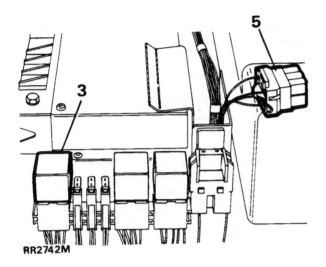

RR2742M

4. Switch on ignition, ABS warning light will illuminate.
5. Connect the prewired plug to the diagnostic plug.
6. Five seconds after connecting diagnostic plug the ABS warning light will extinguish, indicating the start of the blink code cycle.

7. **Start phase:** Observe the ABS warning light, the start phase consists of:
   Pause - 2.5 secs (long)
   Flash - 2.5 secs (long)
   Pause - 2.5 secs (long)
   Flash - 0.5 secs (short)
   (A) shows flash sequence at start of blink cycle.

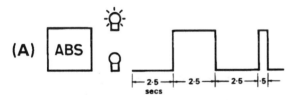

RR2719M

8. **First part of code number:** A pause of 2.5 secs precedes a series of short flashes. Count the flashes until the next long pause occurs, the number obtained is the first part of the code number.
9. **Second part of code number:** A pause of 2.5 secs occurs between first and second parts, before a second series of short flashes occurs. The number of flashes forms the second part of the code number.
   (B) shows flash sequence for code number 3 - 3.

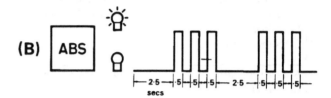

RR2720M

10. The sequence of start phase, first and second parts will continue until terminated by the operator, thus allowing the code obtained to be rechecked.
11. To terminate the sequence disconnect the prewired plug from the diagnostic plug. Wait for cycle to end before code will clear.

    NOTE: Termination will clear the memory of that particular fault. Do not terminate the sequence if unsure of the code number.

12. The memory is capable of storing more than one fault. To search the memory, reconnect the diagnostic plug, and await the next start phase.
13. Repeat procedure until no further faults are stored in the memory. The memory is cleared when a long pause of 7.5 secs occurs after start phase.
    WARNING: Be sure to reconnect the relay after completing test.

FAULT CODE /LOCATION	CAUSE	REMEDY
NOTE: If the ABS warning light illuminates due to a large sensor air gap, the fault will be retained by the ECU memory. Where the wheel sensors have been pushed fully home prior to test, the blink code will indicate a fault that has been rectified.		
2-12 front right 2-13 rear left 2-14 front left 2-15 rear right	Sensor air gap too large -sensor has been pushed outwards by exciter ring	Run-out on sensor rings due to rough roads/potholes, installation Check bearing freeplay, or failure fit new sensor bush, refit sensor
5-12 front right 5-13 rear left 5-14 front left 5-15 rear right	Sensor or wiring has intermittent contact	Carry out multi-meter check -check and repair If rough road causing fault - test vehicle on rough road.
6-12 front right 6-13 rear left 6-14 front left 6-15 rear right	No sensor output Sensor has extremely large air gap	Check sensor installation, bearings, disc mounting fit new sensor bush, refit sensor
4-12 front right 4-13 rear left 4-14 front left 4-15 rear right	Sensor wiring broken or impedance of sensor too high	Check wiring with multi-meter if OK, fit new sensor
2-6 brake light switch	Brake light switch failed, fault in wiring to switch or not connected Fuse A5 blown or not fitted	Check pedal is set back to rear resting position, slowly operate pedal by hand, two clicks must be heard from switch (brake lights on at first click) prior to hissing noise of booster If OK continue with multi-meter check, if not OK check switch and installation. Check fuse A5
2-7	Continuous supply to ECU, with ignition off, faulty valve relay AB14 or wiring	Carry out multi-meter check
2-8	No voltage to ABS solenoid valves, faulty valve relay AB14 or wiring	Carry out multi-meter check

NOTE: After any steering adjustment, bearing replacement/adjustment, brake disc replacement: Check hub end-float and sensor clearance.

NOTE: Having fixed faults clear ALL memory codes and road test vehicle.

FAULT CODE /LOCATION	CIRCUIT DIAGRAM ITEM NUMBER	CAUSE/REMEDY
3-0 inlet front right	AB 23 IV	Open circuit in connection ECU to solenoid valve in booster, or inside ECU - possibly intermittent
3-1 outlet front right	AB 23 OV	
3-2 inlet front left	AB 22 IV	
3-3 outlet front left	AB 22 OV	
3-4 inlet rear right	AB 25 IV	Carry out multi-meter check to: Wiring harness including connectors, booster
3-5 outlet rear right	AB 25 OV	
3-6 inlet rear left	AB 24 IV	
3-7 outlet rear left	AB 24 OV	
3-8 inlet isolating	AB 21 IV	Renew defective component, if all OK fit new ECU. Road test vehicle.
3-9 outlet isolating	AB 21 OV	
4-0 inlet front right	AB 23 IV	Short circuit to ground in connection ECU to solenoid valve in booster - possibly intermittent
4-1 outlet front right	AB 23 OV	
4-2 inlet front left	AB 22 IV	
4-3 outlet front left	AB 22 OV	
4-4 inlet rear right	AB 25 IV	Carry out multi-meter check to: Wiring harness including connectors, booster
4-5 outlet rear right	AB 25 OV	
4-6 inlet rear left	AB 24 IV	
4-7 outlet rear left	AB 24 OV	
4-8 inlet isolating	AB 21 IV	Renew defective component, if all OK fit new ECU. Road test vehicle.
4-9 outlet isolating	AB 21 OV	
5-0 inlet front right	AB 23 IV	Short circuit to 12V in connection ECU to solenoid valve in booster - possibly intermittent
5-1 outlet front right	AB 23 OV	
5-2 inlet front left	AB 22 IV	
5-3 outlet front left	AB 22 OV	
5-4 inlet rear right	AB 25 IV	Carry out multi-meter check to: Wiring harness including connectors, Booster
5-5 outlet rear right	AB 25 OV	
5-6 inlet rear left	AB 24 IV	
5-7 outlet rear left	AB 24 OV	Possible earth fault
5-8 inlet isolating	AB 21 IV	Renew defective component, if all OK fit new ECU. Road test vehicle
5-9 outlet isolating	AB 21 OV	
6-0 inlet front right	AB 23 IV	Short circuit between two connections ECU to solenoid valve in booster - possibly intermittent
6-1 outlet front right	AB 23 OV	
6-2 inlet front left	AB 22 IV	
6-3 outlet front left	AB 22 OV	
6-4 inlet rear right	AB 25 IV	**NOTE: Failure codes for both affected valves will be stored**
6-5 outlet rear right	AB 25 OV	
6-6 inlet rear left	AB 24 IV	
6-7 outlet rear left	AB 24 OV	Carry out multi-meter check to: a) Wiring harness, plug connectors, b) Booster
6-8 inlet isolating	AB 21 IV	
6-9 outlet isolating	AB 21 OV	
		Renew defective component, if all OK fit new ECU. Road test vehicle

Accumulator - check precharge

The accumulator, of the diaphragm type, is precharged with nitrogen at 80 bar, its function is to store hydraulic energy. If a problem is suspected, the following procedure will indicate if the precharge pressure has fallen.

1. Depressurise the brake system fully.
2. Connect a pressure gauge, capable of reading at least 170 bar (2466 psi), to the M10 thread of the accumulator after removing the bleed screw.
3. Switch ignition on and observe the pressure gauge.

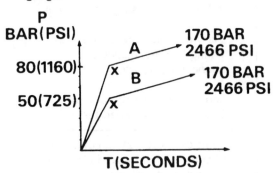

RR 2743M

4. There should be a rapid rise in pressure to accumulator precharge of 80 bar (1160 psi), then a slowing down in the rate of increase as the pressure rises to system pressure, 170 bar (2466 psi) - see graph A.
5. If point x is low as in graph B, ie. 50 bar (725 psi) it indicates that the accumulator has lost its precharge.
6. If faulty, fit a new accumulator.

CONTINUNITY TEST USING A MULTI-METER

Recommended equipment

CAUTION: USE ONLY a multi-meter with compatible male blades to match female spring sockets. Damaged female sockets will necessitate unnecessary component replacement.

To avoid damage to the contacts of the 35 way connector, the manufacturers recommend the use of the adaptor plug shown in the illustrations.
When this adaptor is fully engaged with the 35 way connector, multimeter probes can be inserted into the numbered contacts on the face of the adaptor. The adaptor plug is supplied as a spares item.

MULTI-METER CHECK PROCEDURE

CAUTION: Ensure the multi-meter is correctly set to volts or ohms, dependant on which test is being carried out. Ensure ignition is switched ON or OFF as test requires.

1. Disconnect 35 way connector from ECU, connect adaptor plug. Commence check at appropriate pin on 35 way on wiring harness.
2. Check harness wires for continuity, check fuses and relays.
3. Test related components.
4. If intermittent contact is suspected, attempt to locate the fault by flexing the harness and cables or moving contacts.

TESTS - using a multi-meter

THE following tests are intended as a guide to locating a fault within a circuit. Refer to the ABS circuit diagram for full circuit information.

Key to symbols

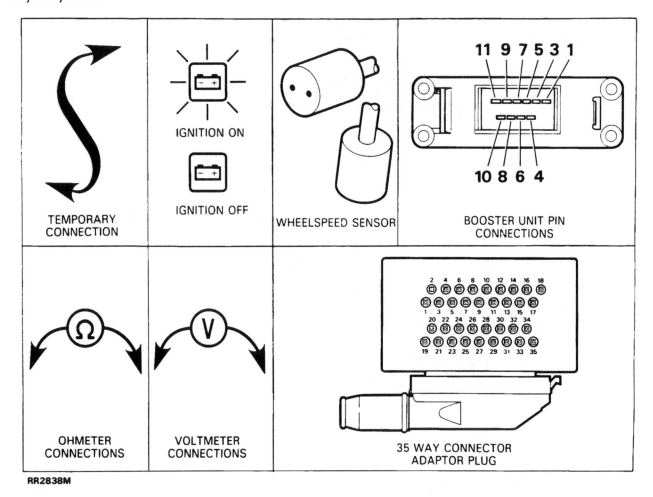

TEMPORARY CONNECTION

IGNITION ON

IGNITION OFF

WHEELSPEED SENSOR

BOOSTER UNIT PIN CONNECTIONS

OHMETER CONNECTIONS

VOLTMETER CONNECTIONS

35 WAY CONNECTOR ADAPTOR PLUG

RR2838M

NOTE: If the correct reading is obtained at the component connector and NOT at the 35 way connector, the harness is at fault.

TEST PROCEDURE

RESULTS/CHECKS

1   Check battery voltage.

Correct result: 10V + Incorrect result: Check fuse AB11, wiring from ignition switch and earth.

1

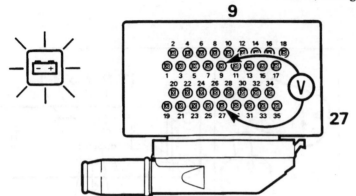

RR2839M

2a   Check valve relay AB14.

Correct result: O V If voltage reading obtained check relay

2a

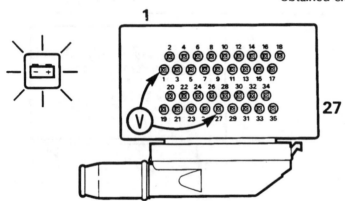

RR2840M

2b   Check valve relay power supply.

Correct result: 10V + Incorrect result: Check wiring to relay, pins 8, 9 and 27 to earth

2b

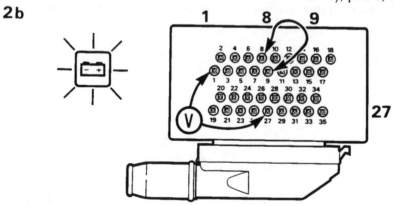

RR2841M

TEST PROCEDURE

RESULTS/CHECKS

3a Check front left wheelspeed sensor
resistance.

Correct result: 1.5 to 2kOhm Incorrect
result at sensor plug. Fit new sensor.

3a

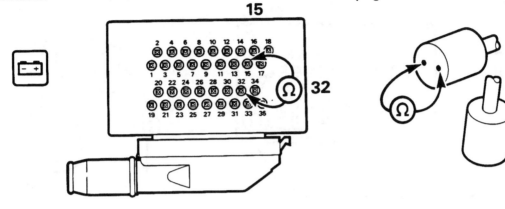

RR2842M

3b Check front left wheelspeed sensor insulation.

Correct result: 100kOhm + Incorrect result at
sensor plug: Fit new sensor.

3b

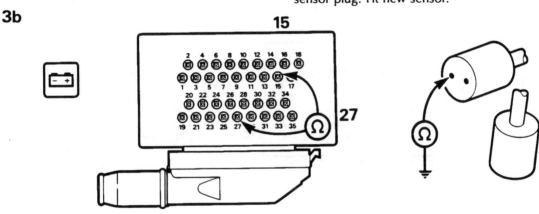

RR2843M

4a Check front right wheelspeed
sensor resistance.

Correct result: 1.5 to 2kOhm Incorrect result at
sensor plug: Fit new sensor.

4a

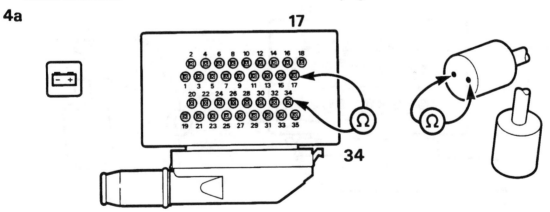

RR2844M

TEST PROCEDURE

RESULTS/CHECKS

4b Check front right wheelspeed
sensor insulation.

Correct result: 100kOhm +
Incorrect result at sensor plug: Fit new sensor.

4b

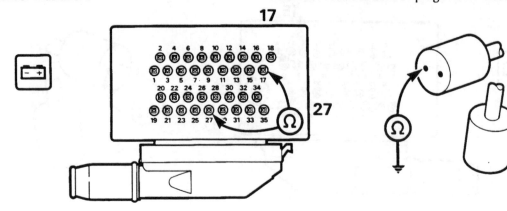

RR2845M

5a Check rear left wheelspeed sensor resistance.

Correct result: 1.5 to 2kOhm
Incorrect result at sensor plug: Fit new sensor.

5a

5b Check rear left wheelspeed sensor insulation.

Correct result: 100kOhm + Incorrect result at
sensor plug: Fit new sensor.

5b

RR2847M

TEST PROCEDURE

RESULTS/CHECKS

6a   Check rear right wheelspeed sensor resistance.

Correct result: 1.5 to 2kOhm
Incorrect result at sensor plug:
Fit new sensor.

6a

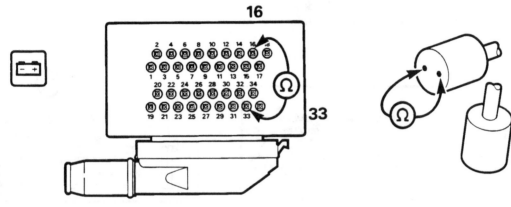

RR2848M

6b   Check rear right wheelspeed sensor insulation.

Correct result: 100kOhm +
Incorrect result at sensor plug:
Fit new sensor.

6b

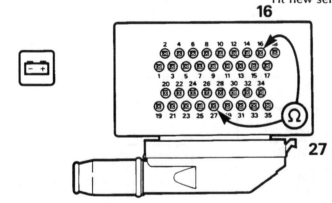

RR2849M

7a   Check isolation valve outlet.

Correct result: 5 to 7 Ohm

(1)   Remove booster harness plug, carry out check
      at booster

(2)   Refit booster harness plug, carry out check at
      35 way

Incorrect result at booster: fit new booster

7a

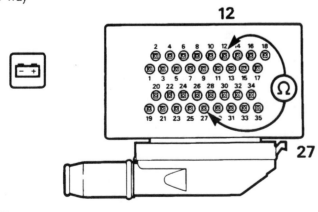
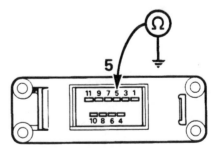

RR2850M

TEST PROCEDURE

7   Check isolation valve, inlet.
(1) Remove booster harness plug, carry out check at booster
(2) Refit booster harness plug, carry out check at 35 way Incorrect result at booster: fit new booster

RESULTS/CHECKS

Correct result: 5 to 7 Ohm

7b

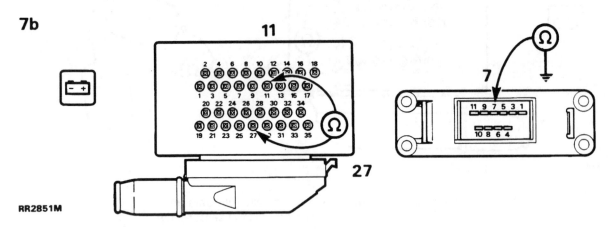

RR2851M

8a   Check ABS solenoid valve front left, outlet.
(1) Remove booster harness plug, carry out check at booster
(2) Refit booster harness plug, carry out check at 35 way

Correct result: 2.5 to 4.5 ohm

Incorrect result at booster: fit new booster

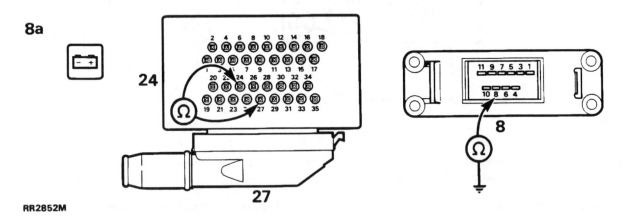

RR2852M

TEST PROCEDURE

RESULTS/CHECKS

8b Check ABS solenoid valve front left, inlet.
(1) Remove booster harness plug, carry out check at booster
(2) Refit booster harness plug, carry out check at 35 way

Correct result: 5 to 7 Ohm

Incorrect result at booster: fit new booster

8b

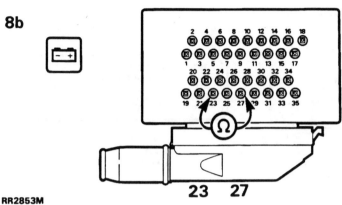

RR2853M

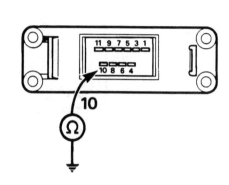

9a Check ABS solenoid valve front right, outlet.
(1) Remove booster harness plug,carry out check at booster
(2) Refit booster harness plug, carry out check at 35 way

Correct result: 2.5 to 4.5 Ohm

Incorrect result at booster: fit new booster

9a

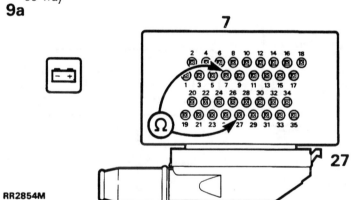

RR2854M

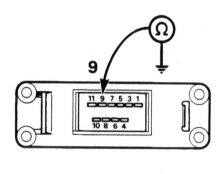

9b Check ABS solenoid valve front right, inlet.
(1) Remove booster harness plug,carry out check at booster
(2) Refit booster harness plug, carry out check at 35 way

Correct result: 5 to 7 Ohm

Incorrect result at booster: fit new booster

9b

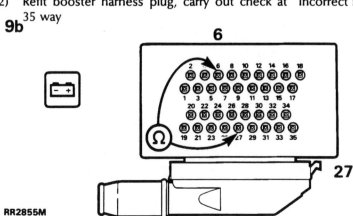

RR2855M

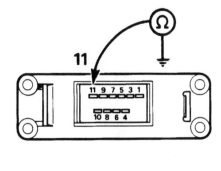

TEST PROCEDURE	RESULTS/CHECKS
10a Check ABS solenoid valve rear left, outlet.	Correct result: 2.5 to 4.5 Ohm
(1) Remove booster harness plug, carry out check at booster	
(2) Refit booster harness plug, carry out check at 35 way	Incorrect result at booster: fit new booster

10a

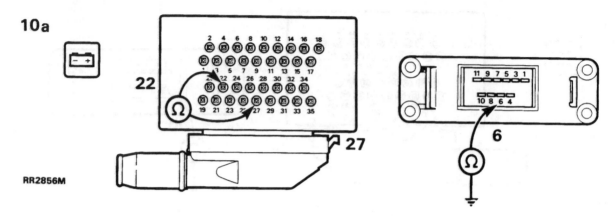

RR2856M

10b Check ABS solenoid valve rear left, inlet.	Correct result: 5 to 7 Ohm
(1) Remove booster harness plug, carry out check at booster	
(2) Refit booster harness plug, carry out check at 35 way	Incorrect result at booster: fit new booster

10b

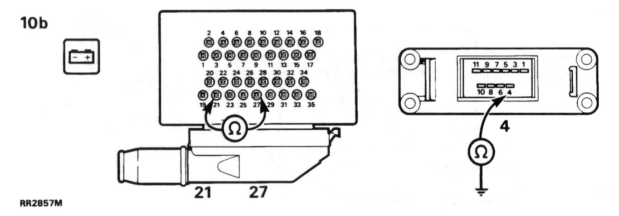

RR2857M

TEST PROCEDURE

RESULTS/CHECKS

11a Check ABS solenoid valve rear right, outlet.

Correct result: 2.5 to 4.5 Ohm

(1) Remove booster harness plug, carry out check at booster

(2) Refit booster harness plug, carry out check at 35 way

Incorrect result at booster: fit new booster

11a

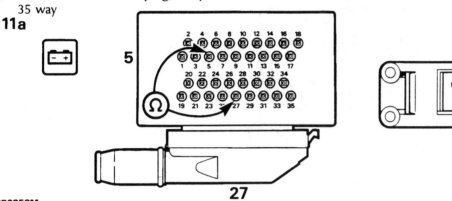

RR2858M

11b Check ABS solenoid valve rear right, inlet.

Correct result: 5 to 7 Ohm

(1) Remove booster harness plug, carry out check at booster

(2) Refit booster harness plug, carry out check at 35 way

Incorrect result at booster: fit new booster

11b

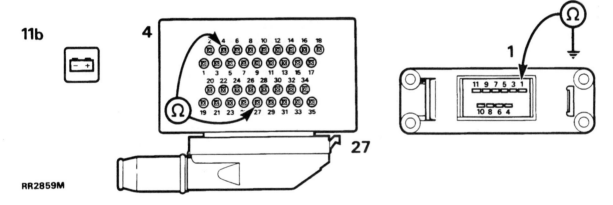

RR2859M

12a Check brake light switch - pedal down.

Correct result: 10V +
This contact must operate first and switch the brake lights.Incorrect reading: fit new brake light switch and recheck. Check cable if fault persists.

12a

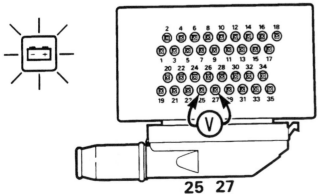

RR2860M

TEST PROCEDURE

12   Check brake light switch - pedal down.

12b

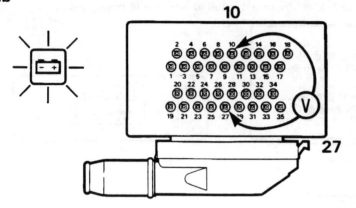

RR2919M

RESULTS/CHECKS

Correct result: 10V+ Incorrect reading: fit new
brake light switch and recheck.
Check cable if fault persists.

FAULT DIAGNOSIS

SYMPTOM	POSSIBLE CAUSE	CHECK	REMEDY
ABS warning light on	ABS electrical fault High sensor air gaps	Check ABS electrical circuit to identify fault	Change component if necessary Push in sensors
Both warning lights ON. Pedal travel and pedal force increased	No booster pressure (fluid loss) No booster pressure (pump not operating) Pump faulty	Check reservoir fluid level and inspect system for leaks Check electrical supply to pump	Rectify as necessary and refill reservoir Rectify electrical supply if necessary Change hydraulic pump
Both warning lights ON (no additional symptoms)	Malfunction of pressure switch	Disconnect pressure switch a) If light remains illuminated vehicle wiring faulty b) If lights extinguish pump defective	 a) Test wiring change harness if necessary b) Change pump
Brake fluid warning light ON	Fluid loss Reservoir fluid level switch malfunction Pressure switch malfunction	Check reservoir fluid level and inspect system for leaks Check fluid level switch Check switch with pressure gauge a) If wiring faulty b) If switch faulty	Rectify leakage, refill reservoir Change reservoir cap/switch a) Replace harness b) Change hydraulic pump
Brake fluid warning light ON. Pedal travel increased, foot pressure normal	Fluid loss from hydrostatic circuit	Check reservoir level and inspect system for leaks	Rectify leakage and refill reservoir Rebleed as necessary

Fault Diagnosis - continued

SYMPTOM	POSSIBLE CAUSE	CHECK	REMEDY
Brake fluid warning light OFF. Pedal travel increased, foot pressure normal	Insufficient bleeding		Rebleed master cylinder circuit
	Master cylinder malfunction		Change booster and bleed system
Hydraulic pump runs constantly	Fluid loss	Check reservoir level and inspect system for leaks	Rectify leakage as necessary, refill reservoir
	Pump non-return valve faulty		Change hydraulic pump
Hydraulic pump runs constantly with warning lights OFF. Pedal travel normal.	Malfunction of pressure switch	Disconnect pressure switch	
	Relay switch malfunction	a) If pump stops	a) Change hydraulic pump
		b) If pump continues running	b) Change relay or cable
Pedal can be moved downwards under constant pressure	Seal leaking in master cylinder	Inspect system for leaks	Change booster unit
	Seal leaking in servo unit		Change booster unit

CHASSIS FRAME

Alignment check - RR2751M

Diagram reference	millimeters	inches
AA Wheelbase reference dimension	2540,00	100.0
BB Centre line of front axle		
CC Centre line of rear axle		
DD Frame datum line		
EE Side member datum line		
FF Datum line		
1	264,525 ± 1,27	10.400 ± .050
2 Frame datum to underside of cross-member	150,80	5.937
3	266,70 ± 2,54	10.500 ± .100
4	237,74 ± 1,27	9.360 ± .050
5	327,81 ± 2,54	12.906 ± .100
6	979,94	38.58
7	2179,73 ± 2,54	85.816 ± .100
8	291,74 ± 2,54	11.486 ± .100
9	707,96 ± 2,54	27.872 ± .100
10	1468,49 ± 2,54	57.815 ± .100
11	1025,27 ± 2,54	40.36 ± .100
12	338,84 ± 2,54	13.34 ± .100
13A	222,25 ± 2,54	8.750 ± .100
13B	240,03 ± 2,54	9.450 ± .100
14 Reference dimension	824,92	32.477
15 To face of boss (both sides)	935,43 ± 2,54	36.828 ± .100
16	838,2 ± 0,38	33.000 ± .015
17 Check figure	630,94 ± 1,27	24.840 ± .050
18	344,17 ± 1,27	13.550 ± .050
19	485,77 ± 2,54	19.125 ± .100
20	485,77 ± 2,54	19.125 ± .100
21	828,68 ± 0,38	32.625 ± .015
22	129,03 ± 2,54	5.080 ± .100
23	2479,45 ± 0,25	97.616 ± .010
24	1290,34 ± 0,38	50.800 ± .015
25	1657,04 ± 0,38	65.238 ± .015
26	2598,44 ± 0,38	102.301 ± .015
27	79,09 ± 0,38	3.114 ± .015
28	465,48 ± 2,54	18.326 ± .100
29	1398,88 ± 0,38	55.074 ± .015
30 Reference dimension	635,00	25.00

CHASSIS FRAME

Diagram reference	millimeters	inches
SECTION W - W		
31 Frame datum line DD		
32	155,91 ± 1,27	6.14 ± .050
33	990,6 ± 0,38	39.00 ± .015
34	825,5 ± 2,54	32.50 ± .100
SECTION X - X		
35 Frame datum line DD		
36	488,95 ± 2,54	19.250 ± .100
37	295,27 ± 2,54	11.625 ± .100
SECTION Y - Y		
38 Frame datum line DD		
39	1320,8 ± 0,38	52.00 ± .015
40	80,39 ± 1,27	3.187 ± .050
SECTION Z - Z		
41 Frame datum line DD		
42	80,39 ± 1,27	3.165 ± .050
43	660,40 ± 0,25	26.000 ± .010
44	9,53 ± 2,54	0.375 ± .100

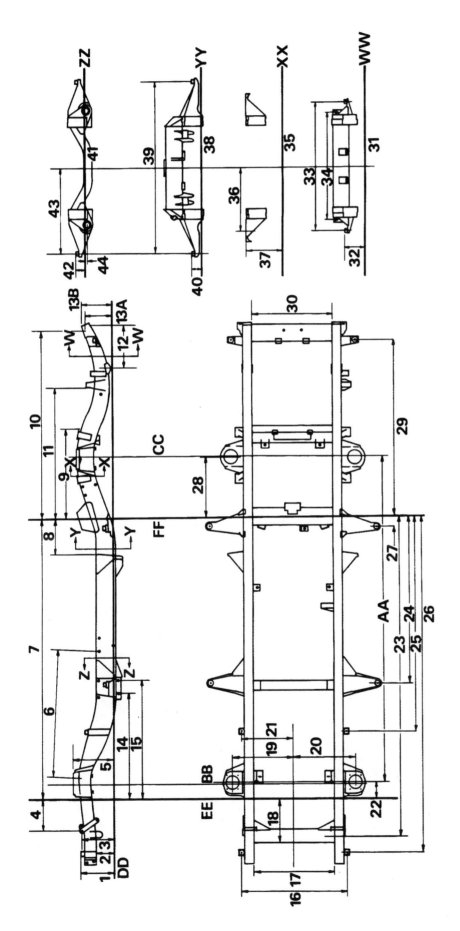

RR2751M

HEATER UNIT 1990 MODEL YEAR

Remove and refit

To remove and refit the heater unit, refer to existing instructions ignoring reference to the thermostat sensor. In addition the following electrical controls from the heater to the air conditioning unit need to be disconnected on removal and connected on refit:-

1. The electrical connector from the heater controls to the electric thermostat, sited at the rear of the evaporator housing.
2. The vent lever microswitch at the multiplug.

RECIRCULATING/FRESH AIR SOLENOID SWITCH
VACUUM UNIT (recirculating/fresh air flaps)

Remove and refit

Remove

1. Disconnect the battery negative lead.
2. Remove the transmission lever surround.
3. Remove the radio mounting console.
4. Remove the centre dash unit and the lower dash panel.
5. **Solenoid switch:** disconnect the electrical leads to the solenoid.
6. Disconnect the two vacuum hoses.
7. Remove the two screws and withdraw the solenoid.
8. **Vacuum unit:** remove the vacuum hose.
9. Remove the actuating rod securing clip.
10. Remove two retaining screws and remove the vacuum unit.

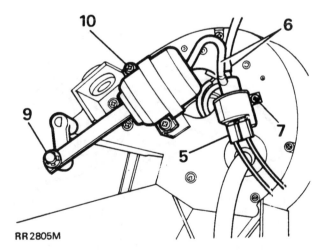

RR2805M

Refit

11. Reverse the removal procedure.

HEATER AND AIR CONDITIONING CONTROLS

Remove and refit

Remove

1. Disconnect the battery negative lead.
2. Remove the transmission lever surround and radio housing.
3. Remove the lower dash panel.
4. Remove the centre dash unit.
5. Disconnect the electrical plugs from the fan speed and recirculate/fresh air switches.
6. **Fan speed switch:** remove fixing screws and withdraw the switch.
7. **Air conditioning / fresh air / recirculating switch:** remove fixing screws and withdraw the switch.
8. **Potentiometer:** disconnect the electrical connector to the electronic thermostat sited at the rear of the evaporator housing.
9. Prise the wire cable connection from the heat control lever.
10. Release the potentiometer from its location.
11. Remove potentiometer with connecting arm to heat control lever. Withdrawing the attached electrical leads through the gommet.
12. **Microswitch:** disconnect the multiplug, lift vent lever, remove the two retaining clips and carefully withdraw the microswitch.

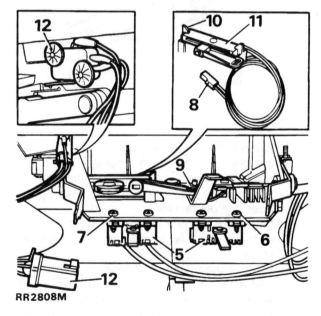

RR2808M

Refit

13. Reverse removal instructions. Check the satisfactory function of the controls before fitting dash and trim panels.

HEATER FAN MOTOR, ROTOR AND RESISTANCE UNIT.

Remove and refit

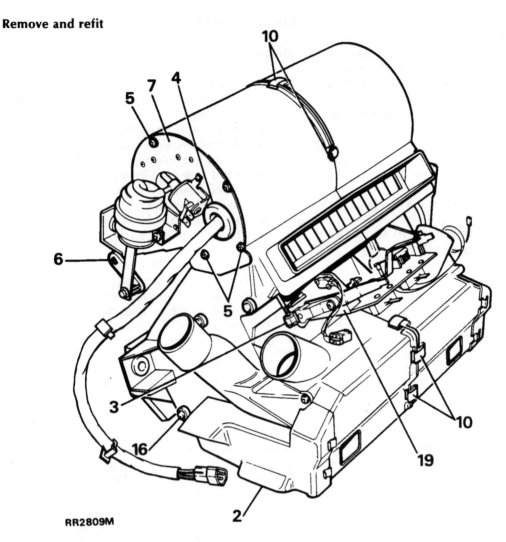

RR2809M

Remove

1. Remove the heater assembly.
2. Remove the left duct to footwell outlet.
3. Mark the position of vent control rod for reassembly. Disconnect by carefully prising open the plastic clip.
4. Disengage the grommet from side cover.
5. Remove the six screws retaining the side cover.
6. Remove the vacuum unit to air flap linkage.
7. Withdraw the side cover to expose the electric wires to the fan motor and resistance unit.
8. Release the resistance unit by tensioning back the metal mounting straps.
9. Remove the side cover feeding the electrical leads and the multiplug through the hole.
10. Remove the ten spring clips, three circlips and the two screws that secure the halves of the heater casing together. Ensure all of the fixings and two foam gaskets are removed.

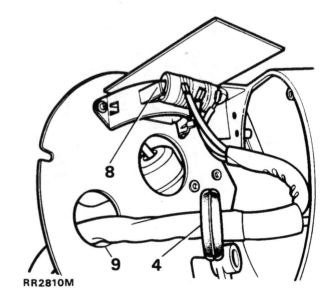

RR2810M

11. Position the flap (A) as shown, prise and slide its lower edge through the gap between motor housing and outer case. While separating each half of the heater casing.

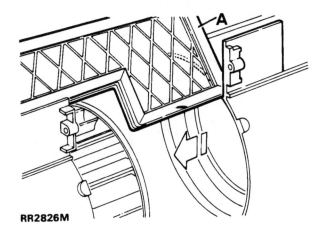

RR2826M

12. Note the location of the air flap pivots, for reassembly.
13. The motor assembly is held into the left half of the casing by two plastic tabs, locate and prise them away from the motor.
14. Note for reassembly the position and layout of the electrical wiring. Then withdraw the motor assembly including attached wires and resistance unit from its housing.

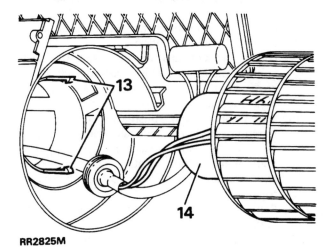

RR2825M

Refit

15. Feed the wiring and resistance unit through the motor housing and fit the motor assembly. Ensure the wires are positioned correctly, to avoid entangling the rotor, and the plastic tabs locate to secure the motor.
16. Mark a white spot on the end of each air flap pivot to be reassembled into the heater casing.
17. Offer the heater casing halves together. Ensure the flap (A) is positioned to reverse instruction 11.
18. Point the remaining air flap pivots in the direction of their location.
19. Locate and slot into the left casing the heater control panel assembly. Examine closely to ensure that both fixings engage and slide into their housing.
20. Slowly and firmly push the casing halves together checking that all components are aligning. Any solid resistance felt suggests a component is not locating correctly. Rectify and continue until the casing halves are together.
21. Refit all of the fixings that hold the heater casing halves together.
22. Reverse removal instructions 4 to 9.
23. Connect the rod to the vent control lever to its marked position.
24. Check all controls operate and flaps seal against the heater casing.
25. Refit the left duct to footwell outlet.
26. Renew the two foam gaskets.
27. Refit the heater assembly.

HEATER CORE

Remove and Refit

Remove

1. Remove the heater assembly.
2. Remove the left duct to footwell outlet.
3. Mark the position of vent control rod, for reassembly. Disconnect by carefully prising open the plastic clip.
4. Remove the ten spring clips, three circlips and the two screws that secure the halves of the heater casing together. Ensure all of the fixings and the two foam gaskets are removed.
5. Remove the pad from around the two coolant hose connections.
6. Position the flap (A) as shown, prise and slide its lower edge through the gap between motor housing and outer case. While separating each half of the heater casing.

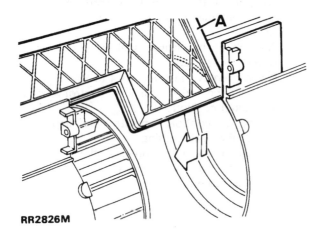

RR2826M

7. Note for reassembly the location of the air flap pivots.
8. Slide out the separate panel.
9. Remove the heater core complete with the sponge packing.

Refit

10. Fit the heater core into the left half of the casing. Slide in the separate panel (8) upto the coolant hose connections.
11. Mark a white spot on the end of each air flap pivot to be reassembled into the heater casing.

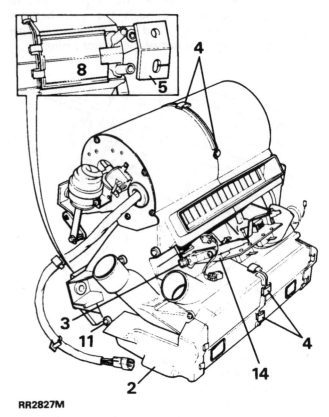

RR2827M

12. Offer the heater casing halves together. Ensure the flap (A) is positioned to reverse instruction 6.
13. Point the remaining air flap pivots in the direction of their location.
14. Locate and slot into the left casing the heater control panel assembly. Examine closely to ensure that both fixings engage and slide into their housing.
15. Slowly and firmly push the casing halves together checking that all components are aligning. Any solid resistance felt suggests a component is not locating correctly. Rectify and continue until the casing halves are together.
16. Refit all of the fixings that hold the heater casing halves together.
17. Connect the rod to the vent control lever to its marked position.
18. Check all controls operate and air flaps seal against the heater casing.
19. Refit the pad around the two coolant hose connections.
20. Refit the left duct to footwell outlet.
21. Renew the two foam gaskets.
22. Refit the heater assembly.

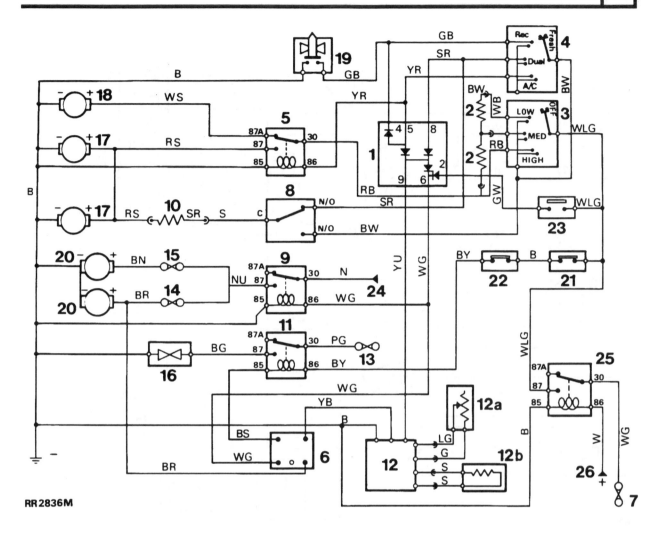

RR2836M

HEATER AND AIR CONDITIONING - EFI vehicles- circuit diagram

1. Diode pack.
2. Resistors.
3. Fan speed switch.
4. Air conditioning/re-circ/fresh air switch.
5. Heater/air conditioning relay.
6. Cable connection to ECU (EFI).
7. Fuse C9 - main fuse panel.
8. Face vent switch.
9. Condenser fan relay.
10. Two level resistor.
11. Compressor clutch relay.
12. Thermostat.
12-
   a. Temperature control potentiometer.

12b Evaporator temperature sensor.
13. Fuse B7.
14. Fuse B8.
15. Fuse B9.
16. Compressor clutch.
17. Air conditioning motors (2) - dashboard unit.
18. Heater motor.
19. Fresh air solenoid.
20. Condenser fan motors.
21. High pressure switch.
22. Low pressure switch.
23. Engine coolant temperature switch.
24. 12V from terminal post.
25. Heater/air con load relay.
26. 12V from ignition load relay.

Cable colour code

B	Black	N	Brown	R	Red	W	White
G	Green	O	Orange	S	Grey	Y	Yellow
L	Light	P	Purple	U	Blue		

The last letter of a colour code denotes the tracer.

NOTE: See EFI circuit diagram for details of air conditioning inputs to ECU.

1

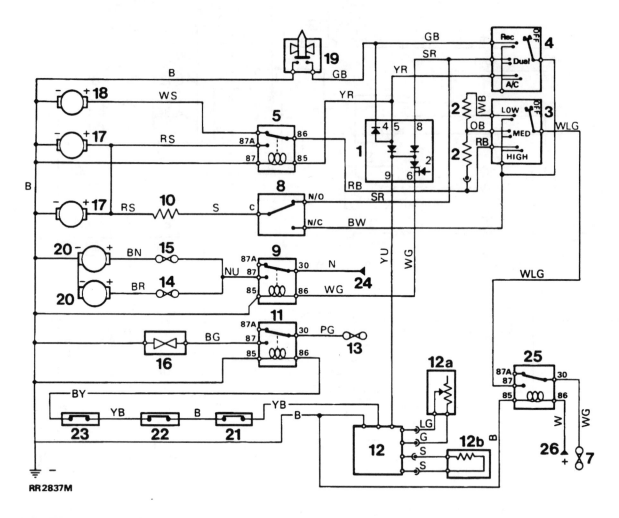

RR2837M

HEATER AND AIR CONDITIONING - DIESEL VEHICLES - circuit diagram

1. Diode pack.
2. Resistors.
3. Fan speed switch.
4. Air conditioning/re-circ/fresh air switch.
5. Heater/air conditioning relay.
6. Not used.
7. Fuse C9 - main fuse panel.
8. Face vent switch.
9. Condenser fan relay.
10. Two level resistor.
11. Compressor clutch relay.
12. Thermostat.
12-
  a. Temperature control potentiometer.

12b Evaporator temperature sensor.
13. Fuse B7.
14. Fuse B8.
15. Fuse B9.
16. Compressor clutch.
17. Air conditioning motors (2) - dashboard unit.
18. Heater motor.
19. Fresh air solenoid.
20. Condenser fan motors.
21. High pressure switch.
22. Low pressure switch.
23. Engine coolant temperature switch.
24. 12V from terminal post.
25. Heater/air con load relay.
26. 12V from ignition load relay.

AIR CONDITIONING

1990 Model year vehicles have modified air conditioning components. Details of which are given here and **must** be used in conjunction with the main workshop manual.

WARNING: All work involving the service and maintenance of the air conditioning requires special equipment, knowledge, experience and a full awareness and adhesion to the safety precautions.

EVAPORATOR ASSEMBLY

Remove and refit

Expansion valve
Remove and refit 1 to 21 and 31 to 49

Hose-Compressor to evaporator
Remove and refit 1 to 19 and 35 to 49

Hose-reciever drier to evaporator
Remove and refit 1 to 19 and 35 to 49

Blower units
Remove and refit 1 to 22 and 30 to 49

Removing
1. Open the bonnet and connect the gauge set.

   WARNING: Wear eye and hand protection when disconnecting components containing refrigerant.Plug all exposed connections immediately.

2. Discharge the system.
3. Disconnect the battery negative lead.
4. Disconnect the evaporator hoses from the compressor and the receiver drier. Use a second wrench to support the hose adaptors.
5. Working underneath the dash unit remove the two screws securing the blower closing panel. Slide the panel out of the two lower retaining clips.
6. Remove the nyloc nut and washer from the evaporator case mounting bracket.

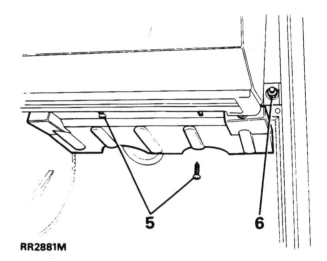

RR2881M

7. Remove the two nyloc nuts securing both centre dash panel and evaporator case mounting bracket.

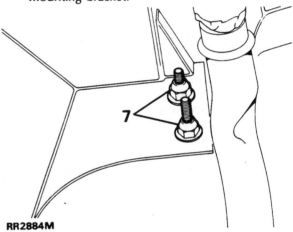

RR2884M

8. Remove the six screws securing the lower edge of the louvre panel to the evaporator case.

   Caution: Care must be taken when removing dash components. They can easily be scratched or damaged by incorrect leverage and excessive force.

9. Pry out, using equal leverage top and bottom, the mirror control switch. Disconnect the two multiplugs.
10. Repeat instruction 9 for removal of the clock. Disconnect electrical leads and the bulb holder.

11. Pry out along the lower edge the four air vents.
12. Remove the nine screws securing the evaporator housing and louvre panel to the dash top.

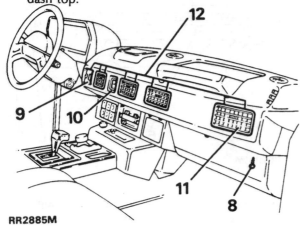

RR2885M

13. Withdraw panel clear of the dash top.
14. Carefully withdraw the refrigerant hoses and evaporator condensation drain tubes through the bulkhead.
15. Remove the air hose from the end of the evaporator case upper.
16. Disconnect electric wiring to the blower motor and electronic thermostat at the multiplugs.
17. Remove the evaporator case assembly from the vehicle and place on a surface that will not scratch the casing.

Dismantling

18. Remove the insulation from the evaporator and expansion valve hose connections.
19. Disconnect the hoses from the expansion valve and evaporator. Use a second wrench to support the hose adaptors and plug the connections.
20. Unclamp the sensor coil from the evaporator outlet pipe.
21. Carefully unscrew the expansion valve from the evaporator. Plug the connection.
22. Remove the eight securing screws and detach the blower units from the evaporator case.

23. Remove the screws securing the upper evaporator casing to the evaporator lower case.
24. Remove the thermister probe and lift off the upper casing.
25. Remove the insulation pad and the screws securing the evaporator to the lower casing.
26. Withdraw the evaporator from the casing.

Assembling

27. Secure the evaporator to the lower casing.
28. Fit the insulation pad.
29. Secure the casing together with the screws and refit the thermister probe.
30. Refit and secure the blower units to the evaporator casing.

Note: Use refrigerant compressor oil on all mating surfaces to assist leakage prevention. Tighten the connections to correct torque.

31. Assemble the expansion valve to the evaporator with the inlet facing downwards.
32. Clamp the sensor coil to the evaporator outlet pipe.
33. Connect the hoses to the evaporator and expansion valve. Use new 'O' rings. See Torque valves.
34. Wrap all exposed metal at the hose connections with prestite tape.

Refitting

35. Place the evaporator assembly on the floor of the vehicle and reconnect two wiring connectors disconnected at instruction 16.
36. Feed the hoses and evaporator condensate tubes through the bulkhead. Ensure that the openings and grommets are adequately sealed against ingress of dust and moisture.
37. Fit the evaporator assembly to its location and reconnect the air hose at the end of the evaporator casing.Ensure the centre dash panel is eased over the evaporator case mounting bracket on the shared fixing point.

EVAPORATOR CASE ASSEMBLY

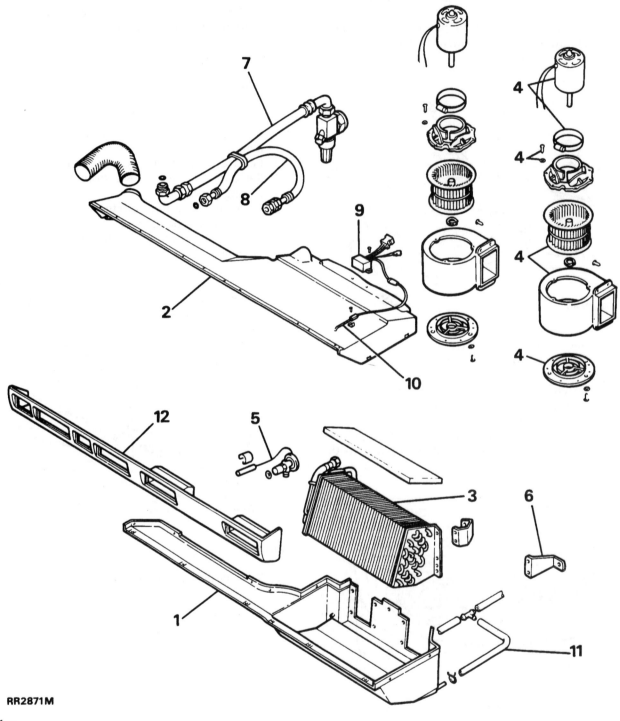

RR2871M

Key

1. Evaporator case lower	4. Blower Assy	7. Hose Assy Suction	10. Thermister Probe
2. Evaporator case upper	5. Expansion Valve	8. Hose Assy Liquid	11. Drain Hose Assy
3. Evaporator	6. Mounting Bracket	9. Thermostat	12. Louvre Panel

38. Feed the electrical connections to the clock and mirror control switch through their apertures in the louvre panel. Refit the louvre panel.
39. Reconnect electrics to the clock and mirror control switch and fit them to louvre panel.
40. Fit the air vents.

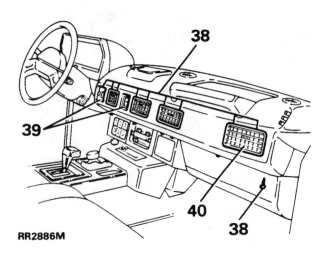

RR2886M

41. Secure, using three new nyloc nuts and plain washers, the evaporator case mounting brackets.
42. Ensure condensation tubes are free from kinks and able to drain off water. Fit the blower closing panel.
43. Connect the two refrigerant hoses to the compressor and receiver drier. Tighten to the correct torque.

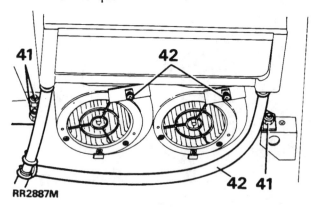

RR2887M

44. Evacuate the system.
45. Charge the complete system.
46. Perform a leak test on any accessible disturbed joints.
47. Perform a functional check.
48. Check compressor oil level.
49. Disconnect the gauge set.

Resistor Unit

The resistor unit is located on the bulkhead closing panel underneath the decker panel.

Remove and refit

Removing

1. Disconnect the battery negative lead and remove decker panel (see body section)
2. Remove the two screws securing the resistor.
3. Release the grommet from the housing.
4. Remove the four screws from the bulkhead closing panel.
5. Trace the resistors electrical wiring to the multiplug and disconnect.
6. Remove the resistor complete with wiring and multiplug.

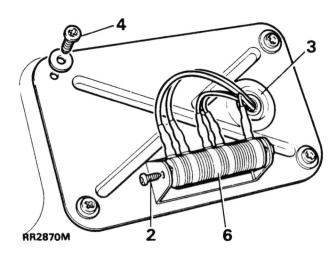

RR2870M

Refitting

7. Reverse the removal instructions.

RECEIVER DRIER

Remove and refit

> CAUTION: Immediate blanking of the receiver drier is important. Exposed life of the unit is only 15 minutes.

Removing

1. Open the bonnet and connect the gauge set.

> WARNING: Wear eye and hand protection when disconnecting components containing refrigerant. Plug all exposed connections immediately.

2. Discharge the system.
3. Disconnect the battery negative lead.
4. Disconnect the electrical leads at the two plug connectors and carefully unscrew, at the hexagon nut, the pressure switches from the receiver drier. Blank the exposed connections immediately.

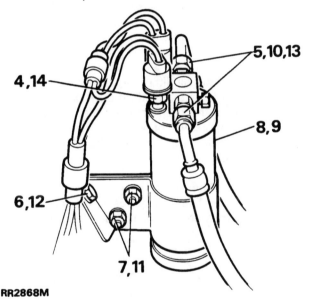

RR2868M

5. Carefully disconnect the two hose connections. Use a second spanner to support the hose adaptor. Blank the exposed connections immediately.
6. Remove one bolt, nut and washers securing the mounting bracket to the wing valance.
7. Remove the clamp bolts, washers and nuts.
8. Withdraw the receiver drier from the mounting bracket.

Refitting

9. Insert the receiver drier into the mounting bracket with this inlet and outlet connections correct to the refrigerant circuit as shown.
10. Connect the two hose connections finger tight. Use refrigerant compressor oil on all mating surfaces to assist leakage prevention.
11. Fit the clamp bolts, washer and nuts.
12. Secure the mounting bracket to the wing valance.
13. Tighten the two hose connections to the correct torque. Use a second spanner to support the hose adaptor.
14. Carefully refit the pressure switches to the receiver drier. Use refrigerant compressor oil on all mating surfaces to assist leakage prevention and tighten the switches to the correct torque. Reconnect the electrical leads.
15. Evacuate the complete system.
16. Charge the complete system.
17. Perform a leak test on any disturbed joints.
18. Carry out a functional check.
19. Check compressor oil level.
20. Disconnect the gauge set.

Compressor Oil Level.

Sanden 709

The compressor specification on petrol and diesel engines is a Sanden 709. It is identified by the label and the oil filler plug located on the side.

Check

It is **NOT** necessary to check the compressor oil level as part of routine maintenance.

NOTE: The compressor oil level should be checked whenever any components, including the compressor are removed and refitted or when a pipe or hose has been removed and reconnected or, if a refrigerant leak is suspected.

All compressors are factory charged with 135 ± 15 ml (4.6 ± 0.5 fl oz) of oil. When the air conditioning equipment is operated some of the oil circulates throughout the system with the refrigerant, the amount varying with engine speed. When the system is switched off the oil remains in the pipe lines and components, so the level of oil in the compressor is reduced, by approximately 30 ml (1 fl oz).

The compressor oil level must finally be checked after the system has been fully charged with refrigerant and operated to obtain a refigerated temperature of the vehicle interior. This ensures the correct oil balance throughout the system.

The compressor is not fitted with an oil level dipstick, and a suitable dipstick must be made locally from 3mm (0.25 in) diameter soft wire in accordance with the accompanying illustration. After shaping, mark the end of the dipstick with sixteen graduations 3mm (0.125in) apart.

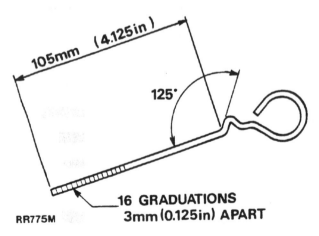

**16 GRADUATIONS
3mm (0.125in) APART**

RR775M

Procedure

1. Open the bonnet.

   Warning: Wear eye and hand protection when disconnecting components containing refrigerant. Plug all exposed connections immediately.

2. Fit the charging and testing equipment.
3. Start the engine and turn the temperature control to maximum cooling position, and the air flow control to HIGH speed. Operate the system for ten minutes at engine speed idle speed.

   NOTE: Open the valve slowly during the following to avoid a sudden pressure reduction in the compressor crankcase, it could cause a large amount of oil to leave the compressor. Refer also to SERVICE VALVES.

4. Reduce the engine speed to idling and **SLOWLY** open the suction side valve on the test equipment until the compound gauge reads 0 or a little below.
5. Stop the engine at this point and quickly open the suction valve and discharge valve.
6. Loosen the oil filter plug and unscrew it slowly by five turns to bleed off crankcase pressure.
7. Remove the oil filler plug. Align the notch on the counterweight with the centre of the oil filler hole. This enables the dipstick to be inserted.

   NOTE: The oil filler plug on compressors fitted to Diesel engines is on the opposite side to that shown. The oil check procedure is the same.

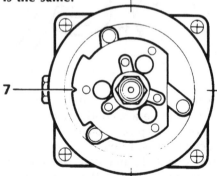

RR2869M

8. Wipe then insert dipstick to its stop position ensuring the angle of the dipstick is flush with the surface of the filler hole.

SD709

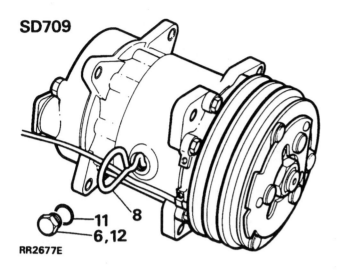

RR2677E

15. Stop the engine.
16. Close all valves on the charging and testing equipment.
17. Disconnect the charging lines from the compressor.
18. Refit the dust caps to the compressor valve stems and gauge connections, and to the charging lines.
19. Close the bonnet.

9. Withdraw the dipstick and count the number of graduations to determine the depth of oil.
10. Oil level SD 709: fifteen to sixteen graduations. Add or remove oil as necessary until the mid-range figure is obtained. It is recommended that a syringe is used for adding or removing oil. Use only the correct compressor oil - see Recommended Lubricants, section 09.
11. Lubricate a new 'O' ring with compressor oil fit it over the threads of the plug without twisting and install the filler plug loosely.
12. Evacuate the air from the compressor using the vacuum pump on the charging and testing equipment, following the equipment manufacturer's instructions. Tighten the filler plug to the correct torque.
13. Close fully the suction and discharge valves.

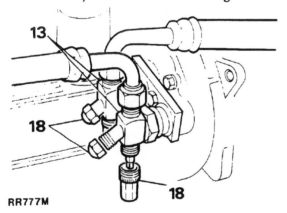

RR777M

14. Start and run the engine at 1,200 rev/min and check for leak at the compressor level plug. Do not overtighten to correct a leak. In the event of a leak isolate the compressor as previously described in items 4 to 6, and check the 'O' ring seats for dirt, etc.

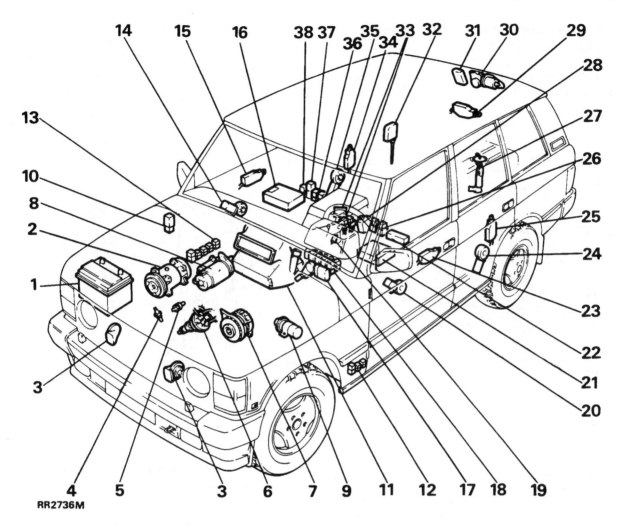

RR2736M

LOCATION OF ELECTRICAL EQUIPMENT - 1990 MODEL YEAR

1. Battery
2. Air conditioning compressor (option)
3. Horns
4. Oil pressure switch
5. Water temperature switch
6. Electronic distributor
7. Alternator
8. Starter motor
9. Coil
10. Headlamp wash timer unit
11. Heater
12. Relays/flasher units
13. Air con relays/diode unit (option)
14. Window lift motor (front RH door)
15. Door lock actuator (front RH door)
16. Electronic control unit (EFI)
17. Wiper motor - front screen
18. Relays/delay units
19. Park brake warning light switch
20. Window lift motor (front LH door)
21. Electronic control unit and relays (ABS) (option)
22. Seat adjustment fusebox (option)
23. Door lock actuator (front LH door)
24. Window lift motor (rear LH door)
25. Door lock actuator (rear LH door)
26. Seat adjustment relays - two (option)
27. Electrical in-tank fuel pump
28. Inertia switch
29. Tailgate lock actuator
30. Wiper motor - rear screen
31. Radio aerial amplifier
32. Fuel filler flap lock actuator
33. Window lift relays and one touch control unit
34. Door lock actuator (rear RH door)
35. Window lift motor (rear RH door)
36. EFI relays (two)
37. Condenser fan timer unit (option)
38. Cruise control relay (option)

NOTE: Left hand drive vehicle shown. Items 10, 12, 13, 17 and 18 located symmetrically opposite on right hand drive vehicles.

**RELAYS, DELAY UNITS, TIMER UNITS, DIODE
PACK - Identification**

Left hand drive vehicle shown, right hand drive
symmetrically opposite.

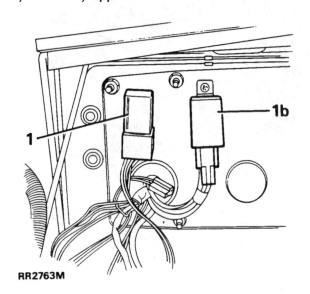

RR2763M

Closure panel viewed from the engine bay
compartment, with protective cover removed.

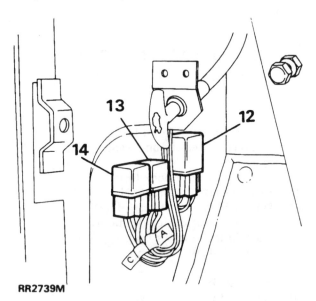

RR2739M

RR2379M shows relays mounted in left hand side of
footwell, trim panel removed, left hand drive.

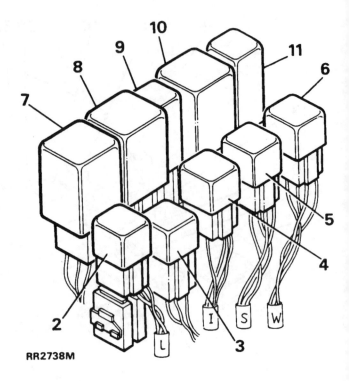

RR2738M

Steering column mounted relays viewed with the
lower dash panel removed.

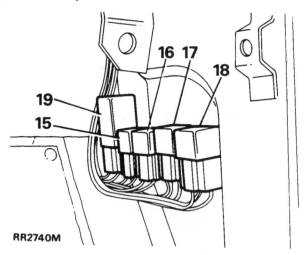

RR2740M

RR2740M shows relays mounted in right hand side
of footwell, trim panel removed, left hand drive

2

Relay/delay/timer/diode unit	Colour	Circuit Diagram Item Number	
		Right hand steer	Left hand steer
1. Headlamp wash timer unit	Black	19.M	18.M
1b. Glow plug timer unit (diesel)	Black	143.M	150.M
2. Headlamp relay	Natural	17.M	16.M
3. Heated front screen relay	Black	3.HF	3.HF
4. Ignition load relay	Natural	1.M	1.M
5. Starter soleniod relay	Natural	6.M	6.M
6. Heated rear window relay	Natural	67.M	64.M
7. Rear wiper delay	Blue	132.M	139.M
8. Interior lamp delay/timer	Red	101.M	99.M
9. Heated front screen timer unit	Grey	2.HF	2.HF
10. Voltage sensitive switch	Yellow	72.M	70.M
11. Front wiper delay	Red	15.M	14.M
12. Flasher/hazard unit	Blue	75.M	73.M
13. Auxiliary lamp relay	Natural	88.M	86.M
14. Sunroof auxiliary relay	Natural	124.M	125.M
15. Air con./heater relay	Natural	5.A	5.A
16. Compressor clutch relay	Natural	11.A	11.A
17. Heater/air con. load relay	Natural	163.M	175.M
18. Condenser fan relay	Natural	9.A	9.A
19. Air con. diode pack	Orange	1.A	1.A
20. Seat adjustment relays - two	Natural	5.6.F	5.6.F
21. Main EFI relay	Silver	22.E	22.E
22. Fuel pump relay	Silver	21.E	21.E
23. Cruise control relay	Natural	16.C	16.C
24. Condenser fan timer unit	Green	33.E	33.E
25. Rear window lift relay	Natural	13.W	13.W
26. Front window lift relay	Natural	14.W	14.W
27. Window lift one touch unit	Black	1.W	1.W
28. Brake check relay (RH steering)	Natural	151.M	. . .

M	Main circuit diagram	**E**	EFI circuit diagram
A	Air conditioning circuit diagram	**SR**	Sunroof circuit diagram
S	Seat adjustment circuit diagram	**W**	Window lift circuit diagram
HF	Heated front screen circuit diagram	**C**	Cruise control circuit diagram

Relays cont'd

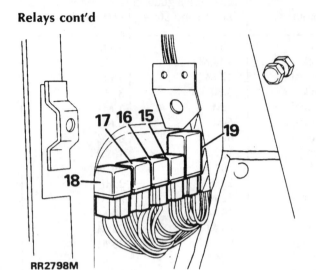

RR2798M

RR2798 shows relays mounted in left hand side of footwell, trim panel removed, right hand drive.

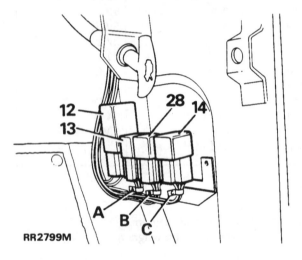

RR2799M

RR2799 shows relays mounted in right hand side of footwell, trim panel removed, right hand drive

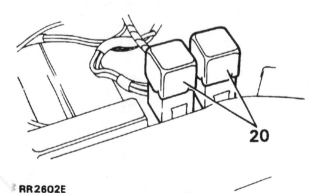

RR2602E

Seat adjustment relays (load control) located beneath the left hand front seat adjacent to fuse box (B).

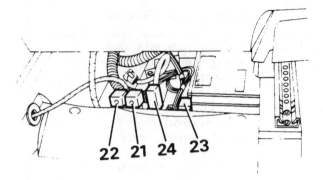

RR2765M

EFI (black terminal block) and fuel pump relays (blue terminal block) mounted beneath right hand front seat (21 and 22).

Condenser fan timer unit (24) mounted beneath right hand front seat.

Cruise control relay (23).

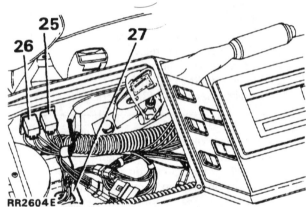

RR2604E

Front (black terminal block) and rear (blue terminal block) window relays. One touch control unit (27) is located inside the glove box, accessible by removing glove box liner.

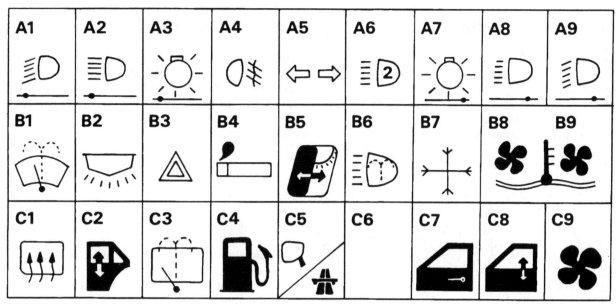

RR2696M

FUSE BOX - RR2696M

FUSE No.	COLOUR CODE	RATING AMPS	IGN. KEY POSITION	FUNCTION
A1	Red	10	II	LH dipped beam
A2	Red	10	II	LH main beam, auxiliary lamp relay
A3	Tan	5	O	LH sidelamps, radio ill., trailer pickup
A4	Red	10	O	Rear fog guard (headlamp switch controlled)
A5	Yellow	20	II	Direction ind., resistor, heated jets, thermo., heated front screen timer, air con. low coolant, speed transducer, interior lamp delay, reverse lights, stop lights
A6	Red	10	II	Auxiliary driving lamps (from main beam)
A7	Tan	5	O	RH sidelamps, rheostat controlled instrument/switch illumination, trailer pick up
A8	Red	10	II	RH main beam
A9	Red	10	II	RH dipped beam (headlamp levelling Germany)
B1	Yellow	20	I	Front wash/wipe, seat relays, window lift relays, antenna amplifier
B2	Yellow	20	O	Interior light, clock, underbonnet ill., elec. seat relays, radio, door lamps
B3	Yellow	20	O	Hazard switch, alarm, main beam/dip flash, horns
B4	Yellow	20	II	Cigar lighters
B5	Yellow	20	II	Sunroof motor
B6	Yellow	20	II	Headlamp wash
B7	Tan	5	II	Air conditioning compressor clutch
B8	Yellow	20	II	Air conditioning/radiator cooling fan
B9	Yellow	20	II	Air conditioning/radiator cooling fan
C1	Green	30	II	Heated rear screen (voltage switch controlled)
C2	Green	30	II	Window lifts - rear
C3	Red	10	II	Rear wash wipe motor, heated rear screen relay, mirror heaters
C4	Red	10	II	Fuel pump
C5	Red	10	II	Mirror motors, cruise control (option)
C6	---	---	---	Not used
C7	Blue	15	O	Central locking
C8	Green	30	II	Window lifts - front
C9	Green	30	II	Heater/air conditioning motor

ALTERNATOR HEAT SHIELD

Remove and refit

Removing

1. Disconnect the battery negative lead.
2. Remove the fixing screw to rocker cover.
3. Remove nut from alternator rear mounting bolt. Remove heat shield.

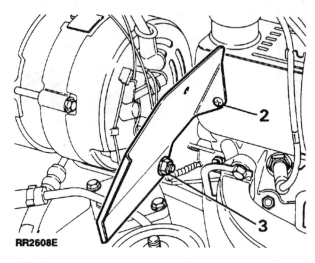

RR2608E

Refitting

4. Reverse removal procedure, check and adjust drive belt tension if required.

CENTRAL DOOR LOCKING - two point

The central door locking system on four door models is now activated from both driver's and passenger's doors. A switch/lock activator unit is fitted in both front doors. The system is controlled by an electronic unit situated on the steering column support bracket

CENTRAL DOOR LOCK CONTROL UNIT

Remove and refit

Removing

1. Disconnect the battery negative lead.
2. Remove the lower fascia panel.
3. Disconnect the harness multi-plug.
4. Remove the securing screws.
5. Remove the control unit.

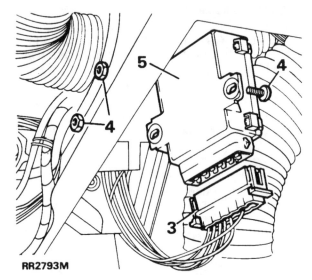

RR2793M

Refitting

6. Reverse the removal procedure.

INSTRUMENT BINNACLE WARNING LIGHT SYMBOLS

 Direction indicator - left turn (green)

 Direction indicator - right turn (green)

 Headlamp main beam on (blue)

 Brake pad wear (amber)

 Trailer connected - flashes with direction indicators (green)

EFI warning light (amber)

 Brake fluid pressure failure/low fluid level, transmission handbrake on (red)

 Low screenwash fluid (amber)

 ABS warning light (red)

 Automatic gearbox oil or transfer box temperature high (red)

Cold start - heater plugs operating (diesel models) (amber)

 Seat belt (red). NOTE: The seat belt warning symbol appears on all binnacles but will only be illuminated when territory regulations require a seat belt warning system to be fitted.

 Ignition on/low charge (red)

 Engine oil pressure low (red)

 Low coolant (red)

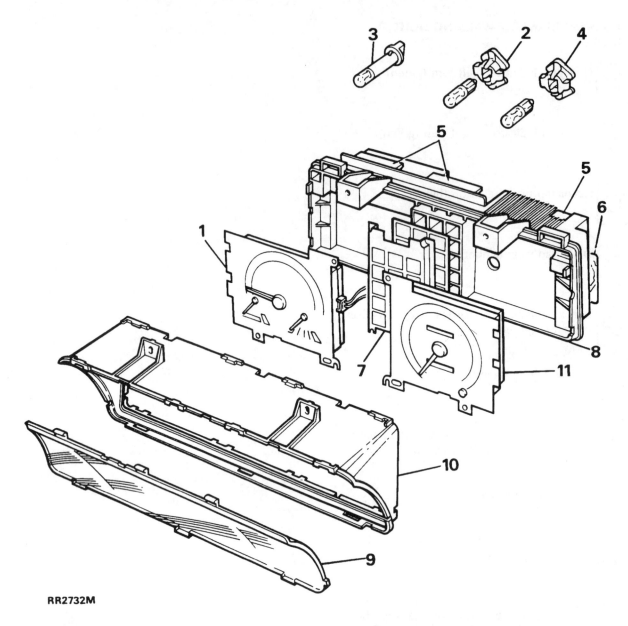

RR2732M

Instrument pack

1. Tachometer, fuel and temperaturte gauge.
2. Ignition warning bulb (with separate blue holder unit)
3. Panel illumination bulb and holder.
4. Warning lights bulb and holder.
5. Printed circuit input tags (for harness connection).
6. Printed circuit.
7. Warning light panel.
8. Instrument case (front).
9. Curved lens.
10. Binnacle housing.
11. Speedometer.

INSTRUMENT BINNACLE

A revised instrument pack is fitted to 1990 model year vehicles. An electronic speedometer is fitted, deleting the requirement for a speedometer cable between speed transducer and speedometer. The instruments are restyled to improve the clarity of graphics.

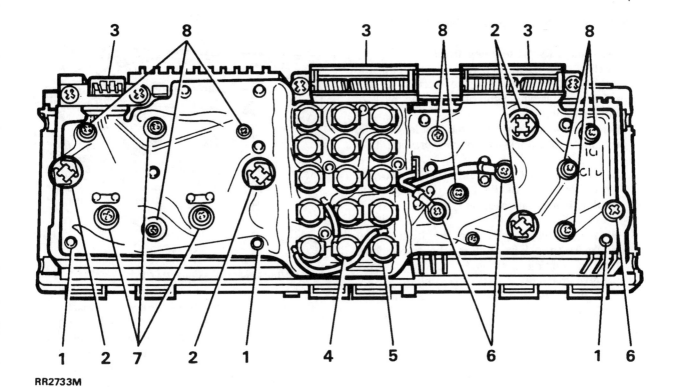

RR2733M

Instrument case (back)

1. Printed circuit locating pegs.
2. Panel illumination bulbs - 4.
3. Harness connectors.
4. Warning light bulbs.
5. No charge warning light bulb (blue holder).
6. Tachometer/fuel/temperature gauge securing screws - 3.
7. Speedometer securing screws - 3.
8. Printed circuit securing screws 8.

PRINTED CIRCUIT HARNESS CONNECTIONS

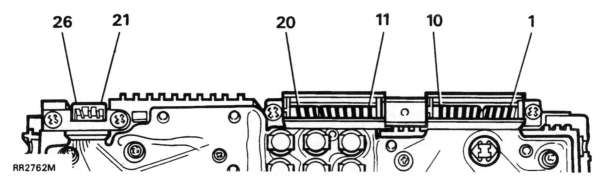

RR2762M

Sequence on connections looking towards the BACK of the instrument case.

RENEWAL OF PANEL AND WARNING LIGHTS

1. Disconnect the battery negative lead.
2. Unclip the back of the cowl from the instrument binnacle to give access to the panel and warning light bulbs in the back of the instrument case.
3. Remove the appropriate bulb holder unit by rotating it anti-clockwise and withdrawing it.

   NOTE: The 'No Charge/Ignition On' warning light, identified by its BLUE coloured bulb holder, is a 2 watt capless type.

4. Fit a new bulb and rotate the bulb holder clockwise to lock in position. The correct bulb type is: warning lights, 1.4 watt capless type, panel illumination, 3 watt capless type.
5. Refit the cowl and refit the battery negative lead.

   NOTE: If difficulty is experienced in changing bulbs due to the limited space available the instrument binnacle fixings should be removed to enable the binnacle to be raised above the fascia as far as other connections permit. See 'Instrument Binnacle - remove and refit' below for details of binnacle mounting bracket fixing.

INSTRUMENT BINNACLE

Remove and refit

Remove

1. Disconnect the battery negative lead.
2. Remove the lower fascia by releasing the six retaining screws.
3. Remove the four nuts (with spring and plain washers) from under the top fascia rail which secure the instrument binnacle to the vehicle.
4. Unclip the binnacle cowl from the rear, and remove.
5. Disconnect the two multi-plugs and the single plug from the printed circuit connectors.
6. Lift the instrument binnacle from the top fascia rail and transfer it to the workbench.

Refitting

7. Reverse the removal instructions 1 to 6.

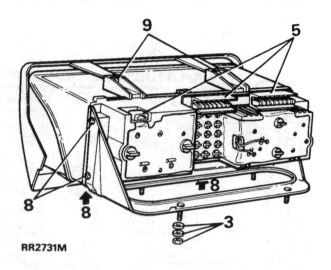

RR2731M

REMOVING INSTRUMENT PACK

8. Having removed the instrument binnacle from the vehicle, detach the binnacle mounting bracket. This is secured to the instrument case by two screws and to the bottom of the binnacle bezel by two smaller screws.
9. Remove the two screws retaining the top of the bezel to the front housing and detach the bezel.
10. Detach the curved lens from the binnacle housing by depressing four tabs and easing the top of the lens out, the depressing three tabs and easing the lower edge of the lens out of its location.
11. Separate the instrument case from the binnacle housing by releasing the upper and lower locating tabs in turn.

Refitting Instrument Pack to Binnacle

12. Reverse removal instructions 9 to 11.

CIRCUIT SERVED

**Numbers refer to pin number on instrument
pack circuit diagram RR2734M**

Coolant temperature 1
Low coolant input 2
Ignition switch 12V+ 3
Ignition warning light 4
Oil pressure warning light 5
Fuel tank unit 6
Transmission oil temperature 7
Cold start warning (diesel) 8
12V+ ignition 9
Tachometer signal 10
Brake fail/handbrake warning light 11
Brake pad wear warning light 12
Low wash fluid 13
Direction indicator - left 14
Zero volts from dimmer 15
Main beam warning light 16
Trailer warning light 17
Direction indicator - right 18
EFI warning light 19
ABS warning light 20
Seat belt warning light 21
Low coolant check 22
Speed signal 23
Not used 24
Panel illumination bulbs (4) 25
Earth -ve 26

Instrument pack

Key

- A. Speedometer
- B. Tachometer
- C. Temperature gauge
- D. Fuel gauge
- E. Low fuel warning unit
- F. Low fuel warning light
- G. Low coolant warning light
- H. Low coolant warning unit

**Removing Tachometer, Fuel and Temperature
Gauge Unit**

**NOTE: The tachometer, fuel and temperature
gauges are replaced as a unit if necessary.**

13. Remove the two panel illumination bulb
    holders.
14. Remove the three larger screws retaining the
    tachometer, fuel and temperature gauges.
    Note the position of the black and white leads
    secured by two of the screws.
15. Carefully manoeuvre the unit from the front of
    the instrument case.

**Refitting the Tachometer, Fuel and Temperature
Gauge Unit**

16. Reverse the removal procedure, items 13 to
    15.

Removing the speedometer

17. Remove the two panel illumination bulb
    holders.
18. Remove the three larger screws securing the
    speedometer.
19. Carefully remove the speedometer from the
    front of the instrument case.

Refitting the speedometer

20. Reverse the removal procedure items 16 to 18.

Removing the Printed Circuit

21. Remove the Speedometer and Tachometer
    units as described above. Removal all warning
    light bulbs before remving the printed circuit.
    Note the position of the no charge warning
    light, identified by its blue coloured bulb
    holder.
22. Remove the two harness connectors, retained
    by four screws to release the printed circuit
    tags and the input plug.
23. Remove the eight screws and plain washers
    securing the printed circuit.
24. Carefully ease the printed circuit from its
    locating pegs.

Refitting the printed circuit

25. Reverse the removal procedure, items 21 to
    24.

AUXILIARY SWITCH PANEL

The auxiliary panel contains five 'push-push' and one single push switch which incorporate integral symbols for identification.

The symbols are illuminated by two bulbs which become operational when the vehicle lights are on.

The rear fog guard lamp (1) and heated front (6) and rear (5) screen switches are also provided with individual warning lights, illuminated when the switches are operated.

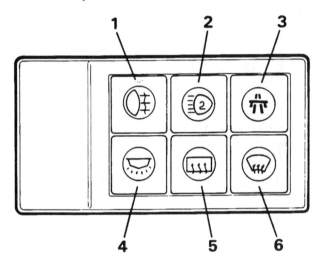

RR2795M

1. Rear fog guard lamps.
2. Auxiliary driving lamps.
3. Cruise control (option).
4. Interior and tailgate lamps.
5. Heated rear screen.
6. Heated front screen (option).

HEATED FRONT SCREEN

The heated front screen will operate when the push switch is operated with engine running. The timer unit, see Relays-identification, will provide a preset time cycle of 7 1/2 minutes ± 20%.
Switching off the ignition, or further operation of the heated front screen switch during the cycle will switch off the screen and cancel, reset and switch off the timer unit.

Fuses

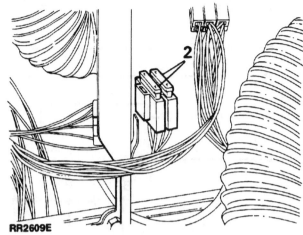

RR2609E

Heated front screen (2) has two 25 amp white, blade type fuses mounted adjacent to the bank of steering column mounted relays.

HEATED FRONT SCREEN

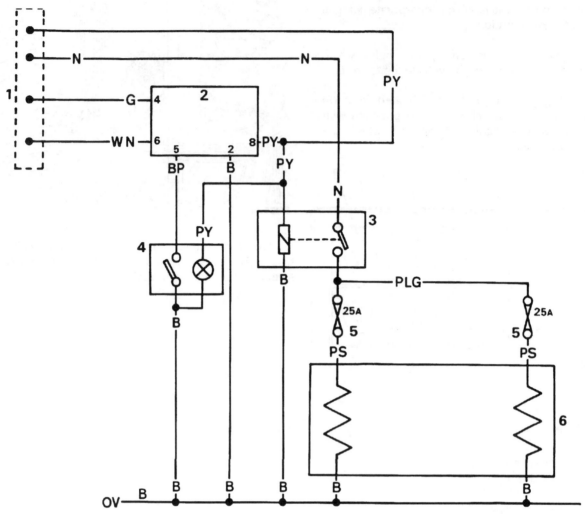

RR2593E

Circuit diagram - RR2593E

1. Main harness connections
   Brown - live positive feed
   Green - ignition positive feed
   Purple/yellow - EFI harness plug
   White/brown - oil pressure switch
   Black - earth
2. Timer unit
3. Load relay
4. Switch/warning light
5. In line fuses - 25 Amp.
6. Heated front screen

Cable colour code

B	Black	**L**	Light	**P**	Purple	**U**	Blue
G	Green	**N**	Brown	**R**	Red	**W**	White
K	Pink	**O**	Orange	**S**	Grey	**Y**	Yellow

The last letter of a colour code denotes the tracer.

CENTRAL DOOR LOCKING

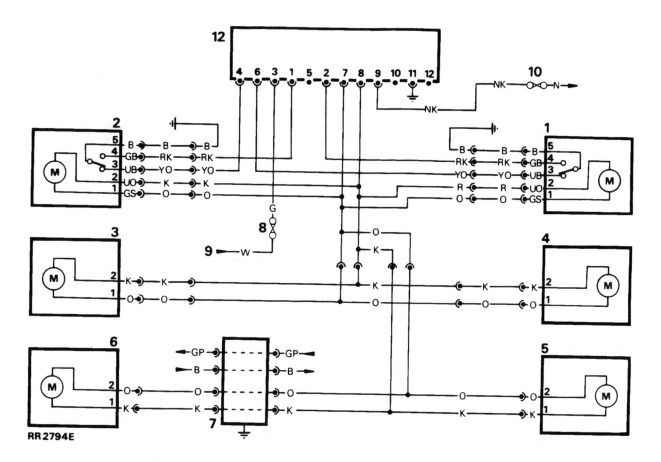

RR 2794E

Circuit diagram - RR2794E

1. Switch/lock unit right hand front door
2. Switch/lock unit left hand front door
3. Lock unit left hand rear door relay
5. Lock unit right hand rear door relay
6. Fuel flap actuator
6. Lock unit tailgail
7. Suppressor
8. Fuse A5
9. Feed from ignition load relay
10. Fuse C7
11. Battery 12V + ve
12. Central door locking control unit

Cable colour code

B	Black	L	Light	P	Purple	U	Blue
G	Green	N	Brown	R	Red	W	White
K	Pink	O	Orange	S	Grey	Y	Yellow

The last letter of a colour code denotes the tracer.

ELECTRIC MIRRORS

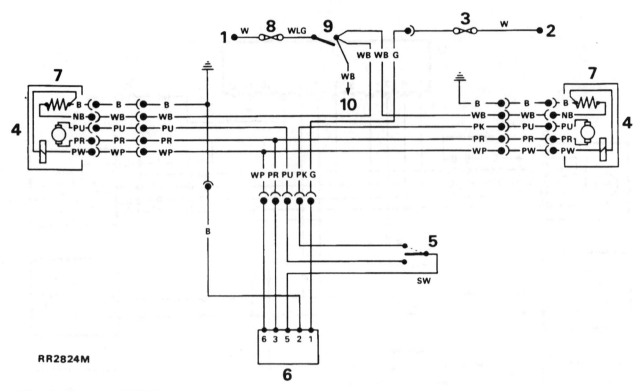

RR2824M

Circuit diagram - RR2824M

1. Ignition 12V.
2. Ignition load relay.
3. Fuse C5 - mirror motors.
4. Mirror motors.
5. Change over switch.
6. Mirror control switch.
7. Mirror heating elements - active with heated rear screen.
8. Fuse C3 - heating elements.
9. Heated rear screen switch.
10. Feed to heated screen relay.

ELECTRIC WINDOW LIFT

Circuit diagram - RR2531E

1. One touch control unit-drivers window
2. Window lift motor-drivers window
3. Window lift motor-front passengers side
4. Window lift motor LH rear
5. Window lift motor RH rear
6. Window lift switch drivers window
7. Window lift switch front passengers window
8. Window lift switch LH rear door
9. Window lift switch RH rear door
10. Isolator switch
11. Window lift switch in LH rear door
12. Window lift switch in RH rear door
13. Relay-rear windows
14. Relay-front windows
15. Clinches
16. Main cable fuses
    - a: Fuse C2
    - b: Fuse C8
    - c: Fuse B1

Cable colour code

B	Black	L	Light	P	Purple	U	Blue
G	Green	N	Brown	R	Red	W	White
K	Pink	O	Orange	S	Grey	Y	Yellow

The last letter of a colour code denotes the tracer.

ELECTRIC WINDOW LIFT

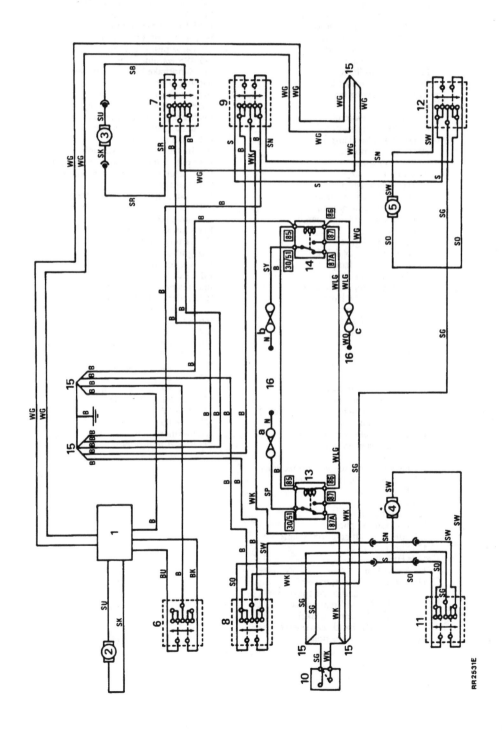

RR2531E

**MAIN CIRCUIT DIAGRAM -
1990 Model year Right hand
steering - RR2830M & RR2831M**

Numerical key

1. Ignition load relay
2. Battery
3. Terminal post
4. Starter solenoid
5. Starter motor
6. Starter relay
7. Starter inhibit switch
7a. Resistor (manual)
8. Ignition switch
9. Tachometer
10. Voltage transformer (dim dip)
11. Ignition warning lamp
12. Alternator
13. Fuse B1
14. Front wipe/wash switch
15. Front wipe delay unit
16. Front wiper motor
17. Headlamp relay
18. Front wash pump
19. Headlamp wash timer unit
20. Headlamp wash pump
21. Main lighting switch
22. Fuse A3
23. Fuse A7
24. LH side lamp
25. LH tail lamp
26. LH number plate lamp
26a. RH number plate lamp
27. High beam dip/flash switch
28. Fuse B2
29. RH side lamp
30. RH tail lamp
31. Rheostat
32. Fuse A8
33. Fuse A2
34. Fuse A9
35. Fuse A1
36. Rear fog switch
37. Fuse A4
38. Switch illumination (2 off)
39. Cigar lighter illumination (2 off)
40. Heater illumination (4 off)
41. Clock illumination
42. Auto gear selector illumination (2 off) - post April 1990 condition
42a. Auto gear selector illumination (2 off) - pre April 1990 condition
43. Instrument illumination (4 off)
43a. Column switch illumination
44. Rear fog warning lamp
45. LH rear fog lamp
46. RH rear fog lamp
47. LH dip beam
48. RH dip beam
49. LH high beam
50. RH high beam
51. High beam warning lamp
52. Fuel gauge
53. Fuel gauge sender unit
54. Water temperature gauge
55. Water temperature sender unit
56. Fuse B3
57. Horn switch
58. RH horn
59. LH horn
60. Under bonnet illumination switch

61. Under bonnet light
62. Clock
63. Fuse C7
64. Fuse C8
65. Pick-up point central locking/window lift
66. Fuse C1
67. Heated rear screen relay
68. Radio aerial amplifier
69. Heated rear screen
70. Heated rear screen switch
71. Heated rear screen warning lamp
72. Voltage sensitive switch
73. Fuse A5
74. Hazard switch
75. Flasher unit
76. Direction indicator switch
77. LH indicator warning lamp
77a. RH indicator warning lamp
78. LH rear indicator lamp
79. LH front indicator lamp
80. LH side repeater lamp
81. RH side repeater lamp
82. RH front indicator lamp
83. RH rear indicator lamp
84. Trailer warning lamp
85. Fuse A6
86. Stop lamp switch
87. Reverse lamp switch
88. Front auxilary lamp relay
89. LH stop lamp
90. RH stop lamp
91. LH reverse lamp
92. RH reverse lamp
93. LH front auxilary lamp
94. RH front auxilary lamp
95. Front auxilary lamp switch
96. Fuse B4
97. Dash cigar lighter
98. Glove box cigar lighter
99. Front interior lamp
100. Rear interior lamp
101. Interior lamp delay unit
102. LH door edge lamp
103. LH puddle lamp
104. RH door edge lamp
105. RH puddle lamp
106. Interior lamp switch
107. LH rear door switch
108. RH rear door switch
109. Tailgate switch
110. LH front door switch
111. RH front door switch
112. Heated washer jets (front screen)
113. Thermostat heated jets
114. Oil pressure warning lamp
115. Oil pressure switch
116. Fuse C4
117. Heated front screen connections
118. Fuel pump (petrol models)
119. Ignition coil
120. Capacitor
121. Distributor
122. EFI Harness plug
123. Fuel shut off solenoid (Diesel)
124. Sun roof relay
124a. Fuse B5
125. Radio fuse
126. Radio and four speakers
    -LF-left hand front speaker
    -LR-left hand rear speaker
    -RF-right front speaker
    -RR-right hand rear speaker
127. Sun roof pick up point

128. Auto transmission and transfer box oil temperature warning lamp
129. Auto transmission oil temperature switch
129a. Transfer box oil temperature switch
130. Fuse C3
131. Rear wash wipe switch
132. Rear wipe delay unit
133. Rear wiper motor
134. Rear screen wash pump
135. Low screen wash fluid level warning lamp
136. Low screen wash switch
137. Low coolant switch
138. Electronic speedo and instrument controls
139. Low coolant level warning lamp
140. Low fuel level warning lamp
141. Glow plug warning lamp (Diesel)
142. E.F.I. warning lamp
143. Glow plug timer unit
144. Glow plugs (Diesel)
145. ABS warning lamp
146. Handbrake/brake fluid level/pressure warning lamp
147. Handbrake warning switch
148. Brake fluid level warning switch
149. Brake pad wear warning lamp
150. Brake pad wear sensors
151. Brake check relay
152. Split charge relay (option)
153. Split charge terminal post (option)
154. Heater/air conditioning connections
155. Fuse C9
156. Coil negative (engine RPM input to ECU)
157. Not used
158. Ignition load relay (+)
159. Battery feed (+)
160. Ignition auxiliary (+)
161. Ignition on (+)
162. Earth (-)
163. Heater/air con. load relay
164. Trailer pick up point
165. Electric seats pick up point (option)
166. Fuse C2
167. Electric mirrors pick up point
168. Alarm pick up point
169. Fuse C5
170. ABS pick up point
171. Fuse B6
172. Fuse B7
173. Condenser fan relay
174. Fuse B8
175. Fuse B9
176. Inertia switch
177. Speed transducer

MAIN CIRCUIT DIAGRAM - Right hand steering RR2830M & RR2831M

Alphabetical key

170.ABS pick up point
145.ABS warning lamp
168.Alarm pick up point
12.Alternator
42.Automatic gear selector illumination (2 off)
129.Automatic transmission oil temperature switch
128.Automatic transmission/transfer box oil temperature warning lamp
2.Battery
148.Brake fluid level warning switch
150.Brake pad wear sensors
149.Brake pad wear warning lamp
151.Brake check relay
120.Capacitor
39.Cigar lighter illumination (2 off)
62.Clock
41.Clock illumination
156.Coil negative, engine speed signal to ECU
43a.Column switch illumination
173.Condenser fan relay
97.Dash cigar lighter
76.Direction indicator switch
121.Distributor
167.Electric mirrors pick up point (option)
165.Electric seats pick up point (option)
138.Electronic speedo and instrument controls
122.EFI Harness plug
142.EFI warning lamp
75.Flasher unit
88.Front auxiliary lamp relay
95.Front auxiliary lamp switch
99.Front interior lamp
18.Front wash pump
15.Front wipe delay unit
14.Front wipe/wash switch
16.Front wiper motor
52.Fuel gauge
53.Fuel gauge sender unit
118.Fuel pump (petrol models)
123.Fuel shut off solenoid (Diesel)
35.Fuse A1
33.Fuse A2
22.Fuse A3
37.Fuse A4
73.Fuse A5
85.Fuse A6
23.Fuse A7
32.Fuse A8
34.Fuse A9
13.Fuse B1
28.Fuse B2
56.Fuse B3
96.Fuse B4
124a.Fuse B5
171.Fuse B6
172.Fuse B7
174.Fuse B8
175.Fuse B9
66.Fuse C1
166.Fuse C2
130.Fuse C3
116.Fuse C4
169.Fuse C5

63.Fuse C7
64.Fuse C8
155.Fuse C9
98.Glove box cigar lighter
144.Glow plugs (Diesel)
143.Glow plug timer unit (Diesel)
141.Glow plug warning lamp (Diesel)
146.Handbrake/brake fluid level/pressure warning lamp
147.Handbrake warning switch
74.Hazard switch
17.Headlamp relay
20.Headlamp wash pump
19.Headlamp wash timer unit
117.Heated front screen connections
69.Heated rear screen
67.Heated rear screen relay
70.Heated rear screen switch
71.Heated rear screen warning lamp
112.Heated washer jets
40.Heater illumination (4 off)
154.Heater/air con. connections
163.Heater/air con. load relay
27.High beam dip/flash switch
51.High beam warning lamp
57.Horn switch
119.Ignition coil
1.Ignition load relay
8.Ignition switch
11.Ignition warning lamp
176.Inertia switch
43.Instrument illumination (4 off)
101.Interior lamp delay unit
106.Interior lamp switch
47.LH dip beam
102.LH door edge lamp
93.LH front auxiliary lamp
110.LH front door switch
79.LH front indicator lamp
49.LH high beam
59.LH horn
77.LH indicator warning lamp
25.LH number plate lamp
103.LH puddle lamp
107.LH rear door switch
45.LH rear fog lamp
78.LH rear indicator lamp
91.LH reverse lamp
24.LH side lamp
80.LH side repeater lamp
89.LH stop lamp
25.LH tail lamp
139.Low coolant level warning lamp
137.Low coolant switch
140.Low fuel level warning lamp
135.Low screen wash fluid level warning lamp
136.Low screen wash switch
21.Main lighting switch
115.Oil pressure switch
114.Oil pressure warning lamp
65.Pick up point-central locking/window lift
68.Radio aerial amplifier
126.Radio and four speakers
125.Radio fuse
36.Rear fog switch
44.Rear fog warning lamp
100.Rear interior lamp
134.Rear screen wash pump
131.Rear wash wipe switch
132.Rear wipe delay unit
133.Rear wiper motor
7a.Resistor (manual)
87.Reverse lamp switch
48.RH dip beam
104.RH door edge lamp
94.RH front auxiliary lamp

111.RH front door switch
82.RH front indicator lamp
50.RH high beam
58.RH horn
77a.RH indicator warning lamp
26a.RH number plate lamp
105.RH puddle lamp
108.RH rear door switch
46.RH rear fog lamp
83.RH rear indicator lamp
92.RH reverse lamp
29.RH side lamp
81.RH side repeater lamp
90.RH stop lamp
30.RH tail lamp
31.Rheostat
177.Speed transducer
152.Split charge relay (option)
153.Split charge terminal post (option)
7.Starter inhibit switch
5.Starter motor
6.Starter relay
4.Starter solenoid
86.Stop lamp switch
127.Sunroof pick up point
124.Sunroof relay
38.Switch illumination (2 off)
9.Tachometer
109.Tailgate switch
3.Terminal post
113.Thermostat - heated washer jets
164.Trailer pick up point
84.Trailer warning lamp
129a.Transfer box oil temperature switch
60.Under bonnet illumination switch
61.Under bonnet light
72.Voltage sensitive switch
10.Voltage transformer (dim-dip)
54.Water temperature gauge
55. Water temperature sender unit

MAIN CIRCUIT DIAGRAM
Right hand steering RR2830M of RR2831M

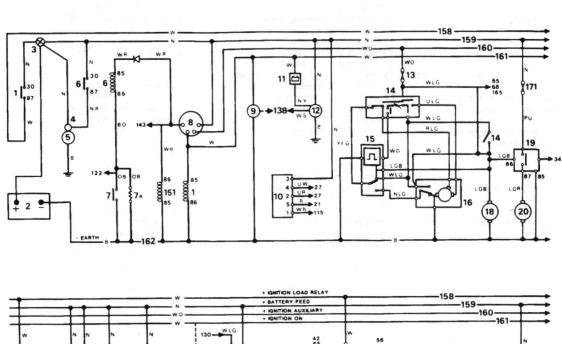

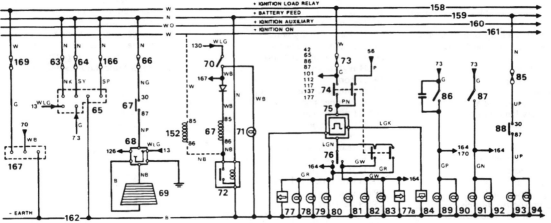

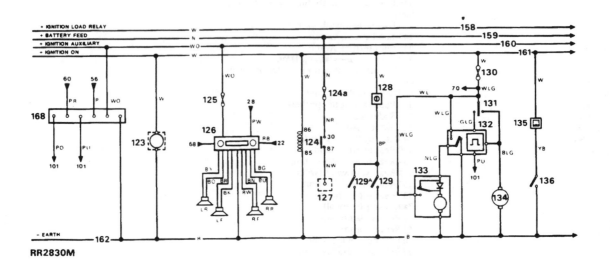

RR2830M

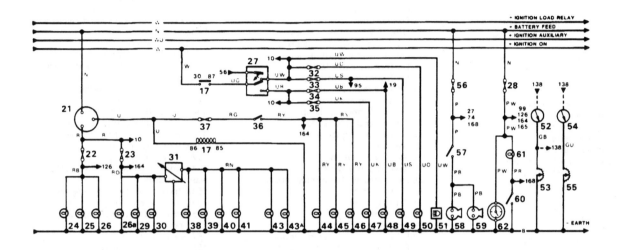

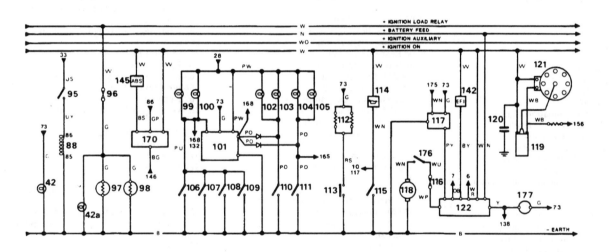

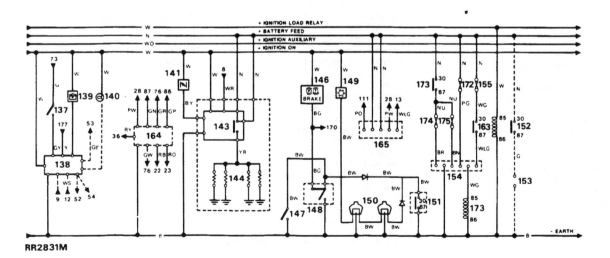

RR2831M

**MAIN CIRCUIT DIAGRAM -
1990 Model year Left hand
steering - RR2828M & RR2829M**

1. Ignition load relay
2. Battery
3. Terminal post
4. Starter solenoid
5. Starter motor
6. Starter relay
7. Starter inhibit switch (auto)
7a. Resistor (manual transmission)
8. Ignition switch
9. Tachometer
10. Ignition warning lamp
11. Alternator
12. Fuse B1
13. Front wipe/wash switch
14. Front wipe delay unit
15. Front wiper motor
16. Headlamp relay
17. Front wash pump
18. Headlamp wash timer unit
19. Headlamp wash pump
20. Main lighting switch
21. Fuse A3
22. Fuse A7
23. LH side lamp
24. LH tail lamp
25. LH number plate lamp
25a. RH number plate lamp
26. High beam dip/flash switch
27. RH side lamp
28. RH tail lamp
29. Rheostat
30. Fuse A8
31. Fuse A2
32. Fuse A9
33. Fuse A1
34. Rear fog switch
35. Fuse A4
36. Switch illumination (2 off)
36a. Headlamp levelling switch illumination (Germany)
37. Cigar lighter illumination (2 off)
38. Heater illumination (4 off)
39. Clock illumination
40. Auto gear selector illumination (2 off) - post April 1990 condition
40a. Auto gear selector illumination (2 off) - pre April 1990 condition
41. Instrument illumination (4 off)
41a. Column switch illumination
42. Rear fog warning lamp
43. LH rear fog
44. RH rear fog
45. LH dip beam
46. RH dip beam
47. LH high beam
48. RH high beam
49. High beam warning lamp
50. Fuel gauge
51. Fuel gauge sender unit
52. Water temperature gauge
53. Water temperature sender unit
54. Fuse B2
55. Horn switch
56. RH horn
57. LH horn
58. Under bonnet illumination switch
59. Under bonnet light
60. Clock
61. Fuse C7
62. Fuse C2

63. Pick-up point central locking/window lift
64. Heated rear screen relay
65. Fuse C1
66. Radio aerial amplifier
67. Heated rear screen
68. Heated rear screen switch
69. Heated rear screen warning lamp
70. Voltage sensitive switch
71. Fuse A5
72. Hazard switch
73. Flasher unit
74. Direction indicator switch
75. LH indicator warning lamp
75a. RH indicator warning lamp
76. LH rear indicator lamp
77. LH front indicator lamp
78. LH side repeater lamp
79. RH side repeater lamp
80. RH front indicator lamp
81. RH rear indicator lamp
82. Trailer warning lamp
83. Fuse A6
84. Stop lamp switch
85. Reverse lamp switch
86. Front auxilary lamp relay (option)
87. LH stop lamp
88. RH stop lamp
89. LH reverse lamp
90. RH reverse lamp
91. LH front auxilary lamp (option)
92. RH front auxilary lamp (option)
93. Front auxilary lamp switch
94. Fuse B4
95. Dash cigar lighter
96. Glove box cigar lighter
97. Front interior lamp
98. Rear interior lamp
99. Interior lamp delay unit
100. LH door edge lamp
101. LH puddle-lamp
102. RH door edge lamp
103. RH puddle lamp
104. Interior lamp switch
105. LH rear door switch
106. RH rear door switch
107. Tailgate switch
108. LH front door switch
109. RH front door switch
110. Heated washer jets (front screen)
111. Thermostat-heated washer jets
112. Oil pressure warning lamp
113. Oil pressure switch
114. Fuse C4
115. Inertia switch
116. Fuel pump (petrol models)
117. Ignition coil (petrol models)
118. Capacitor (petrol models)
119. Distributor (petrol models)
120. EFI Harness plug
121. Speed transducer
122. Trailer pick up point
123. Radio fuse
124. Radio and four speakers
-LF-left hand front speaker
-LR-left hand rear speaker
-RF-right front speaker
-RR-right hand rear speaker
125. Sun roof relay
125a. Fuse B5
126. Alarm pick up point
127. Overspeed warning (Saudi only)
128. Fuse B6
129. Fuse C5
130. Fuel shut off solenoid (Diesel)
131. Seat buckle switch (Saudi only)
132. Overspeed monitor (Saudi only)
133. Heated front screen pick up point (option)

134. Sunroof pick up point (option)
135. Auto transmission/transfer box oil temperature warning lamp
136. Auto transmission oil temperature switch
136a. Transfer box oil temperature switch
137. Fuse C3
138. Rear wash wipe switch
139. Rear wipe delay unit
140. Rear wiper motor
141. Rear screen wash pump
142. Low screen wash fluid level warning lamp
143. Low screen wash switch
144. Low coolant switch
145. Electronic speedo and instrument controls
146. Low coolant level warning lamp
147. Low fuel level warning lamp
148. E.F.I. warning lamp
149. Glow plug warning lamp (Diesel)
150. Glow plug timer unit(Diesel)
151. Glow plugs (Diesel)
152. ABS warning lamp
153. Handbrake/brake fluid level/pressure warning lamp
153a. Brake fluid level warning switch
154. Handbrake warning switch
155. Brake pad wear warning lamp
156. Brake pad wear sensors
157. Brake check unit
158. Split charge relay (option)
159. Split charge terminal post (option)
160. Heater/air conditioning connections
161. Fuse C9
162. Coil negative (engine RPM input to ECU)
163. Ignition load relay (+)
164. Battery feed (+)
165. Ignition auxiliary (+)
166. Ignition on (+)
167. Earth (-)
168. Warning lights supply common earth (-)
169. Warning lights supply (+)
170. Electric seats pick up point
171. Fuse B3
172. Fuse B8
173. Fuse C8
174. Electric mirrors pick up point (option)
175. Heater/air conditioning load relay
176. Cruise control pick up points (option)
177. Fuse B9
178. Condenser fan relay
179. Fuse B7
180. ABS pick up point
181. Headlamp levelling switch connection (German)
182. Headlamp levelling actuator (2) (German)

MAIN CIRCUIT DIAGRAM - Left hand steering RR2828M & RR2829M

Alphabetical key

180.ABS pick up point
152.ABS warning lamp
126.Alarm pick up point
11.Alternator
40.Automatic gear selector illumination (2 off)
136.Automatic transmission oil temperature switch
135.Automatic transmission/transfer box oil temperature warning lamp
2.Battery
153a.Brake fluid level warning switch
157.Brake check unit
156.Brake pad wear sensors
155.Brake pad wear warning lamp
118.Capacitor (petrol models)
37.Cigar lighter illumination (2 off)
60.Clock
39.Clock illumination
162.Coil negative, engine speed signal to ECU
41a.Column switch illumination
178.Condenser fan relay
176.Cruise control pick up point (option)
95.Dash cigar lighter
74.Direction indicator switch
119.Distributor (petrol models)
174.Electric mirrors pick up point (option)
170.Electric seats pick up point (option)
145.Electronic speedo and instrument controls
120.EFI harness plug
148.EFI warning lamp
73.Flasher unit
86.Front auxiliary lamp relay (option)
93.Front auxiliary lamp switch
97.Front interior lamp
17.Front wash pump
14.Front wipe delay unit
13.Front wipe/wash switch
15.Front wiper motor
50.Fuel gauge
51.Fuel gauge sender unit
116.Fuel pump (petrol models)
130.Fuel shut off solenoid (Diesel)
33.Fuse A1
31.Fuse A2
21.Fuse A3
35.Fuse A4
71.Fuse A5
83.Fuse A6
22.Fuse A7
30.Fuse A8
32.Fuse A9
12.Fuse B1
54.Fuse B2
171.Fuse B3
94.Fuse B4
125a.Fuse B5
128.Fuse B6
179.Fuse B7
172.Fuse B8
177.Fuse B9
65.Fuse C1
162.Fuse C2

137.Fuse C3
114.Fuse C4
129.Fuse C5
61.Fuse C7
173.Fuse C8
161.Fuse C9
96.Glove box cigar lighter
151.Glow plugs (Diesel)
150.Glow plug timer unit (Diesel)
149.Glow plug warning lamp (Diesel)
153.Handbrake/brake fluid level/pressure warning lamp
154.Handbrake warning switch
72.Hazard switch
182.Headlamp levelling actuator (2) (Germany)
181.Headlamp levelling switch connection (Germany)
36a.Headlamp levelling switch illumination (Germany)
16.Headlamp relay
19.Headlamp wash pump
18.Headlamp wash timer unit
133.Heated front screen pick up point (option)
67.Heated rear screen
64.Heated rear screen relay
68.Heated rear screen switch
69.Heated rear screen warning lamp
110.Heated washer jets
38.Heater illumination (4 off)
160.Heater/air con. connections
175.Heater/air con. load relay
26.High beam dip/flash switch
49.High beam warning lamp
55.Horn switch
117.Ignition coil
1.Ignition load relay
8.Ignition switch
10.Ignition warning lamp
115.Inertia switch
41.Instrument illumination (4 off)
99.Interior lamp delay unit
104.Interior lamp switch
45.LH dip beam
100.LH door edge lamp
91.LH front auxiliary lamp
108.LH front door switch
77.LH front indicator lamp
47.LH high beam
57.LH horn
75.LH indicator warning lamp
25.LH number plate lamp
101.LH puddle lamp
105.LH rear door switch
43.LH rear fog lamp
76.LH rear indicator lamp
89.LH reverse lamp
23.LH side lamp
78.LH side repeater lamp
87.LH stop lamp
24.LH tail lamp
146.Low coolant level warning lamp
144.Low coolant switch
147.Low fuel level warning lamp
142.Low screen wash fluid level warning lamp
143.Low screen wash switch
20.Main lighting switch
113. Oil pressure switch
112.Oil pressure warning lamp
132.Overspeed monitor (Saudi only)
127.Overspeed warning (Saudi only)
63.Pick up point-central locking/window lift
66.Radio aerial amplifier
124.Radio and four speakers
123.Radio fuse
34.Rear fog switch
42.Rear fog warning lamp
98.Rear interior lamp
141.Rear screen wash pump
138.Rear wash wipe switch

139.Rear wipe delay unit
140.Rear wiper motor
7a.Resistor (manual)
85.Reverse lamp switch
46.RH dip beam
102.RH door edge lamp
92.RH front auxiliary lamp
109.RH front door switch
80.RH front indicator lamp
48.RH high beam
56.RH horn
75a.RH indicator warning lamp
25a.RH number plate lamp
103.RH puddle lamp
106.RH rear door switch
44.RH rear fog lamp
81.RH rear indicator lamp
90.RH reverse lamp
27.RH side lamp
79.RH side repeater lamp
88.RH stop lamp
28.RH tail lamp
29.Rheostat
121.Speed transducer
158.Split charge relay (option)
159.Split charge terminal post (option)
7.Starter inhibit switch
5.Starter motor
6.Starter relay
4.Starter solenoid
84.Stop lamp switch
134.Sunroof pick up point
125.Sunroof relay
36.Switch illumination (2 off)
9.Tachometer
107.Tailgate switch
3.Terminal post
111.Thermostat - heated washer jets
122.Trailer pick up point
82.Trailer warning lamp
136a.Transfer box oil temperature switch
58.Under bonnet illumination switch
59.Under bonnet light
70.Voltage sensitive switch
52.Water temperature gauge
53.Water temperature sender unit

MAIN CIRCUIT DIAGRAM
Left hand steering RR2828M of RR2829M

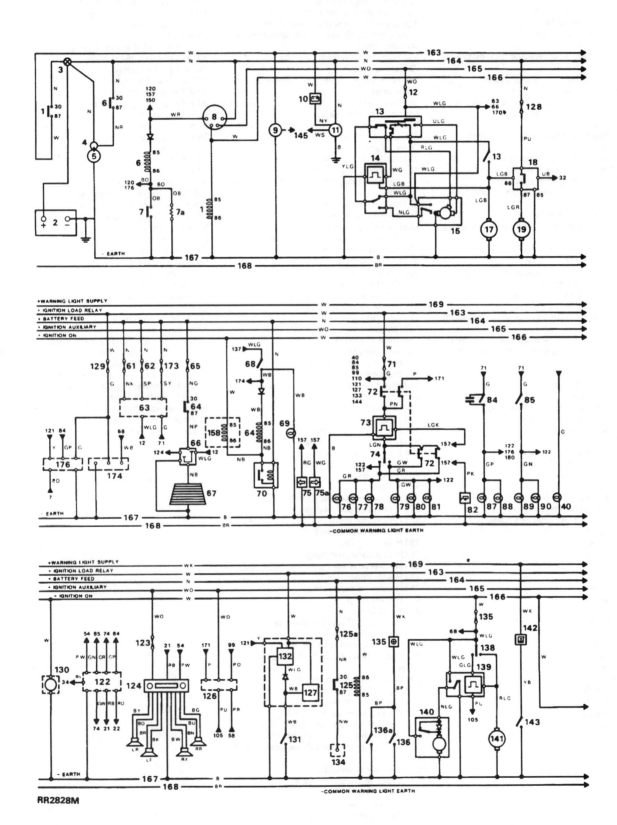

RR2828M

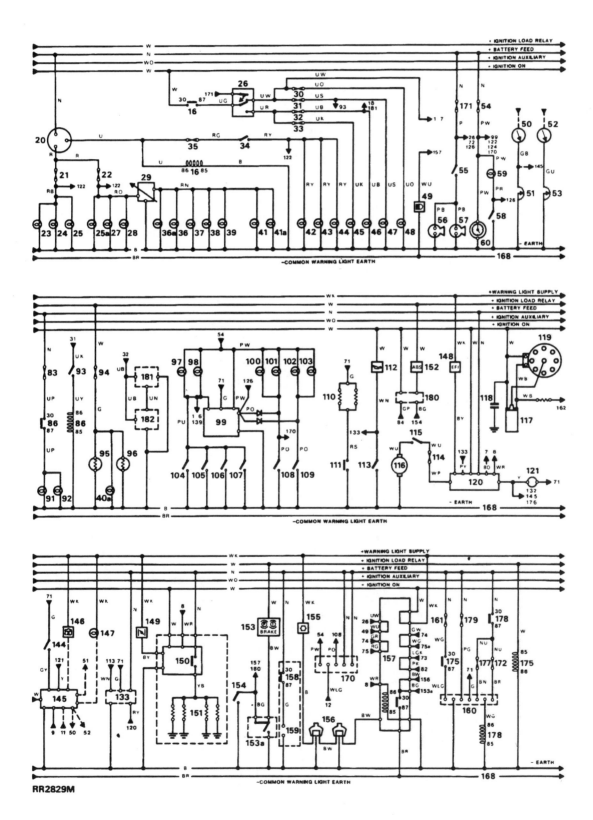

RR2829M

LAND-ROVER **RANGE ROVER**

RANGE ROVER
1991 MODEL YEAR

WORKSHOP MANUAL SUPPLEMENT

Publication Number LSM180WS6

Published by the
Technical Publications Department of

1991 Model Year Supplement

CONTENTS

CONTENTS

INTRODUCTION

In line with Land Rover's policy of constantly improving its model range, a number of additions to the Range Rover model is made for 1991 model year.

These improvements include:

- Revised fuel system with a new driver operated petrol filler flap release.
- Cruise control option for right hand drive vehicles. Service details for cruise control were included in 1990 model year supplement LSM 180 WS5.
- New glass slide and tilt sunroof option
- Heated door locks - both front doors on 4 door vehicles
- Suspension anti-roll bars, front and rear
- Improved vehicle suspension damping
- Recessed rear seat belt anchorage
- Headlamp levelling option
- High mounted rear stop lamp, fitted as a teritorial requirement
- Glare control rear view mirror option

Included in the introduction section of this supplement is a revised procedure for fuel handling including 'Hot fuel handling precautions'. Revised instructions for servicing fuel system components are included to cover both existing and 1991 model fuel systems.

Also included is the procedure for adjusting the kick down cable and gear selector cable on the ZF automatic gearbox.

FUEL HANDLING PRECAUTIONS

The following information provides basic precautions which must be observed if fuel is to be handled safely. It also outlines the other areas of risk which must not be ignored.
This information is issued for basic guidance only, and in any case of doubt, appropriate enquiries should be made of your local Fire Marshal or Fire Department.

Fuel vapour is highly flammable and in confined spaces is also very explosive and toxic.
When fuel evaporates it produces 150 times its own volume in vapour, which when diluted with air becomes a readily ignitable mixture. The vapour is heavier than air and will always fall to the lowest level. It can readily be distributed throughout a workshop by air current, consequently, even a small spillage of fuel is very dangerous.

Always have a fire extinguisher containing **FOAM CO₂ GAS**, or **POWDER** close at hand when handling fuel, or when dismantling fuel systems and in areas where fuel containers are stored.

WARNING: It is imperative that the battery is not disconnected during fuel system repairs as arcing at the battery terminal could ignite fuel vapour in the atmosphere. Always disconnect the vehicle battery BEFORE carrying out work on a fuel system. Whenever fuel is being handled, transferred or stored, or when fuel systems are being dismantled all forms of ignition must be extinguished or removed, any head-lamps used must be flameproof and kept clear of spillage.

NO ONE SHOULD BE PERMITTED TO REPAIR COMPONENTS ASSOCIATED WITH FUEL WITHOUT FIRST HAVING HAD FUEL SYSTEM TRAINING.

HOT FUEL HANDLING PRECAUTIONS

WARNING: Before commencing any operation requiring fuel to be drained from the fuel tank, the following procedure must be adhered to:

1. Allow sufficient time for the fuel to cool, thus avoiding contact with hot fuels.
2. Vent the system by removing the fuel filler cap in a well ventilated area. Refit the filler cap until the commencement of fuel drainage.

FUEL TRANSFER

WARNING: FUEL MUST NOT BE EXTRACTED OR DRAINED FROM ANY VEHICLE WHILE IT IS STANDING OVER A PIT.

The transfer of fuel from the vehicle fuel tank must be carried out in a well ventilated area. An approved transfer tank must be used according to the transfer tank manufacturer's instructions and local regulations, including attention to grounding of tanks.

FUEL TANK REMOVAL

A **FUEL VAPOUR** warning label must be attached to the fuel tank upon removal from the vehicle.

FUEL TANK REPAIR

Under no circumstances should a repair to any tank be attempted.

Base idle speed

See setting procedure .... 525 ± 25 rev/min.

Fuel tank capacity .... 81,8 litres, 18 gals

FUEL FILTER - 1991 MODEL YEAR

Remove and refit

WARNING: Ensure that the fuel handling precautions given in Section 01 - Introduction regarding fuel handling are strictly adhered to when carrying out the following instructions.

WARNING: The spilling of fuel is unavoidable during this operation. Ensure that all necessary precautions are taken to prevent fire and explosion.

Removing

1. Depressurise the fuel system.
2. The fuel filter is located on the right-hand chassis side member forward of the fuel tank filler neck. Access to the filter is gained through the right-hand rear wheel arch.
3. Clamp the inlet and outlet hoses to prevent the minimum of fuel spillage when disconnecting the hoses.
4. Loosen the two fuel unions and remove the hoses from the filter canister.
5. Release the single nut and bolt securing the filter and clamp and remove the filter.

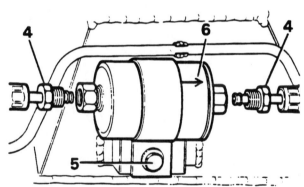

RR2966E

Refitting

6. Fit a new filter observing the direction of flow arrow on the canister.
7. Tighten the single nut and bolt.
8. Fit the inlet and outlet hoses. Tighten the unions to a torque of 20-25 ft lb(27-34Nm).
9. Refit the fuel pump relay. Reconnect the battery.
10. Start the engine and inspect for fuel leaks around the hose connections.

LUBRICATE FRONT AND REAR PROPELLER SHAFT UNIVERSAL AND SLIDING JOINTS

1. Clean all the grease nipples on the front and rear propeller shafts.
2. Charge a low pressure hand-grease gun with grease of a recommended make and grade and apply to the grease nipples at the front and rear propeller shaft universal and sliding joints.

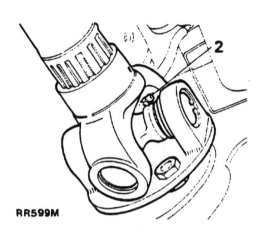

RR599M

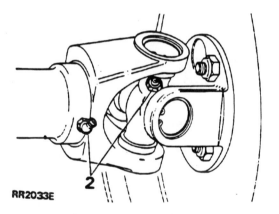

RR2033E

EVAPORATIVE CONTROL SYSTEM - 1991 model year

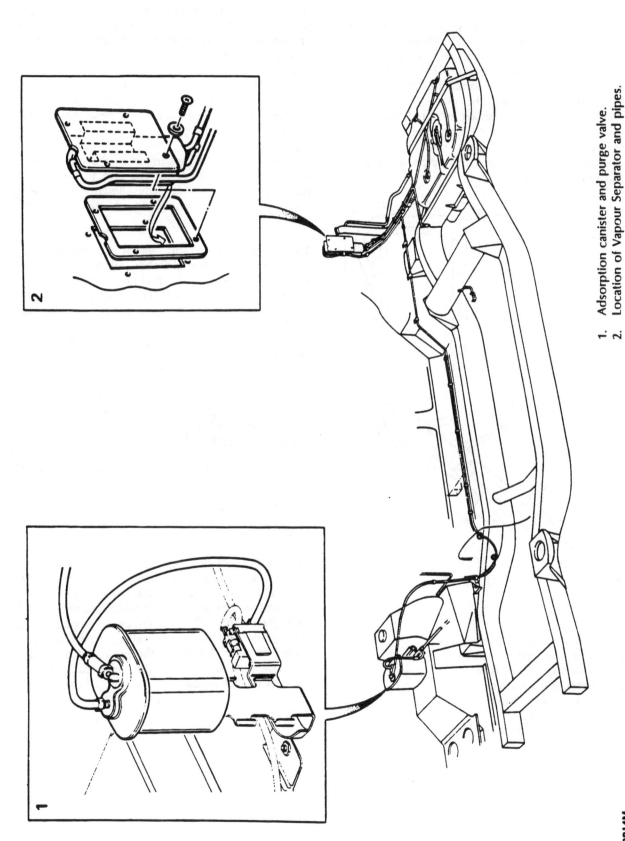

1. Adsorption canister and purge valve.
2. Location of Vapour Separator and pipes.

ST2814M

1

Evaporative emission control system - 1991 model year

The system is designed to prevent harmful fuel vapour from escaping to the atmosphere. The system consists of a new vapour separator tank connected to the fuel tank, and located between the body inner and outer panels on the right hand side of the vehicle near the rear wheel arch. An adsorption canister, containing activated charcoal, is positioned in the engine compartment attached to the front right hand fender valance. The two components are connected by a pipe running the length of the chassis.

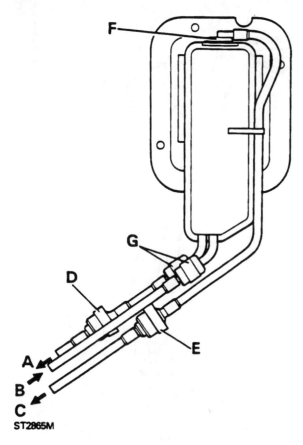

ST2865M

A   Pressure relief to atmosphere.
B   From fuel tank to separator.
C   To adsorption canister.
D   Pressure relief valve.
E   Pressure relief valve.
F   Shut-off valve.
G   "Speed Fit" connectors.

A pressure relief valve is fitted in the hose open to atmosphere, which would act as a safety valve should a build-up of pressure occur in the system, for example if a hose became blocked or kinked. The volume of vapour emitted, in such an instance, would be acceptable.

A pressure relief valve is also fitted in the hose to the adsorption canister and releases vapour to the canister when the pressure in the separator reaches between .75 and 1.0 psi.

In the top of the separator a shut-off valve is incorporated in the vapour exit port to prevent the possible presence of any liquid fuel being transmitted to the adsorption canister should the vehicle roll over.

The adsorption canister, which is connected by hose to the plenum chamber, adsorbs and stores the fuel vapour from the fuel tank while the engine is not running. The vapour is purged from the canister by air drawn through an orifice in the base of the canister and by the influence of vacuum at the top. The vapour drawn into the plenum chamber through a solenoid operated purge valve is finally burnt in the combustion chambers.

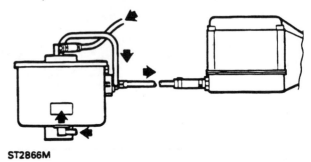

ST2866M

The purge valve, which is attached to the adsorption canister support bracket, is controlled by the fuel injection E.C.U. which determines the most emission acceptable time at which purging should take place. This will normally be at engine speeds above idle and when the vehicle is in motion. A signal from the E.C.U. to the purge valve operates the solenoid and opens the valve to purge the canister of fuel vapour.

VAPOUR SEPARATOR

Remove

WARNING: Ensure that all necessary precautions are taken against fuel spillage and fuel vapour to prevent fire or explosion.

1. Disconnect the battery negative terminal.
2. Working from beneath the vehicle, disconnect the evaporative control pipes from the green end of the "speedfit" connectors. To achieve this, manufacture a suitable tool with a forked end to fit into the two slots in the end of the connector as shown in the illustration below. Press down on the collet and while depressed pull the pipe from the connector.

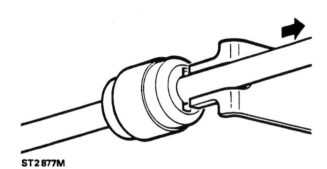

ST2877M

3. Remove the four screws securing the vapour separator support plate to the body panel situated in the right hand side of the load space.
4. Withdraw the separator and pressure relief valves from the vehicle.

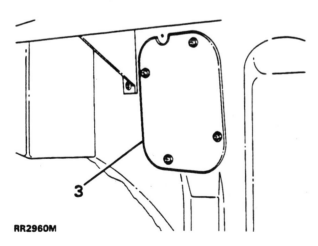

RR2960M

NOTE: While the pressure relief valves are renewable, the shut-off valve in the top of the separator is only available complete with a new separator assembly.

Fitting vapour separator.

5. Fit the separator and pipes into the vehicle side panel, if necessary using a new seal. Fit the self adhesive side to the separator. Secure with the four screws.
6. From beneath the vehicle, fit the pipes from the separator to the connectors. Push each pipe into the corresponding connector as far as it will go so that it is locked by the collet. Check that the pipes are free and not trapped or kinked. Secure the pipes to the under body clips.

TESTING EVAPORATIVE EMISSION CONTROL

The following pressure test procedure is intended to provide a method for ensuring that the system does not leak excessively and will effectively control evaporative emissions.

Equipment required.

Nitrogen cylinder (compressed air may be used to pressure the system when there has NEVER been fuel present in the fuel or evaporative control systems).

Water manometer (0 - 30" H2O or more).

Pipework and a "T" piece.

Method.

1. Ensure that there is at least two gallons of fuel in the fuel tank unless there has never been any fuel in the system.
2. Disconnect, at the adsorption canister, the pipe to the vapour separator.
3. Connect this pipe to the nitrogen cylinder and the water manometer using the "T" piece.
4. Pressurise the system to between 26.5 and 27.5 inches of water, allow the reading to stabilize, then turn off the nitrogen supply.

5. Measure the pressure drop within a period of 2 minutes 30 seconds. If the drop is greater than 2.5 inches of water the system has failed the test. Note that a fully sealed system will show a slight increase in pressure.
6. Should the system fail the test, maintain the pressure in the system and apply a soap solution round all the joints and connections until bubbles appear to reveal the source of the leak.
7. Repeat the test and if successful, dismantle the test equipment and reconnect the pipe to the adsorption canister.

FUEL SYSTEM 1991 MODEL YEAR

A revised fuel system is fitted to 1991 model year vehicles. The major change is the fitting of a new plastic fuel tank with improved breather system. The remote expansion tank is now deleted.

Where territorial regulations apply a vapour separator is fitted in the evaporative loss system.

A further improvement is the fitting of a combined fuel pump and sender unit. A panel in the floor of the vehicle permits access to the fuel pump/sender unit.

On diesel vehicles a sender unit only is fitted in the fuel tank.

E.F.I. WARNING SYMBOL 1990/91 VEHICLES

NOTE: From VIN No.451997 fuel injection ECU part no. PRC8702 replaced PRC7081. This ECU will NOT illuminate the EFI warning symbol when a fault code is stored in the ECU memory.

BASE IDLE SPEED SETTING

NOTE: the base idle speed is set at the factory. It should not require further adjustment unless the plenum chamber is changed. The adjustment screw is sealed with a plug to prevent unauthorised alteration. Check the ignition timing before attempting the following procedure, since this will affect the idle speed.

Equipment required

Two blanking hoses. It is recommended that these are manufactured using a new air by-pass valve hose - Part No.ETC7874. Cut two equal pieces 90mm (3 1/2 inches) long from the hose and seal one end of each, using 13mm (1/2 inch) diameter bar. A suitable clamp can be used to ensure an air tight seal

Checking procedure

1. Drive the vehicle for at least two miles until the engine and transmission are hot. Switch off the engine.
2. Check that all electrical loads are off including air conditioning.
3. Remove the air by-pass valve hose.
4. Fit the blanking hoses to both the plenum chamber and the air by-pass valve. Ensure the hoses are securely fitted to prevent air leaks. Note that the throttle cable and cruise control actuator have been omitted from the illustration for clarity.

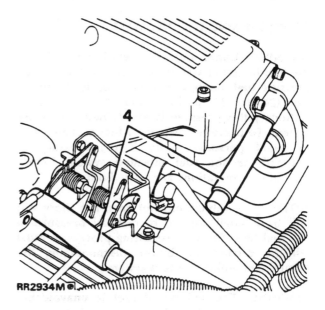

RR2934M

5. Start the engine and check that the idle speed is within the limits specified in Section 05 - Engine Tuning Data.

Adjusting base idle speed

6. Remove the tamper proof plug that protects the idle speed screw. Drill the plug and insert a self tapping screw to enable the plug to extracted.

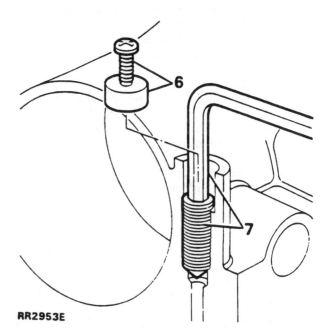

RR2953E

7. Start the engine, and using a suitable Allen key, adjust the idle screw clockwise to decrease or counter-clockwise to increae the idle speed.
8. Stop the engine, remove blanking hoses and reconnect the hose to the plenum chamber.
9. Fit a new tamper proof plug.

DEPRESSURISING THE FUEL SYSTEM

WARNING: Under normal operating conditions the fuel injection system is pressurised by a high pressure fuel pump, operating at up to 2.3 to 2.5 bar (34 to 37 p.s.i.). When the engine is stationary this pressure is maintained within the system. To prevent pressurised fuel escaping and to avoid personal injury it is necessary to depressurise the fuel injection system before any service operations are carried out.

NOTE: If the vehicle has not been run there will still be a small amount of residual pressure in the fuel line. The depressurising procedure must still be carried out before disconnecting the component within the fuel system.

WARNING: The spilling of fuel is unavoidable during this operation. Ensure that all necessary precautions are taken to prevent fire and explosion.

1. The fuel pump relay is located under the front right hand seat.
2. Pull the fuel pump relay off its multi-plug (see Electronic Fuel Injection Relays-Section 19, Page 28).
3. Start and run the engine.
4. When sufficient fuel has been used up causing the fuel line pressure to drop, the injectors will become inoperative, resulting in engine stall. Switch the ignition off.
5. Disconnect the battery negative terminal.

   NOTE: Fuel at low pressure will remain in the system. To remove this low pressure fuel, place an absorbent cloth around the fuel feed hose at the fuel rail and release the fuel feed hose at the appropriate end.

6. Disconnect either:
   a) The nut and ferrule at the fuel rail
   OR
   b) The hose at the inlet end of the fuel filter.

Refitting

7. Refit the fuel feed hose.
8. Refit the fuel pump relay, reconnect the battery.
9. Crank the engine (engine will fire within approximately 6 to 8 seconds).

FUEL SYSTEM 1991 MODEL YEAR

A revised fuel system is fitted to 1991 model year vehicles. The major change is the fitting of a plastic fuel tank with improved breather system. The remote expansion tank is now deleted.

A further improvement is the fitting of a combined fuel pump and sender unit. A panel in the floor of the vehicle permits access to the fuel pump/sender unit

FUEL PUMP/SENDER UNIT

SENDER UNIT - Diesel vehicles

WARNING: Ensure that the Fuel Handling Precautions given in Section 01 - Introduction regarding fuel handling are strictly adhered to when carrying out the following instructions.

CAUTION: Before disconnecting any part of the fuel system, it is imperative that all dust, dirt and debris is removed from around the components to prevent ingress of foreign matter into the fuel system.

Special Tool - LST131, pump retaining ring spanner

- LST 144 -'Speedfit' disconnector

NOTE: The retaining rings are colour coded as follows:
        RED - High pressure pump/sender unit
        BLACK - Diesel sender unit

Remove and refit

Removing

1. Depressurise the fuel system.
2. Disconnect battery negative lead.
3. Syphon at least 9 litres (2 gallons) of fuel from the fuel tank using a suitable container that can be sealed afterwards.

4. Remove carpet from loadspace floor and tailgate.
5. Fold back the sound insulation to reveal the access panel.
6. Remove the securing screws and detach the access panel from the floor.
7. Disconnect the electrical connections at the multi-plug.
8. Remove the insulation sealant from around the ground lead, and disconnect the ground lead.
9. Disconnect the two fuel line unions from the fuel pump.
10. Using Special Tool No. LST131, remove pump assembly retaining ring and withdraw the pump from the fuel tank.

WARNING: A quantity of fuel will be retained in the body of the unit, care must be taken to prevent fuel spillage when the unit is removed.

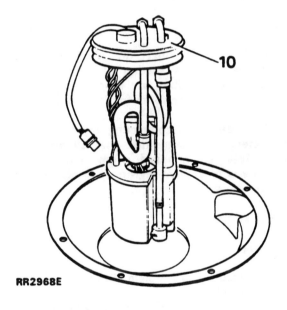

RR2968E

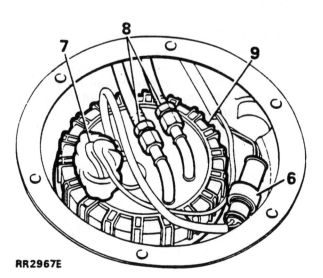

RR2967E

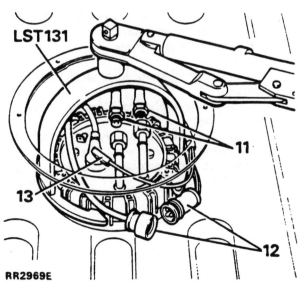

RR2969E

Refitting

11. Insert the fuel pump into the tank. Fit the retaining ring and tighten to a torque of 45-50 Nm (34-37 lbf ft).
12. Connect the fuel lines to the pump.
13. Connect the electrical leads at the multi-plug.
14. Connect the ground lead to the pump and insulate with suitable sealant.
15. When the fuel system has been reassembled check all fuel pipes, sealing rings and hose connections are secure.
16. Run the engine to check for fuel leaks before final assembly.
17. Inspect the access panel seal, fit a new seal if necessary.
18. Fit the access panel and secure to the floor with the screws.
19. Reverse operations 4 - 5 to refit the sound insulation and carpet.

FUEL TANK

WARNING: Ensure that the Fuel Handling Precautions given in Section 01 - Introduction regarding fuel handling are strictly adhered to when carrying out the following instructions.

CAUTION: Before disconnecting any part of the fuel system, it is imperative that all dust, dirt and debris is removed from around the components to prevent ingress of foreign matter into the fuel system.

Remove and refit

Removing

1. Depressurise fuel system. Disconnect battery negative lead.
2. Syphon the fuel tank into a suitable container that can be sealed afterwards. **ENSURE THAT THE TANK IS DRAINED COMPLETELY.** (refer to Warning concerning fuel vapour and spillage at start of this procedure).
3. Remove carpet from loadspace floor and tailgate.
4. Fold back the sound insulation to reveal the access panel.
5. Remove the securing screws and detach the access panel from the floor.
6. Disconnect the electrical connections at the multi-plug.

7. Remove the insulation sealant from around the ground lead, and disconnect the ground lead.
8. Disconnect the two fuel line unions from the fuel pump.
9. Working underneath the vehicle, remove the rear anti-roll bar straps, and allow the bar to swing down clear of the tank.

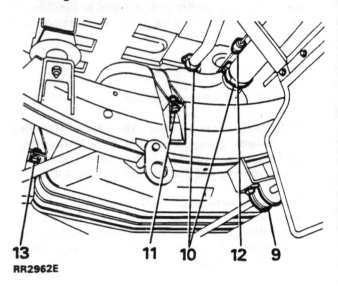

13   **11**   **10**   **12**   **9**
RR2962E

10. Remove the tank filler and vent hoses at the fuel tank.
11. Remove the nut and bolt securing the right hand side of the fuel tank strap.
12. Disconnect the evaporative control pipe at the green end of the 'speedfit' connector.

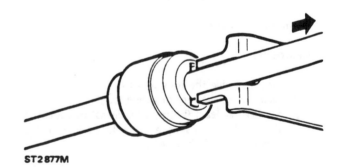

ST2877M

NOTE: To disconnect the 'speedfit' connector, forked end into the two slots of the connector as shown in the illustation above. Press down on the collet and simultaneously pull the pipe from the connector. Special tool LST 144 is available for this operation.

3. Clamp the inlet and outlet hoses to prevent the minimum of fuel spillage when disconnecting the hoses.
4. Loosen the two fuel line unions and remove the hoses from the filter canister.
5. Release the single nut and bolt securing the filter and clamp and remove the filter.

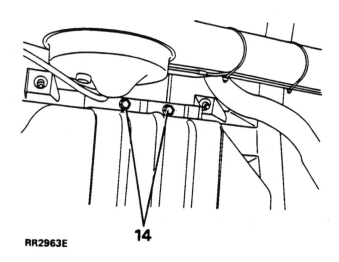

RR2963E

13. Remove the back two bolts and nut plates securing the fuel tank cradle.
14. Remove the front nuts, bolts and washers, and remove the fuel tank cradle.
15. With the aid of an assistant, tilt the right hand side of the tank upwards and manouver the tank through the chassis to remove.

Refitting

16. Reverse the removal procedure, ensuring that the sealing ring, fuel pipe and hose connections are secure.
17. Run the engine and re-check all connections to ensure no fuel leaks exist. Reverse the remaining removal procedure.

FUEL FILTER

Remove and refit

WARNING: ENSURE THAT THE FUEL HANDLING PRECAUTIONS GIVEN IN SECTION 01 - INTRODUCTION REGARDING FUEL HANDLING ARE STRICTLY ADHERED TO WHEN CARRYING OUT THE FOLLOWING INSTRUCTIONS.

WARNING: THE SPILLING OF FUEL IS UNAVOIDABLE DURING THIS OPERATION. ENSURE THAT ALL NECESSARY PRECAUTIONS ARE TAKEN TO PREVENT FIRE AND EXPLOSION.

Removing

1. Depressurise the fuel system.
2. The fuel filter is located on the right-hand chassis side member forward of the fuel tank filler neck. Access to the filter is gained through the right-hand rear wheel arch.

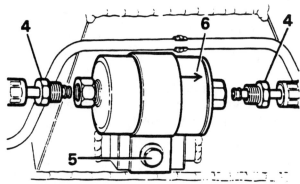

RR2966E

Refitting

6. Fit a new filter observing the direction of flow arrow on the canister.
7. Tighten the single nut and bolt.
8. Fit the inlet and outlet hoses. Tighten the unions to a torque of 20-25 ft lb(27-34Nm).
9. Refit the fuel pump relay, reconnect the battery.
10. Start the engine and inspect for fuel leaks around the hose connections.

FUEL FILLER FLAP RELEASE BUTTON

The fuel filler flap is no longer part of the central locking system on 1991 model year vehicles. The filler flap is permanently locked. To release the flap press the button situated on the steering column shroud. On closing, the filler flap will be locked automatically. Note that the release button will only work with ignition switched OFF.

Remove and refit

Removing

1. Disconnect the battery negative lead.
2. Carefully pry the release button from the steering column shroud.

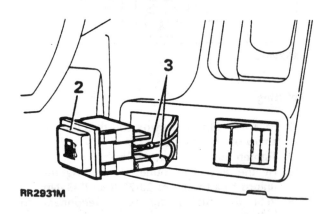

RR2931M

3. Remove the release button from the shroud and disconnect the two wiring connectors. Ensure that the wires protrude through the shroud to facilitate reassembly.

Refitting

4. Reverse the removal procedure.

FUEL FILLER FLAP RELEASE ACTUATOR

Remove and refit

Removing

1. Ensure that the fuel filler flap is released. Disconnect the battery negative lead.
2. Remove eight screws, and withdraw the closure panel, situated in the right hand side of the load space.
3. Release two screws and manoeuvre the actuator clear of its mounting.
4. Disconnect the wiring plug.
5. Withdraw the actuator.

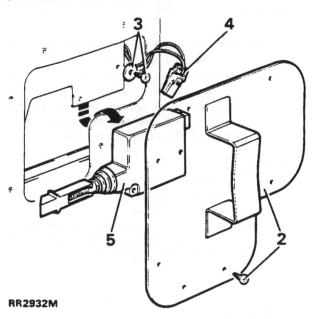

RR2932M

Refitting

6. Reverse the removal procedure.

FUEL SYSTEM - pre 1991 vehicles

The following procedures have been amended to include new fuel handling precautions.

FUEL PUMP

Remove and refit

Removing

WARNING: Ensure that the Fuel Handling Precautions given in Section 01 - Introduction regarding fuel handling are strictly adhered to when carrying out the following instructions.

1. Drive the vehicle onto a suitable hoist.
2. Depressurise the fuel pump system. (see depressurising procedure-page 34)
3. Disconnect the battery negative terminal.
4. Remove the fuel tank from the chassis frame. (see fuel tank remove and refit-page 38)
5. Place the tank in a safe area.
6. Disconnect the fuel supply hose from the pump.
7. Remove any previous sealant from the top of the pump flange.
8. Remove the five screws and withdraw the pump from the tank.

Refitting

9. Clean the immediate area around the pump opening in the fuel tank.
10. Fit a **NEW** pump seal.
11. Secure the pump to the tank and tighten the screws securely.
12. Liberally coat the heads of the screws and flange of the fuel pump with Sikaflex 221 flexible adhesive sealant.
13. Reverse the removal procedure, ensuring that the sealing ring, fuel line and hose connections are secure.
14. Run the engine and re-check all connections to ensure no fuel leaks exist. Reverse the remaining removal procedure.

FUEL TANK GAUGE UNIT

Remove and refit

Service tool - 18G 1001 Locking spanner

Removing

WARNING: Ensure that the Fuel Handling Precautions given in Section 01 - Introduction regarding fuel handling are strictly adhered to when carrying out the following instructions.

CAUTION: Before disconnecting any part of the fuel system, it is imperative that all dust, dirt and debris is removed from around the components to prevent ingress of foreign matter into the fuel system.

1. Disconnect the battery. Chock the front wheels, raise the rear wheels clear of the ground and support the vehicle on stands.
2. Remove the drain plug from the bottom of the fuel tank and drain the fuel into a suitable container that can be sealed afterwards, refit the drain plug.

ENSURE THAT THE TANK IS DRAINED COMPLETELY. Refit the drain plug. (refer to Warning concerning fuel vapour and spillage at start of this procedure).

3. Remove the left side rear wheel to provide easy access to the gauge unit which is fitted in the side of the fuel tank.
4. Disconnect the electrical leads from the gauge unit.
5. Using tool 18G 1001 release the tank unit locking ring.
6. Remove the gauge unit and sealing washer.

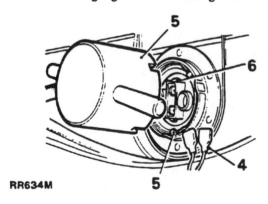

RR634M

Refitting

7. Coat the mating faces with Bostik 662 and fit a **NEW** sealing washer and locate the gauge unit in the tank ensuring that the notch in the periphery of the gauge unit locates with the register in the gauge aperture of the tank.
8. Refit the electrical leads.
   Green/Black lead to top terminal.
   Black lead to lower terminal.
9. Reverse the removal procedure, ensuring that the sealing ring, fuel pipe and hose connections are secure.
10. Run the engine and recheck all connections to ensure no fuel leaks exist.

FUEL TANK

Remove and refit

Removing

WARNING: Ensure that the Fuel Handling Precautions given in Section 01 - Introduction regarding fuel handling are strictly adhered to when carrying out the following instructions.

CAUTION: Before disconnecting any part of the fuel system it is imperative that all dust, dirt and debris is removed from around the components to prevent ingress of foreign matter into the fuel system.

1. Drive the vehicle onto a suitable hoist.
2. Depressurise the fuel system. (see depressurizing procedure-page 34)
3. Disconnect the battery negative terminal.
4. Disconnect the electrical leads to the fuel tank sender unit. Disconnect the fuel pump electrical multiplug, access to which is gained through the left hand rear wheel arch, the plug is located between the underside of the body and chassis side member.
5. Raise the hoist.
6. Remove the drain plug from the bottom of the fuel tank and drain the fuel into a suitable container that can be sealed afterwards. **ENSURE THAT THE TANK IS DRAINED COMPLETELY.**
   Refit the drain plug (refer to Warning concerning fuel handling at start of this procedure.

From underneath the vehicle

7. Disconnect the fuel hose from the inlet side of the fuel filter.
8. Disconnect the fuel return pipe to the fuel tank.

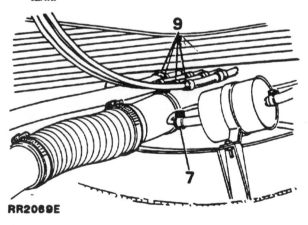

RR2069E

9. Remove the breather hose and three evaporative loss hoses from the fuel tank, seal all hose and pipe openings to prevent ingress of foreign matter.
10. Release the two large hose clamps, securing the inter-connecting hose to tank and filler tube, manoeuvre the hose up the outside of the filler tube to enable it to be withdrawn from the tank filler neck.
11. With assistance from a second person supporting the fuel tank, remove the four tank fixings.

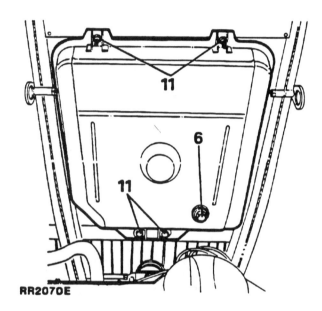

RR2070E

12. Tilt the left hand side of the tank downwards and manoeuvre it out of the chassis frame. Care should be taken to ensure that the fuel feed pipe to filter is not damaged when lowering the tank.
13. Place the tank in a safe area and ensure that all necessary precautions are undertaken to make all personnel within the vicinity aware that the tank will give off residual fuel fumes.
14. If necessary remove the fuel pump from the tank. (See Fuel Pump remove and refit).

Refitting

15. Refit the fuel tank to the chassis, taking care to relocate the fuel feed pipe grommets between the fuel tank and chassis.
16. Reverse the removal procedure, ensuring that the sealing ring, fuel line and hose connections are secure.
17. Run the engine and re-check all connections to ensure no fuel leaks exist. Reverse the remaining removal procedure.

KICKDOWN CABLE ADJUSTMENT

Kickdown cable must be checked and adjusted as follows:

> **NOTE: The kickdown cable must be adjusted while the vehicle is running at idle.**

1. Adjust the outer cable to achieve a crimp gap of 0.25 to 1.25mm (.010 to .050 in) dimension 'A'.
2. Hold the outer cable while tightening the locknuts.

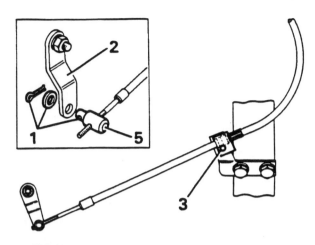

RR2981M

6. Tighten the outer cable clamp to 22 - 28Nm (16 - 21ft lb).
7. Reconnect the battery leads.
8. Ensuring the vehicle is on level ground with the parking brake applied, check the oil level while engine is running at idle with neutral selected, after selecting each gear.

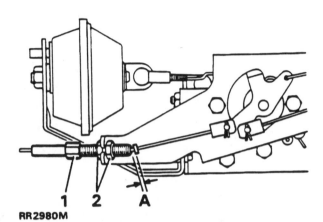

RR2980M

GEAR LEVER SELECTOR CABLE SETTING

Working underneath the vehicle:

1. Remove the split pin and washer securing the trunnion to the gear change lever at the gearbox and disconnect the trunnion from the lever.
2. Select neutral gear at the gearbox using the gear change lever.
3. Release the clamp securing the outer selector cable, the clamp is attached to a bracket which is mounted on the side of the gearbox extension housing.
4. Select neutral gear, at the gear shift, within the vehicle.
5. Rotate the trunnion clockwise or counter clockwise, until the trunnion will engage with the gear change lever at the gearbox, fit the trunnion and secure in position using a **NEW** split pin and washer.

OVERHAUL FRONT STUB AXLE, CONSTANT VELOCITY JOINT AND SWIVEL ASSEMBLY ON VEHICLES FITTED WITH ABS

Note: The following text applies to both 1990 and 1991 model year vehicles fitted with ABS. Instructions refer to both model years except where otherwise stated.

Service tools:
18G 284AAH extractor.
LST 132 bearing installer.
LST 133 seal installer.
LST 141 steering torque test adaptor.

Remove stub axle, axle shaft and constant velocity joint.

1. Remove the hub complete as described in the operation to overhaul the hub assembly on ABS fitted vehicles.
2. Drain the swivel pin housing and refit plug.
3. Remove the six bolts retaining the stub axle to the swivel housing.
4. Remove the mud shield.
5. Remove the stub axle and joint washer.

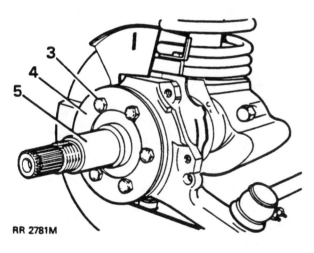

RR 2781M

6. Pull out the axle shaft and constant velocity joint from the axle casing.

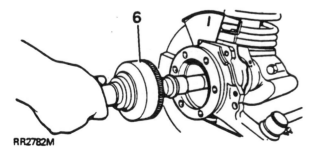

RR2782M

Remove constant velocity joint from axle shaft

7. Hold the axle shaft firmly in a soft jawed vice.
8. Using a soft mallet drive the constant velocity joint from the shaft.
9. Remove the circlip and collar from the axle shaft.

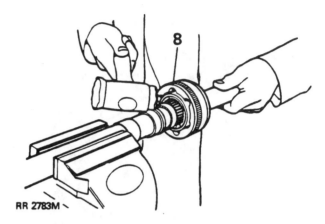

RR 2783M

Dismantle the constant velocity joint

10. Mark the relative positions of the constant velocity joint inner and outer race and the cage for correct reassembly.
11. Tilt and swivel the cage and inner race to remove the balls.

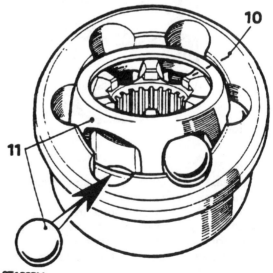

ST1025M

12. Swivel the cage into line with the axis of the joint and turn it until two opposite windows coincide with two lands of the joint housing.
13. Withdraw the cage.
14. Turn the inner track at right angles to the cage with two of the lands opposite the cage openings and withdraw the inner race.

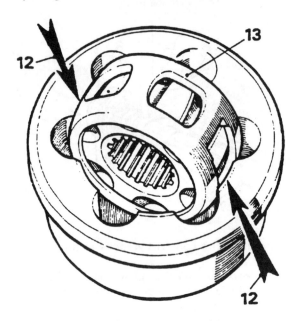

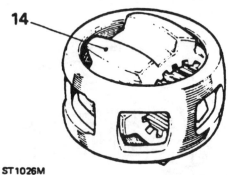

ST1026M

15. Degrease and examine all components for general wear and condition.
16. Examine the inner and outer track, cage balls and bearing surfaces of the constant velocity joint for damage and excessive wear.
17. To assemble the constant velocity joint, reverse the dismantling instructions and lubricate with a recommended oil.
18. Check that the end-float of the assembled joint does not exceed 0,64 mm (0.025 in).

Fit constant velocity joint to axle

19. Fit the collar and a new circlip.
20. Engage the constant velocity joint on the axle shaft splines and using a soft mallet, drive the joint home.

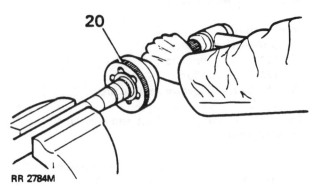

RR 2784M

Renew stub axle, thrust ring, oil seal and bearing

21. Drill and chisel off the thrust ring taking care to avoid damaging the stub axle.
22. Remove the bearing and oil seal using special tool 18G 284AAH and slide hammer. Ensure that the fingers of the tool locate behind the bearing to drive it out. Repeat for the oil seal.

18G 284 AAH

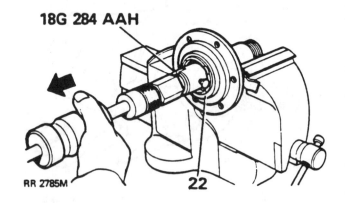

RR 2785M

Refit

23. Lubricate the seal and lip with EP90 oil and with the cavity side leading press in a new oil seal using special tool LST 133.

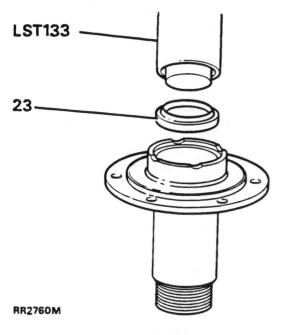

LST133 —

23 —

RR2760M

24. Using special tool LST 132, fit bearing with its part number visible when fitted, and flush with the end face of the stub axle.

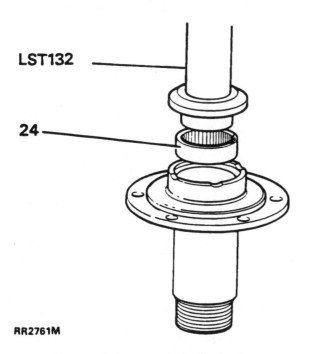

LST132 —

24 —

RR2761M

25. Press fit a new thrust ring onto the stub axle.

Remove swivel pin housing.

26. Remove the brake shield secured at the bottom by one nut and bolt, and midway by the lock stop nut.
27. Disconect the track-rod end ball joint from the housing.
28. Disconnect the drag-link ball joint.
29. Disconnect the jump hoses from the brake jump hose bracket.
30. Remove the ABS brake sensor.
31. Remove the six bolts securing the oil seal and retaining plate to the swivel pin housing. Prise the seal from the swivel pin housing.

   NOTE: The oil seal and retaining plate cannot be removed until the swivel pin bearing housing is removed.

32. Remove the two countersunk screws securing the brake damper/shield bracket, and the lower swivel pin to the housing.
33. Withdraw the lower swivel pin and joint washer by tapping the small protruding lug.
34. Remove the top swivel pin retaining bolts complete with the brake jump hose bracket.
35. Withdraw the top swivel pin and shims.
36. Remove the swivel pin housing while retrieving the lower taper bearing.
37. If the swivel pin housing is to be renewed, the drain, level and filler plugs and lock-stop bolt.

Remove and overhaul swivel pin bearing housing

38. Remove the seven bolts securing the swivel pin bearing housing to the axle case. Remove the swivel pin bearing housing.
39. Remove and discard the oil seal and joint washer.
40. Drift out the lower swivel pin bearing track.
41. Press out the top swivel pin bush housing assembly. Discard the thrust washer. From 1991 model year, discard the thrust washers and bearing.
42. If worn, pitted or damaged, renew the swivel pin bearing housing.
43. Press in a new lower swivel pin bearing track.

44. Press in a new bush and bush housing. Ensure that the relieved lip of the bush housing faces towards the rear oil seal, as shown.

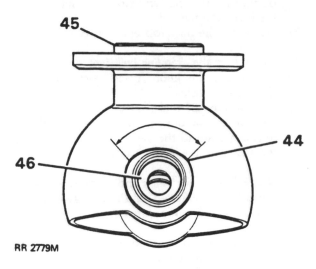

RR 2779M

45. With the seal lips trailing press the axle shaft oil seal flush into the rear of the housing. Grease the lips.
46. Fit a new thrust washer into the top swivel pin bush with the black P.T.F.E. coating uppermost. Check it is in position when fitting the top swivel pin. From 1991 model year fit new thrust washers and thrust bearing.
47. Hang the swivel pin bearing housing oil seal and retainer plate over the back of the housing. Ensure they are in the correct assembly order.
48. Fit a new joint washer and secure the swivel pin bearing housing to the axle. Starting with the top fixing dowel bolt. Tighten evenly to the correct torque.

Fit swivel pin housing

49. Grease and fit the lower swivel pin bearing to the bearing housing.
50. Place the swivel pin housing in position over the swivel pin bearing housing.
51. Using a new joint washer, fit the lower swivel pin with lip outboard. Do not secure with screws at this stage.
52. Fit a new sensor bush and new oil seal, lip side leading to the top swivel pin.
53. Lubricate with a recommended oil and fit the top swivel pin with existing shims.
54. Coat the threads of the top swivel pin bolts with Loctite 542. Fit the bolts and jump hose bracket (do not tighten).
55. Coat the threads of the lower swivel pin screws with Loctite 270 and fit, together with the damper and shield bracket. Tighten to the correct torque.
56. Tighten the top swivel pin and brake jump hose bracket securing bolts to the correct torque.

Check and adjust preload on bearings 1990 model year

57. The preload on bearings to be 0,18 to 0,23 mm (0.007 to 0.009 ins), **without** the swivel housing oil seal and axle fitted, and reading from the centre of the swivel pin. The torque required to turn the swivel assembly from lock to lock to be 5.1 to 7.3 Nm (45 to 65 in.lbs). Adjust by removing or adding shims to the top swivel pin.

Check and adjust preload on bearings 1991 model year on

The preload on bearings to be 0,25 to 0,30 mm (0.010 to 0.012 ins), **without** the swivel housing oil seal and axle fitted, and reading from the centre of the swivel assembly from lock to lock to be 2.0 to 2.8 Nm (18 to 25 in.lbs). Adjust by removing or adding shims to the top swivel pin.

58. To take a reading use special tool LST 141 torque test adaptor, with a torque wrench and extension as shown.

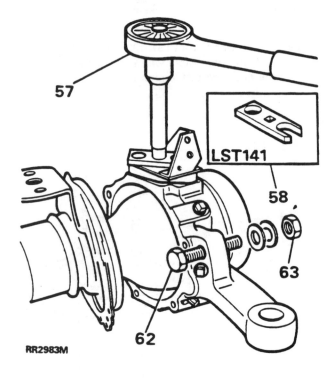

RR2983M

Fit remaining components

59. Liberally apply (do not pack) a recommended grease between the lips of the swivel housing oil seal.
60. Secure the oil seal with the retaining plate and securing bolts tightening evenly to the correct torque.

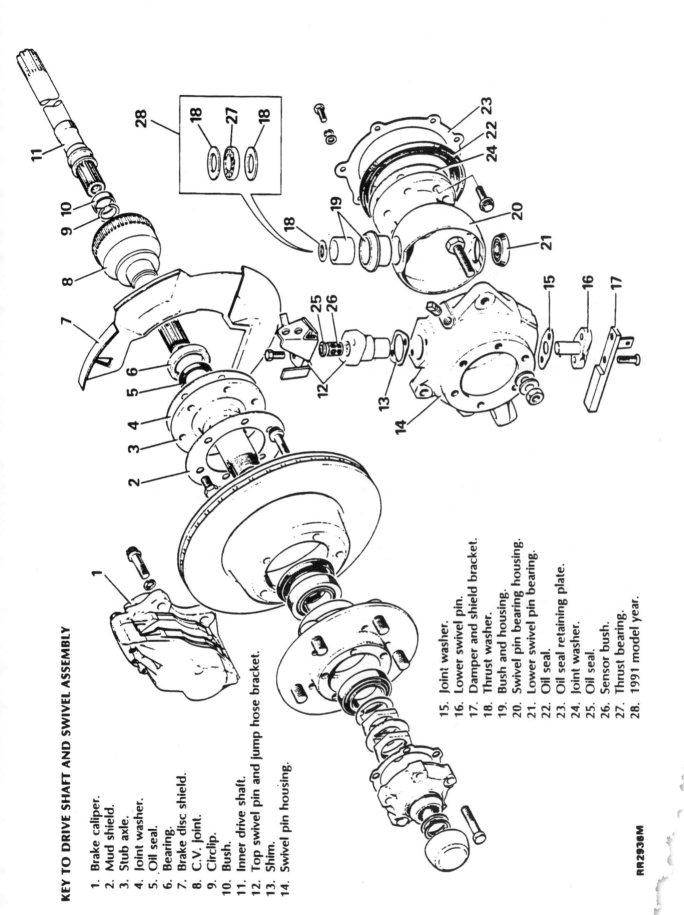

KEY TO DRIVE SHAFT AND SWIVEL ASSEMBLY

1. Brake caliper.
2. Mud shield.
3. Stub axle.
4. Joint washer.
5. Oil seal.
6. Bearing.
7. Brake disc shield.
8. C.V. joint.
9. Circlip.
10. Bush.
11. Inner drive shaft.
12. Top swivel pin and jump hose bracket.
13. Shim.
14. Swivel pin housing.
15. Joint washer.
16. Lower swivel pin.
17. Damper and shield bracket.
18. Thrust washer.
19. Bush and housing.
20. Swivel pin bearing housing.
21. Lower swivel pin bearing.
22. Oil seal.
23. Oil seal retaining plate.
24. Joint washer.
25. Oil seal.
26. Sensor bush.
27. Thrust bearing.
28. 1991 model year.

RR2936M

61. Fit the track-rod and drag link and secure with new split pins.
62. Loosely fit the lock stop bolt for later adjustment.
63. Fit the brake disc shield. Leaving the middle fixing nut loose until the lock stop has been set.

Fit drive shaft and stub axle

64. Insert the axle shaft, and when the differential splines are engaged, push the assembly home.

    CAUTION: Take care not to damage the axle shaft oil seals.

65. Place a new joint washer in position on the swivel pin housing to stub axle mating face. Coat the threads of the stub axle bolts with Loctite 270.
66. Fit the stub axle with the keyway at the 12 o'clock position.

    CAUTION: Ensure that the constant velocity joint bearing journal is butted against the thrust ring on the stub axle. Before the stub axle is secured.

67. Place the mud shield in position and secure the stub axle to the swivel pin housing with the six bolts and tighten evenly to the correct torque.
68. Fit the brake jump hoses to the brake jump hose bracket.
69. To complete the assembly, follow instructions to fit front hub on ABS fitted vehicles.
70. Check that the swivel pin housing oil drain plug is tightly fitted and remove the filler and level plugs.
71. Inject approximately 0,35 litres (0.6 pints) of recommended oil until the oil reaches the level hole. Fit and tighten the filler and level plugs and wipe away any surplus oil.
72. Set the steering lock-stop bolt to provide a clearance of 20mm (0.787in) between the tyre wall and radius arm. Tighten the locknut which also secures the brake disc shield.
73. Fit the ABS brake sensor following the instructions in the brake section.

ANTI-ROLL BAR ASSEMBLY FRONT

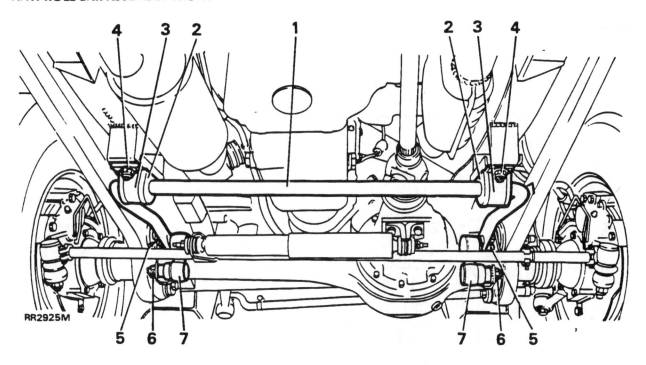

RR2925M

KEY

1. Anti-roll bar
2. Rubber bush
3. Strap
4. Nut, bolt, washer

5. Nut and washer
6. Castellated nut and split pin
7. Ball joint link arm

ANTI-ROLL BAR FRONT

Remove and refit

Remove

1. Mark for reassembly position of rubber bushes on the anti-roll bar.
2. Remove the four nuts, bolts and washers securing the two bush straps.
3. Remove the nuts, bolts, washers and rubber bushes from the ball joint links and remove anti-roll bar.

Refit

4. Position bushes on the anti-roll bar. Ensure the split points towards axle.
5. Fit the anti-roll bar with the two straps. To ensure correct fit the angled sides of the bar should point down as shown. Loosely fit the bolts, washers and nyloc nuts.
6. Fit bolt, washers and rubber bushes. Using new nuts fit anti-roll bar to ball joint links. Tighten to a torque of 68 Nm.
7. Tighten to a torque of 30 Nm the nuts securing the straps.

ANTI-ROLL BAR BALL JOINT LINKS-FRONT

Remove and refit

Remove

1. Remove the two nuts, bolts, washers and rubber bushes from the ball joint links.
2. Remove split pin and loosen castellated nut a few turns.
3. Release ball joint using special tool 18G 1063A as shown.
4. Remove castellated nut and ball joint link.

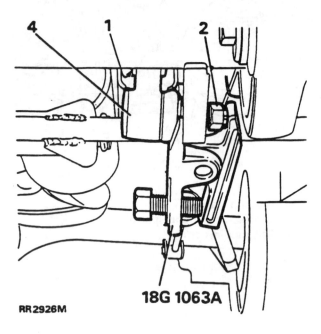

RR 2926M   18G 1063A

Refit

5. Fit ball joint link and castellated nut. Ensure the ball joint link arm points up. Tighten to a torque of 40 Nm and fit new split pin.
6. Align anti-roll bar to ball joint links.
7. Fit bolts, washers and rubber bushes using new self locking nuts secure anti-roll bar to ball joint links. Tighten to a torque of 68 Nm.

ANTI-ROLL BAR ASSEMBLY REAR

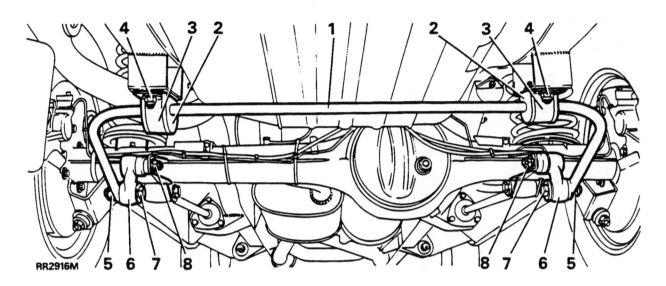

RR2916M

KEY

1. Anti-roll bar
2. Rubber bush
3. Strap
4. Nut, bolt, washer

5. Nut and washer
6. Ball joint link arm
7. Bolt and washer
8. Castellated nut and split pin

ANTI-ROLL BAR REAR

Remove and refit

Remove

1. Note for reassembly, the position of rubber bushes on the anti-roll bar.
2. Remove the four nuts, bolts and washers securing the two bush straps.
3. Remove the nuts, bolts, washers and rubber bushes from the ball joint links and remove anti-roll bar.

Refit

4. Position the rubber bushes on the anti-roll bar. Ensure the split points towards axle.
5. Fit the anti-roll bar with the two straps. Ensure the ball joint link arms point down as shown. Loosely fit, the bolts, washers and new nyloc nuts.
6. Fit bolt, washers and rubber bushes. Using new nuts fit anti-roll bar to ball joint links. Tighten to a torque of 68 Nm.
7. Tighten to a torque of 30 Nm the nuts securing the straps.

ANTI-ROLL BAR BALL JOINT LINKS-REAR

Remove and refit

Remove

1. Remove the two nuts, bolts, washers and rubber bushes from the ball joint links and lower anti-roll bar to clear links.
2. Remove split pin and loosen castellated nut a few turns.
3. Release ball joint using special tool 18G 1063A as shown.
4. Remove castellated nut and ball joint link.

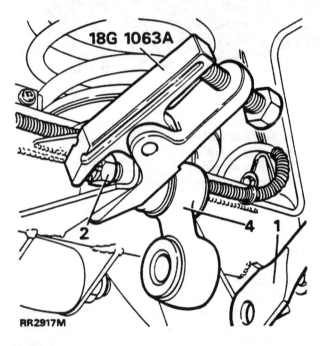

RR2917M

Refit

5. Fit ball joint link arm and castellated nut. Ensuring the ball joint link arm points down as shown.Tighten to a torque of 40 Nm and fit new split pin.
6. Align anti-roll bar to ball joint links.
7. Fit bolts, washers and rubber bushes using new self locking nuts secure anti-roll bar to ball joint links. Tighten to a torque of 68 Nm.

GLASS SUNROOF 1991 MODEL YEAR

Operation

The sunroof operates in a tilt and slide action controlled by a rocker switch near the interior lamp.

A drive motor and control unit is located behind the switch and interior lamp panel. The control units function is to stop the drive motor at the full tilt and slide positions.

The removal and refit of the sunroof assemblies shown can be carried out without removing the complete sunroof assembly.

GLASS SUNROOF ASSEMBLY.

Remove refit and adjust

Remove

1. Open the sunroof to the tilt position.
2. Remove the two mechanism covers. Slide rearwards to disengage from their location and lift out.
3. Remove two screws from each side as shown.
4. Remove glass sunroof.

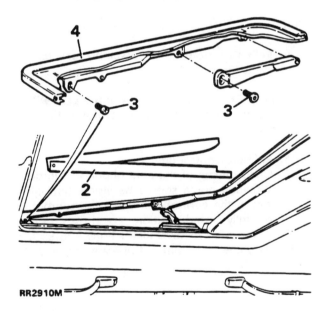

RR2910M

Refit and adjust

5. Replace the glass sunroof
6. Fit the four screws firmly but do not tighten.
7. Close the sunroof

8. Check the height of the sunroof panel against the roof aperture. The trimmed edge of the glass sunroof should stand approximately 1mm proud of the roof aperture.
9. Adjust by releasing the four screws and moving the sunroof up or down as required. Tighten the screws.
10. Fit the two mechanism covers.
11. Fully check the sunroof operates correctly.

SUNROOF WIND DEFLECTOR ASSEMBLY

Remove, refit and adjust

Remove

1. Open sunroof.
2. Remove the two screws accessed through the slot in the deflector
3. Remove the wind deflector assembly

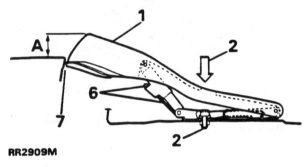

RR2909M

Refit

4. Replace the wind deflector assembly
5. Fit the two screws firmly but do not tighten.

Adjust

Note: Adjustment and attachment of the deflector is by the same two screws.

6. Adjust the wind deflector rearwards or forwards into the position shown. At the same time adjust the height A' to 15mm by moving the slotted metal strip rearwards or forwards. Tighten the two screws.
7. Ensure the deflector does not catch the front edge of the roof aperture when operated.
8. On completion fully check that the sunroof operates correctly.

Manual operation.

If the sunroof fails to operate by electrical means the sunroof can be opened or closed manually with the key provided.

1. Remove the two turnbuckles to access the sunroof motor spindle located behind the switch plate.
2. Engage the key into the motor spindle and turn to open or close the sunroof panel.
3. On completion of manual operation the motor spindle MUST BE TURNED BACK A QUARTER TURN TO ENSURE ENGAGEMENT TO THE ELECTRICAL DRIVE MOTOR.

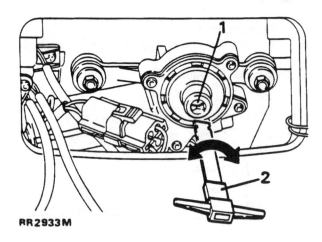

RR2933M

MOTOR DRIVE ASSEMBLY AND CONTROL UNIT

NOTE: The following servicing of the sunroof assembly can be carried out without removing the complete sunroof assembly.

Remove and refit

Remove

1. Fully close the sunroof then disconnect the battery negative terminal.
2. Turn to release the two turnbuckles to access the motor drive assembly and control unit, located behind the switchplate.
3. Remove the switchplate and disconnect the two multiplugs from the switch and courtesy light.

4. Release the front of the headlining sufficiently to access the motor drive assembly and control unit.
5. Disconnect the two multiplugs from the control unit to the motor drive unit and to the main harness.

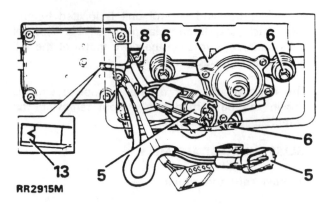

RR2915M

6. Remove the three screws securing the motor drive assembly.
7. Remove the motor drive assembly.
8. To remove the control unit undo the fixing screw. Lower then move the control box inwards to release from mounting.
9. Inspect the motor drive assembly and control unit for wear and damage, renew as necessary.

Refit

10. Refit the motor drive assembly ensuring the metal insert is fitted.

CAUTION:The motor drive assembly gear will not mesh correctly with the drive cables if the metal insert is NOT refitted.

11. Refit the control unit.
12. Check timing of the control unit to sunroof. A V'shaped notch should be visible through the slot in the control unit when the sunroof is in the fully closed position.
13. Reverse the removal instructions 2 to 5.
14. Fully check the sunroof operates correctly.

GLASS SUNROOF COMPLETE ASSEMBLY

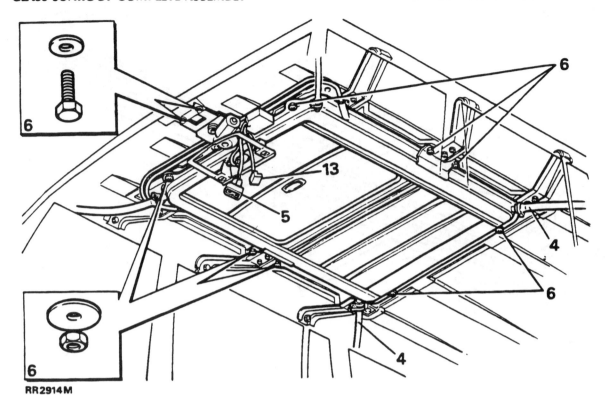

RR 2914 M

Remove and refit

Remove

1. Fully open the sunroof rearwards then disconnect the battery negative terminal.
2. Remove the switchplate and disconnect the two multiplugs from the switch and courtesy light
3. Remove the headlining completely from the vehicle
4. Remove the four clips and disconnect the drain tubes
5. Disconnect the multiplug from the control unit to the main harness.
6. With assistance remove the eight nuts and washers and two bolts. Lower the complete sunroof assembly to enable it to be removed through the rear of the vehicle.

Refit

7. Manually operate the sunroof to the fully closed position. On completion of manual operation the motor spindle MUST BE TURNED BACK A QUARTER TURN TO ENSURE ENGAGEMENT TO THE ELECTRICAL DRIVE MOTOR.

8. With assistance lift the complete sunroof assembly to the roof panel.
9. Locate and fit loosely the eight retaining nuts and washers and two bolts.
10. Ensure the closed sunroof now fits equally positioned in the roof panel aperture. Tighten the retaining nuts and bolts, recheck fit.
11. Reconnect the electrical multiplugs to the main harness and sunroof switch.
12. Fully check the sunroof operates correctly and leave in the open position.
13. Disconnect the sunroof switch
14. Fit and secure the drain tubes with retaining clips. Water test to ensure a watertight seal.
15. Fit the headlining and sunroof trim.
16. Reconnect electrical multiplugs to sunroof switch and interior light then fit switchplate.
17. Close glass sunroof and draw sunshade.

SLIDE AND GUIDE CHANNEL ASSEMBLIES OR SUNSHADE PANEL.

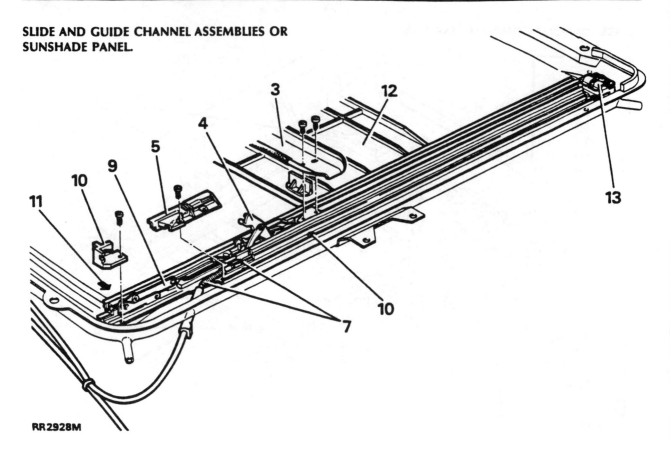

RR2928M

Remove and refit

NOTE: The following servicing of the sunroof assembly can be carried out without removing the complete sunroof assembly.
The sunshade panel is removed by releasing, either the left or right slide and guide channel assembly, instructions 1. to 12.

Remove

1. Remove glass panel assembly.
2. Remove sunroof wind deflector assembly.
3. Remove rear crossmember drainchannel.
4. Move the tilt slide rearwards until the location cam is clear of the locator block.
5. Remove the locator block.

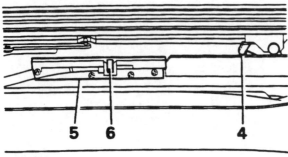

RR2929M

6. Move the tilt slide forwards until the location cam has reached the position it would normally locate into the locator block. Manually adjust the cam outwards to allow the tilt slide to pass and to attain the full tilt position.

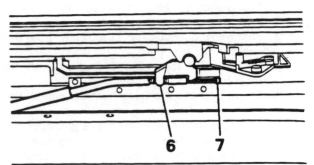

RR2930M

7. The drive cable end is now accessible. Disconnect drive cable from the slide assembly.
8. Push the tilt slide rearwards reversing instruction 6.
9. Push complete slide assembly rearwards approximately 2".
10. Remove front end stop and the attaching screw from centre of guide channel.

11. Push guide channel assembly out sideways to release guide channel from the roof panel.
12. Slide the sunshade panel forward and lift out of runner to remove.

Continue for removal of slide and guide channel assembly.

13. With the aid of a flashlight directed between the roof panel and sunroof assembly. Observe for reassembly the guide channel rear spring fixing point.
14. Pull the guide channel forward to release from the rear spring fixing point. Remove the guide channel asembly

Refit

15. Reverse the removal instructions
16. Fully check the sunroof operates correctly.

TIMING OF CONTROL UNIT TO SUNROOF OPERATION.

The timing of control unit to sunroof operation will be disturbed:-
If the sunroof position is altered when the control unit is removed.
Or the control unit is removed and the control unit gear is moved manually.

1. To check timing of the control unit to sunroof. A V'shaped notch should be visible through the slot in the control unit when the sunroof is in the fully closed position.

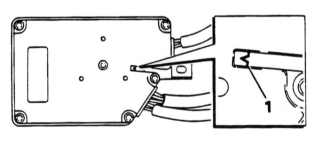

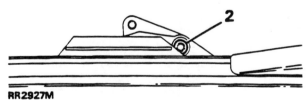

RR2927M

2. To check timing of the control unit when the glass sunroof panel is removed. A V'shaped notch should be visible through the slot in the control unit when the sunroof tilt mechanism is in the position shown.

HEATED FRONT DOOR LOCK ASSEMBLY

Remove and refit

Remove

1. Disconnect battery negative lead.
2. Remove outside front door handle assembly.

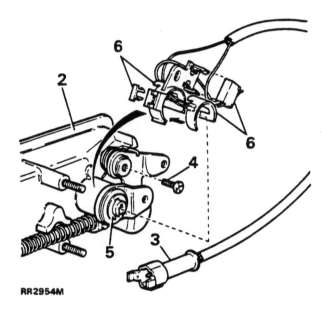

RR2954M

3. Disconnect the heaters electrical wiring at the multiplug.
4. Remove heater retaining bracket screw.
5. Remove 'C' clip and colored cam link from end of barrel assembly.
Caution: Ensure the loose barrel assembly remains in position, to avoid components falling apart.
6. Remove heater retaining bracket, complete with de-icing element, switch and wiring assembly.

Refit

7. Hold de-icing element in position and fit heater retaining bracket assembly.
8. Reverse removal instructions 1 to 5.

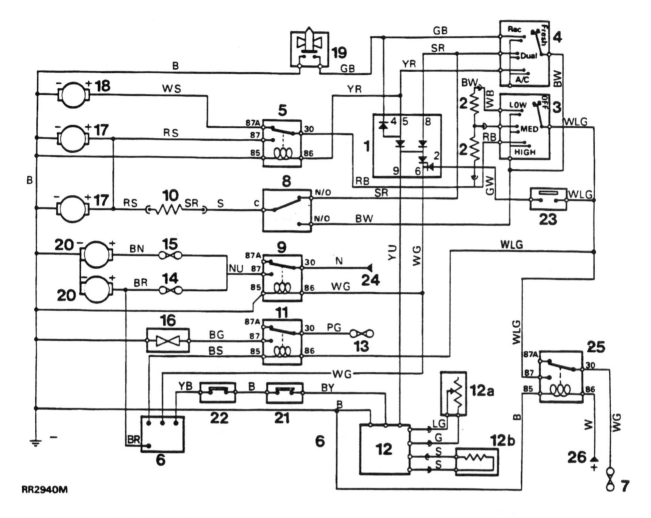

RR2940M

HEATER AND AIR CONDITIONING - circuit diagram - 1991 model year

1. Diode pack.
2. Resistors.
3. Fan speed switch.
4. Air conditioning/re-circ/fresh air switch.
5. Heater/air conditioning relay.
6. Cable connection to ECU (EFI).
7. Fuse C9 - main fuse panel.
8. Face vent switch.
9. Condenser fan relay.
10. Two level resistor.
11. Compressor clutch relay.
12. Thermostat.
12a. Temperature control potentiometer.
12b. Evaporator temperature sensor.
13. Fuse B7.

14. Fuse B8.
15. Fuse B9.
16. Compressor clutch.
17. Air conditioning motors (2) - dashboard unit.
18. Heater motor.
19. Fresh air solenoid.
20. Condensor fan motors.
21. High pressure switch.
22. Low pressure switch.
23. Engine coolant temperature switch.
24. 12V from terminal post.
25. Heater/air con load relay.
26. 12V from ignition load relay.

NOTE: See EFI circuit diagram for details of air conditioning inputs to ECU.

Cable colour code

B	Black	L	Light	P	Purple	U	Blue
G	Green	N	Brown	R	Red	W	White
K	Pink	O	Orange	S	Grey	Y	Yellow

The last letter of a colour code denotes the tracer.

RR2985M

LOCATION OF ELECTRICAL EQUIPMENT - 1991 MODEL YEAR

1. Battery
2. Air conditioning compressor (option)
3. Horns
4. Oil pressure switch
5. Water temperature switch
6. Electronic distributor
7. Alternator
8. Starter motor
9. Coil
10. Headlamp wash timer unit
11. Heater
12. Relays/flasher units
13. Air con relays/diode unit (option)
14. Window lift motor (front RH door)
15. Door lock actuator (front RH door)
16. Electronic control unit (EFI)
17. Wiper motor - front screen
18. Relays/delay units
19. Park brake warning light switch
20. Window lift motor (front LH door)
21. Electronic control unit and relays (ABS) (option)

22. Seat adjustment fusebox (option)
23. Door lock actuator (front LH door)
24. Window lift motor (rear LH door)
25. Door lock actuator (rear LH door)
26. Seat adjustment relays - two (option)
27. Electrical in-tank fuel pump
28. Inertia switch
29. Tailgate lock actuator
30. Wiper motor - rear screen
31. Radio aerial amplifier
32. Fuel filler flap lock actuator
33. Window lift relays and one touch control unit
34. Door lock actuator (rear RH door)
35. Window lift motor (rear RH door)
36. EFI relays (two)
37. Condenser fan timer unit (option)
38. Cruise control relay (option)
39. Dimming mirror (option)
40. RH door lock heater
41. LH door lock heater

NOTE: Left hand drive vehicle shown. Items 10, 12, 13, 17 and 18 located symmetrically opposite on right hand drive vehicles.

1

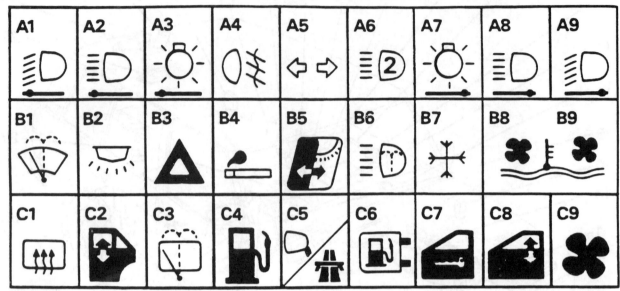

RR2984M

FUSE BOX - RR2984M

FUSE No.	COLOUR CODE	RATING AMPS	IGN. KEY POSITION	FUNCTION
A1	Red	10	II	LH dipped beam
A2	Red	10	II	LH main beam, auxiliary lamp relay
A3	Tan	5	O	LH sidelamps, radio ill., trailer pickup
A4	Red	10	O	Rear fog guard (headlamp switch controlled)
A5	Yellow	20	II	Direction ind., resistor, heated jets, thermo., heated front screen timer, air con. low coolant, speed transducer, interior lamp delay, reverse lights, stop lights, dimming rear view mirror
A6	Red	10	II	Auxiliary driving lamps (from main beam)
A7	Tan	5	O	RH sidelamps, rheostat controlled instrument/switch illumination, trailer pick up
A8	Red	10	II	RH main beam
A9	Red	10	II	RH dipped beam, headlamp levelling (option)
B1	Yellow	20	I	Front wash/wipe, seat relays, window lift relays, antenna amplifier
B2	Yellow	20	O	Interior light, clock, underbonnet ill., elec. seat relays, radio, door lamps, heated door locks
B3	Yellow	20	O	Hazard switch, alarm, main beam/dip flash, horns
B4	Yellow	20	II	Cigar lighters
B5	Yellow	20	II	Sunroof motor
B6	Yellow	20	II	Headlamp wash
B7	Tan	5	II	Air conditioning compressor clutch
B8	Yellow	20	II	Air conditioning/radiator cooling fan
B9	Yellow	20	II	Air conditioning/radiator cooling fan
C1	Green	30	II	Heated rear screen (voltage switch controlled)
C2	Green	30	II	Window lifts - rear
C3	Red	10	II	Rear wash wipe motor, heated rear screen relay, mirror heaters
C4	Red	10	II	Fuel pump
C5	Red	10	II	Mirror motors, cruise control (option)
C6	Tan	5	O or I	Fuel filler flap
C7	Blue	15	O	Central locking
C8	Green	30	II	Window lifts - front
C9	Green	30	II	Heater/air conditioning motor

AUTOMATIC DIMMING REARVIEW MIRROR (OPTION)

Description

The dimming rearview mirror is designed to eliminate dangerous and annoying glare during any driving situation. Using light sensing electronics, the mirror automatically monitors and controls the reflection of glaring light from the rear of the vehicle.

Forward and rear facing sensors monitor ambient lighting conditions. When the rear facing sensor in the glass senses glare, for example, from a following vehicle, it causes the glass to darken and absorb light. As glare subsides the glass returns to its normal clear state.

The mirror is controlled by a three position switch:
In the **OFF** position there is no power to the mirror and the glass returns to its normal clear state.
HI position can be used to eliminate the glare from distant headlamps.
LO position can be used for city driving if the driver's eyes are not so sensitive to glare.
In either **HI** or **LO** position the mirror is operational with ignition switched **ON**.

Reverse override

When reverse gear is selected the mirror will return to its clear state.

Mirror adjustment

To alter the position of the mirror, always grasp it in the middle and adjust it gently as shown in the illustration.

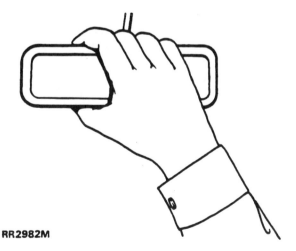

RR2982M

Function test

To check mirror function:

1. Switch ignition ON, select transmission Park or Neutral.
2. Move mirror sensitivity switch to the HI or LO position.
3. Mask the front sensor, located on the right hand side of the mirror back, using a piece of black cloth. The glass should now darken.
4. Remove the cloth, or select reverse gear, the glass should now return to its clear state.
5. Repeat the procedure using HI and LO switch positions to ensure correct operation.

Fault diagnosis

If mirror does not function:

1. Check ignition is switched ON, transmission in Park or Neutral.
2. Check mirror sensitivity switch is in the HI or LO position.
3. Check switch controls are illuminated. If not, the most likely fault is in the wiring to the mirror.

HIGH LEVEL STOP LAMP - Territorial requirement

Remove and refit

Remove

1. Disconnect the battery negative lead.

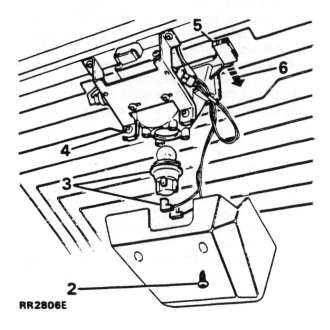

RR2806E

2. Remove the two cover retaining screws and remove the cover.
3. Disconnect the electrical leads to the bulb holder. Remove the bulbholder and the bulb with a counter clockwise twist.
4. Remove the two mounting plate to brake light screws.
5. Observe position of stop lamp on the rear screen. Carefully release the assembly tabs on the stop lamp from the rear screen mountings.
6. Slide the stop lamp out.

Refit

7. Renew the bulb if necessary, the correct bulb is a 12V, 21 watt, bayonet type.
8. Reverse the removal instructions.

DOOR LOCKS/FUEL FILLER FLAP

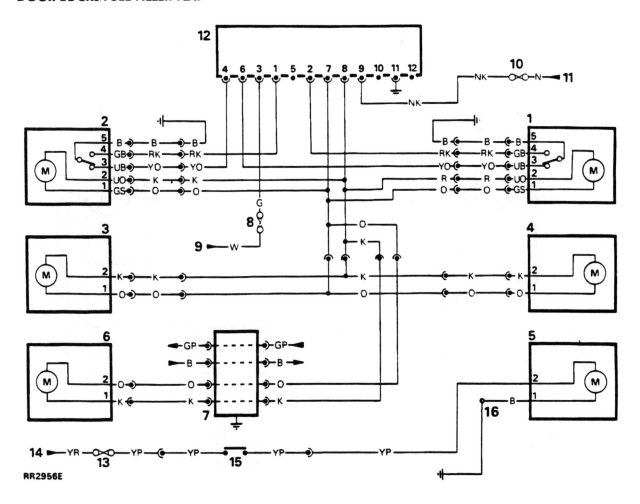

RR2956E

Circuit diagram - RR2956E

1. Switch/lock unit right hand front door
2. Switch/lock unit left hand front door
3. Lock unit left hand rear door relay
4. Lock unit right hand rear door
5. Fuel flap actuator
6. Lock unit tailgate
7. Suppressor
8. Fuse A5
9. Feed from ignition load relay - pin 87
10. Fuse C7
11. Battery 12V +ve
12. Central door locking control unit

13. Fuse C6
14. Feed from ignition load relay - pin 87A
15. Fuel flap release switch
16. Fuel tank filler pipe earth

Cable colour code

B	Black	**L**	Light	**P**	Purple	**U**	Blue
G	Green	**N**	Brown	**R**	Red	**W**	White
K	Pink	**O**	Orange	**S**	Grey	**Y**	Yellow

HEADLAMP LEVELLING

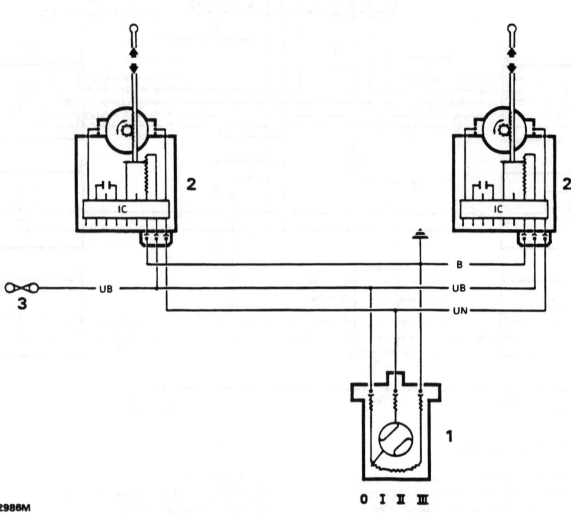

ı RR2986M

Circuit diagram - RR2986M

1. Headlamp levelling switch
2. Headlamp levelling actuator/motor
3. Fuse A9

Cable colour code

B	Black	**L**	Light	**P**	Purple	**U**	Blue
G	Green	**N**	Brown	**R**	Red	**W**	White
K	Pink	**O**	Orange	**S**	Grey	**Y**	Yellow

SUNROOF/AUTOMATIC DIMMING MIRROR

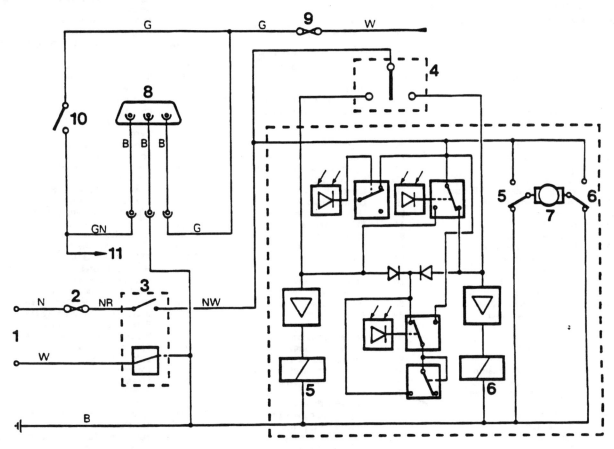

RR2958E

Circuit diagram - RR2958E

1. Main harness connections
   Brown - live positive feed
   White - ignition positive feed
   Black - ground
2. Fuse B5
3. Auxiliary relay
4. Operating switch
5. Relay - tilt, open to closed
   - slide, closed to open
6. Relay - slide, open to closed
   - tilt, closed to open
7. Drive motor
8. Mirror connection
9. Fuse A5
10. Reverse lamps switch
11. Reverse lamps

CABLE COLOUR CODE

B	Black
U	Blue
N	Brown
P	Purple
G	Green
R	Red
W	White
Y	Yellow

The last letter of a colour code denotes the tracer colour.

------- Denotes component enclosure

MAIN CIRCUIT DIAGRAM. - 1991 Model year Right hand steering - RR2976M & RR2977M

Numerical key

1. Ignition load relay
2. Battery
3. Terminal post
4. Starter solenoid
5. Starter motor
6. Starter relay
7. Starter inhibit switch
7a. Resistor (manual)
8. Ignition switch
9. Tachometer
10. Voltage transformer (dim dip)
11. Ignition warning lamp
12. Alternator
13. Fuse B1
14. Front wipe/wash switch
15. Front wipe delay unit
16. Front wiper motor
17. Headlamp relay
18. Front wash pump
19. Headlamp wash timer unit
20. Headlamp wash pump
21. Main lighting switch
22. Fuse A3
23. Fuse A7
24. LH side lamp
25. LH tail lamp
26. LH number plate lamp
26a. RH number plate lamp
27. High beam dip/flash switch
28. Fuse B2
29. RH side lamp
30. RH tail lamp
31. Rheostat
32. Fuse A8
33. Fuse A2
34. Fuse A9
35. Fuse A1
36. Rear fog switch
37. Fuse A4
38. Switch illumination (2 off)
39. Cigar lighter illumination (2 off)
40. Heater illumination (4 off)
41. Clock illumination
42. Auto gear selector illumination
43. Instrument illumination (4 off)
43a. Column switch illumination
44. Rear fog warning lamp
45. LH rear fog lamp
46. RH rear fog lamp
47. LH dip beam
48. RH dip beam
49. LH high beam
50. RH high beam
51. High beam warning lamp
52. Fuel gauge
53. Fuel gauge sender unit
54. Water temperature gauge
55. Water temperature sender unit
56. Fuse B3
57. Horn switch
58. RH horn
59. LH horn
60. Under bonnet illumination switch

61. Under bonnet light
62. Clock
63. Fuse C7
64. Fuse C8
65. Window lift pick-up point
66. Fuse C1
67. Heated rear screen relay
68. Radio aerial amplifier
69. Heated rear screen
70. Heated rear screen switch
71. Heated rear screen warning lamp
72. Voltage sensitive switch
73. Fuse A5
74. Hazard switch
75. Flasher unit
76. Direction indicator switch
77. LH indicator warning lamp
77a. RH indicator warning lamp
78. LH rear indicator lamp
79. LH front indicator lamp
80. LH side repeater lamp
81. RH side repeater lamp
82. RH front indicator lamp
83. RH rear indicator lamp
84. Trailer warning lamp
85. Fuse A6
86. Stop lamp switch
87. Reverse lamp switch
88. Front auxilary lamp relay
89. LH stop lamp
90. RH stop lamp
91. LH reverse lamp
92. RH reverse lamp
93. LH front auxilary lamp
94. RH front auxilary lamp
95. Front auxilary lamp switch
96. Fuse B4
97. Dash cigar lighter
98. Glove box cigar lighter
99. Front interior lamp
100. Rear interior lamp
101. Interior lamp delay unit
102. LH door edge lamp
103. LH puddle lamp
104. RH door edge lamp
105. RH puddle lamp
106. Interior lamp switch
107. LH rear door switch
108. RH rear door switch
109. Tailgate switch
110. LH front door switch
111. RH front door switch
112. Heated washer jets (front screen)
113. Thermostat heated jets
114. Oil pressure warning lamp
115. Oil pressure switch
116. Fuse C4
117. Heated front screen connections
118. Fuel pump (petrol models)
119. Ignition coil
120. Capacitor
121. Distributor
122. EFI Harness plug
123. Fuel shut off solenoid (Diesel)
124. Sun roof relay
124a. Fuse B5
125. Radio fuse
126. Radio and four speakers
   -LF-left hand front speaker
   -LR-left hand rear speaker
   -RF-right front speaker
   -RR-right hand rear speaker
127. Sun roof pick up point

128. Auto transmission and transfer box oil temperature warning lamp
129. Auto transmission oil temperature switch
129a. Transfer box oil temperature switch
130. Fuse C3
131. Rear wash wipe switch
132. Rear wipe delay unit
133. Rear wiper motor
134. Rear screen wash pump
135. Low screen wash fluid level warning lamp
136. Low screen wash switch
137. Low coolant switch
138. Electronic speedo and instrument controls
139. Low coolant level warning lamp
140. Low fuel level warning lamp
141. Glow plug warning lamp (Diesel)
142. E.F.I. warning lamp
143. Glow plug timer unit
144. Glow plugs (Diesel)
145. ABS warning lamp
146. Handbrake/brake fluid level/pressure warning lamp
147. Handbrake warning switch
148. Brake fluid level warning switch
149. Brake pad wear warning lamp
150. Brake pad wear sensors
151. Brake check relay (Australia only)
152. Split charge relay (option)
153. Split charge terminal post (option)
154. Heater/air conditioning connections
155. Fuse C9
156. Coil negative (engine RPM input to ECU)
157. Fuel filter flap (see door cable circuit diagram)
158. Ignition load relay (+)
159. Battery feed (+)
160. Ignition auxiliary (+)
161. Ignition on (+)
162. Earth (-)
163. Heater/air con. load relay
164. Trailer pick up point
165. Electric seats pick up point (option)
166. Fuse C2
167. Electric mirrors
168. Alarm pick up point
169. Fuse C5
170. ABS pick up point
171. Fuse B6
172. Fuse B7
173. Condenser fan relay
174. Fuse B8
175. Fuse B9
176. Inertia switch
177. Speed transducer
178. Central locking
179. Fuse C6
180. Cruise control pick-up point (option)

MAIN CIRCUIT DIAGRAM - Right hand steering RR2976M & RR2977M

Alphabetical key

170.	ABS pick up point	63.	Fuse C7	46.	RH rear fog lamp
145.	ABS warning lamp	64.	Fuse C8	83.	RH rear indicator lamp
168.	Alarm pick up point	155.	Fuse C9	92.	RH reverse lamp
12.	Alternator	98.	Glove box cigar lighter	29.	RH side lamp
42.	Automatic gear selector illumination (2 off)	144.	Glow plugs (Diesel)	81.	RH side repeater lamp
		143.	Glow plug timer unit (Diesel)	90.	RH stop lamp
129.	Automatic transmission oil temperature switch	141.	Glow plug warning lamp (Diesel)	30.	RH tail lamp
		146.	Handbrake/brake fluid level/pressure warning lamp	31.	Rheostat
128.	Automatic transmission/transfer box oil temperature warning lamp			177.	Speed transducer
		147.	Handbrake warning switch	152.	Split charge relay (option)
		74.	Hazard switch	153.	Split charge terminal post (option)
2.	Battery	17.	Headlamp relay		
148.	Brake fluid level warning switch	20.	Headlamp wash pump	7.	Starter inhibit switch
150.	Brake pad wear sensors	19.	Headlamp wash timer unit	5.	Starter motor
149.	Brake pad wear warning lamp	117.	Heated front screen connections	6.	Starter relay
151.	Brake check relay (Australia only)	69.	Heated rear screen	4.	Starter solenoid
120.	Capacitor	67.	Heated rear screen relay	86.	Stop lamp switch
178.	Central locking	70.	Heated rear screen switch	127.	Sunroof pick up point
39.	Cigar lighter illumination (2 off)	71.	Heated rear screen warning lamp	124.	Sunroof relay
62.	Clock	112.	Heated washer jets	38.	Switch illumination (2 off)
41.	Clock illumination	40.	Heater illumination (4 off)	9.	Tachometer
156.	Coil negative, engine speed signal to ECU	154.	Heater/air con. connections	109.	Tailgate switch
		163.	Heater/air con. load relay	3.	Terminal post
43a.	Column switch illumination	27.	High beam dip/flash switch	113.	Thermostat - heated washer jets
173.	Condenser fan relay	51.	High beam warning lamp	164.	Trailer pick up point
180.	Cruise control pick-up point (option)	57.	Horn switch	84.	Trailer warning lamp
		119.	Ignition coil	129a.	Transfer box oil temperature switch
97.	Dash cigar lighter	1.	Ignition load relay		
76.	Direction indicator switch	8.	Ignition switch	60.	Under bonnet illumination switch
121.	Distributor	11.	Ignition warning lamp		
167.	Electric mirrors	176.	Inertia switch	61.	Under bonnet light
165.	Electric seats pick up point (option)	43.	Instrument illumination (4 off)	72.	Voltage sensitive switch
		101.	Interior lamp delay unit	10.	Voltage transformer (dim-dip)
138.	Electronic speedo and instrument controls	106.	Interior lamp switch	54.	Water temperature gauge
		47.	LH dip beam	55.	Water temperature sender unit
122.	EFI Harness plug	102.	LH door edge lamp	65.	Window lift pick-up point
142.	EFI warning lamp	93.	LH front auxiliary lamp		
75.	Flasher unit	110.	LH front door switch		
88.	Front auxiliary lamp relay	79.	LH front indicator lamp		
95.	Front auxiliary lamp switch	49.	LH high beam		
99.	Front interior lamp	59.	LH horn		
18.	Front wash pump	77.	LH indicator warning lamp		
15.	Front wipe delay unit	25.	LH number plate lamp		
14.	Front wipe/wash switch	103.	LH puddle lamp		
16.	Front wiper motor	107.	LH rear door switch		
52.	Fuel gauge	45.	LH rear fog lamp		
53.	Fuel gauge sender unit	78.	LH rear indicator lamp		
118.	Fuel pump (petrol models)	91.	LH reverse lamp		
123.	Fuel shut off solenoid (Diesel)	24.	LH side lamp		
157.	Fuel filler flap	80.	LH side repeater lamp		
35.	Fuse A1	89.	LH stop lamp		
33.	Fuse A2	25.	LH tail lamp		
22.	Fuse A3	139.	Low coolant level warning lamp		
37.	Fuse A4	137.	Low coolant switch		
73.	Fuse A5	140.	Low fuel level warning lamp		
85.	Fuse A6	135.	Low screen wash fluid level warning lamp		
23.	Fuse A7				
32.	Fuse A8	136.	Low screen wash switch		
34.	Fuse A9	21.	Main lighting switch		
13.	Fuse B1	115.	Oil pressure switch		
28.	Fuse B2	114.	Oil pressure warning lamp		
56.	Fuse B3	68.	Radio aerial amplifier		
96.	Fuse B4	126.	Radio and four speakers		
124a.	Fuse B5	125.	Radio fuse		
171.	Fuse B6	36.	Rear fog switch		
172.	Fuse B7	44.	Rear fog warning lamp		
174.	Fuse B8	100.	Rear interior lamp		
175.	Fuse B9	134.	Rear screen wash pump		
66.	Fuse C1	131.	Rear wash wipe switch		
166.	Fuse C2	132.	Rear wipe delay unit		
130.	Fuse C3	133.	Rear wiper motor		
116.	Fuse C4	7a.	Resistor (manual)		
169.	Fuse C5	87.	Reverse lamp switch		
179.	Fuse C6	48.	RH dip beam		
		104.	RH door edge lamp		
		94.	RH front auxiliary lamp		
		111.	RH front door switch		
		82.	RH front indicator lamp		
		50.	RH high beam		
		58.	RH horn		
		77a.	RH indicator warning lamp		
		26a.	RH number plate lamp		
		105.	RH puddle lamp		
		108.	RH rear door switch		

MAIN CIRCUIT DIAGRAM
Right hand steering RR2976M and RR2977M

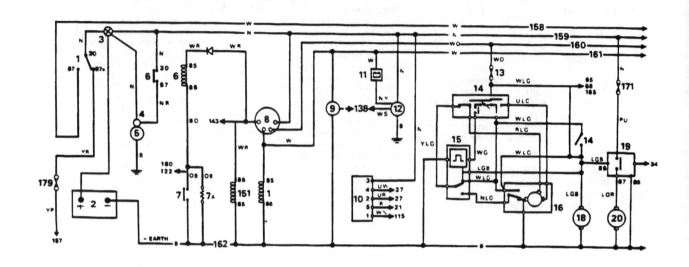

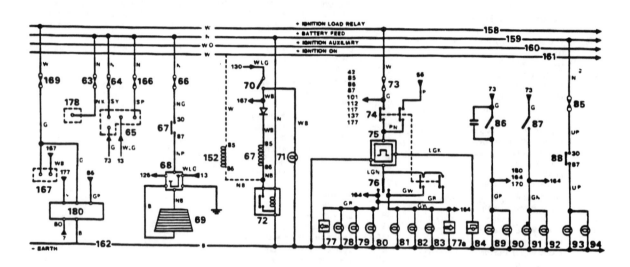

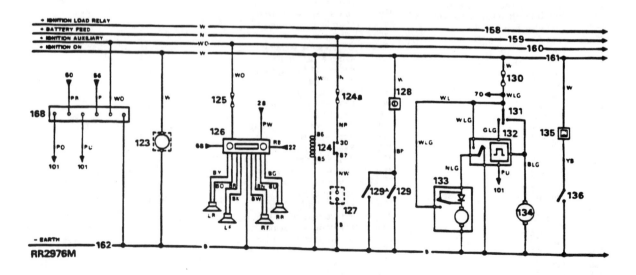

RR2976M

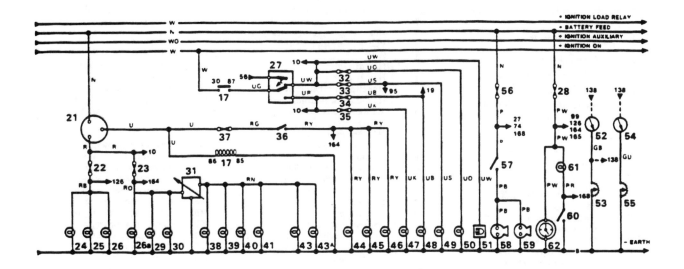

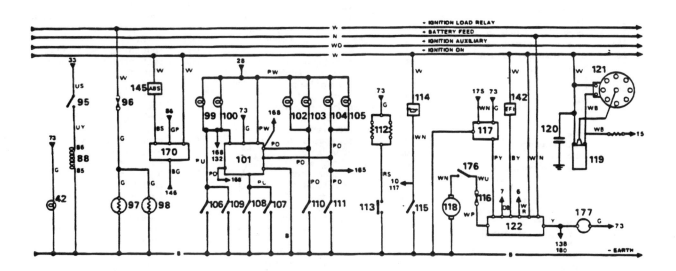

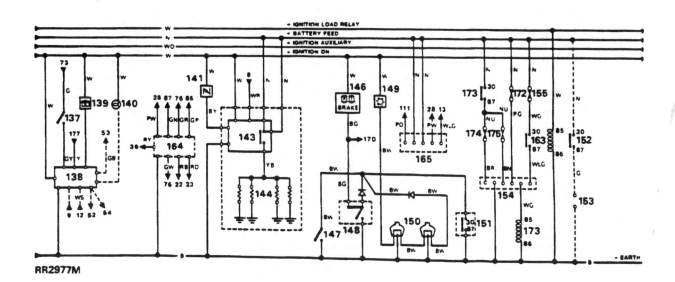

RR2977M

MAIN CIRCUIT DIAGRAM - 1991 Model year Left hand steering - RR2978M & RR2979M

1. Ignition load relay
2. Battery
3. Terminal post
4. Starter solenoid
5. Starter motor
6. Starter relay
7. Starter inhibit switch (auto)
7a. Resistor (manual transmission)
8. Ignition switch
9. Tachometer
10. Ignition warning lamp
11. Alternator
12. Fuse B1
13. Front wipe/wash switch
14. Front wipe delay unit
15. Front wiper motor
16. Headlamp relay
17. Front wash pump
18. Headlamp wash timer unit
19. Headlamp wash pump
20. Main lighting switch
21. Fuse A3
22. Fuse A7
23. LH side lamp
24. LH tail lamp
25. LH number plate lamp
25a. RH number plate lamp
26. High beam dip/flash switch
27. RH side lamp
28. RH tail lamp
29. Rheostat
30. Fuse A8
31. Fuse A2
32. Fuse A9
33. Fuse A1
34. Rear fog switch
35. Fuse A4
36. Switch illumination (2 off)
36 a.Headlamp levelling switch illumination (Germany)
37. Cigar lighter illumination (2 off)
38. Heater illumination (4 off)
39. Clock illumination
40. Auto gear selector illumination (2 off)
41. Instrument illumination (4 off)
41a. Column switch illumination
42. Rear fog warning lamp
43. LH rear fog
44. RH rear fog
45. LH dip beam
46. RH dip beam
47. LH high beam
48. RH high beam
49. High beam warning lamp
50. Fuel gauge
51. Fuel gauge sender unit
52. Water temperature gauge
53. Water temperature sender unit
54. Fuse B2
55. Horn switch
56. RH horn
57. LH horn
58. Under bonnet illumination switch
59. Under bonnet light
60. Clock
61. Fuse C7
62. Fuse C2
63. Pick-up point central locking/window lift

64. Heated rear screen relay
65. Fuse C1
66. Radio aerial amplifier
67. Heated rear screen
68. Heated rear screen switch
69. Heated rear screen warning lamp
70. Voltage sensitive switch
71. Fuse A5
72. Hazard switch
73. Flasher unit
74. Direction indicator switch
75. LH indicator warning lamp
75a. RH indicator warning lamp
76. LH rear indicator lamp
77. LH front indicator lamp
78. LH side repeater lamp
79. RH side repeater lamp
80. RH front indicator lamp
81. RH rear indicator lamp
82. Trailer warning lamp
83. Fuse A6
84. Stop lamp switch
85. Reverse lamp switch
86. Front auxilary lamp relay (option)
87. LH stop lamp
88. RH stop lamp
89. LH reverse lamp
90. RH reverse lamp
91. LH front auxilary lamp (option)
92. RH front auxilary lamp (option)
93. Front auxilary lamp switch
94. Fuse B4
95. Dash cigar lighter
96. Glove box cigar lighter
97. Front interior lamp
98. Rear interior lamp
99. Interior lamp delay unit
100. LH door edge lamp
101. LH puddle lamp
102. RH door edge lamp
103. RH puddle lamp
104. Interior lamp switch
105. LH rear door switch
106. RH rear door switch
107. Tailgate switch
108. LH front door switch
109. RH front door switch
110. Heated washer jets (front screen)
111. Thermostat-heated washer jets
112. Oil pressure warning lamp
113. Oil pressure switch
114. Fuse C4
115. Inertia switch
116. Fuel pump (petrol models)
117. Ignition coil (petrol models)
118. Capacitor (petrol models)
119. Distributor (petrol models)
120. EFI Harness plug
121. Speed transducer
122. Trailer pick up point
123. Radio fuse
124. Radio and four speakers
 -LF-left hand front speaker
 -LR-left hand rear speaker
 -RF-right front speaker
 -RR-right hand rear speaker
125. Sun roof relay
125a. Fuse B5
126. Alarm pick up point
127. Overspeed warning (Saudi only)
128. Fuse B6
129. Fuse C5
130. Fuel shut off solenoid (Diesel)
131. Seat buckle switch (Saudi only)
132. Overspeed monitor (Saudi only)
133. Heated front screen pick up point (option)

134. Sunroof pick up point (option)
135. Auto transmission/transfer box oil temperature warning lamp
136. Auto transmission oil temperature switch
136a. Transfer box oil temperature switch
137. Fuse C3
138. Rear wash wipe switch
139. Rear wipe delay unit
140. Rear wiper motor
141. Rear screen wash pump
142. Low screen wash fluid level warning lamp
143. Low screen wash switch
144. Low coolant switch
145. Electronic speedo and instrument controls
146. Low coolant level warning lamp
147. Low fuel level warning lamp
148. E.F.I. warning lamp
149. Glow plug warning lamp (Diesel)
150. Glow plug timer unit(Diesel)
151. Glow plugs (Diesel)
152. ABS warning lamp
153. Handbrake/brake fluid level/pressure warning lamp
153a. Brake fluid level warning switch
154. Handbrake warning switch
155. Brake pad wear warning lamp
156. Brake pad wear sensors
157. Fuse C6
158. Split charge relay (option)
159. Split charge terminal post (option)
160. Heater/air conditioning connections
161. Fuse C9
162. Coil negative (engine RPM input to ECU)
163. Ignition load relay (+)
164. Battery feed (+)
165. Ignition auxiliary (+)
166. Ignition on (+)
167. Earth (-)
168. Fuel filler flap (see door locks circuit diagram)
169. Central locking
170. Electric seats pick up point
171. Fuse B3
172. Fuse B8
173. Fuse C8
174. Electric mirrors
175. Heater/air conditioning load relay
176. Cruise control pick up points (option)
177. Fuse B9
178. Condenser fan relay
179. Fuse B7
180. ABS pick up point
181. Headlamp levelling switch connection (option)
182. Headlamp levelling actuator (2) (option)

MAIN CIRCUIT DIAGRAM - Left hand steering RR2978M & RR2979M

Alphabetical key

180.	ABS pick up point
152.	ABS warning lamp
126.	Alarm pick up point
11.	Alternator
40.	Automatic gear selector illumination (2 off)
136.	Automatic transmission oil temperature switch
135.	Automatic transmission/transfer box oil temperature warning lamp
2.	Battery
153a.	Brake fluid level warning switch
156.	Brake pad wear sensors
155.	Brake pad wear warning lamp
118.	Capacitor (petrol models)
169.	Central locking
37.	Cigar lighter illumination (2 off)
60.	Clock
39.	Clock illumination
162.	Coil negative, engine speed signal to ECU
41a.	Column switch illumination
178.	Condenser fan relay
176.	Cruise control pick up point (option)
95.	Dash cigar lighter
74.	Direction indicator switch
119.	Distributor (petrol models)
174.	Electric mirrors
170.	Electric seats pick up point (option)
145.	Electronic speedo and instrument controls
120.	EFI harness plug
148.	EFI warning lamp
73.	Flasher unit
86.	Front auxiliary lamp relay (option)
93.	Front auxiliary lamp switch
97.	Front interior lamp
17.	Front wash pump
14.	Front wipe delay unit
13.	Front wipe/wash switch
15.	Front wiper motor
168.	Fuel filler flap
50.	Fuel gauge
51.	Fuel gauge sender unit
116.	Fuel pump (petrol models)
130.	Fuel shut off solenoid (Diesel)
33.	Fuse A1
31.	Fuse A2
21.	Fuse A3
35.	Fuse A4
71.	Fuse A5
83.	Fuse A6
22.	Fuse A7
30.	Fuse A8
32.	Fuse A9
12.	Fuse B1
54.	Fuse B2
171.	Fuse B3
94.	Fuse B4
125a.	Fuse
128.	Fuse
179.	Fuse
172.	Fuse B8
177.	Fuse B9
65.	Fuse C1
162.	Fuse C2

137.	Fuse C3
114.	Fuse C4
129.	Fuse C5
157.	Fuse C6
61.	Fuse C7
173.	Fuse C8
161.	Fuse C9
96.	Glove box cigar lighter
151.	Glow plugs (Diesel)
150.	Glow plug timer unit (Diesel)
149.	Glow plug warning lamp (Diesel)
153.	Handbrake/brake fluid level/pressure warning lamp
154.	Handbrake warning switch
72.	Hazard switch
182.	Headlamp levelling actuator (2) (Germany)
181.	Headlamp levelling switch connection (option)
36a.	Headlamp levelling switch illumination (option)
16.	Headlamp relay
19.	Headlamp wash pump
18.	Headlamp wash timer unit
133.	Heated front screen pick up point (option)
67.	Heated rear screen
64.	Heated rear screen relay
68.	Heated rear screen switch
69.	Heated rear screen warning lamp
110.	Heated washer jets
38.	Heater illumination (4 off)
160.	Heater/air con. connections
175.	Heater/air con. load relay
26.	High beam dip/flash switch
49.	High beam warning lamp
55.	Horn switch
117.	Ignition coil
1.	Ignition load relay
8.	Ignition switch
10.	Ignition warning lamp
115.	Inertia switch
41.	Instrument illumination (4 off)
99.	Interior lamp delay unit
104.	Interior lamp switch
45.	LH dip beam
100.	LH door edge lamp
91.	LH front auxiliary lamp
108.	LH front door switch
77.	LH front indicator lamp
47.	LH high beam
57.	LH horn
75.	LH indicator warning lamp
25.	LH number plate lamp
101.	LH puddle lamp
105.	LH rear door switch
43.	LH rear fog lamp
76.	LH rear indicator lamp
89.	LH reverse lamp
23.	LH side lamp
78.	LH side repeater lamp
87.	LH stop lamp
24.	LH tail lamp
146.	Low coolant level warning lamp
144.	Low coolant switch
147.	Low fuel level warning lamp
142.	Low screen wash fluid level warning lamp
143.	Low screen wash switch
20.	Main lighting switch
113.	Oil pressure switch
112.	Oil pressure warning lamp
132.	Overspeed monitor (Saudi only)
127.	Overspeed warning (Saudi only)
63.	Pick up point-central locking/window lift
66.	Radio aerial amplifier
124.	Radio and four speakers
123.	Radio fuse
34.	Rear fog switch
42.	Rear fog warning lamp

98.	Rear interior lamp
141.	Rear screen wash pump
138.	Rear wash wipe switch
139.	Rear wipe delay unit
140.	Rear wiper motor
7a.	Resistor (manual)
85.	Reverse lamp switch
46.	RH dip beam
102.	RH door edge lamp
92.	RH front auxiliary lamp
109.	RH front door switch
80.	RH front indicator lamp
48.	RH high beam
56.	RH horn
75a.	RH indicator warning lamp
25a.	RH number plate lamp
103.	RH puddle lamp
106.	RH rear door switch
44.	RH rear fog lamp
81.	RH rear indicator lamp
90.	RH reverse lamp
27.	RH side lamp
79.	RH side repeater lamp
88.	RH stop lamp
28.	RH tail lamp
29.	Rheostat
121.	Speed transducer
158.	Split charge relay (option)
159.	Split charge terminal post (option)
7.	Starter inhibit switch
5.	Starter motor
6.	Starter relay
4.	Starter solenoid
84.	Stop lamp switch
134.	Sunroof pick up point
125.	Sunroof relay
36.	Switch illumination (2 off)
9.	Tachometer
107.	Tailgate switch
3.	Terminal post
111.	Thermostat - heated washer jets
122.	Trailer pick up point
82.	Trailer warning lamp
136a.	Transfer box oil temperature switch
58.	Under bonnet illumination switch
59.	Under bonnet light
70.	Voltage sensitive switch
52.	Water temperature gauge
53.	Water temperature sender unit

MAIN CIRCUIT DIAGRAM
Left hand steering RR2978M & RR2979M

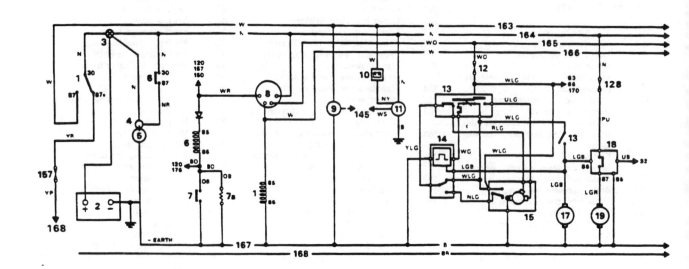

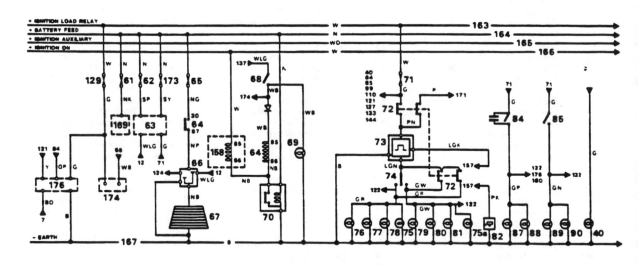

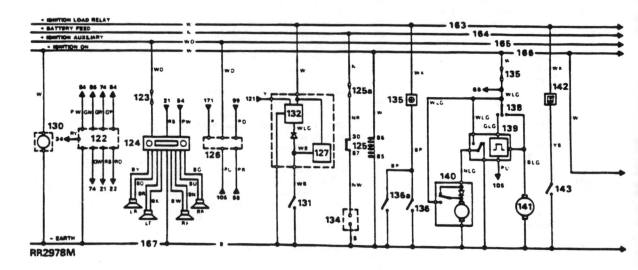

RR2978M

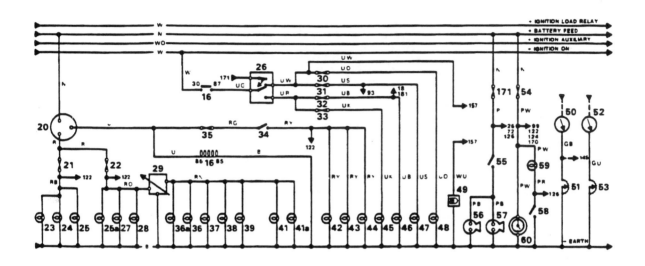

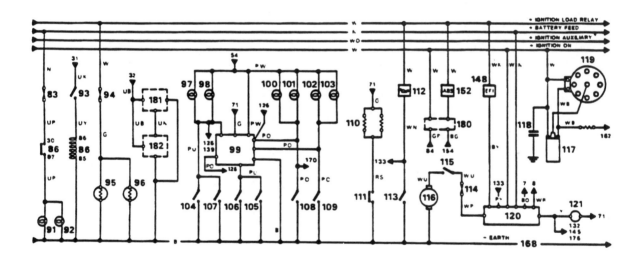

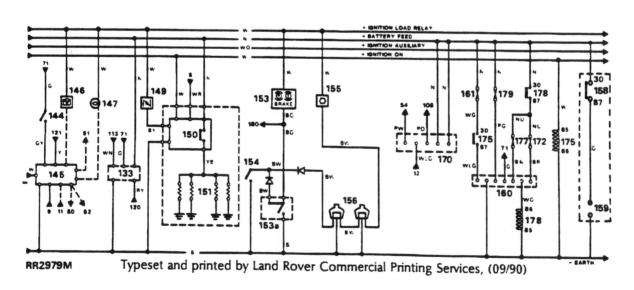

RR2979M   Typeset and printed by Land Rover Commercial Printing Services, (09/90)

RANGE ROVER

RANGE ROVER
POWER STEERING

WORKSHOP MANUAL SUPPLEMENT

Publication Number LSM180WS8

Published by the
Technical Publications Department of

Power Steering Supplement

CONTENTS

INTRODUCTION

RANGE ROVER POWER STEERING

The following workshop manual supplement covers the steering system for all Range Rovers fitted with the Adwest Varamatic power steering box and Holborn Series 200 steering pump.

This information updates that given in Section 57 of the current workshop manual, and is intended to replace the existing section as a whole.

This supplement contains a new procedure for centralising the steering box, which must be carried out when the steering box and steering components have been removed. It is essential that this procedure is followed whenever steering components are removed.

The procedures include instructions for vehicles fitted with the cruise control option. It is essential to follow the procedure to prevent the cruise control cassette being damaged when steering components are disconnected. These instructions should be ignored for vehicles without cruise control.

This supplement also contains service procedures for a new lower steering shaft introduced in January 1991. This shaft is identified by having the flexible coupling fitted to the lower end of the shaft.

Note that there is an improved procedure for pressure testing the steering system, which requires removing the pressure hose from the steering pump, instead of the steering box.

STEERING	Nm	lbf ft	lbf in
Ball joint nuts	40	30	-
Clamp bolt nuts	14	10	-
Steering column bracket nuts	27	20	-
Steering wheel nut	38	28	-
Universal joint pinch bolt	35	26	-
PAS box			
- Drop arm nut	176	130	-
- Sector shaft cover to steering box	22-27	16-20	-
- Steering box to chassis	81	60	-
- Steering box fluid pipes 14mm thread	15	11	-
- Steering box fluid pipes 16mm thread	20	15	-
- Tie bar to steering box	81	60	-
PAS pump			
- High pressure fluid pipe	20	15	-
- Power steering pump mounting	35	26	-
- Pulley bolts, power steering pump	8-12	6-9	-
- Hose clamp	3	-	27
PAS reservoir			
- Hose clamp	3	-	27

POWER STEERING FLUID PIPES

CAUTION: When fluid pipes are removed for any reason, it is essential that the pipe ends and fluid ports in steering box, pump and fluid reservoir are plugged to prevent ingress of foreign matter. The following procedures must be followed when refitting fluid pipes:

Power steering pump

1. Remove plugs from pipes and pump, place clamp on feed hose.

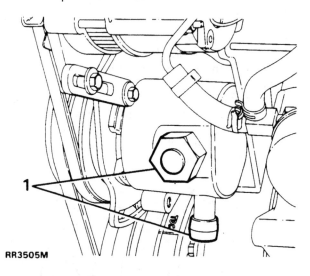

RR3505M

2. Push hose fully onto pump.
3. Hold clamp in position, torque clamp to 3 Nm (2 lbf ft)
4. Fit high pressure union into pump finger tight.
5. Hold pipe in correct position, and torque union to 20Nm (15 lbf ft)

Power steering box

1. Remove plugs from pipes and steering box ports and immediately refit pipes fingertight.

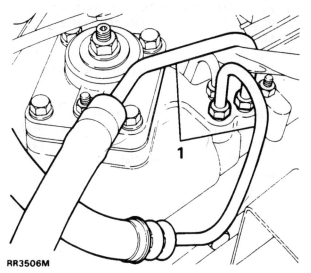

RR3506M

2. Finally tighten to the correct torque: 16mm thread - 20 Nm (15 lbf ft), 14mm thread - 15Nm (11 lbf ft).

Power steering reservoir

1. Remove plugs from pipes and reservoir and immediately refit pipes and clamps.

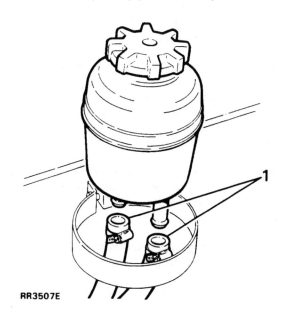

RR3507E

2. Hold clamps in position, torque clamps to 3 Nm (2 lbf ft)

1

POWER STEERING BOX

Remove and refit

Service tools:
Drop arm extractor-MS252A

NOTE: It is important that whenever any part of the system, including the flexible piping, is removed or disconnected, that the utmost cleanliness is observed.

All ports and hose connections must be suitably sealed off to prevent ingress of dirt, etc. If metallic sediment is found in any part of the system, the complete system should be checked, the cause rectified and the system thoroughly cleaned.

Under no circumstances must the engine be started until the reservoir has been filled. Failure to observe this rule will result in damage to the pump.

Metric pipe fittings are used with 'O' ring pipe ends on the fittings to the steering box.

Follow normal 'O' ring replacement procedure whenever pipes are disconnected.

Ensure that compatible metric components are used when fitting replacement pipes.

CAUTION: PRIOR TO REMOVING ANY OF THE COMPONENTS INCORPORATED IN THE STEERING LINKAGE, IT IS IMPERATIVE THAT THE ROAD WHEELS ARE IN A STRAIGHT AHEAD POSITION AND THAT THE STEERING WHEEL IS THEN REMOVED TO PREVENT THE CRUISE CONTROL SPIRAL CASSETTE BEING WOUND UP OR DAMAGED IF THE STEERING LINKAGE IS INADVERTENTLY MOVED OR ROTATED.

AFTER REFITTING STEERING LINKAGE COMPONENTS, THE CORRECT PROCEDURE MUST BE FOLLOWED TO ENSURE THAT THE ROAD WHEELS, STEERING BOX AND STEERING WHEEL ARE ALL IN THE CORRECT POSITION RELATIVE TO EACH OTHER WHEN IN THE STRAIGHT AHEAD CONDITION. IF IT IS FOUND THAT THE STEERING WHEEL REQUIRES REPOSITIONING, IT IS IMPORTANT TO ENSURE THAT THE DRIVE PEGS ON THE CRUISE CONTROL CASSETTE ARE IN THE CORRECT POSITION BEFORE THE STEERING WHEEL IS REPLACED.

THIS WILL ENSURE THAT THE DRIVE PEGS LOCATE IN THEIR RESPECTIVE HOLES IN THE REAR OF THE STEERING WHEEL.

AFTER FINAL ALIGNMENT RECONNECT THE MULTI-PLUG TO THE CASSETTE, TIGHTEN THE STEERING WHEEL SECURING NUT AND FIT THE TRIM PAD.

NOTE: WHEN THE DRAG LINK IS DISCONNECTED FROM THE STEERING BOX THE TRAVEL AVAILABLE AT THE STEERING WHEEL TO EACH FULL LOCK IS NOT THE SAME, I.E. THE STEERING BOX IS ASSYMETRIC. THEREFORE THE CORRECT PROCEDURE MUST BE USED TO SET THE BOX ON CENTRE.

Removing

1. Park the vehicle on a level surface.
2. Prop open the hood.
3. Remove the filler cap from the power steering fluid reservoir.
4. Disconnect the fluid pipes from the pump. Drain and discard the fluid. Replace the filler cap.
5. Disconnect the fluid feed and return pipes from the steering box.

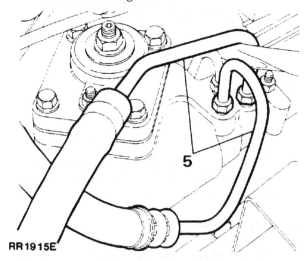

RR1915E

6. **PLUG ALL PIPE ENDS AND STEERING BOX PORTS TO PREVENT INGRESS OF FOREIGN MATTER.**
7. Jack up and support the chassis front end with axle stands. Alternatively, raise the vehicle on a hoist.

WARNING: Whichever method is adopted, it is essential that the wheels are chocked, the parking brake is applied, and low range selected with differential lock engaged. (if applicable)

8. Disconnect the drag link from the drop arm using a suitable extractor.
9. Remove the pinch bolt attaching the universal joint to the power steering box.
10. Loosen the nut securing the tie bar to the panhard rod mounting bracket.
11. Remove the bolts securing the tie bar to the steering box and move the tie bar aside.
12. Remove the fixings attaching the power steering box to the chassis side member.
13. Withdraw the power steering box.

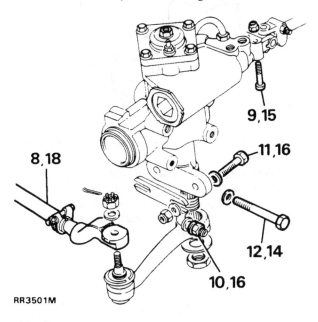

9,15
11,16
8,18
12,14
10,16
RR3501M

Refitting

14. Refit the steering box to the chassis side member and tighten the four bolts to the correct torque (81 Nm, 60 lbf ft).
15. Reconnect the pinch bolt attaching the universal joint to the power steering box, and tighten to the correct to the correct torque.
16. Refit the tie bar, tighten the three fixings starting with the tie bar to panhard rod, then loosen all three by one complete turn.
17. Check, and if necessary, adjust the steering box (see power steering box - adjust page 14).
18. Refit the drag link and secure.
19. Lower the vehicle to the ground.
20. Remove the sealing plugs and immediately refit the pipes to the steering box, fingertight. Finally tighten to the correct torque: 16mm thread - 20 Nm 15 lbf ft, 14mm thread - 15Nm 11 lbf ft.
21. Remove the filler cap from the power steering fluid reservoir. fill the reservoir to the oil level mark on the dipstick attached to the filler cap with the recommended fluid (see section 09) and bleed the power steering system (see power steering system - bleed page 12).

22. Check the fluid level and replace the filler cap.
23. Test the steering system for leaks with the engine running, by holding the steering hard on full lock in both directions.

CAUTION: Do not maintain this pressure for more than 30 seconds in any one minute, to avoid causing the oil to overheat and possible damage to seals.

24. Close the hood.
25. Carefully drive the vehicle, using full lock in both directions, a short distance within the dealer premises to settle the steering components. If possible, drive the vehicle over speed bumps and include harsh braking.

CAUTION: Do not drive the vehicle on the public highway.

26. On nearing the end of step 25, ensure that the vehicle is driven in a straight line on level ground and brought to a stop.
27. Tighten the tie bar to the panhard rod mounting arm to the correct torque (110 Nm, 81 lbf ft).
28. Tighten the two fixings securing the tie bar to the steering box to the correct torque (81 Nm, 60 lbf ft).
29. Ensure that the steering wheel is correctly aligned when the wheels are in the straight ahead position.

NOTE: It may be necessary to remove the steering wheel and reposition on the splines to obtain this position.(see steering wheel - remove and refit page 22).

30. Road test the vehicle.

POWER STEERING BOX OVERHAUL

Service tools:
LST120 - 'C' Wrench
LST119 - Worm adjusting wrench
MS252A - Drop arm extractor
606602 - Ring expander
606603 - Ring compressor
606604 - Seal saver, sector shaft
RO1015 - Seal saver, valve and worm
RO1016 - Torque setting tool

Dismantle

1. Remove the steering box from the vehicle, and withdraw the drop arm.

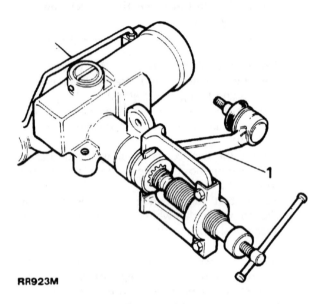

RR923M

2. Rotate the retainer ring, as necessary, until one end is approximately 12 mm (0.500 in) from the extractor hole.
3. Lift the cover retaining ring from the groove in the cylinder bore, using a suitable pointed drift applied through the hole provided in the cylinder wall.
4. Complete the removal of the retainer ring, using a screwdriver.
5. Turn on left lock until the piston pushes out the end cover.

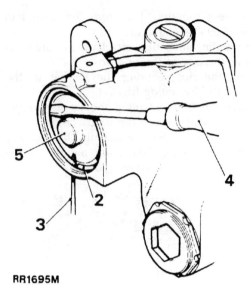

RR1695M

6. Loosen the set screw retaining the rack pad adjuster.
7. Remove the rack pad adjuster.
8. Remove the sector shaft adjuster locknut.
9. Remove the sector shaft cover fixings.
10. Screw in the sector shaft adjuster until the cover is removed.
11. Slide out the sector shaft.

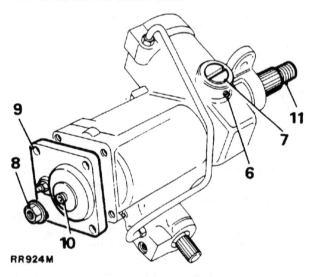

RR924M

12. Withdraw the piston, using a suitable bolt screwed into the tapped hole in the piston.

13. Remove the worm adjuster locknut using 'C' Wrench, LST120.
14. Remove the worm adjuster using wrench LST119.

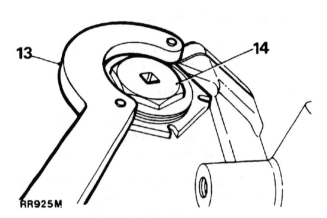

RR925M

15. Tap the splined end of the shaft to free the bearing.
16. Withdraw the bearing cup and caged ball bearing assembly.
17. Withdraw the valve and worm assembly.
18. Withdraw the inner bearing ball race and shims.
19. Retain the shims for reassembly

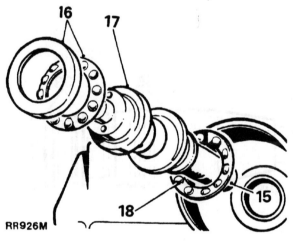

RR926M

Steering box seals

20. Remove the circlip and seals from the sector shaft housing bore.

   NOTE: Do not remove the sector bushes from the casing. Replacement parts are not available.

21. Remove the circlip and seals from the input shaft housing bore.

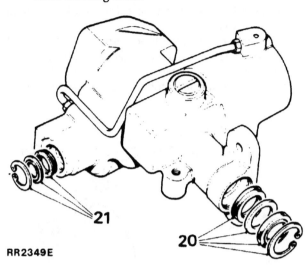

RR2349E

Inspecting

22. Discard all rubber seals and provide replacements.

   NOTE: A rubber seal is fitted behind the plastic ring on the rack piston. Discard the seal and also the plastic ring and provide replacements.

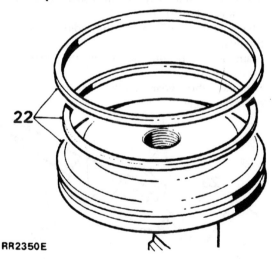

RR2350E

Steering box casing

23. Examine the piston bore for traces of scoring and wear.
24. Examine the inlet tube thread for damage. If repair is necessary this can be undertaken by using a suitable tap.
25. Examine the feed tube for signs of cracking.

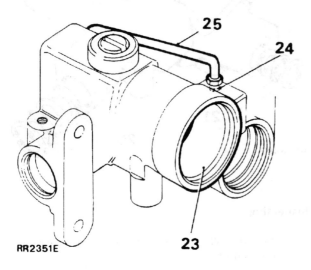

RR2351E

Sector shaft assembly

26. Check that there is no side play on the rollers.
27. If excessive side play on the roller does exist fit a new sector shaft.
28. Check the condition of the adjuster screw threads.
29. Examine the bearing areas on the shaft for excessive wear.
30. Examine the gear teeth for uneven or excessive wear.

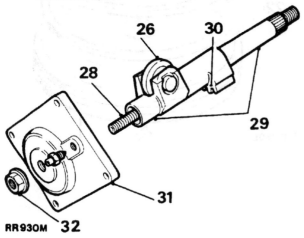

RR930M

Sector shaft cover assembly

31. The cover, bush and seal are supplied as a complete assembly for replacement purposes.

Sector shaft adjuster locknut

32. The locknut functions also as a fluid seal, a new nut must be fitted at overhaul.

Valve and worm assembly

33. Examine the valve rings which must be free from cuts, scratches and grooves. The valve rings should be a loose fit in the valve grooves.
34. Remove the damaged rings ensuring that no damage is done to the seal grooves.
35. If required, fit replacement rings, using the ring expander 606602. Warm the rings and expander tool to aid assembly, using hot water for this purpose. Fit the rings to the expander, slide the expander over the valve and worm assembly, in turn fit the rings to their respective grooves. Remove the expander, slide the valve and worm assembly into the ring compressor 606603 and allow the rings to cool.

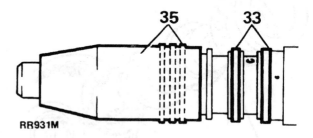

RR931M

NOTE: The expander will not pass over rings already fitted. The rings must be discarded to allow access and then new rings must be fitted.

36. Examine the bearing areas for wear. The areas must be smooth and not indented.
37. Examine the worm track which must be smooth and not indented.
38. Check for wear on the torsion bar assembly pins; no free movement should exist between the input shaft and the worm.

NOTE: Any sign of wear makes it essential that a new valve and worm assembly is fitted.

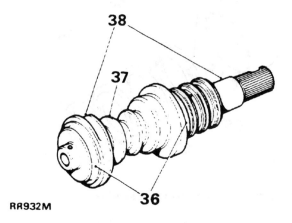

RR932M

Ball bearing and cage assemblies

39. Examine the ball races and cups for wear and general condition.
40. If the ball cage has worn against the bearing cup, fit replacements.
41. Bearing balls must be retained by the cage.
42. Bearings and cage repair are carried out by the complete replacement of the bearings and cage assembly.

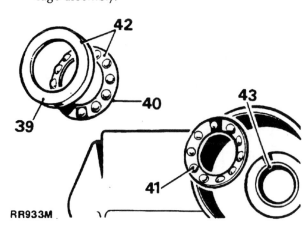

RR933M

43. To remove the inner bearing cup and shim washers, jar the steering box on the work bench, or use a suitable extractor.

NOTE: Should difficulty be experienced at this stage, warm the casing and the bearing assembly. Cool the bearing cup using a suitable mandrel and jar the steering box on the bench.

Rack thrust pad and adjuster

44. Examine the thrust pad for scores.
45. Examine the adjuster for wear in the pad seat.
46. Examine the nylon pad for distortion and adjuster set screw assembly for wear.

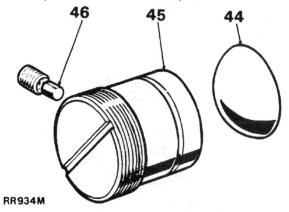

RR934M

Rack and piston

47. Examine for excessive wear on the rack teeth.
48. Ensure the thrust pad bearing surface is free from scores and wear.
49. Ensure that the piston outer diameters are free from burrs and damage.
50. Examine the seal and ring groove for scores and damage.

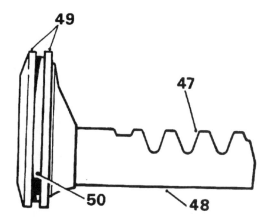

RR935M

7

51. Fit a new rubber ring to the piston. Warm the white nylon seal and fit this to the piston.
52. Slide the piston assembly into the cylinder with the rack tube outwards. Allow to cool.

Reassemble

NOTE: When fitting replacement oil seals, these must be lubricated with recommended fluid. Also ensure that absolute cleanliness is observed during assembly.

Input shaft oil seal

53. Fit the seal, lipped side first, into the housing. When correctly seated, the seal backing will lie flat on the bore shoulder.
54. Fit the extrusion washer and secure with the circlip.

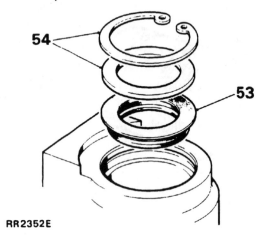

RR2352E

Sector shaft seal

55. Fit the oil seal, lipped side first.
56. Fit the extrusion washer.
57. Fit the dust seal, lipped side last.
58. Fit the circlip.

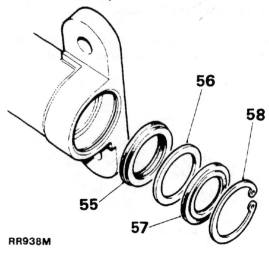

RR938M

Fitting the valve and worm assembly

59. If removed, refit the original shim washer(s) and the inner bearing cup. Only Petroleum Jelly may be used as an aid to assembling the bearings.

    NOTE: If the original shims are not available, fit shim(s) of 0.76 mm (0.030 in) nominal thickness.

60. Fit the inner cage and bearings assembly.
61. Fit the valve and worm assembly, using seal saver RO1015 to protect the input shaft seal.
62. Fit the outer cage and bearings assembly.
63. Fit the outer bearing cup.

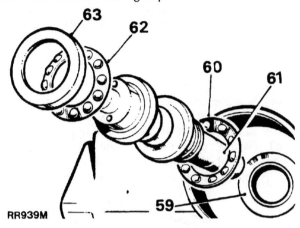

RR939M

64. Fit a new worm adjuster sealing ring and loosely screw the adjuster into the casing. Fit the locknut, but do not tighten.
65. Turn in the worm adjuster until the end-float at the input is almost eliminated.
66. Measure and record the maximum rolling resistance of the valve and worm assembly, using a spring balance and cord coiled around the torque setting tool RO1016.
67. Turn in the worm adjuster to increase the figure recorded in instruction 66 by 1.8 to 2.2 kg (4 to 5 lb) at 1.250 in (31.7 mm) radius to settle the bearings, then back off the worm adjuster until the figure recorded in instruction 66 is increased by 0.9 to 1.3 kg (2 to 3 lb) only, with locknut tight. Use worm adjusting wrench LST119 and 'C' wrench LST120.

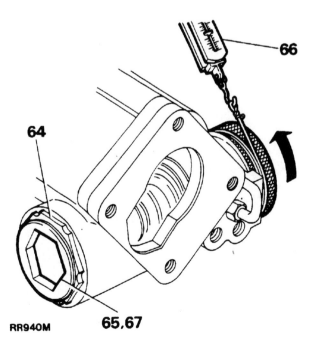

RR940M

Fitting the rack and piston

68. Screw a slave bolt into the piston head for use as an assembly tool.
69. Fit the piston and rack assembly so that the piston is 63.5 mm (2.5 in) approximately from the outer end of the bore.
70. Feed in the sector shaft using seal saver 606604 aligning the centre gear pitch on the rack with the centre gear tooth on the sector shaft. Push in the sector shaft, and, at the same time rotate the input shaft about a small arc to allow the sector roller to engage the worm.

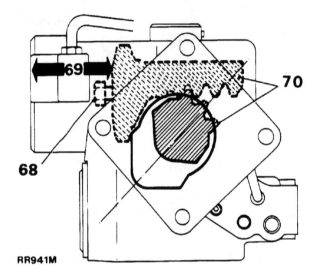

RR941M

Fitting the rack adjuster

71. Fit the sealing ring to the rack adjuster.
72. Fit the rack adjuster and thrust pad to engage the rack. Back off a half turn on the adjuster.
73. Loosely fit the nylon pad and adjuster set screw assembly to engage the rack adjuster.

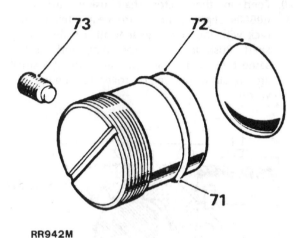

RR942M

Fitting the sector shaft cover

74. Fit the sealing ring to the cover.
75. Screw the cover assembly fully on to the sector shaft adjuster screw.
76. Position the cover on to the casing.
77. Tap the cover in place. If necessary back off on the sector shaft adjuster screw to allow the cover to joint fully with the casing.

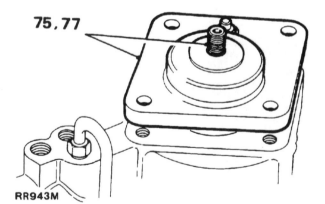

RR943M

NOTE: Before tightening the fixings, rotate the input shaft about a small arc to ensure that the sector roller is free to move in the valve worm.

78. Fit the cover fixings and tighten to the correct torque (22 - 27 Nm, 16 - 20 lbf ft).

Fitting the cylinder cover

79. Fit the square section seal to the cover.
80. Remove the slave bolt fitted at operation 68 and press the cover into the cylinder just sufficient to clear the retainer ring groove.
81. Fit the retainer ring to the groove with one end of the ring positioned 12 mm (0.5 in) approximately from the extractor hole.

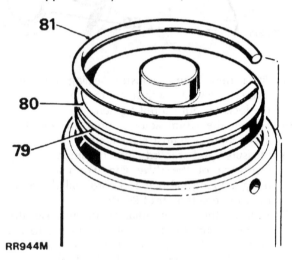

RR944M

Adjusting the sector shaft

NOTE: If adjustment of the sector shaft is being carried out, and the drop arm has been removed, refit and secure the drop arm with the nut so that no backlash is present between the drop arm and sector shaft

82. To set the worm on centre, rotate the input shaft to the full inner-lock (i.e. full right lock for a left hand drive vehicle, full left lock for a right hand drive vehicle.

NOTE: if this is carried out on the vehicle, the drag link must be disconnected. Rotate the input shaft back towards the centre exactly two full turns. The box is now on centre and can be adjusted.

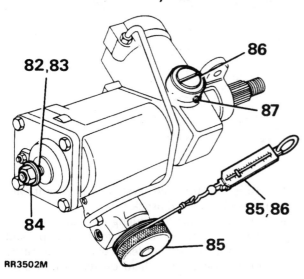

RR3502M

83. Hold the input shaft and rock the drop arm to obtain the 'feel' of the backlash present. Continue rocking while an assistant slowly turns the sector shaft adjusting screw. Continue rotating the adjuster srew until the backlash has almost been eliminated.
84. Refit the locknut and tighten. This action should remove any residual backlash. If it does not, loosen the lock nut and repeat steps 83 and 84 from the beginning.

NOTE. It is important that the steering box is correctly centralised before any backlash adjustments are made.

Adjusting the rack adjuster.

85. Measure and record the maximum rolling resistance at the input shaft, using a spring balance, cord and torque tool R01016.
86. Turn in the rack adjuster to increase the figure recorded in 85 by 0.9 to 1.3 kg (2 to 3 lb). **The final figure may be less than but must not exceed 7.25 kg (16 lb).**

87. Lock the rack adjuster in position with the grub screw.

Torque peak check

With the input shaft rotated from lock-to-lock, the rolling resistance torque figures should be greatest across the centre position and equally disposed about the centre position.

The condition depends on the value of shimming fitted between the valve and worm assembly inner bearing cup and the casing. The original shim washer value will give the correct torque peak position unless major components have been replaced.

Procedure

88. With the input coupling shaft toward the operator, turn the shaft fully counter-clockwise.
89. Check the torque figures obtained from lock-to-lock using a spring balance cord and torque tool R01016.

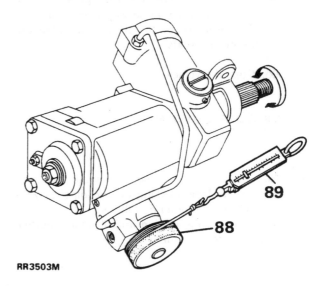

RR3503M

Adjustments

90. Note where the greatest figures are recorded relative to the steering position. If the greatest figures are not recorded across the centre of travel (i.e. steering straight-ahead position), adjust as follows:

If the torque peak occurs **before** the centre position, **add** to the shim washer value; if the torque peak occurs **after** the centre position, **subtract** from the shim washer value.

Shim washers are available as follows:
0.03mm, 0.07mm, 0.12mm and 0.24mm (0.0015 in, 0.003 in, 0.005 in and 0.010 in).

NOTE: Adjustment of 0.07mm (0.003 in) to the shim value will move the torque peak area by 1/4 turn approximately on the shaft.

91. Fit the drop arm to the steering box using a new tab washer. Tighten the nut to the correct torque (176 Nm, 130 lbf ft) and bend over tab.
92. Refit the steering box to the vehicle.
93. Replenish the system with the correct grade of fluid. Refer to Recommended Lubricants and Power Steering System-bleed.
94. Test the system for leaks, with the engine running at 1000 rev/min by holding the steering hard on full lock in both directions.

    NOTE: Do not maintain this pressure for more than 30 seconds in any one minute to avoid overheating the fluid and possibly damaging the seals.

95. Road test the vehicle.

POWER STEERING SYSTEM

Bleed

1. Fill the steering fluid reservoir to the appropriate level marking on the dipstick with one of the recommended fluids.
2. Start and run the engine until it attains normal operating temperature.

3. Check and correct the reservoir fluid level.

    NOTE: During the carrying out of items 4, 5 and 6, ensure that the steering reservoir is kept full. Do not increase the engine speed or move the steering wheel.

4. Run the engine at idle speed, loosen the bleed screw. When fluid seepage past the bleed screw is observed, retighten the screw.

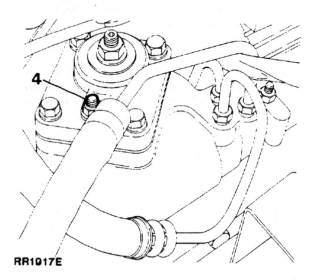

RR1017E

5. Ensure that the fluid level is in alignment with the mark on the dipstick.
6. Wipe off all fluid lost during bleeding.
7. Check all hose connections, pump and steering box for fluid leaks under pressure by holding the steering hard on full lock in both directions.

    CAUTION: Do not maintain this pressure for more than 30 seconds in any one minute, to avoid causing the oil to overheat and possible damage to the seals. The steering should be smooth lock-to-lock in both directions, that is, no heavy or light spots when changing direction when the vehicle is stationary.

8. Carry out a short road test. If necessary, repeat the complete foregoing procedure.

POWER STEERING SYSTEM

Test

If there is a lack of power assistance for the steering the pressure of the hydraulic pump should be checked first before fitting new components to the system. The fault diagnosis chart should also be used to assist in tracing faults in the power steering system.

SERVICE TOOLS

HY23   -Pressure gauge
JD10-2 -Test adaptor
LST10-11-Thread adaptor

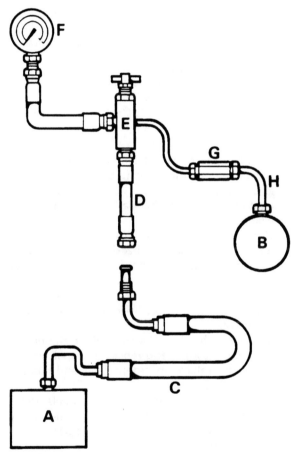

RR3609M

A. Steering box.
B. Steering pump.
C. Existing hose, steering box to pump.
D. Test adaptor LST10-12.
E. Test adaptor JD10-2.
F. Pressure gauge HY23.
G. Thread adaptor LST10-12.
H. Test adaptor LST10-12.

Procedure

1. The hydraulic pressure gauge in conjunction with the test adaptor is used for testing the power steering system. This gauge is calibrated to read up to 140 kgf/cm² (2000 p.s.i.) and the maximum pressure which may be expected in the power steering system is 77 kgf/cm² (1100 p.s.i.).
2. Under certain fault conditions of the hydraulic pump it is possible to obtain pressures up to 105 kgf/cm² (1500 p.s.i.). Therefore, it is important to realise that the pressure upon the gauge is in direct proportion to the pressure being exerted upon the steering wheel. When testing, apply pressure to the steering wheel very gradually while carefully observing the pressure gauge.
3. Check, and if necessary replenish, the fluid reservoir.
4. Examine the power steering units and connections for leaks. All leaks must be rectified before attempting to test the system.
5. Check the steering pump drive belt for condition and tension, rectify as necessary.
6. Assemble the test equipment and fit to the vehicle, as shown in the diagram.
7. Open the tap in the adaptor.
8. Bleed the system but exercise extreme care when carrying out this operation so as not to overload the pressure gauge.
9. With the system in good condition, the pressures should be as follows:

   (a) Steering wheel held hard on full lock and engine running at 1,000 rev/min, the pressure should be 70 to 77 kgf/cm² (1000 to 1100 p.s.i.).
   (b) With the engine idling and the steering wheel held hard on full lock, the pressure should be 28 kgf/cm² (400 p.s.i.) minimum.

These checks should be carried out first on one lock, then on the other.

CAUTION: Under no circumstances must the steering wheel be held on full lock for more than 30 seconds in any one minute, otherwise there will be a tendency for the oil to overheat and possible damage to the seals may result.

10. Release the steering wheel and allow the engine to idle. The pressure should be below 7 kgf/cm² (100 p.s.i.).
11. If the pressures recorded during the foregoing tests are outside the specified range, or pressure imbalance is recorded, a fault exist in the system. To determine if the fault is in the steering box or the pump, close the adaptor tap for a period not exceeding five seconds.
12. If the gauge fails to register the specified pressure, the pump is at fault and a new unit must be fitted.
13. Repeat the foregoing test after fitting a new pump and bleeding the system. If pump delivery is satisfactory but low pressure or a substantial imbalance exists, the fault must be in the steering box valve and worm assembly.

ADJUST POWER STEERING BOX

NOTE: The condition of adjustment which must be checked is one of no backlash when the steering box is in the central position, ie 'on-centre'. ADJUSTMENTS OF THE STEERING BOX WOULD NOT NORMALLY BE REQUIRED ON A BOX THAT IS STILL WITHIN ITS WARRANTY PERIOD. IF A BOX IS CONSIDERED STIFF OR TIGHT AND IT IS STILL WITHIN ITS WARRANTY PERIOD, IT MUST BE REMOVED FOR RETURN TO THE MANUFACTURERS. IN ANY EVENT NO ATTEMPT MUST BE MADE TO INTRODUCE BACKLASH TO COUNTER STIFFNESS IN THE SYSTEM AS A WHOLE.

1. Jack up the front of the vehicle until the wheels are clear of the ground and support the chassis using axle stands.

   WARNING: Before jacking apply park brake, engage 'P' in automatic transmission, 'L' in transfer box (engage diff-lock if applicable) chock wheels.

2. Disconnect the drag link from the steering drop arm.
3. Set the steering box 'on-centre'. This is achieved by turning the steering wheel to the full 'inner' lock. (ie full left lock for a right hand drive vehicle or full right lock for a left hand drive vehicle). Then turn the steering wheel back towards the centre EXACTLY two full turns.

NOTE: If the steering wheel is not straight it can be refitted at this stage in accordance with the correct procedure.

4. Without moving its position, gently rock the drop arm to obtain the 'feel' of the lash present.

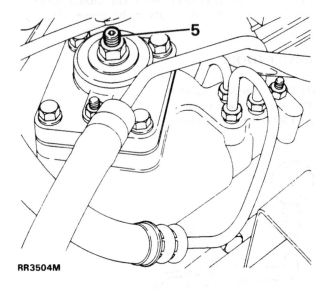

RR3504M

5. Continue the rocking action while an assistant slowly tightens the steering box adjuster screw after loosening the locknut. Continue tightening until the backlash has almost been eliminated.
6. Tighten the locknut. This action should remove the remaining backlash. If backlash is still present loosen the locknut and repeat step 5.
7. Rotate the steering wheel from lock to lock and check that no excessive tightness exists at any point.
8. Reconnect the drag link and tighten the nut to the correct torque and replace the split pin.
9. Lower the vehicle to ground level and remove the wheel chocks.
10. Check alignment of the front wheels using suitable equipment and adjust if necessary (See Front Wheel Alignment - page 31).
11. Road test the vehicle.
12. If the steering wheel is offset during straight-ahead running the drag link length must be adjusted to compensate (Note: the steering wheel was set correct relative to the steering box in step three.

POWER STEERING FLUID RESERVOIR

Remove and refit

Removing

1. Place a drain tray beneath the power steering box.
2. Prop open the hood.
3. Remove the reservoir filler cap.
4. Disconnect the return hose from the steering box. Drain the fluid completely from the reservoir, reconnect the hose.

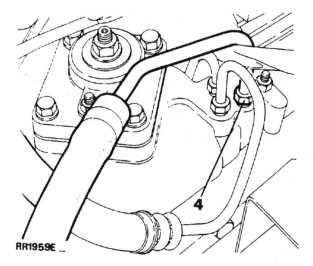

RR1959E

CAUTION: Power steering fluid is harmful to paintwork Should any fluid seep onto body, chassis, or any other components immediately wipe clean. It is most important that fluid drained from the power steering system is not re-used.

5. Refit the return hose to the steering box.
6. Release the pinch bolt and remove the reservoir from the bracket.
7. Release the hose clamps and remove the flexible hoses, withdraw the reservoir from the engine compartment.

NOTE: If the reservoir is not to be refitted immediately, the hoses must be sealed to prevent the ingress of foreign matter.

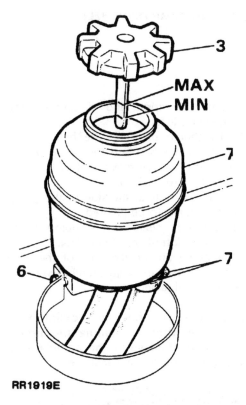

RR1919E

NOTE: The reservoir contains an integral filter which is not serviceable, however, in normal use the reservoir unit should last the life of the vehicle. Should the power steering system malfunction and under inspection it is found that the steering fluid has been contaminated by foreign matter a new FLUID RESERVOIR MUST be fitted.

Refitting

8. Reconnect the flexible hoses to the reservoir. Finally tighten the hose clamps to 3 Nm (2lbf ft).
9. Refit the reservoir to the bracket and tighten the pinch bolt securely.
10. Fill the reservoir to the prescribed level on the dipstick with one of the recommended fluids (Section 09) and bleed the power steering system. See Power Steering System-bleed.
11. Fit the reservoir filler cap.
12. Close the hood.

POWER STEERING PUMP DRIVE BELT

Adjust

Procedure

1. Prop open the hood and disconnect the battery negative lead.
2. Check, by thumb pressure, the belt tension between the crankshaft and the pump pulley. There should be a free movement of between 4 to 6mm (0.16 to 0.25 in).
3. Loosen the two nuts at the side of the pump to allow the pump to be pivoted.
4. Loosen the bolt securing the pump lower bracket to the slotted adjustment link.
5. Pivot the pump (in the direction of the bold arrow) as necessary and adjust until the correct belt tension is obtained.

CAUTION: **Do not use the pump casing as a point of leverage when tensioning the power steering drive belt. Damage to the pump casing may be caused leading to fluid leakage.**

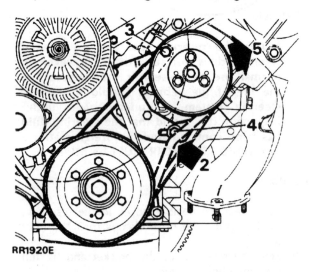

RR1920E

6. Maintaining the tension, tighten the pump adjusting bolt and the top pivot nuts.

NOTE: **Check the alternator drive belt tension after adjusting the power steering pump belt.**

7. Reconnect the battery negative lead and close the hood.

NOTE: **Check adjustment after running engine at fast idle speed for 3 to 5 minutes if a new belt has been fitted.**

POWER STEERING PUMP DRIVE BELT

Remove and refit

Removing or preparing for the fitting of a new belt.

1. Prop open the hood and disconnect the battery negative lead.
2. Loosen the idler pulley bolt and remove the fan belt.
3. Loosen the alternator mountings and remove the drive belt.
4. Loosen the power steering pump mountings.
5. Pivot the pump and remove the drive belt.

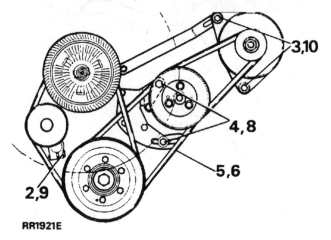

RR1921E

Refitting

6. Locate the driving belt over the crankshaft and pump pulleys.
7. Adjust the position of the pump to give a driving belt tension of 4 to 6mm (0.16 to 0.25 in) movement when checked by thumb pressure midway between the crankshaft and pump pulleys.

CAUTION: **Do not use the pump casing as a point of leverage when tensioning the power steering drive belt. Damage to the pump casing may be caused leading to fluid leakage.**

8. Maintaining the tension, tighten the pump adjusting bolt and the top pivot nut.
9. Refit the fan belt and adjust the tension to give 4 to 6mm (0.16 to 0.25 in) movement when checked by thumb pressure midway between the crankshaft and water pump pulleys.

10. Refit the alternator drive belt and adjust to give 4 to 6mm (0.16 to 0.25 in) movement when checked midway between the power steering pump and alternator pulleys.
11. Reconnect the battery negative lead and close the hood.

   NOTE: Check adjustment after running engine at fast idle speed for 3 to 5 minutes if a new belt has been fitted.

STEERING PUMP

NOTE: The power steering pump is not a serviceable item. In the event of failure or damage a new pump must be fitted.

Remove and refit

Removing

1. Disconnect the battery negative lead.
2. Loosen the alternator pivot bolts and adjustment link bolts, pivot the alternator inwards and remove the drive belt.
3. Loosen the water pump drive belt idler pulley and remove the drive belt.
4. Remove the left hand bank spark plug leads and detach the distributor cap, place the leads and cap to one side.
5. Disconnect the electrical plug from the distributor amplifier unit.
6. Loosen the two nuts securing the power steering pump pivot bracket.
7. Release the three bolts securing the pulley to the steering pump, do not remove them at this stage.
8. Release the bottom adjustment bolt below the steering pump and pivot the pump inwards towards the water pump to enable the drive belt to be removed.

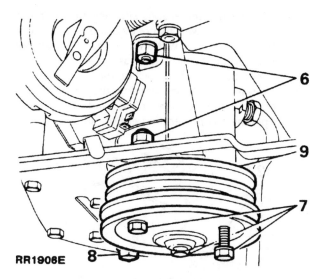

RR1906E

9. Remove the three bolts with plain washers retaining the pulley to the pump and withdraw the pulley.

   NOTE: Place a drain tray underneath the vehicle to catch any power steering fluid which will seep from the pump when the fluid pipe is disconnected.

   CAUTION: Power steering fluid is harmful to paintwork. Should any fluid seep onto the body, chassis, or any other components immediately wipe clean. It is most important that fluid drained from the power steering system is not re-used.

10. Disconnect the fluid pipe from the side of the pump, plug the pipe and pump openings to prevent ingress of dirt.

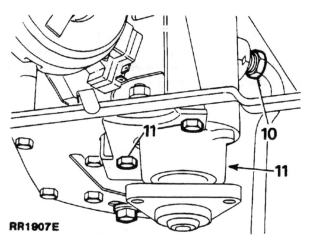

RR1907E

11. Remove the three bolts securing the pump to the pivot bracket, manoeuvre the pump out of the bracket and withdraw it from the engine compartment as far as the remaining connected fluid hose will permit.

12. Release the clamp securing the hose to the pump, remove the hose and plug both openings to prevent ingress of dirt.

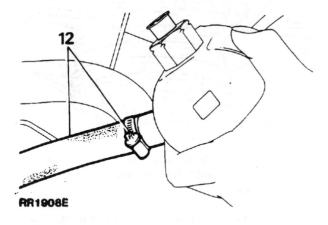

RR1908E

Refitting

13. Remove the plug from the feed hose and secure the hose to a NEW pump. Tighten the hose clamp to 3 Nm (2 lbf ft).

14. The pump into the pivot bracket and secure in position with the three retaining bolts. Tighten the bolts to the specified torque (35 Nm, 26 lbf ft).

15. Remove the plugs from the pressure pipe and steering pump openings. Fit the pipe, fingertight, hold the pipe in correct position and finally tighten the pipe to 20 Nm (15 lbf ft).

CAUTION: Care should be taken to ensure that the high pressure fluid pipe is well clear of both the drive belt and the top of the power steering box.

16. Fit the pulley to the steering pump drive flange, coat the three bolts with Loctite and fit to the steering pump, do not fully tighten the bolts at this stage.

17. Refit the crankshaft to steering pump drive belt, pivot the steering pump outwards to tension the belt, tighten the pivot bolts securely. Check that the belt deflects approximately 4 to 6 mm (0.16 to 0.25in) when checked by thumb pressure midway between the crankshaft and pump pulleys.

18. Tighten the three steering pump pulley retaining bolts to the specified torque (8-12 Nm, 6-9 lbf ft).

19. Reverse the remaining removal instructions.

20. Bleed the power steering system.

21. Test the power steering system for leaks with the engine running, holding the steering on full lock in both directions.

CAUTION: Do not maintain this pressure for more than 30 seconds in any one minute, to avoid causing the oil to overheat and possible damage to the seals.

22. Close the hood.
23. Road test the vehicle.

POWER STEERING

FAULT DIAGNOSIS

SYMPTOM	CAUSE	TEST ACTION	CURE
INSUFFICIENT POWER ASSISTANCE WHEN PARKING	(1) Lack of fluid	Check hydraulic fluid tank level	If low, fill and bleed the system
	(2) Driving belt	Check belt tension	Adjust the driving belt
	(3) Defective hydraulic pump	(a) Fit pressure gauge between high pressure hose and steering pump with steering held hard on full lock, see Note 1 and 'Power Steering System Test'	If pressure is outside limits (high or low) after checking items 1 and 2, see Note 2
		(b) Release steering wheel and allow engine to idle. See 'Power Steering System Test'	If pressure is greater, check box for freedom and self- centering action
POOR HANDLING WHEN VEHICLE IS IN MOTION	Lack of castor action (wheels will not return to centre)	This can be caused by stiffness or tightness in one or more of the components in the steering sytem as a whole i.e. column, swivel housing etc.	Each individual component must be tested in isolation to the others and reworked as necessary. Backlash MUST NOT be introduced into the steering box to counter stiffness in other components
HYDRAULIC FLUID LEAKS	Damaged pipework, loose connecting unions etc.	Check by visual inspection; leaks from the high pressure lines are best found while holding the steering on full lock with engine running at fast idle speed (See Note 1)	Tighten or renew as necessary
NOTE: Leaks from the steering box tend to show up under low pressure conditions, that is, engine idling and no pressure on steering wheel		Check 'O' rings on pipework	Renew as necessary

SYMPTOM	CAUSE	TEST ACTION	CURE
EXCESSIVE NOISE	(1) If the high pressure hose is allowed to come into contact with the body shell, or any component not insulated by the body mounting, noise will be transmitted to the car interior	Check the loose runs of the hoses	Alter hose route or insulate as necessary
	(2) Noise from hydraulic pump	Check oil level and bleed system	If no cure, change hydraulic pump

Note 1. Never hold the steering wheel on full lock for more than 30 seconds in any one minute, to avoid causing the oil to overheat and possible damage to the seals.

Note 2. High pressure-   In general it may be assumed that excessive pressure is due to a fault in the hydraulic pump.

Low pressure-   Insufficient pressure may be caused by one of the following:

1. Low fluid level in reservoir   } Most usual cause of
2. Pump belt slip   } insufficient pressure
3. Leaks in the power steering system
4. Hydraulic pump not delivering correct pressure
5. Fault in steering box valve and worm assembly
6. Leak at piston sealing in steering box
7. Worn components in either steering box or hydraulic pump

Steering pump

Make/type .... Hobourn series 200
Operating pressure - straight ahead position - at idle ...... 7 kgf/cm² (100 p.s.i.) maximum
Full lock (left or right) at idle .... 28 kgf/cm² (400 p.s.i.) minimum
Full lock (left or right) 1000 rev/min .... 70-77 kgf/cm² (1000-1100 p.s.i.)

LOWER STEERING SHAFT AND UNIVERSAL JOINTS

NOTE: A new lower steering shaft was introduced in Jan 1991, see page 32, Section 57 for details.

Remove and refit

CAUTION: PRIOR TO REMOVING ANY OF THE COMPONENTS INCORPORATED IN THE STEERING LINKAGE, IT IS IMPERATIVE THAT THE ROAD WHEELS ARE IN A STRAIGHT AHEAD POSITION AND THAT THE STEERING WHEEL IS THEN REMOVED TO PREVENT THE CRUISE CONTROL SPIRAL CASSETTE BEING WOUND UP OR DAMAGED IF THE STEERING LINKAGE IS INADVERTENTLY MOVED OR ROTATED.

AFTER REFITTING STEERING LINKAGE COMPONENTS, THE ROAD WHEELS MUST BE RE-POSITIONED STRAIGHT AHEAD BEFORE FITTING THE STEERING WHEEL, DO NOT RECONNECT THE MULTI-PLUG TO THE CASSETTE OR FIT THE TRIM PAD AT THIS STAGE. IF, AFTER THE VEHICLE HAS BEEN DRIVEN, IT IS FOUND THAT THE STEERING WHEEL REQUIRES RE-POSITIONING, REMOVE THE WHEEL. RE-ALIGN THE DRIVE PEGS ON THE CRUISE CONTROL CASSETTE BY SLIGHTLY ROTATING THE UPPER PART OF THE CASSETTE IN THE APPROPRIATE DIRECTION UNTIL THE PEGS LIE HORIZONTAL TO THE STEERING COLUMN.

FIT THE STEERING WHEEL ENSURING THAT THE DRIVE PEGS LOCATE IN THEIR RESPECTIVE HOLES ON THE REAR OF THE STEERING WHEEL.

AFTER FINAL ALIGNMENT RE-CONNECT THE MULTI-PLUG TO THE CASSETTE, TIGHTEN THE STEERING WHEEL SECURING NUT AND FIT THE TRIM PAD.

Removing
1. Ensure the road wheels are in the straight ahead position.

   NOTE: To gain access to the coupling shaft it is necessary to remove the air flow sensor and air filter canister.

2. Remove one pinch bolt from the top universal joint to the steering column.
3. Remove two pinch bolts from the lower universal joint.
4. Manoeuvre the shaft upper universal joint up the steering column splines to release the lower joint from the steering box splines. Withdraw the shaft from the steering column splines.
5. Withdraw the lower universal joint from the shaft.

NOTE: Do not dismantle the upper coupling joint. The steering shaft, rubber coupling and top universal joint is only available as an assembly.

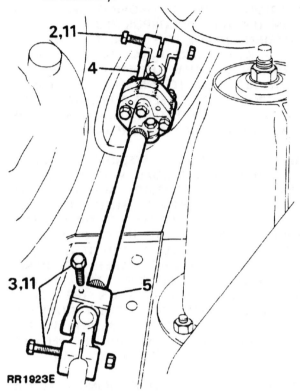

RR1923E

6. Inspect both universal joints for wear and excessive play, fit new joints if necessary.
7. Inspect the rubber coupling for condition - rubber deterioration, fit a new assembly if necessary.

Refitting

NOTE: When refitting the universal joints to their respective components ensure that the pinch bolt holes line up with their respective grooves.

8. Position the lower universal joint on the shaft.
9. Position the shaft assembly onto the steering column, manoeuvre the assembly up the steering column splines until it is possible to locate the lower universal joint onto the steering box splines.
10. Locate the bolt holes in the universal joints with their respective grooves in the steering column, shaft and steering box splines.
11. Fit the pinch bolts, and tighten to the correct torque (35 Nm, 26 lbf ft).

STEERING WHEEL

Remove and refit

CAUTION: PRIOR TO REMOVING ANY OF THE COMPONENTS INCORPORATED IN THE STEERING LINKAGE, IT IS IMPERATIVE THAT THE ROAD WHEELS ARE IN A STRAIGHT AHEAD POSITION AND THAT THE STEERING WHEEL IS THEN REMOVED TO PREVENT THE CRUISE CONTROL SPIRAL CASSETTE BEING WOUND UP OR DAMAGED IF THE STEERING LINKAGE IS INADVERTENTLY MOVED OR ROTATED.

AFTER REFITTING STEERING LINKAGE COMPONENTS, THE ROAD WHEELS MUST BE RE-POSITIONED STRAIGHT AHEAD BEFORE FITTING THE STEERING WHEEL, DO NOT RECONNECT THE MULTI-PLUG TO THE CASSETTE OR FIT THE TRIM PAD AT THIS STAGE. IF, AFTER THE VEHICLE HAS BEEN DRIVEN, IT IS FOUND THAT THE STEERING WHEEL REQUIRES RE-POSITIONING, REMOVE THE WHEEL. RE-ALIGN THE DRIVE PEGS ON THE CRUISE CONTROL CASSETTE BY SLIGHTLY ROTATING THE UPPER PART OF THE CASSETTE IN THE APPROPRIATE DIRECTION UNTIL THE PEGS LIE HORIZONTAL TO THE STEERING COLUMN.

FIT THE STEERING WHEEL ENSURING THAT THE DRIVE PEGS LOCATE IN THEIR RESPECTIVE HOLES ON THE REAR OF THE STEERING WHEEL.

AFTER FINAL ALIGNMENT RE-CONNECT THE MULTI-PLUG TO THE CASSETTE, TIGHTEN THE STEERING WHEEL SECURING NUT AND FIT THE TRIM PAD.

Removing

Service Tools:
18G 1014 Steering wheel remover
18G 1014-2 Adaptor pins

> NOTE: The steering column is of a 'safety' type and incorporates shear pins. Therefore do not impart shock loads to the steering column during removing and refitting the steering wheel or at any time.

1. Disconnect the battery negative lead.
2. Ensure the road wheels are in the straight ahead position to enable the steering wheel to be fitted in its correct location on re-assembly.
3. Carefully ease the centre trim pad off the steering wheel.

4. Disconnect the cruise control electrical multi-plug located in the small opening below the centre retaining nut.
5. While holding the steering wheel remove the retaining nut and serrated washer.
6. Extract the steering wheel using service tool 18G 1014. Ensure the extractor pins are inserted in the threads up to shoulder of the pins.

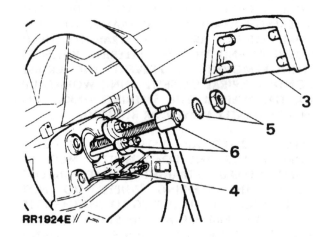

RR1924E

CAUTION: IT IS IMPERATIVE THAT THE UPPER PART OF THE CRUISE CONTROL CASSETTE IS NOT ROTATED AFTER THE STEERING WHEEL IS REMOVED. TO PREVENT ROTATION SECURE THE UPPER AND LOWER PART OF THE CASSETTE IN POSITION WITH ADHESIVE TAPE.

Refitting

7. Ensure the road wheels are in the straight ahead position.
8. Place the steering wheel on the column splines and remove the previously applied adhesive tape to the spiral cassette.
9. Ensure the two drive pegs on the upper part of the cassette align with their respective location holes on the underside of the steering wheel, ease the wheel onto the pegs.

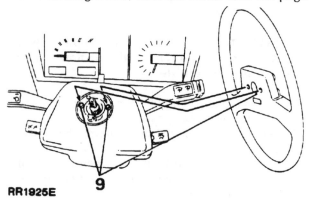

RR1925E

Continued

CAUTION: Do not apply shock loads to the steering wheel.

10. Fit the nut and washer and tighten to the specified torque (38 Nm, 28 lbf ft).
11. Reconnect the cruise control multi-plug and refit the steering wheel centre cover.
12. Reconnect the battery.

STEERING COLUMN

NOTE: The steering column assembly is not a serviceable component.

Remove and refit

Service tool:
18G1014 - Extractor for steering wheel.
18G1014 - 2 Adaptor pins.

CAUTION: The steering column is of a 'safety' type and incorporates shear pins. Therefore do not impart shock loads to the steering column at any time.

CAUTION: PRIOR TO REMOVING ANY OF THE COMPONENTS INCORPORATED IN THE STEERING LINKAGE, IT IS IMPERATIVE THAT THE ROAD WHEELS ARE IN A STRAIGHT AHEAD POSITION AND THAT THE STEERING WHEEL IS THEN REMOVED TO PREVENT THE CRUISE CONTROL SPIRAL CASSETTE BEING WOUND UP OR DAMAGED IF THE STEERING LINKAGE IS INADVERTENTLY MOVED OR ROTATED.

AFTER REFITTING STEERING LINKAGE COMPONENTS, THE ROAD WHEELS MUST BE RE-POSITIONED STRAIGHT AHEAD BEFORE FITTING THE STEERING WHEEL, DO NOT RECONNECT THE MULTI-PLUG TO THE CASSETTE OR FIT THE TRIM PAD AT THIS STAGE. IF, AFTER THE VEHICLE HAS BEEN DRIVEN, IT IS FOUND THAT THE STEERING WHEEL REQUIRES RE-POSITIONING, REMOVE THE WHEEL. RE-ALIGN THE DRIVE PEGS ON THE CRUISE CONTROL CASSETTE BY SLIGHTLY ROTATING THE UPPER PART OF THE CASSETTE IN THE APPROPRIATE DIRECTION UNTIL THE PEGS LIE HORIZONTAL TO THE STEERING COLUMN.

FIT THE STEERING WHEEL ENSURING THAT THE DRIVE PEGS LOCATE IN THEIR RESPECTIVE HOLES ON THE REAR OF THE STEERING WHEEL.

AFTER FINAL ALIGNMENT RE-CONNECT THE MULTI-PLUG TO THE CASSETTE, TIGHTEN THE STEERING WHEEL SECURING NUT AND FIT THE TRIM PAD.

Removing

1. Remove the steering wheel using extractor 18G1014 and adaptor pins.

   CAUTION: IT IS IMPERATIVE THAT THE UPPER PART OF THE CRUISE CONTROL CASSETTE IS NOT ROTATED AFTER THE STEERING WHEEL IS REMOVED. TO PREVENT ROTATION SECURE THE UPPER AND LOWER PART OF THE CASSETTE IN POSITION WITH ADHESIVE TAPE.

2. Remove the lower dash panel and unclip the lower trim pad from the driver's side.
3. Disconnect the electrical multi-plugs from the steering column switches and release the electrical wiring from the retaining clip located half way down the steering column.
4. Remove the steering column shroud fixings and manoeuvre the shroud off the column switches.
5. Remove the top pinch bolt, universal joint to steering column.
6. Remove the fixings, steering column to floor board.
7. Remove the fixings, steering column to dash bracket.
8. Withdraw the steering column assembly.

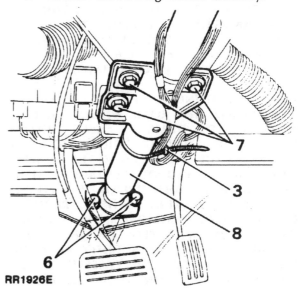

RR1926E

Refitting

9. Position the sealing gasket on the end of the column assembly.
10. Feed the steering shaft through the floor board and engage the drive splines at the coupling shaft.
11. Fit the column upper fixings, do not fully tighten at this stage.
12. Fit the column lower fixings, do not fully tighten at this stage.
13. Tighten the lower fixings to the specified torque (27 Nm, 20 lbf ft).
14. Fit universal joint pinch bolt, and tighten to the correct torque (35 Nm, 26 lbf ft).
15. Tighten the column upper fixings to the specified torque (27 Nm, 20 lbf ft).
16. Reverse 1 to 4.

STEERING COLUMN LOCK ASSEMBLY

Remove and refit

Service tool:
18G1014 - Extractor for steering wheel.
18G1014 - 2 Adaptor pins.

For ignition/starter switch-remove and refit as described in Electrical Section 86.

CAUTION: PRIOR TO REMOVING ANY OF THE COMPONENTS INCORPORATED IN THE STEERING LINKAGE, IT IS IMPERATIVE THAT THE ROAD WHEELS ARE IN A STRAIGHT AHEAD POSITION AND THAT THE STEERING WHEEL IS THEN REMOVED TO PREVENT THE CRUISE CONTROL SPIRAL CASSETTE BEING WOUND UP OR DAMAGED IF THE STEERING LINKAGE IS INADVERTENTLY MOVED OR ROTATED.

AFTER REFITTING STEERING LINKAGE COMPONENTS, THE ROAD WHEELS MUST BE RE-POSITIONED STRAIGHT AHEAD BEFORE FITTING THE STEERING WHEEL, DO NOT RECONNECT THE MULTI-PLUG TO THE CASSETTE OR FIT THE TRIM PAD AT THIS STAGE. IF, AFTER THE VEHICLE HAS BEEN DRIVEN, IT IS FOUND THAT THE STEERING WHEEL REQUIRES RE-POSITIONING, REMOVE THE WHEEL. RE-ALIGN THE DRIVE PEGS ON THE CRUISE CONTROL CASSETTE BY SLIGHTLY ROTATING THE UPPER PART OF THE CASSETTE IN THE APPROPRIATE DIRECTION UNTIL THE PEGS LIE HORIZONTAL TO THE STEERING COLUMN.

FIT THE STEERING WHEEL ENSURING THAT THE DRIVE PEGS LOCATE IN THEIR RESPECTIVE HOLES ON THE REAR OF THE STEERING WHEEL.

AFTER FINAL ALIGNMENT RE-CONNECT THE MULTI-PLUG TO THE CASSETTE, TIGHTEN THE STEERING WHEEL SECURING NUT AND FIT THE TRIM PAD.

Removing

1. Disconnect the battery negative lead.
2. Carefully detach the steering wheel centre cover and using service tool 18G1014 and adaptor pins remove the steering wheel.

   CAUTION: IT IS IMPERATIVE THAT THE UPPER PART OF THE CRUISE CONTROL CASSETTE IS NOT ROTATED AFTER THE STEERING WHEEL IS REMOVED. TO PREVENT ROTATION SECURE THE UPPER AND LOWER PART OF THE CASSETTE IN POSITION WITH ADHESIVE TAPE.

3. Release the fixings securing the shroud to the steering column and withdraw the shroud.
4. Release the column switches from the switch housing to gain access to the column lock fixings.
5. Using a sharp punch and a hammer, lightly tap the head of the shear pins in a counter-clockwise direction to release them from the column lock housing.

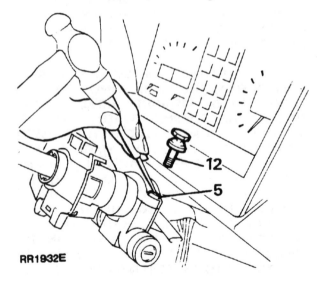

RR1932E

6. Remove the sheared bolts.
7. Detach the upper cap.
8. Withdraw the lower column lock assembly.

Continued

Refitting

9. Position the steering lock upper cap on the outer column, locating the spigot in the hole provided.
10. Place the lower lock assembly into the column.
11. Fit the shear bolts to retain the cap and lock.
12. Tighten the bolts sufficient to shear off the heads.
13. Reverse 1 to 4.

DROP ARM

Remove and refit

Service tools:
MS252A Drop arm extractor

Removing

1. Place the vehicle on a suitable hydraulic hoist, alternatively raise the front of the vehicle using a hydraulic floor jack and install axle stands under the front axle, remove the floor jack.
2. Disconnect the drag link from the drop arm ball joint, using a suitable extractor.

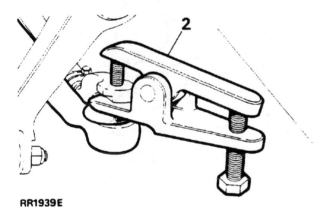

RR1939E

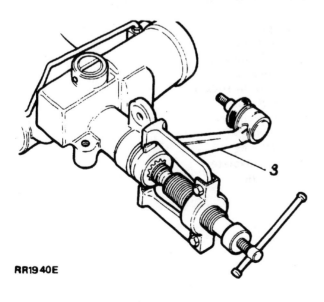

RR1940E

3. Remove the drop arm from the steering box rocker shaft, using extractor MS252A.

NOTE: The drop arm ball joint is integral with the drop arm.

Refitting

4. Set the steering box "on-centre". This is achieved by rotating the steering wheel to the full inner lock (ie full left lock for a right hand drive vehicle or full right lock for a left hand drive vehicle). Then turn the steering wheel back towards the centre exactly two full turns.
5. Fit the drop arm in position, aligning the master splines.
6. Fit the drop arm fixing and tighten to the correct torque (176 Nm, 130 lbf ft).
7. Fit the drag link and tighten to the correct torque (40 Nm, 30 lbf ft).

DROP ARM BALL JOINT

Overhaul

The drop arm ball joint can be overhauled with a repair kit available which consists of the the following items:

Ball pin	Ball lower socket
Retainer	Spring
Spring rings	'O' ring
Dust cover	Cover-plate
Ball top socket	Circlip

Dismantle

1. Remove the drop arm from the vehicle and clean the exterior.
2. Remove the spring rings and prise off the dust cover.
3. In the interests of safety, position the ball joint under a press to relieve the spring tension and support the housing both sides of the ball pin, as illustrated. Apply pressure to the cover plate and remove the circlip and slowly release the pressure.

WARNING: Personal injury could result if the circlip is removed without pressure being applied and maintained to the cover plate.

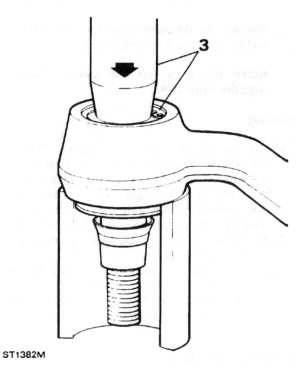

ST1382M

4. Remove the spring, top socket and 'O' ring.
5. Since the ball pin cannot be removed with the retainer in position, tap the threaded end of the ball pin to release the retainer and to remove the pin from the housing.

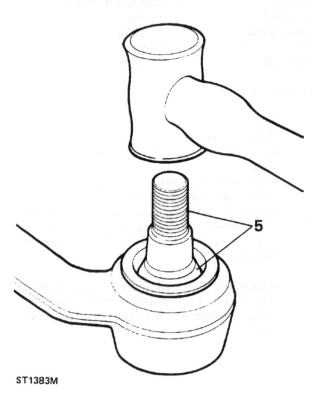

ST1383M

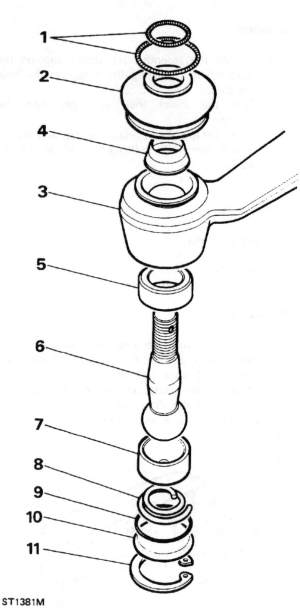

ST1381M

KEY TO BALL JOINT

1. Spring rings
2. Dust cover
3. Ball housing
4. Retainer
5. Bottom socket
6. Ball pin
7. Top socket
8. Spring
9. 'O' ring
10. Cover-plate
11. Circlip

6. Using a sharp-edged punch or chisel, drive the ball lower socket from the housing.
7. Clean the housing and remove any burrs.

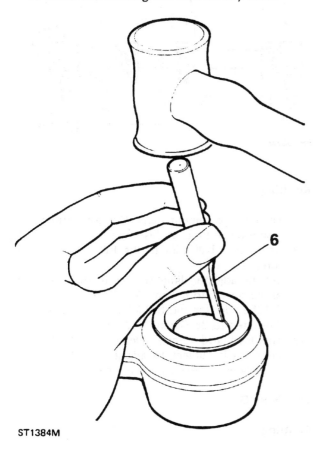

ST1384M

Assemble

8. Press in the lower socket squarely up to the shoulder.
9. Dip the ball in Duckhams LB10 grease, or equivalent and fit to the housing and pack with grease.
10. Fit the top socket.
11. Fit the spring, small diameter towards the ball.
12. Fit the 'O' ring and using the same method as for removing the circlip, compress the cover plate and secure with the circlip. Ensure that the circlip is fully seated in the machined groove

13. Press the retainer onto the ball pin so that the top edge is level with the edge of the taper.

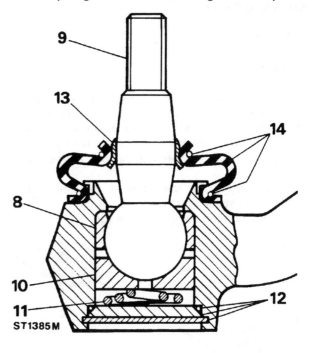

ST1385M

14. Fit the dust cover and retain with the two spring rings.
15. Fit the drop arm to the steering box using a new lock washer. Tighten the retaining nut to the correct torque (176 Nm, 130 lbf ft) and bend over the lock washer.
16. Assemble the ball pin to the drag link, see instructions for fitting drag link and track rod, tighten the castle nut to the correct torque (40 Nm, 30 lbf ft)and secure with a new cotter pin.

TRACK ROD AND LINKAGE

Remove and refit

TRACK ROD

Removing

1. Place the vehicle on a suitable hydraulic hoist, alternatively raise the front of the vehicle using a hydraulic floor jack and install axle stands under the front axle, remove the floor jack.
2. Disconnect the steering damper at the track rod.
3. Disconnect the track rod at the ball joints, using a suitable extractor.
4. Withdraw the complete track rod.

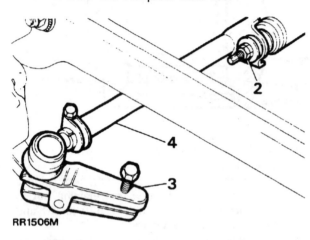

RR1506M

LINKAGE

Removing

5. Loosen the clamp bolts.
6. Unscrew the ball joints.
7. Unscrew the track rod adjuster, left hand thread.

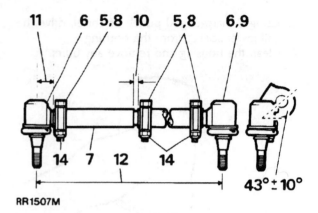

RR1507M

Refitting

8. Fit the replacement parts. Do not tighten the clamp pinch bolts at this stage.
9. Screw in a ball joint to the full extent of the threads.
10. Set the adjuster dimensionally to the track rod as illustrated, to 8.9mm (0.350 in).
11. Set the adjuster end ball joint dimensionally, as illustrated to 28.57mm (1.125 in).
12. The track rod effective length of 1230.0mm (48.4 in) is subject to adjustment during the subsequent wheel alignment check.

TRACK ROD

Refitting

13. Fit the track rod and tighten the ball joint nuts to the correct torque (40 Nm, 30 lbf ft).
14. Check the front wheel alignment.
15. Reverse 1 and 2.

CAUTION: A new track rod must be fitted if the existing track rod is damaged or bent. No attempt should be made to repair or straighten it.

STEERING DAMPER

Remove and refit

Removing

1. Place the vehicle on a suitable hydraulic hoist, alternatively raise the front of the vehicle using a hydraulic floor jack and place axle stands under the front axle, remove the floor jack.
2. Remove the fixings at the differential case bracket.
3. Remove the fixings at the track rod bracket.
4. Withdraw the steering damper.

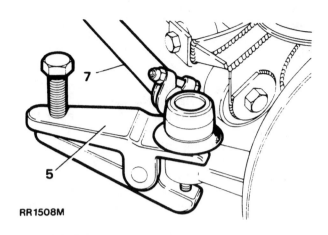

RR1508M

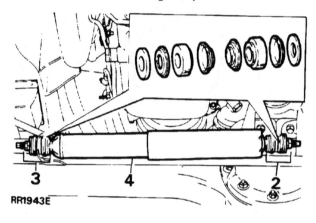

RR1943E

Refitting

5. Reverse 1 to 4.

DRAG LINK AND DRAG LINK ENDS

Remove and refit

Service tool 18G 1063 - Extractor for ball joint

Removing

1. Check alignment of front wheels.
2. Ensure wheels are in the straight-ahead position, and remain so during the following procedure.
3. Place the vehicle on a suitable hydraulic hoist, alternatively raise the front of the vehicle using a hydraulic floor jack and place axle stands under the front axle-remove the floor jack.
4. Remove the right hand front road wheel.
5. Disconnect the drag link ball joint at the swivel housing arm, using a suitable extractor.
6. Disconnect the drag link end at the drop arm ball joint, using a suitable extractor.
7. Withdraw the drag link.

DRAG LINK ENDS

Removing

8. Loosen the clamp bolts.
9. Unscrew the ball joint.
10. Unscrew the offset end.

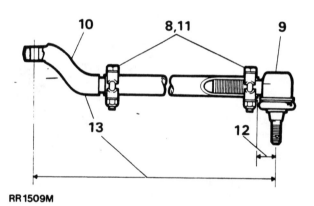

RR1509M

Refitting

11. Fit the replacement ends. Do not tighten the clamp bolts at this stage.
12. Set the ball joint dimensionally to the drag link, as illustrated, to 28.57mm (1.125 in).
13. Adjust the offset end to obtain the nominal overall length of 919.0mm (36.2 in). The final length is adjusted during refitting.
14. Set the steering box "on-centre". This is achieved by rotating the steering wheel to the full inner lock (i.e. full left lock for right hand drive vehicle or full right lock for a left hand drive vehicle). Then turn the steering wheel back **exactly** two full turns. The box is now centralised.
15. Remove the steering wheel, if necessary, and refit in the straight ahead position (see Steering Wheel, Remove and Refit - page 22).

DRAG LINK

Refitting

16. Fit the drag link. Tighten the ball-joint nuts to the correct torque (40 Nm, 30 lbf ft).
17. Check, and if necessary, set the steering lock stops.
18. Turn the steering and ensure that full travel is obtained between the lock stops. Adjust the drag link length to suit.
19. Using a mallet, tap the ball joints in the direction indicated so that both pins are in the same angular plane.
20. Tighten the clamp bolts to the correct torque (14 Nm, 10 lbf ft).

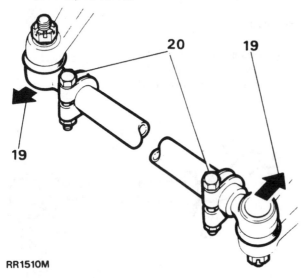

RR1510M

21. Reverse 3 and 4.
22. Road test the vehicle. If, when driving in the straight ahead position, it is found that the steering wheel is offset by 0° to ±5° in either direction, the drag link length can be adjusted to compensate for this deviation. NO attempt, must be made to correct for steering wheel deviations greater than ±5°. In this case the steering wheel should be removed and refitted when the road wheels are in the straight ahead position (see Steering Wheel, Remove and Refit - page22).

CAUTION: A new drag link must be fitted if the existing drag link is damaged or bent. No attempt should be made to repair or straighten it.

STEERING LOCK STOPS

Check and adjust

Checking

1. Measure the clearance between tyre wall and radius arm at full lock. This must be 20 mm (0.787 in).

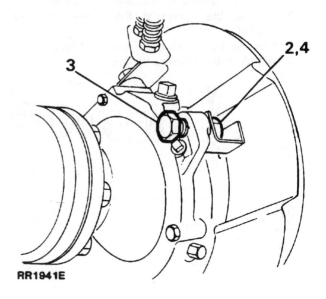

RR1941E

Adjusting

2. Loosen the stop bolt locknut.
3. Turn the stop bolt in or out as required.
4. Tighten the locknut.
5. Check the clearance between tyre wall and radius arm on each lock.

FRONT WHEEL ALIGNMENT

Check and adjust

Checking

Toe-out dimensions

NOTE: No Adjustment is provided for castor, camber or swivel pin inclinations.

1. Set the vehicle on level ground with the road wheels in the straight-ahead position.
2. Push the vehicle back then forwards for a short distance to settle the linkage.
3. Measure the toe-out at the horizontal centre-line of the wheels.
4. Check the tightness of the clamp bolt fixings for the correct torque (14 Nm, 10 lbf ft).

Adjusting

6. Loosen the adjuster sleeve clamp.
7. Rotate the adjuster to lengthen or shorten the track rod.
8. Check the toe-out setting as in instructions 1 to 4. When the toe-out is correct lightly tap the steering linkage ball joint, in the directions illustrated, to the maximum of their travel to ensure full unrestricted working travel.
9. Finally, tighten the clamp bolts to correct torque (14 Nm, 10 lbf ft).

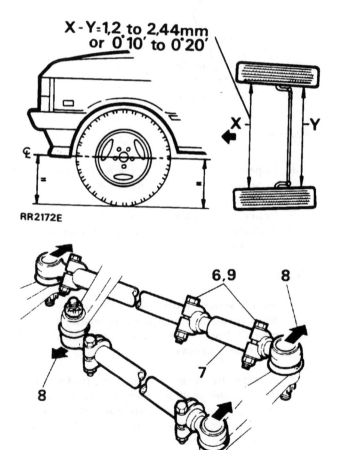

X - Y = 1,2 to 2,44mm
or 0°10' to 0°20'

RR2172E

RR1512M

LOWER STEERING SHAFT AND UNIVERSAL JOINTS

JAN 1991 introduction

Remove and refit

CAUTION: PRIOR TO REMOVING ANY OF THE COMPONENTS INCORPORATED IN THE STEERING LINKAGE, IT IS IMPERATIVE THAT THE ROAD WHEELS ARE IN A STRAIGHT AHEAD POSITION AND THAT THE STEERING WHEEL IS THEN REMOVED TO PREVENT THE CRUISE CONTROL SPIRAL CASSETTE BEING WOUND UP OR DAMAGED IF THE STEERING LINKAGE IS INADVERTENTLY MOVED OR ROTATED.

AFTER REFITTING STEERING LINKAGE COMPONENTS, THE ROAD WHEELS MUST BE RE-POSITIONED STRAIGHT AHEAD BEFORE FITTING THE STEERING WHEEL, DO NOT RECONNECT THE MULTI-PLUG TO THE CASSETTE OR FIT THE TRIM PAD AT THIS STAGE. IF, AFTER THE VEHICLE HAS BEEN DRIVEN, IT IS FOUND THAT THE STEERING WHEEL REQUIRES RE-POSITIONING, REMOVE THE WHEEL. RE-ALIGN THE DRIVE PEGS ON THE CRUISE CONTROL CASSETTE BY SLIGHTLY ROTATING THE UPPER PART OF THE CASSETTE IN THE APPROPRIATE DIRECTION UNTIL THE PEGS LIE HORIZONTAL TO THE STEERING COLUMN.

FIT THE STEERING WHEEL ENSURING THAT THE DRIVE PEGS LOCATE IN THEIR RESPECTIVE HOLES ON THE REAR OF THE STEERING WHEEL.

AFTER FINAL ALIGNMENT RE-CONNECT THE MULTI-PLUG TO THE CASSETTE, TIGHTEN THE STEERING WHEEL SECURING NUT AND FIT THE TRIM PAD.

Removing

1. Ensure the road wheels are in the straight ahead position.

   NOTE: To gain access to the lower steering shaft it is necessary to remove the air flow sensor and air filter canister.

2. Remove two pinch bolts from the upper universal joint to the steering column.
3. Remove one pinch bolt from the lower universal joint.
4. Manoeuvre the whole shaft assembly up the steering column splines to release the lower joint from the steering box splines. Withdraw the shaft from the steering column splines.
5. Withdraw the upper universal joint from the shaft.

NOTE: Do not dismantle the lower coupling joint. The lower steering shaft, is only available as an assembly.

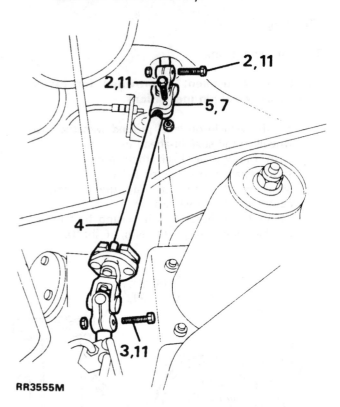

RR3555M

6. Inspect both universal joints for wear and excessive play, fit new components if necessary.
7. Inspect the rubber coupling for condition - rubber deterioration, fit a new rubber steering shaft if necessary.

Refitting

NOTE: When refitting the universal joints to their respective components ensure that the pinch bolt holes line up with their respective grooves.

8. Position the lower universal joint on the shaft.
9. Position the shaft assembly toward the end of the steering column, manoeuvre the assembly up the steering column splines until it is possible to locate the lower universal joint onto the steering box splines.
10. Locate the bolt holes in the universal joints with their respective grooves in the steering column, shaft and steering box splines.
11. Fit the pinch bolts, and tighten to the correct torque (35 Nm, 26 lbf ft).

Typeset and Printed by Land Rover Printing Services, (02/91)

RANGE ROVER
LT77S GEARBOX

WORKSHOP MANUAL SUPPLEMENT

Publication Number LSM 180 EN WS 9

Published by the
Technical Publications Department of

© Copyright Land Rover 1991

37 - MANUAL GEARBOX

CONTENTS

CONTENTS

GEAR CHANGE HOUSINGS

1. Separate main gearbox from transfer box, remove bell housing, drain oil, and clean exterior.
2. Remove gear change housing cover.

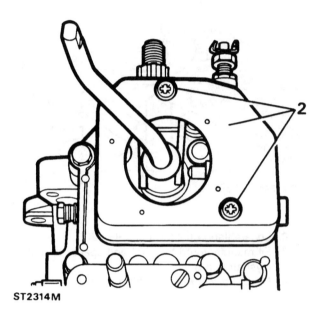

ST2314M

3. Remove transfer gear change housing.
4. Remove main gear change housing.

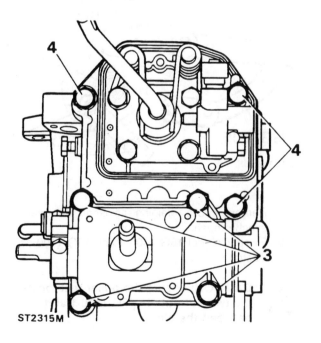

ST2315M

Extension housing

1. Remove snap ring retaining oil seal collar.

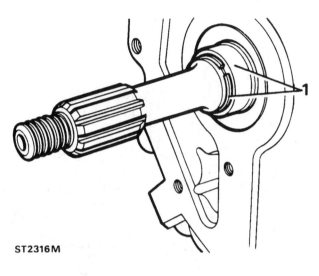

ST2316M

2. Using service tools 18G 705 and 18G 705-1A withdraw oil seal collar.

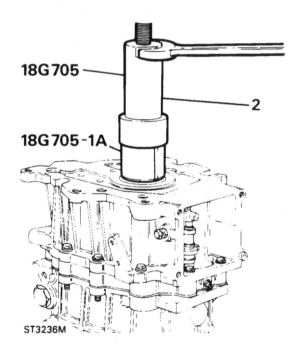

ST3236M

3. Remove fifth gear extention housing.
4. Secure centre plate to gearcase with two 8 x 35mm bolts.
5. Remove selector yoke from selector shaft.

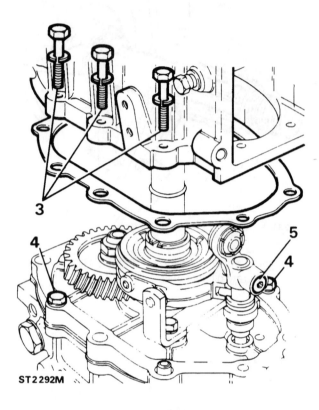

ST2292M

Mainshaft and layshaft fifth gears.

1. Remove mainshaft "O" ring.
2. Remove oil pump drive shaft.
3. Remove "E" clips from selector fork.
4. Remove fifth gear selector spool.
5. Remove selector fork bracket.

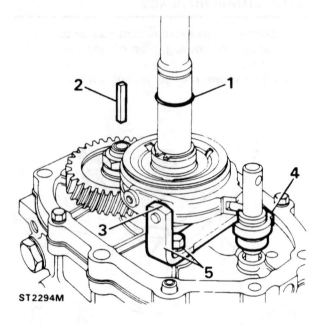

ST2294M

6. Locate flange holder tool 18G 1205.
7. Fit manufactured tool "A" and spacer to restrain layshaft fifth gear.
8. De-stake and remove fifth gear nut.

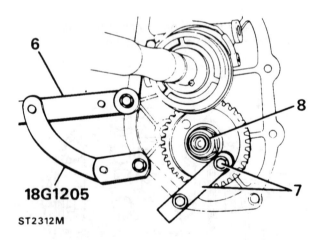

18G1205

ST2312M

9. Remove circlip retaining mainshaft fifth gear synchromesh.
10. Fit special tool 18G 1400-1 and 18G 1400 as illustrated.

 CAUTION: ensure the puller feet locate in the two cut-outs in 18G 1400-1 and between the pins.

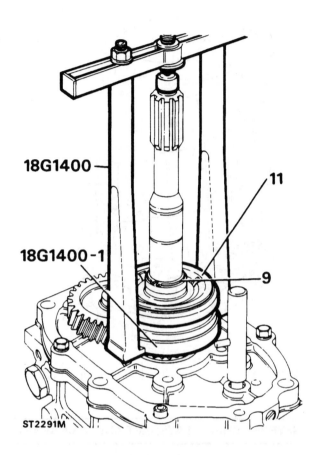

18G1400

18G1400-1

11

9

ST2291M

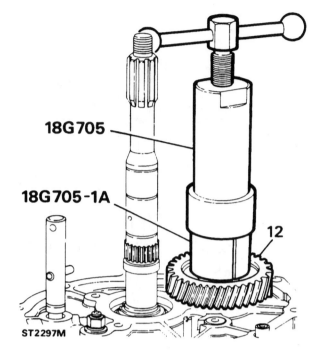

18G705

18G705-1A

12

ST2297M

Main gear case.

1. Secure reverse shaft retainer, manufactured tool "A", to centre plate.
2. Fit studs, manufactured tool "B" to gear case.

11. Remove fifth gear synchromesh.

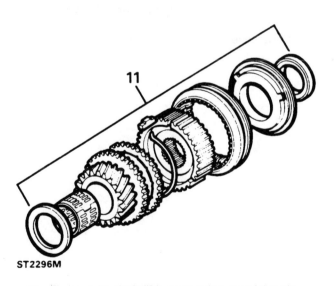

11

ST2296M

12. Remove layshaft fifth gear using special tools 18G 705 and 18G 705-1A.

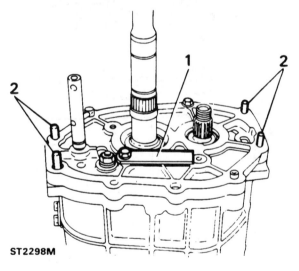

2

1

2

2

ST2298M

3. Invert gear case and locate studs in workstand holes.
4. Remove selector shaft spool retainer.

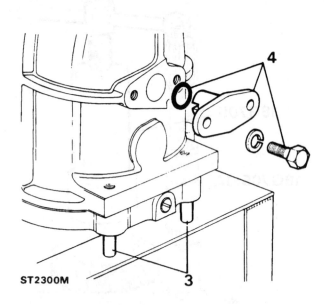

ST2300M   3

5. Remove front cover and gasket.
6. Retrieve selective washers.

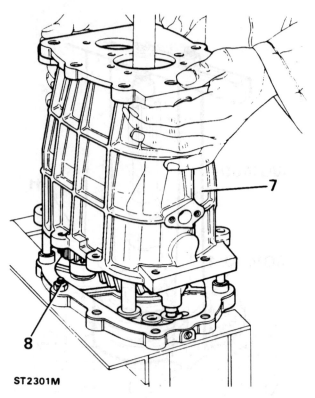

ST2301M

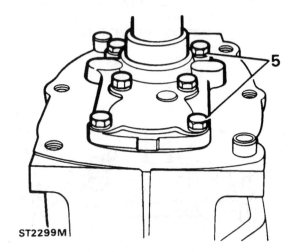

ST2299M

7. Remove bolts and lift-off gear case.
8. Secure centre plate with nut and bolt.

REVERSE SHAFT, LAYSHAFT AND MAINSHAFT

1. Remove retainer (tool "A") and reverse shaft.
2. Remove thrust washer, reverse gear and spacer.
3. Remove reverse lever pin with "E" clip attached.
4. Remove lever and slipper pad.

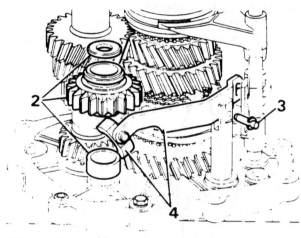

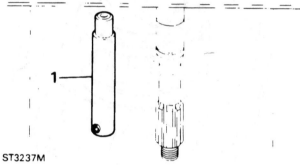

ST3237M

5. Remove input shaft and fourth gear baulk ring.
6. Remove layshaft by tilting, as illustrated and lifting mainshaft.

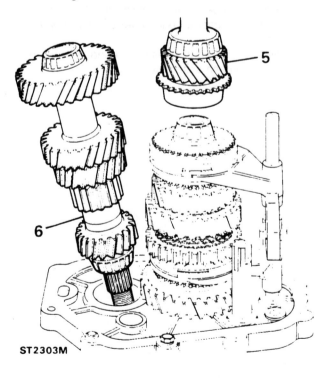

ST2303M

7. Unscrew plug and remove spring and outboard detent ball.
8. Align fifth gear selector pin with centre plate slot.
9. Remove mainshaft, gears, selectors and forks.
10. Remove selector fork assembly from gears.

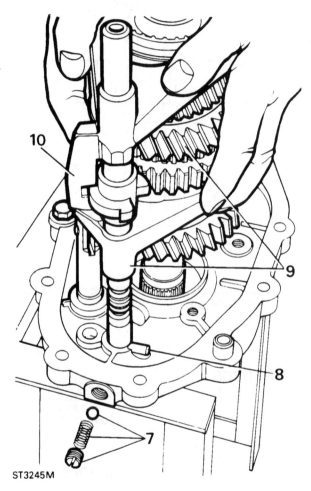

ST3245M

11. Collect inboard detent ball and spring from centre plate.

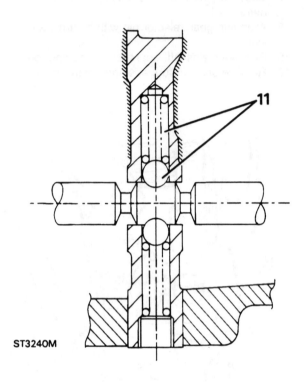

ST3240M

12. Using extractor tool 18G 705 and collets 18G 705-7, withdraw layshaft bearings.

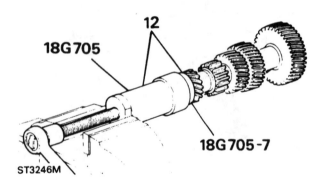

18G 705

12

18G 705-7

ST3246M

DISMANTLE MAINSHAFT

1. Remove circlip retaining first gear assembly.

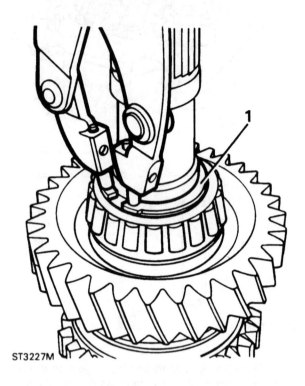

ST3227M

2. Remove taper bearing, bush, needle bearing, first gear spacer, cone, inner and outer baulk rings.
3. Remove circlip to release first and second gear synchromesh assembly.

4. With MS 47 press first gear assembly from mainshaft.
5. Remove first and second synchromesh baulk rings.
6. Using MS 47 and support bars under 2nd gear, press off pilot bearing, third, fourth synchromesh second and third gear assembly.

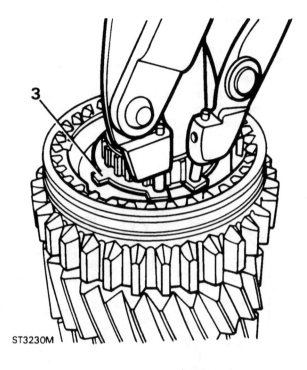

ST3230M

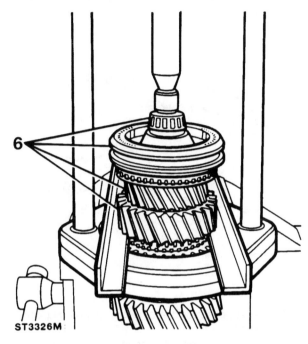

ST3326M

7. Remove washer, third, fourth synchromesh, third gear baulk ring, split needle rollers, bush, needle bearing and second gear.
8. Remove snap ring, spacer, second gear cone and circlip.

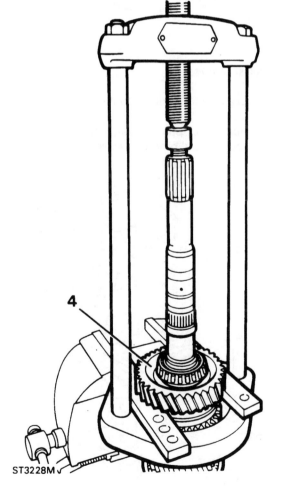

ST3228M

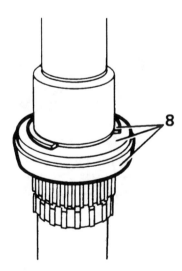

ST3234M

GEARBOX CASINGS AND OIL PUMP

Degrease and clean all components and discard gaskets and seals.

Gearbox casing

1. Remove mainshaft and layshaft bearing tracks.
2. Remove plastic scoop from inside the casing.

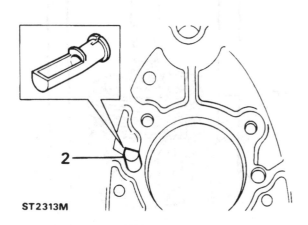

ST2313M

3. Inspect case for damage, cracks and stripped threads.
4. Fit a new scoop with scoop side towards top of casing.

Front cover

1. Remove oil seal from cover. Do not fit a new seal at this stage

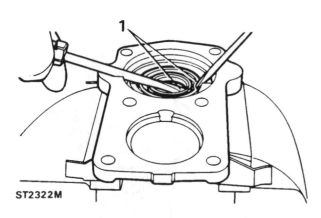

ST2322M

Centre plate

1. Remove bearing tracks.
2. Inspect for damage and selector rail bore for wear.
3. Temporally fit reverse shaft gear and lever and check clearance between slipper and lever does not exceed 0,20 mm (0.008 in).

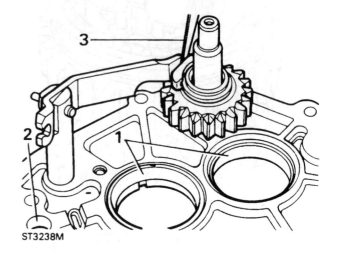

ST3238M

Extension case

1. Examine for damage to threads and machined faces.
2. Remove oil pump cover, inspect gears and housing and renew if required.

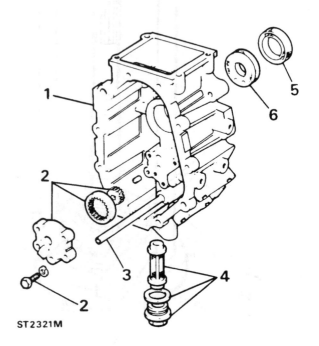

ST2321M

3. Check oil pick up pipe for obstruction but do not remove.
4. Remove drain plug assembly. Clean and renew filter and washers if necessary.
5. Renew oil seal.
6. Renew Ferrobestos bush.

 WARNING: This bush contains abestos. Do not attempt to clean it. see INTRODUCTION, Information, Poisonous substances.

7. Fit new bush with drain holes towards bottom of casing.

⚠ **CAUTION: If drain holes are not positioned correctly oil may build up behind oil seal and cause a leak.**

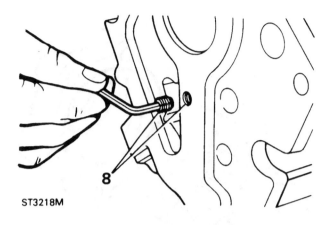

ST3218M

9. Fit oil seal to housing, lip side leading, using 18G 1422. Apply SAE 40 oil to lip.

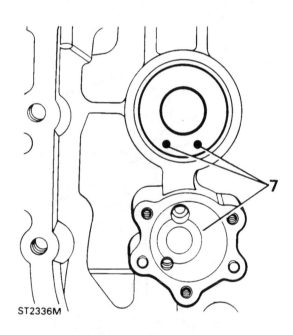

ST2336M

8. If extension housing is being renewed transfer grub screw to new housing. Apply Loctite to threads.

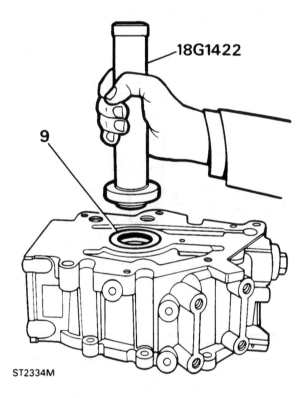

18G1422

ST2334M

10. Assemble gears to oil pump and fit cover.

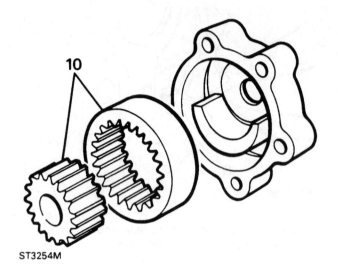

ST3254M

11. Examine gate plate and renew if worn or damaged.

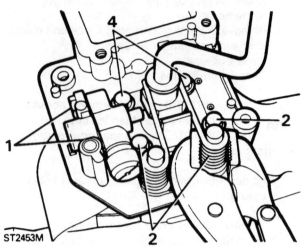

ST2453M

5. Check for wear in cross pin slots in housing and wear in lower gear lever.

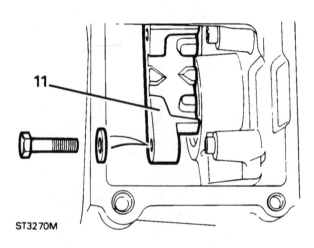

ST3270M

GEAR CHANGE HOUSING

1. Remove reverse plunger and retain shims.
2. Remove bolts retaining bias springs.

 WARNING: To avoid personal injury, restrain each spring in turn with a pair of grips while the bolts are being removed.

3. Remove the two springs.
4. Remove remaining bolts to release lower gear lever assembly.

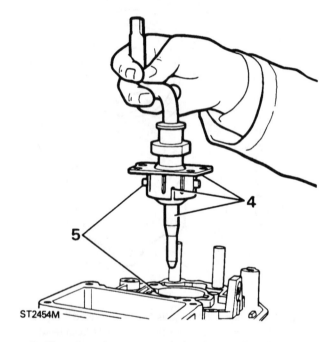

ST2454M

6. Turn housing over and check security of spool guide bolts.
7. Remove oil seal and fit a replacement, lip side leading.

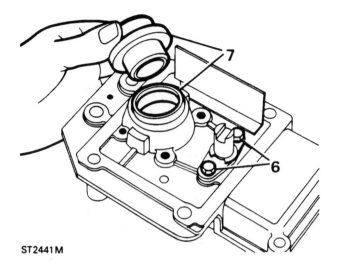

ST2441M

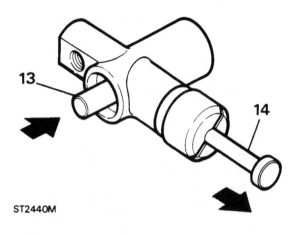

ST2440M

8. Examine bias springs and renew if weak or distorted.
9. Grease lower gear lever ball with Shell Alvina R3 and fit new Railko bush.
10. Fit gear lever to housing.
11. Fit adjustment plate.

 NOTE: Apply Hylomar PL 32 or Loctite 290 to threads of two short bolts and fit them forward of the gear lever. Tighten bolts to prevent plate moving while springs are being fitted.

12. Fit bias springs locating long end against gear lever.

NOTE: Apply above sealant to threads of spring retaining bolts. Use grips to compress springs to enable bolts to be fitted.

13. Examine and test reverse gear plunger.

NOTE: Apply a load of 45 to 55 kg (100 to 120 lb) to plunger nose. If it functions within these limits it is satisfactory. The plunger is only available as a complete assembly.

14. Check that the reverse switch plunger operates when reverse plunger is depressed.

SYNCHROMESH ASSEMBLIES

Third-fourth and fifth gear synchromesh.

NOTE: the above assemblies are the same except that fifth gear synchromesh has a retainer plate.

1. Mark relationship of inner and outer members.
2. Remove wire clip from both sides of assembly.

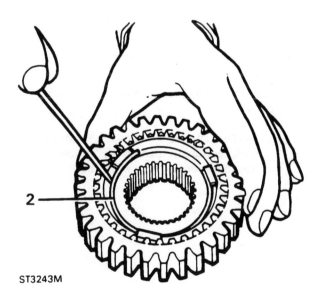

ST3243M

3. Remove slippers and separate the two members.
4. Examine all parts for damage and wear including wire clips for tension.
5. Check no radial movement exists between inner members and mainshaft splines. (except fifth gear synchromesh).
6. Examine inner and outer splines for wear.

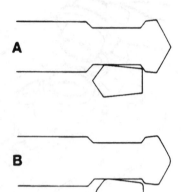

ST2449M

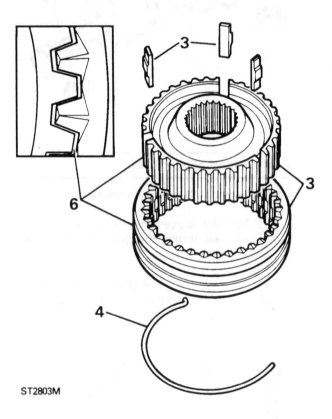

ST2803M

7. Examine the dog teeth on all gears for wear and damage.

 NOTE: example"A" shows a tooth in good condition. Example"B" shows the rounded corners of a worn tooth.

First-second synchromesh

8. Repeat instructions 1 to 6 for third-fourth synchromesh.
9. Examine step in each of outer splines.
10. Check that the step on both sides of the internal splines are sharp not rounded.

 NOTE: this applies only to splines on selector groove side of member.

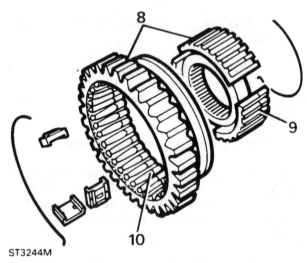

ST3244M

11. Fit inner member to outer so that the wide splines of inner member are under the spur gear teeth.

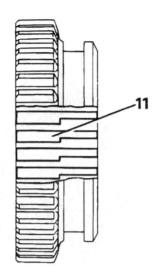

ST3247M

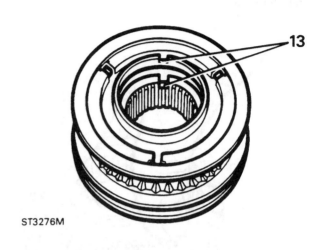

ST3276M

12. Fit the slippers and secure with a spring each side of the synchromesh.

⚠ **NOTE: The hooked end of each spring must locate in the same slipper with the free ends running in opposite directions and resting against the remaining slippers.**

CHECKING BAULK RING CLEARANCES

Check clearance of all baulk rings and gears by pressing the baulk ring against the gear and measuring the gap. The minimum clearance should be 0,38mm (0.015in).

First gear

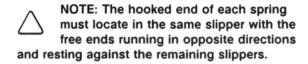

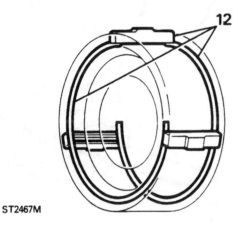

ST2467M

13. Assemble third-fourth and fifth gear synchromesh components as in instruction 12.

⚠ **NOTE: The back plate for fifth gear is fitted to the rear of the assembly with the single tag locating in a slot in the inner member.**

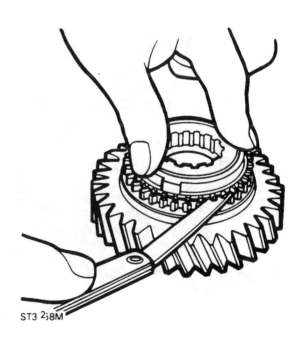

ST3 258M

second gear

fourth gear

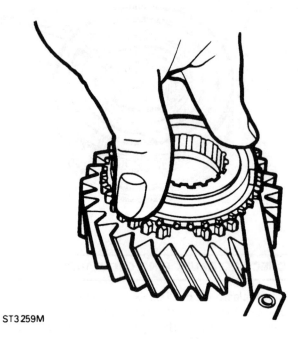

ST3259M

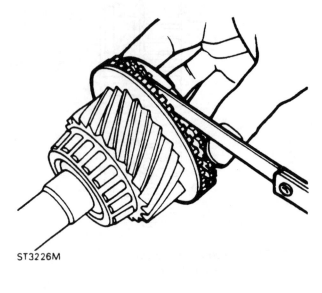

ST3226M

Fifth gear

Third gear

ST3260M

ST3261M

INPUT SHAFT

1. Examine the gear and dog teeth for wear and damage.
2. Polish oil seal track if necessary.
3. Using 18G 284 AAH and 18G 284 remove pilot bearing track.

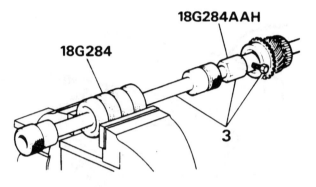

ST3278M

4. Using 18G 47BA and MS 47 remove taper bearing.

⚠ **NOTE: ensure that the bearing is supported by the lip inside 18G 47 BA.**

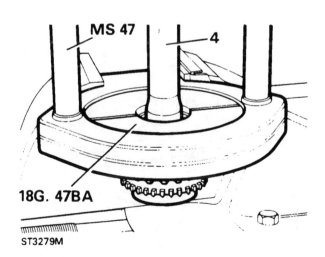

ST3279M

5. Support the shaft under MS 47 and press in a new track.
6. Using Press MS 47, Collets 18G 47B and adaptor 18G 47 BAX fit a new taper bearing.

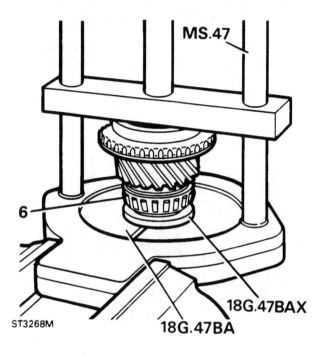

ST3268M

MAINSHAFT

1. Examine bearing journals for wear and scores.
2. Check condition of circlip grooves.
3. Examine splines for wear and damage.
4. Use an air line to check that the main oil feed from the pump is clear and feed to spigot bearing.
5. Check oil feed holes to roller bearings are clear.

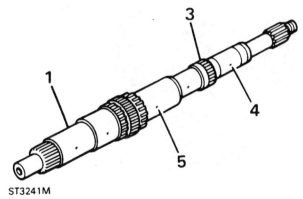

ST3241M

MAINSHAFT GEAR END FLOAT CHECKS

1. Hold mainshaft in vice front end downwards.
2. Fit front circlip for first-second synchromesh.
3. Fit second gear cone.
4. Fit spacer.
5. Fit snap ring.

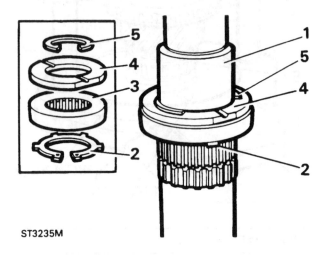

ST3235M

Second gear end-float.

1. Fit needle roller and second gear.
2. Fit third gear bush.

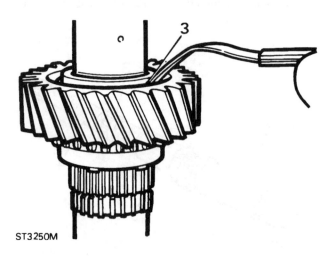

ST3250M

3. Check clearance between second gear and bush flange. Not to exceed 0,20 (0.008in).
4. Remove above components.

Third gear end-float.

1. Fit needle roller to third gear.
2. fit third gear bush to third gear.
3. Place gear on flat surface, bush flange downwards, and with a straight edge across gear check clearance between straight edge and gear. Not to exceed 0,20 (0.008in).

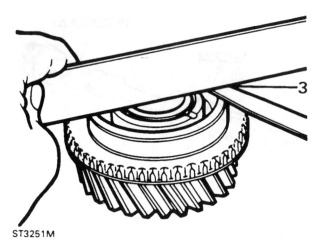

ST3251M

First gear bush end-float.

1. Invert mainshaft rear end uppermost.
2. Fit inner and outer second gear baulk rings.

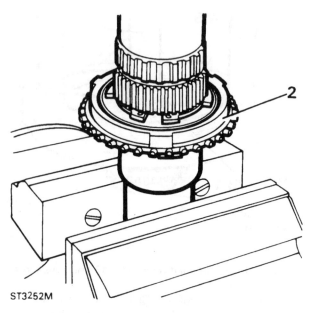

ST3252M

3. Fit first-second synchromesh hub, fork groove uppermost.
4. Fit circlip.

5. Fit first gear inner and outer baulk ring.
6. Fit cone.
7. Fit spacer.
8. Fit first gear bush.
9. Fit dummy bearing.
10. Fit circlip.
11. Check clearance between dummy bearing and bush. Not to exceed 0,75mm (0.003in).
12. Remove circlip, dummy bearing and bush.

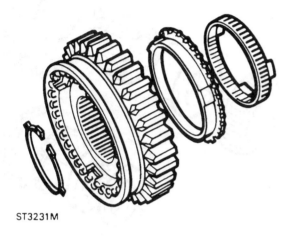

ST3231M

First-second synchromesh assembly

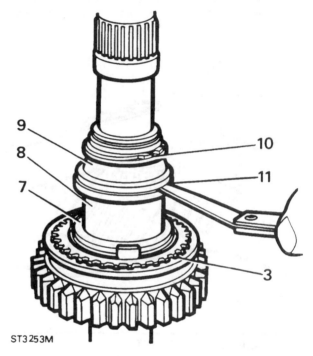

ST3253M

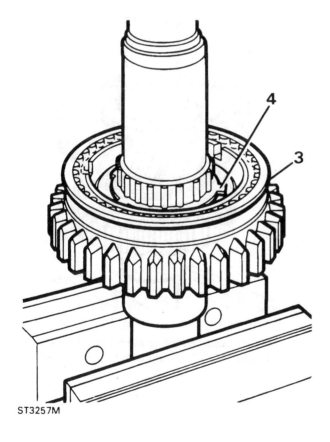

ST3257M

Selective first gear bush

Part number	Thickness
FTC2005	30,905/30,955
FTC2006	30,955/31,005
FTC2007	31,005/31,055
FTC2008	31,055/31,105
FTC2009	31,105/31,155

Check first gear to bush end-float.

1. Fit roller bearing and bush to first gear.
2. Place bush flange side downwards on a raised block on a flat surface.

⚠️ **NOTE: the block should be approximately the same diameter as the bush flange so that the gear is suspended and does not rest on the flat surface.**

3. Place straight edge across gear and check clearance between gear and straight edge. Not to exceed 0,20mm (0.008in).

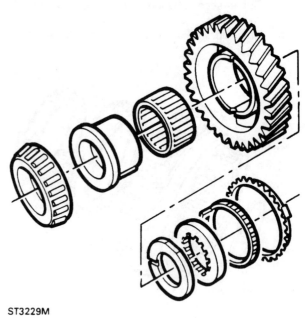

ST3229M

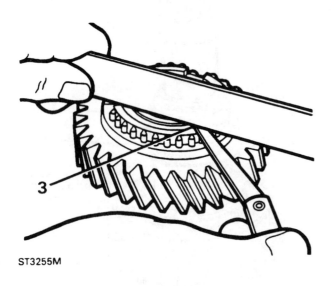

ST3255M

ASSEMBLING MAINSHAFT

1. With the first-second synchromesh hub and spacer in position, assemble the rear end of the shaft.
2. Fit the roller bearing and bush to first gear.
3. Fit first gear to mainshaft.

First gear assembly

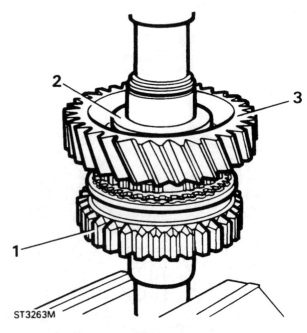

ST3263M

4. Fit the taper bearing to mainshaft using MS 47, collets 18G 47 BA and adaptor 18G 47 BAX.

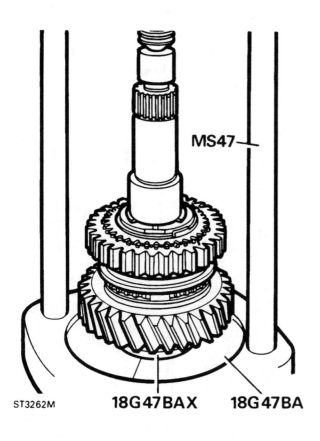

ST3262M   **18G47BAX**   **18G47BA**

⚠ **CAUTION: Ensure that the slots in the baulk ring align with the synchromesh slippers while pressing on the bearing.**

5. Invert mainshaft and press assembly back against circlip.

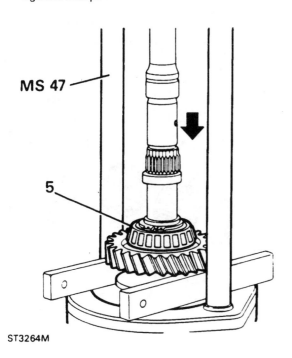

MS 47

5

ST3264M

⚠ **NOTE: Instruction 5 is necessary since it is probable that when pressing on the bearing it will have clamped the first gear bush preventing it from turning.**

6. Reposition mainshaft in vice and using a screw driver blade check that the first gear bush is free to turn.

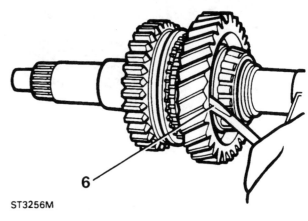

6

ST3256M

7. Position mainshaft in vice, rear end downwards and fit second gear needle roller, and second gear.
8. Fit third gear bush.
9. Fit third gear needle rollers.
10. Fit third gear.
11. Fit third gear baulk ring.

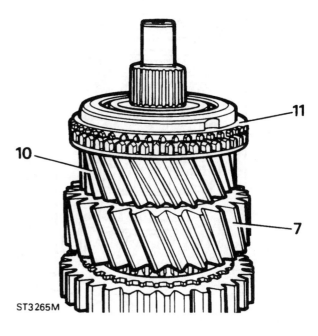

11

10

7

ST3265M

ST3233M

Third-fourth synchomesh assembly

12. Fit third-fourth gear synchromesh hub.
13. Using MS 47 with supports under first gear, press the spigot bearing on to shaft.

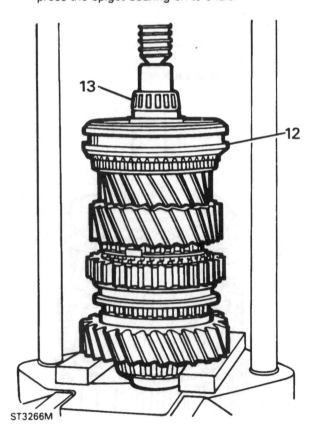

ST3266M

LAYSHAFT

1. Examine the layshaft for wear and damage.
2. Press bearings on to layshaft using MS 47 and supporting bars.

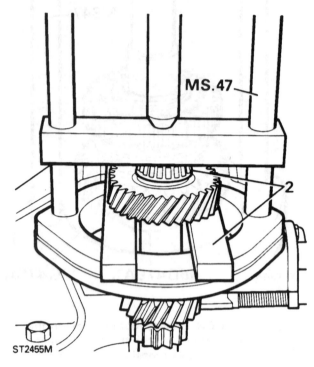

MS.47

ST2455M

REVERSE GEAR AND SHAFT

1. Remove one circlip from the idler gear and remove bearings.

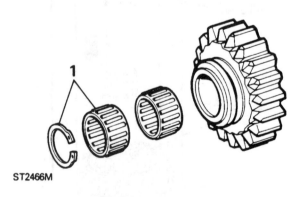

ST2466M

⚠ **NOTE: One bearing cage is twisted in manufacture. The twist causes the gear to tilt on the shaft forcing the gear into engagement. Renew bearings if worn or if the gear jumps out of engagement.**

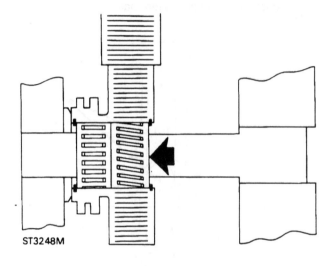

ST3248M

2. Fit the bearings either way round and secure with the circlip.
3. Check condition of idler gear and mating teeth on layshaft and synchromesh outer member.

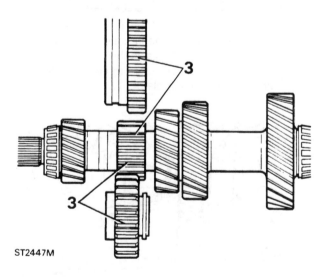

ST2447M

4. Examine idler shaft for wear, scores and pitting.

SELECTORS

1. Examine selector rail and pins for wear and damage.
2. Examine first-second selector fork for wear cracks and damage.

⚠ **NOTE: The the selector rail and fork is only supplied as a complete assembly.**

3. Examine third-fourth selector fork for wear, cracks and damage.
4. Examine fifth gear selector fork, pads and pivot pins.
5. Examine interlock spools for wear and damage.

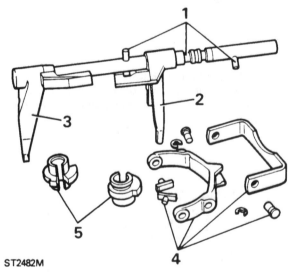

ST2482M

6. Remove snap ring and examine selector yoke assembly.

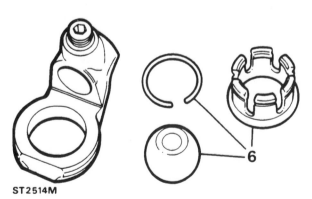

ST2514M

Assembling selectors.

7. Rest first-second fork and shaft assembly on bench and locate pin in jaw of fork.
8. Fit interlock spool and third-fourth fork and engage spool in jaw of fork.

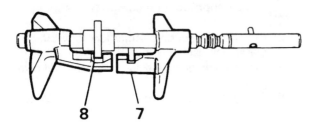

ST2488M

9. Slide spool and fork towards first- second selector until slot in spool locates over pin keeping the spool engaged in third-fourth fork jaw.

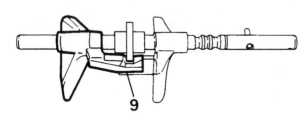

ST2487M

ASSEMBLING GEARBOX SHAFTS TO CENTRE PLATE

Fitting gears to centre plate

1. Secure centre plate to workstand, fit bearing tracks and inboard detent ball and spring.

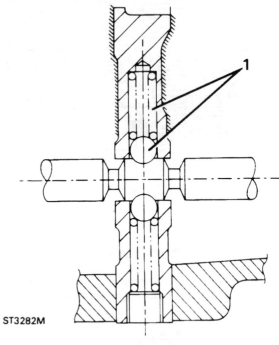

ST3282M

2. Check both synchromesh units are in neutral and fit selector shaft assembly.
3. Fit mainshaft and selectors to centre plate and align pin with slot in plate.

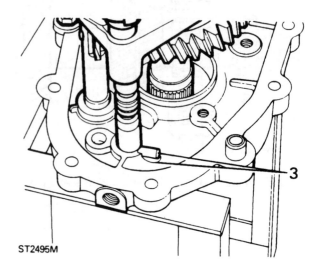

ST2495M

4. Fit layshaft While lifting mainshaft to clear layshaft rear bearing.
5. Turn selector shaft and interlock spool to allow reverse lever to engage spool flange.
6. Fit reverse lever to pivot post and secure with pin and circlip.
7. Fit slipper pad to lever.
8. Fit reverse gear shaft, spacer and gear.
9. Fit slipper to reverse gear and ensure roll pin in shaft engages in slot in centre plate.

10. Secure reverse shaft with manufactured tool "A".
11. Fit reverse gear thrust washer to shaft.
12. Fit fourth gear baulk ring.
13. Lubricate spigot bearing and fit input shaft.
14. Remove centre plate workstand bolt and fit gasket.

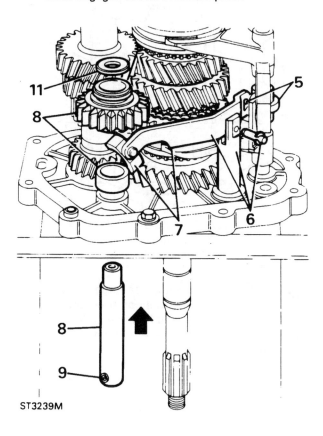

ST3239M

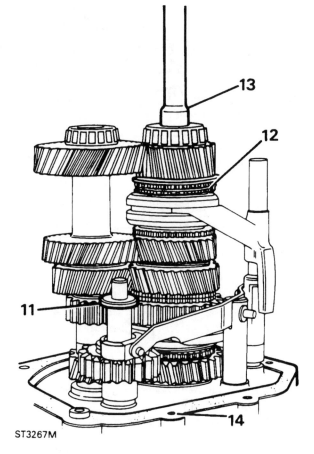

ST3267M

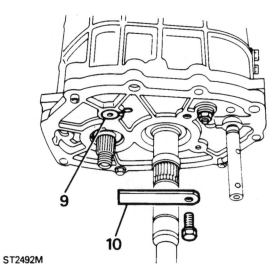

ST2492M

FITTING GEARBOX CASING

1. Turn selector shaft and spool to neutral position.
2. Fit out-board detent ball and spring and secure with plug.

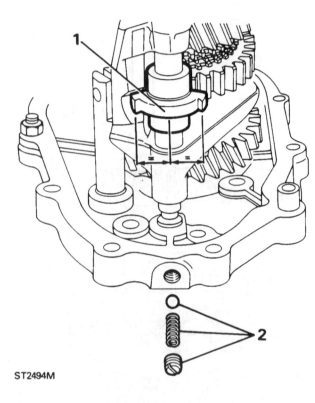

ST2494M

3. Fit guide studs to casing and check oil scoop is correctly fitted.
4. Without using force, fit gearcase.

 NOTE: Ensure that the centre plate dowels and selector shaft are properly located.

5. Secure centre plate and gearcase to workstand with two 8 x 35mm bolts.
6. Apply PL 32 to joint face and bolt threads and fit spool retainer.

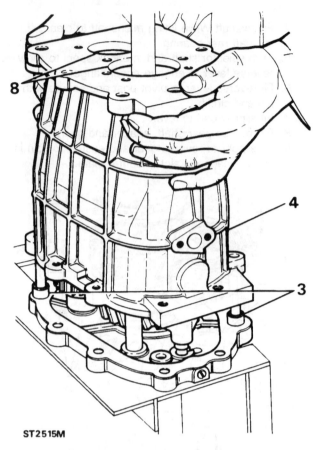

ST2515M

⚠️ **CAUTION: Do not use force to fit retainer. Provided the spool has not been disturbed the retainer will slide into position. If not, remove the gear case and reposition spool or shaft.**

7. Remove detent plug, apply Loctite 290 or Hylomar PL 32 to thread, refit and stake.
8. Fit layshaft and input shaft bearing tracks.

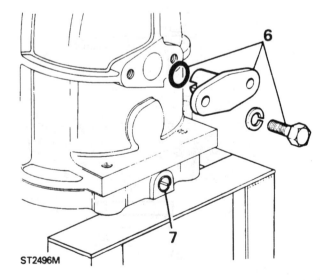

ST2496M

FITTING FIFTH GEAR

⚠ **CAUTION: Since the fifth gear is a tight fit on the layshaft, the force, when pressing the gear, must not be transfered to the layshaft front bearing. Tool"D"and packing disc should be made to the dimensions given to absorb the force. The plate also retains the input shaft bearing outer track.**

1. Secure the plate with two 8x25mm bolts. Insert disc between plate and layshaft.

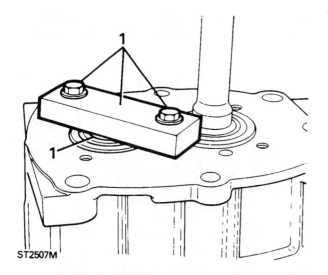

ST2507M

2. Release and invert gearbox and remove reverse shaft retainer plate.
3. With the extraction groove uppermost, drive fifth gear on to layshaft using 18G 1422.

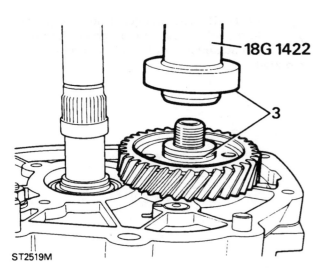

ST2519M

4. Fit a new stake nut but do not tighten.
5. Fit fifth gear assembly to mainshaft.

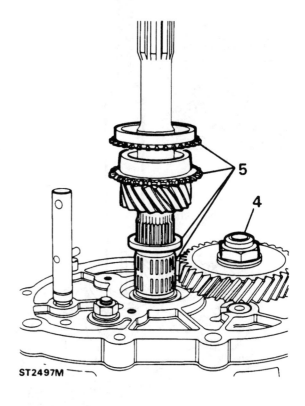

ST2497M

6. Press fifth gear synchromesh assembly to mainshaft using 18G 1431.

⚠ **CAUTION: Before pressing the assembly fully home, ensure that the slipper pads locate in the baulk ring slots.**

Part number	Thickness
FRC 5284	5,10
FRC 5286	5,16
FRC 5288	5,22
FRC 5290	5,58
FRC 5292	5,34
FRC 5294	5,40
FRC 5296	5,46
FRC 5298	5,52
FRC 5300	5,58
FRC 5302	5,64

7. Fit the thinnest washer and secure with circlip.
8. Measure clearance between circlip and washer.

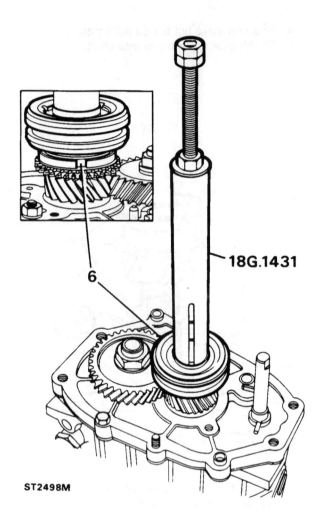

ST2498M

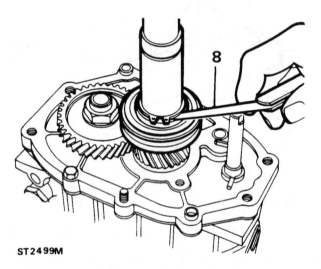

ST2499M

⚠ **NOTE: Only limited movement of the synchromesh inner member on the main-shaft is permissable. The maximum clearance is 0,005mm to 0,055mm (0.0002in) to (0.002in and to achieve this the following selective washers are available.**

9. Tighten layshaft stake nut using 18G 1205.

⚠ **CAUTION: The practice of locking gears to provide a restraint to tighten the nut is not acceptable due to high torque figure required.**

10. Secure tool "A" to gear and gear case and using a suitable torque wrench tighten the nut to the correct torque.

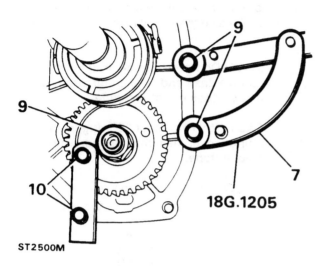

ST2500M

18G.1205

11. Using a round nose punch, form the collar into the layshaft slots.

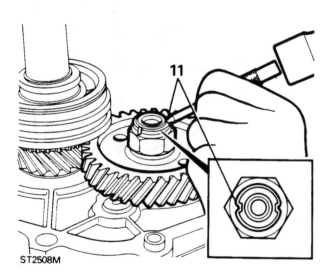

ST2508M

FIFTH GEAR SELECTOR FORK ASSEMBLY

1. Fit fifth gear selector fork bracket.
2. Fit the fifth gear spool long end towards centre plate.

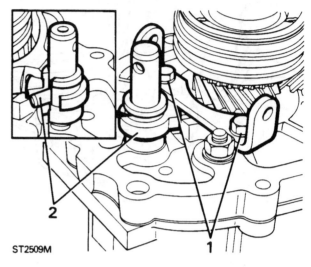

ST2509M

3. Fit slippers to selector fork.
4. Fit fork to synchromesh and secure with pins and "E" clips.

⚠ **NOTE: Before fitting pins and clips cover holes in centre plate to prevent them falling into casing.**

5. Engage tongue of spool in selector fork.
6. Fit oil pump drive to layshaft.

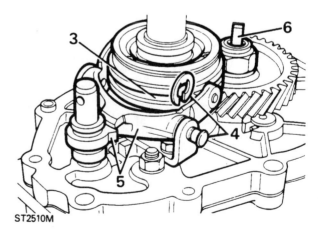

ST2510M

7. Fit yoke to selector shaft and secure with a new Loctite encapsulated grub screw.

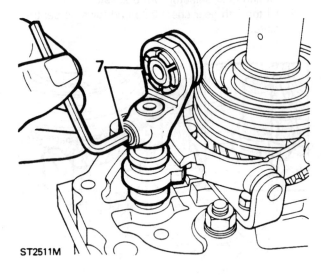

ST2511M

EXTENSION CASE

1. Release centre plate from workstand and fit gasket on joint face.
2. Fit extension case while aligning oil pick-up pipe. Remove guide studs and secure to main case.

 NOTE: Do not use force, if necessary remove case and re-align oil pump drive if case does not fit first time.

 CAUTION: To protect "O" ring while fitting, cover mainshaft splines with smooth tape.

3. Fit "O" ring to mainshaft groove.

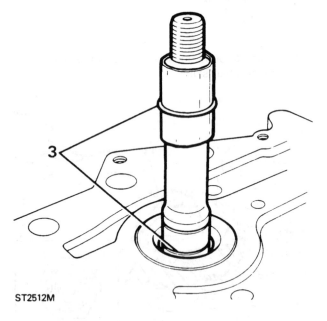

ST2512M

4. Fit "O" ring collar to mainshaft using 18G 1431.

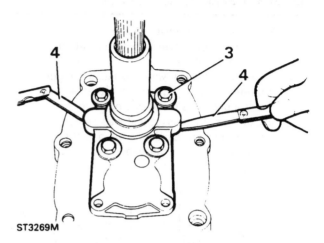

ST3269M

18G 1431

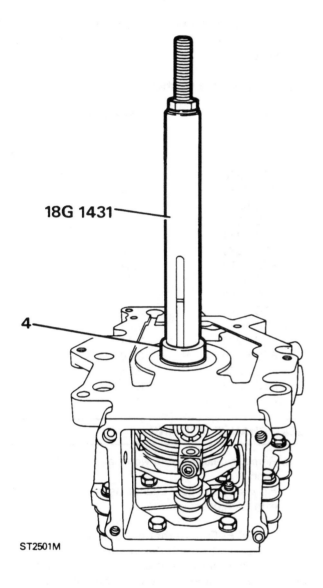

ST2501M

Input-Mainshaft bearing adjustment.

1. Turn gearbox over with input shaft uppermost. Remove layshaft support plate.

⚠ **NOTE: Correct shimming of the input shaft bearing is vital to ensure that the mainshaft assembly has the design intended end float, and the bearings are not pre-loaded.**

2. Measure the thickness of a new front cover gasket.
3. Place the original shim on mainshaft bearing and finger tighten the bolts.
4. Measure the clearance between front cover and gearcase with two feeler gauges.

5. If required, change the selective washer to provide a clearance of 0,35mm to 0,085mm (0.001 to 0.003ins) less than the gasket thickness.

⚠ **NOTE: This will ensure that when the gasket and cover is fitted to the correct torque, the input and mainshaft bearings will have no pre-load and not more than 0,06mm (0.0025in) end float.**

6. Remove front cover and keep gasket and selective washer together.

Mainshaft selective washers

Part number	Thickness(mm)
FRC 4327	1,51
FRC 4329	1,57
FRC 4331	!,63
FRC 4333	1,69
FRC 4335	1,75
FRC 4337	1,81
FRC 4339	1,87
FRC 4341	1,93
FRC 4343	1,99
FRC 4345	2,05
FRC 4347	2,11
FRC 4349	2,17
FRC 4351	2,23
FRC 4353	2,29
FRC 4355	2,35
FRC 4357	2,41
FRC 4359	2,47
FRC 4361	2,53
FRC 4363	2,59
FRC 4365	2,65
FRC 4367	2,67
FRC 4369	2,77

LAYSHAFT BEARING ADJUSTMENT

1. Place original selective washer on layshaft bearing, fit front cover without gasket, and finger tighten bolts.
2. Measure clearance, with two feeler gauges, between cover and gearcase. Select a shim that will provide a clearance equal to the thickness of the gasket that was selected and measured when calculating the adjustment of the input and mainshaft bearing.

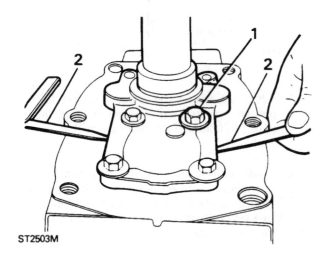

ST2503M

⚠️ **NOTE: This will ensure zero layshaft bearing end float and not more than 0,025mm (0.001in) pre-load once the cover and gasket are fitted and bolts correctly torqued.**

3. Remove cover and selected washer and fit new oil seal, lip towards gearcase.
4. Fit mainshaft and layshaft selected washers and gasket.

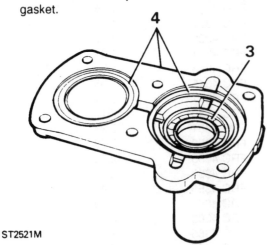

ST2521M

5. Wrap protective tape round input shaft splines.
6. Apply Hylomar PL 32 to bolt threads and secure cover.

Layshaft selective washers.

Part number	Thickness(mm)
FTC 0262	1,36
FTC 0264	1,42
FTC 0266	1,48
FTC 0268	1,54
FTC 0270	1,60
FTC 0272	1,66
FTC 0274	1,72
FTC 0276	1,78
FTC 0278	1,84
FTC 0280	1,90
FTC 0282	1,96
FTC 0284	2,02
FTC 0286	2,08
FTC 0288	2,14
FTC 0290	2,20
FTC 0292	2,26
FTC 0294	2,32
FTC 0296	2,38

GEAR CHANGE HOUSING

1. Remove gearbox from workstand and place on bench.
2. Fit gasket and gear change assembly to extension housing.

⚠️ **NOTE: Ensure that the gear lever pin passes through the centre of the yoke and engages in the gate plate. Also, the spool retainer must locate over the fifth gear spool.**

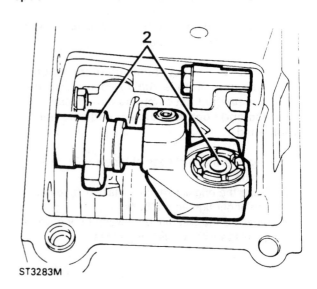

ST3283M

Bias adjustment plate setting.

1. Slacken bias adjustment plate bolts. Select fourth gear and move lever fully to right.
2. Tighten adjustment plate bolts.
3. Check adjustment is correct by selecting third gear then fourth.

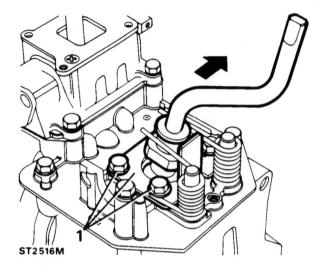

ST2516M

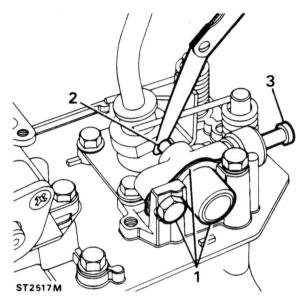

ST2517M

4. Fit sealing rubber to gear change housing and fit cover.
5. Fit and adjust reverse lamp switch, **see** **ELECTRICAL, Adjustment,**
6. Fit bell housing.

Setting reverse gear plunger.

1. Fit plunger and original shims to gear change housing.
2. Select first gear and measure clearance between reverse plunger and flat on side of gear lever.

 NOTE: The clearance should be 0,6mm to 0,85mm (0.024in to 0.034in). Adjust by adding or removing shims.

3. Fit reverse lamp switch plunger.

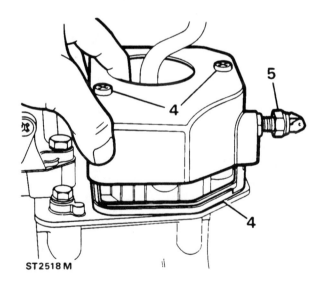

ST2518M

DATA

Reverse lever and slipper pad clearance	0,725 mm
Reverse gear plunger operating load	45 to 55 kg
Synchromesh assemblies push through load	8,2 to 10 kgf
Clearance between baulk rings and gears	0,38 mm
Fifth gear end float	0,020 mm
Third gear end float	0,020 mm
Second gear end float	0,020 mm
First gear bush end float	0.7 mm
First gear end float	0,20 mm
Fifth gear synchromesh end float	0,005 to 0,055 mm
Reverse gear plunger clearance	0,6 to 0.85 mm (0.024 to 0.034 in)

TORQUE VALUES

△ **NOTE: Torque wrenches should be regularly checked for accuracy to ensure that all fixings are tightened to the correct torque.**

	Nm
Bottom cover to clutch housing	7 - 10
Oil pump to extension case	7 - 10
Clip, clutch release lever	7 - 10
Spool retainer to gearcase	7 - 10
Extension case to gearcase	22 - 28
Pivot, clutch lever to bell housing	22 - 28
Guide, clutch release sleeve	22 - 28
Slave cylinder to bell housing	22 - 28
Front cover to gearcase	22 - 28
Fifth gear support bracket	22 - 28
Bell housing to gearbox	65 - 80
Oil drain plug	47 - 54
Oil filter plug	65 - 80
Breather	14 - 16
Oil level plug	25 - 35
Gear lever extension to lower lever	22 - 28
Fifth gear layshaft stake nut	204 - 231
Gear change housing to extension case	22 - 28
Reverse plunger to gear change housing	22 - 28
Adjustment plate to gear change housing	22 - 28
Cover to gear change housing	7 - 10
Bell housing to cylinder block	36 - 45
Yoke to selector shaft	22 - 28
Reverse lever pivot post nut	22 - 28
Plug detent ball and spring	22 - 28

SERVICE TOOLS

△ **NOTE: Where the use of special tools is specified, only these tools should be used to avoid the possibility of personal injury and or damage to components.**

18G 705   Puller, bearing remover

18G.705

18G 705-1A   Adaptor for mainshaft oil seal track and layshaft fifth gear

18G.705 – 1A

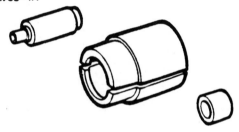

18G 705-7   Adaptor for layshaft bearings

18G.705 – 7

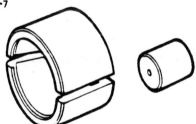

18G.1400

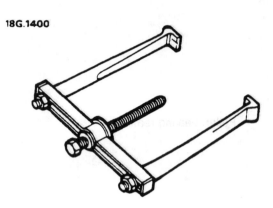

18G 1400   Remover synchromesh hub and gear cluster

18G 1400-1   Adaptor mainshaft fifth gear

18G.1400-1

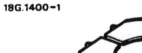

MS 47   Hand press

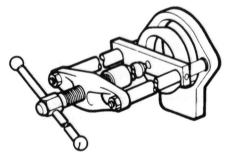

MS47

18G 47BA   Adaptor input shaft bearing

18G.47BA

18G 47BAX   Conversion kit

18G.47BAX

18G 284   Impulse extractor

18G.284(MS.284)

18G 284AAH   Adaptor for input shaft pilot bearing track

18G284AAH

18G 1422   Mainshaft rear oil seal replacer

18G.1422

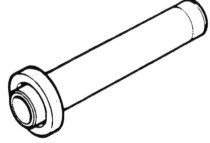

18G 1431   Mainshaft rear oil seal replacer

18G.1431

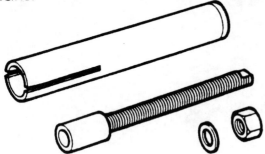

18G 1205   Flange holder

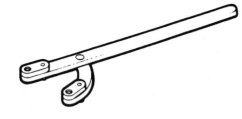

18G1205

LOCALLY MANUFACTURED TOOLS

In addition to the special service tools, the following tools can be locally made to assist the dismantling and assembly of the gearbox. The following overhaul procedure is based upon the assumption that these tools are available.

Tool 'A'. Dual purpose tool. Reverse shaft retainer to prevent the shaft falling out when the gearbox in inverted. Also, a layshaft fifth gear retainer to hold the fifth gear whilst releasing stake nut. Use 5mm mild steel to manufacture the tool. When using the tool for the layshaft nut, a suitable spacer is required 20mm diameter 23mm long, with an 8mm diameter clearance hole.

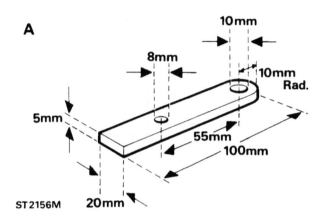

ST2156M

Tool 'B'. Four pilot studs with an 8mm thread for locating in the four counter sunk blind holes in the workstand.

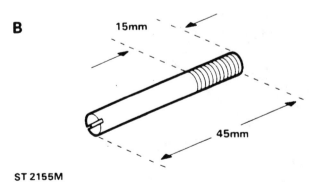

ST 2155M

Tool 'C'. Mild steel dummy centre bearing for the selection of first gear bush.

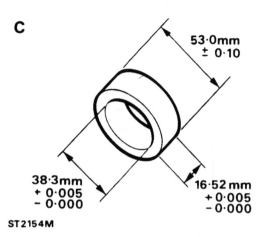

ST2154M

Tool 'D'. Layshaft support plate is fitted with two 8 x 25mm bolts and washers to the front of the gearbox case. It also supports the input shaft bearing outer track.

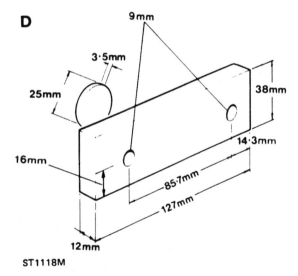

ST1118M

Tool 'E'. Workstand for securely locating the gearbox during overhaul. Manufacture from 30mm x 30mm angle iron. The single hole marked 'A' should be drilled through the material with a 10mm drill.

The four counter sunk blind holes marked 'B' should also be made with a 10mm drill, but must not be drilled through the material.

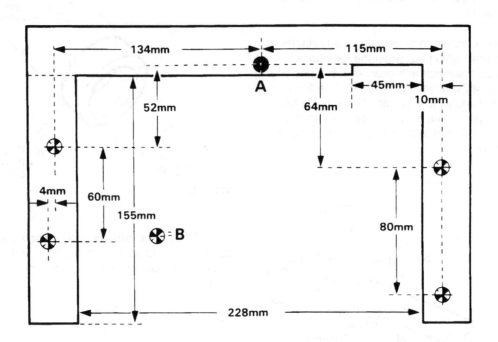

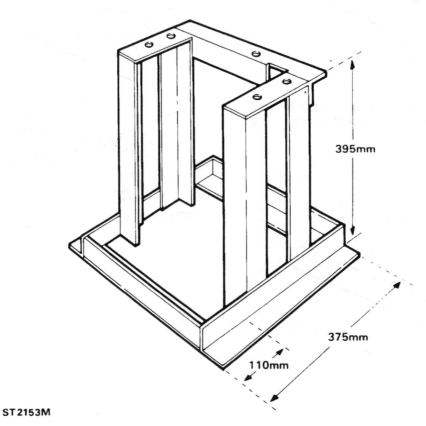

ST 2153M

GEARS AND SHAFTS

1. Third - fourth selector fork.
2. Interlock spool.
3. First - second fork and selector rail assembly.
4. First - second synchromesh.
5. First gear synchromesh outer baulk ring.
6. First gear synchromesh inner baulk ring.
7. Cone.
8. Thrust washer.
9. First gear.
10. Needle roller bearings.
11. First gear selective bush.
12. Centre taper roller bearing.
13. Circlip.
14. Thrust washer.
15. Fifth gear.
16. Fifth gear baulk ring.
17. Fifth gear synchromesh.
18. Fifth gear synchromesh back plate.
19. Fifth gear synchromesh selective washer.
20. Circlip.
21. "O" ring.
22. Oil seal collar.
23. Snap ring.
24. Fourth gear baulk ring.
25. Pilot taper bearing.
26. Spacer.
27. Third - fourth synchromesh.
28. Third gear baulk ring.
29. Third gear.
30. Third gear bush.
31. Second gear.
32. Thrust washer.
33. Cone.
34. Second gear synchromesh inner baulk ring.
35. Second gear synchromesh outer baulk ring.
36. Mainshaft.
37. Input shaft bearing track and selective washer.
38. Input shaft.
39. Input shaft taper bearing.
40. Fourth gear.
41. Selective shim.
42. Taper bearing.
43. Layshaft fourth gear.
44. Layshaft third gear.
45. Layshaft second gear.
46. Layshaft reverse gear.
47. Layshaft first gear.
48. Taper bearing.
49. Layshaft fifth gear.
50. Layshaft fifth gear retaining stake nut.
51. Circlips retaining first gear and first-second gear synchromesh.
52. Snap ring retaining second gear cone and spacer.
53. Spacer.
54. Snap ring.
55. Reverse idler gear.
56. Thrust washer.
57. Snap ring.
58. Fifth gear spool.
59. Gear change lever yoke.
60. Gear change ball and retaining ring.
61. Gear change Nylon seating.

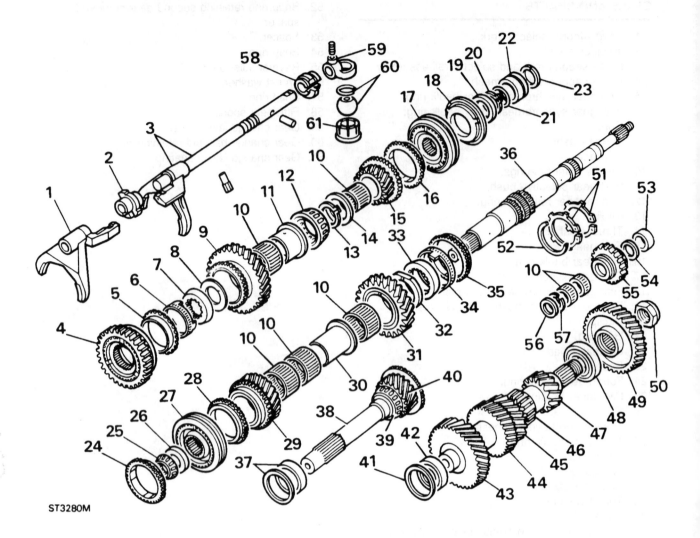

ST3280M

GEARBOX CASING

1. Front cover.
2. Front cover oil seal.
3. Front cover gasket.
4. Oil drain plug and washer.
5. Oil level plug.
6. Gearbox main casing.
7. Spool retainer.
8. Gasket.
9. Inboard detent ball and spring.
10. Reverse lever and slipper.
11. Locating dowels - centre plate to maincase.
12. Reverse lever pivot post.
13. Centre plate.
14. Selector plug, detent ball and spring.
15. Gasket.
16. Fifth gear selector bracket.
17. Fifth gear selector fork.
18. Reverse gear shaft.
19. Oil pick-up pipe.
20. Oil pump drive shaft.
21. Oil pump gears and cover.
22. Fifth gear extension housing.
23. Fifth gear extension housing drain plug and filter.
24. Ferrobestos bush.
25. Oil seal.

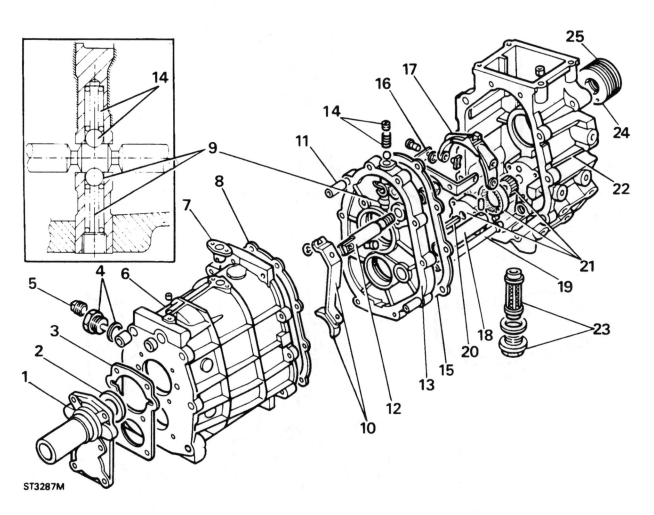

ST3287M

GEAR CHANGE HOUSING ASSEMBLY

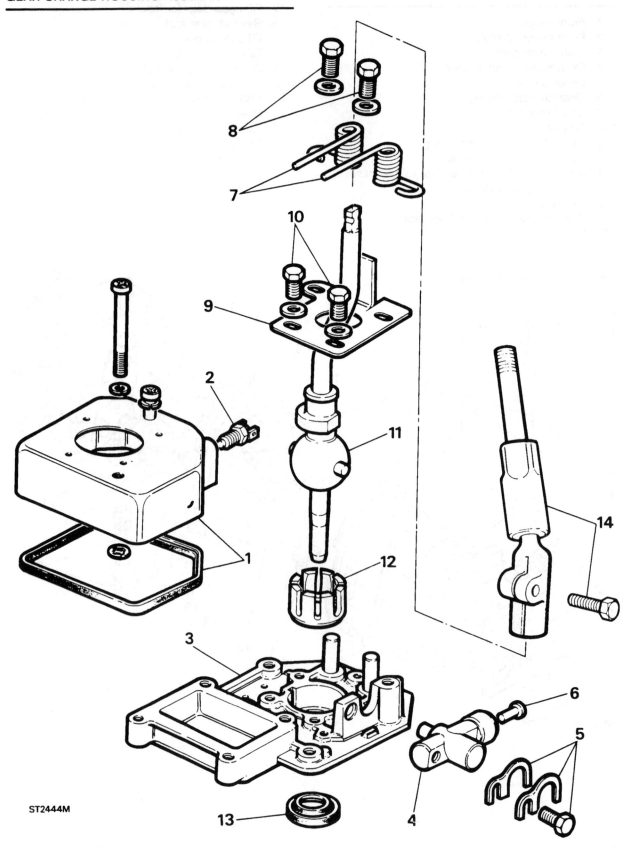

ST2444M

KEY TO GEAR CHANGE HOUSING ASSEMBLY

---

1. Gear change housing cover and gasket
2. Reverse lamp switch
3. Gear change housing
4. Reverse gear plunger
5. Reverse gear plunger shims and bolt
6. Reverse lamp plunger
7. Bias springs
8. Bias spring retaining bolts
9. Bias adjustment plate
10. Bias adjustment plate bolts
11. Lower gear lever
12. Railko bush
13. Lower gear lever housing oil seal
14. Upper gear lever pinch bolt

RANGE ROVER

RANGE ROVER
1992 MODEL YEAR

WORKSHOP MANUAL SUPPLEMENT

Publication Number LSM 180 EN WS 10

Published by the
Technical Publications Department of

CONTENTS

INTRODUCTION

For 1992 model year, the specification of Range Rovers is further improved by the inclusion of the following features:

Memory driver's seat and external mirrors. Heated front seats. Dimming rear view mirror with map reading lights.

Improvements to the vehicle electrical system have also been made, including the use of fusible cables in the positive battery lead and new connectors.

Also included in this publication is the new alternator positive belt tensioner incorporated on 1990 model vehicles.

The purpose of this supplement is to cover the 1992 model differences, and should be used in conjunction with the main workshop manual.

SYNTHETIC RUBBER

Many 0-ring seals, flexible pipes and other similar items which appear to be natural rubber are made of synthetic materials called Fluoroelastomers. Under normal operating conditions this material is safe, and does not present a health hazard. However, if the material is damaged by fire or excessive heat, it can break down and produce highly corrosive Hydrofluoric acid which can cause serious burns on contact with skin. Should the material be in a burnt or overheated condition handle only with seamless industrial gloves. Decontaminate and dispose of the gloves immediately after use.

If skin contact does occur, remove any contaminated clothing immediately and obtain medical assistance without delay. In the meantime, wash the affected area with copious amounts of cold water or limewater for fifteen to sixty minutes.

RECOMMENDED SEALANTS

A number of branded products are recommended in this manual for use during maintenance and repair work.

These items include: **HYLOMAR GASKET AND JOINTING COMPOUND** and **HYLOSIL RTV SILICON COMPOUND.**

They should be available locally from garage equipment suppliers. If there is any problem obtaining supplies, contact one of the following companies for advice and the address of the nearest supplier.

MARSTON LUBRICANTS LTD.
Hylo House,
Cale lane,
New Springs,
Wigan WN2 1JR,

0942 824242

COPYRIGHT

RECOMMENDED LUBRICANTS AND FLUIDS

Use only the recommended grades of oil set out below.
These recommendations apply to climates where operational temperatures are above -10°C.

Petrol engine sump Oil can	BP Visco 2000 plus Castrol Syntron X Castrol GTX -2 Castrolite TXT Duckhams Hypergrade Motor Oil Esso Superlube EX2 Mobil Super Duckhams QXR Mobil 1 Rally Formula Esso Vitra	Fina Supergrade Motor Oil Fina First Shell Super Motor Oil Shell Gemini Havoline X1 Havoline multigrade UK only - Land Rover Parts 15W/40
Diesel engine sump **	BP Vanellus C3 Extra (15W/40) Castrol Turbomax (15W/40) Duckhams Fleetmaster SHPD (15W/40) Esso Super Diesel Oil TD (15W/40) The following list of oils to MIL - L - 2104D or CCMC D2 or API Service levels CD are for emergency use only if the above oils are not available. They can be used for topping up without detriment, but if used for engine oil changing, they are limited to a maximum of 5,000 km (3,000 miles) between oil and filter changes. BP Vanellus C3 Multigrade (15W/40) Castrol RX Super (15W/40) Duckhams Hypergrade (15W/50) Esso Essolube XD - 3 plus (15W/40) Mobil Delvac Super (15W/40)	Mobil Delvac 1400 Super (15W/40) Fina Kappa LDO (15W/40) Shell Myrina (15W/40) Texaco URSA Super TD (15W/40) UK only - Land Rover Parts SHPD Fina Dilano HPD (15W/40) Shell Rimula X (15W/40) Texaco URSA Super Plus (15W/40)
Automatic gearbox	BP Autran DX2D Castrol TQ Dexron IID Duckhams Fleetmatic CD Duckhams D - Matic Esso ATF Dexron IID	Mobil ATF 220D Fina Dexron IID Shell ATF Dexron IID Texamatic Fluid 9226 UK only - Land Rover Parts ATF Dexron II
Manual gearbox	BP Autran G Castrol TQF Duckhams Q - Matic Esso ATF Type G Mobil ATF 210	Fina Purfimatic 33G Shell Donax TF Texamatic Type G or Universal UK only - Land Rover Parts ATF Type 'G'
Front and Rear differential Swivel pin housings	BP Gear Oil SAE 90EP Castrol Hypoy SAE 90EP Duckhams Hypoid 90 Esso Gear Oil GX (85W/90) Mobil Mobilube HD90	Fina Pontonic MP SAE (80W/90) Shell Spirax 90EP Texaco Multigear Lubricant EP (85W/90) UK only - Land Rover Parts EP90

** **Other approved oils include:** Agip Sigma Turbo, Aral OL P327, Autol Valve - SHP, Aviation Turbo, Caltex RPM Delo 450, Century Centurion, Chevron Delo 450 Multigrade, Divinol Multimax Extra, Ecubsol CD Plus, Elf Multiperformance 4D, Esso Special Diesel, Fanal Indol X, Fuchs Titan Truck 1540, Gulf Superfleet Special, IP Taurus M, Total Rubia TIR XLD, Valvoline Super HD 4D LD, Veedol Turbostar, Gulf Superfleet (GB), Silkolene Turbolene D, Kuwait Q8 T700.

Propeller shaft Front and Rear	BP Energrease L2 Castrol LM Grease Duckhams LB 10 Esso Multi - purpose Grease H	Mobil Grease MP Fina Marson HTL 2 Shell Retinax A Marfak All Purpose Grease
Power steering box and fluid Reservoir Transfer Gearbox	BP Autran DX2D BP Autran G Castrol TQ Dexron IID Castrol TQF Duckhams Fleetmatic CD Duckhams Q - matic Esso ATF Dexron IID Esso ATF Type G Mobil ATF 220D Mobil ATF 210	Fina Dexron IID Fina Purfimatic 33G Shell ATF Dexron IID Shell Donax TF Texamatic Fluid 9226 Texamatic Type G or 4291A Universal UK only - Land Rover Parts ATF Dexron II or Type G
Brake and clutch reservoirs	Brake fluids having a minimum boiling point of 260°C (500°F) and complying with FMVSS 116 DOT4	
Lubrication nipples (hubs, ball joints etc.)	BP Energrease L2 Castrol LM Grease Duckhams LB 10 Esso Multi - purpose Grease H	Mobil Grease MP Fina Marson HTL 2 Shell Retinax A Marfak All Purpose Grease
Ball joint assembly Top Link	BPL21M Castrol M53 Shell Retirax AM	Duckhams LBM10 Esso MP Mobil Supergrease
Seat slides Door lock striker	BP Energrease L2 Castrol LM Grease Duckhams LB 10 Esso Multi - purpose Grease H Mobil Grease MP	Fina Marson HTL 2 Shell Retinax A Marfak All purpose grease NLGI - 2 Multi - purpose Lithium - based Grease

Recommended lubricants and fluids - All climates and conditions

COMPONENT	SPECIFICATION	VISCOSITY	AMBIENT TEMPERATURE °C
Petrol models Engine sump Oil can	Oils must meet: RES.22.OL.G-4 or CCMC G-4 API service level SG	5W/30	─30 to ~35
		5W/40 5W/50	─30 to 50
		10W/30	─20 to ~30
		10W/40 10W/50	─20 to 50
		15W/40 15W/50	─15 to 50
		20W/40 20W/50	─10 to 50
		25W/40 25W/50	─5 to 50
Diesel models Engine sump	RES 22 OLD-5 CCMC D-5 API CE	15W/40 10W/30	15W/40: ─15 to 50; 10W/30: ─20 to ~35
* Emergency use:	MIL - L - 2104D, CCMCD2 or API CD	10W/30	─20 to 40
Main Gearbox Automatic	ATF Dexron IID		─30 to 50
Main Gearbox manual	ATF M2C33 (F or G)		─30 to 50
Final drive units Swivel pin housings	API GL4 or GL5 MIL - L - 2105 or MIL - L - 21-05B	90 EP	─20 to 50
		80W EP	─30 to 10
Power steering Borg Warner Transfer Box	ATF M2C 336 or ATF Dexron IID		─30 to 50

* Diesel Models - Engine Sump

Oils for emergency use only if the SHPD oils are not available. They can be used for topping up without detriment, but if used for engine oil changing, they are limited to a maximum of 5,000 km (3,000 miles) between oil and filter changes. (See previous page)

Engine cooling system	Use an ethylene glycol based anti-freeze (containing no methanol) with non-phosphate corrosion inhibitors suitable for use in aluminium engines to ensure the protection of the cooling system against frost and corrosion in all seasons. Use one part anti-freeze to one part water for protection down to -36°C. **IMPORTANT: Coolant solution must not fall below proportions one part anti-freeze to three parts water, i.e. minimum 25% anti-freeze in coolant otherwise damage to engine is liable to occur.**
Battery lugs, Earthing surfaces where paint has been removed	Petroleum jelly. **NOTE: Do not use Silicone Grease**
Air Conditioning System Refrigerant	**METHYLCHLORIDE REFRIGERANTS MUST NOT BE USED** Use only with refrigerant 12. This includes 'Freon 12' and 'Arcton 12'
Compressor Oil	Shell Clavus 68 BP Energol LPT68 Sunisco 4GS Texaco Capella E Wax/Free 68. Castrol Icematic 99
ABS Sensor bush-rear	Silicone grease: Staborags NBU - Wabco 830 502,0634 Wacker chemie 704 - Wabco 830 502,0164 Kluber GL301

ANTI-FREEZE

ENGINE TYPE	MIXTURE STRENGTH	PERCENTAGE CONCENTRATION	PROTECTION LOWER TEMPERATURE LIMIT
V8 (aluminium) Diesel VM	One part anti-freeze One part water	50%	
Complete protection Vehicle may be driven away immediately from cold			- 36°C
Safe limit protection Coolant in mushy state. Engine may be started and driven away after warm-up period			- 41°C
Lower protection Prevents frost damage to cylinder head, block and radiator. Thaw out before starting engine			- 47°C

DRIVE BELTS - ADJUST OR FIT NEW BELTS

**WARNING: Disconnect battery negative terminal
before adjusting drive belts to avoid possibility
of vehicle being started.**

COMPRESSOR DRIVE BELT

Belt must be tight with not more than 4 to 6mm total
deflection when checked by hand midway between
pulleys on longest run.

Where belt has stretched beyond limits, a noisy
whine or knock will often be evident during
operating, adjust as follows:

1. Loosen idler pulley securing bolt.
2. Adjust position of idler pulley until correct
   tension is obtained.
3. Tighten securing bolt and recheck belt tension.

ILLUSTRATION A

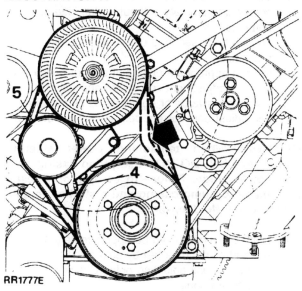

RR1777E

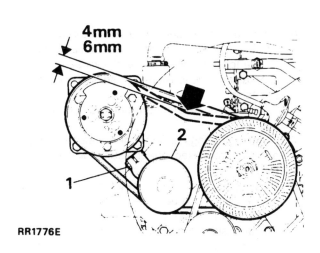

RR1776E

**Check driving belts, adjust or fit new belts as
necessary.**

1. Examine following belts for wear and condition,
   fit new belts if necessary:

   (A) Crankshaft-Idler pulley-Water Pump
   (B) Crankshaft-Steering Pump
   (C) Steering Pump-Alternator

ILLUSTRATION B

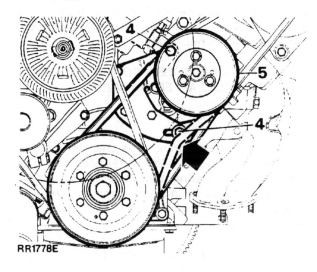

RR1778E

ILLUSTRATION C

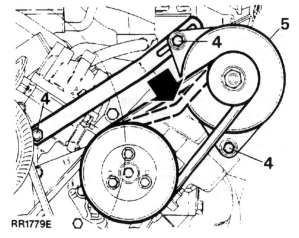

RR1779E

1

2. Each belt should be sufficiently tight to drive appropriate auxiliary without undue load on bearings.
3. Loosen bolts securing unit to its mounting bracket.
4. Loosen appropriate pivot bolt or idler pulley and fixing at adjustment link where applicable.
5. Pivot unit inwards or outwards as necessary and adjust until correct belt tension is obtained.

CAUTION: When tensioning power steering pump drive belt DO NOT use pump casing as a point of leverage. Failure to comply may result in damage to pump casing and distortion to seal face causing fluid leakage.

6. Belt deflection should be approximately 4 to 6mm at points denoted by bold arrows.
7. Tighten all unit adjusting bolts. Check adjustment again.

CAUTION: When fitting a new drive belt, tension belt as described above. Reconnect battery and start and run engine for 3 to 5 minutes at fast idle, after which time belt must be re-checked, re-tension belt if necessary.

ALTERNATOR DRIVE BELT/POWER STEERING BELT - VEHICLES AFTER VIN 602813

Adjust

NOTE: A positive drive tensioner is fitted to these vehicles to provide greater accuracy when setting power steering and alternator drive belts. The tensioner eliminates the need to lever both power steering pump and alternator when adjusting belt tension.

1. Loosen alternator pivot bolt and bolt securing alternator to tensioner.
2. Loosen two tensioner nuts and bolt securing tensioner to water pump bracket.
3. Rotate tensioner lead screw anti-clockwise, remove drive belt.
4. Disconnect left hand bank plug leads and coil lead.
5. Release distributor cap retaining clip, place cap to one side.
6. Remove plug from distributor amplifier.
7. Loosen power steering pump adjuster bolt and pump pivot nuts.
8. Remove power steering belt.
9. Ensure pump is free to rotate on its mounting, DO NOT lever pump, further loosen fixings if necessary

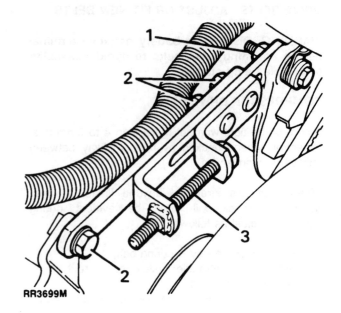

RR3699M

10. Check both drive belts, renew if necessary.
11. Fit power steering and alternator drive belts.
12. Rotate tensioner lead screw clockwise until alternator belt is tensioned to specified figure, see table.
13. Check steering belt is tensioned to specified figure.
14. Tighten all fixings on tensioner, steering pump and alternator. Reconnect distributor cap and leads.
15. Run engine at fast idle speed for 3 to 5 minutes if a new belt has been fitted. Check tension, re-adjust if necessary.
16. Adjust position of top radiator hose to give 20 to 30 mm clearance between hose and alternator fan guard.

BELT TENSION

Fitting alternator or steering belt

Tension or retension belts to:

Alternator	Steering
110 - 120 lbf	85 - 105 lbf
470 - 500 N	380 - 465 N

Refitting used belts

90 - 95 lbf	75 - 95 lbf
400 - 420 N	335 - 420 N

MEMORY SEAT SYSTEM

Description

To provide owners with greater convenience when positioning the driving seat. The Electronic Control Memory Unit (ECU) allows two different driving seat positions to be stored in its memory, which may be recalled by either of two driver's depressing the appropriate switch. The ECU is connected only to the driving seat circuit, the passenger seat has no ECU in the control circuit and therefore will require adjustment by each individual passenger.

As the position of both exterior mirrors and the driving seat are closely related, the mirrors are also connected to the drivers seat ECU.

When the vehicle is stationary and for driver access, the seat control circuit allows the position driver's seat to be adjusted while the driver's door is open. To adjust the position of the passenger seat the start/ignition switch must be turned to the 'I' or 'II' position.
Both seats remain fully adjustable with the vehicle in motion, but at speeds above 6 KPH the drivers seat memory functions become inoperative.

Operation

Refer to illustration RR3684M

Adjusting the front seats (and mirrors) to a comfortable position, should only be carried out when the vehicle is stationary and with the driver's door open or with the ignition switch turned to position 'I' or 'II' using the appropriate multi position control switches, 8 passenger seat or 6 drivers seat. The four electric motors A B D C in both seats may be driven clockwise or anti-clockwise by a pair of switch contacts housed within control switch 8 and 6. Each pair of contacts move in unison in the same direction when operated, to drive the motor as required. The passenger seat motors are connected directly to the control switch 8 but the drivers seat motors 6 are operated indirectly through 18 the ECU. Each motor in the drivers seat also drives a sensor 7- A B C D which send signals to 18 in order for the ECU to calculate and memorize the seat position. Any mirror adjustments signalled by the potentiometers 21 are also memorized by the ECU.

For reasons of safety and to prevent accidental selection of the wrong driving seat position when the vehicle is in motion, the ECU receives road speed transducer signals via connection 14.

At speeds above approximately 6 KPH the signal deactivates the memory recall facility but continues to allow normal seat or mirror adjustments to be carried out. Once the vehicle speed is below 6 KPH the original memorized positions may be recalled by momentary depressing memory switches 9 or 11. If the vehicle battery or the ECU is disconnected for a period of four weeks or more the memory will have been erased and therefore will require initialising as follows:-

WARNING: The initialisation procedure will cause the seat to move to its maximum travel in all directions through a programmed sequence of manoeuvres before coming to rest in the optimum mid adjustment position.

CALIBRATION/INITIALISATION PROCEDURE

1. With the vehicle safely parked and the hand brake securely applied, ensure that subsequent full movement of the drivers seat and both exterior mirrors is not obstructed.
2. Turn the ignition switch to position 'I' or 'II' and depress the green memory set switch 9, five times in succession, then immediately key in 2112 using the memory switches. The drivers seat and mirrors will now commence to move through the programmed sequence of manoeuvres before coming to rest in the optimum mid adjustment position.

The memory of the ECU is now ready to receive and store two positional combinations for the driver's seat and exterior mirrors. Positional adjustment of the seat and mirrors may be carried out with the vehicle moving or stationary, but the ECU will only memorize the settings when the the vehicle is stationary and by momentarily depressing the green memory set switch 9 and one of the numbered switches simultaneously.

When the memory has stored the required positional combinations and if the driver inadvertently recalls the incorrect seat setting by depressing the wrong memory recall switch, and finds the seat moving to an uncomfortable or dangerous driving position, operating the seat control switch will halt the movement and override the memory without erasing it.

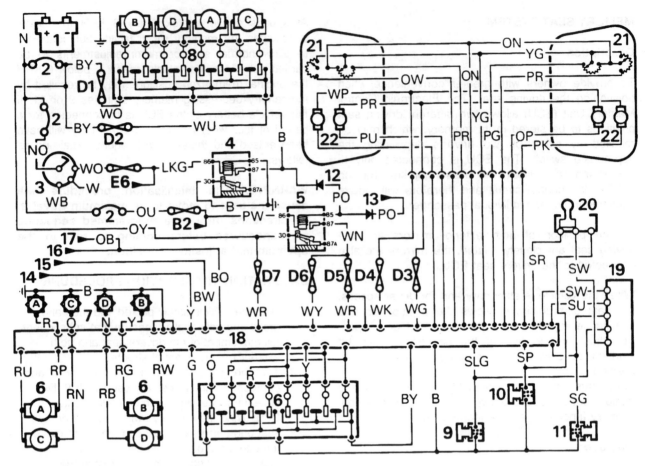

RR3684M

1. Battery
2. Fusible links (3)
3. Ignition switch
4. Passenger's seat relay
5. Driver's seat relay
6. Driver's seat control switch and adjustment motors
   - A Base height front
   - B Base height rear
   - C Recline
   - D Seat fore and aft
7. Driver's seat position sensors one per motor A B C D
8. Passenger's seat control switch and adjustment motors
   - A Base height front
   - B Base height rear
   - C Recline
   - D Seat fore and aft
9. Memory set push button
10. Memory recall push button 1
11. Memory recall push button 2

12. Diode
13. Diode and connection to the driver's door interior light switch
14. Vehicle speed signal, input
15. Park brake signal, input
16. Park/Neutral switch signal input
17. EFI control unit connection
18. Electronic control memory unit, ECU
19. Mirror control switch
20. Mirror change over switch
21. Mirror potentiometers, LH/RH
22. Mirror motors, LH/RH
D1. 30 amp fuse, passenger seat
D2. 30 amp fuse, passenger seat
D3. 3 amp fuse, mirrors LH/RH
D4. 3 amp fuse, mirrors LH/RH
D5. 30 amp fuse, drivers seat
D6. 30 amp fuse, drivers seat
D7. 3 amp fuse, clipped to box (memory maintenance fuse)
E6. 10 amp fuse, also feeds other circuits
B2. 15 amp fuse, also feeds other circuits

MEMORY STORE OR RECALL

Memory store or recall is available with
a) Ignition in position 1 or 2 with park/neutral or park brake engaged.
OR
b) Driver's door open with park/neutral or park brake engaged.

Store selected setting

1. Park vehicle with park/neutral engaged or park brake on, with door open or ignition in position 1 or 2.
2. Select required seat/mirror position.
3. Press circular button, keep depressed while pressing one of rectangular buttons (1 or 2) to store setting.
4. Setting will remain stored until procedure repeated.

Recall stored setting

1. Park vehicle with park/neutral engaged or park brake on, with door open or ignition in position 1 or 2.
2. Press rectangular button for required setting. Seat and mirrors will move to stored position.

NOTE: Operating one of seat/mirror switches will stop movement before stored position is reached.

COMPONENT LOCATION

Memory system ECU, located under driver's seat.
Control switch, on inboard side of driver's seat.
For location of seat system fuses and relays, Electrical Section 86.

FAULT DIAGNOSIS

CALIBRATION/INITIALISATION PROCEDURE

If a fault is suspected in the memory seat system, the calibration/initialisation procedure may be followed to establish that a fault does exist and its possible cause. This procedure must also be followed if new system components have been fitted. Park vehicle with driver's door open, ignition position 1 and park, neutral or park brake engaged.

WARNING: Stand clear of seat during calibration sequence.

To start the sequence, fully press green circular button 5 times, followed by rectangular buttons in the order 2 - 1 - 1 - 2
The sequence will put seat through full travel in all planes of seat function, and mirrors through full travel in all planes of mirror movement. After completion of sequence, seat and mirrors will stop in mid-travel position, this indicates that the system is functioniong correctly.

This sequence checks following items:

1. Inputs from memory function buttons.
2. All outputs to, and feedbacks from, motors
3. Checks to point of failure, that is where no feedback is received from motor driving in that specific plane. If there is no motor movement, electrical drive to motor is inoperative. If motor moves in demanded plane, then stops, no feedback is indicated.

MEMORY SEAT/MIRROR SYSTEM SERVICE CHECK

THE CORRECT OPERATION OF MEMORY POSITION STORE AND RECALL MUST BE CHECKED TO ENSURE CORRECT AND SAFE OPERATION OF MEMORY SYSTEM

Manual transmission vehicles

Memory position, store and recall is only possible when following conditions apply:

- Driver's door open **OR** ignition AUX or IGN, **AND** park brake applied, vehicle speed less than 6 kph.

CAUTION: It is potentially hazardous if memory store or recall is possible without park brake applied or with vehicle speed above 6 kph. The cause must be immediately investigated, see MEMORY SEAT SYSTEM CONTINUITY CHECK.

1. If memory position recall/store is possible without park brake applied (vehicle stationary), it is essential to check following:

   - Park brake signal to ECU
   - ECU

2. If memory recall is possible when vehicle speed is over 6 kph, regardless of park brake position, it is essential to check following:

   - Speed signal to ECU
   - Park brake signal to ECU
   - ECU

3. Memory position store/recall function inoperative when park brake applied, check following:

   - Park brake signal to ECU
   - ECU.

Automatic transmission vehicles:

Memory position, store and recall is only possible when following conditions apply:

Driver's door open OR ignition AUX or IGN, AND park brake applied, OR park/neutral engaged, vehicle speed less than 6 kph.

CAUTION: It is potentially hazardous if memory store or recall is possible without park brake or park/neutral applied or with vehicle speed above 6 kph. The cause must be immediately investigated, see MEMORY SEAT SYSTEM CONTINUITY CHECK.

1. If memory position recall/store is possible without park brake applied (vehicle stationary), it is essential to check following:

   - Park brake signal to ECU
   - Park/neutral signal to ECU
   - ECU

2. If memory recall is possible with park brake applied or park/neutral engaged, and vehicle speed above 6 kph, it is essential to check following:

   - Park/neutral signal to ECU
   - Speed signal to ECU
   - ECU.

3. If memory position store/recall function is NOT possible after applying park brake or engaging park/neutral, check following:

   - Park brake signal system continuity check
   - Park/neutral signal
   - ECU

FAULT FINDING

NOTE: The following chart lists care points referring to possible faults/remedies in the memory seat system.

FAULTS/SYMPTOMS	CAUSE	REMEDY
Seat or mirrors inoperative	Fuses blown, not inserted or drivers seat load relay	Reinsert or replace fuses under seat and courtesy light fuse, main fuse panel. Refit or fit new relay.
System only operative with door open	Passenger seat relay	Refit or replace
Mirrors and clock inoperative	Mirror/clock harness not connected to main harness	Connect mirror/clock harness behind mirror switch pack and dash
Mirror or mirrors inoperative	Pins backed out in 5-way Espa connector	Repair connector in mirror mounting
Mirrors inoperative	Non connection of 24-way Sumitomo connector	Connect 24-way to memory seat ECU under driver's seat
Mirrors operative but in wrong planes	Mirror switch assy in wrong position or elevation	Fit mirror switch in correct elevation
System partially functional	ECU link harness broken	Replace ECU
Seat inoperative	Non connection of 10-way Sumitomo connector	Reconnect, under driver's seat

Continued

Seat operating in different planes and travels to that demanded	Wrongly handed link harness fitted in seat	Fit correct link harness, between seat switch and ECU
Seat pulsing to position in more than one plane	Non connection of 6-way Sumitomo Connect	6-Way, under driver's seat
Seat pulsing to position	No connection at sensor/gear box (ECU input or output)	Make connection to sensor unit, at relevant gearbox

IMPORTANT: Refer to UNDERSEAT HARNESS LAYOUT for correct wiring installation.

Refer to MEMORY SEAT/MIRROR SYSTEM FAULT DIAGNOSIS if fault has not been located.

MEMORY SEAT/MIRROR SYSTEM FAULT DIAGNOSIS

Manual and memory seat/mirror system totally inoperative - 1.

Seat system losing memory position - 7.

Memory recall function inoperative - 12.

Incorrect manual electric seat control operation - 17.

Incorrect manual mirror operation/movement - 28.

Service checks - 44.

Manual and memory seat/mirror system totally inoperative

1. Are 30 amp fuses and fuse B2 inserted correctly and intact?
   Yes, go to 2.
   No, replace fuse or reinsert, check system.
2. Is drivers seat load relay inserted correctly?
   Yes, go to 3.
   No, insert correctly, check system.
3. Does system operate after replacing drivers seat load relay?
   Yes, check system.
   No, go to 4.
4. Is fusible link inserted correctly and intact?
   Yes, go to 6.
   No, go to 5.
5. Upon replacing fusible link does system operate correctly?
   Yes, check system.
   No, go to 6.
6. See memory seat system continuity checks: 4, 5, 6, 7 8 and 9.

Seat system losing memory position

7. Does the seat system lose memory positions upon IGN/AUX being switched off and door closed?
   Yes, go to 8.
   No, check system.
8. Is 3A stand alone fuse inserted correctly and intact?
   Yes, go to 9.
   No, check 11.
9. Is fusible link intact?
   Yes, go to 10.
   No, go to 11.
10. See memory seat system continuity check 3.
11. Does system retain position 24 hours after replacing or reinserting fuse or fusible link?
    Yes, check system
    No, go to 10.

Memory recall function inoperative

12. Does system attempt to go through calibration sequence?
    Yes, is recall function inoperative? Go to 7.
    No, go to 13.
13. Does system attempt to go through calibration sequence after replacing original seat switch?
    Yes, check system. Clean original switch, and recheck - See seat switch - clean.
    No, go to 14.
14. Are connectors/connections to seat switch via seat switch harness to ECU intact?
    Yes, go to 16.
    No, go to 15.
15. Does system attempt to go through calibration sequence after repairing connections to base of seat switch or reconnecting /replacing seat switch link harness, (between switch and ECU)?
    Yes, check system.
    No, go to 16.
16. See memory seat system continuity check. Incorrect manual electric seat control operation

Incorrect manual electric seat control operation

17. Are 30 amp fuses intact and inserted correctly?
Yes, go to 18.
No, reinsert/replace fuses correctly, check system

18. Is fusible link intact and inserted correctly?
Yes, go to 20.
No, reinsert/replace fusible link correctly, check system.

19. Does seat operate or attempt to operate under calibrate sequence.
Yes, go to 20.
No, go to 13, then 21.

20. Does seat move under manual electric control in all demanded directions? (pulsing or not pulsing to demanded position)?
Yes, go to 22.
No, go to 21.

21. Does seat switch move seat under manual electric control in all demanded directions, after replacing seat switch?
Yes, check system
No, go to 14 or check seat motor operation.

22. Observe non movement of seat in plane/s where seat did not go through full movement or stop at mid positions under calibrate routine.
Go to 23

23. Does manual electric seat movement in this plane pulse to position demanded?
Yes, go to 24.
No, check motor operation.

24. Are connections between gearbox sensor unit and ECU secure (and electrically sound)?
Yes, go to 25.
No, go to 26.

25. Does manual movement in this plane pulse in demanded direction after replacing gearbox sensor unit?
Yes, check 27.
No, check system

26. Secure connections, re-check 22. and 23.

27. See memory seat system continuity check.

Incorrect manual mirror operation or movement

28. Are 3 amp fuses under driver's seat inserted correctly and intact?
Yes, go to 29.
No, replace or reinsert fuse, check system.

29. Do mirrors work correctly under calibrate sequence (both mirrors going through full movement and stopping near mid position)?
Yes, go to 30.
No, go to 33, 37, and 41.

30. Is mirror switch assembly mounted in correct elevation in dash?
Yes, go to 31
No, mount mirror correctly.

31. Does L.H. mirror work correctly under manual control without pulsing to position?
Yes/No, go to 32.

32. Does R.H. mirror work correctly under manual control without pulsing to position?
Yes/No, go to 33.

33. Is same fault common to both L.H. and R.H. mirrors?
Yes, go to 34.
No, go to 37.

34. Is connection made from manual mirror switches to main harness?
    Yes, go to 35.
    No, re-make connection and check system.
35. Do mirrors work correctly after replacing mirror joystick?
    Yes, check system
    No, go to 36.
36. See continuity checks.
37. Are connections to mirror faulty? (check for pin backout on 5 way ESPA connector)?
    Yes, re-make connections and check system
    No, go to 38.
38. Does mirror function correctly upon replacing mirror?
    Yes, check system
    No, go to 39.
39. Does mirror still exhibit same fault after replacing mirror changeover switch?
    Yes, go to 41.
    No, check system
40. See continuity checks
41. Does mirror movement still pulse in demanded direction under manual mirror electric control?
    Yes, possible feed back from mirror missing, go to 40.
    No, check system
42. Does mirror move, pulsing in opposite direction to that demanded under manual mirror electric control?
    Yes, possible feedback short to vehicle ground, check 40, continuity to vehicle ground
    No, check system
43. Are mirror or mirrors still inoperative?
    Yes, go to 40.

Service checks

44. Do seats operate under manual control when driver's door is open?
    Yes, check system fully, go to 47.
    No, go to 45.
45. Is interior light on when driver's door is open?
    Yes, check 30 amp fuses, then go to 46.
    No, go to 48.
46. Does door switch have a tendency to stick in off position when opening door?
    Yes, replace switch, check system
    No, go to 48.
47. Do manual electric seats operate when door open, but NOT when either IGN or AUX are engaged and door closed?
    Yes, check fuse and seat relays, go to 53.
    No, check 48.
48. Are connections to door switch made, including fuse B2?
    Yes, check 49.
    No, make connections, check system.
49. Does door switch make a good electrical contact
    Yes, go to 53.
    No, replace switch, check system.
50. Does memory position recall function operate when park brake or park/neutral is not engaged?
    Yes, go to 53.
    No, is system OK?
51. Does memory position recall function operate when either park brake or park/neutral engaged?
    Yes, is system OK?
    No, go to 53.
52. Does speed signal inhibit memory recall function?
    Yes, is system OK?
    No, go to 53.
53. See memory seat system continuity check.

MEMORY SEAT SYSTEM CONTINUITY CHECK

Carry out the following checks as directed from the fault diagnosis chart.

Note that the checks should be carried out in conjunction with schematic diagrams RR3721M, RR3722M, and circuit diagram RR3684.

All tests are caried out with ECU disconnected. Note that tests state ignition key position, multi-meter set to volts or ohms.

RR3721M - Right hand drive

MEMORY SEAT SCHEMATIC WIRING DIAGRAM

These diagrams show wiring details from 10 way and 24 way connectors to mirror and driver's seat connections.

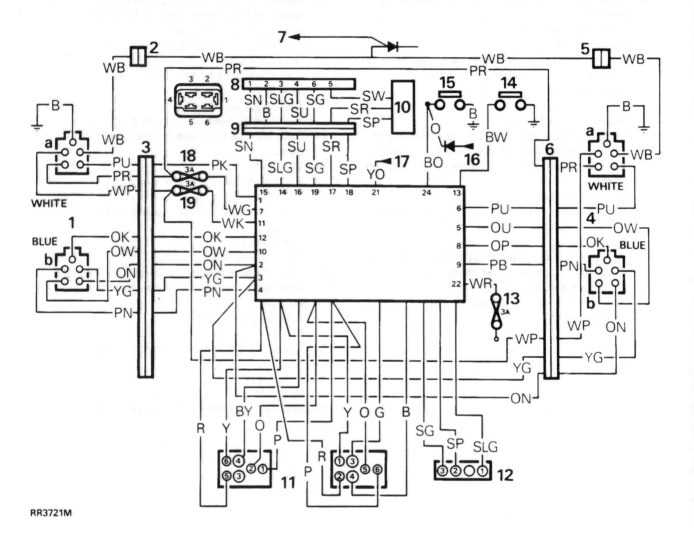

RR3721M

RR3722M - Left hand drive

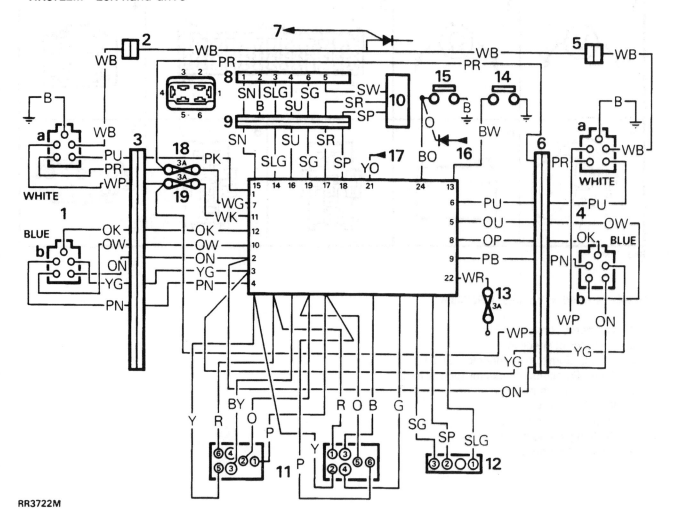

RR3722M

Key to RR3721M and RR3722M

1. Driver's mirror connectors, a) white, b) blue
2. 8 way connector, driver's door to main harness
3. 13 way connector, driver's door to main harness
4. Passenger's mirror connectors, a) white, b) blue
5. 8 way connector, passenger's door to main harness
6. 13 way connector, passenger's door to main harness
7. To heated rear screen switch
8. Mirror switch

9. Mirror/clock harness to main harness
10. Mirror cross over switch 11. Driver's seat switch connectors
12. Memory button connector
13. 3 amp fuse, permanent battery feed
14. Park brake switch
15. Park/neutral switch
16. EFI ECU
17. Signal from speed buffer
18. Fuse D3, 3 amp
19. Fuse D4, 3 amp

NOTE: Pin numbers 1 to 24 refer to 24 way Sumitomo connector.

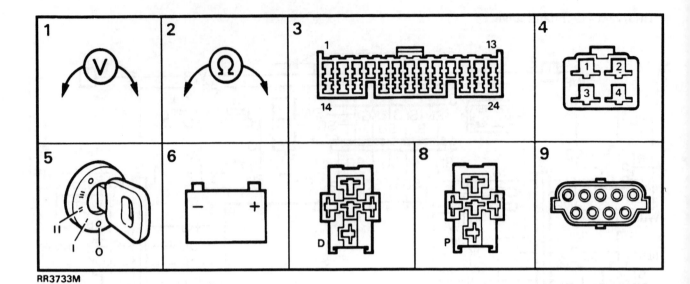

RR3733M

Symbols used in checks, RR3733M:

1. Voltmeter connection
2. Ohmeter connection
3. 24 way Sumitomo connector (ECU)
4. 4 way Sumitomo connector (power feed)
5. Ignition switch position
6. Vehicle battery
7. Driver's seat load relay
8. Passenger's seat load relay
9. Seat motor connector

CONTINUITY CHECK

1. a) Check park brake input voltage to ECU pin 13.
   b) Check park/neutral input voltage to ECU pin 24.

1

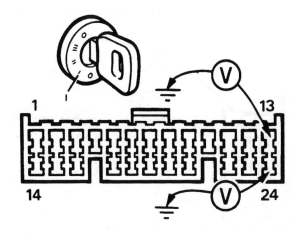

RR3734M

Correct result:
   a) Park brake applied, 0 volts. Park brake off.
   b) Park/neutral engaged, 0 volt. Not engaged, 5 volt.

2. a) Check resistance park brake input to ground.
   b) Check resistance park/neutral input to ground.

2

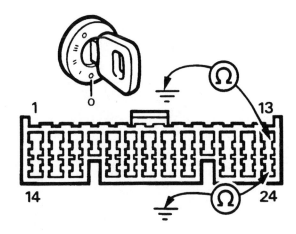

RR3735M

Correct result:
   a) Park brake applied short circuit. Not applied open circuit.
   b) Park/neutral engaged, short circuit. Not engaged, open circuit.

3. Check permanent battery feed to pin 22.

3

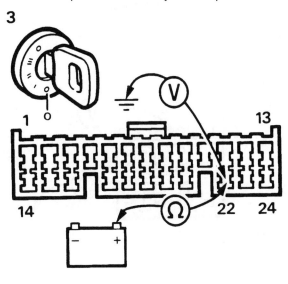

RR3736M

Correct result:
   Voltage, battery connected, 12 volt.
   Resistance, short circuit.

4. a) Check voltage at ECU enable feed, 4-way Sumitomo, pin 2 and 3.
   b) Check resistance at ECU enable feed, 4-way Sumitomo, pin 2 and ground.

4

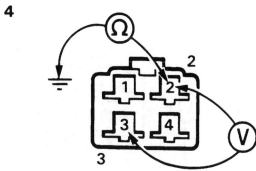

RR3737M

Correct result:
   a) Voltage 12 volt, driver's door open, ignition or auxiliary on.
   b) Resistance, short circuit.

5. a)   Check voltage at ECU power drive feed,
         4-way Sumitomo, pin 1 and 2.
   b)   Check resistance between pin 1 and
         battery negative terminal.

5

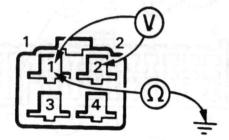

RR3738M

Correct result:
   a)   Voltage, 12 volt.
   b)   Resistance, short circuit. Readings only
         obtained with driver's door open or ignition
         on or auxiliary.

6. a)   Check voltage at ECU power drive feed,
         4-way Sumitomo, pin 3 and 4.
   b)   Check resistance between pin 3 and
         battery negative terminal.

6

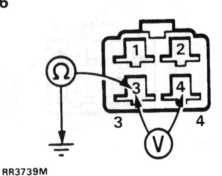

RR3739M

Correct result:
   a)   Voltage, 12 volt.
   b)   Resistance, short circuit. Readings only
         obtained with driver's door open or ignition
         on or auxiliary.

7. Check continuity to driver's seat load relay,
    tests carried out at relay base.
   a)   Check voltage, pin 87 to ground.
   b)   Check continuity, pin 87 to battery positive
         terminal. Readings only obtained with
         driver's door open, ignition or auxiliary on
         and relay inserted.
   c)   Check voltage, pin 30 to ground.
   d)   Check continuity, pin 30 to battery positive
         terminal.

7

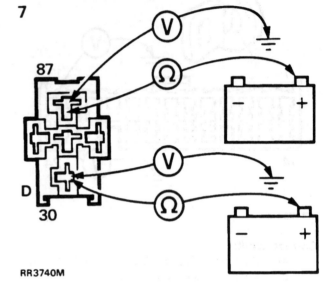

RR3740M

Correct result:
      a) and c) 12 volt, b) and d) short circuit.

8. Check continuity to driver's seat relay pin 85, relay inserted.
   System armed i.e. driver's door open or ignition or auxiliary on.

   a)   Check voltage pin 85 to ground.
   b)   Check resistance pin 85 to ground.

8

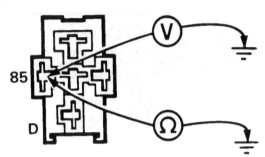

RR3741M

Correct result:
> a) 0 volt b) Short circuit.

> System not armed.
> c)   Check voltage, pin 85 to ground.
> d)   Check resistance.

Correct result:
> c) 12 volt, d) Open circuit.

9. Check continuity to driver's seat relay pin 86. System armed or disarmed.

   a)   Check voltage pin 86 to ground.
   b)   Check resistance pin 86 to battery positive.

9

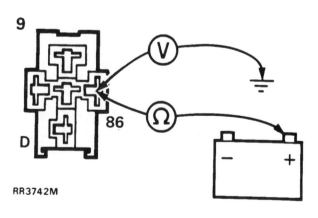

RR3742M

Correct result:
> a) 12 volt, b) Short circuit.

10. Check continuity to passenger's seat load relay, tests carried out at relay base.

   a)   Check voltage, pin 85 to ground.
   b)   Check continuity, pin 85 to ground.
   c)   Check voltage, pin 30 to ground.
   d)   Check continuity, pin 30 to ground.

10

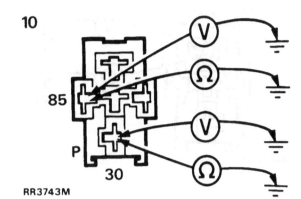

RR3743M

Correct result:
> a) and c) 0 volt, b) and d) short circuit.

11. Check continuity to passenger's seat relay pin 86.

   Driver's door open or shut, ignition or auxiliary on.
   a)   Check voltage pin 86 to ground.

11

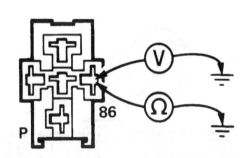

RR3744M

Correct result:
> a) 12 volt.

> Driver's door open or shut, ignition or auxiliary off.
> b)   Check voltage, pin 86 to ground.
> c)   Check resistance, pin 86 to ground.

Correct result:
> b) 0 volt c) 26.2 ohms.

12. Check continuity to passenger's seat relay pin 87.
    System not active.

    a)   Check voltage pin 87 to ground.

12

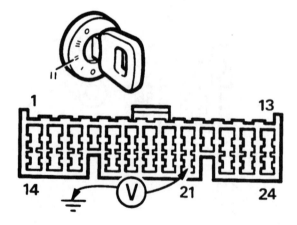

RR3745M

14. Seat motor resistance check. Disconnect blue motor harness connector, check resistance of each motor.

14

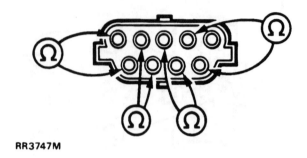

RR3747M

Correct result:
    a) 12 volt.

    Ignition or auxiliary on.
    b)   Check voltage pin 87 to ground.
    c)   Check continuity pin 87 to ground.

Correct result:
    b) 0 volt c) Short circuit.

13. Check input from speed buffer.

    Check voltage between pin 21, 24-way, and ground.

13

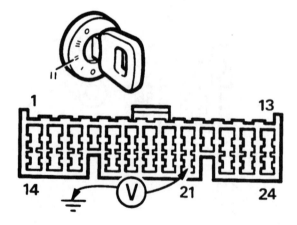

RR3746M

Correct result:
    Switching from 12 volt to 0 volt, 12 pulses per wheel revolution, as vehicle is pushed forward.

Correct result:
    1 to 0.7 ohm (not open circuit or closed circuit).

MEMORY SEAT SYSTEM REPAIRS

MEMORY SEAT FAILURE

NOTE: Carry out following procedure if seat failure occurs with seat obscuring fixing bolts.

1. Check 30A fuses and courtesy lamp fuse B2.
2. Disconnect 9 way connector between seat ECU and motors. Power motor from a seperate battery source.
3. If partial failure occurs in forward and reverse travel only, change drive cable as required to move seat to desired position.
4. If 2. and 3. not possible, move seat by driving cables manually.

DRIVER'S SEAT

Remove and refit

Removing

1. Remove two screws, remove side trim panel.
2. Remove four screws, remove front trim panel.
3. Remove three fixings, remove seat cushion side trim. Remove seat belt securing bolt.
4. Move seat to most rearward position. If seat will not move, see MEMORY SEAT FAILURE.
5. Remove two front fixings.
6. Move seat to most forward position.
7. Remove four rear fixings.
8. Disconnect battery negative terminal.
9. Release main cable clip, disconnect connections under seat including heated seat and seat belt audible warning.
10. Remove seat from vehicle.

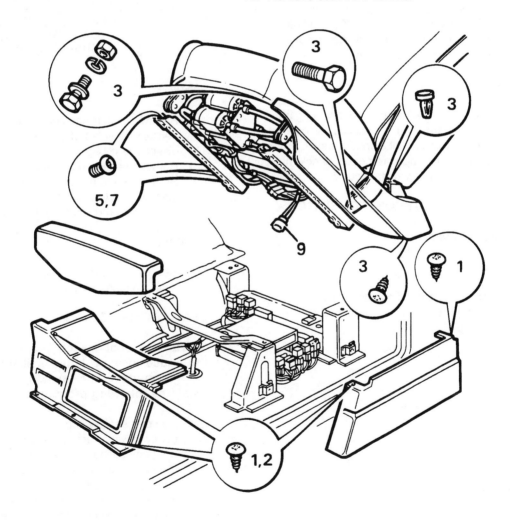

RR3749M

Refitting

11. Reverse removal instructions.
12. Arreange electrical leads beneath seat to ensure they do not become trapped by seat mechanism.

DRIVE CABLE

Remove and refit

Removing

1. Remove seat.
2. Cut cable tie, remove drive cable securing clips.
3. Remove drive cable from gearbox.
4. Remove drive cable from motor by unscrewing ferrule.
5. Cut cable ties from drive cable. Note position for reassembly.
6. Remove drive cable. If cable has failed, 'twist' may have occurred in seat. To rectify this, use a small screwdriver to turn gearbox of failed cable until twist is removed.

Refitting

8. Reverse removal procedure, ensuring new cable ties are fitted in original positions.
9. Operate seats to full extent of travel. To ensure that 'twist' has been removed, check that both gearboxes stop simultaneously.

SEAT ADJUSTMENT CONTROL SWITCH

Remove and refit

Removing

1. Disconnect battery negative lead.
2. Pry finger tip controls from top of switch housing.

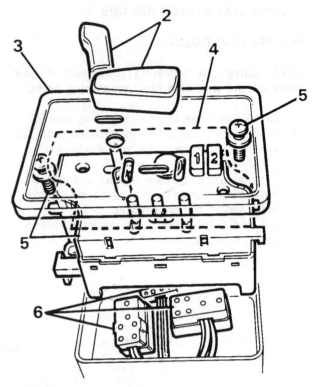

RR3762M

3. Remove switch housing cover by lightly depressing sides of switch housing to disengage clips.
4. Remove sealing diaphragm.
5. Remove switch securing screws, lift switch to gain access to multiplugs.
6. Disconnect multiplugs and remove switch.

Refitting

7. Reverse removal instructions, fitting a new sealing diaphragm.

SEAT SWITCH - CLEAN

NOTE: If a seat switch problem is diagnosed, the cause may be liquid spillage or ingress of foreign matter. The switch may be cleaned using the following procedure.

1. Remove seat switch, see seat adjustment control switch remove and refit.
2. Discard sealing membrane.
3. Clean affected area of switch using a slightly damp clean cloth.
4. If contamination still exists, clean switch using a clean cloth slightly dampened with methylated spirits.
5. Allow switch to dry completely.
6. Refit switch using a new membrane.
7. Check seat switch for satisfactory operation.

EXTERIOR MIRROR CONTROL SWITCHES

Remove and refit

Removing

1. Disconnect battery negative lead.
2. Remove air vent adjacent to switches.
3. Carefully pry button from mirror adjustment switch.

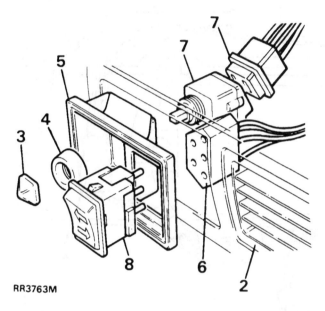

RR3763M

4. Unscrew locking ring from switch.
5. Withdraw switch retaining panel, noting position of adjustment switch in panel retaining clip.
6. Disconnect multiplug at rear of changeover switch, remove panel.
7. Disconnect multiplug to remove mirror adjustment switch.
8. Depress two spring clips and remove change over switch.

Refitting

9. Reverse operations 1 to 8.

NOTE: The mirror adjustment switch is located so that the multiplug connector is in the 12 o'clock position. (On non memory mirrors this connector is in the 9 o'clock position).

ELECTRONIC CONTROL UNIT (ECU)

Remove and refit

Removing

1. Remove driver's seat.
2. Disconnect connector from seat.

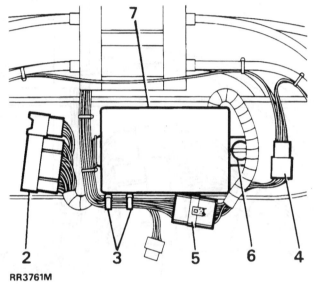

RR3761M

3. Remove cable ties.
4. Disconnect sensor and seat switch multiplug, remove from seat.
5. Disconnect seat motor multiplug.
6. Turn ECU retaining turnbuckle half a turn.
7. Remove ECU.

Refitting

8. Reverse removal procedure, ensuring cable retaining clips are correctly located, see UNDERSEAT HARNESS LAYOUT.
9. Initialise system, see CALIBRATION/INITIALISATION PROCEDURE.

UNDERSEAT HARNESS LAYOUT

**WARNING: To prevent damage to wiring under
driver's seat and subsequent failure, the wiring
must be installed as shown in RR3748M**

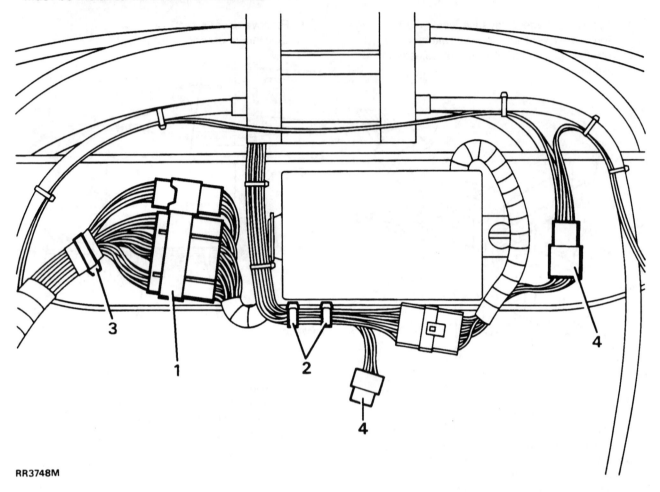

RR3748M

1. ECU link harness connector has retaining clip
   to seat base.
2. Link harness has two cable ties to seat motor
   harness, one if which is secured to seat base.
3. Main harness has P-clip securing it to seat
   base.
4. Sensor connector to link harness has retaining
   clip to seat base.

DIMMING REARVIEW MIRROR WITH MAPLIGHTS

Operation

The dimming mirror is supplied through fuse E6 when the ignition switch is in the I or II position. The mirror unit has two light sensors, one facing forward and one to the rear. The sensors monitor and compare the light intensity and lighten or darken the mirror accordingly. As the mirror darkens the green LED located to the left of the glare control, will become brighter, indicating that the mirror is operating. A slide control switch marked from OFF to MAX allows the driver to adjust the mirror glare to suit prevailing light conditions.

The mirrors which are different for left and right hand drive vehicles, can be identified by removing the right hand map reading light which will reveal a label indicating LH or RH steering.

The mirror and reverse lights circuits are interconnected, this ensures when vehicle is reversed the mirror clears.

The reverse lights are supplied by fuse E4 via the ignition load relay 4, which is energized through the ignition switch 3 and fuse B4.

Dimming mirrors have passenger and driver map reading lights which are supplied by fuse E6 and independently switched.

CAUTION: When parking vehicle overnight or for a prolonged period. Do not leave dimming mirror switch and ignition switch 'ON'

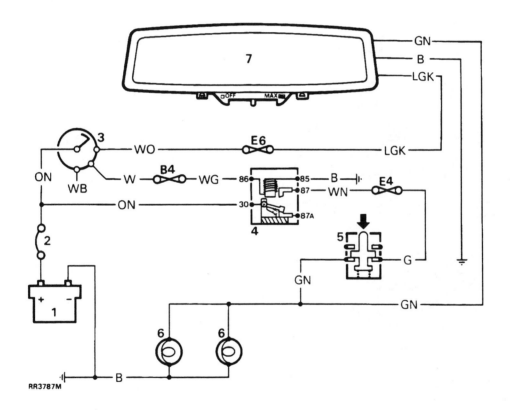

RR3787M

Circuit diagram including reverse lights

1. Battery
2. Fuse links
3. Ignition switch
4. Ignition load relay
5. Reverse light switch
6. Reverse lights
7. Mirror
B4. Fuse 10 amp
E6. Fuse 10 amp
E4. Fuse 20 amp

See section 86 electrical for fuse and relay location

Function test

To check mirror function:

1. Check that the mirror is the correct hand/type for the vehicle.
2. Switch ignition ON, select Park or Neutral gear.
3. Move mirror slide switch to MAX.
4. Mask front sensor, located on back of mirror assembly with black cloth. Providing light is hitting mirror glass it should slowly darken, and LED will illuminate
5. Remove masking, or select reverse gear, glass should now clear - and the LED will dim.
6. Repeat procedure using lower switch position to ensure correct operation.

Fault diagnosis

If mirror does not function repeat function test or refer to circuit diagram.

Map light bulb renewal.

1. Disconnect battery negative lead.

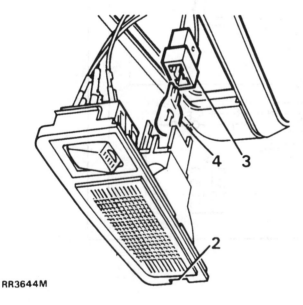

RR3644M

2. Pry slot to open cover.
3. Remove bulbholder.
4. Remove bulb from holder.
5. Replace bulb with 12v 5w capless.

Refit

6. Reverse removal instructions.

HEATED SEAT

Description

The front seat cushion and squab are fitted with heating elements bonded to the seat foams. They are connected by a two way connector located on the inboard side of the seat base.

They are protected from overheating by a thermostat located in the rear centre of the cushion pad.

The thermostat will open (switch off) when the surrounding foam reaches +36°C. It will not close (switch on) until temperaure falls to +26°C. Tolerance on both figures +3°C.

NOTE: It is essential to note that following initial use, vehicle interior temperature, duration of seat occupancy and trim material can greatly influence point at which seat foam cools sufficiently to allow subsequent heating cycles to occur.

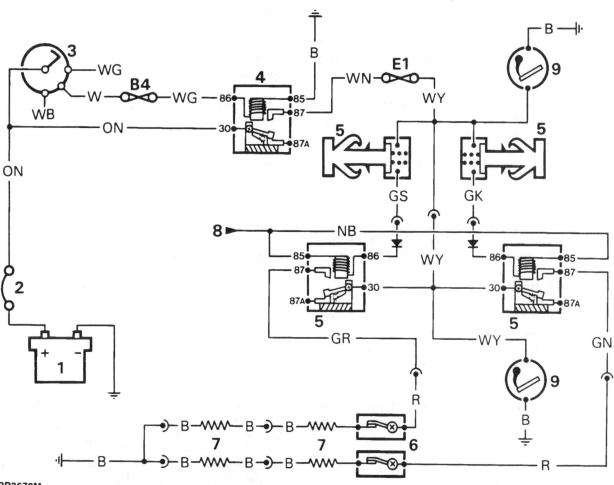

RR3678M

1. Battery
2. Fuse link
3. Ignition switch
4. Ignition load relay
5. Seat heater switches and relays
6. Thermostats
7. Seat heater elements
8. Earth connection via 'Load Shed' circuit
9. Cigar lighter elements

NOTE: Each thermostat is centrally located along cushion rear edge, under the cushion cover. Relay location is shown in section 86 electrical.

FRONT SEAT HEATED CUSHION AND SQUAB

Operation

Electrical heating elements fitted to a vehicle for what ever purpose, may in certain operating conditions cause a voltage drop in the power supply to more essential services.

So the seat heating circuit and the rear window demist circuit, are monitored and earthed by the 'Load Shed' circuit. The operation of the heated seat circuit should be studied in conjunction with the 'Load Shed' circuit.

Provided the overall electrical load is not causing a voltage drop, and seat cushion is below 26°C. The seat heater relays 5 earthed through load shed connection 8 allow relays 5 to operate and seat elements to be energized.

The cigar lighter element though supplied via the same fuse as the seat heaters, are not earthed or monitored by load shed circuit.

HEATED SEAT CONTINUITY CHECK

Initial check

Check for battery voltage at main two way heated seat connector, with ignition and heated seat switch on. Ensure all ancilliary equipment is switched off.

Thermostat check

Switch heated seats on, if seat element heats up, check thermostat opens, i.e. switches off.
To facilitate this a container of hot water should be placed on the seat, in area of thermostat. Allow time for heat to soak into seat base.

CAUTION: Care must be taken NOT to damage seat trim during the operation.

Check thermostat closes, i.e. switches on when cooled down. To facilitate cooling, apply an ice pack to seat in area of thermostat.

If heated seats do not work:

Check continuity of heating elements at main heated seat connector, correct resistance of approximately 1.6 Ohms.

Incorrect result i.e. open circuit indicates heating element or thermostat faulty.

Check continuity of squab and cushion circuits:

Check squab to cushion connector on inboard side of squab base. If connection correct check continuity of cushion circuit:

Disconnect squab to cushion connector.

Bridge connector to seat cushion, check continuity at main connector, correct resistance of approximately 1 Ohm.

Incorrect result i.e. open circuit indicates heating element or thermostat in cushion faulty.

Check seat squab element continuity cushion to squab connector, correct result aproximately 0.6 Ohms.

Incorrect result i.e. open circuit indicates heating element in squab faulty.

Remove heated cushion.

1. Remove front seat assembly, See front seat remove and refit.

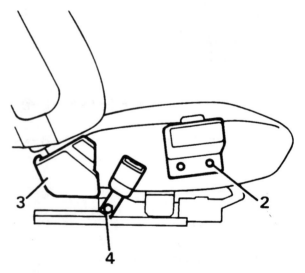

RR3645M

2. Remove two screws securing seat control adjustment unit.
3. Remove two screws securing corner trim.
4. Release seat belt buckle bracket.

Continue for removal of heated squab.

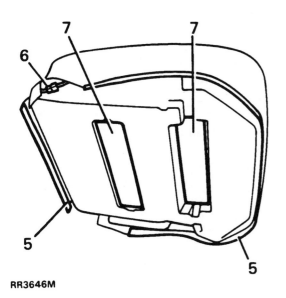

RR3646M

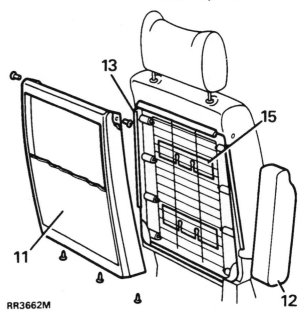

RR3662M

5. Release trim from seat frame.
6. Disconnect heater wiring at multiplug to seat squab. Remove cushion and trim from seat frame.
7. Turn 90° two seat trim retention plates and push through slot in cushion foam.

10. Remove headrest.
11. Remove squab panel rear. Three screws at base. Peel back trim to remove screw from each top corner.
12. Remove armrest assembly.
13. Release trim from edge of seat frame.
14. Remove squab foam with trim from seat frame.
15. Turn 90° two trim retention plates and push through slot in foam.
16. Fold trim over squab foam to reveal two wire retention rods.

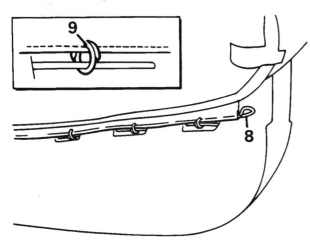

RR3647M

8. Fold seat trim over cushion to reveal stapled wire retention rods.
9. Pry open staples and release seat trim from seat cushion.

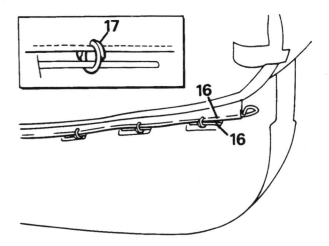

RR3663M

17. Pry open staples and release trim from squab cushion.

Refit

18. Reverse removal instructions.

A1	A2	A3	A4	A5	A6	A7	A8	A9

B1	B2	B3	B4	B5	B6	B7	B8	B9

C1	C2	C3	C4	C5	C6	C7	C8	C9

RR3780M

FUSE BOX - RR3780

Fuse No.	Colour Code	Fuse Value	Key Position	Function
A1	Red	10A	'II'	LH headlamp dipped beam.
A2	Red	10A	'II'	LH headlamp main beam, front auxiliary lamps relay, main beam warning lamp (LH STG).
A3	Red	10A	'O'	LH sidelamps & numberplate lights.
A4	Red	10A	'O'	Rear fog lamps.
A5	Red	10A	'II'	Direction indicators.
A6	Yellow	20A	'II'	Front auxiliary lamps*, dim-dip*(UK only).
A7	Red	10A	'O'	RH sidelamps.
A8	Red	10A	'II'	RH main beam, main beam warning lamp (RH STG).
A9	Red	10A	'II'	RH dip beam.
B1	Red	10A	'II'	Stop lamps.
B2	Blue	15A	'O'	Interior lamps, clock, underbonnet lamp, electric seat relays*, CD player*, radio memory, door edge lamps, heated door locks.
B3	Yellow	20A	'O'	Hazard switch, horns, headlamp flash.
B4	Red	10A	'II'	Instrument pack, ignition relay, speed signal unit, reverse lamps.
B5	Yellow	20A	'II'	Electric sunroof*.
B6	Yellow	20A	'II'	Headlamp wash pump.
B7	Red	10A	'II'	Air conditioning compressor*.
B8	Yellow	20A	'II'	Air conditioning radiator fan*.
B9	Yellow	20A	'II'	Air conditioning radiator fan*.
C1	Green	30A	'II'	Heated rear window (Voltage sensitive).
C2	Green	30A	'II'	Rear window lifts* (4-door).
C3	Red	10A	'II'	Petrol:- ignition coil. Diesel:- fuel shut-off solenoid and glowplug timer.
C4	Yellow	20A	'II'	*Petrol injection unit, petrol pump relay. *Fuel heater (diesel).
C5	Yellow	20A	'II'	Front wash/wipe.
C6	Red	10A	'O'-'I'	Fuel flap release.
C7	Blue	15A	'O'	Central locking, voltage-sensitive switch, alarm .
C8	Green	30A	'II'	Front window lifts.
C9	Green	30A	'II'	Heating and air-conditioning unit*.

* Where applicable

Auxiliary fuse box (D)
- Fig. RR3781

An auxiliary fusebox for the electrically-operated seats and memory drivers seat and mirrors is located inside the rear of the driver's seat base. Access to the fusebox is improved if the seat can be moved fully forward.

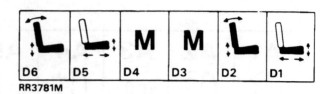

RR3781M

Access to the fuses is by lifting off the top cover of the fusebox. Fuse D1 is at the inboard end of the box.

Fuse No	Colour Code	Fuse Value	Function
D1	**Green**	30 amp	Passenger's seat base/height front
D2	**Green**	30 amp	Passenger's seat recline/height rear
D3	**Violet**	3 amp	Mirror motors (memory)
D4	**Violet**	3 amp	Mirror motors (memory)
D5	**Green**	30 amp	Driver's seat base/height front
D6	**Green**	30 amp	Driver's seat recline/height rear

Clipped to fusebox:

D7	**Violet**	3 amp	Memory maintenance

Auxiliary fusebox (E) - Fig. RR3782

Located inside the rear of the front passenger seat base, this fusebox is more easily accessible if the seat can be moved fully forward.
Access to the fuses is by lifting off the top cover of the fusebox. Fuse E1 is at the inboard end of the box.

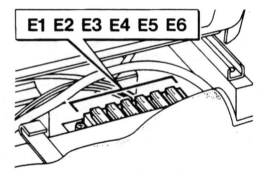

RR3782M

Fuse No.	Colour Code	Fuse Value	Key Position	Function
E1	Yellow	20A	'II'	Seat heaters* (voltage sensitive), cigar lighters.
E2	Red	10A	'II'	Door mirrors, cruise control*, emission maintenance reminder*(Canada), central locking unit, Alarm.
E3	Red	10A	'II'	Heated rear window switch, mirror switch, mirror heaters, split charge*, rear wash/wipe, heater relay, sunroof relay*, load shedding relay.
E4	Yellow	20A	'II'	Heated jets, front heated screen timer*, airconditioning*, low oil and low coolant warning lamps*, interior lamp delay unit, auto-transmission graphics illumination, overspeed warning* (Gulf).
E5	Red	10A	'I'	Power amplifier* (Canada).
E6	Red	10A	'I'	Seat relays*, window lift relays, aerial amplifier, radio, auto dimming mirror* and map lamps*.

* Where Applicable

Miscellaneous fuses under front right seat -

One 10A Red	- Fuel pump (Petrol only)
One 20A Yellow	- EFI

Fuses on steering column reinforcing bracket -

Two 30A Green	- Heated front screen
One 10A Red	- Warning light bulb check relay (right hand drive only) or glow plug timer unit (diesel)

RELAYS

Right hand steering

Closure panel viewed from engine bay, protective cover removed

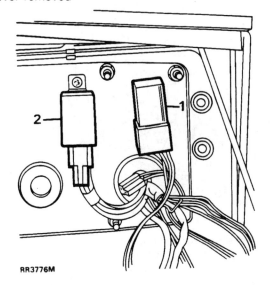

RR3776M

Relay

1. Headlamp wash timer unit
2. Glow plug timer unit (Diesel)

Relays mounted in right hand side footwell

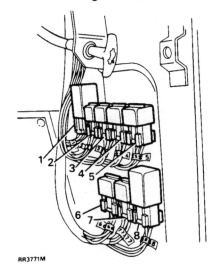

RR3771M

Relay, Colour - relay, base

1. Speed buffer, White, White
2. Diesel heater, Yellow, Yellow
3. Sunroof, Yellow, Yellow
4. Brake check (Australia), Yellow, Yellow
5. Auxiliary lamps, Yellow, Yellow
6. Cruise control, Green, Green
7. Load shed, Yellow, Yellow
8. Heated front screen timer, Grey, White

Relays mounted in left hand side footwell

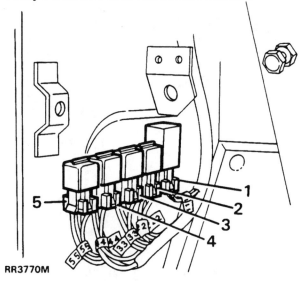

RR3770M

1. Air con. diode unit, Orange, Red
2. Heater/air con. changeover, Green, Green
3. Air con. clutch, Yellow, Yellow
4. Air con. fan, Yellow, Yellow
5. Heater/air con. Yellow, Yellow

Steering column mounted relays Right hand steering

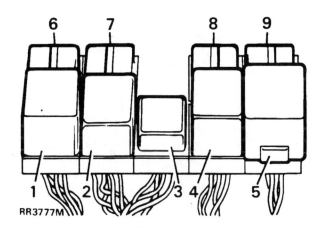

RR3777M

Relays shown with lower dash panel removed.

NOTE: Relay bases are black with a coloured top corresponding to relay colours.

1. Rear wipe delay, Blue, Blue
2. Front wipe delay, Red, Red
3. Heated front screen, Black, Black
4. Interior lamps, Black, Black
5. Voltage sensitive switch, Yellow, Yellow
6. Starter motor, Yellow, Yellow
7. Heated rear screen, Yellow, Yellow
8. Headlamp relay, Yellow, Yellow
9. Ignition load relay, Green, Green
10. Flasher unit, Black, Blue

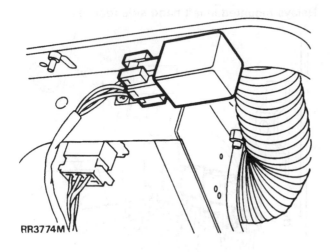

RR3774M

RR3774M shows flasher unit mounted on steering column support bracket.

Left hand steering

Closure panel viewed from engine bay, protective cover removed

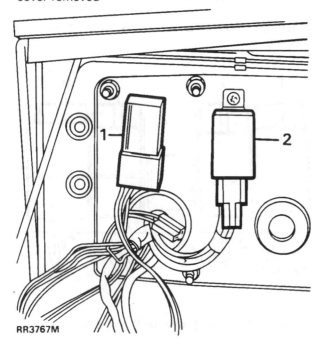

RR3767M

Relay - Colour, relay, base

1. Headlamp wash timer, Black, Black
2. Glow plug timer (Diesel), Black, Black

Relays mounted in left hand side footwell

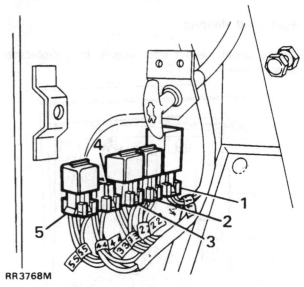

RR3768M

1. Speed buffer, White, White
2. Diesel, Yellow, Yellow
3. Sunroof, Yellow, Yellow
4. Not used
5. Auxiliary lamps, Yellow, Yellow

Relays mounted in right hand side footwell

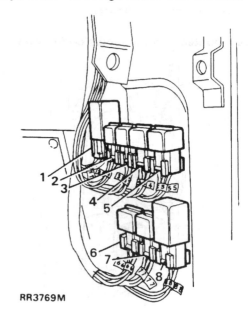

RR3769M

1. Air con. diode unit, Orange, Red
2. Heater/air con. changeover, Green, Green
3. Air con. clutch, Yellow, Yellow
4. Air con. fan, Yellow, Yellow
5. Heater/air con. Yellow, Yellow
6. Cruise control, Green, Green
7. Load shed, Yellow, Yellow
8. Heated front screen timer, Grey, White

Steering column mounted relays Left hand steering

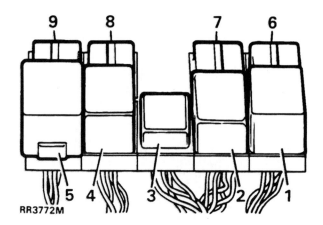

RR3772M

Relays shown with lower dash panel removed.

NOTE: Relay bases are black with a coloured top corresponding to relay colours.

1. Rear wipe delay, Blue, Blue
2. Front wipe delay, Red, Red
3. Heated front screen, Black, Black
4. Interior lamps, Black, Black
5. Voltage sensitive switch, Yellow, Yellow
6. Starter motor, Yellow, Yellow
7. Heated rear screen, Yellow, Yellow
8. Headlamp relay, Yellow, Yellow
9. Ignition load relay, Green, Green

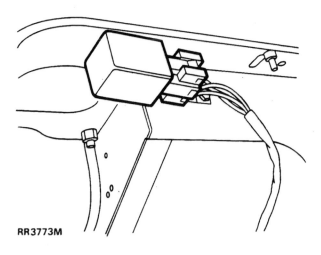

RR3773M

RR3773M shows flasher unit mounted on steering column support bracket.

Glove box and under seat mounted relays.

Relays mounted inside glove box, accessible by removing glove box liner.

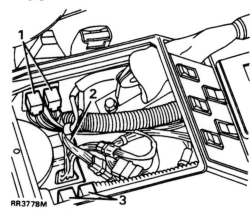

RR3778M

1. Window lift relays, yellow, yellow
2. Window lift control unit
3. Heated seat relays, yellow, yellow

Relays mounted under front seats

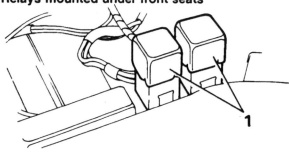

RR3784M

1. Seat adjust relays (2) underneath left hand front seat - L.H. steering

Relays underneath right hand front seat

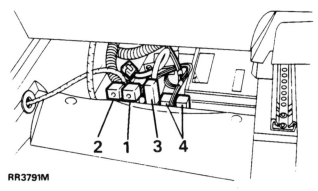

RR3791M

1. EFI, black base
2. Fuel pump, blue base
3. Condenser fan timer
4. Seat adjust relays RH steering only

RANGE ROVER

**RANGE ROVER
1993 MODEL YEAR**

WORKSHOP MANUAL SUPPLEMENT

Publication Number LSM 180 EN WS 11

1993 Model Year Supplement

Published by the
Technical Communication Department of

CONTENTS

01 - INTRODUCTION

CONTENTS

Page

INFORMATION

INTRODUCTION

Range Rover LSE

An important addition to the model range is the long wheelbase (108 inch) Range Rover LSE. A new 4.2 litre V8 engine is fitted to this vehicle.

1993 model year

In line with its policy of continual vehicle improvement, Land Rover has introduced a number of vehicle enhancements for 1993 model year Range Rovers.

Specification of individual vehicles may vary, but all models will include some of the new features summarised below:

- Electronic air suspension giving improved ride quality, automatic self levelling and varying height settings.

- Electronic traction control, giving improved traction when one rear wheel spins while the other has good grip.

- 3.9 litre high compression engine available with catalytic converters.

- Improved in car entertainment, three specification levels including new head units, CD player, speakers and sub-woofer.

- Cruise control system improvements, now available on manual vehicles.

- Electrical improvements - "One shot" window extended to passenger door. After switching off ignition a modified controller will give roof and window closing for 45 secs. Inhibited if door is opened and closed. A new 100 amp alternator is also used where required.

This workshop manual supplement includes service and repair information for the new features. It should be used in conjunction with the existing Workshop Manual LSM 180ENWM.

LOCATION OF IDENTIFICATION NUMBERS

Engine serial number - V8 engine

Stamped on a cast pad on the cylinder block, between numbers 3 and 5 cylinders.

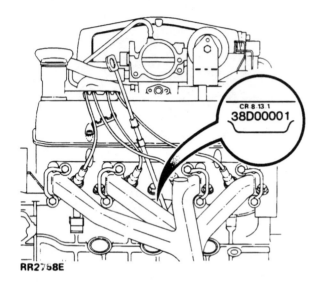

RR2758E

3.9 Litre: Engines are identified by the prefix:

35D. - 9.35:1 compression, manual transmission
36D. - 9.35:1 compression, automatic transmission
37D. - 8.13:1 compression, manual transmission
38D. - 8.13:1 compression, automatic transmission
40D. - 8.94.1 compression, automatic transmission

Main gearbox LT77 - 5 speed

Stamped on a cast pad on the bottom right hand side of the gearbox.

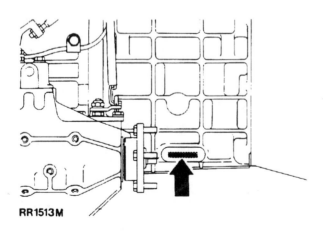

RR1513M

Automatic gearbox ZF4HP22

Stamped on a plate riveted to the bottom left hand side of the gearbox casing.

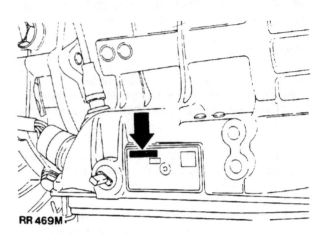

RR 469M

Transfer gearbox-Borg Warner

Stamped on a plate attached to the gearbox casing, between filler/level and drain plug.

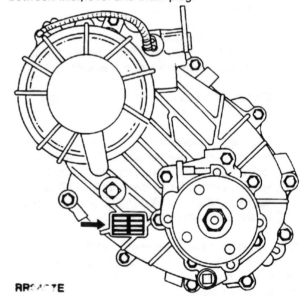

RR〰〰7E

Front and rear axle

Stamped on the top of the left hand axle tubes.

Vehicle identification number (VIN)

Stamped on right hand side of chassis ahead of rear
wheel.

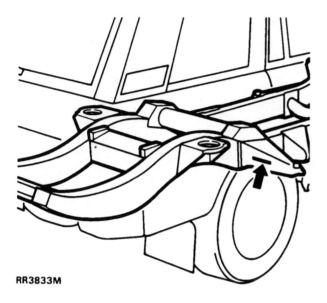

RR3833M

Vehicle identification number (VIN)

Stamped on right hand side of chassis ahead of rear wheel.

INTRODUCTION

04 - GENERAL SPECIFICATION DATA

CONTENTS

Page

INFORMATION

CONTENTS

ENGINE 4.2 V8

Type	V8
Number of cylinders	Eight, two banks of four
Bore	94.00 mm
Stroke	77.00 mm
Capacity	4275 cc
Valve operation	Overhead by push-rod
Compression ratio	8.94:1
Maximum power	149kW at 4850 rev/min

Crankshaft

Main journal diameter....................................	58.409-58.422 mm
Minimum regrind diameter	57.393-57.406 mm
Crankpin journal diameter	50.800-50.812 mm
Minimum regrind diameter	49.784-49.797 mm
Crankshaft end thrust/(end float)	Taken on thrust washers of centre main bearing 0.10-0.20 mm

Main bearings

Number and type	5, Vandervell shells
Material	Lead-indium
Diametrical clearance....................................	0.010-0.048 mm
Undersize bearing shells	0.254 mm, 0.508 mm

Connecting rods

Type	Horizontally split big-end, plain small-end
Length between centres	143.81-143.71 mm

Big-end bearings

Type and material	Vandervell VP lead-indium
Diametrical clearance....................................	0.015-0.055 mm
End-float crankpin	0.15-0.36mm
Undersize bearing shells	0.254 mm, 0.508 mm

Piston pins

Diameter	22.215-22.220 mm
Fit-in connecting rod	Press fit
Clearance in piston	0.002-0.007 mm

Pistons

Clearance in bore, measured at bottom
of skirt at right angles to piston pin .... 0.018-0.041 mm

Piston rings

Number of compression rings 2
Number of control rings 1
No 1 compression ring .... Molybdenum barrel faced
No 2 compression ring .... Tapered and marked 'T' or 'TOP'
Width of compression rings .... 1.478-1.49 mm
Compression ring gap .... 0.40-0.65 mm
Oil control ring type .... Hepworth and Grandage
Oil control ring width .... 3.0 mm
Oil control ring rail gap .... 0.38-1.40 mm

Camshaft

Location .... Central
Bearings .... Non serviceable
Number of bearings 5
Drive .... Chain 9.52 mm pitch x 54 pitches.

Tappets .... Hydraulic-self-adjusting

Valves

Length:	Inlet	116.59-117.35 mm
	Exhaust	116.59-117.35 mm
Seat angle:	Inlet	45° to 45 1/2°
	Exhaust	45° to 45 1/2°
Head diameter:	Inlet	39.75-40.00 mm
	Exhaust	34.226-34.480 mm
Stem diameter:	Inlet	8.664-8.679 mm
	Exhaust	8.651-8.666 mm
Stem to guide clearance:	Inlet	0.025-0.066 mm
	Exhaust	0.038-0.078 mm
Valve lift (Inlet and Exhaust)...		9.49 mm
Valve spring length fitted		40.4 mm at pressure of 29.5 kg

Lubrication

System type.. Wet sump, pressure fed
Oil pump type .... Gear
Oil pressure .... 2.11 to 2.81 kg/cm^2 (30 to 40 p.s.i) at 2400 rev/min
with engine warm
Oil filter-internal... Wire screen, pump intake filter in sump
Oil filter-external .... Full flow, self-contained cartridge

VEHICLE WEIGHTS AND PAYLOAD

When loading a vehicle to its maximum (Gross Vehicle Weight), consideration must be taken of the vehicle kerb weight and the distribution of the payload to ensure that axle loadings do not exceed the permitted maximum values. It is the customer's responsibility to limit the vehicle's payload in an appropriate manner such that neither maximum axle loads nor Gross Vehicle Weight are exceeded.

Petrol-engined models		Front Axle kg	Rear Axle kg	Total kg
Manual				
2 door	EEC Kerb weight	955	969	1924
	Gross Vehicle Weight*	1100	1510	2510
4 door	EEC Kerb weight	967	993	1960
	Gross Vehicle Weight*	1100	1510	2510
Catalytic model	EEC Kerb weight	973	994	1967
	Gross Vehicle Weight*	1100	1510	2510
Automatic				
2 door	EEC Kerb weight	982	973	1955
	Gross Vehicle Weight*	1100	1510	2510
4 door	EEC Kerb weight	983	1021	2004
	Gross Vehicle Weight*	1100	1510	2510
Catalytic model	EEC Kerb weight	989	1022	2011
	Gross Vehicle Weight*	1100	1510	2510
Long wheelbase models	EEC Kerb weight	1070	1080	2150
	Gross Vehicle Weight*	1200	1620	2620

⚠ **NOTE: EEC KERB WEIGHT is the minimum vehicle specification, plus full fuel tank and 75 kg driver. GROSS VEHICLE WEIGHT is the maximum all-up weight of the vehicle including driver, passengers, and equipment. This figure is liable to vary according to legal requirements in certain countries.**

When **air conditioning** is fitted, 42 kg must be added to the above front axle weights and total weights.

VEHICLE DIMENSIONS

Overall length 4.45m
   - Long wheelbase vehicles 4.65m
Overall width 1.82m
Overall height 1.80m
Wheelbase 2.54m
   - Long wheelbase vehicles 2.74m
Track: front and rear 1.49m
Ground clearance: under differential 190mm
Turning circle 11.89m
   - Long wheelbase vehicles 13.64m
Loading height 749mm
Maximum cargo height 1.028m
Rear opening height 0.87m
Usable luggage capacity, rear seat folded 2.00m³
Usable luggage capacity, rear seat in use
   - four door vehicles 1.03m³
   - two door vehicles 1.17m³
Maximum roof rack load .... 75 kg

TYRE PRESSURES

Pressures: Check with tyres cold	Normal on and off-road use. All speeds and loads		Off-road 'emergency' soft use maximum speed of 40 kph (25 mph)	
	Front	Rear (*)	Front	Rear
bars	1.9	2.4 (2.6)	1.2	1.8
lbf/in²	28	35 (3.8)	17	25
kgf/cm²	2.0	2.5 (2.7)	1.2	1.8

(*) Long wheelbase vehicles (108")

The pressure of tyres must be increased be 2.8 bars (3 lbf in² 0.2 kgf/cm²). For use with sustained driving speeds above 160 km/hr (100 miles/hour) or with heavy axle loads.
Normal operating pressures should be restored as soon as reasonable road conditions or hard ground is reached.
After any usage off the road, tyres and wheels should be inspected for damage particularly if high cruising speeds are subsequently to be used.

Towing: When the vehicle is used for towing, the reduced rear tyre pressures for extra ride comfort are not applicable.

 WARNING: Vehicles fitted with tubeless alloy road wheels as original equipment, note that these wheels DO NOT accept inner tubes and tubed tyres MUST NOT be fitted.

05 - ENGINE TUNING DATA

CONTENTS

Page

INFORMATION

ENGINE 3.9 V8

⚠ **NOTE: A high compression catalyst engine is available for 1993 model year**

Type .... 3.9 Litre V8

Firing order 1-8-4-3-6-5-7-2

Cylinder Numbers
Left bank 1-3-5-7
Right bank 2-4-6-8

No 1 Cylinder location .... Pulley end of left bank

Timing marks .... On crankshaft vibration damper

Spark plugs
Make/type(8.13:1 Compression) .... Champion RN12YC
Gap .... 0.84-0.96mm (0.033-0.038 in)
Make/type(9.35:1 Compression) .... Champion RN9YC
Gap .... 0.84-0.96mm (0.033-0.038 in)

Coil
Make/type .... Bosch 0-221-122-392, (ETC 6574)

Compression ratio .... 8.13:1 or 9.35:1

Fuel injection system .... Lucas 14 CUX Hot-wire air flow sensor system electronically controlled

Valve Timing	Inlet	Exhaust
Opens	32° BTDC	70° BBDC
Closes	73° ABDC	35° ATDC
Duration	285°	285°
Valve peak	104° ATDC	114° BTDC

Idle speed - controlled by EFI system
- all loads off in neutral .... 672 to 728 rev/min
- auto gearbox in gear, air con operating .... 650±28 rev/min
- auto gearbox in gear, air con off .... 600±28 rev/min
- manual gearbox .... 700±28 rev/min
- manual gearbox, air con operating .... 750±28 rev/min

Base idle speed .... See setting procedure - 525 ± 25 rev/min.

Ignition Timing - dynamic at 800 rev/min max, vacuum disconnected
8.13:1 compression, non catalyst .... 2° BTDC ± 1°
8.13:1 catalyst .... 6° BTDC ± 1°
9.35:1 compression, non catalyst .... 4° BTDC ± 1°
9.35:1 compression, catalyst .... 5° BTDC ± 1°

Exhaust gas
CO content at idle .... 0.5 to 1.0% max.

Distributor

Make/type .... Lucas 35DLM8 electronic
Rotation .... Clockwise
Air gap 0.20-0.35mm

Part number	Lucas	Rover
8.13:1, non catalyst	42518A	ERR 1250
8.13:1, catalyst	42648	ETC 6268
9.35:1, non catalyst	42510A	ERR 0744
9.35:1, catalyst	42543A	ERR 2986

Centrifugal Advance
Decelerating check-vacuum hose disconnected
Distributor rpm decelerating speeds

8.13:1 non catalyst

2000	Distributor advance	5° 30' to 8° 30'
1400		6° 18' to 8° 30'
800		2° to 4°

8.13:1 catalyst

1600 - 2300	Distributor advance	8° 54' to 11°
1400		8° 36' to 10° 36'
600		1° 18' to 3° 18'

9.35:1 non catalyst

2200	Distributor advance	7° to 10°
1400		7° 48' to 10°
650		1° to 3°

9.35:1 catalyst

2200	Distributor advance	5° 30' to 8° 30'
1400		6° 18' to 8° 30'
800		2° to 4°

Fuel

8.13:1, non catalyst .... 91 RON minimum unleaded
8.13:1, catalyst .... 95 RON minimum unleaded
9.35:1, non catalyst .... 95 RON minimum unleaded
9.35:1, catalyst .... 95 RON minimum unleaded
USA vehicles .... CLC or AKI 90 octane minimum

Australian market variations

Fuel .... 91 RON minimum
Compression ratio 8.13:1
Spark plug .... Champion RN12YC
Spark plug gap .... 0.84-0.96mm (0.033-0.038 in)
Ignition Timing at 800 rev/min max
(vacuum pipe disconnected) .... 2° BTDC ± 1°
Exhaust gas idle CO .... 1% max (hot)

ENGINE 4.2 V8

Type .... 4.2 Litre V8

Firing order 1-8-4-3-6-5-7-2

Cylinder Numbers
Left bank 1-3-5-7
Right bank 2-4-6-8

No 1 Cylinder location .... Pulley end of left bank

Timing marks .... On crankshaft vibration damper

Spark plugs
Make/type .... Champion RN11YCC
Gap .... 0.84-0.96mm (0.033-0.038 in)

Coil
Make/type .... Bosch 0-221-122-392, (ETC 6574)

Compression ratio 8.94:1

Fuel injection system .... Lucas 14 CUX Hot-wire air flow sensor system
electronically controlled

Valve Timing	Inlet	Exhaust
Opens	28° BTDC	72° BBDC
Closes	64° ABDC	20° ATDC
Duration	272°	272°
Valve peak	108° ATDC	116° BTDC

Idle speed - controlled by EFI system
- all loads off in neutral .... 672 to 728 rev/min
-auto gearbox in gear, air con operating............. 650±28 rev/min
-auto gearbox in gear, air con off .... 600±28 rev/min
-manual gearbox .... 700±28 rev/min
-manual gearbox, air con operating .... 750±28 rev/min

Base idle speed .... See setting procedure - 525 ± 25 rev/min.

**Ignition Timing - dynamic at 800 rev/min max,
vacuum disconnected**
8.94:1, catalyst .... 8° BTDC ± 1°

Exhaust gas
CO content at idle.. 0.5 to 1.0% max.

Distributor

Make/type .... Lucas 35DLM8 electronic
Rotation .... Clockwise
Air gap 0.20-0.35mm

Part number	Lucas	Rover
8.94:1, catalyst	42510A	ERR 0744

Centrifugal Advance
Decelerating check-vacuum hose disconnected
Distributor rpm decelerating speeds

8.94:1 catalyst

2200	Distributor advance	7° to 10°
1400		7° 48' to 10°
800		1° to 3°

Fuel

8.94:1, catalyst .... 95 RON minimum unleaded
USA vehicles .... CLC or AKI 90 octane minimum

10 - MAINTENANCE

CONTENTS

Page

MAINTENANCE

CONTENTS

Page

MAINTENANCE

ALTERNATOR AND STEERING PUMP DRIVE BELTS.

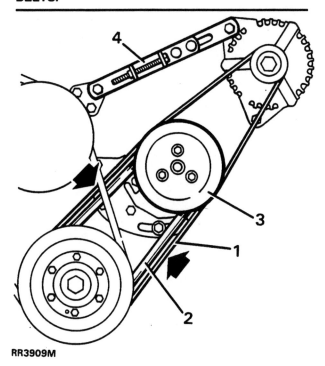

RR3909M

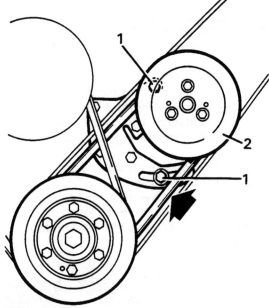

RR3910M

1. Alternator drive belt
2. Steering pump drive belt
3. Steering pump and guide pulley
4. Alternator drive belt tensioner

A new alternator drive belt is used, driven from the crankshaft pulley. A guide pulley on the power steering pump guides the belt in this area. Alternator and power steering belts have individual adjustment, but PAS belt must be adjusted before alternator belt.

STEERING PUMP DRIVE BELT

Adjust

 NOTE: Loosen alternator drive belt to facilitate accurate adjustment of the PAS drive belt.

1. Loosen steering pump adjuster bolt and pivot nuts.
2. Ensure pump is free to rotate on mounting. **DO NOT** lever pump, loosen fixings further if necessary.

3. Carefully lever against pump bracket to tension belt. On left hand drive models, where access is restricted, a lever with one end cranked at 5° to 10°, may be fed down between water pump and distributor. Place lever against steering pump bracket, carefully levering from water pump/front cover.

 CAUTION: DO NOT lever against steering pump casing. Damage to casing may result in oil leaks.

4. Check tension using a recognised belt tensioning gauge.

   Belt tension using a Clavis gauge:
   - 142 - 152 Hz.

When checked with normal hand pressure at the mid-point of the longest span, the belt should deflect 0,5 mm per 25 mm of belt run between pulley centres.

5. Tighten steering pump fixings.
6. Recheck belt tension
7. Adjust alternator belt, *see alternator drive belt.*

 CAUTION: When fitting a new drive belt, tension belt as described above. Reconnect battery and start and run engine for 3 to 5 minutes at fast idle, after which time belt must be re-checked, re-tension belt if necessary.

ALTERNATOR DRIVE BELT

Adjust

⚠ **NOTE: The steering pump pulley is used as a guide pulley for the alternator belt. Adjust steering belt before adjusting alternator belt,** *see steering pump drive belt.*

1. Loosen alternator pivot bolt and bolt securing alternator to tensioner.
2. Loosen two tensioner nuts and bolt securing tensioner to water pump bracket.
3. Rotate tensioner lead screw clockwise to tension belt.

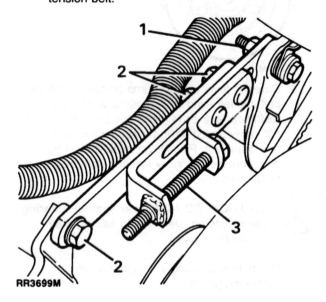

RR3699M

4. heck tension using a recognised belt tensioning gauge applied midway between crank and slider pulley.

   Belt tension using a Clavis gauge:
   - 152 - 158 Hz.

When checked with normal hand pressure at the mid-point of the longest span, the belt should deflect 0,5 mm per 25 mm of belt run between pulley centres.

5. Tighten alternator fixings.
6. Recheck belt tension.

⚠ **CAUTION: When fitting a new drive belt, tension belt as described above. Reconnect battery and start and run engine for 3 to 5 minutes at fast idle, after which time belt must be re-checked, re-tension belt if necessary.**

17 - EMISSION CONTROL

CONTENTS

Page

REPAIR

Charcoal canister 93 Model Year

Remove

1. Disconnect battery negative lead.
2. Pry out purge valve.
3. Disconnect pipe.
4. Loosen bolt.
5. Remove charcoal canister.

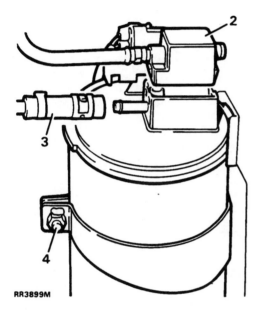

RR3899M

Refit

6. Reverse removal procedure.

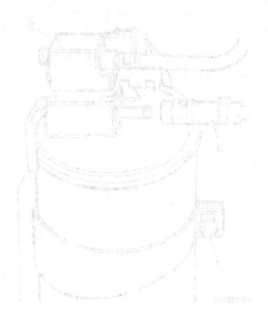

19 - FUEL SYSTEM

CONTENTS

Page

DESCRIPTION AND OPERATION

FAULT DIAGNOSIS

REPAIR

CRUISE CONTROL SYSTEM-HELLA GR66

Description

The cruise control system consists of electro-mechanical devices, and comprises of the following components. A 1993 model year introduction is the inclusion of cruise control on manual vehicles.

Electronic control unit (ECU)

The electronic control unit is located behind the lower dash panel. The microprocessor based E.C.U. evaluates the signals provided by the driver controls, brake pedal switch, clutch pedal switch on 1993 manual models, and the road speed transducer. The ECU activates the vacuum pump as required. The E.C.U. also has a memory function for set speed storage.

Driver operated switches

The main cruise control switch is located in the auxiliary switch panel and activates the cruise control system. The steering wheel switches provide 'set/accelerate' and 'resume/decelerate' features. These switches provide the interface between driver and cruise control system.

Brake pedal switch

The brake pedal switch is located under the lower dash attached to the brake pedal mounting bracket. The switch provides for fast disengagement of the cruise control system and rapid return of the throttle levers to the idle position when the brake pedal is applied.

Clutch pedal switch - 1993 introduction

The clutch pedal switch is located under the lower dash attached to the clutch pedal mounting bracket. The switch provides for fast disengagement of the cruise control system and rapid return of the throttle levers to the idle position when the clutch pedal is applied.

Road speed transducer

The road speed transducer is mounted on a bracket located on the left hand chassis side member adjacent to the rear engine mounting. The transducer provides road speed data to the E.C.U. The cruise control system cannot be engaged until the road speed exceeds 45 km/h, (28 mph) the system will automatically disengage at a road speed of 42 km/h (26 mph).

Vacuum pump

The vacuum pump is located in the engine compartment, attached to the left hand valance. The vacuum pump is energised when the main cruise control switch is operated, and is actuated by the steering wheel and brake pedal switches. The pump provides a vacuum source to the cruise control actuator at the throttle levers. A control valve in the pump provides for steady increase of road speed or purge of the system when the brake pedal is applied.

Actuator

The actuator is located in the engine compartment and is bolted to the throttle lever bracketry. The actuator provides the servo mechanism link between the cruise control system and throttle linkage and is operated by vacuum from the vacuum pump.

Neutral lockout relay-cruise control - Automatic vehicles

The relay is located under the rear of the front right hand seat. Access is gained through the opening at the bottom of the seat when the seat is in its fully forward position.

1993 models - the relay is located in the right hand side footwell, accessible by removing the trim panel.

The function of the relay is to disengage the cruise control system if neutral, or park, is selected in the main gearbox, when the system is engaged.

Engine speed trip ECU - Manual vehicles

This unit is located in the right hand side footwell, accessible by removing the trim panel.

The function of the unit is to disengage cruise control if engine speed exceeds 5000 rev/min.

CRUISE CONTROL - CIRCUIT DIAGRAM - 1990/92

1. Cruise control ECU
2. Vacuum pump
3. Brake switch/vent valve
4. Stop lamps
5. Brake switch
6. Steering wheel set and reset switches
7. Fuse A5
8. Main cruise control switch-auxiliary panel
9. Fuse C5 (10A)
10. 12V + supply to transducer
11. Speed transducer
12. Ignition load relay-item 1 main circuit diagram
13. Battery feed
14. Cruise control harness multi-plug identification
15. Ignition switch-item 8 main circuit diagram
16. Relay - neutral lockout
17. Start inhibit switch
18. Diode
--- Denotes existing main cable

Cable colour code

B	Black	L	Light	P	Purple	U	Blue
G	Green	N	Brown	R	Red	W	White
K	Pink	O	Orange	S	Grey	Y	Yellow

The Last letter of a colour denotes the tracer colour.

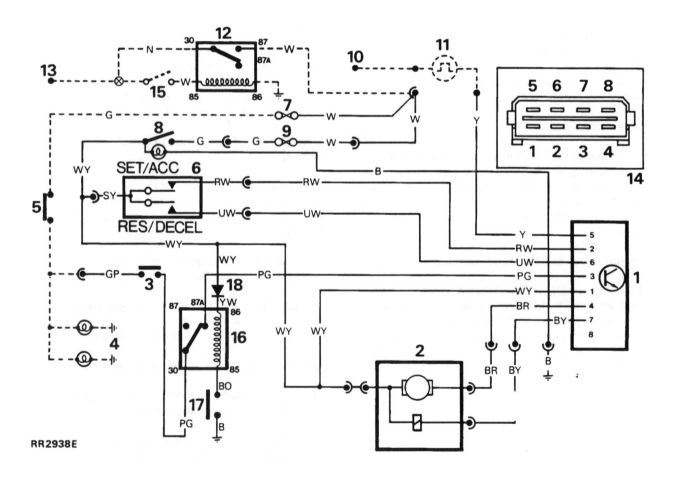

RR2938E

**CRUISE CONTROL - CIRCUIT DIAGRAM -
AUTOMATIC VEHICLES - 1993 Model year**

1. Cruise control ECU
2. Vacuum pump
3. Brake switch/vent valve
4. Brake light switch
5. Steering wheel set and reset switches
6. Neutral lock out relay
7. Main cruise control switch-auxiliary panel
8. Speed buffer
9. Speed transducer
10. Fuse B4 10A

11. Ignition feed
12. Fuse E2 10A
13. Ignition feed from load relay
14. Vehicle alarm
15. Park/neutral switch
16. Diode
17. Ignition feed
18. Fuse B1 10A
19. Stop lamps
--- Denotes existing main cable

Cable colour code

B	Black	L	Light	P	Purple	U	Blue
G	Green	N	Brown	R	Red	W	White
K	Pink	O	Orange	S	Grey	Y	Yellow

The Last letter of a colour denotes the tracer colour.

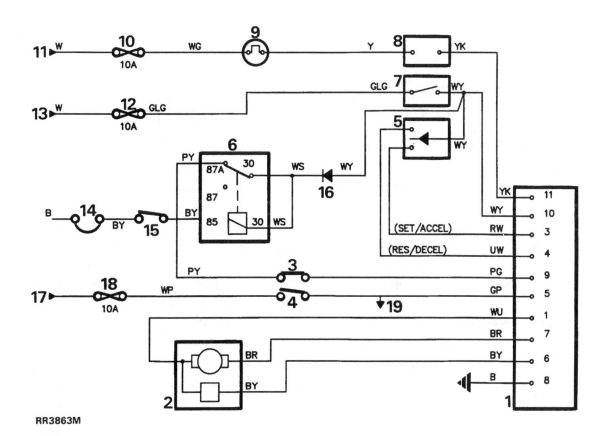

RR3863M

**CRUISE CONTROL - CIRCUIT DIAGRAM -
MANUAL VEHICLES - 1993 Model year**

1. Cruise control ECU
2. Vacuum pump
3. Brake switch/vent valve
4. Brake light switch
5. Clutch switch
6. Steering wheel set and reset switches
7. Engine trip ECU
8. Main cruise control switch-auxiliary panel
9. Speed buffer
10. Speed transducer
11. Fuse B4 10A
12. Ignition feed
13. Fuse E2 10A
14. Ignition feed from load relay
15. Speed signal from ignition module
16. 6.8 Kohm resistor
17. Diode
18. Ignition feed
19. Fuse B1 10A
20. Stop lamps
--- Denotes existing main cable

Cable colour code

B	Black	L	Light	P	Purple	U	Blue
G	Green	N	Brown	R	Red	W	White
K	Pink	O	Orange	S	Grey	Y	Yellow

The Last letter of a colour denotes the tracer colour.

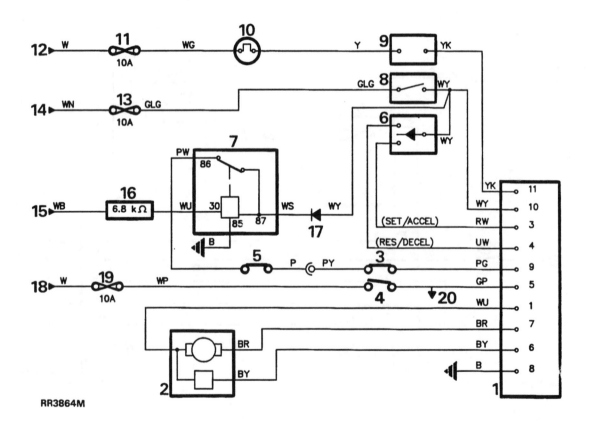

RR3864M

ROAD TEST - Pre 1993 models

 CAUTION: Do not engage cruise control when vehicle is being used in low transfer gear or reverse.

 WARNING: The use of cruise control is not recommended on winding, snow covered or slippery roads or in heavy traffic conditions where a constant speed cannot be maintained.

1. Start engine, depress main control switch to actuate cruise control system. Accelerate to approximately 50 km/h, (30 mph), operate 'set/acc' switch, immediately release switch, remove foot from accelerator pedal. Vehicle should maintain speed at which 'set/acc' switch was operated.
2. Operate 'set/acc' switch and hold at that position, vehicle should accelerate smoothly until switch is released. Vehicle should now maintain new speed at which 'set/acc' switch was released.
3. Apply 'res/decel' switch while vehicle is in cruise control mode, cruise control should disengage. Slow to approximately 55 km/h, (35 mph) operate 'res/decel' switch, immediately release switch and remove foot from accelerator, vehicle should smoothly accelerate to previously set speed. Increase speed using accelerator pedal, release pedal, vehicle should return to previously set speed.

4. Operate brake pedal, cruise control system should immediately disengage returning vehicle to driver control at accelerator pedal. Operate 'res/decel' switch, vehicle should accelerate to previously set speed without driver operation of accelerator pedal.
5. Operate 'res/decel' switch and allow vehicle to decelerate to below 42 km/h, (26 mph). Operate 'res/decel' switch, cruise control system should remain disengaged.
6. Operate 'set/acc' switch below 45 km/h, (28 mph), cruise control system should remain disengaged. Accelerate, using accelerator pedal to above 45 km/h, (28 mph), operate 'res/decel' switch, and remove foot from accelerator pedal, vehicle should smoothly adjust to previously memorised speed.
7. Depress main control switch in control system should immediately disengage and erase previously set speed from E.C.U. memory *see ETM, For Fault Diagnosis.*

ROAD TEST 1993 models

 CAUTION: Do not engage cruise control when vehicle is being used in low transfer gear or reverse.

 WARNING: The use of cruise control is not recommended on winding, snow covered or slippery roads or in heavy traffic conditions where a constant speed cannot be maintained.

1. Start engine, depress main control switch to actuate cruise control system. Accelerate to approximately 50 km/h, (30 mph), operate **'set/acc'** switch, immediately release switch, remove foot from accelerator pedal. Vehicle should maintain speed at which **'set/acc'** switch was operated.

2. Operate **'set/acc'** switch and hold at that position, vehicle should accelerate smoothly until switch is released. Vehicle should now maintain new speed at which **'set/acc'** switch was released.

3. Momentarily touch and release 'set/acc' switch, vehicle speed should increase 1.6 km/h (1 mph) for each touch. Note that five touches will increase speed 8 km/h (5 mph).

4. Apply **'res/decel'** switch while vehicle is in cruise control mode, cruise control should disengage. Slow to approximately 55 km/h, (35 mph) operate **'res/decel'** switch, immediately release switch and remove foot from accelerator, vehicle should smoothly accelerate to previously set speed. Increase speed using accelerator pedal, release pedal, vehicle should return to previously set speed.

5. Operate brake pedal, cruise control system should immediately disengage returning vehicle to driver control at accelerator pedal. Operate **'res/decel'** switch, vehicle should accelerate to previously set speed without driver operation of accelerator pedal.

6. Operate **'res/decel'** switch and allow vehicle to decelerate to below 42 km/h, (26 mph). Operate **'res/decel'** switch, cruise control system should remain disengaged.

7. Operate **'set/acc'** switch below 40 km/h, (28 mph), cruise control system should remain disengaged. Accelerate, using accelerator pedal to above 45 km/h, (28 mph), operate **'res/decel'** switch, and remove foot from accelerator pedal, vehicle should smoothly adjust to previously memorised speed.

8. **Automatic vehicles**- select neutral, system should disengage. **Manual vehicles**- depress clutch, system should disengage.

9. Cruise at 80 km/h (50 mph), declutch, select neutral, remove foot from clutch. Operate **'res/decel'** switch. Engine should rev to 5000 rev/min, cruise control disengages, engine returns to idle.

10. Engage forward gear. Operate **'res/decel'** switch. Remove foot from accelerator. Speed should accelerate to previous set speed.

11. Depress main control switch in control system should immediately disengage and erase previously set speed from E.C.U. memory *see ETM, For Fault Diagnosis.*

BRAKE PEDAL SWITCH/VENT VALVE

Service repair no - 19.75.35

Remove

1. Remove lower dash panel, *see CHASSIS AND BODY, Repair, lower dash panel.*
2. Disconnect electrical multi-plug from brake pedal switch.
3. Pull vent hose from switch.
4. Loosen locknut, unscrew switch from bracket.

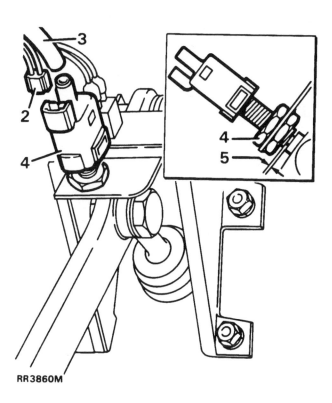

RR3860M

Refit

5. Fit switch. Adjust switch to provide a clearance of 1.0 mm between switch body and contact button.
6. Tighten locknut.
7. Fit hose and multi-plug securely.
8. Reverse remaining removal instructions.

CLUTCH PEDAL SWITCH/VENT VALVE - 1993 model year addition

Service repair no - 19.75.34

Remove

1. Remove lower dash panel, *see CHASSIS AND BODY, Repair, lower dash panel.*
2. Disconnect electrical multi-plug from clutch pedal switch.
3. Pull vent hose from switch.
4. Unscrew adjusting nut, remove switch.

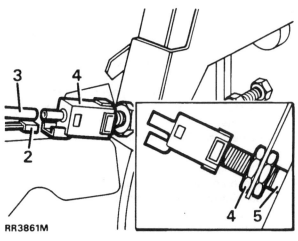

RR3861M

Refit

5. Refit switch, fit adjusting nut. Adjust valve to provide zero clearance between valve body and inside shoulder of contact button.
6. Tighten adjusting nut
7. Fit hose and multi-plug securely.
8. Reverse remaining removal instructions.

MAIN CONTROL SWITCH

Service repair no - 19.75.30

Remove and refit of main control switch and bulb replacement is included in Electrical Section 86, **see ELECTRICAL, Repair, auxiliary switch panel.**

DRIVER OPERATED CRUISE CONTROL SWITCHES-STEERING WHEEL

Service repair no -
  Set - 19.75.36
  Resume - 19.75.37

Remove

1. Disconnect battery negative terminal.
2. Pry centre trim pad off steering wheel.
3. Disconnect electrical multi-plug located in small opening below steering wheel retaining nut.
4. Carefully pry switch(es) out of steering wheel spoke(s).
5. Release small switch button from opening within spoke(s).
6. Carefully pull switch and electrical leads through spoke until access is gained to electrical connections beneath switch.
7. Disconnect electrical leads from switch and withdraw switch(es).

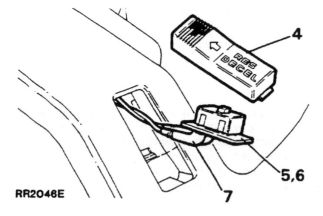

RR2046E

Refit

8. Reverse removal procedure ensuring electrical leads are fitted securely.

SPIRAL CASSETTE

Service repair no - 19.75.54

The spiral cassette is located behind steering wheel. Access to unit is gained by removing steering wheel and steering column shroud.

⚠ **NOTE: To enable steering wheel to be refitted in correct radial position, ensure front road wheels are in straight ahead position.**

Remove

Service Tools:
LRT-57-014 Steering wheel remover
LRT-57-015 Adaptor pins

1. Disconnect battery negative terminal.
2. Remove steering wheel centre trim panel.
3. Disconnect electrical multi-plug located in small opening in centre of steering wheel.
4. Remove steering wheel securing nut and serrated washer, using service tool LRT-57-014 and adaptor pins, withdraw steering wheel.

⚠ **CAUTION: Apply adhesive tape to upper and lower halves of spiral cassette to prevent upper half rotating after steering wheel is removed. Failure to do this will result in damage to flexible tape inside cassette.**

5. Remove six lower fixings securing steering column shroud.
6. Release either left hand or right hand fixing securing top of shroud.

7. Ease halves of shroud apart until access is gained to electrical multi-plug on cassette. Disconnect multi-plug.
8. Remove cassette from steering column.

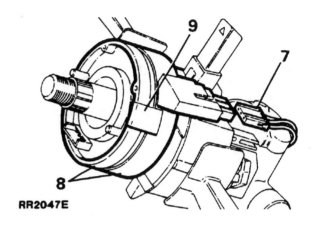

RR2047E

Refit

9. Remove adhesive tape retaining halves of spiral cassette.

⚠ **NOTE: Ensure that two pegs on spiral cassette locate in two holes on underside of steering wheel before securing steering wheel.**

10. Reverse removal instructions, ensuring that electrical leads within steering column shroud are not trapped between shroud mating faces.

ACTUATOR

Service repair no - 19.75.12

 NOTE: The actuator is non serviceable, fit a new unit if failure or damage occurs.

Remove

1. Disconnect battery negative terminal.
2. Pull rubber elbow from actuator.
3. Remove nut securing actuator to throttle bracket.
4. Remove actuator, and manoeuvre actuator operating link off throttle lever.
5. Withdraw actuator.

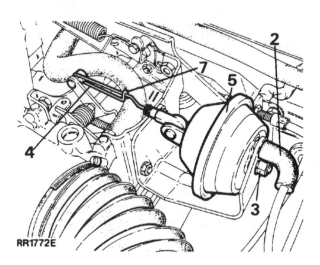

RR1772E

Refit

6. Inspect rubber diaphragm. Fit a new actuator assembly if diaphragm is damaged.
7. Reverse removal procedure, fitting hook uppermost

ACTUATOR LINK-SETTING

Service repair no - 19.75.21

 NOTE: Setting procedure is carried out at minimum throttle condition only.

1. Ensure ignition is switched 'OFF'.

2. Check clearance between inside edge of actuator link and recessed diameter of throttle lever. Clearance should be 0.2 to 2.0 mm.

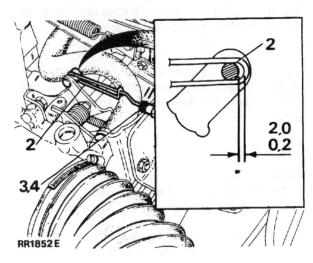

RR1852E

Link - adjust

3. Remove link from actuator.
4. Rotate socket joint adjuster as necessary.
5. Refit link to actuator and recheck clearance between link and lever.
6. With throttle fully open, check a gap of at least 3mm exists between side of link ("A" in illustration) and side of small spring ("B" in illustration). Realign link by bending to achieve correct gap. Recheck clearance at closed throttle/open throttle. Check link slides smoothly in groove of throttle lever.

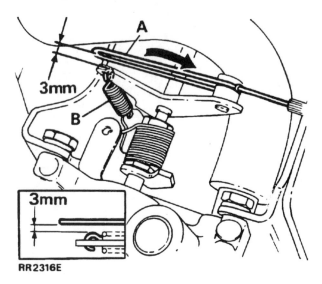

RR2316E

VACUUM PUMP

Service repair no - 19.75.06

 NOTE: The vacuum pump is non serviceable, fit a new unit if failure or damage occurs.

Remove

1. Disconnect battery negative terminal.
2. Disconnect multi-plug from top of vacuum pump.
3. Disconnect vacuum feed hose from vacuum pump.
4. Withdraw three vacuum pump rubber mountings.

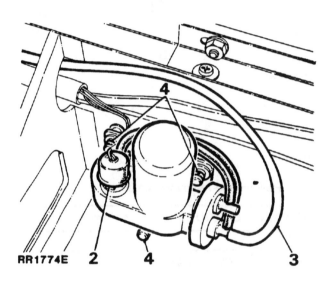

RR1774E 2   4   3

5. Remove vacuum pump.

Refit

6. Reverse removal procedure ensuring all hose and electrical connections are secure.

ELECTRONIC CONTROL UNIT (ECU) - CRUISE CONTROL- Pre 1993

Service repair no - 19.75.49

Remove

1. Remove lower dash panel, see CHASSIS AND BODY, Repair, lower dash panel.
2. Remove two fixings, lower ECU to access multi-plug.
3. Disconnect ECU multi-plug, remove unit from vehicle.

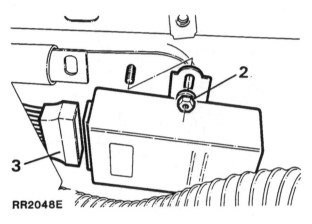

RR2048E

Refit

4. Reverse removal instructions ensuring that electrical multi-plug is securely reconnected.

ELECTRONIC CONTROL UNIT (ECU) - CRUISE CONTROL - 1993

Service repair no - 19.75.49

Remove

1. Remove lower dash panel, *see CHASSIS AND BODY, Repair, lower dash panel.*
2. Release wire clip.
3. Disconnect ECU multi-plug.
4. Remove ECU fixing.
5. Remove ECU.

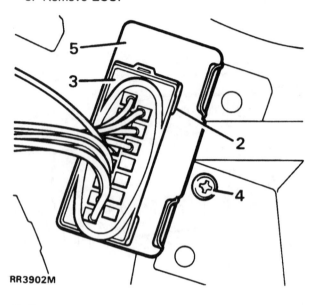

RR3902M

Refit

6. Reverse removal instructions ensuring that electrical multi-plug is securely reconnected.

NEUTRAL LOCKOUT RELAY - Pre 1993

Remove

1. Adjust seat fully forward.
2. Disconnect battery negative terminal.
3. Pull relay from terminal block.

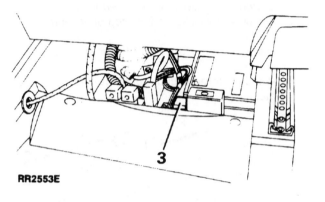

RR2553E

Refit

4. Reverse the removal instructions.

NEUTRAL LOCKOUT RELAY - Automatic

SPEED TRIP ECU - Manual - 1993

> **NOTE: The neutral lock out relay/speed trip ECU is mounted in the right hand side footwell. To identify components, see 1993 Range Rover Electrical Troubleshooting Manual.**

68 - AIR SUSPENSION

CONTENTS

Page

DESCRIPTION AND OPERATION

REPAIR

68 - AIR SUSPENSION

CONTENTS

Page

RANGE ROVER ELECTRONIC AIR SUSPENSION - (EAS)

Description

The electronic air suspension is a versatile microprocessor controlled system that exploits the advantages of air suspension. It provides a variable spring rate which achieves near constant ride frequency for all load conditions, giving:

• Improved ride quality.
• Continuity of ride quality, laden or unladen.
• Constant ride height.
• Improved headlamp levelling.

The function of the system is to provide five height modes, each of which is automatically maintained at the given height by the system logic with the minimum of driver involvement. Vehicle height is sensed by four rotary potentiometer type height sensors. Vehicle height information from each potentiometer signals the ECU to adjust each air spring by switching the solenoid valves to hold, add or release air. The system provides five height settings and automatic self levelling as follows:

Standard - standard ride height i.e. 790mm ± 7mm, measured from centre of wheelarch eyebrow to floor.

Low profile: 20 mm below standard.

Access: 60 mm below standard.

High profile: 40 mm above standard.

Extended profile: 20 to 30 mm above high profile.

Self levelling

The system provides self levelling under varying vehicle loads. The vehicle will self level to the lowest corner height level for 20 seconds after switching off engine, exiting vehicle and closing doors.

Standard

Vehicle ride height is the same as with conventional suspension, but is maintained under all load conditions. This also provides improved headlamp levelling.

Low profile

This position gives improved handling and fuel consumption at high speed. When the vehicle speed exceeds 80 kph (50 mph) for more than 30 seconds, with INHIBIT switch off, the vehicle will enter the low profile position. The vehicle will return to standard height when vehicle speed drops below 56 kph (35 mph) for more than 30 seconds, unless vehicle stops, in which case it returns to standard when driven away. The LOWER lamp is illuminated in this condition.

Access

This position makes passenger boarding and luggage loading easier. With the vehicle stationary, park brake on (manual), P selected (automatic), footbrake off, doors closed and INHIBIT switch off, pressing the LOWER switch will select the ACCESS position. It is possible to select access for 15 seconds after switching engine off. The LOWER lamp flashes until access position is reached, when it remain constantly illuminated

 NOTE: Opening a door will freeze vehicle position.

From access the vehicle will return to standard ride height if the RAISE switch is pressed, OR inhibit switched on OR park brake released, OR the vehicle driven off.

High profile

This position is used to improve approach and departure angles and when wading. Pressing the RAISE switch will select this position provided the road speed is below 56 kph (35 mph) with INHIBIT off. The vehicle will return to standard position when road speed exceeds 56 kph (35 mph) or LOWER switch is pressed. The RAISE lamp is illuminated in this condition.

NOTE: When raising ride height, rear of vehicle will raise by 70% of movement first followed by 70% of front. Rear will raise remaining 30% before front. Lowering will be achieved by lowering front of vehicle first. This will ensure that, with headlamps illuminated, there is no inconvenience from headlamp dazzle to other road users. BUT, lowering to access position will be achieved by the fastest possible means, by opening all air valves at the same time.

Extended profile

This position is achieved when vehicle is off road in standard or high profile and the chassis is grounded leaving wheels unsupported. Initial ECU reaction is to deflate (lower) affected springs. After a timed period ECU detects no height change, therefore it reinflates springs in an attempt to regain traction. The RAISE lamp will flash in this mode. After ten minutes system will return to high profile, unless LOWER switch is pressed.

LOCATION OF COMPONENTS (RR3856M)

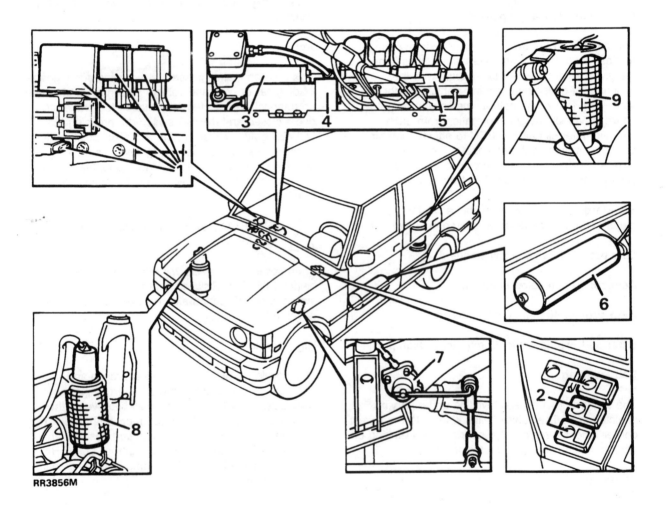

RR3856M

1. Electronic control unit (ECU), relays, fuses and disable switch.
2. Control switches
3. Compressor
4. Air dryer
5. Valve block

6. Reservoir
7. Height sensors (4)
8. Front air spring
9. Back air spring

DESCRIPTION OF COMPONENTS
- see RR3868M

Electrical control unit - ECU

The ECU is located underneath the right hand front seat, on top of the fuel ECU. It maintains the requested vehicle ride height by adjusting the volume of air in each air spring. It is connected to the cable assembly by a 35 way connector. To ensure safe operation the ECU has extensive on board diagnostic and safety features. The ECU is non-serviceable, in case of failure it must be replaced.

Relays, fuses - RR3857M

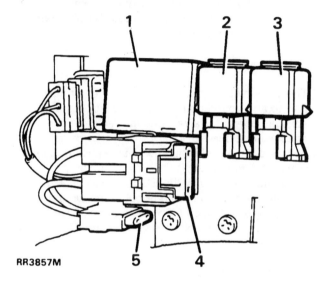

RR3857M

Power supply for the system consists of the following components:

1. Delayed power turn off relay. This remains powered up for 20 seconds after exiting vehicle to allow self levelling.
2. Compressor relay, 4 pin.
3. Warning light relay, 5 pin.
4. 30 amp 'maxifuse' for compressor power.
5. 15 amp fuse for ECU pin 1.

Disable switch - RR3862M

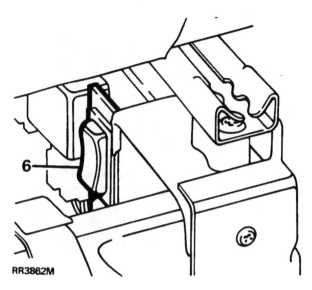

RR3862M

The disable switch 6. is mounted under the right hand front seat. The switch has no markings, in the DISABLE position the bottom of the switch is pushed in. It is used to disable system when vehicle is being delivered, or when working on the system after depressurising. The switch disables the system at speeds below 56 kph (35 mph).

Height sensors

Four potentiometer type height sensors signal vehicle height information to the ECU. The potentiometers are mounted on the chassis and activated by links to the front radius arms and rear trailing links. In case of height sensor failure the assembly must be replaced.

Control switches - see RR3516M

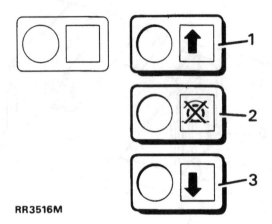

RR3516M

Mounted on the lower fascia, three control switches are arranged thus:

1 - Raise - momentary touch switch.

2 - Inhibit - self latching switch, when switched on the vehicle will remain at standard ride height. This position is used when the automatic height adjustment is not required i.e. when towing. Self levelling will continue to function.

3 - Lower - momentary touch switch.

The switches incorporate a warning lamp. When engine is started all three warning lamps will illuminate for three seconds as part of bulb check. The switches are illuminated when the vehicle lights are on, controlled by the dimmer switch.

The following components, AIR COMPRESSOR, AIR DRYER and VALVE BLOCK are contained in the AIR SUPPLY UNIT mounted on the right hand chassis side.

Air compressor

The air compressor provides system pressure. A thermal switch is incorporated which switches off the compressor relay earth at 130°C. The compressor has an air intake silencer mounted behind rear mud flap. The air intake filter is located adjacent to the fuel filler flap. The filter is renewed every 40,000 kms/24,000 miles/24 months. (30,000 miles USA).

Air dryer

The air dryer is connected into the air line between compressor and reservoir. It removes moisture from pressurised air entering the system. When air is exhausted from the system it passes through the dryer in the opposite direction. The air dryer is regenerative in that air absorbs moisture in the dryer and expells it to atmosphere.

The air dryer unit is non-serviceable, designed to last the life of the vehicle. However if water is found in the system when reservoir drain plug is removed, the air dryer must be changed.

 CAUTION: If the air dryer is removed from the vehicle the ports must be plugged to prevent moisture ingress.

Valve block

The valve block controls the direction of air flow. Air flow to and from the air springs is controlled by six solenoid operated valves, one for each air spring, one inlet and one exhaust. A diaphragm valve operated by the solenoid outlet valve ensures that all exhausted air passes through the air dryer. In response to signals by the ECU, the valves allow high pressure air to flow in or out of the air springs according to the need to increase or decrease pressure. The valve block is non-serviceable, in case of failure it must be replaced.

Non-return valves

The valve block contains three non-return valves. NRV1 retains compressor air pressure by preventing flow back to the compressor. NRV2 prevents loss of pressure in the system if reservoir pressure drops. It also ensures correct flow through the inlet valve. NRV3 ensures correct flow through the exhaust valve.

Reservoir

The 10 litre reservoir is mounted on the left hand side of the chassis. One connection acts as inlet and outlet to the rest of the system. It stores compressed air between set pressure levels. The reservoir drain plug requires removing every 40,000 kms/24,000 miles/24 months. (30,000 miles USA) to check for moisture in the system, *see Repair, air reservoir - drain.*

Pressure switch

Mounted on the reservoir is a pressure switch which
senses air pressure and signals the ECU to operate
the compressor when required. The compressor will
operate when pressure falls to between 7.2 and 8.0
bar. It will cut out at a rising pressure of between 9.5
and 10.5 bar.

Air springs - see RR3887M

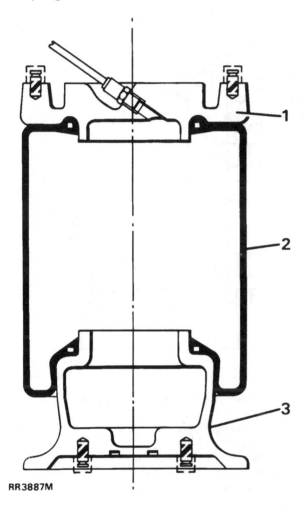

RR3887M

Air springs components

1. Top plate
2. Rolling rubber diaphragm
3. Piston

The air springs are mounted in the same position as
conventional coil springs.

Front and back air springs are of similar construction,
but are not interchangeable.

The diaphragm is NOT repairable, if failure occurs
the complete unit must be replaced.

PNEUMATIC SYSTEM DIAGRAM

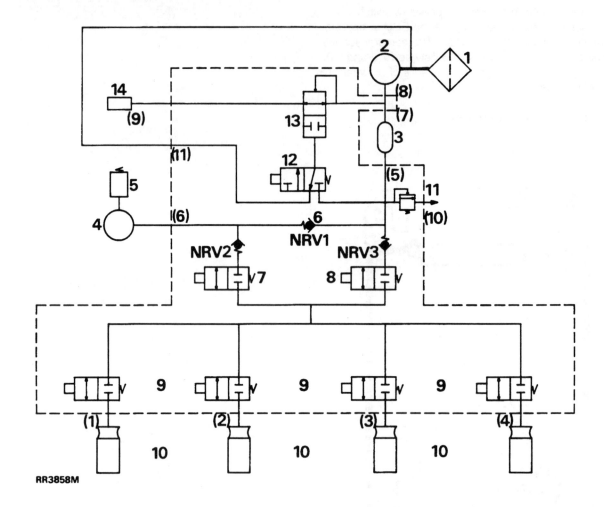

RR3858M

Key to RR3858M

1. Inlet filter
2. Compressor
3. Air dryer
4. Reservoir
5. Pressure switch

Valve block comprises items 6. to 12.

6. One way valves NRV1, 2 and 3.
7. Inlet solenoid valve
8. Exhaust solenoid valve
9. Air spring solenoid valves
10. Air springs
11. Pressure relief valve
12. Solenoid diaphragm valve
13. System air operated diaphragm valve
14. Silencer

Valve block port numbers (1) TO (11)

(1) Air spring - back left
(2) Air spring - back right
(3) Air spring - front left
(4) Air spring - front right
(5) Dryer outlet
(6) Reservoir in/out
(7) Dryer inlet
(8) Compressor inlet
(9) Outlet
(10) Pressure relief valve vent
(11) Diaphragm outlet (to compressor inlet)

-------------- denotes valve block

AIR PIPE COLOUR CODES

The following pipes have a coloured band to aid assembly:

Component .... Colour

Back left spring .... Red
Back right spring .... Blue
Front left spring.. Yellow
Front right spring .... Green
Reservoir .... Brown
Exhaust.. Violet

SYSTEM OPERATION - see RR3858M

Air is drawn through the inlet filter 1. to the compressor 2., where it is compressed to 10.0 ± 0.5 bar.

Compressor operation activates the diaphragm solenoid valve 12. to prevent air going straight to atmosphere.

Compressed air passes to the air dryer 3. Moisture is removed as air flows through the dryer dessicant. The dessicant in the dryer becomes wet.

Dried air passes to the valve block, through NRV1 to the reservoir 4.

The three non-return valves 6. ensure correct air flow. They also prevent loss of spring pressure if total loss of reservoir pressure occurs.

A pressure switch 5. maintains system pressure between set limits by switching the compressor on and off via an ECU controlled relay.

For air to be admited to any spring or springs, inlet valve 7. and the relevant air spring solenoid valve or valves 9. must be energised.

For air to be exhausted from any spring, the exhaust valve 8. and the relevant air spring solenoid valve or valves must be energised.

The diaphragm solenoid valve ensures that air exhausted to atmosphere passes through the dryer. This action purges moisture from the dessicant and regenerates the air dryer.

Air is finally exhausted through the system air operated diaphragm valve 13. and to atmosphere through a silencer 14. at the chassis rear crossmember.

ECU INPUTS

The air suspension system is controlled by the ECU, which operates dependant on driver selected inputs plus those listed below. In each mode the ECU maintains the requested ride height by adjusting the volume of air in one or more of the air springs.

Battery - 12 volt supply from ignition load relay.

Engine - from alternator phase tap, signals engine speed to ECU. Note that engine must be running for all height changes, except access and self-levelling when parked. The compressor will be disabled if engine speed falls below 500 rev/min. This is to prevent the compressor drawing current from the battery when the alternator is not charging.

Height sensors - four potentiometer height sensors provide suspension height signals to the ECU.

Road speed - the road speed transducer provides information enabling height changes to occur at correct road speed. Input speed signal to ECU is from a buffer unit located in the driver's side footwell.

Interior light delay unit - signals ECU if any door, not tailgate, is opened, which immediately suspends all height changes.

Parkbrake switch, manual vehicles - the parkbrake must be ON to enter ACCESS.

Gearbox inhibit switch, automatic vehicles - the transmission must be in park to enter access, parkbrake on or off.

Footbrake switch (brake light) - when footbrake is applied, and for one second after release, all height levelling is suspended below 1.6 kph (1 mph) and above 8 kph (5 mph). The purpose of this is to prevent the system reacting to suspension movement caused by weight transfer during braking and to prevent suspension wind up during height change. Note that this inhibit function is removed after sixty seconds e.g. if footbrake is held on for this time.

Delayed turn off relay - remains energised after switching engine off and exiting vehicle, enables self levelling to occur for 20 secs. If vehicle is stationary, the ECU will energise the relay every six hours to allow self levelling to occur if necessary.

Reservoir pressure switch - when the ECU detects an output from the pressure switch indicating low pressure, the ECU will operate the compressor relay until the pressure switch indicates normal pressure.

Diagnostic plug ground - note that the two halves of the diagnostic plug are normally connected. When disconnected the system will not operate. It will remain frozen at its current height until reconnected.

Disable switch - In the disable position the switch sends a door open signal to the ECU. This freezes the system in position at speeds below 56 kph (35 mph).

SYSTEM FUNCTION

The following table indicates conditions required for various air suspension modes.

⚠ **NOTE: That the engine must be running unless indicated, and that ACCESS may be selected for 15 seconds after switching engine off.**

Function	Condition		Warning lamp on

1. Automatic functions - Inhibit switch OFF.

Function	Condition		Warning lamp on
High profile to standard	Over 56kph (35mph)		No
Standard to low profile	Over 80kph (50 mph) for 30 secs		Lower
Low profile to standard	Below 56kph (35 mph) for 30 secs (but above 1.6 kph (1 mph))		No
Access to standard	Park brake off or drive away		No

2. Driver select functions - Inhibit switch OFF.

Function	Condition		Warning lamp on
Standard to high profile	Raise switch below 56kph (35 mph)		Raise
High profile to standard	Lower switch below 56kph (35 mph)		No
Standard to access	Lower switch	)Stationary/)park brake on	Lower
Low profile to access (where vehicle has not returned to standard	Lower switch	)- manual/)transmission P)- automatic/	Lower
High to Access	Press lower switch twice	)doors shut	No
Access to standard	Raise switch		Lower
Access to high	Press raise switch twice		Raise

3. Inhibit switch ON

Function	Condition		Warning lamp on
High profile to standard	Below 56kph (35 mph)		Inhibit
Low profile to standard			Inhibit
Access to standard	Stationary/park brake on		Inhibit

4. Self levelling

Function	Condition		Warning lamp on
Vehicle levelling for 20 secs, and every 6 hrs	Stationary/engine off/ exit vehicle		No

DIAGNOSTICS AND FAULT RECOVERY

The ECU incorporates Fault Recovery Strategies to minimise the effect of a system failure. A serial data link is provided to allow diagnostic information to be retrieved using the Lucas hand held tester. This is also used to set height sensor datum when required. Note that the serial link connector is coloured black for identification purposes. Any faults stored in the ECU memory, from the previous or current running period will cause the ECU to flash the RAISE and LOWER lamps for 30 secs. followed by continuous illumination.

If the ECU registers a system fault, it will store the fault in the memory. The fault recovery programme will operate the system depending on the nature of the fault as follows:

Speed sensor fault - the ECU will place the system in standard height and activate inhibit.

Height sensor fault - the ECU will place the system in standard height and activate inhibit. Note that if more than one height sensor fails, the ECU will deflate the air springs to the bump stops.

⚠ **WARNING: If any two failure occur the system deflates and lowers vehicle to its bump stops, it is possible to drive the vehicle provided that great caution is exercised. The vehicle ride will be extremely uncomfortable and only low speeds will be possible. It is essential that the vehicle fault is rectified as soon as possible.**

Pressure switch fault - the ECU will register pressure switch failure if it detects that the compressor has worked for a programmed time with normal air spring operation possible. The ECU will periodically operate the compressor as air is required. The vehicle will be inhibited to standard.

Compressor fault - the ECU will register compressor failure if it detects that the compressor has worked for a programmed time with normal air spring operation not possible. The ECU will attempt to place the system in standard ride height, or a safe lowered position (which could be system deflated). The system will be inhibited from further ride height changes.

Air leaks - during normal operation the ECU correlates the operating time of the compressor with air usage. If compressor use is greater than programmed, the ECU will register an air leak and attempt to place the system in standard ride height, or a safe lowered position (which could be system deflated). The system will be inhibited from further ride height changes.

Valve block fault - the control of each air spring is monitored to determine that every valve is working correctly.

1. If the ECU detects an air valve stuck open it will attempt to adjust the vehicle to standard height or a safe lowered position (which could be system deflated). The system will be inhibited from further ride height changes.
2. If an air valve is stuck closed above standard height the ECU will deflate the other three air springs.
3. If an air valve is stuck closed, at or below standard height, the ECU will attempt to adjust the other springs to the same height and activate inhibit

AIR SUSPENSION CIRCUIT DIAGRAM
- RR3859M

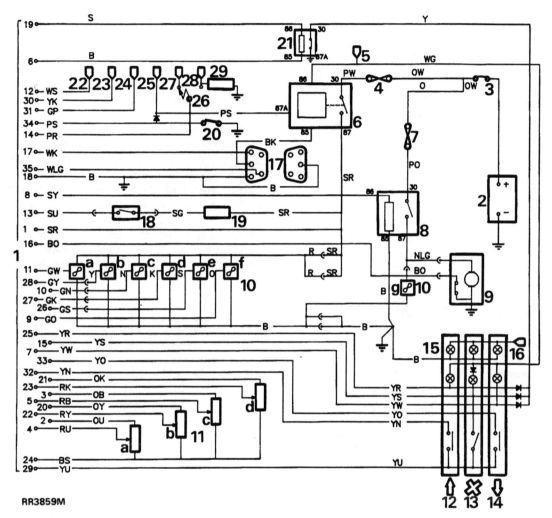

RR3859M

Key to RR3859M

1. ECU
2. Battery
3. Fusible link
4. 15 amp fuse
5. Ignition feed
6. Delayed turn off relay
7. 30 amp maxi fuse
8. Compressor relay
9. Compressor and thermal switch
10. Solenoid valves
   a. back left
   b. back right
   c. front left
   d. front right
   e. inlet
   f. exhaust
   g. outlet
11. Height sensors
   a. back left
   b. back right

c. front left
d. front right
12. RAISE switch
13. INHIBIT switch
14. LOWER switch
15. Warning lamps
16. Switch illumination from panel lamps
17. Diagnostic plug
18. Pressure switch
19. 1 Kohm resistor (in harness)
20. Disable switch
21. Warning light relay
22. Engine speed input from alternator
23. Road speed input from speed buffer
24. Brake switch input
25. Door open input
26. Manual/auto select link
27. Park brake input
28. Park neutral switch input
29. 1 Kohm resistor (in harness)

ECU HARNESS PLUG WIRING DETAILS
- see RR3692M

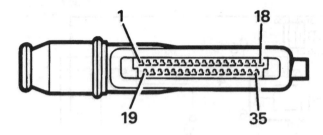

RR3692M

1. Slate/red	19. Slate/red
2. Orange/slate	20. Orange/red
3. Orange/blue	21. Orange/purple
4. Orange/pink	22. Orange/brown
5. Orange/green	23. Orange/Yellow
6. Black/slate	24. Black/pink
7. Yellow/white	25. Yellow/pink
8. Slate/yellow	26. Green/orange
9. Green/slate	27. Green/pink
10. Green/black	28. Green/yellow
11. Green/white	29. Yellow/blue
12. White/slate	30. Yellow/pink
13. Slate/blue	31. Green/pink
14. Black/blue	32. Yellow/brown
15. Yellow/slate	33. Yellow/orange
16. Not used	34. Purple/slate
17. White/pink	35. White/light green

SYSTEM CALIBRATION - height sensor datum

Equipment required:

Lucas hand held test unit and air suspension memory card

⚠ **NOTE: This procedure must be carried out when a new ECU or height sensor has been fitted.**

Calibration will also be required if any part affecting damper relationship to body is changed i.e. damper mounts, axles, chassis unit and body panels. The vehicle can be calibrated laden or unladen, but Gross Vehicle Weight must not be exceeded. Tyres must all be the same size and at correct pressures.

IMPORTANT: The floor used for calibration must be level and smooth in all directions to enable procedure to be carried out successfully.

RECOMMENDED EQUIPMENT

Lucas hand held tester .... RTC 6834
Adaptor lead, air suspension .... STC 1089

Memory card, air suspension:
    English .... STC 590
    French .... STC 591
    German .... STC 592
    Italian.. STC 593
    Spanish .... STC 594
    Dutch .... STC 595
    Jananese .... STC 598

Pressure test equipment .... LRT 60.001
Pipe cutter .... LRT 60.002
Leak detection spary .... STC 1090
35 way 'pin out' box .... STC 644

SUSPENSION COMPONENTS

This section gives repair procedures for air suspension components. It is essential to note that repairs to other suspension and transmission components are affected by air suspension.

To remove the following components DEPRESSURISE the system: front axle, panhard rod, radius arms, rear top and bottom links and rear axle.

 WARNING: The air spring must be restricted by suspension loading, with dampers fitted before inflation. Unrestricted movement of a pressurised air spring will result in failure of the assembly, causing component and possible personal injury.

DEPRESSURISE SYSTEM

Service repair no - 60.50.38

Service tool:
RTC 6834 - Lucas hand held tester

 WARNING: Air suspension is pressurised up to 10 bar. Dirt or grease must not enter the system. Wear hand, ear and eye safety standard protection when servicing system.

1. Depressurising system will lower body on to bump stops.
2. Connect hand held tester and follow manufacturer's instructions to depressurise complete system.
3. Ensure system is completely depressurised. Check that all air springs are deflated, and vehicle has dropped evenly to the bump stops. If a spring, or springs, remains inflated possibly due to a stuck solenoid valve, it will be necessary to disconnect the pressurised pipe at air spring.

 WARNING: Wear hand, ear and eye safety standard protection. For extra protection wrap a clean cloth around pipe to be disconnected. Note that vehicle will lower to bump stops when pipe is disconnected.

4. Disconnect air pipe *see disconnect/connect air pipe.*
5. Disable system using switch under right hand front seat.

Repressurise

6. Switch disable switch OFF.
7. Run engine to repressurise system.

AIR RESERVOIR - DRAIN

Service repair no - 50.50.24

The reservoir is drained every 40,000 Kms (24,000 miles) - USA 30,000 miles.

1. Depressurise system, *see Depressurise system.*
2. Clean area around reservoir drain plug.
3. Partially open drain plug, allow residual air to escape.

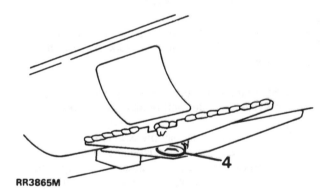

RR3865M

4. Remove drain plug, NO water should be present. If water is present, air dryer unit must be changed *see air dryer.*
5. Fit drain plug, checking sealing washer. Tighten to *70 Nm.*
6. Repressurise system.

AIR SPRINGS/HEIGHT SENSORS - INSPECT

Visually check air springs for cuts, abrasions and stone damage to alloy end plates. Check security of retention clips. Check height sensors for damage to housing, operating links and cable assembly.

AIR HARNESS INSPECT

Check air harness (pipes) for damage and security over its full length around vehicle.

LEAK TEST PROCEDURE

Service repair no - 60.50.35

If an air leak is suspected the use of a proprietery leak detection spray is recommended. This procedure should also be used where pneumatic components have been disturbed.

The spray used must have a corrosion inhibitor, and must not cause damage to paintwork, plastics, metals and plastic pipes.

Recommended leak detection spray is GOTEC LDS. This is available under part number STC1090.

1. Ensure system is fully pressurised.
2. Clean around area of suspected leak.
3. Using manufacturer's instructions, spray around all component joints and air springs, working systematically until source of leak is found.
4. If a component eg: air spring, air dryer is leaking. rectify by fitting a new component.
5. If an air pipe connection is leaking cut 5 mm off end of pipe. Fit new collet, *see air pipe connection collet and 'O' rings.*
6. Reinflate system, carry out leak test.

OPERATING SWITCH WARNING LIGHT AND ILLUMINATION

Service repair no - 60.50.17

 NOTE: Each switch contains a warning light bulb, and an illumination bulb.

Remove and refit

Remove

1. Remove centre dash panel, *see CHASSIS AND BODY, Repair, centre dash panel.*
2. Depress locating tags of switch to remove switch.

RR3888M

3. Remove bulb by turning anti-clockwise and releasing from switch.

Refit

4. Fit new bulb and turn anti-clockwise until fully located.
5. Reverse removal procedure.

DISCONNECT/CONNECT AIR PIPE

Remove and refit

Remove

 WARNING: Air suspension is pressurised up to 10 bar. Dirt or grease must not enter the system. Wear hand, ear and eye safety standard protection when servicing system.

1. Depressurise complete system, *see Depressurise system.*

 CAUTION: Air pipes may be damaged if not disconnected correctly, resulting in possible leaks.

2. Clean air pipe connection with stiff brush and soapy water. Peel back rubber boot.
3. To disconnect air pipes apply equal downward pressure on collet at 'A' as shown.

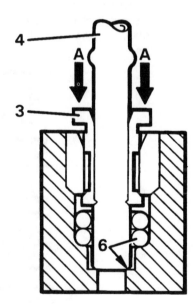

RR3592M

4. Pull air pipe firmly out through centre of collet.
5. Inspect disconnected end of air pipe for damage and scores. Rectify as necessary.

△ **NOTE: Air pipe may be trimmed if sufficient straight pipe remains. Ensure pipe end is cut square, without distortion or frays to obtain air tight seal. Use service tool LRT 60 - 002. Lightly chamfer pipe using a pencil sharpener after cutting. DO NOT CUT PIPES MORE THAN TWICE.**

Refit

6. Push pipe firmly through two 'O' rings until it contacts base of housing as shown. Gently pull pipe to ensure connection. The collet will retain some movement while depressurised. Refit rubber boot.
7. Pressurise system, *see Depressurise system.*
8. Leak test connection, *see Leak test procedure.*

AIR PIPE CONNECTION COLLET AND 'O' RINGS

Remove and refit

Remove

  WARNING: Air suspension is pressurised up to 10 bar. Dirt or grease must not enter the system. Wear hand, ear and eye safety standard protection when servicing system.

1. Clean area with stiff brush and soapy water.
2. Depressurise system, *see Depressurise.*
3. Disconnect air pipe, *see Disconnect/Connect air pipe*

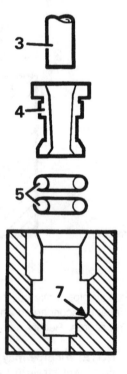

RR3593M

4. Remove collet.
5. Carefully pry out two 'O' rings, using a smooth plastic hook, eg: a crochet hook.

⚠ **CAUTION: Avoid scratching inside wall of housing, creating possible leak path.**

Refit

6. Lightly grease new 'O' rings.
7. Fit 'O' rings into recess. Use a crochet hook to avoid damage to 'O' rings and housing.
8. Locate collet legs into housing, push fully home.
9. Inspect end of air pipe for damage and scores rectify by trimming.

△ **NOTE: Air pipe may be trimmed if sufficient straight pipe remains. Ensure pipe end is cut square, without distortion or frays to obtain air tight seal. Use service tool LRT 60 - 002. Lightly chamfer pipe using a pencil sharpener after cutting. DO NOT CUT PIPES MORE THAN TWICE.**

10. Connect air pipe, *see Disconnect/connect air pipe.*
11. Pressurise system, *see Depressurise system.*
12. Leak test connection, *see Leak testing procedure.*

FRONT DAMPER

Service repair no - 60.30.02

Remove and refit

Remove

 WARNING: Air suspension is pressurised up to 10 bar. Dirt or grease must not enter the system. Wear hand, ear and eye safety standard protection when servicing system.

WARNING: Unrestricted movement of a pressurised air spring will result in failure of assembly, causing component damage and possible personal injury. It is possible to remove damper assembly without depressurising air springs, providing distance between axle and chassis is held as if damper assembly were still fitted. This is achieved by supporting vehicle on stands with a jack under the axle.

1. Disconnect battery negative lead.
2. Remove wheel, *see WHEELS AND TYRES, Repair, WHEEL.*
3. Support chassis on axle stands.
4. Support front axle with jack.

⚠ **CAUTION: Do not lower axle when damper is removed, this may result in damage to air springs.**

5. Remove top and bottom damper fixings.

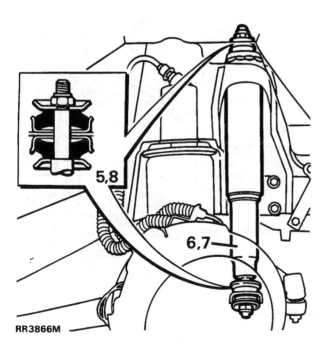

RR3866M

6. Remove damper.

Refit

7. Fit damper.
8. Fit top and bottom fixings, ensuring mounting rubbers are fitted as shown.
9. Tighten fixings to *38Nm.*
10. Reverse removal instructions 1 to 4.

REAR DAMPER

Service repair no - 64.31.02

Remove and refit

Remove

⚠ **WARNING: Air suspension is pressurised up to 10 bar. Dirt or grease must not enter the system. Wear hand, ear and eye safety standard protection when servicing system.**

⚠ **WARNING: Unrestricted movement of pressurised air spring will result in failure of assembly, causing component damage and possible personal injury. It is possible to remove damper assembly without depressurising air springs, providing distance between axle and chassis is held as if damper assembly were still fitted. This is achieved by supporting vehicle on stands with a jack under the axle.**

1. Disconnect battery negative lead.
2. Remove wheel, *see WHEELS AND TYRES, Repair, WHEEL.*
3. Support chassis on stands.
4. Support axle with jack.

⚠ **CAUTION: Do not lower axle when damper is removed, this may result in damage to air springs.**

5. Remove damper top and bottom fixings.

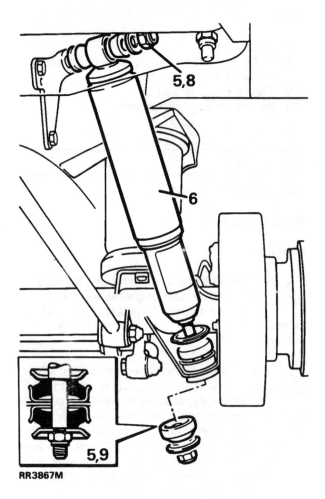

RR3867M

6. Remove damper.

Refit

7. Fit damper.
8. Fit top fixings, tighten to *82Nm*
9. Fit bottom fixings, ensure mounting rubbers are fitted as shown, tighten to *38Nm*
10. Reverse removal instructions 1 to 4.

FRONT AIR SPRING

Service repair no - 60.21.01

Remove and refit

Remove

⚠️ **WARNING: Air suspension is pressurised up to 10 bar. Dirt or grease must not enter the system. Wear hand, ear and eye safety standard protection when servicing system.**

⚠️ **WARNING: The air spring must be restricted by suspension loading, with dampers fitted before inflation. Failure to observe this warning could cause air spring failure, resulting in component damage or personal injury. DO NOT ATTEMPT TO DISMANTLE AIR SPRING**

1. Depressurise system, *see Depressurise system.*
2. Disconnect battery negative lead.
3. Remove wheel, *see WHEELS AND TYRES, Repair, WHEEL.*
4. Support chassis on axle stands.
5. Support front axle with jack.
6. Peel back rubber boot. Disconnect air pipe from air spring, *see Disconnect/Connect air pipe assembly.*

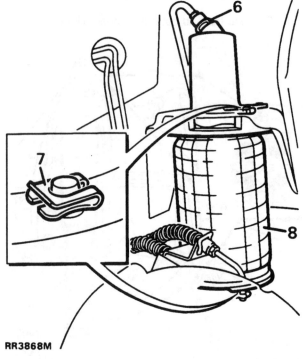

RR3868M

7. Remove four retaining clips from upper and lower fixing.
8. Remove air spring assembly.

Refit

9. Locate air spring assembly onto lower fixing, ensure air pipe connection points rearwards.
10. Connect air pipe to air spring assembly, *see Disconnect/Connect air pipe assembly, fitting rubber boot.*
11. Raise axle to locate air spring assembly into upper fixing, if required.
12. Fit new retaining clips to fixing points.
13. Reverse removal instructions 1 to 6.
14. Leak test air spring and around conections, *see Leak test.*

REAR AIR SPRING ASSEMBLY

Service repair no - 64.21.01

Remove and refit

Remove

 WARNING: Air suspension is pressurised up to 10 bar. Dirt or grease must not enter the system. Wear hand, ear and eye safety standard protection when servicing system.

 WARNING: The air spring must be restricted by suspension loading, with dampers fitted before inflation. Failure to observe this warning could cause air spring failure, resulting in component damage or personal injury. DO NOT ATTEMPT TO DISMANTLE AIR SPRING

1. Depressurise system, *see Depressurise system.*
2. Disconnect battery negative lead.
3. Remove wheel *see WHEELS AND TYRES, Repair, WHEEL.*
4. Support chassis on axle stands.
5. Support axle with jack.
6. Remove four retaining clips from upper and lower fixing.

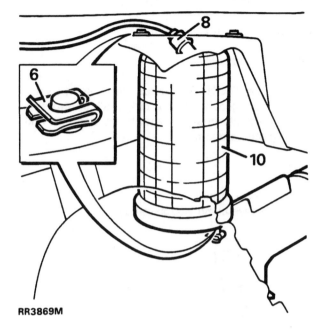

RR3869M

7. Lower axle for access to air pipe connection at top of air spring.
8. Clean connection with a stiff brush and soapy water. Peel back rubber boot.
9. Disconnect air pipe, *see Disconnect/Connect air pipe, seal all ends.*
10. Remove air spring assembly.

Refit

11. Locate air spring assembly onto lower fixing. Ensure air pipe connection points towards rear.
12. Connect air pipe to air spring assembly, fitting rubber boot, *see Disconnect/Connect air pipe.*
13. Raise axle to locate air spring assembly into upper fixing, if required.
14. Fit four new retaining clips to fixing points.
15. Reverse removal instructions 1 to 5.
16. Leak test air spring and connector, *see Leak test.*

BUMP STOP

Service repair no - 60.30.10

Remove and refit

⚠ CAUTION: Air suspension system uses 'progessive' bump stops, which must not be interchanged with those used on coil spring suspension.

Remove

1. Remove fixings.
2. Remove bump stop assembly.

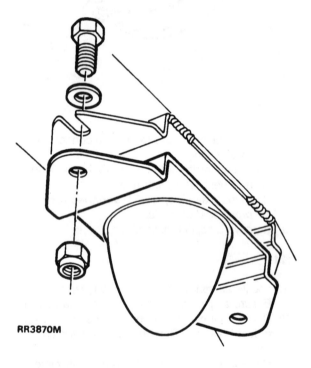

RR3870M

Refit

3. Position fixing bolts in chassis bracket.
4. Fit bump stop.
5. Tighten fixings.

HEIGHT SENSOR

Service repair no - 60.36.01 - Front

Service repair no - 64.36.01 - Back

Remove and refit

Remove

1. Disconnect battery negative lead.
2. Remove wheel *see WHEELS AND TYRES, Repair, wheel.*
3. Disconnect height sensor multiplug.
4. Remove height sensor lower link fixing.

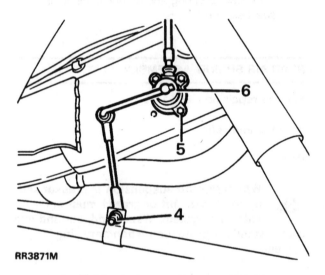

RR3871M

⚠ CAUTION: Back height sensors have longer lower link than the front sensors.

5. Remove height sensor fixings.
6. Remove height sensor.

Refit

7. Reverse removal instructions.
8. Recalibrate system *see Adjustment, recalibrate system.*
9. Attain standard ride height.

PRESSURE RELIEF VALVE

Remove and refit

⚠ **WARNING: Air suspension is pressurised up to 10 bar. Dirt or grease must not enter the system. Wear hand, ear and eye safety standard protection when servicing system.**

Remove

1. Remove valve block *see valve block.*
2. Clean around pressure relief valve with a stiff brush and soapy water.
3. Remove pressure relief valve.

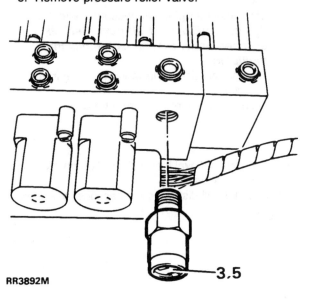

RR3892M

Refit

4. Coat threads of pressure relief valve with Loctite 572.
5. Fit valve, tighten to *12 Nm.*
6. Reverse removal instructions.

COMPRESSOR INLET FILTER.

Service repair no - 60.50.12

Remove and refit

The inlet filter is changed every 40,000 Kms (24,000 miles) - USA 30,000 miles.

⚠ **NOTE: Compressor inlet filter is situated adjacent to the fuel filler flap. Access is gained by removing the closure plate situated in the right hand side of load space.**

Remove

1. Remove sub woofer, (if fitted) *see ELECTRICAL, Repair, sub woofer.*
2. Remove eight screws. Remove closure panel.

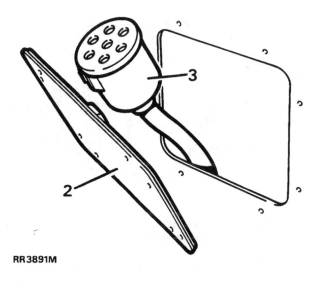

RR3891M

3. Remove inlet filter from mounting bracket.
4. Remove filter from pipe.

Refit

5. Fit new filter.
6. Reverse removal instructions.

AIR SUPPLY UNIT.

Service repair no - 60.50.23

Remove and refit

Mounted on the chasis this unit contains compressor, air dryer and valve block. The unit must be removed before removing these components.

⚠️ **WARNING: System is pressurised up to 10 bar. Dirt or grease must not enter the system. Wear hand,ear and eye safety standard protection when servicing system.**

Remove

1. Depressurise system *see Depressurise system.*
2. Disconnect battery negative lead.
3. Remove air supply unit side cover plate.

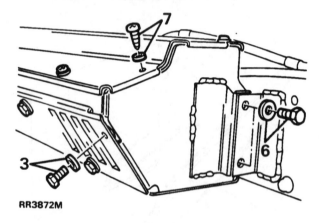

RR3872M

4. Disconnect multiplug.
5. Disconnect compressor inlet pipe, seal all exposed ends.
6. Support air supply unit. Remove four mounting bolts.

⚠️ **CAUTION: DO NOT allow unit to hang on pipes or electrical leads.**

7. Remove air supply assembly top cover plate.

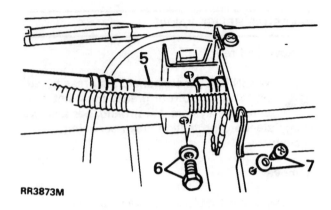

RR3873M

8. Clean all components. Identify air pipe connections.
9. Disconnect air pipe connections, *see Disconnect/Connect air pipe, Seal all exposed ends. Disconnect remaining multiplug.*
10. Remove air pipes and wiring harness from assembly.
11. Remove air supply unit from vehicle.

Refit

12. Reverse removal instructions, tighten mounting bolts to *24Nm.*
13. Leak test all disturbed connections *see leak test.*

AIR DRYER

Service repair no - 60.50.09

Remove and refit

Remove

⚠ WARNING: Air suspension is pressurised up to 10 bar. Dirt or grease must not enter the system. Wear hand, ear and eye safety standard protection when servicing system.

1. Remove air supply unit *see air supply unit.*
2. Disconnect two air pipes from air dryer, *see Disconnect/Connect air pipe.*

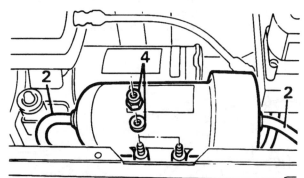

RR3874M

3. Seal dryer connections to prevent moisture intake.
4. Remove fixings.
5. Remove dryer.

Refit

6. Inspect air pipes. If damaged fit new pipes. DO NOT ATTEMPT TO TRIM DRYER PIPES.
7. Reverse removal instructions tighten nuts to *12 Nm*
8. Leak test connections, *see Leak test.*

AIR COMPRESSOR

Service repair no - 60.50.10

Remove and refit

Remove

⚠ WARNING: The air compressor assembly becomes hot when running. Avoid personal contact or allow to cool.

1. Remove air supply unit, *see air supply unit.*
2. Remove compressor outlet pipe, seal all exposed ends.

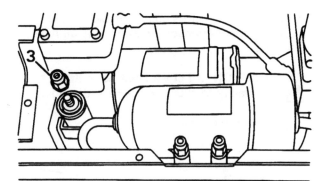

RR3875M

3. Remove four fixing nuts.
4. Remove compressor assembly.

Refit

5. Inspect compressor mountings, replace if necessary.
6. Reverse removal instructions, tighten nuts to *7Nm*
7. Check operation of compressor.
8. Leak test connections, *see Leak test.*

VALVE BLOCK

Service repair no - 60.50.11

Remove and refit

Remove

 WARNING: Air suspension is pressurised up to 10 bar. Dirt or grease must not enter the system. Wear hand, ear and eye safety standard protection when servicing system.

1. Remove air supply assembly *see air supply unit.*
2. Disconnect air pipes from valve block, *see Disconnect/Connect air pipe , seal all pipe ends.*

⚠ **CAUTION: Air pipes must be refitted correctly to avoid component damage.**

3. Remove four fixing bolts.

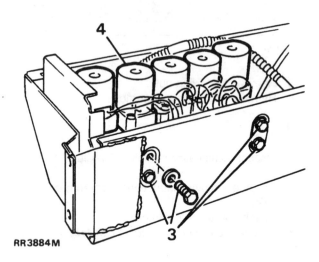

RR3884M

4. Remove valve block assembly.

Refit

5. Reverse removal instructions.
6. Leak test connections, *see Leak test.*

RESERVOIR PRESSURE SWITCH

Service repair no - 60.50.07

Remove and refit

Remove

 WARNING: Air suspension is pressurised up to 10 bar. Dirt or grease must not enter the system. Wear hand, ear and eye safety standard protection when servicing system.

1. Depressurise system, *see Depressurise system.*
2. Disconnect battery negative lead.
3. Clean around pressure switch with stiff brush and soapy water.
4. Disconnect pressure switch multiplug.

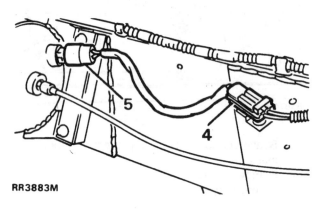

RR3883M

5. Unscrew and remove pressure switch.

⚠ **CAUTION: Protect opening from ingress of dirt.**

Refit

6. Apply Loctite 572 to thread of pressure switch.
7. Fit pressure switch and tighten to a torque of **23 Nm.**
8. Connect multiplug and battery.
9. Start engine to re-pressurise system.
10. Attain standard ride height.
11. Leak test pressure switch, *see Leak test.*

AIR RESERVOIR

Service repair no - 60.50.03

Remove and refit

Remove

⚠️ WARNING: Air suspension is pressurised up to 10 bar. Dirt or grease must not enter the system. Wear hand, ear and eye safety standard protection when servicing system.

1. Depressurise reservoir, *see Depressurise system.*
2. Clean around air pipe connection and drain plug with stiff brush and soapy water.
3. Open drain plug to release any residual pressure.
4. Disconnect air pipe, *see Disconnect/Connect air pipe.*

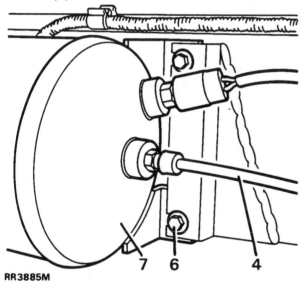

RR3885M

5. Disconnect pressure switch multi-plug.
6. Release four fixing bolts.
7. Remove reservoir.

Refit

7. Fit reservoir. Tighten bolts to *24Nm.*
8. Connect air pipe, fitting rubber boot, *see Disconnect/Connect air pipe.*
9. Connect pressure switch multi-plug.
10. Tighten drain plug to *70 Nm.*
11. Start engine to repressurise system.
10. Leak test reservoir, *see Leak test.*

ELECTRONIC CONTROL UNIT

Service repair no - 60.50.04

Remove and refit

Remove

1. Remove front trim from right hand front seat base.
2. Adjust seat rearward and upward.
3. Disconnect battery negative lead.
4. Release retaining clip from upper ECU plug.

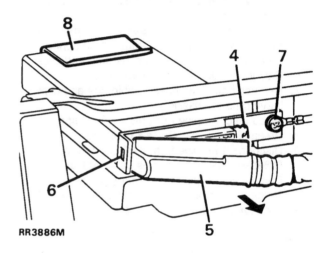

RR3886M

5. Move plug in direction of arrow.
6. Detach hooked end of plug from retaining post.
7. Remove retaining screw.
8. Remove ECU from retaining clip.

Refit

9. Fit ECU into retaining clip.
10. Fit retaining screw.
11. Connect ECU harness plug. Ensure plug retaining clip engages.
12. Reverse remaining removal procedure.
13. If fitting a new ECU, recalibrate height settings, *see Adjustment, Calibrate system.*

AIR HARNESS

Service repair no - 60.50.21

Remove and refit

Remove

⚠ **CAUTION: Thoroughly clean around all connections before disconnecting air pipes. Seal all exposed components against ingress of dirt and moisture.**

1. Place vehicle on a wheel free ramp.
2. Remove wheels, *see WHEELS AND TYRES, Repair, wheels.*
3. Remove air supply unit, *see air supply unit.*
4. Disconnect air pipe from front left air spring.
5. Release front left chassis cable ties and clips.
6. Disconnect air pipe from reservoir.
7. Release back left chassis cable ties and clips, leave clips in chassis.
8. Disconnect air pipe from back left air spring.
9. Release three rear chassis cable ties.
10. Disconnect air pipe from back right air spring.
11. Release back right chassis cable ties and clips.
12. Disconnect air pipe from front right air spring.
13. Release front right chassis cable ties and clips.
14. Remove air harness from vehicle.

Refit

15. Layout air harness, identifying routing and connections.
16. Route air harness around chassis.
17. Remove sealing plugs, reconnect left front air spring.
18. Secure left front chassis ties and clips.
19. Working around chassis, reverse removal procedure.

70 - BRAKES

CONTENTS

Page

DESCRIPTION AND OPERATION

REPAIR

WARNING LIGHTS

Brake fluid pressure/level and parking brake warning light - (red) - 1

The warning light situated in instrument binnacle indicates insufficient pressure in system and/or low fluid level. Warning light will illuminate when ignition is switched ON as part of initial bulb check, and when parking brake is applied.

If pressure in hydraulic system is lower than cut-in pressure for warning light, light will illuminate. When light is on hydraulic pump will start. Note, if light remains illuminated after bulb check and releasing park brake, DO NOT drive vehicle until light extinguishes.

⚠️ **WARNING: If light illuminates while vehicle is in motion, investigate fault immediately. Braking will be available after loss of pressure, but greater force will be required at pedal to slow vehicle.**

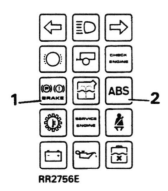

1 ———   ——— 2

RR2756E

ABS warning light - (amber) - 2 USA vehicles - (red) - 2

⚠️ **WARNING: Power assisted braking is not available if ignition is switched off. An increase in effort at brake pedal will be required to apply brakes.**

The ABS warning light situated in instrument binnacle indicates a failure in ABS system. Warning light will illuminate when ignition is switched ON, it will extinguish when vehicle speed exceeds 7 km/h (5 mph). This indicates that system self monitoring check was successful, and system performs correctly.

If light remains on or subsequently illuminates with ignition ON a fault in ABS system is indicated. The self monitoring procedure is repeated frequently while ignition is ON. If a fault is detected during self monitoring, light will illuminate indicating that one or more wheels are not under ABS control.

⚠️ **WARNING: Reduced ABS control is possible with ABS warning light illuminated depending on severity and type of fault. If both ABS and brake failure warning lights are illuminated, loss of system pressure or hydraulic pump failure is indicated. IT IS ESSENTIAL THAT FAULT IS IMMEDIATELY INVESTIGATED.**

ABS warning light - 1993 introduction

On 1993 model year vehicles a feature has been added to indicate whether or not the ABS ECU has recorded any faults which have not been repaired. If no faults are recorded the ABS warning light will switch off for half a second after ignition is switched on and the ECU has completed its self checks. This will occur during the time that the light is on between switching on and driving above 7 kph (5 mph). This enables a vehicle tester to check ABS without driving the vehicle.

⚠️ **NOTE: On a small number of early American vehicles, the bulb check masks the feature.**

ELECTRONIC TRACTION CONTROL - ETC

- WABCO DIFFERENTIAL BRAKING

WABCO, manufacturers of Range Rover ABS brake system have developed a differential braking system, ETC available as an extension to ABS. The system operates on the rear axle only, to help prevent loss of traction where one wheel has more grip than the other.
The system works by applying the brake to a spinning rear wheel. This transfers torque to the wheel with the grip. The brake supplies the torque resistance which the wheel cannot.

An example of when the system would operate is where one side of the vehicle is on ice and the other side on tarmac. ETC will control the spinning rear wheel.

 WARNING: If both wheels spin the system does not operate, as braking one wheel will not aid traction.

The system switches itself out at 50 kph (30 mph) since a vehicle travelling above this speed will not need ETC.

System operation is smooth and continuous and will not affect the comfort of the vehicle.

ETC is inhibited when the brakes are applied.

COMPONENTS

As ETC is an extension of the ABS unit it is only available on ABS equipped vehicles.

ECU - the system uses an extended ABS ECU. The same ECU is used on both ETC and non ETC vehicles. If ETC valve block is not connected electrically the ECU assumes the vehicle does not have ETC.

Two solenoid valves - similar to ABS control valves, incorporated in a valve block fitted to the ABS booster. In case of failure the valve block may be removed from the booster unit and a new unit fitted.

Brake pipes - three additional brake pipes to the ETC valve block are required.

ETC Warning light (1) - situated in the instrument binnacle, the warning light works in three different ways:

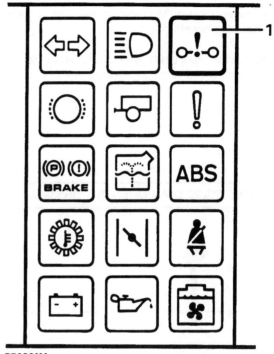

RR3901M

ETC active - The light will illuminate for a minimum of two seconds or as long as the system is active. In practice this time will rarely exceed ten seconds. This warns the driver that traction is becoming limited.

Protection mode - In the unlikely event that the system remains active continuously for more than sixty seconds, the system shuts down to protect brakes and solenoid valves from overheating. The warning light will flash at half second intervals for a minimum of ten seconds while ETC is shut down. If ETC is shut down, but NOT required by conditions, the light will not flash.

ETC fault - If a fault occurs which disables ETC, the warning light is constantly illuminated, (even when there is no wheel spin,) until ignition is switched off.

Bulb check - The light will illuminate for three seconds when ignition is switched on and ABS/ETC self checks completed.

USA - early vehicles - the warning light will be illuminated as part of warning light bulb check.

USA - later vehicles - the warning light will NOT be illuminated as part of warning light bulb check.

Changes to accomodate ETC

PCRV valve - moved to below booster unit, mounted on inner wing panel.

Accumulator - has direct feed to ETC valve block. Accumulator bleed valve is relocated to ETC valve block.

FAULT DIAGNOSIS

Diagnosis is by Wabco Diagnostic Controller - STC 2 with new software card, for both ETC and non ETC vehicles. See also Range Rover Electrical Trouble Shooting Manual.

Memory cards ABS/ETC:

English	STC 1080
French	STC 1081
German	STC 1082
Italian	STC 1083
Spanish	STC 1084

ETC HYDRAULIC COMPONENTS - RR3893M

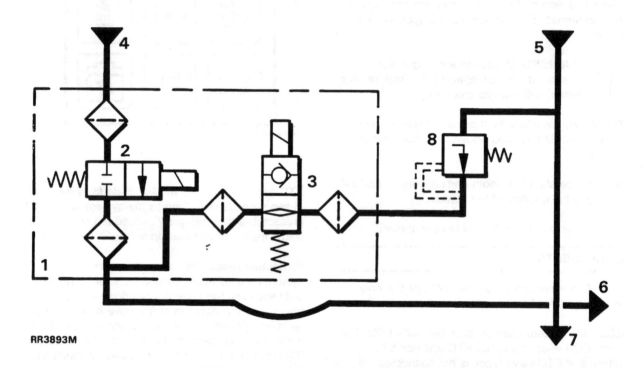

RR3893M

For full details of ABS components, *see ABS brakes, HYDRAULIC COMPONENTS*

1. ETC valve block
2. Power circuit solenoid valve - normally closed
3. Master cylinder isolating solenoid valve - normally open
4. From accumulator
5. From master cylinder power valve
6. Power circuit to rear brakes
7. Power circuit to front brakes
8. PCRV valve

ETC OPERATION - see RR3893M

When the wheelspeed sensors detect a rear wheel is spinning at above vehicle speed, solenoid valve 3. closes, isolating the master cylinder from the rear brakes. Solenoid valve 2. is pulsed open, allowing accumulator pressure to the rear brakes. The rear brake ABS valves operate to apply or release the brake at the spinning wheel as required.

ETC VALVE BLOCK

Remove and refit

Removing

1. Disconnect battery negative lead.
2. Depressurise brake system, **see ABS Brakes, depressurise system.**
3. Remove three hydraulic pipes from ETC valve block.

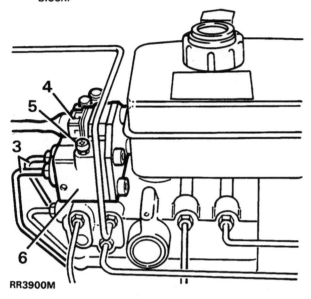

RR3900M

4. Disconnect ETC multi-plug.
5. Remove two valve block securing bolts.
6. Remove ETC valve block.

Refitting

7. Reverse removal procedure.
8. Bleed brakes, **see ABS brakes, brake system bleed (ABS).**

 NOTE: Bleed screw on ETC valve block is used when bleeding accumulator.

ETC VALVE BLOCK

Remove and refit

Remaining

1. Disconnect earth lead (negative lead).
2. Depressurise accumulator, see ABS Brakes, depressurise system.
3. Remove four hydraulic pipes from ETC valve block.

4. Disconnect electrical connector.
5. Remove two valve block retaining bolt.
6. Remove valve block.

Refitting

7. Reverse removal procedure.
8. Bleed brakes and ABS brakes, under specifications.

NOTE: Bleed screw on ETC valve block is used when bleeding accumulator.

86 - ELECTRICAL

CONTENTS

CONTENTS

Page

DESCRIPTION AND OPERATION

ANTI THEFT ALARM SYSTEM

For 1993 models a vehicle alarm system is available as original equipment. The main function of the system is to offer easy to use remote locking and unlocking of the vehicle without having to actively select the alarm function.

ALARM COMPONENTS

ANTI-THEFT SYSTEM FUNCTION

Perimetric protection

Using the key in the correct sequence will turn on and off perimetric protection only. When fully perimetrically armed, all doors, tailgate, and bonnet are protected against unauthorised access. If the door key is used in the normal manner the driver will be unaware of the door key sequence. The time taken to lock or unlock with the key must be less than 5 seconds. To prevent unauthorised tampering, the alarm will sound if the key is held in the unlocked position for longer than 5 seconds when armed. Cranking is disabled when perimetric protection is armed.

 NOTE: When key is turned left or right the keyswitch input will be activated, in conjunction with the sill button switch when links are operated.

1. Electronic control unit (ECU) and relays
2. Bonnet switch
3. Tailgate switch
4. Alarm horn
5. Light emitting diode (LED)

6. Ultrasonic unit
7. Door switches
8. Lock barrel, sill buttons
9. Handset transmitter (two supplied)

Volumetric protection

Using the handset transmitter will turn on and off volumetric protection. In volumetric mode the vehicle interior is protected using the ultrasonic sensor. Using the handset also arms and disarms the vehicle perimetrically. Cranking is disabled when volumetric and perimetric protection is armed.

 NOTE: If armed volumetrically the vehicle CANNOT be disarmed using the key.

Alarm horn

When an intrusion is detected the alarm horn will sound intermittently (Switzerland and Denmark continuous horn sound) and the hazard lights flash (where territorial regulations allow) for 30 seconds. The alarm must be retriggered before alarm horn will sound again.

Vehicle status indication

Vehicle status is indicated by up to three devices: (a) alarm horn, (b) hazard lights, (c) dash board LED. When the vehicle arms in either mode the hazard lights will flash three times and the LED will flash rapidly for 10 seconds. LED will then flash at a slower rate while vehicle is armed. When the vehicle disarms, hazard lights will flash once and LED will extinguish. If LED remains lit, it indicates that the alarm has been triggered. Turning on ignition or arming the alarm will extinguish LED. The LED will give a long pulse flash to indicate the ultrasonic unit being activated.

Radio frequency system

The RF system uses four frequencies according to market. If the coaxial aerial is not fitted system performance will be impaired. Both ECU and handset have a colour coded label.

Central locking

Central locking is controlled by the alarm ECU and may be operated by the key, sill button(s) or handset. The system works on both front doors on four door vehicles or driver's door on two door vehicles.

 NOTE: The central door locking system will shut down for a short period after more than 15 consecutive operations.

Inertia switch

An inertia switch is incorporated in the alarm system ECU. If ignition is on and the vehicle receives an impact sufficient to activate the inertia switch, the ECU will signal to unlock central locking actuators and flash hazard lights. Central locking will remain disabled for 30 seconds. To reset turn ignition off and then on after the 30 second period has elapsed.

Ultrasonic unit

The unit operates by emitting an air pressure carrier wave and receiving the wave back. Any disturbance within the vehicle which disturbs the wave will be detected, triggering the alarm.
When the volumetric sensor is activated it monitors movement within the vehicle for 15 seconds before detecting and responding to intrusions. If the sensor detects movement within the vehicle it delays arming until a 15 seconds quiet period has elapsed. If continuous movement is detected the alarm will not arm volumetrically.

Frequency	Colour ECU/Handset	Territory
418.0 MHz	Pink/pink	UK, Ireland
224.5 MHz,	Yellow/yellow	France
433.92 MHz	Blue/blue	Europe, not France, Switzerland, Italy, Denmark
433.92 MHz	White/Blue	Switzerland, Denmark
315.0 MHz	Green/green	Rest of world, Italy, Australia
315.0 MHz	Orange/Green	Gulf, Japan

Partially armed mode

If a door, tailgate or bonnet is left open when the system is armed, the LED will not light for 10 seconds indicating a mislock condition. Hazard lights will not flash. If an open door or tailgate is causing the mislock, the starter motor is disabled. The alarm will sound if ignition is turned to start position. If an open bonnet is causing the mislock the starter motor is disabled. The alarm will arm the volumetric part of the system. If the door tailgate or bonnet is subsequently closed, after a 5 second delay, the doors will unlock and immediately lock and the system will fully arm.

Handset transmitter

The handset LED will give one short flash when button is pressed momentarily.
If button is held down the LED will light again after 2 seconds for 2 seconds, and extinguish until button is released and repressed. The handset contains unique information distinguishing it from other transmitters. It also contains a set of 'random' rolling codes programmed into the ECU before leaving the factory. Each time the handset is pressed a different code is transmitted to the ECU.
If handset is operated more than four times outside the vehicle range (6 metres) or power supply is removed, it will be necessary to re-sychronise handset and the ECU by pressing the handset three times within range and within 5 seconds.

⚠ NOTE: If both handsets are lost or damaged when system is armed it will be necessary to fit a new ECU with two matching handsets.

Handset batteries

If handset LED flashes continuously when button is pressed, the batteries need replacing. The hazard lights will flash one 3 second pulse, instead of three times upon arming vehicle.

Power up mode

The alarm system always remembers the state it was left in when power was removed. If the alarm powers up in an armed state and is subsequently triggered it will give a warning that it will fully trigger unless disarmed. This warning consists of short horn pulses every two seconds for 15 seconds.

New born mode

When the ECU is first produced, it will be in its 'new born' mode. In this mode it will respond to any remote of the right frequency. This mode will be cancelled when the ECU has received ten valid handset signals without power interruption.

Engine cranking

It is only possible to crank the engine when ignition is ON and alarm disabled.

BUILT IN TEST PROCEDURE

The built in test procedure is accessed as follows:

1. Starting conditions: ignition off, doors unlocked, bonnet switch depressed.
2. Carry out instructions 3 to 7 within 8 seconds.
3. Release bonnet switch
4. Switch ignition ON.
5. Lock doors.
6. Switch ignition OFF.
7. Switch ignition ON.

If alarm is correctly accessed, horn will sound and LED will flash. The following checks can be made:

8. Open and close any door or tailgate - LED will light.
9. Depress bonnet switch - hazards will flash.
10. Check engine cranking is disabled. Do not turn off ignition.
11. Check ultrasonic by operating handset, LED will emit one 5 second flash, and will flash if interior is disturbed.

⚠ NOTE: If ECU is in new born mode any handset of the right frequency will work. If not an initialised handset is required see Handset Initialisation.

12. Turn OFF ignition or press handset to end test procedure. Horn will sound as before to indicate end of test mode.

2

ELECTRICAL

RANGE ROVER

IN CAR ENTERTAINMENT (ICE)

For 1993 model year three levels of factory fitted in car entertainment are available.

New features are as follows:
Side screen antenna, new head units, subwoofer assembly, new speakers and new CD autochanger.

The Mid/low line radio has the following features:
Radio data system (RDS), electronic tuning, one touch memory, automatic programme control (APC), Dolby, subwoofer line output, CATS coded, manual tape deck.

High line radio is as above with the following exceptions:
Logic tape deck, blank skip/repeat, 5 channel line output, CD ready (this unit is fitted when the CD option is called for).

Subwoofer

The subwoofer unit is located in the right hand side of the luggage compartment. It amplifies frequencies between 20 and 150 Hz to give an enhanced bass sound.

Subwoofer amplifier

The amplifier is fitted on top of the subwoofer unit.

Speaker amplifier

A remote 4 x 20 amp speaker amplifier is part of high line ICE specification.
This is also fitted on top of the subwoofer.

Side screen antenna

The antenna is now printed into the rear side screen on four door models. For America and Japan the element is fitted in both rear side screens, known as diversity antenna system. Other markets have a single element in the right hand side screen only. Diversity reception means that if vehicle movement results in a loss of signal due to reflections from buildings (known as multipath distortion), the radio will switch to the antenna receiving the strongest signal. This results in less interference and better stereo performance.

Antenna amplifiers

New antenna amplifiers are located behind the headlining above the side screen antenna(s). Right hand side fitment is an FM + AM amplifier, left hand side, diversity, is an FM only amplifier.

Speakers

Trim level 1 - Two door vehicles have two front twin cone speakers Four door vehicles have two coaxial front speakers and two twin cone rear speakers.
Trim level 2 - Four coaxial speakers, two front, two rear and a subwoofer.
Trim level 3 - Four coaxial speakers, two front, two rear, two bass speakers and crossover unit front, a subwoofer and amplifier. Twin cone speakers have a mid range and tweeter cone driven by the same coil. Coaxial speakers have two cones and two coils. Where front doors have bass speakers a crossover unit is fitted which effectively splits the frequency between bass and coaxial.

CD autochanger

The CD autochanger is fitted underneath the subwoofer unit.

DESCRIPTION AND OPERATION

HANDSET INITIALISATION

⚠ **NOTE: New handsets are supplied in pairs. If a new handset is required, it will require initialisation to the ECU using the following procuedure:**

1. Starting conditions: ignition off, doors unlocked, bonnet switch depressed.
2. Carry out instructions 3. to 9. within 8 seconds.
3. Switch ignition ON.
4. Switch ignition OFF.
5. Lock doors.
6. Unlock doors.
7. Release bonnet switch.
8. Switch ignition ON.
9. Switch ignition OFF.

If alarm is correctly accessed, horn will sound and LED will light. It is now possible to programme two handsets of correct frequency to vehicle alarm ECU. This must be carried out within two minutes.

10. Press and hold down button on first handset until dash LED flashes.
11. Repeat instruction 10. for second handset.
12. The LED will extinguish if both handsets have been initialised correctly.

HANDSET BATTERIES

Replace

1. Gently prise handset apart using a coin or small flat bladed screwdriver.
2. Hold the board in one hand, cup other hand, clap hands together to jar batteries from clip.
3. Leave batteries out, operate handset by pressing button for 10 seconds to allow integrated circuit to reset itself.

⚠ **CAUTION: Handle new batteries as little as possible. Hands should be clean, dry and free from grease.**

4. Fit new batteries in clip, positive side uppermost.
5. Clip handset case together.

ALARM ECU

Service repair no - 86.77.01

Remove and refit

Remove

1. Remove lower dash panel, see CHASSIS AND BODY, Repair, lower dash panel.
2. Remove multiplugs and aerial lead from ECU.

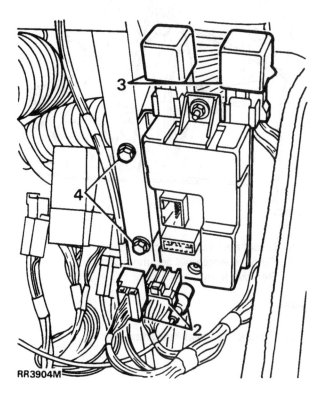

RR3904M

3. Remove relays and bases from bracket.
4. Remove ECU bracket fixings.
5. Remove ECU with bracket.

Refit

6. Reverse removal procedure. Ensure aerial and multiplugs are fitted securely to ensure alarm functions correctly.

ALARM HORN

Remove and refit

Remove

1. Remove decker panel, *see CHASSIS AND BODY, Repair, decker panel.*

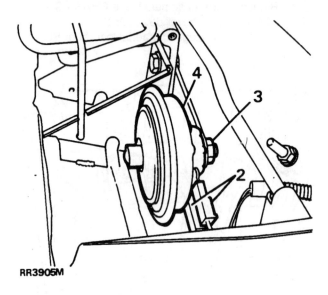

RR3905M

2. Disconnect two lucar connectors.
3. Remove single nut securing horn.
4. Remove horn.

Refit

5. Reverse removal instructions

ANTENNA AMPLIFIER

Remove and refit

Remove

1. Remove headlining sufficiently to gain access to signal amplifier. *see CHASSIS AND BODY, Repair, headlining.*
2. Remove 'RF in' lead from antenna.

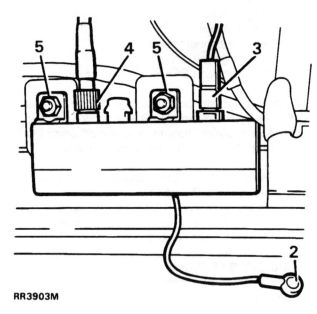

RR3903M

3. Remove '+ VE' lead from amplifier.
4. Unscrew 'RF out' lead, disconnect.
5. Remove two securing nuts.
6. Remove amplifier.

Refit

7. Reverse removal instructions. To ensure 'RF out' lead is correctly located, hold centre lead down in position while tightening knurled nut.

SUBWOOFER BOX

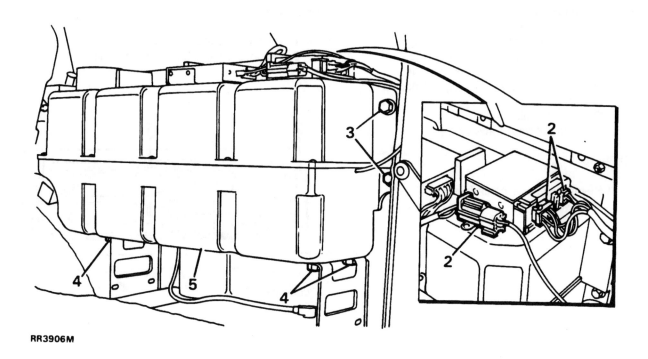

RR3906M

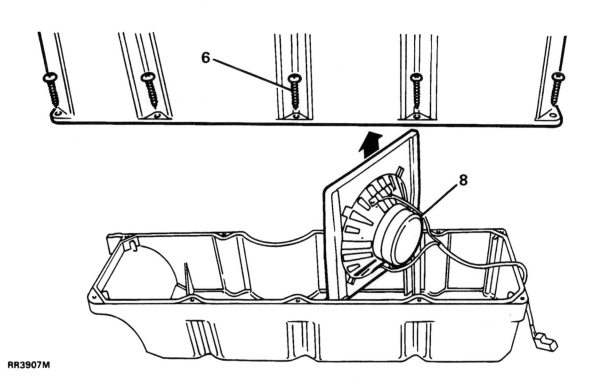

RR3907M

Remove and refit

Remove

1. Disconnect battery negative lead.
2. Disconnect electrical leads.
3. Remove four bolts from upper fixing.
4. Remove four bolts from lower fixing.
5. Remove subwoofer box from vehicle.
6. Remove ten screws securing two halves of subwoofer.
7. Removetop half of unit.
8. Remove subwoofer speaker.

Refitting

9. Reverse removal procedure.

RADIO

Remove and refit

Remove

1. Disconect battery negative lead.
2. Remove access covers from radio.

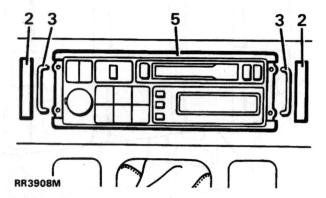

RR3908M

3. Insert suitable radio removal tools e.g. SMD 4091 into access holes.
4. Press removal tools to release radio.
5. Remove radio, disconnect aerial and multiplugs from rear of radio.

Refit

6. Reverse radio code.
7. Reactivate radio code.

RANGE ROVER

RANGE ROVER
2.4 & 2.5 TURBO DIESEL ENGINES

WORKSHOP MANUAL SUPPLEMENT

Publication Number LSM180WS4 Ed 2

Published by the
Technical Publications Department of

2.4 & 2.5 Turbo Diesel Engine Supplement

CONTENTS

CONTENTS

INTRODUCTION

This supplement supersedes publication No's. LSM227 WS, LSM180 WS4 and combines the existing 2.4 litre Diesel Engine with the introduction of the new 2.5 Litre Diesel Engine for the Range Rover. It should be used in conjunction with the existing Range Rover Workshop Manual publication No. LSM180 WM.

SYNTHETIC RUBBER

Many 0-ring seals, flexible pipes and other similar items which appear to be natural rubber are made of synthetic materials called Fluoroelastomers. Under normal operating conditions this material is safe, and does not present a health hazard. However, if the material is damaged by fire or excessive heat, it can break down and produce highly corrosive Hydrofluoric acid which can cause serious burns on contact with skin. Should the material be in a burnt or overheated condition handle only with seamless industrial gloves. Decontaminate and dispose of the gloves immediately after use.

If skin contact does occur, remove any contaminated clothing immediately and obtain medical assistance without delay. In the meantime, wash the affected area with copious amounts of cold water or limewater for fifteen to sixty minutes.

RECOMMENDED SEALANTS

A number of branded products are recommended in this manual for use during maintenance and repair work.

These items include: **HYLOMAR GASKET AND JOINTING COMPOUND** and **HYLOSIL RTV SILICON COMPOUND.**

They should be available locally from garage equipment suppliers. If there is any problem obtaining supplies, contact one of the following companies for advice and the address of the nearest supplier.

MARSTON LUBRICANTS LTD.
Hylo House,
Cale lane,
New Springs,
Wigan WN2 1JR,

0942 824242

COPYRIGHT

MODEL: DIESEL RANGE ROVER 2.5 LITRE ENGINE.

Type	95 A VM type HR 4924 HI	
Number of cylinders	4	
Bore	92 mm	3.62 in
Stroke	94 mm	3.7 in
Capacity	2500 cm³	152.32 in³
Injection order	1 - 3 - 4 - 2	
Compression ratio	22.5 : 1 (± 0.5)	

Crankshaft

Front main journal diameter	62,995 to 63,010 mm	2.4801 to 2.4807 in
Clearance in main bearing	0,05 to 0,115 mm	0.0019 to 0.0045 in
Minimum regrind diameter	62,495 mm	2.4604 in
Central main journal diameter	63,005 to 63,020 mm	2.4805 to 2.4811 in
Clearance in main bearing	0,03 to 0,088 mm	0.0012 to 0.0034 in
Minimum regrind diameter	62,52 mm	2.4614 in
Rear main journal diameter	69,985 to 70,00 mm	2.7551 to 2.7559 in
Clearance in main bearing	0,040 to 0,070 mm	0.0015 to 0.0027 in
Minimum regrind diameter	69,485 mm	2.7354 in
Crankpin journal diameter	53,94 to 53,955 mm	2.123 to 2.124 in
Clearance in big end bearing	0,022 to 0,076 mm	0.0008 to 0.0030 in
Minimum regrind diameter	53,44 mm	2.104 in
End float	0,153 to 0,304 mm	0.006 to 0.0119 in
Adjustment	Thrust washers	
Thrust washers available	2,311 to 2,362	0.090 to 0.093 in
	2,411 to 2,462 mm	0.095 to 0.097 in
	2,511 to 2,562 mm	0.099 to 0.101 in

Thrust spacer

Thickness	7,9 to 8,1 mm	0.311 to 0.319 in
Diameter	89,96 to 90 mm	3.542 to 3.543 in

Main bearings
Standard
Internal diameter:

Front	63,060 to 63,11 mm	2.4872 to 2. 4845 in
Centre	63,050 to 63,09 mm	2.4823 to 2.4838 in
Rear	70,040 to 70,055 mm	2.7574 to 2.7580 in

Bearing undersizes:
0,25 mm (0.01 in) and 0,5 mm (0.02 in) less than the dimensions given.

Main bearing carriers
Internal diameter:

Front	67,025 to 67,050 mm	2.639 to 2.640 in
Centre	66,67 to 66,687 mm	2.624 to 2.625 in
Rear	75,005 to 75,030 mm	2.953 to 2.954 in
Piston oil jet opening pressure	1,5 to 2,0 kg/cm²	22 to 29 lb/in²

2.5 LITRE ENGINE CONTINUED

Liners
Internal diameter:
White

Standard	92,000 to 92,010 mm	3.6220 to 3.6224 in

Red

Standard	92,010 to 92,020 mm	3.6224 to 3.6228 in
Protrusion	0,01 to 0,06 mm	0.0004 to 0.002 in
Adjustment	Shims	
Shims available	0,15 mm	0.006 in
	0,20 mm	0.008 in
	0,23 mm	0.009 in
Maximum ovality	0,100 mm	0.004 in
Maximum taper	0,100 mm	0.004 in

Cylinder heads

Minimum thickness	89,95 to 90,05 mm	3.541 to 3.545 in

Gaskets

Free thickness	Identity		
Number STC 654	No notch	1,51 to 1,59 mm	0.059 to 0.062 in
Number STC 656	1 notch	1,75 to 1,83 mm	0.069 to 0.072 in
Number STC 655	2 notches	1,65 to 1,73 mm	0.065 to 0.068 in
Fitted thickness			
Number STC 654		1,42 mm ± 0,04	0.056 in ± 0.001575
Number STC 656		1,62 mm ± 0,04	0.064 in ± 0.001575
Number STC 655		1,52 mm ± 0,04	0.059 in ± 0.001575

End plates

Height	91,26 to 91,34 mm	3.593 to 3.596 in

Connecting rods
Weights (connecting rod complete with small end bush, big-end cap and big-end bolts, but without the big-end shell).

Letter Code		
L	1156 to 1172 gr	Fully machined balanced

Pistons
Skirt diameter:
(measured at approximately 15 mm (0.6 in) above
the bottom of the skirt).

Class A	91,92 to 91,93mm	3.6188 to 3.6192 in
Class B	91,93 to 91,94mm	3.6192 to 3.6196 in
Piston skirt wear limit	0,05 mm	0.0019 in
Maximum ovality of gudgeon pin bore	0,05mm	0.0019 in
Piston clearance.		
Top of piston to cylinder head	0,95 to 1,04mm	0.0374 to 0.0409 in
Piston protrusion above crankcase	0,38 to 0,47mm	0.0149 to 0.0185 in
	Fit gasket 1,42	
....	0,58 to 0,67mm	0.0228 to 0.0263 in
	Fit gasket 1,62	
....	0,48 to 0,57mm	0.0189 to 0.0224 in
	Fit gasket 1,52	
Maximum piston to liner clearance	0,15mm	0.006 in

2.5 LITRE ENGINE CONTINUED

Small end bush
Internal diameter:
  Minimum .... 30,030 mm   1.1823 in
  Maximum .... 30,045 mm   1.1828 in
  Wear limit between bush
  and gudgeon pin .... 0,100 mm   0. 004 in

Big-end bearings
Standard
  Internal diameter .... 53,977 to 54,016 mm   2.125 to 2.126 in
  Bearing undersizes:
    0,25 mm (0.01 in) and 0,5 mm (0.02 in) less than the dimensions given.

Piston rings
Clearance in groove:
  Top .... 0,080 to 0,130 mm   0.0031 to 0.0051 in
  Second .... 0,070 to 0,102 mm   0.0027 to 0.004 in
  Oil control .... 0,040 to 0,072 mm   0.0015 to 0.0028 in
Fitted gap:
  Top .... 0,25 to 0,50 mm   0.0098 to 0.0196 in
  Second .... 0,25 to 0,45 mm   0.0098 to 0.0177 in
  Oil control .... 0,25 to 0,58 mm   0.0098 to 0.0228 in

Gudgeon Pins
Type .... Fully floating
Diameter .... 29,990 to 29,996 mm   1.180 to 1.181 in
Clearance in connecting rod .... 0,034 to 0,055 mm   0.0013 to 0.0022 in
Wear limit between gudgeon
pin and connecting rod bush .... 0,100 mm   0.004 in

Camshaft
Journal diameter: Front .... 53,495 to 53,51 mm   2.1061 to 2.1067 in
  Bearing clearance .... 0,030 to 0,095 mm   0.0012 to 0.0037 in
  Centre .... 53,45 to 53,47 mm   2.1043 to 2.1051 in
  Bearing clearance .... 0,07 to 0,14 mm   0.0027 to 0.0055 in
  Rear .... 53,48 to 53,50 mm   2.1055 to 2.1063 in
  Bearing clearance .... 0,04 to 0,11 mm   0.0016 to 0.0043 in

Cam lobe minimum dimensions:

RR1578M

Inlet (A)
  (c) .... 38,5 mm   1.516 in
  (d) .... 45,7 mm   1.799 in
Exhaust (B)
  (c) .... 37,5 mm   1.476 in
  (d) .... 45,14 mm   1.777 in
Thrust plate thickness .... 3,95 to 4,05 mm   0.155 to 0.159 in

2.5 LITRE ENGINE CONTINUED

Tappets

Outside diameter	14,965 to 14,985 mm	0.589 to 0.590 in

Rocker gear

Shaft diameter	21,979 to 22,00 mm	0.865 to 0.866 in
Bush internal diameter	22,020 to 22,041 mm	0.867 to 0.868 in
Assembly clearance	0,020 to 0,062 mm	0.0.0008 to 0.0024 in
Wear limit between bush and shaft	0,2 mm	0.008 in

Valves

Face angle:		
Inlet	55° 30'	
Exhaust	45° 30'	
Head diameter:		
Inlet	40,05 to 40,25 mm	1.576 to 1.584 in
Exhaust	33,80 to 34,00 mm	1.331 to 1.338 in
Head stand down:		
Inlet	0,80 to 1,20 mm	0.0315 to 0.0472 in
Exhaust	0,79 to 1,19 mm	0.0311 to 0.468 in
Stem diameter:		
Inlet	7,940 to 7,960 mm	0.312 to 0.313 in
Exhaust	7,920 to 7,940 mm	0.311 to 0.312 in
Clearance in guide:		
Inlet	0,040 to 0,075 mm	0.0016 to 0.0029 in
Exhaust	0,060 to 0,095 mm	0.0024 to 0.0037 in

Valve guides

Inside diameter	8 to 8,015 mm	0.314 to 0.315 in
Fitted height (above spring plate counterbore)	13,5 to 14 mm	0.531 to 0.551 in

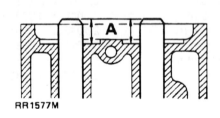

RR1577M

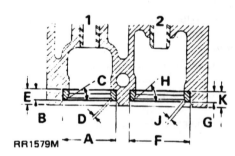

RR1579M

Valve seat inserts

Machining dimensions

Exhaust (1)

A	36,066 to 36,050 mm	1.4199 to 1.4193 in
B	7,00 to 7,05 mm	0.275 to 0.277 in
C	44°30'	
D	1,65 to 2,05 mm	0.065 to 0.080 in
E	10,15 to 10,25 mm	0.399 to 0.403 in

Inlet (2)

F	42,070 to 42,086 mm	1.6536 to 1.6569 in
G	7,14 to 7,19 mm	0.281 to 0.283 in
H	34° 30'	
J	1,8 to 2,2 mm	0.071 to 0.086 in
K	10,3 to 10,4 mm	0.405 to 0.409 in

2.5 LITRE ENGINE CONTINUED

Valve springs

Free length	44,65 mm	1.76 in
Fitted length	38,6 mm	1.52 in
Load at fitted length	34 ± 3% Kg	75 ± 3% lbf.
Load at top of lift	92,5 ± 3% Kg	204 ± 3% lbf.
Number of coils	5,33	

Valve timing

Rocker clearance: Timing

Inlet	0,30 mm	0.012 in
Exhaust	0,30 mm	0.012 in

Inlet valve:

Opens	22° ± 5° B.T.D.C.
Closes	48° ± 5° A.B.D.C.

Exhaust valve:

Opens	60° ± 5° B.B.D.C.
Closes	24° ± 5° A.T.D.C.

Lubrication

System pressure with oil at 90-100° C

at 4,000 rev/min	3,5 to 5,0 kgf/cm²	50 to 70 lbf/in².
Pressure relief valve opens	6.38 kgf/cm²	91 lbf/in².

Pressure relief valve spring

- free length	57,5 mm	2.26 in.

Oil pump:

Outer rotor end float	0,04 to 0,087 mm	0.0015 to 0.0034 in.
Inner rotor end float	0,04 to 0,087 mm	0.0015 to 0.0034 in.
Outer rotor to body		
diametrical clearance	0,130 to 0,230 mm	0.005 to 0.009 in.
Rotor body to drive gear		
clearance (pump not fitted)	0,15 to 0,25 mm	0.0059 to 0.0098 in

COOLING SYSTEM

Thermostat	80°C ± 2°C	
Pressure cap	1,05 kgf cm²	15 lb f/in²

DRIVE BELT TENSIONING

Installed drive belts using a recognised driving belt
tension gauge to be :-

Air conditioning compressor	450N	95 lbf
Power steering pump	400N	90 lbf
Alternator/water pump	490N	110 lbf

FUEL SYSTEM

Fuel lift pump .... mechanical, driven by camshaft
Turbo charger:
    Shaft radial clearance .... 0,35 mm   0.0137 in
    Shaft axial clearance .... 0,10 mm   0.0039 in
Waste gate valve:
    Opening pressure .... 0,9 kgf cm^2 13 lbf/in^2

CLUTCH

Make and type .... Valeo, diaphragm
Diameter .... 235mm   9.25 in

GEARBOX

Model .... LT77 (manual)
Type .... Five speed, single helical constant
mesh with synchromesh on all
forward gears

TRANSFER GEARBOX

Model .... BORG WARNER
Type .... 13-61 with viscous controlled unit

STARTER MOTOR

Make and type .... BOSCH 0.001. 362.092

ALTERNATOR

Make and type .... Magnetti Marelli A127 - 65A
On Diesel Vogue Range Rover .... Magnetti Marelli A133 - 80A

MODEL: 2.4 LITRE DIESEL RANGE ROVER ENGINE

Type .... 11A VM type HR 492 HI
Number of cylinders 4
Bore .... 92 mm   3.62 in
Stroke .... 90 mm   3.54 in
Capacity .... 2393 cm³   146.03 in³
Injection order .... 1 - 3 - 4 - 2
Compression ratio .... 21.5 : 1 (± 0.5)

Crankshaft
Front main journal diameter .... 62,98 to 63 mm   2.4795 to 2.4803 in
   Clearance in main bearing .... 0,06 to 0,13 mm   0.0023 to 0.005 in
   Minimum regrind diameter .... 62,48 mm   2.4498 in
Central main journal diameter .... 62,98 to 63 mm   2.4795 to 2.4803 in
   Clearance in main bearing .... 0,05 to 0,113 mm   0.0019 to 0.0044 in
   Minimum regrind diameter .... 62,48 mm   2.4498 in
Rear main journal diameter .... 69,98 to 70 mm   2.7551 to 2.7559 in
   Clearance in main bearing .... 0,06 to 0,105 mm   0.0023 to 0.0041 in
   Minimum regrind diameter .... 69,48 mm   2.7354 in
Crankpin journal diameter .... 53,92 to 53,94 mm   2.1228 to 2.1236 in
   Clearance in big end bearing .... 0,035 to 0,094 mm   0.0014 to 0.0037 in
   Minimum regrind diameter .... 53,42 mm   2.1032 in
End float .... 0,12 to 0,323 mm   0.005 to 0.0127 in
Adjustment .... Thrust washers
   Thrust washers available .... 2,311 to 2,362 mm   0.090 to 0.093 in
                                      2,411 to 2,462 mm   0.095 to 0.097 in
                                       2,511 to 2,562 mm   0.099 to 0.101 in

Thrust spacer
Thickness .... 7,9 to 8,1 mm   0.311 to 0.319 in
Diameter .... 89,96 to 90 mm   3.542 to 3.543 in

Main bearings
Standard
Internal diameter:
Front .... 63,060 to 63,11 mm   2.4872 to 2. 4845 in
Centre .... 63,050 to 63,09 mm   2.4823 to 2. 4838 in
Rear .... 70,060 to 70,085 mm   2.7582 to 2.7592 in
Bearing undersizes:
0,25 mm (0.01 in) and 0,5 mm (0.02 in) less than the dimensions given.

Main bearing carriers
Internal diameter:
Front/centre .... 66,67 to 66,687 mm   2.624 to 2.625 in
Rear .... 75,005 to 75,030 mm   2.953 to 2.954 in
Piston oil jet opening pressure .... 1,5 to 2,0 kg/cm²   22 to 29 lb/ in²

2.4 LITRE ENGINE CONTINUED

Liners
Internal diameter:
White
Standard .... 92,000 to 92,010 mm   3.6220 to 3.6224 in
Red
Standard .... 92,010 to 92,020 mm   3.6224 to 3.6228 in
Protrusion .... 0 to 0,05 mm   0 to 0.002 in
Adjustment .... Shims
Shims available .... 0,15 mm   0.006 in
                                                                   0,20 mm   0.008 in
                                                                   0,23 mm   0.009 in
Maximum ovality .... 0,100 mm   0.004 in
Maximum taper .... 0,100 mm   0.004 in

Cylinder heads
Minimum thickness .... 89,95 to 90,05 mm   3.541 to 3.545 in
Gaskets

Free thickness	Identity		
Number STC 654	No notch	1,60 mm	0.063 in
Number STC 656	1 notch	1,80 mm	0.071 in
Number STC 655	2 notches	1,70 mm	0.067 in

Fitted thickness
Number STC 654 .... 1,42 mm   0.056 in
Number STC 656 .... 1,62 mm   0.064 in
Number STC 655 .... 1,52 mm   0.059 in

End plates
Height .... 91,26 to 91,34 mm   3.593 to 3.596 in

Connecting rods
Weights (connecting rod complete with small end bush, big-end cap and big end bolts, but without the big-end shell).

Letter Code		
A	1100 to 1109 gr	38.80 to 39.12 oz
B	1110 to 1119 gr	39.15 to 39.47 oz
C	1120 to 1129 gr	39.51 to 39.82 oz
D	1130 to 1139 gr	39.86 to 40.17 oz
E	1140 to 1149 gr	40.21 to 40.53 oz
F	1150 to 1159 gr	40.56 to 40.88 oz
G	1160 to 1169 gr	40.92 to 41.23 oz
H	1170 to 1179 gr	41.27 to 41.58 oz
I	1180 to 1189 gr	41.62 to 41.94 oz

Small end bush
Internal diameter:
Minimum .... 30,030 mm   1.1823 in
Maximum .... 30,045 mm   1.1828 in
Wear limit between bush
and gudgeon pin .... 0,100 mm   0.004 in

Big-end bearings
Standard
Internal diameter .... 53,975 to 54,014 mm   2.125 to 2.126 in
Bearing undersizes:
    0,25 mm (0.01 in) and 0,5 mm (0.02 in) less than the dimensions given.

2.4 LITRE ENGINE CONTINUED

Pistons

Skirt diameter:
(measured at approximately 15 mm (0.6 in) above the bottom of the skirt).

Class A	91,965 to 91,975 mm	3.6207 to 3.6211 in
Class B	91,975 to 91,985 mm	3.6211 to 3.6214 in
Piston skirt wear limit	0,05 mm	0.0019 in
Maximum ovality of gudgeon pin bore	0,05 mm	0.0019 in

Piston clearance.

Top of piston to cylinder head	0,85 to 0,94 mm	0.0335 to 0.0370 in
Piston protrusion above crankcase	0,48 to 0,57 mm Fit gasket 1,42	0.0189 to 0.0224 in
Piston protrusion above crankcase	0,68 to 0,77 mm Fit gasket 1,62	0.0268 to 0.0303 in
Piston protrusion above crankcase	0,58 to 0,67 mm Fit gasket 1,52	0.0228 to 0.0263 in
Maximum piston to liner clearance	0,15 mm	0.006 in

Piston rings

Clearance in groove:

Top	0,080 to 0,130 mm	0.0031 to 0.0051 in
Second	0,070 to 0,102 mm	0.0027 to 0.004 in
Oil control	0,030 to 0,062 mm	0.0012 to 0.0024 in

Fitted gap:

Top	0,40 to 0,65 mm	0.0157 to 0.0256 in
Second	0,25 to 0,45 mm	0.0098 to 0.0177 in
Oil control	0,25 to 0,58 mm	0.0098 to 0.0228 in

Gudgeon Pins

Type	Fully floating	
Diameter	29,990 to 29,996 mm	1.180 to 1.181 in
Clearance in connecting rod	0,034 to 0,055 mm	0.0013 to 0.0022 in
Wear limit between gudgeon pin and connecting rod bush	0,100 mm	0.004 in

Camshaft

Journal diameter	53,48 to 53,50 mm	2.105 to 2. 106 in
Clearance in bearings	0,040 to 0,11 mm	0.0016 to 0.0043 in

Cam lobe minimum dimensions:

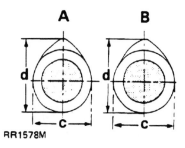

RR1578M

Inlet (A)		
(c)	38,5 mm	1.516 in
(d)	45,7 mm	1.799 in
Exhaust (B)		
(c)	37,5 mm	1.476 in
(d)	45,14 mm	1.777 in
Thrust plate thickness	3,95 to 4,05 mm	0.155 to 0.159 in.

2.4 LITRE ENGINE CONTINUED

Tappets

Outside diameter	14,965 to 14,985 mm	0.589 to 0.590 in

Rocker gear

Shaft diameter	21,979 to 22,00 mm	0.865 to 0.866 in
Bush internal diameter	22,020 to 22,041 mm	0.867 to 0.868 in
Assembly clearance	0,020 to 0,062 mm	0.0.0008 to 0.0024 in
Wear limit between bush and shaft	0,2 mm	0.008 in

Valves

Face angle:		
Inlet	55° 30'	
Exhaust	45° 30'	
Head diameter:		
Inlet	40,05 to 40,25 mm	1.576 to 1.584 in
Exhaust	33,80 to 34,00 mm	1.331 to 1.338 in
Head stand down:		
Inlet	0,80 to 1,20 mm	0.0315 to 0.0472 in
Exhaust	0,79 to 1,19 mm	0.0311 to 0.468 in
Stem diameter:		
Inlet	7,940 to 7,960 mm	0.312 to 0.313 in
Exhaust	7,920 to 7,940 mm	0.311 to 0.312 in
Clearance in guide:		
Inlet	0,040 to 0,075 mm	0.0016 to 0.0029 in
Exhaust	0,060 to 0,095 mm	0.0024 to 0.0037 in

Valve guides

Inside diameter	8 to 8,015 mm	0.314 to 0.315 in
Fitted height (above spring plate counterbore)	13,5 to 14 mm	0.531 to 0.551 in

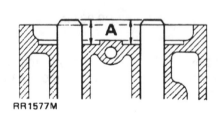

RR1577M

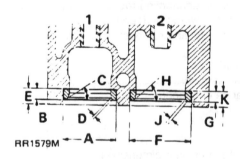

RR1579M

Valve seat inserts

Machining dimensions

Exhaust (1)

A	36,066 to 36,050 mm	1.4199 to 1.4193 in
B	7,00 to 7,05 mm	0.275 to 0.277 in
C	44° 30'	
D	1,70 to 1,80 mm	0.067 to 0.071 in
E	10,00 to 10,10 mm	0.393 to 0.397 in

Inlet (2)

F	42,070 to 42,086 mm	1.6536 to 1.6569 in
G	7,14 to 7,19 mm	0.281 to 0.283 in
H	34° 30'	
J	1,9 to 2,0 mm	0.075 to 0.079 in
K	10,25 to 10,35 mm	0.403 to 0.407 in

2.4 LITRE ENGINE CONTINUED

Valve springs

Free length	44,65 mm	1.76 in
Fitted length	38,6 mm	1.52 in
Load at fitted length	34 ± 3% Kg	75 ± 3% lbf.
Load at top of lift	92,5 ± 3% Kg	204 ± 3% lbf.
Number of coils	5,33	

Valve timing

Rocker clearance: Timing

Inlet	0,30 mm	0.012 in
Exhaust	0,30 mm	0.012 in

Inlet valve:

Opens	22° ± 5° B.T.D.C.
Closes	48° ± 5° A.B.D.C.

Exhaust valve:

Opens	60° ± 5° B.B.D.C.
Closes	24° ± 5° A.T.D.C.

Lubrication

System pressure with oil at 90 - 100°C

at 4,000 rev/min	3,5 to 5,0 kgf/cm²	50 to 70 lbf/in².
Pressure relief valve opens	4 to 4,5 kgf/cm ²	57 to 64 lbf/in².
Pressure relief valve spring		
- free length	57,5 mm	2.26 in.

Oil pump:

Outer rotor end float	0,081 to 0,097 mm	0.003 to 0.004 in.
Inner rotor end float	0,081 to 0,097 mm	0.003 to 0.004 in.
Outer rotor to body		
diametrical clearance	0,130 to 0,230 mm	0.005 to 0.009 in.
Rotor body to drive gear		
clearance	0,050 to 0,070 mm	0.0 02 to 0.003 in.

COOLING SYSTEM

Thermostat	83°C ± 2°C	
Pressure cap	1,05 kgf cm²	15 lb f/in²

DRIVE BELT TENSIONING

On 'V' type installed drive belts using a recognised
driving belt tension gauge to be :-

On 12,7 mm wide belts	450N	....	95 lbf

"In field" Tensioning - No gauge available

Deflection of belt run between longest belt
centres to be:- .... 0,5 mm per 25 mm of belt run

FUEL SYSTEM

Fuel lift pump	mechanical, driven by camshaft	
Turbo charger:		
Shaft radial clearance	0,42 mm	0.016 in
Shaft axial clearance	0,15 mm	0.006 in
Waste gate valve:		
Opening pressure	0,9 kgf/cm^2	13 lbf/in^2

CLUTCH

Make and type	Valeo, diaphragm	
Diameter	235,0 mm	9.25 in

ENGINE TUNING DATA

Model: Diesel Range Rover .... **1990 MODEL YEAR 2.5 LITRE ENGINE**

Engine

Type	95A VM Type HR 4924 HI	
Capacity	2500 cm³	152.32 in³
Compression pressure	24 to 26 kgf/cm²	340 to 370 lbf/in²
Injection order	1 - 3 - 4 - 2	
Idling speed at running temperature	750 - 800 rev/min	
Idling speed cold start temperature	1000 - 1100 rev/min	
Maximum light running speed	4700 to 4730 rev/min	
Maximum governed road speed	4200 rev/min	
Valve rocker clearances (cold)		
Inlet	0,30 mm	0.012 in
Exhaust	0,30 mm	0.012 in

Fuel injection pump

Make and type	Bosch Rotary VE 4 10F 2100 L269
Injection pump timing	3° -0 + 1° B.T.D.C.

Injectors

Make and type	Bosch KBE 58 S 4/4
Nozzle type	DNO SD 263 or SDV 4011379
Opening pressure	150 +8/-0 BAR

Heater plugs

Make and type	Bosch 0.250.201.012
Nominal voltage	11 volts

ENGINE TUNING DATA

Model: Diesel Range Rover .... **1986 MODEL YEAR 2.4 LITRE ENGINE**

Engine
Type .... 11A VM Type HR 492 HI
Capacity .... 2393 cm³   146.03 in³
Compression pressure at crank speed 150 rev/min ... 32 to 35 kgf/cm²   450 to 500 lbf/in²
Injection order .... 1 - 3 - 4 - 2
Idling speed at running temperature .... 750 - 800 rev/min
Maximum light running speed .... 4700 to 4730 rev/min
Maximum governed road speed .... 4200 rev/min
Valve rocker clearances (cold)
Inlet .... 0,30 mm   0.012 in
Exhaust .... 0,30 mm   0.012 in

Fuel injection pump
Make and type .... Bosch Rotary VE L 168-1
Injection pump timing .... 3° B.T.D.C.

Injectors
Make and type .... Bosch KBE 58 S 4/4
Nozzle type .... DNO SD 263
Opening pressure .... 150 + 8/-0 BAR

Heater plugs
Make and type .... Bosch 0.250.201.012
Nominal voltage .... 11 volts

TORQUE WRENCH SETTINGS

ENGINE	Nm
Camshaft screws	24
Connecting rod bolts	81 *
Crankshaft pulley nut	152
Cylinder head bolts	SEE SPECIAL PROCEDURE
Cylinder head oil pipe unions	8
Engine coolant rail bolts	8
Engine mountings	49
Engine sump bolts	11
Engine sump pan bolts	11
Exhaust manifold nuts	32
Exhaust pipe flange bolts	27
Flywheel bolts	108
Flywheel housing bolts	49
Fuel line unions	19
Heater plugs	23
Idler gear screws 2.4 litre engine	27
Injection pump mounting nut	31
Injection pump gear nut	88
Injector nut	27
Inlet manifold nuts	32
Main bearing carrier bolts	42
Oil drain plugs	79
Oil filter base	38
Oil pump screws	27
Oil thermostat	74
Rear main bearing carrier nuts	27
Rocker cover nuts	9
Rocker shaft pedestal nuts	108 *
Timing cover screws	12
Turbo charger to manifold nuts	26
Vacuum pump nuts	21
Vacuum pump screws 2.5 Litre Engine	28
Valve gear oil pipe unions	8
Water pump screws	24

ELECTRICAL	Nm
Alternator tie rod	49
Alternator bracket to crankcase	54
Alternator pulley nut	54
Alternator bottom fixing	54
Starter motor to flywheel housing	68

* Apply Molyguard to threads before fitting.

RECOMMENDED LUBRICANTS AND FLUIDS

Use only the recommended grades of oil set out below.
These recommendations apply to climates where operational temperatures are above -10°C.

Petrol engine sump Oil can	BP Visco 2000 plus Castrol Syntron X Castrol GTX -2 Castrolite TXT Duckhams Hypergrade Motor Oil Esso Superlube EX2 Mobil Super Duckhams QXR Mobil 1 Rally Formula Esso Vitra	Fina Supergrade Motor Oil Fina First Shell Super Motor Oil Shell Gemini Havoline X1 Havoline multigrade UK only - Land Rover Parts 15W/40
Diesel engine sump **	BP Vanellus C3 Extra (15W/40) Castrol Turbomax (15W/40) Duckhams Fleetmaster SHPD (15W/40) Esso Super Diesel Oil TD (15W/40) The following list of oils to MIL - L - 2104D or CCMC D2 or API Service levels CD are for emergency use only if the above oils are not available. They can be used for topping up without detriment, but if used for engine oil changing, they are limited to a maximum of 5,000 km (3,000 miles) between oil and filter changes. BP Vanellus C3 Multigrade (15W/40) Castrol RX Super (15W/40) Duckhams Hypergrade (15W/50) Esso Essolube XD - 3 plus (15W/40) Mobil Delvac Super (15W/40)	Mobil Delvac 1400 Super (15W/40) Fina Kappa LDO (15W/40) Shell Myrina (15W/40) Texaco URSA Super TD (15W/40) UK only - Land Rover Parts SHPD Fina Dilano HPD (15W/40) Shell Rimula X (15W/40) Texaco URSA Super Plus (15W/40)
Automatic gearbox	BP Autran DX2D Castrol TQ Dexron IID Duckhams Fleetmatic CD Duckhams D - Matic Esso ATF Dexron IID	Mobil ATF 220D Fina Dexron IID Shell ATF Dexron IID Texamatic Fluid 9226 UK only - Land Rover Parts ATF Dexron II
Manual gearbox	BP Autran G Castrol TQF Duckhams Q - Matic Esso ATF Type G Mobil ATF 210	Fina Purfimatic 33G Shell Donax TF Texamatic Type G or Universal UK only - Land Rover Parts ATF Type 'G'
Front and Rear differential Swivel pin housings	BP Gear Oil SAE 90EP Castrol Hypoy SAE 90EP Duckhams Hypoid 90 Esso Gear Oil GX (85W/90) Mobil Mobilube HD90	Fina Pontonic MP SAE (80W/90) Shell Spirax 90EP Texaco Multigear Lubricant EP (85W/90) UK only - Land Rover Parts EP90

** **Other approved oils include:** Agip Sigma Turbo, Aral OL P327, Autol Valve - SHP, Aviation Turbo, Caltex RPM Delo 450, Century Centurion, Chevron Delo 450 Multigrade, Divinol Multimax Extra, Ecubsol CD Plus, Elf Multiperformance 4D, Esso Special Diesel, Fanal Indol X, Fuchs Titan Truck 1540, Gulf Superfleet Special, IP Taurus M, Total Rubia TIR XLD, Valvoline Super HD 4D LD, Veedol Turbostar, Gulf Superfleet (GB), Silkolene Turbolene D, Kuwait Q8 T700.

Propeller shaft Front and Rear	BP Energrease L2 Castrol LM Grease Duckhams LB 10 Esso Multi - purpose Grease H	Mobil Grease MP Fina Marson HTL 2 Shell Retinax A Marfak All Purpose Grease
Power steering box and fluid Reservoir Transfer Gearbox	BP Autran DX2D BP Autran G Castrol TQ Dexron IID Castrol TQF Duckhams Fleetmatic CD Duckhams Q - matic Esso ATF Dexron IID Esso ATF Type G Mobil ATF 220D Mobil ATF 210	Fina Dexron IID Fina Purfimatic 33G Shell ATF Dexron IID Shell Donax TF Texamatic Fluid 9226 Texamatic Type G or 4291A Universal UK only - Land Rover Parts ATF Dexron II or Type G
Brake and clutch reservoirs	Brake fluids having a minimum boiling point of 260°C (500°F) and complying with FMVSS 116 DOT4	
Lubrication nipples (hubs, ball joints etc.)	BP Energrease L2 Castrol LM Grease Duckhams LB 10 Esso Multi - purpose Grease H	Mobil Grease MP Fina Marson HTL 2 Shell Retinax A Marfak All Purpose Grease
Ball joint assembly Top Link	BPL21M Castrol M53 Shell Retinax AM	Duckhams LBM10 Esso MP Mobil Supergrease
Seat slides Door lock striker	BP Energrease L2 Castrol LM Grease Duckhams LB 10 Esso Multi - purpose Grease H Mobil Grease MP	Fina Marson HTL 2 Shell Retinax A Marfak All purpose grease NLGI - 2 Multi - purpose Lithium - based Grease

Recommended lubricants and fluids - All climates and conditions

COMPONENT	SPECIFICATION	VISCOSITY	AMBIENT TEMPERATURE °C (Approx. range)
Petrol models Engine sump Oil can	Oils must meet: RES.22.OL.G-4 or CCMC G-4 API service level SG	5W/30	-30 to +35
		5W/40 5W/50	-30 to +50
		10W/30	-20 to +35
		10W/40 10W/50	-20 to +50
		15W/40 15W/50	-10 to +50
		20W/40 20W/50	0 to +50
		25W/40 25W/50	+5 to +50
Diesel models Engine sump	RES 22 OLD-5 CCMC D-5 API CE	15W/40 10W/30	15W/40: -10 to +50 / 10W/30: -20 to +35
* Emergency use:	MIL - L - 2104D, CCMCD2 or API CD	10W/30	-20 to +50
Main Gearbox Automatic	ATF Dexron IID		-30 to +50
Main Gearbox manual	ATF M2C33 (F or G)		-30 to +50
Final drive units Swivel pin housings	API GL4 or GL5 MIL - L - 2105 or MIL - L - 21-05B	90 EP	-20 to +50
		80W EP	-30 to +10
Power steering Borg Warner Transfer Box	ATF M2C 336 or ATF Dexron IID		-30 to +50

* Diesel Models - Engine Sump

Oils for emergency use only if the SHPD oils are not available. They can be used for topping up without detriment, but if used for engine oil changing, they are limited to a maximum of 5,000 km (3,000 miles) between oil and filter changes. (See previous page)

Engine cooling system	Use an ethylene glycol based anti-freeze (containing no methanol) with non-phosphate corrosion inhibitors suitable for use in aluminium engines to ensure the protection of the cooling system against frost and corrosion in all seasons. Use one part anti-freeze to one part water for protection down to -36°C. **IMPORTANT: Coolant solution must not fall below proportions one part anti-freeze to three parts water, i.e. minimum 25% anti-freeze in coolant otherwise damage to engine is liable to occur.**
Battery lugs, Earthing surfaces where paint has been removed	Petroleum jelly. **NOTE: Do not use Silicone Grease**
Air Conditioning System Refrigerant	**METHYLCHLORIDE REFRIGERANTS MUST NOT BE USED** Use only with refrigerant 12. This includes 'Freon 12' and 'Arcton 12'
Compressor Oil	Shell Clavus 68 BP Energol LPT68 Sunisco 4GS Texaco Capella E Wax/Free 68. Castrol Icematic 99
ABS Sensor bush-rear	Silicone grease: Staborags NBU - Wabco 830 502,0634 Wacker chemie 704 - Wabco 830 502,0164 Kluber GL301

ANTI-FREEZE

ENGINE TYPE	MIXTURE STRENGTH	PERCENTAGE CONCENTRATION	PROTECTION LOWER TEMPERATURE LIMIT
V8 (aluminium) Diesel VM	One part anti-freeze One part water	50%	
Complete protection Vehicle may be driven away immediately from cold			- 36°C
Safe limit protection Coolant in mushy state. Engine may be started and driven away after warm-up period			- 41°C
Lower protection Prevents frost damage to cylinder head, block and radiator. Thaw out before starting engine			- 47°C

SUPPLEMENTARY MAINTENANCE SCHEDULE FOR DIESEL - RANGE ROVER

The following supplementary schedule should be used together with the schedule in the main Workshop Manual, for the complete maintenance of Range Rover Diesel models.

The maintenance intervals in this schedule are for European highway driving conditions, for change intervals of engine oil and all filters, under severe abnormal operating conditions, consult your nearest Land Rover Dealer.

Every 500 km (250 miles)

- Check engine oil level

After first 1,500 km (1000 miles)

- Tighten inlet manifold, exhaust manifold and turbo-charger bolts
  (See **Section 06** for torque wrench settings)
- Change engine oil and filter
- Check engine coolant level
- Check drive belt tension
- General check for fluid leaks
- Check tappet clearance

Every 10,000 km (6,000 miles)

- Change engine oil and oil filter
- Drain sedimenter
- Change fuel filter
- Check for fluid leaks
- Check drive belt tension

Every 20,000 km (12,000 miles)

- Clean lift pump filter
- Clean fuel sedimenter
- Clean fuel tank breather pipe
- Change air filter element
- Check engine cold idle speed

Every 40,000 km (24,000 miles)

- Check tappet clearance
- Check glow plug operation (continuity)
- Remove diesel injectors, spray test and refit

Every 80,000 km (48,000 miles)

- Remove intercooler element and flush out using 'GENKLENE' produced by ICI Ltd

Every 96,000 km (60,000 miles)

- Check turbo-charger impeller shaft axial and radial clearance
  (See **Section 04** General Specification Data)
- Check wastegate operation

SPECIAL MAINTENANCE INSTRUCTION

First 40,000Km (24,000 miles) only

NOTE: These instructions must be carried out at the first 40,000 Km (24,000 miles) service. The use of new type gasket eliminates the need to retorque head bolts at 1,500 Km (1,000 miles).

1. Centre bolts, starting with bolt A: Without slackening bolts, tighten each bolt in sequence through 10 - 15°.
2. Side bolts: Without slackening bolts cheque that torque of each bolt is 85 - 90 Nm. first M1 then M2.

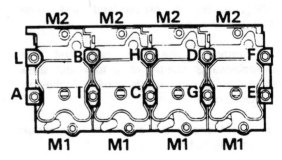

RR3804M

ENGINE COOLANT

The level of coolant in the expansion tank should be checked daily or weekly dependent on the operating conditions.

The expansion tank is located in the engine compartment and:-

On 2.4 litre engines is fitted with a spring loaded filler cap. (1) Fig. RR1154

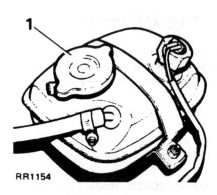

On 2.5 litre engines is fitted with a plastic filler cap and combined coolant level sensor.
(2) Fig. RR2729M

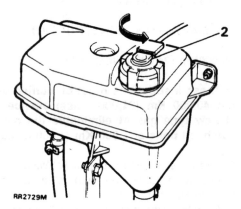

WARNING: Do not remove the expansion tank filler cap when the engine is hot, because the cooling system is pressurised and personal scalding could result.

When removing the filler cap, first turn it anti-clockwise a quarter of a turn and allow all pressure to escape, before turning further in the same direction to lift off.

With a cold engine the expansion tank should be approximately half full.

When replacing the filler cap, it is important that it is tightened down fully. Failure to tighten the filler cap properly may result in water loss, with possible damage to the engine through overheating.

Frost precautions and engine protection.

To prevent corrosion of the aluminium alloy engine parts it is imperative that the cooling system is filled with the specified strength solution of clean water and the correct type of anti-freeze, winter and summer.

The cooling system should be drained and flushed out and refilled with anti-freeze every 40,000 km (24,000 miles) or sooner where the purity of the water is questionable.

After the second winter the system should be drained and thoroughly flushed by using a hose inserted in the radiator filler orifice.

NOTE: Whenever the cooling system has been drained and refilled, the vehicle should be run for approximately 20 minutes to ensure that the thermostat is open. Recheck the coolant level top up as necessary.

**ENGINE OIL LEVEL CHECKING AND TOPPING
UP - Fig. RR1155**
Withdraw the dipstick (1) and wipe the blade clean.

Re-insert the dipstick fully, then withdraw it and
check the oil level indication, which must be
between the 'MAX' (top) and 'MIN' (bottom) mark.

RR1155

To top-up, remove the filler cap (2) and top-up the
engine with new oil, then repeat the checking and
topping-up procedure until the oil level is correct. Do
not overfill. Do not forget to replace the filler cap.

Oil draining and refilling - Fig RR1156
The oil should be drained after a run when the
engine is warm. The oil filter can be renewed while
the oil is draining.

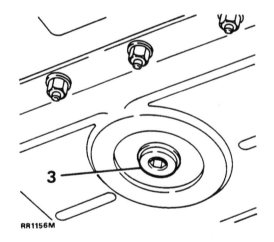

RR1156M

Place a container under the engine that has a
capacity of at least 7 litres (12 pints)

Unscrew the drain plug (3) and drain the oil. Clean
the drain plug; use a new sealing washer if
necessary and refit the drain plug.

Fill the engine with the correct quantity of new oil
and recheck the level.

ENGINE OIL REFILL AND FILTER RENEWAL
Following any drain and refill of the engine oil or
renewal of the engine oil filter cartridge the engine
must be run at idle speed for a short period to allow
oil pressure to build up in the turbo-charger.

**CAUTION: Serious damage to the turbo-charger
will result if the engine is run above idling speed
before oil pressure is restored.**

Oil filter cartridge renewal - Fig. RR1157
Slacken the clip and disconnect the air intake hose
from the turbo-charger.

Clean the area around the filter head, and place a
container beneath the engine.

Unscrew the oil filter cartridge (1) and discard it.

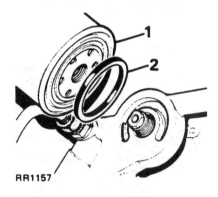

RR1157

Wet the seal (2) of the new oil filter with engine oil.

Screw the new filter into position, using hand force
only.

Check the engine oil level.

Refit the air intake hose to the turbo-charger and
tighten the clip.

Start the engine and check for leaks.

Stop the engine, wait a few minutes, then check the
oil level and top-up if necessary.

MAIN FUEL FILTER - Fig. RR1161

Draining off water and sediment
It is essential that any water and sediment in the fuel filter is drained off, as water in the fuel can result in damage to the injection pump.

Hold a small receptacle beneath the drain cock.

Unscrew the drain cock (1) at the bottom of the filter half a turn.

Drain off water and sediment.

Immediately fuel starts to flow from the drain cock tighten the drain cock.

NOTE: Any delay in tightening the drain cock when the fuel starts to flow could possibly mean bleeding the fuel system.

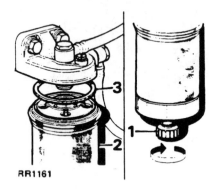

RR1161

Renewing the fuel filter element

Clean the area around the filter head, and place a container beneath the filter.

Unscrew the filter (2) - a quantity of fuel will be released - and discard the filter. A hexagon is formed on the base of the filter for unscrewing it with a spanner.

Wet the seal (3) of the new filter with fuel.

Screw the new filter into position and tighten with a spanner.

Ensure that the drain cock at the bottom of the filter is screwed up tight.

CLEANING FUEL TANK BREATHER PIPE - Fig. RR1168

The fuel tank breather pipe must be cleaned regularly to prevent diesel oil residue and road dust causing blockage. The pipe is located underneath the vehicle and runs down the body panel joint, to the rear of the fuel tank filler neck.

Clean the pipe at the intervals specified in the maintenance schedule, or more frequently if operating in dusty or muddy conditions.

Wipe clean the end of the breather pipe (1) and use a stout piece of wire to clear the inside.

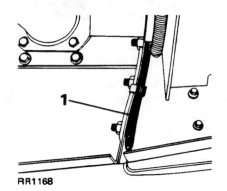

RR1168

FUEL SEDIMENTER

The sedimenter is attached to the left-hand side of the chassis frame near the fuel tank, and increases the working life of the fuel filter by the larger droplets of water and larger particles of foreign matter from the fuel.

Drain off water as follows:

Drain off water - Fig. RR1159

Slacken off drain plug (1) and allow water to run out. When pure diesel fuel is emitted, tighten the drain plug.

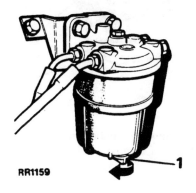

RR1159

Clean element - Fig. RR1160

If fuel is used from dubious storage facilities, the sedimenter should be removed and cleaned as circumstances require or as specified in the maintenance schedule.

Disconnect the fuel inlet pipe from the sedimenter and raise pipe above the the level of the fuel tank and support in this position to prevent fuel draining from the tank.

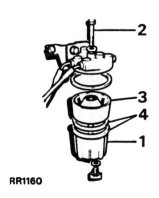

RR1160

Support the sedimenter bowl (1), unscrew the bolt (2) on the top of the unit and remove the bowl.

Remove the sedimenter element (3) and clean all parts in kerosene. Fit new seals (4) and reassemble the sedimenter.

Slacken off the drain plug, when pure diesel fuel runs out, tighten plug. Start the engine and check the sedimenter for leaks.

**RENEW AIR CLEANER ELEMENT
- Figs. RR1158/RR1171**

Disconnect the hose (1) from the air cleaner. Release the retaining strap (2) and lift up the air cleaner assembly.

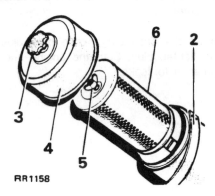

RR1158

Unscrew the knob (3) and remove the end cover (4) from the air cleaner casing. Unscrew the wing nut (5), discard the element (6) and wipe clean the casing and cover.

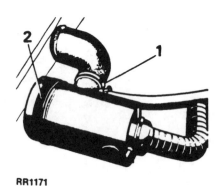

RR1171

**CHECK AIR CLEANER DUMP VALVE
- Fig. RR1169**

Squeeze open the dump valve (7) and check that the interior is clean. Also, check that the rubber is flexible and in good condition. If necessary, remove the dump valve to clean the interior. Fit a new valve if the original is in poor condition

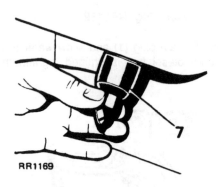

RR1169

Fit a new element, rubber seal end first, and reassemble the air cleaner.

TAPPET ADJUSTMENT - Fig. RR1164

The correct clearance is: inlet and exhaust 0,30 mm (0.012 in) engine cold.

Remove rocker cover
Unscrew the centre retaining bolts and remove the rocker covers for each cylinder, taking care not to lose the seals from the top of the rocker cover.

Check and adjust the tappets
Turn the engine over until number 1 valve (counting from front of engine) is fully open.

Using a 0,30 mm (0.012 in) feeler gauge (1) check the clearance between the valve tip and rocker pad of number 7 valve.

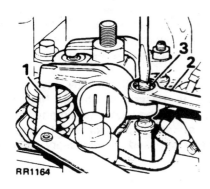

RR1164

Adjust the clearance by slackening the lock nut (3) and turning the tappet adjusting screw clockwise to reduce clearance and anti-clockwise to increase clearance. Recheck the clearance after tightening the lock nut.

Continue to check and adjust the remaining tappets in the following sequence:

With No.1 valve fully open adjust No.7 valve.
With No.8 valve fully open adjust No.2 valve.
With No.5 valve fully open adjust No.3 valve.
With No.4 valve fully open adjust No.6 valve.
With No.7 valve fully open adjust No.1 valve.
With No.2 valve fully open adjust No.8 valve.
With No.3 valve fully open adjust No.5 valve.
With No.6 valve fully open adjust No.4 valve.

Refitting the rocker covers
Clean the rocker cover gasket seating face.

Inspect the rocker cover gaskets; renew if damaged.

Position the rocker cover with the oil filler cap on No.1 cylinder, and the rocker cover with the breather pipe to No.3 cylinder

Check that the collars and seals are located on the top of the rocker covers, then fit the rocker covers and tighten the retaining nuts.

INJECTORS - Fig. RR1165

To locate a faulty injector, slacken the feed pipe union nut on the suspected injector and run the engine slowly. if there is no change in engine performance or if a faulty condition, such as a smoky exhaust, has disappeared, it can be assumed that the injector is faulty and a replacement injector should be fitted.

Unscrew the retaining nut and remove the rocker cover adjacent to the injector to be removed.

Disconnect the fuel leak-off pipe (1) and the high pressure pipe (2) from the injector.

Unscrew the mounting nut (3), and remove the mounting clamp, injector (4) and sealing washer.

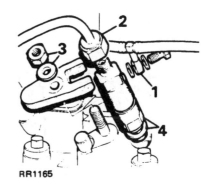

RR1165

Before fitting an injector fit a new sealing washer.

Fit the injector, its mounting clamp and tighten the injector retaining nut to a torque of 1,7 kg/m.

Refit the high pressure feed pipe and leak-off pipe.

Refit the rocker cover; renew gasket if it is damaged; check that the collars and seals are located on top of the rocker cover before fitting and tightening the rocker cover.

NOTE: Fit the rocker cover with the oil filler cap on No.1 cylinder and the rocker cover with the breather pipe to No. 2 and 3 cylinders.

CHECK DRIVE BELTS - adjust or renew

Right-hand steering - Fig. RR1162

Left-hand steering - Fig. RR1163

WARNING: Disconnect the battery to prevent any possibility of the starter motor being operated.

The procedure for checking and adjusting the drive belts for the alternator (1), power steering pump (2) and the optional, air conditioning compressor (3) is similar. Examine all belts for wear and renew if necessary.

NOTE: Any marks on the outside of the air conditioning drive belt, caused by belt slipper bracket, can be ignored.

Check the tension of each drive belt, the belts should fit within the following dimensions, when checked at mid-point between the pulleys on the longest side of the belt.

Using a recognised drive belt tensioning gauge the tensions to be:-

On 'V' type drive belts:-
    12,7mm wide belts .... 450N .... 95 lbf

On poly 'V' drive belts 2.5 Litre Engines:-
    Power steering pump .... 400N .... 90 lbf
    Alternator/water pump .... 490N ..... 110 lbf

"In field" Tensioning-No gauge available

Using normal hand pressure to check deflection, the belt should be tensioned to give a deflection of 0,5 mm per 25 mm of belt run between belt centres.

If any of the drive belts require adjustment, slacken the applicable pivot bolt (4) and the adjusting bracket nut and screw (5), pull the driven unit away from the engine until the belt is tight. Tighten the adjusting bracket then tighten the pivot bolt. Check the belt tension and readjust if necessary.

CAUTION: When fitting a new drive belt, tension the belt as described above. Reconnect the battery, start and run the engine for 3 to 5 minutes at fast idle, after which time the belt must be re-checked. If necessary retension the belt.

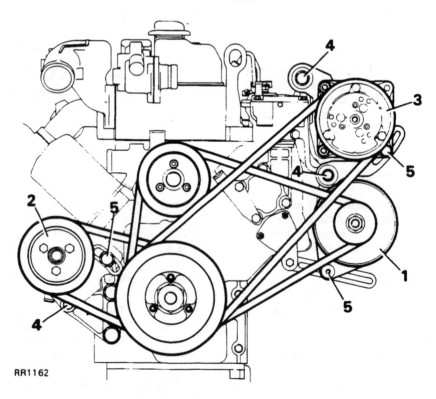

RR1162

RIGHT HAND STEERING

LEFT HAND STEERING

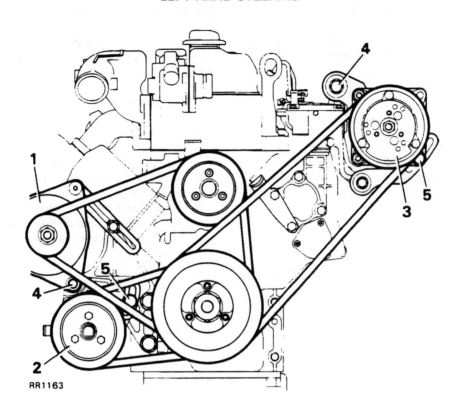

RR1163

CHECK COLD START ADJUSTMENT AND COLD IDLE SPEED 2.4 LITRE ENGINE

NOTE: It is important that these checks are only carried-out when the engine is cold.

Cold start adjustment

1. Check dimension 'A' which should be 3mm to 4mm.
   If adjustment is required slacken the cable clamp nut and move the clamp forward or rearward as necessary to achieve the correct dimensions and tighten the clamp nut.

Cold idle speed

2. The cold idle speed should be between 1000 and 1100 r.p.m. If adjustment is required slacken the nut and move the lever stop (3) to increase or decrease the speed accordingly and tighten the nut.

CHECK AND ADJUST FAST IDLE SETTING PROCEDURE 2.5 LITRE ENGINE.

NOTE: It is important that these checks are carried-out when the engine is warm - above 40°C.

Fast idle adjustment

1. Dimension 'A' should be 4.5 mm. Adjust the lever inserting a 4.5mm distance piece into the gap to hold this dimension.
2. Move the accelerator lever to achieve engine speed 1000 to 1100 r.p.m. (no load).
3. Release and move the lever stop until it rests against the stop tab on the accelerator lever. Retighten the lever stop. Remove the distance piece.

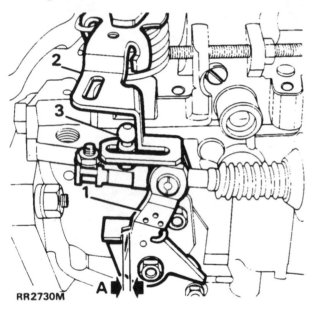

RR2730M

18G.1367A

Remover crankshaft pulley

18G.1367-1A

Adaptor crankshaft gear remover

18G.1368

Remover and holder
injection pump drive gear 2.4
engine

18G.1374

Replacer crankshaft rear oil seal

18G.1375

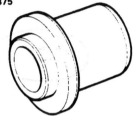

Replacer timing cover oil seal

18G.1377

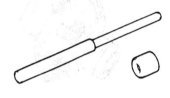

Remover/replacer valve guide

18G.1378B

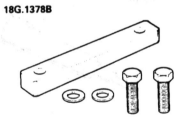

Retainer beam and gauge block
cylinder liner

18G.1369A

Timing gauge

18G.1370B

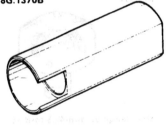

Remover/replacer sleeve
crankshaft

18G.1371

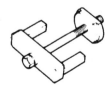

Remover cylinder liner

18G.1372B

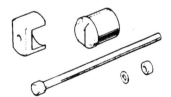

Remover/replacer crankshaft
bearings

18G.1372BX

Thrust pad

1

18G.1373

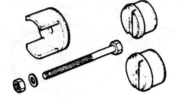

Remove/replacer front and rear crankshaft bearings

MS.76B

Basic handle set valve seat cutter

MS.150-8

Dia. 7.9 mm-8.5 mm

Adjustable pilot

MS.621

Dia. Range 28.5 mm-44mm 15° & 45°

Adjustable valve seat cutter

LST 122

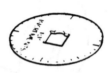

Angle gauge

MS.690

Dia. Range 52 mm-42.5 mm 35°

Adjustable cutter

18G.79

Clutch centralising tool

MS.107

Adaptor timing injector fuel pump

LST-139

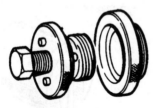

Remover and holder injection pump drive gear 2.5 engine.

DIESEL ENGINE FAULT DIAGNOSIS

SYMPTOMS

Engine will not start
Start with check No. 1 and proceed as directed

Engine lacks power (ensure that the vehicle is not overloaded)
Start with check No. 34 and proceed as directed

Incorrect idling
Start with check No. 26 and proceed as directed

Excessive exhaust
Start with check No. 17 and proceed as directed

Engine misfires
Start with check No. 29 and proceed as directed

ENGINE FAULT DIAGNOSIS

CHECK:	ACTION:

1. Does the starter motor turn the engine?
    YES: Check 2
    NO: Check 4

2. Does the starter turn the engine at normal starting speed?
    YES: Check 6
    NO: Check 3

3. Is the engine oil of the correct grade?
    YES: Check 4
    NO: Change the oil

4. Is the battery charged and in good condition?
    YES: Check 5
    NO: Charge or renew the battery as necessary

5. Are all the cables and connections in the starter and solenoid circuit satisfactory?
    YES: Suspect faulty starter or solenoid
    NO: Repair as necessary

6. Are the heater plugs operating?
    YES: Check 8
    NO: Check 7

7. Is the heater plug electrical circuit satisfactory?
    YES: Check the heater plug
    NO: Repair the circuit

8. Does the manual cold start advance operate correctly?
    YES: Check 9
    NO: Renew cold start device

9. Is fuel reaching the injectors?
    YES: Check 17
    NO: Check 10

10. Is the fuel cut-off solenoid working?
    YES: Check 12
    NO: Check 11

11. Is the solenoid electrical circuit satisfactory?
    YES: Suspect faulty solenoid
    NO: Repair as necessary

12. Is there a supply of clean fuel in the tank?
    YES: Check 13
    NO: Fill the tank and bleed the system

13. Are there leaks at fuel pipes or connections?
    YES: Repair the leaks and bleed the system
    NO: Check 14

14. Is there a blockage in the fuel system?
    YES: Clear the blockage or renew the filter system
    NO: Check 15

15. Is the fuel lift pump operating?
    YES: Check 16
    NO: Renew the lift pump

16. Does the fuel system require bleeding?
    YES: Bleed the fuel system
    NO: Suspect faulty injection pump

17. Are the injector pipes connected in the correct firing order?
    YES: Check 18
    NO: Correct the firing order

18. Are the correct injectors fitted?
    YES: Check 19
    NO: Fit correct injectors

ENGINE FAULT DIAGNOSIS

CHECK:		ACTION:

19. Are the injectors fitted correctly

    YES: Check 20
    NO: Rectify the error

20. Is the injection timing correct?

    YES: Check 21
    NO: Re-set the timing

21. Is the air cleaner or trunking blocked?

    YES: Clear the blockage
    NO: Check 22

22. Is the injector spray pattern, opening pressure and test performance satisfactory?

    YES: Check 23
    NO: Clean or renew injectors as necessary

23. Are valve clearances correct?

    YES: Check 24
    NO: Adjust the valve clearances

24. Are the cylinder compression pressures satisfactory?

    YES: Check 25
    NO: Locate and correct the fault

25. Is the injection pump delivery correct?

    YES: Suspect faulty turbo-charger
    NO: Adjust or renew the injection pump

26. Does the throttle cable operate correctly

    YES: Check 27
    NO: Repair or renew the throttle cable

27. Does the throttle cable have at least 1.5 mm (1/16") free play?

    YES: Check 28
    NO: Adjust the throttle cable

28. Is the idle speed screw setting correct?

    YES: Check 29
    NO: Adjust the engine idle speed

29. Is the fuel tank air vent restricted?

    YES: Clear the restriction
    NO: Check 30

30. Are there leaks at the fuel pipes or connections?

    YES: Repair the leaks and bleed the system
    NO: Check 31

31. Is there a blockage in the fuel system?

    YES: Clear the blockage and bleed the system
    NO: Check 32

32. Is the lift pump operating correctly?

    YES: Check 33
    NO: Renew the lift pump

33. Does the fuel system require bleeding?

    YES: Bleed the system
    NO: Check 17

34. Are the brakes binding?

    YES: Adjust the brakes
    NO: Check 35

35. Is the throttle cable transmitting full travel to the throttle lever?

    YES: Check 17
    NO: Adjust the throttle cable

REMOVING AND REFITTING ENGINE

The procedure for engine remove and refit is similar to the petrol engine. The major component differences are highlighted in the following procedure. All instructions refer to both 2.4 and 2.5 engines unless otherwise stated.

CAUTION: Seal all pipe ends against the ingress of dirt after disconnecting oil, fuel, fluid, vacuum or air conditioning pipelines.

Removing

1. Remove the radiator and intercooler unit. The radiator unit has a built in engine oil cooler, access to the lower union is possible when the fan cowl is removed.
2. Remove the air cleaner assembly and connecting hoses.
3. Remove the power steering pump outlet and inlet hoses.
4. Disconnect the engine harness multiplug and, if the vehicle has air conditioning, the wiring to the compressor clutch.
5. (Air conditioning vehicles only) turn the high and low pressure compressor service valves to the OFF position (fully clockwise). Depressurise the compressor and remove the high and low pressure hoses.
6. Disconnect the heater return hose at the water pump and draw it clear.
7. Remove the heater inlet hose at the bulkhead connection.
8. Remove the split pin securing the inner throttle cable to the fuel injection pump.
9. Depress the tags on the outer cable adjusting screw to release the cable from the mounting bracket.
10. Disconnect the vacuum pipe from the vacuum pump.
11. Disconnect the glow plug feed wire.
12. Remove the main fuel line at the fuel pump, retaining the washers.

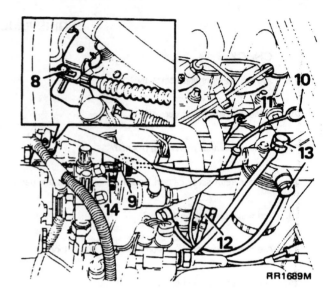

RR1689M

13. Remove the inlet and outlet fuel lines at the filter assembly.
14. Remove the spill return pipe union at the fuel injection pump.
15. Remove the exhaust manifold heat shield.
16. Release the exhaust flange nuts and disconnect the exhaust down pipe.
17. Remove the starter motor heat shield, wiring connections and fixings to the bell housing. Leave the starter motor attached to the engine block.
18. Remove one centre engine mounting nut from each side.
19. Remove the fixings securing the bell housing to the engine.
20. Attach a suitable lifting chain and hoist to the engine lifting hooks.
21. Raise the engine clear of the mountings and support the gearbox.
22. Remove the right hand engine mounting.

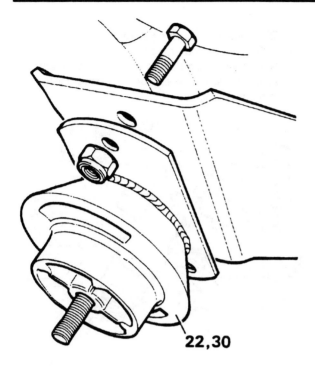

22,30

23. Remove the centre bolt from the left hand engine mounting.

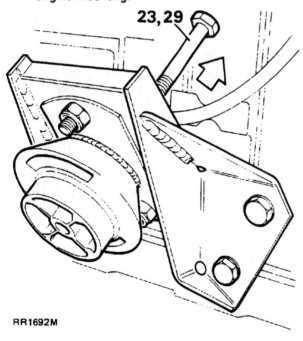

23,29

RR1692M

24. Withdraw the engine from the gearbox and release the gearbox and transfer box breather pipes from their securing clip.
25. Lift the engine clear of the vehicle.

Refitting.

Before refitting the engine

Smear the splines of the primary pinion, the clutch centre and withdrawal unit abutment faces with molybdenum disulphide grease, Rocol MTS.1000. Smear the engine to gearbox joint faces with Hylomar jointing compound.

26. Attach a lifting chain and hoist to the engine lifting hooks.
27. Lower the engine into the engine bay and locate the gearbox and transfer box breather pipes in their securing clip.
28. Locate the primary pinion into the clutch and secure the engine to the bell housing with at least two bolts.
29. Fit the left hand centre engine mounting bolt.
30. Fit the right hand engine mounting and centre bolt.
31. Lower the engine on to the mountings.
32. Secure the fixings at both front engine mountings.
33. Remove the lifting equipment and the gearbox support.
34. Reverse instructions 1 to 17.
35. Prime the fuel system.

CYLINDER HEADS

NOTE: Before removing cylinder heads check alignment of heads, evidence of head gasket or manifold gasket blowing and evidence of water leaks.

Remove and refit

Removing

1. Disconnect battery negative lead.
2. Remove expansion tank filler cap. Drain coolant.
3. Disconnect breather hoses from rocker covers. Disconnect brake servo hose.
4. Disconnect air conditioning temperature switch.

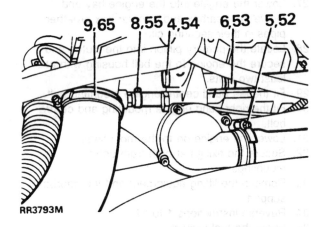

RR3793M

5. Disconnect by-pass hose and top hose at thermostat housing.
6. Disconnect cold start hose at water rail.
7. Disconnect bleed hose at water rail.

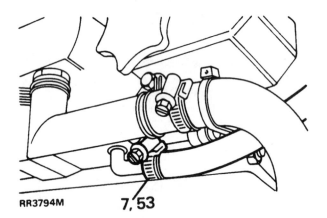

RR3794M

8. Disconnect vacuum pipe from inlet manifold.
9. Remove intercooler pipe.
10. Remove fuel feed pipes from injector. Remove all injectors, with spill pipe, lay aside. Retain injector dowels.

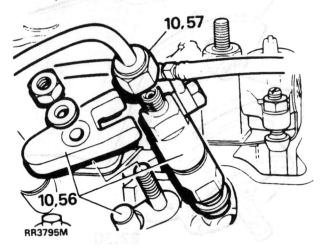

RR3795M

11. Remove heater plug feed wire.
12. Remove cold start hose from cylinder head.
13. Disconnect temperature sensor connector.

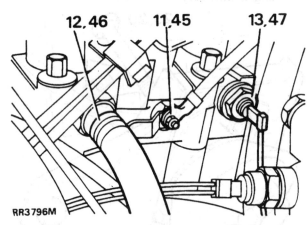

RR3796M

14. Remove rocker covers.
15. Remove rocker assemblies. Remove push rods, inspect.
16. Remove eight bolts securing water rail. Lay water rail aside on heater hose.

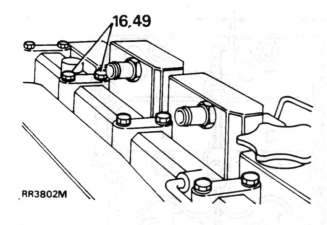

RR3802M

17. Remove oil feed banjo bolts from cylinder heads.
18. Remove exhaust heat shield.

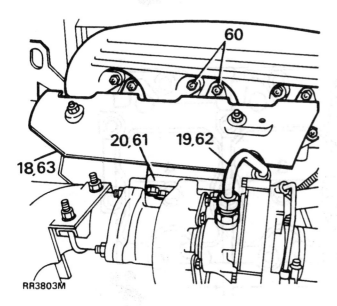

RR3803M

19. Remove turbocharger oil feed pipe
20. Remove four nuts securing turbocharger to exhaust manifold.
21. Remove outer cylinder head bolts.
22. Remove centre cylinder head bolts.
23. Lay cylinder head oil feed pipe against bulkhead.
24. Remove cylinder heads complete with manifolds.
25. Remove inlet and exhaust manifolds, discard gaskets. Inspect cylinder heads

INSPECT CYLINDER HEADS

Inspect cylinder heads, using the checks below.
Any head that fails one or more check must be replaced with a new component, retaining those heads which pass all the checks.

a) Minimum width - 109 mm.

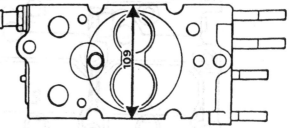

RR3810M

b) Height - 90 mm ± 0.05mm.
c) Inspect for cracks across valve bridge.
d) Distortion of mating faces.
e) Indentation of upper face caused by clamps.
f) Coolant leakage.
g) Measure end plate height - 91,26 to 91,43 mm.

If components pass above checks they may be refitted, using latest gasket and new centre bolts.

26. If new heads are being fitted, remove heater plugs, oil feed dowels, coolant adaptor and temperature transmitter. Fit these items to new cylinder heads. Fit new injector shrouds. Using an airline, check rocker oil feed drilling is free of obstruction.
27. Inspect gaskets, attempt to determine area of failure. Remove old gaskets from block. Thoroughly clean all traces of old gasket material from face of block. Check liner protrusion, see **LINER PROTRUSION CHECK.**

WARNING: Failure to clean block face thoroughly could lead to head gasket failure.

28. Remove oil filter, catching any oil spillage.
29. Remove fan asembly, left hand thread.

Refitting

30. Fit inlet manifold loosely. Fit exhaust manifold loosely, fitting lifting eye.
31. Thoroughly clean face of new cylinder heads.
32. Determine thickness of head gasket required - see **HEAD GASKET SELECT.** Fit gaskets to cylinder block correctly.
33. Fit cylinder head assembly to block, locating studs to turbocharger.
34. Align head assembly with gaskets.
35. Ensure head side holes align with gasket and holes in block. Gaps between heads should be parallel, see RR3809M.

NOTE: 2.4 litre models, where bulkhead clearance is limited, fit number 8 push rod into cylinder head before fitting head assembly. To ensure push rod does NOT protrude below face of cylinder head, tape it in place.

7

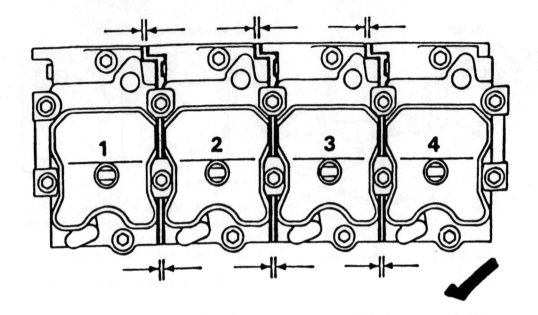

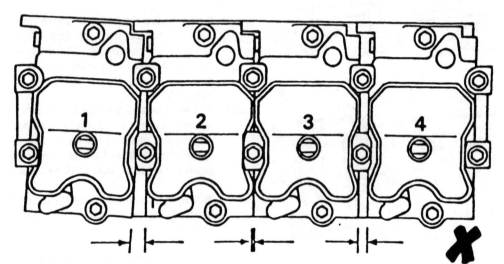

RR3809M

36. Lubricate side bolts (without washers) with engine oil, fit loosely.
37. Ensure inlet manifold is fitted square to cylinder heads to bring heads into alignment.
38. Lubricate threads and underside of central bolt heads with Molybdenum Disulphide. Fit centre bolts loosely, with end plates at front and rear. Align oil feed pipe.
39. Partially tighten centre bolts, holding end plates flush with cylinder heads. Ensure gasket positions are square and have not moved.

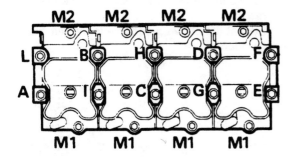

RR3804M

40. Centre bolts:
    a) Torque centre bolts to 30 Nm in sequence shown, starting from bolt A. REPEAT procedure for each bolt.
    b) Tighten each bolt through an angle of 70°, in sequence.
    c) Tighten each bolt an additional 70° in sequence.

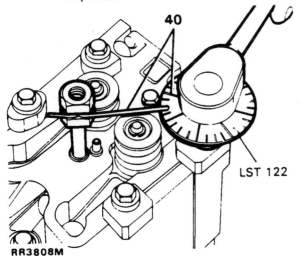

LST 122

RR3808M

41. Torque side bolts to 80 Nm, in the sequence bolts M1 then bolts M2.
42. Fit oil feed pipe, tighten bolts to 8 Nm.
43. Fit push rods and rocker assemblies, tighten single fixing to 108 Nm.

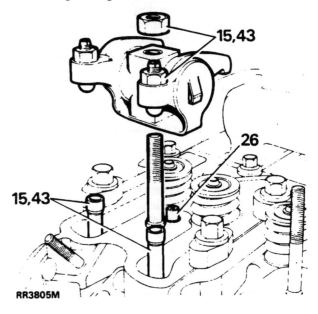

RR3805M

44. Adjust tappets.
45. Fit heater plug feed wire, tighten connector plates.
46. Fit cold start hose to cylinder head.
47. Connect temperature sensor connector.
48. Fit fan assembly.
49. Fit two rear bolts to water rail. Fit water rail attaching by pass hose. Tighten eight bolts to 8 Nm.
50. Tighten by pass hose clip.
51. Fit cold start hose to water rail, tighten clip.
52. Fit top hose, tighten clip.
53. Fit bleed hose to water rail, tighten clip.
54. Connect air conditioning temperature switch.
55. Connect vacuum pipe from inlet manifold, tighten clip.
56. Fit injectors with copper sealing washers. Locate dowels, tighten clamp nuts to 26 Nm.
57. Fit fuel supply pipes to injectors, tighten to 19 Nm.
58. Fit rocker covers, tighten to 9 Nm.
59. Fit breather pipes to rocker covers. Connect brake servo hose.
60. Tighten exhaust and inlet manifold nuts to 32 Nm.
61. Tighten four turbocharger to manifold nuts to 25 Nm.
62. Fit and tighten turbocharger oil feed pipe.
63. Fit exhaust heat shield
64. Fit oil filter.
65. Fit intercooler pipe, tighten clip.

Coolant refill

66. Remove coolant pipe from top of radiator.
67. Fill system through expansion tank until radiator is full.
68. Refit pipe to radiator and tighten.
69. Start engine, run until operating temperature is achieved, top up expansion tank as necessary.
70. Fit expansion tank filler cap, run engine for twenty minutes.

Retorque cylinder heads

71. Allow engine to cool completely.
72. Drain coolant.
73. Remove rocker covers.
74. Remove water rail.
75. Centre bolts, starting with bolt A:
    a) Loosen bolt, torque to 30 Nm,
    b) Tighten bolt through an angle of 120°.

    NOTE: 120° may be achieved by tightening through 60°, immediately followed by a further 60°. The total 120° MUST BE ACHIEVED BEFORE proceeding to next bolt.

    c) Repeat for each bolt in sequence shown.
76. Retorque outer bolts to 90 Nm. without loosening, first M1 then M2.
77. Fit rocker assemblies, tighten single fixing to 108 Nm.
78. Adjust tappets.
79. Fit water rail using new gaskets.
80. Fit hoses, tighten clips.
81. Check top up oil.
82. Refill cooling system. Run engine until operating temperature is reached, top up if necessary.

RETORQUE CYLINDER HEADS

First 40,000Km (24,000 miles) only

NOTE: These instructions must be carried out at the first 40,000 Km (24,000 miles) service OR 40,000 Km (24,000 miles) AFTER the above procedure has been carried out. The use of new type gasket eliminates the need to retorque head bolts at 1,500 Km (1,000 miles).

1. Centre bolts, without slackening bolts, start with bolt A, tighten each bolt in sequence through 10 - 15°.
2. Side bolts: Without slackening bolts cheque that torque of each bolt is 85 - 90 Nm. first M1 then M2.

LINER PROTRUSION CHECK

1. Ensure face is clean
   Correct reading:
   2.4 Litre and 2.5 Litre - 0,00 to 0,06 mm

2. To obtain the correct liner protrusion, attach special tool 18G 1378 B as illustrated, to the cylinder block and tighten the bolts to 30 Nm. Fit a dial test indicator so that the stylus rests in a loaded condition on the external rim of the liner and set the dial to zero. Slide the stylus across to the cylinder block and note the reading.
   Repeat the above procedure to the remaining cylinders.

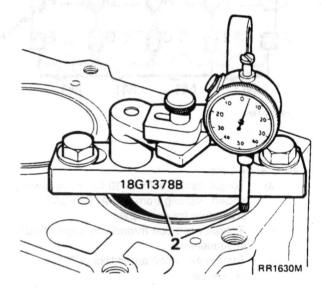

3. Remove the liners and add shims as required to achieve the protrusion.

HEAD GASKET SELECT

1. Before fitting the cylinder heads it is necessary to determine the thickness of gasket that must be used to achieve the correct clearance between each piston crown and cylinder head. Three thicknesses of gasket are available, see table below. The following procedure should be used to determine which size to fit. However, only one thickness of gasket must be used on all four cylinders, this being the one for the cylinder which calls for the thickest gasket.

Identification	Part no.	Fitted thickness
No notch	STC 654	142mm ± 0.04
One notch	STC 656	162mm ± 0.04
Two notches	STC 655	152mm ± 0.04

2. Turn the crankshaft to bring number one piston to T.D.C.

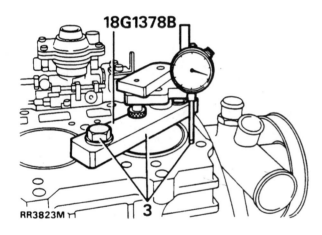

RR3823M

3. Fit special tool 18G 1378B to the cylinder block and tighten the bolts to 30 Nm Attach the dial test indicator to the tool, as illustrated, and position the stylus, in a loaded condition, on the cylinder block and zero the gauge. Slide the indicator over so that the stylus rests on the piston crown and note the reading.

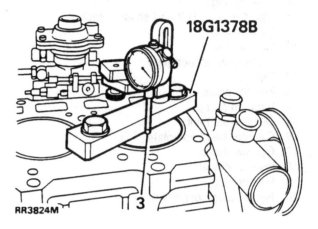

RR3824M

Example
Required piston clearance .... 0,85 to 0,94 mm
Plus measured height 0,60   0,60 mm
_____
Thickness of gasket required .... 1,45 to 1,54 mm

The nearest compressed thickness of gasket available is 1,52 mm part number STC655

4. Repeat the above instruction on the remaining cylinders. The thickest gasket required is the one which must be fitted to all cylinders.

ENGINE EXTERNAL COMPONENTS 2.4 LITRE ENGINE

1. Inlet manifold
2. Engine coolant rail
3. Turbo-charger
4. Engine lifting eye
5. Heat shield
6. Exhaust manifold
7. Sealing rings
8. Cylinder head bolt and spacer block
9. Oil filler cap
10. Rocker cover
11. Valve gear oil feed pipe
12. Dipstick
13. Injector pipes
14. Vacuum pump
15. Oil filter element
16. Cylinder head end-plate
17. Cylinder head
18. Injector dowel
19. Heater plug
20. Heater plug copper link
21. Turbo-charger support bracket
22. Coolant thermostat
23. Oil thermostat
24. Vacuum pump gear
25. Retaining clamp - vacuum pump
26. Oil filter base adapter
27. Cylinder block
28. Fuel injection pump
29. 'O' ring
30. Flywheel housing
31. Flywheel
32. Water pump
33. Crankshaft pulley
34. Timing cover
35. Oil pressure relief valve
36. Sump
37. Sump pan
38. Fuel lift pump
39. Cold start device

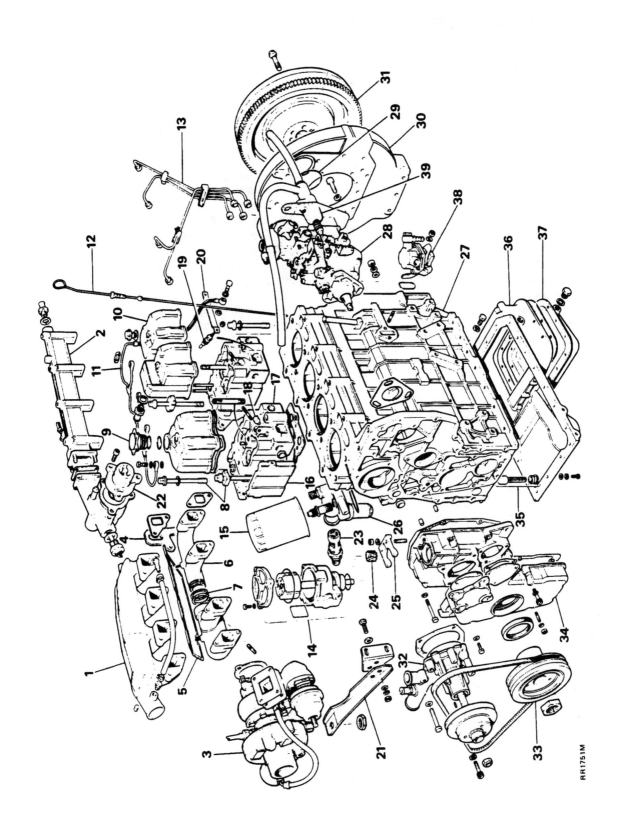

2.4 LITRE ENGINE

ENGINE EXTERNAL COMPONENTS 2.5 LITRE ENGINE

1. Inlet manifold
2. Engine coolant rail
3. Turbo-charger
4. Engine lifting eye
5. Heat shield
6. Exhaust manifold
7. Sealing rings
8. Cylinder head bolt and spacer block
9. Oil filler cap
10. Rocker cover
11. Valve gear oil feed pipe
12. Dipstick
13. Injector pipes
14. Screw plug
15. Oil filter element
16. Cylinder head end-plate
17. Cylinder head
18. Injector dowel
19. Heater plug
20. Heater plug copper link
21. Turbo-charger support bracket
22. Coolant thermostat
23. Oil thermostat
24. Support bracket
25. Bolt
26. Oil filter base adapter
27. Cylinder block
28. Fuel injection pump
29. 'O' ring
30. Flywheel housing
31. Flywheel
32. Water pump
33. Crankshaft pulley
34. Timing cover
35. Oil pressure relief valve
36. Sump
37. Sump bolt
38. Fuel lift pump
39. Cold start device

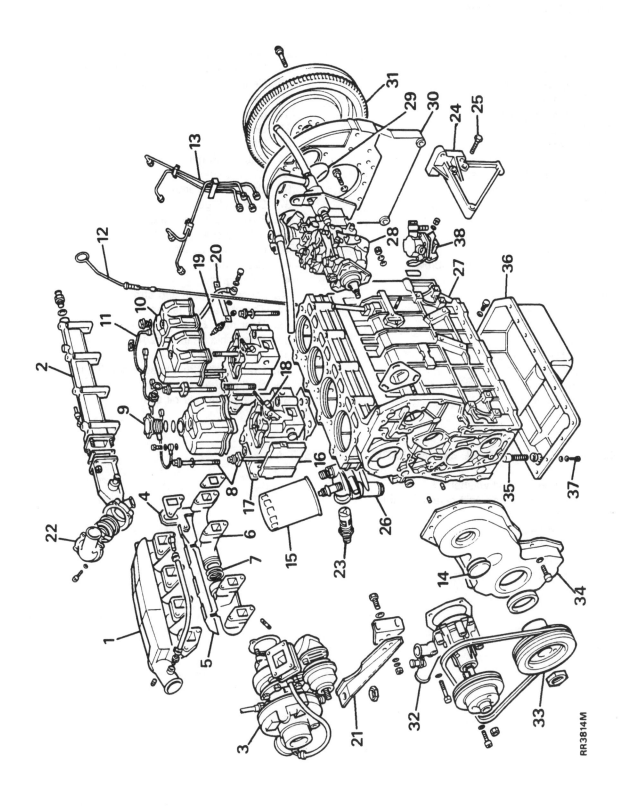

2.5 LITRE ENGINE

RR3814M

KEY TO ENGINE INTERNAL PARTS

1. Liner
2. Shim
3. 'O' ring seals
4. Compression rings
5. Oil control ring
6. Valve spring cap
7. Valve guide
8. Rocker shaft bush
9. Inlet rocker arm
10. Rocker shaft (pedestal)
11. Exhaust rocker arm
12. Push rod
13. Injector
14. Snap ring
15. Gudgeon pin
16. Valve clearance adjusting screw
17. Piston
18. Inlet valve
19. Exhaust valve
20. Spring clip
21. Tappet
22. Oil pressure switch
23. Small end bush
24. Thrust plate
25. Connecting rod
26. Camshaft bearings
27. Connecting rod bearing shell
28. Carrier location and lubrication shaft
29. Central main bearing carrier
30. Central main bearing shell
31. Camshaft
32. Gear retaining nut (injection pump)
33. Idler gear
34. Crankshaft gear
35. 'O' ring seal
36. Oil pump assembly
37. Camshaft gear
38. Fuel injection pump gear
39. 'O' ring seal
40. Front main bearing
41. Crankshaft
42. 'O' ring seal
43. Oil pick-up pipe and strainer
44. Thrust washer halves
45. Rear main bearing
46. Rear main bearing carrier
47. 'O' ring seal
48. Crankshaft thrust spacer and 'O' ring seal
49. Socket headed screw
50. Crankshaft rear oil seal

KEY TO 2.5 LITRE DIESEL ENGINE VARIATIONS INSET A

32. Retaining nut and washer
33. Vacuum pump and split gear assembly
34. Crankshaft gear
35. 'O'-ring seal
36. Oil pump assembly
37. Camshaft gear
38. Fuel injection pump gear

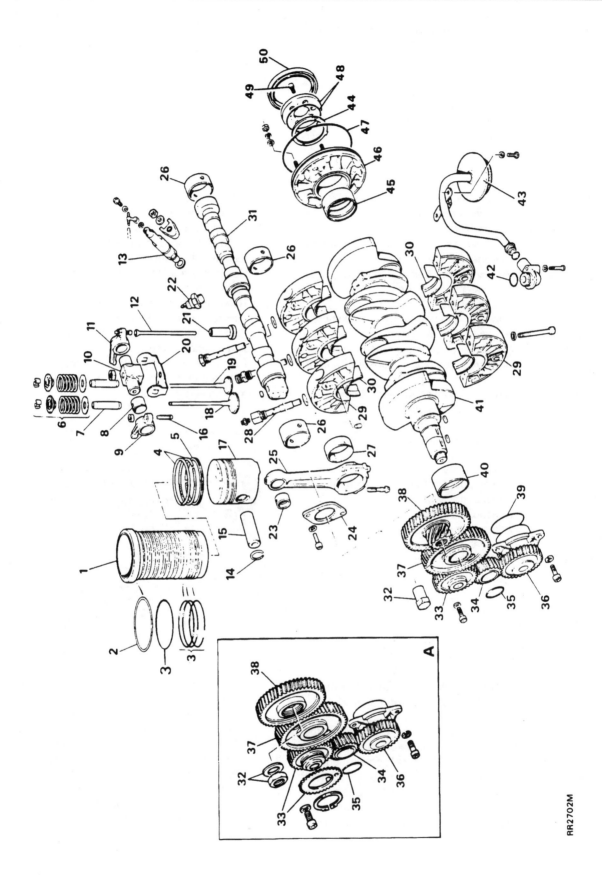

RR2702M

DISMANTLING, OVERHAUL AND REASSEMBLY

Special Tools

18G 29	Valve lapping tool
18G 55A	Piston ring compressor
18G 79	Clutch centralising tool
18G 106A	Valve spring compressor
18G 257	Circlip pliers (large)
18G 284	Impulse extractor
18G 284-10	Adaptor remover injector
18G 1004	Circlip pliers (small)
18G 1367	Remover crankshaft pulley
18G 1367-1A	Adaptor remover gear
18G 1368	Remover and holder injection pump drive gear 2.4 engine
LST - 139	Remover and holder injection pump drive gear 2.5 engine
18G 1369A	Timing marker
18G 1370B	Remover replacer sleeve crankshaft
18G 1371	Remover cylinder liner
18G 1372B	Remover replacer camshaft bearings
18G 1373	Remover replacer crankshaft front and rear main bearings
18G 1374	Replacer crankshaft rear oil seal
18G 1375	Replacer timing cover oil seal
18G 1377	Remover replacer valve guides
18G 1378B	Retainer cylinder liner
MS 70	Oil filter wrench
MS 76	Basic handle set
MS 107	Timing adaptor fuel injection pump
MS 150-7	Expandable pilot
MS 150-8	Expandable pilot
MS 621	Adjustable valve seat cutter
MS 690	Adjustable valve seat cutter
LST 122	Cylinder head bolt angle gauge

DISMANTLING

Removing ancilliary equipment

NOTE: All instructions refer to both 2.4 and 2.5 litre diesel engines unless otherwise stated.

Remove the engine from the vehicle. Clean the exterior and in the interests of safety and efficient working, secure the engine to a recognised engine stand and drain the oil from the sump. Before commencing make a careful note of the position of brackets, clips, harnesses, pipes, hoses, filters and other miscellaneous items to facilitate re-assembly.

1. Remove the alternator and mounting bracket.
2. Remove the starter motor.
3. Remove the power steering pump.
4. Remove the Air Conditioning Compressor and mounting brackets.
5. Remove the oil filter cartridge.
6. Remove the oil drain pipe from the turbo-charger and engine block union.
7. Remove the two socket headed bolts securing the turbo-charger support bracket to the cylinder block.
8. Disconnect the oil feed to the turbo-charger.
9. Remove the four bolts and release the turbo-charger from the exhaust manifold.
10. Remove the inlet and exhaust manifolds.
11. Remove the special nuts and lift off the four rocker covers and joint washers.
12. Release the six bolts and remove the coolant rail, complete with thermostat housing.
13. Disconnect the injector pipes from the injectors and injector pump.
14. Release the clamp nuts and remove the injectors complete with spill rail and collect the four dowels.

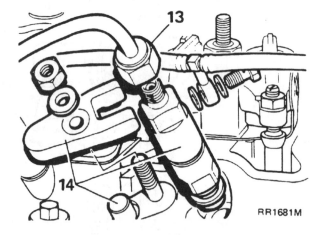

15. Turn the crankshaft in a clockwise direction to bring number one piston to T.D.C. on the firing stroke with number four cylinder valves on the "rock". This condition is necessary for removal of the injection pump at a later stage.
16. Remove the four single nuts and lift off each rocker assembly keeping them identified with their respective cylinder heads. Check that the oil feed dowels are in position in the heads and not inside the pedestals. Remove the push-rods.

17. Remove all cylinder head bolts and clamps. Lift of each cylinder head and gasket and number it according to the bore from which it was removed.
18. Withdraw the four bolts and remove the water pump complete with pulley.

NOTE: Instructions 19 and 20 refer to 2.4 Litre engines only.

19. Remove the vacuum pump oil feed pipe.
20. Remove the two nuts and clamp plate and withdraw the vacuum pump.

Remove injection pump 2.4 litre engines

1. Remove the injection pump drive gear access plate from front cover.
2. Remove the injection pump drive gear retaining nut.

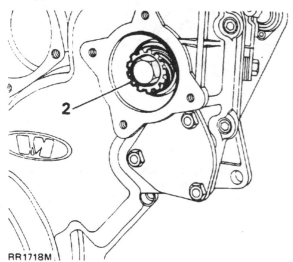

RR1718M

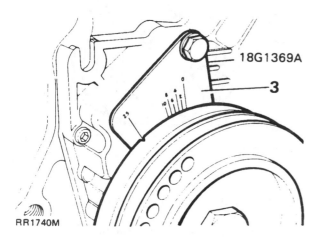

RR1740M

3. Fit the timing marker 18G 1369A to the front cover. The 'O' on the scale should line-up with the groove in the crankshaft pulley.
4. Turn the crankshaft anti-clockwise, beyond the 25° mark on the scale, to remove backlash, and then turn it clockwise until the groove in the crankshaft pulley is aligned with the 25° B.T.D.C. mark. The key on the injection pump shaft should now be at the 11 o'clock position.
5. Fit special tool 18G 1368 to the front cover. Lock the flywheel, and slacken the three nuts that secure the injection pump flange to the engine block.
6. Turn the centre bolt of the tool until the gear releases from the taper. Remove the tool, and pump retaining nuts and withdraw the pump complete with cold start device.

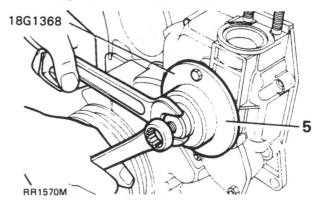

RR1570M

7. Lock the flywheel and remove the crankshaft pulley securing nut.
8. Using special tool 18G 1367A withdraw the crankshaft pulley.

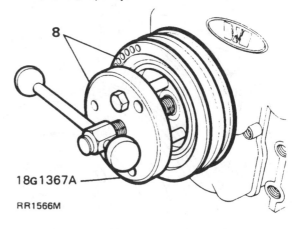

RR1566M

9. Remove the timing cover and retrieve the injector pump drive gear.

Remove injection pump 2.5 litre engines

1. Using the pegged component, item 6 of special tool LST - 139 remove the injection pump drive gear access plate from front cover.
2. Remove the injection pump drive gear retaining nut and washer.

CAUTION: Ensure the washer is removed to prevent it from dropping inside the timing cover.

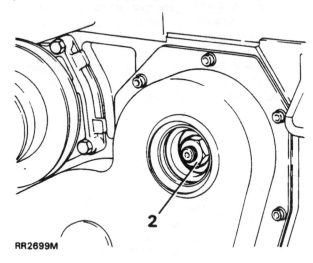

RR2699M

3. Remove bolt from timing cover, using a 47 mm tube spacer and M6 x 55 mm bolt, fit timing gauge 18G 1369A to front cover. The 'O' on the scale should line-up with the groove in the crankshaft pulley.

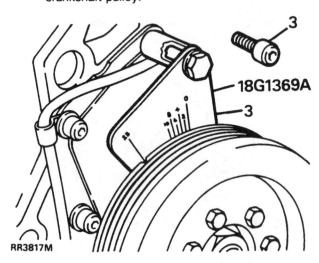

18G1369A

RR3817M

4. Turn the crankshaft anti-clockwise, beyond the 25° mark on the scale, to remove backlash, and then turn it clockwise until the groove in the crankshaft pulley is aligned with the 25° B.T.D.C. mark. The key on the injection pump shaft should now be at the 11 o'clock position viewed from the front of the engine.

5. Fit item 5 of special tool LST - 139 flush to the front cover. Lock the flywheel, and slacken the three nuts that secure the injection pump flange to the engine block.
6. Fit item 6 into the injection pump drive gear. Ensure a flush fit against item 5 and the centre bolt is fully retracted.
7. Turn the centre bolt of the tool until the gear releases from the taper. Retain the gear on the tool. Remove the injection pump retaining nuts and withdraw the pump complete with cold start device.

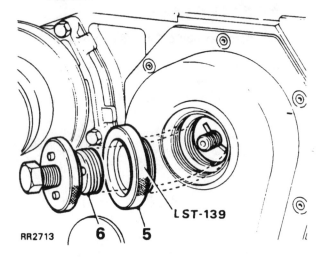

LST-139

RR2713   6   5

8. Lock the flywheel and remove the crankshaft pulley securing nut.
9. Using special tool 18G 1367A withdraw the crankshaft pulley.

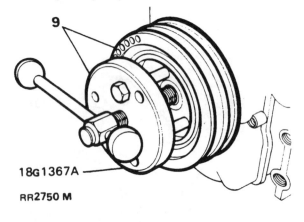

18G1367A

RR2750 M

10. Remove the timing cover with injection pump drive gear.
11. Remove the special tool from the timing cover and injection pump drive gear.
12. Reassemble the special tool LST - 139.

Remove remaining components both 2.4 & 2.5 engines

1. Remove the clutch pressure plate and centre plate.
2. Remove the three bolts and withdraw the spigot bearing plate.
3. Remove the six bolts and lift off the flywheel.
4. To assist with the removal of the flywheel fit two 8 mm bolts approximately 100 mm (4.0") long into the clutch retaining bolt holes, diametrically opposite, and lift the flywheel from the engine.

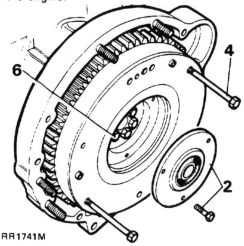

RR1741M

5. Remove the nine bolts and six nuts and withdraw the flywheel housing.
6. Remove the single socket-headed screw and withdraw the crankshaft thrust plate and outer thrust washer halves.

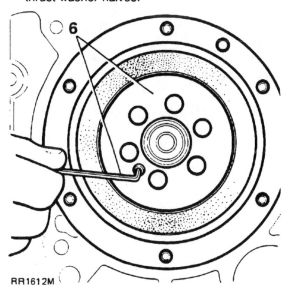

RR1612M

7. Remove the oil filter adaptor housing.
8. Remove the sump oil pan.
9. Remove the twenty-one screws and remove the sump.
10. Remove the three bolts and remove the oil pump pickup pipe and strainer and '0' ring.

NOTE: Before performing the next instruction mark the top of each piston with the number of the bore commencing at the front of the engine. Unlike most engines the connecting rods are not numbered relative to the bores.

11. Turn the crankshaft to bring numbers one and four connecting rod caps to an accessible position. Remove each cap and lower bearing shell, in turn, and push the connecting rod and piston up the bore and withdraw from the top. Immediately refit the cap to the connecting rod with the number on the same side. Repeat the procedure for numbers two and three connecting rod assemblies.
12. Using a suitable piece of timber drift-out the rear main bearing carrier assembly complete with bearing shells and oil seal.
13. Remove the three screws retaining the oil pump to the crankcase and withdraw the pump complete with drive gear.
14. Position the cylinder block horizontal with the crankcase uppermost and remove the two screws securing the camshaft retaining plate to the cylinder block and carefully withdraw the camshaft complete with gear. It is necessary to have the cylinder block inverted so that the tappets will not drop, and foul the cams.

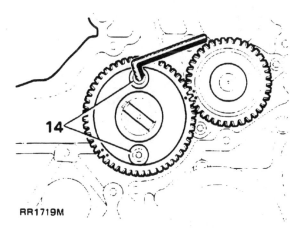

RR1719M

15. Remove the three screws and :-
    - On 2.4 Litre engines remove the idler gear.
    - On 2.5 Litre engines remove the vacuum pump and gear assembly.

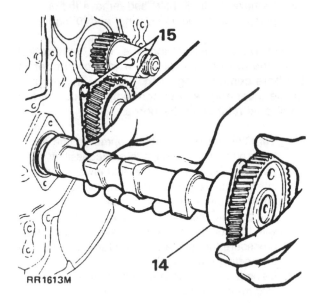

RR1613M

16. Mark for re-assembly and remove from the left hand side of the cylinder block the three main bearing oil feed and carrier location shafts, and identify for re-assembly. Remove the oil pressure switch.

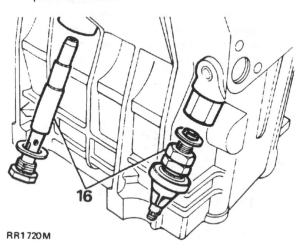

RR1720M

17. To remove the crankshaft and main bearing carrier assembly from the crankcase, slide special tool 18G 1370B over the crankshaft gear, as illustrated, and with assistance withdraw the complete assembly rearwards.

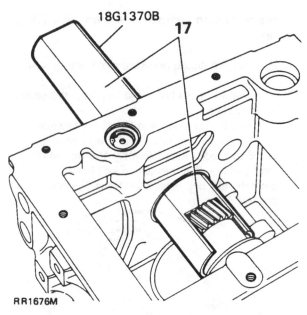

RR1676M

18. Should difficulty be experienced in removing the complete assembly as described above, slide the assembly rearwards sufficiently to gain access to the main bearing carrier bolts. Mark the carriers for assembly and remove the bolts, two for each carrier.

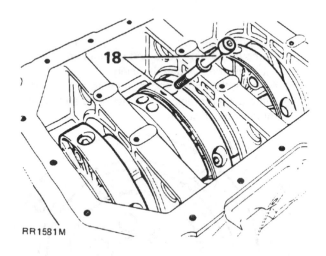

RR1581M

19. Separate the two halves of each carrier, remove from the crankshaft and temporarily re-assemble the carriers. Withdraw the crankshaft through the rear of the crankcase.

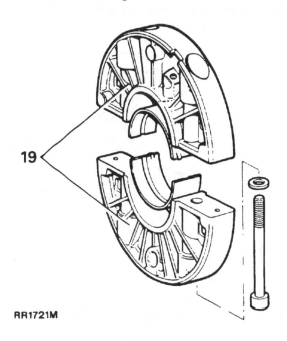

RR1721M

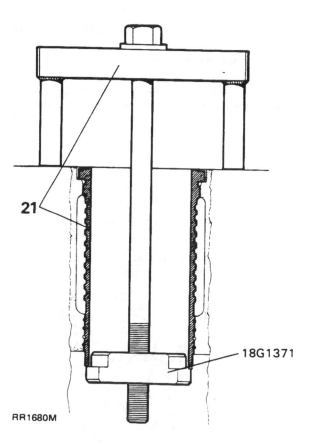

21

18G1371

RR1680M

20. Remove the cam followers and identify for possible re-assembly to their original locations.
21. If after inspection it is necessary to renew the cylinder liners then they should be removed as follows: position special tool 18G 1371 as illustrated and turn the centre bolt clockwise to withdraw each liner from the cylinder block. Each liner is fitted with three red 'O' rings; the lower one for oil sealing and the others for coolant sealing. The shim under the lip is for achieving the correct protrusion of the liner above the cylinder block face.

22. Remove the pressure relief valve assembly by removing the circlip which will release the cap, spring and relief valve.

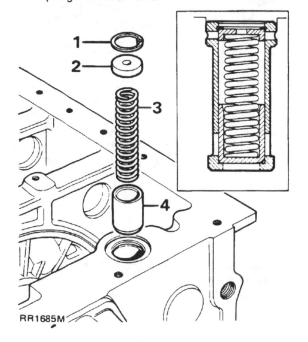

RR1685M

1 Circlip   3 Spring
2 Cap   4 Plunger

12 VM DIESEL ENGINE

RANGE ROVER

INSPECTION AND OVERHAUL OF COMPONENTS

Cylinder head assemblies

Ensure that the marks made when the cylinder heads were removed are maintained and that during the following instructions the various parts of the cylinder heads are similarly identified.

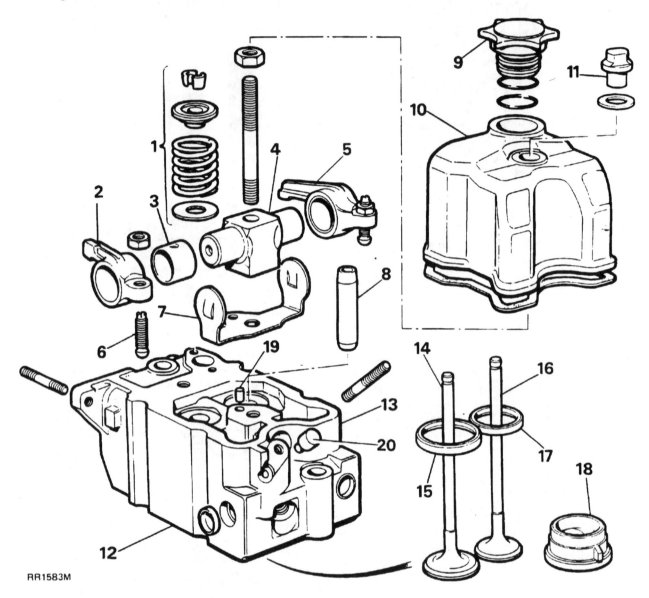

RR1583M

Key to cylinder head and associated components.

1. Valve spring, cap seat and cotters.
2. Inlet valve rocker.
3. Bush.
4. Rocker shaft. (Pedestal)
5. Exhaust valve rocker.
6. Rocker adjusting screw.
7. Spring clip.
8. Valve guide.
9. Oil filler cap.
10. Rocker cover.

11. Rocker cover nut.
12. Cylinder head.
13. Injector locating dowel.
14. Inlet valve.
15. Inlet valve seat.
16. Exhaust valve.
17. Exhaust valve seat.
18. Pre-combustion chamber.(Hot plug.)
19. Pedestal lubrication dowel.
20. Injector clamp dowel

24

1. Using valve spring compressor 18G 106A or
   suitable alternative remove the collets, spring
   cups, springs and valves.
2. Remove the rocker arm pedestal stud and
   manifold studs.
3. Degrease and remove carbon deposits from the
   cylinder heads. Examine the cylinder head
   mating face for cracks pitting and distortion.
   Renew if necessary.

**CAUTION: The cylinder heads are plated
therefore the face must not be machined.**

4. Cracked or burned hot plugs can be removed
   by heating the cylinder head uniformly in an
   oven to 150°C. Tap out the hot plug using a
   thin drift inserted through the injector hole.
   Clean-out the hot plug pocket in the cylinder
   head.
5. Measure the depth of seat (D) and the new hot
   plug height (B) to establish they meet the fitted
   tolerance detailed below. If necessary machine
   the outer face of the hot plug to suit.
6. To fit the new hot-plug cool in liquid nitrogen
   whilst maintaining the cylinder head at the
   above temperature fit the hot plug. Ensure that
   the small pip on the side of the hot plug locates
   in the groove in the side of the pocket. Allow
   the cylinder head to cool slowly.

Hot plug diameter	A	30,380 to 30,395 mm
Hot plug height	B	23,350 to 23,440 mm
Hot plug seat dia.	C	30,340 to 30,370 mm
Depth of seat	D	23,570 to 23,730 mm

Maximum protrusion above cylinder head	0,02 mm
Maximum depth below cylinder head	0,03 mm

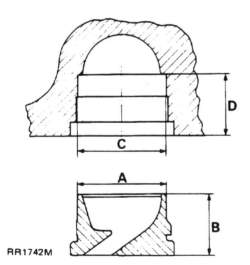

RR1742M

Valves

1. Clean the valves and renew any that are bent,
   have worn stems, or are burnt and damaged.
   Valves that are satisfactory for further service
   can be refaced. This operation should be
   carried out using a valve grinding machine.
   Only the minimum of material should be
   removed from the valve face to avoid thinning
   of the valve edge which must be not less than
   1,30 mm (dimension A). Check the valves
   against the dimensions given in the data
   section. In addition dimensions B should be as
   follows:-

D. Inlet valve	2,73 to 3,44 mm
E. Exhaust valve	2,45 to 3,02 mm

Angle C
Of inlet valve D. .... 55° 30'
Of exhaust valve E. .... 45° 30'

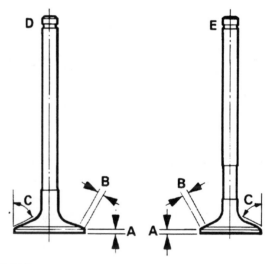

RR1702M

Valve guides

1. Visually examine the guides for damage, cracks, scores and seizure marks. Insert the appropriate servicable or new valve in the guides and check that the stem-to-guide clearance is within the tolerance given in the data.
2. To renew valve guides, heat the cylinder head to a temperature of between 80°C and 90°C and using special tool 18G 1377 without height gauge 18G 1377/2 press the guides out through the top of the cylinder head.

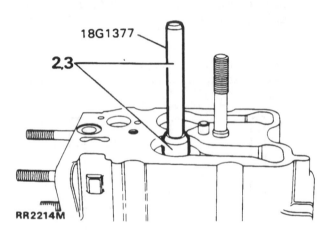

18G1377

2,3

RR2214M

3. Whilst maintaining the above temperature and using the same tool, but with height gauge 18G 1377/2 drive-in new guides from the top of the cylinder head to the distance determined by the gauge or to dimensions in the data.

Valve seat inserts

1. Examine the valve seat inserts for damage, wear and cracks. the seats can be restored provided they are not abnormally wide due to refacing operations. If the seat cutting operation, however, excessively lowers the valve recess or if the seat cannot be narrowed to within the limits given in the data, the insert should be renewed.
2. To recut an inlet valve seat use an expandable pilot M.S. 150-8 loosely assemble the collet, expander and nut. Ensure that the chamfered end of the expander is towards the collet. Insert the assembled pilot into the valve guide from the combustion face side of the cylinder head until the shoulder contacts the valve guide and the whole of the collet is inside the valve guide. Expand the collet in the guide by turning the tommy bar clockwise whilst holding the knurled nut.

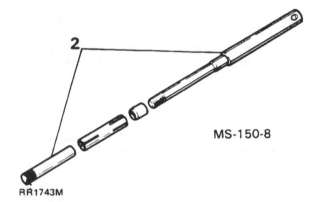

2

MS-150-8

RR1743M

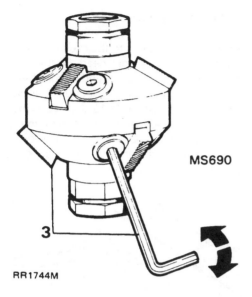

MS690

3

RR1744M

3. Select cutter MS 690 and ensure that the cutter blades are correctly fitted to the cutter head with the angled end of the blade downwards facing the work, as illustrated. Check that the cutter blades are adjusted so that the middle of the blade contacts the area of material to be cut. Use the key provided in the hand set MS 76.

4. Fit the wrench to the cutter head, apply it to the seat to be refaced and turn clockwise using only very light pressure. Continue cutting until the width of the seat is in accordance with the dimension J in data.

5. To check the effectiveness of the cutting operation use engineer's blue or a feeler gauge made from cellophane.

6. Smear a quantity of engineer's blue round the valve seat and revolve a properly ground valve against the seat. A continuous fine line should appear round the valve. If there is a a gap of not more than 12 mm it can be corrected by lapping.

7. Alternatively, insert a strip of cellophane between the valve and seat, hold the valve down by the stem and slowly pull out the cellophane. If there is a drag the seal is satisfactory at that spot. Repeat this in at least eight places. Lapping in will correct a small open spot.

8. Perform the above instructions to recut an EXHAUST valve seat using cutter MS 621 until the seat width is in accordance with dimension D in data. Check that the valve head recess is within the data limits.

9. To remove either an inlet or exhaust valve seat, hold the cylinder head firmly in a vice, wear protective goggles and grind the old insert away until thin enough to be cracked and prised out. Take care not to damage the insert pocket. Remove any burrs and swarf from the pocket. Failure to do this could cause the new insert to crack when being fitted.

10. Heat the cylinder head, uniformly in an oven, to a temperature of 150°C cool the new seat insert by dipping into liquid Nitrogen. This will enable the seat to be positioned without the use of pressure. Allow the cylinder head to cool naturally to avoid distortion.

Lapping in valves

1. To ensure a gas tight seal between the valve face and the valve seat it is necessary to lap-in the appropriate valve to its seat. It is essential to keep the valve identified with its seat once the lapping in operation has been completed.

2. Unless the faces to be lapped are in poor condition it should only be necessary to use fine valve lapping paste. Smear a small quantity of paste on the valve face and lubricate the valve stem with engine oil.

3. Insert the valve in the appropriate guide and using a suction type valve lapping tool employ a light reciprocating action while occasionally lifting the valve off its seat and turning it so that the valve returns to a different position on the seat.

4. Continue the operation until a continuous matt grey band round the valve face is obtained. To check that the lapping operation is successful, wipe off the valve paste from the valve and seat and make a series of pencil lines across the valve face. Insert the valve into the guide and while pressing the valve onto the seat revolve the valve a quarter turn a few times. If all the pencil lines are cut through no further lapping is required.
5. Wash all traces of grinding paste from the valves and cylinder head seats.

Valve springs.

1. Examine the valve springs for damage and overheating and discard any that are visually faulty.
2. New and used valve springs, in the interests of uniformity, should be subjected to load and height tests as shown in the table and diagram below.
   The amount of distortion D must not exceed 2,0 mm (0.078 in).

	Test load (Kg)		Height (mm)	Condition
A	0.00	H1	43.20	Free height
B	33-35	H2	37.00	Closed valve
C	88-94	H3	26.61	Open valve

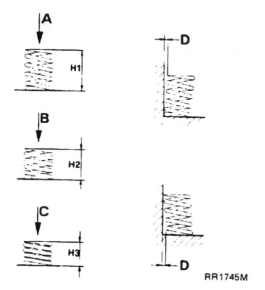

RR1745M

Assembling the cylinder head

1. Assemble the valves to their respective positions in the cylinder head. Fit the spring plates, springs and cups and secure the assembly with the split collets using valve spring compressor 18G 106A or equivalent.
2. Using feeler gauges check the inlet and exhaust valve head stand down i.e clearance of valve heads below cylinder head combustion face, see data.

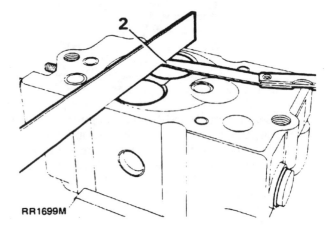

RR1699M

3. When renewing the cylinder head water jacket plugs secure them in position with Loctite 601
4. Renew the manifold retaining studs and when fitting a new pedestal stud secure it with Loctite 270.
5. Fit the rocker pedestal location and lubrication dowel into each cylinder head and ensure that the oil hole is clear. Place the heads to one side ready for assembly to the cylinder block at a later stage.

Rocker assembly and push rods.

1. Remove the spring clip and slide the rockers from the shaft.
2. Clean and examine the rocker shafts and check for ovality, overall wear taper, and surface condition. Compare the dimensions with those given in data.
3. Examine the rockers and renew any that have worn rocker pads. It is not permissible to grind a pad in an attempt to restore a rocker.
4. Examine the rocker adjusting screws and renew any that are worn.
5. Check the internal dimensions of the bushes against the figures in data. If necessary renew the bushes ensuring that the oil hole in the bush aligns with the hole in the rocker arm. Check that the rocker arm to shaft clearance is within the figures in data.
6. Assemble the rocker-arms to the shaft noting that they are handed and that when assembled the pad ends point inwards. Retain the assembly with the spring clip and place to one side for fitting to the cylinder head at a later stage.

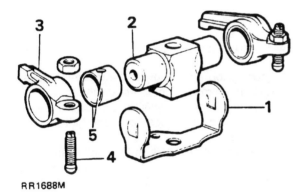

RR1688M

7. Examine the push rods and discard any that are bent or have worn or pitted ends.

Cylinder block

1. Clean the cylinder block with kerosene or suitable solvent and blow dry with compressed air all oil passages and water ways. Carry out a careful visual examination checking for cracks and damage.
2. Measure the cylinder liner bores for ovality, taper and general wear using any suitable equipment. An inside micrometer is best for checking ovality and a cylinder gauge for taper.
3. Check the ovality of each bore by taking measurements at the top of the cylinder just below the ridge at two points diametrically opposite. The difference between the two figures is the ovality of the top of the bore. Similar measurements should be made approximately 50 mm (2.0 in) up from the bottom of the bore so that the overall ovality may be determined.
4. The taper of each cylinder is determined by taking measurements at the top and bottom of each bore at right angles to the gudgeon pin line. The difference between the two measurements is the taper.
5. To establish maximum overall bore wear, take measurements at as many points possible down the bores at right angles to the gudgeon pin line. The largest recorded figure is the maximum wear and should be compared with the original diameter of the cylinder liner. (See **Section 04** General specification data).
6. If the cylinder bores are excessively worn outside the limits the cylinder liners must be renewed. See ENGINE ASSEMBLY.
7. Alternatively, if the overall wear, taper and ovality are well within the acceptable limits and the original pistons are serviceable new piston rings may be fitted. It is important however, that the bores are deglazed, with a hone, to give a cross-hatched finish to provide a seating for the new rings. It is vital to thoroughly wash the bores afterwards to remove all traces of abrasive material.

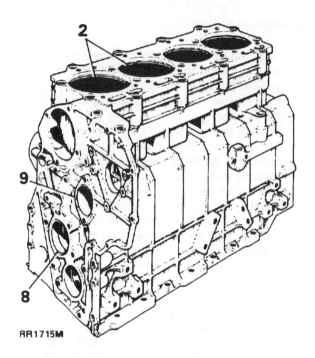

RR1715M

8. Using an inside micrometer check the front main bearings for general condition, overall wear, taper and ovality. If outside the limits given in data remove the bearing. Use special tool 18G 1373 to renew the bearing, see ENGINE ASSEMBLY.

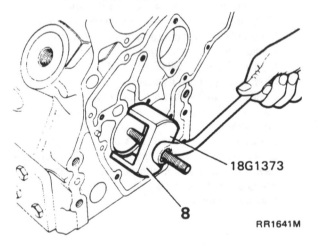

18G1373

8

RR1641M

9. Measure the internal diameter of each camshaft bearing at several points using an internal micrometer. A comparison of the bearing diameters with those of the respective camshaft journals will give the amount of clearance. The bearings should be renewed if the clearance is excessive or if they are scored or pitted. Use special tool 18G 1372B as illustrated, to remove the bearings.

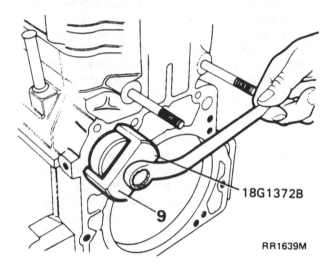

18G1372B

9

RR1639M

Crankshaft

1. Identify for reassembly and remove the main bearing carriers from the crankshaft.
2. Degrease the crankshaft and clear out the oil ways, which can become clogged after long service.
3. Mount the crankshaft on "V" blocks and examine visually, the crankpins and main bearing journals, for obvious wear, scores, grooves and overheating.
4. With a micrometer, measure and note the ovality and taper of each main bearing journal and crankpin as follows:
   Ovality - Take two readings at right-angles to each other at various intervals.
   Taper - Take two readings parallel to each other at both ends of the main bearing journal and crankpin.

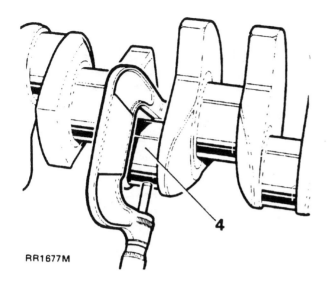

RR1677M

5. If the overall wear exceeds 0,01 mm (0.004 ins) for both main bearing journals and crankpins regrind and fit undersize bearings. When regrinding do not remove any material from thrust faces.

6. After grinding it is important to restore the journal fillet radii as illustrated.

A = 2.7 to 3.00mm
B = 2.5mm

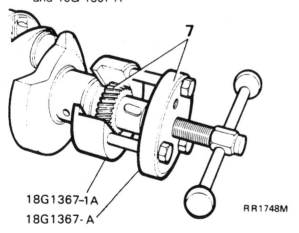

RR1678M

7. Examine the timing gear teeth and if worn remove the gear with special tool 18G 1367-1A and 18G 1367-A

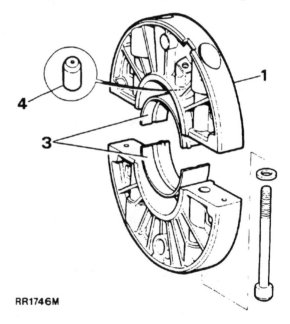

18G1367-1A
18G1367-A

RR1748M

8. To fit a new gear, heat in an oven to 180°C to 200°C, and press-on to the shaft up to the shoulder. Fit a new key for the crankshaft pulley.

Crankshaft carriers

1. Assemble the three main bearing carriers with the bearings fitted and tighten to the correct torque.

2. Using an internal micrometer check the internal diameters of the bearings against the figures in data and renew if necessary or in any event if the crankshaft is being reground.

3. Remove the bearings from the carriers, reassemble and tighten bolts to correct torque. With an internal micrometer check the carrier bore against the figures in data, and for excessive ovality.

4. Check that the piston oil jets in the carriers open at the correct pressure and renew if necessary. Drift the old jet out through the carrier bore, apply a thin coat of Loctite AVX Special around the new jet before fitting.

RR1746M

Rear main bearing carrier

1. Extract the oil seal taking care not to damage the carrier bore.
2. Using an internal micrometer check the bearing dimensions against the figures in data.
3. If required remove the bearing using special tool 18G 1373, as illustrated.

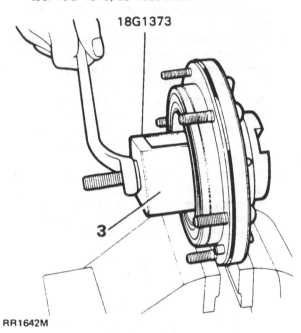

18G1373

3

RR1642M

4. Check the carrier bearing bore for wear against the figures in data.
5. With special tool 18G 1374 fit a new oil seal to the rear carrier, lipside leading.

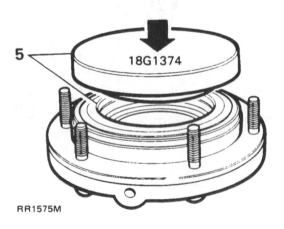

5

18G1374

RR1575M

Thrust spacer

1. Examine the spacer thrust face for damage, scratches, cracks and seizure marks. Ensure that outer diameter on which the seal runs is free from imperfections.
2. With micrometers check the thickness A and the diameter B at four diametrically opposite points and compare with the figures in data.

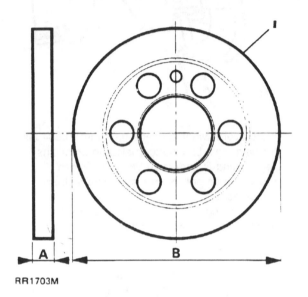

A B

RR1703M

Flywheel

1. Examine the flywheel clutch face for cracks, grooves and signs of over-heating. If excessive damage is evident renew or reface the fly-wheel.

Flywheel face run-out

2. The above check should be carried out during engine assembly. See fitting flywheeel.

Camshaft

1. Carry-out a visual examination of the cam lobes and bearing surfaces. If these are worn, scored or cracked the shaft should be renewed.
2. If visually satisfactory, carry out the dimensional checks detailed in the data section to the cams and bearing journals.
3. Check the camshaft for straightness, by mounting between centres and checking with a dial test gauge on the centre bearing journal. The shaft may be straightened under a press if the bend exceeds 0,05 mm (0.002 in). This work, however, should be entrusted to a specialist.
4. Examine the gear teeth and if worn or damaged press the shaft from the gear, together with the thrust plate.
5. Before fitting a new gear, check the thrust plate thickness at the four points illustrated. Renew the plate if the dimensions do not conform to the limits in data.

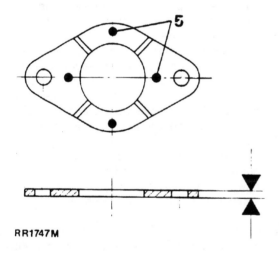

RR1747M

6. Heat the new gear in an oven to 180°C to 200°C, fit the thrust plate and press the gear onto the shaft until the gear is hard against the shoulder. If, when the gear has cooled the thrust plate turns freely on the shaft the camshaft end-float will be correct when fitted.

Cam followers (Tappets)

1. Examine the cam followers and discard any that are worn, pitted or scored on the cam contact face. Check also the cups in which the push rods seat.
2. Check the stem diameter for general wear, ovality and taper. Take measurements at several points round the circumference and along the length of the stem.

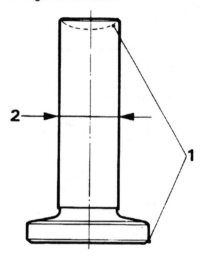

RR1710M

Connecting rods and pistons

1. Whilst keeping each piston and connecting rod identified for possible refitting, separate the pistons from the rods and remove the piston rings. Degrease and decarbonise the pistons and rings ready for examination. Likewise prepare the connecting rods for inspection.

RR1683M

Pistons and rings

1. Examine the pistons for scores, cracks signs of overheating and general wear.
2. If visually satisfactory measure the piston skirt at right angles to the gudgeon pin 15 mm above the bottom of the piston skirt. If the wear is in excess of the maximum permitted in data and the piston to liner clearance is in excess of 0,15 mm (0.006 in) new pistons and liners must be fitted.

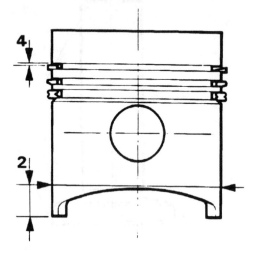

RR1714M

3. Check the gudgeon pins for wear, scores, pitting and signs of overheating. Check the gudgeon pin bore for ovality.

4. Examine the piston rings for damage, wear and cracks. Fit the rings to the pistons as illustrated and using a feeler gauge check the side clearance in the grooves.

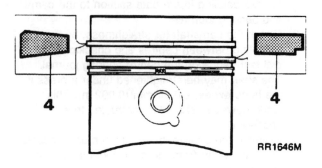

RR1646M

5. To check the piston ring fitted gap insert the ring squarely into the bottom of the bore at the lowest point of piston travel. To ensure squareness push the ring down the bore with a piston. Using an appropriate feeler gauge check the gaps of all the rings in turn. The correct gaps are given in data. If any gap is less than that specified, remove the ring and file the ends square whilst holding the ring in a filing jig or vice.
6. The previous instruction should also be carried out when new pistons and rings are fitted to new liners but the rings may be inserted squarely in any position in the bore.

NOTE: The difference in weight between the four pistons must not exceed 5 grams. When renewing pistons and liners they should all belong to the same classification A or B.

Connecting rods

1. Examine the connecting rods and caps for cracks using a recognised crack testing process.
2. Assemble the cap and rod and tighten to the correct torque. Check the crank pin bore using an inside micrometer and three different points. the bore must be 57,563 to 57,582 mm. Renew rods if the tolerance exceeds 0,02 mm.
3. Examine the connecting rod shells and discard if worn, scored or show signs of overheating. Assemble the rods, caps and shells and tighten to the correct torque. Check the internal diameter against the figures in data.
4. Inspect the small end bush for wear against the figures in data. Check that the wear limit between bush and gudgeon pin does not exceed 0,100 mm (0.004 in). When renewing the bush ensure that the oil hole aligns with the connecting rod hole.

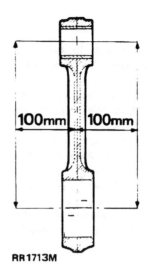

RR1713M

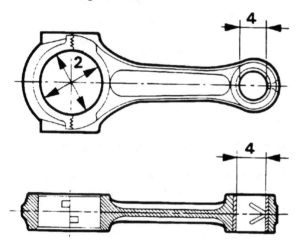

RR1712M

5. Check the rod for bend and twist, taking measurements at approximately 100 mm from the centre of the rod using a recognised alignment gauge. Twist or bend must not exceed 0,5 mm (0.019 in).

6. If it is necessary to renew connecting rods check that the weight difference between them does not exceed 10 grams, see letter code in data (2.4 Litre engines only).
7. Slightly warm the pistons and assemble to the connecting rods ensuring that the recess in the piston crown is on the same side as the number on the connecting rod big end. Insert the gudgeon pins and secure with the circlips.

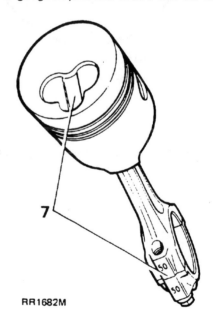

RR1682M

8. Fit the connecting rod bearing shells ensuring that the tags locate in the cutouts.

Oil pump

NOTE: The oil pump is only supplied as an assembly complete with drive gear.

1. Dismantle the oil pump and clean with kerosene or solvent. Examine the rotors and body for wear and pitting.
2. Assemble the oil pump noting that the chamfered side of the outer rotor is fitted downwards towards the drive gear.
3. Check, with a feeler gauge, the clearance between the inner and outer rotor A.
4. Check the clearance between the pump body and outer rotor B and compare the figures in data.

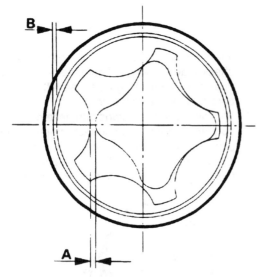

RR1711M

5. Examine the gear teeth for wear, chips and pitting.

Oil pressure relief valve

1. Examine the plunger for scores and pitting. If necessary the valve plunger may be lapped to its seat, to restore efficiency, using fine valve grinding compound. Make sure that all trace of the compound is removed before assembling valve to the crankcase.
2. Check the free length of the spring against the figure in data.

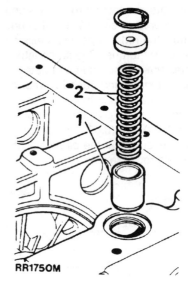

RR1750M

Idler gear assembly 2.4 litre engine only

1. Check the idler gear for wear and damage and for wear in the bushes. Check that the lubrication hole at the back of the mounting plate is clear. If the gear is unservicable the complete unit should be renewed.

Vacuum pump and gear assembly 2.5 litre engine only

1. Inspect the gear for wear and damage. Check the vanes for wear. Examine the vacuum pump housing for scouring or damage.
   If the unit is worn or damaged the complete assembly should be renewed.

Injection pump drive gear

1. Check the injection pump gear (and combined vacuum pump gear on 2.4 litre engines) for damage, wear and pitting. Examine the bore and keyways for wear. Renew if any gear is unsatisfactory.

Oil filter adaptor housing

1. This housing contains a by-pass valve which opens to maintain oil circulation when a difference in pressure exists between the filter base outlet to the oil cooler and the main oil gallery due to a restriction in the oil cooling system. A thermostat which opens at 80°C, to allow oil to pass to the oil cooler is also incorporated in the housing.

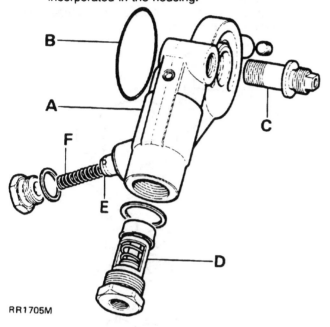

RR1705M

A   Adaptor housing.
B   'O' ring
C   Oil filter and adaptor
    housing union screws
D   Thermostat
E   By-pass plunger
F   By-pass plunger spring

2. Remove the thermostat and check the opening temperature. Place the thermostat in vessel containing water and a thermometer. Appply heat and observe the temperature at which the thermostat opens. Refit or renew as necessary, using a new sealing washer.
3. Remove the by-pass valve plug and remove the spring and plunger. Check the plunger for scores and pitting. Refit or renew as necessary using a new sealing washer.

Vacuum pump 2.4 litre engines only

1. Remove the three screws and withdraw the top cover and "O" ring seal.
2. Check the rotor and vanes for wear.
3. Examine the drive gear for wear.

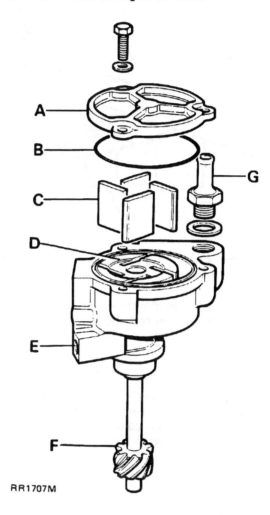

RR1707M

A   Cover
B   'O' ring
C   Vanes
D   Rotor
E   Lubrication port
F   Drive gear
G   Vacuum hose adapter
    and non return valve

4. Check the rotor end float by placing a straight edge across the pump body and with a feeler gauge measure the clearance between the machined outer diameter and straight edge. The end float should be 0,07 to 0,14 mm (0.002 to 0.004 in).

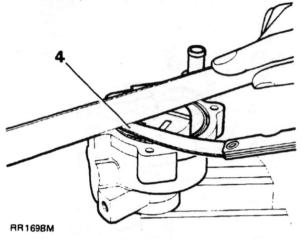

RR1698M

5. Fit the vanes, noting that the round edge must face outwards.

6. Check operation of vacuum non return valve.
7. Fit a new "O" ring seal and secure the cover with the three screws.

Water pump

1. Since the water pump is not serviceable the complete assembly should be renewed if the impeller is worn and corroded or if there is excessive end float or side movement in the impeller shaft.

Fuel lift pump

1. Mark the relationship of the pump cover to the body to facilitate reassembly.
2. Remove the six retaining screws and lift-off the cover.
3. Remove the valve plate.
4. Press down on the diaphragm and twist to release the diaphragm from the body.
5. Remove the diaphragm spring.
6. Clean and examine all parts. The diphragm can be renewed if faulty.

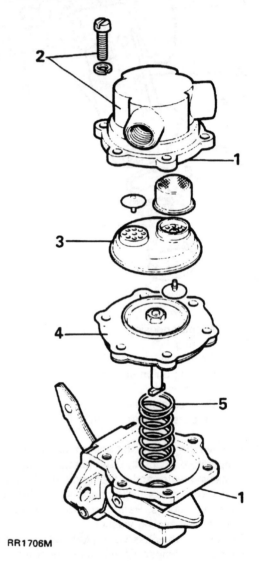

RR1706M

7. Reassemble the pump reversing the above procedure.

Thermostat and housing 2.4 litre engine only

1. Remove the three socket headed screws and withdraw the thermostat and body from the water rail.

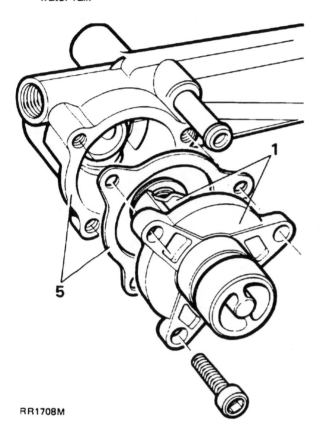

RR1708M

2. Hold the body in a vice and press down upon the two "ears" of the thermostat and twist to release it from the body.

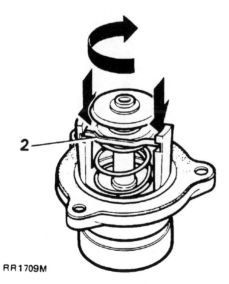

RR1709M

3. To test the thermostat, note the opening temperature stamped on the end of the thermostat and place it in a vessel containing water and a thermometer. Apply heat and observe the temperature at which the thermostat opens. Renew if necessary.
4. Fit the thermostat to the body, reversing the removal instructions.
5. Using a new joint washer, fit the thermostat and body to the water rail.

Thermostat and housing 2.5 litre engine only

1. Remove the four socket headed screws and lift the outlet elbow clear to remove the thermostat with its fitted seal from the thermostat housing.

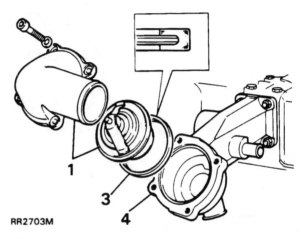

RR2703M

2. To test the thermostat, remove the seal (3) note the opening temperature stamped on the end of the thermostat and place it in a vessel containing water and a thermometer. Apply heat and observe the temperature at which the thermostat opens. Renew if necessary.
3. Fit a new joint seal onto the edge of the thermostat ensuring it is fitted evenly.
4. Refit the thermostat ensuring location of the seal into the recess of the thermostat housing.
5. Refit the outlet elbow and tighten the screws, evenly.

Inlet and exhaust manifold

1. Examine the manifold for damage and cracks.
2. Check the mating faces with the cylinder head
   for distortion by mounting on a surface plate
   and checking with feeler gauges. If necessary,
   the flange faces may be machined to restore
   maximum surface contact with the cylinder
   head.
3. The exhaust manifold is manufactured in two
   sections and piston ring type seals are used to
   provide a flexible gas tight seal. Renew the
   rings if cracked and assemble the two sections
   using Vaseline on the rings to facilitate
   assembly.

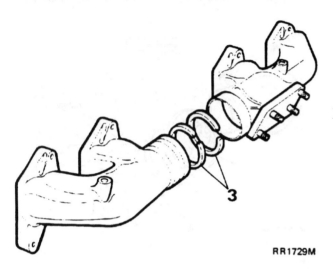

RR1729M

ASSEMBLING ENGINE

Fitting cylinder liners

1. Clean the liners and the cylinder block areas of contact. Fit the liners without 'O' rings. The liners should drop into position under their own weight, if not, further cleaning is necessary.
2. To obtain the correct liner protrusion, attach special tool 18G 1378,B as illustrated, to the cylinder block and tighten the bolts to 30 Nm (22 lbf/ft). Fit a dial test indicator so that the stylus rests in a loaded condition on the external rim of the liner and set the dial to zero. Slide the stylus across to the cylinder block and note the reading.
   Repeat the above procedure to the remaining cylinders.

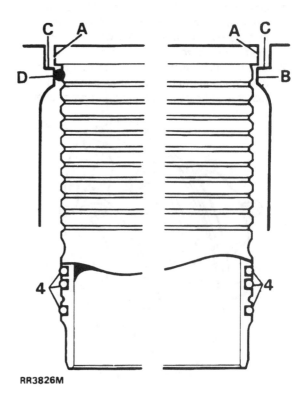

RR3826M

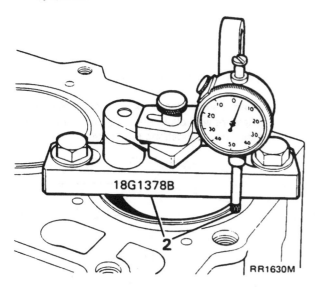

18G1378B

RR1630M

3. Remove the liners and add shims as required to achieve the protrusion given in the data **Section 04**.
4. Remove the liners and fit three new 'O' rings. Apply molybdenum disulphide grease, such as 'Marston's Molycote' to the 'O' ring contact area in the cylinder block.
5. Apply 'Loctite 275' to areas A and B. Avoid any sealant contacting the shim and face C.
   An 'O' ring is fitted to top of liner, on later 2.5 engines or when fitting new liners to 2.4 and early 2.5 engines. Fit 'O' ring seal to position D and apply Loctite to area A only. Avoid sealant contacting the shim, face C and 'O' ring.

6. Fit the liners to the cylinder block and hold them in using the cylinder head spacers and slave bolts, tighten the bolts to 30 Nm (22 lb/ft), leave the spacers and slave bolts in position for approximately two hours until the Loctite is set.

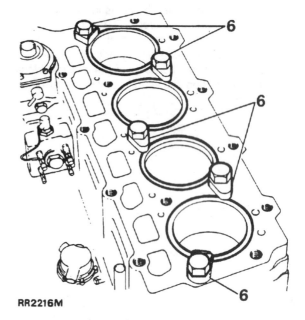

RR2216M

Fitting front and rear main bearings.

1. Use special tool 18G 1373 to refit the front main bearings to the cylinder block, ensuring that the oil hole in bearing aligns with oil hole in the bearing bore.
2. Use the same tool 18G 1373 to refit the rear main bearings to the carrier assembly, ensuring that the oil holes in bearing and carrier align.

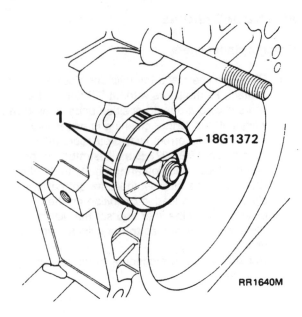

RR1640M

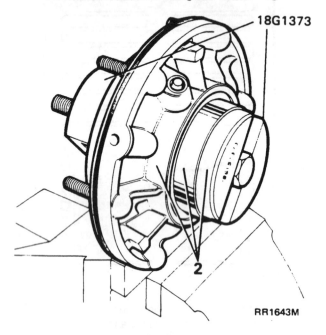

RR1643M

Camshaft bearings

1. Renew the camshaft bearings in the cylinder block using special tool 18G 1372.
2. Each bearing shell has two oil holes and it is essential that these align exactly with the corresponding oil drillings in the cylinder block. The illustration shows the camshaft rear bearing being fitted.

Fitting camshaft and followers

1. Invert the cylinder block and smear the cam followers with clean engine oil and fit them to their original locations in the cylinder block.

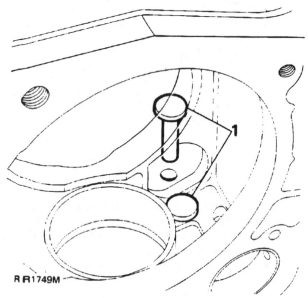

R R1749M

2. Smear the camshaft journals with clean engine oil and and carefully insert the camshaft complete with thrust plate and gear. Temporarily secure the camshaft to the cylinder block with the two screws.

Fitting crankshaft and carrier assembly.

1. Fit new main bearing shells to each of the carrier halves.
2. Assemble the carriers to the crankshaft journals, ensuring that the same carriers are fitted to their original locations and that the piston jet cut-a-way is towards the front of the crankshaft. Secure each carrier with the two bolts tightening evenly to the correct torque. Check that the oil jet is in position.

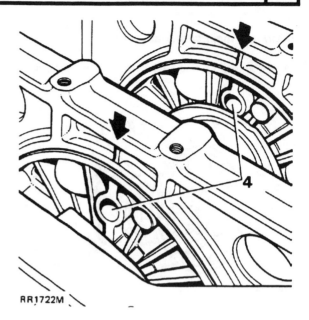

RR1722M

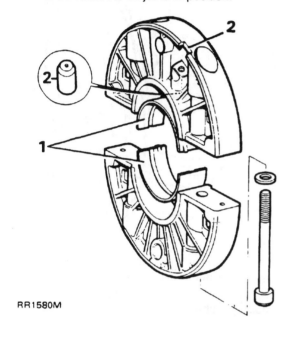

RR1580M

3. Slide special tool 18G 1370 over the crankshaft gear and, if necessary, with assistance insert the crankshaft and carrier assembly into the crankcase in the same manner as for removal.
4. Align the holes in the lower carriers, as illustrated, with the centre of the crankcase webs.

5. Secure each carrier assembly to the crankcase with the appropriate oil feed and carrier location shaft. Ensure that the shafts are fitted to their original locations with new washers.
   The correct locations are as follows:-
   Front carrier shaft - Oil feed to vacuum pump.
   Centre carrier shaft -Oil feed to turbo-charger.
   Rear carrier shaft -Blank
   Tighten the shafts to the correct torque.
6. Fit the oil pressure switch.

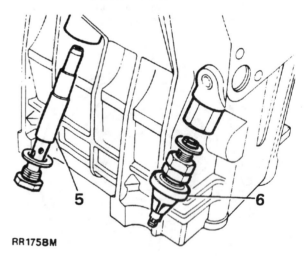

RR1758M

Fitting rear main carrier assembly.

1. Fit a new 'O' ring seal to the rear main carrier.

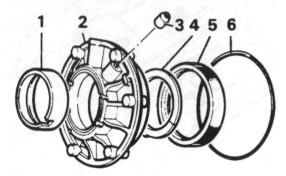

RR2776M

1	Bearing
2	Carrier
3	Oil jet
4	Outer thrust washers
5	Oil seal
6	'O' ring seal

2. Fit new outer thrust halves to the oil seal side with the oil grooves outwards. Ensure that both halves are of the same thickness value and that the thrust with the tag locates in the keyway in the carrier. Hold the thrusts in position with Vaseline.

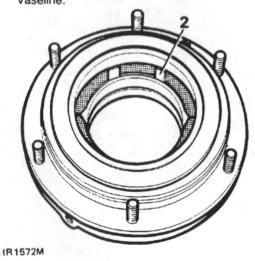

RR1572M

3. With the cylinder block still in the inverted position, lubricate the oil seal with clean engine oil and fit the carrier assembly to the crankcase. Ensure that the oil hole in the crankcase is aligned with the oil hole in the carrier as illustrated.

RR1611M

4. When correctly aligned the dowel in the carrier must be at the 1 o'clock position. Final alignment will be achieved when the flywheel housing is fitted.

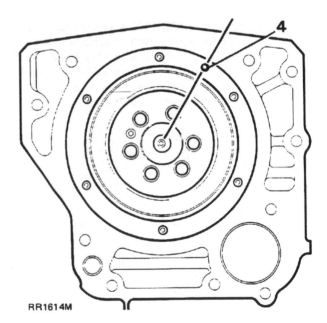

RR1614M

5. Fit a new 'O' ring seal to the rear of the flywheel housing.

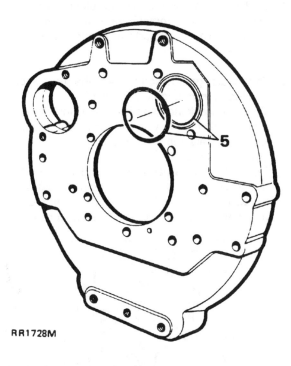

RR1728M

6. Fit the flywheel housing and secure with the nine bolts, tightening evenly to the correct torque. Fit and evenly tighten, to the correct torque, the six carrier retaining nuts.

7. Fit the thrust spacer and a new 'O' ring seal and secure with the socket headed screw.

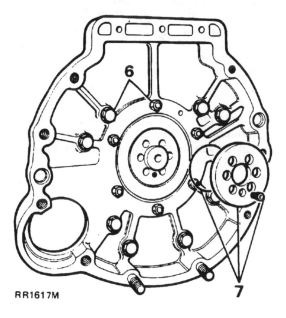

RR1617M

8. To check the crankshaft end-float, insert two flywheel bolts in the crankshaft using spacers equivalent to thickness of the flywheel and tighten to the correct torque. Mount a dial test indicator with the stylus resting, in a loaded condition, on the thrust spacer. Lever the crankshaft back and forth and note the reading. Adjust the end-float, if necessary, by substituting with washers of an appropriate thickness, see data section for available washers.

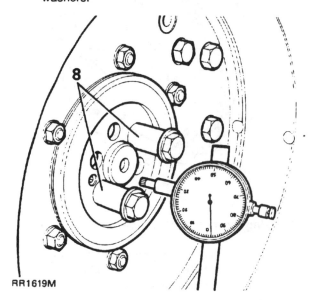

RR1619M

Fitting flywheel

1. Fit the flywheel using the same method as for removal. Fit and evenly tighten the six retaining bolts to the correct torque.

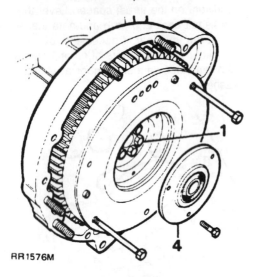

RR1576M

Checking flywheel face run-out

2. Mount a dial test indicator on the flywheel housing with the stylus positioned in a loaded condition on the flywheel face and zero the gauge.
3. Turn the flywheel and take readings every 90°. The difference between the highest and lowest readings taken at all four points should not exceed 0,10 mm (0.004 in) which is the maximum permissible run-out.
4. Fit the spigot bearing and plate and secure with the three bolts.

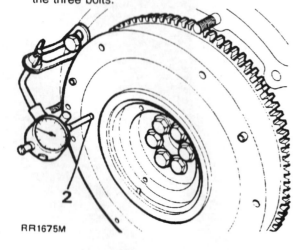

RR1675M

Fitting idler gear and oil pump 2.4 litre engine.

1. Whilst maintaining the cylinder block in the inverted position, remove the two socket headed screws and partially withdraw the camshaft.

2. Fit the idler gear assembly with the three socket headed screws and tighten evenly.
3. Turn the crankshaft and idler gear until the dots align, as illustrated, with the single dot on the idler gear between the two dots on the crankshaft gear.
4. Refit the camshaft and align the gears so that the single dot on the camshaft gear is between the two dots on the idler gear, as illustrated. Fit and tighten the two camshaft retaining screws.

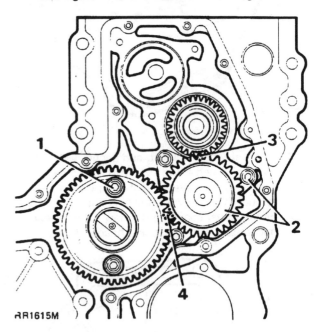

RR1615M

5. Using a new 'O' ring seal fit the oil pump assembly and secure with the three socket headed screws tightening evenly to the correct torque.

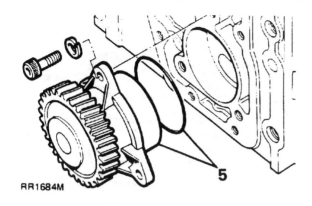

RR1684M

Fitting vacuum and oil pumps 2.5 litre engine.

1. Whilst maintaining the cylinder block in the inverted position, remove the two socket headed screws and partially withdraw the camshaft.
2. Using a new 'O' ring seal offer the vacuum pump and gear assembly into its location.
3. Turn the crankshaft and vacuum pump gear until the dots align, as illustrated, with the single dot on the vacuum pump gear between the two dots on the crankshaft gear. Fully house the vacuum pump, tightening the three socket headed screws to the correct torque.

NOTE: The screw with the smaller diameter head should be fitted closest to the camshaft gear.

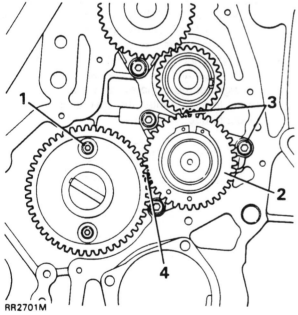

RR2701M

4. Refit the camshaft and align the gears so that the single dot on the camshaft gear is between the two dots on the vacuum pump gear, as illustrated. Fit and tighten the two camshaft retaining screws.
5. Fit the oil pump assembly and secure with the three socket headed screws tightening evenly to the correct torque.

Fitting oil pressure relief valve

1. Clean the valve seating in the crankcase and fit the relief valve, spring and cap and secure with the circlip using 18G 257 or suitable alternative pliers.

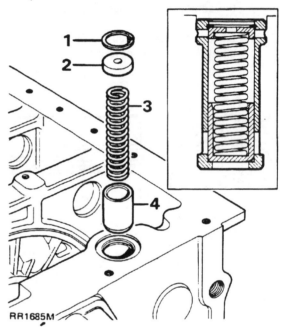

RR1685M

1   Circlip
2   Cap
3   Spring
4   Plunger

Fitting connecting rods and pistons

1. If the original pistons and connecting rods are being refitted ensure that they are returned to their original locations.
2. Turn the cylinder block over to an upright position.
3. Turn the crankshaft to bring numbers one and four crankpins to the B.D.C position.
4. Stagger the piston ring gaps as follows :__

   A   Compression ring gap 30° to the right of the combustion chamber recess.

   B   Scraper ring gap on the opposite side of the combustion chamber recess.

   C   oil control rings gap 30° to the left of the combustion chamber recess.

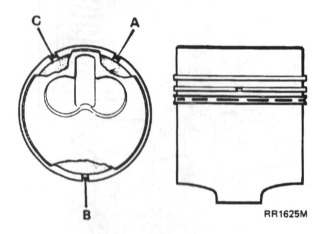

RR1625M

5. Check that the recess area in the piston crown is on the same side as the figures on the connecting rod. Fit the connecting rod bearing shells. Using piston ring compressor 18G 55A or a suitable alternative, insert number one and number four pistons into the cylinder bores ensuring that the recess area in the piston crown is toward the camshaft side of the engine. Tap the pistons into position in the bores.

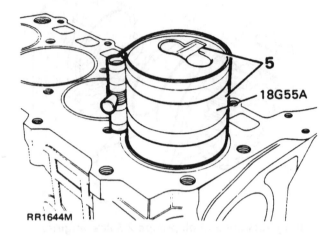

RR1644M

6. Turn the cylinder block over and fit the connecting rod caps so that the figures are on the same side. Apply 'Molyguard' to the threads of the NEW bolts and tighten to the correct torque.
7. Repeat the above instructions to fit number two and three pistons.

Fitting oil strainer and sump.

1. Fit a new 'O' ring seal to the oil pick-up pipe and insert into the crankcase. Secure the strainer end of the pipe to the crankcase with two bolts. See items 42 and 43 on illustration of engine internal components.
2. Clean the sump and crankcase mating faces and apply 'Loctite 518' to both surfaces. Secure the sump with the twenty-one bolts tightening evenly to the correct torque.
3. Apply 'Hylosil RTV' to the oil pan and sump mating faces and secure the pan to the sump with eighteen nuts and evenly tighten to the correct torque. Tighten the drain plug to the correct torque.

Fitting cylinder heads.

1. The fitting of the cylinder heads requires a precise sequence of instructions to be carried out. It includes - checking cylinder liner protrusion - selecting head gasket thickness and tightening the head bolts in the correct order.

   For these details see: **CYLINDER HEADS** remove and refit. Section 12 pages 6 to 11.

Fitting and timing fuel injector pump.

1. Temporarily fit the timing cover and crankshaft pulley and turn the crankshaft until the T.D.C. mark on the cover aligns with the groove in the crankshaft pulley so that number one piston is at T.D.C. on the compression stroke, with number four valves 'rocking'.
2. Attach the special timing gauge 18G 1369A to the timing cover and turn the crankshaft anti-clockwise until the pulley groove aligns with the 25° B.T.D.C. mark on the scale.

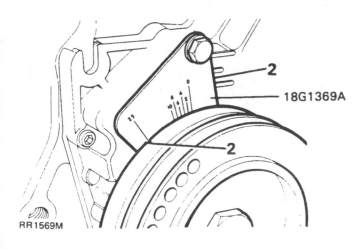
RR1569M

3. Remove the pulley and timing cover and mesh the injection pump and camshaft gears so the tooth marked '4' is offset from the two camshaft teeth marked with dots, also the two keyways positioned exactly as illustrated.

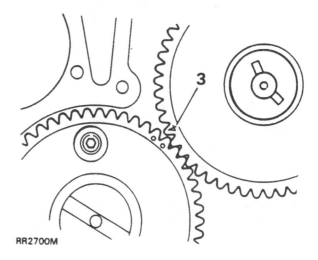
RR2700M

4. Whilst holding the gear in this position fit the injection pump with a new joint washer ensure the key on the shaft is at the 11 o'clock position viewed from front of engine. Secure the three nuts, finger tight only. Fully tighten the injection pump gear retaining nut to the correct torque.
5. Release the screw on the cold start cable and turn the trunnion 90° until the lever is fully released.

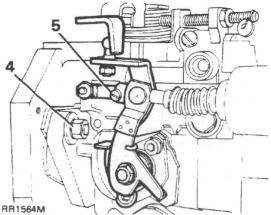
RR1564M

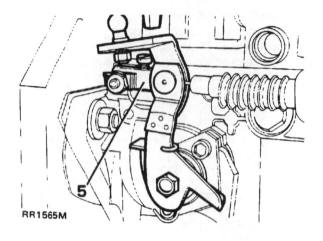

RR1565M

6. Fit the special tool MS107 and dial test indicator to the rear of the pump.

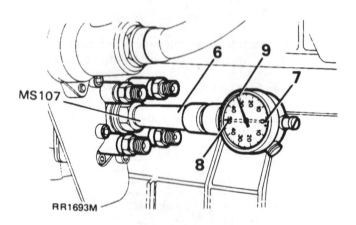

MS107

RR1693M

7. Fit the timing cover and scale and crankshaft pulley and turn the crankshaft to T.D.C. Then turn crankshaft anti-clockwise until the indicator needle stops and zero the indicator. The groove on the pulley should now be approximately aligned with the 25° B.T.D.C. mark.

8. Turn the crankshaft clockwise so that the pulley groove is aligned with the 3° B.T.D.C. mark. Turn the injector pump body, clockwise or anti-clockwise as necessary until the indicator reads 50 (0,5 mm).

9. Tighten the pump body retaining nuts and turn crankshaft to T.D.C. and check that the dial reads 68 (0,68 mm)

10. Move the cold start lever rearward to the normal running position prior to instruction 5, and tighten the screw. **See Maintenance Section 10** for cold start adjustment.

11. Turn the crankshaft until the T.D.C. mark on the cover or timing gauge aligns with the pulley groove.

12. Remove the pulley and timing cover and fit a new joint washer and 'O' ring seal to the crankshaft.

NOTE: Hylosil RTV is used in place of a joint washer on 2.5 Litre engines.

13. At the same time check that the timing marks on the gear train all align, as illustration.

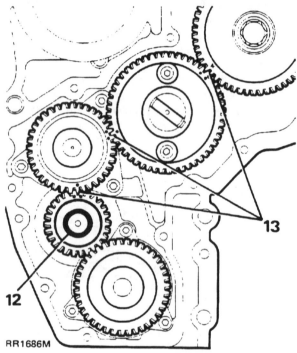

RR1686M

14. Fit the timing cover and secure with the twelve socket-headed screws and one bolt and tighten evenly to the correct torque. Using special tool 18G 1375 drive in a new timing cover seal, cavity side leading.

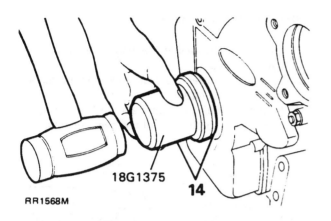

18G1375

14

RR1568M

15. Fit the pump drive gear cover plate using a new
'O' ring seal. Secure with the four bolts and
tighten evenly.
16. Fit the crankshaft pulley and tighten the nut to
the correct torque.

Fitting vacuum pump 2.4 litre engine

Fit the vacuum pump with a new 'O' ring seal and
secure with the clamp and two nuts and tighten to
the correct torque. Check that the backlash between
the vacuum pump drive gear and worm drive does
not exceed 0,200 mm (0.008 in).

Fitting water pump

1. Using a new joint washer fit the water pump
and pulley assembly and secure with the four
bolts, tightening evenly to the correct torque.

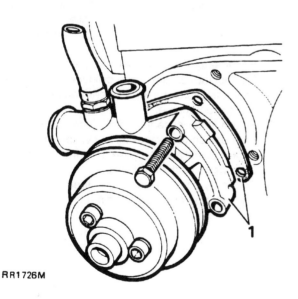

RR1726M

Fitting valve rocker assemblies

1. Check that the oil feed dowels are in position in
each cylinder head.
2. Fit the push rods ensuring that the ball-end
locates correctly in the cam follower cup.
3. Slacken-off the tappet adjusting screws. Fit the
valve rocker assemblies to the cylinder head
over the oil feed dowels and locate the tappet
adjusting screws in the push rod cups. Secure
with the single nut and tighten to the correct
torque.

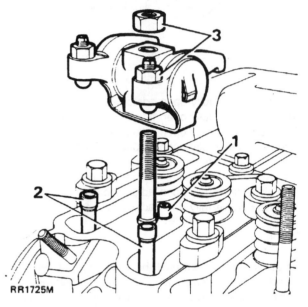

RR1725M

4. Adjust the inlet and exhaust valve tappet
clearances to 0,30 mm (0.012 in) in the
following manner and sequence. The feeler
gauge should be a sliding fit between the rocker
and valve tip. Slacken the rocker adjusting
screw locknut and turn the screw clockwise to
decrease or anti-clockwise to increase the
clearance. When correct hold the screw against
rotation and tighten the locknut. Two sequences
to adjust the clearances may be used.

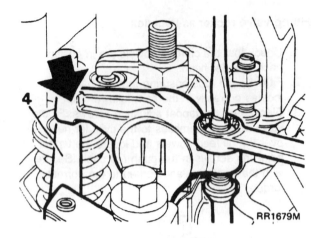

RR1679M

Sequence A

With No.1 valve fully open adjust No.7 valve.
With No.8 valve fully open adjust No.2 valve.
With No.5 valve fully open adjust No.3 valve.
With No.4 valve fully open adjust No.6 valve.
With No.7 valve fully open adjust No.1 valve.
With No.2 valve fully open adjust No.8 valve.
With No.3 valve fully open adjust No.5 valve.
With No.6 valve fully open adjust No.4 valve.

Sequence B

Rotate the crankshaft until the valves of number four cylinder are rocking then adjust the clearance of number one valve. Adjust the remaining valve clearances in the following order:-

Adjust:-
Valves of No. 3 cyl with No. 2 valves rocking
Valves of No. 4 cyl with No. 1 valves rocking
Valves of No. 2 cyl with No. 3 valves rocking

Fitting injectors and pipes

1. Fit the sealing washer the the injector to the cylinder head.
2. Locate the dowel and clamp and tighten the nut to the correct torque.
3. Fit the remaining injectors and spill rail using a new washer both sides of the banjo unions.

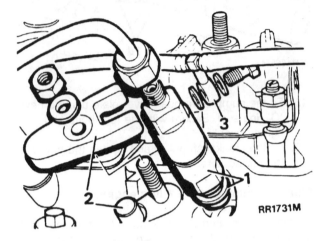

RR1731M

4. Fit the heater plugs and three connecting terminal bars.
5. Fit the supply pipes to the injectors and injector pump. Do not overtighten the union nuts.

Fit rocker covers and coolant rail

1. Using new gaskets fit the rocker covers noting that the tallest covers are fitted to numbers two and three cylinders and the oil filler cap to number one cylinder. Tighten the special nuts to the correct torque.
2. Fit the engine coolant rail complete with thermostat housing to the cylinder heads using new gaskets. Tighten the eight bolts evenly to the correct torque.
3. Fit the water hose from the injector pump cold start device to number three cylinder head rocker cover and the hose from the thermostat housing to cold start device.
4. Fit the by-pass hose between thermostat housing and and water pump.

Fit oil filter adaptor

1. Fit the oil filter adaptor, using a new 'O' ring seal, to the cylinder block. Ensure that the adaptor is fitted, as illustrated, with the elongated cavity on the side facing the cylinder block at the bottom. Secure with the union screw to the correct torque.

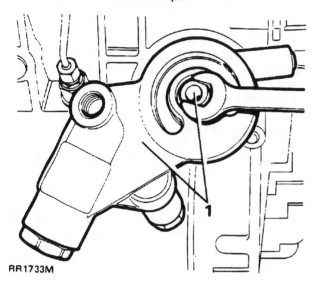

RR1733M

2. Smear the oil filter canister seal with clean engine oil and screw the canister on to the adaptor until contact then turn a further half turn by hand only. See maintenance **Section 10.**
3. Connect the oil feed pipe to the front main bearing carrier adaptor union and the banjo hose end to the vacuum pump.

Fit fuel lift pump

1. Using a new gasket fit the fuel lift pump to the cylinder block. Ensure that the actuating lever rides on top of the cam.

RR1694M

Fit the turbocharger

1. Fit the turbocharger support bracket to the cylinder block attachment bracket.
2. Also fit the starter motor heat shield rear support bracket which shares a common fixing point on the cylinder block.

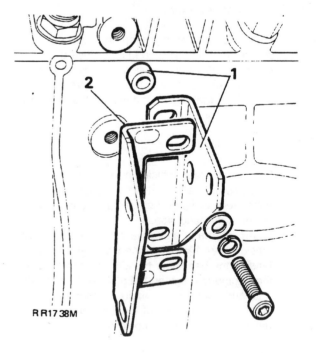

R R1738M

3. Fit the oil feed hose to the centre union on the cylinder block.
4. Fit the oil return hose to the crankcase union.
5. Fit a new gasket to the exhaust manifold and fit the turbo-charger and tighten the four nuts evenly to the correct torque.
6. Connect the oil feed and oil return pipes to the turbocharger.

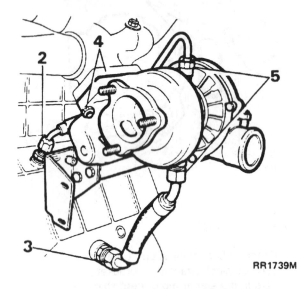

RR1739M

7. Fit the heat shield to the exhaust manifold.

Fit power steering pump

1. Fit the power steering pump and support bracket to the engine and fit the drive belt. Adjust the drive belt tension. **See Maintenance Section 10.** To tension the belt move the pump away from the engine and tighten the pivot and adjusting bolts.

Fit the alternator

1. Right hand steer vehicles have the alternator mounted on the left side of the engine. On left hand steer vehicles the alternator is mounted on the right hand side.
2. Fit the alternator and drive belt. Adjust the belt tension. **See Maintenance Section 10.** To tension the belt, lever the alternator away from the engine and tighten the pivot and adjusting nuts and bolts. Do not apply pressure to the stator or slip ring end of the alternator, whilst tensioning, or damage could result.

Fit the air conditioning compressor

1. Fit the mounting bracket to the cylinder block and attach the compressor, noting that on R.H.S. vehicles the compressor and alternator share a common pivot belt. Fit and tension the drive belt. **See Maintenance Section 10.** Pivot the compressor anti-clockwise and tighten the pivot and adjusting nuts and bolts.

CAUTION: When fitting a new drive belt, tension the belt as described above. Start and run the engine for 3 to 5 minutes at fast idle, after which time the belt must be re-checked. If necessary retension the belt.

Fitting starter motor

1. Fit the starter motor to the flywheel housing and secure with either two bolts or two nuts. Also attach the heat shield to the lower fixing, together with the earth strap.
2. Secure the rear-end of the starter motor to the rear support bracket, fitted earlier, with two bolts and attach the rear of the heat shield to the top bolt.

Fitting clutch

1. Clean the flywheel and clutch assembly faces.
2. Place the clutch centre friction plate in position on the flywheel with the flat side towards the flywheel.
3. Fit the clutch assembly and loosely secure with the six bolts.
4. Centralise the centre plate using special tool 18G 79 or a spare primary shaft and tighten the six bolts evenly to the correct torque.
5. Smear the splines of the centre plate with a Molybdenum disulphide grease.

TURBOCHARGER DESCRIPTION

A turbocharger is a simple but efficient means of increasing engine power. It consists of an exhaust gas driven air compressor that delivers high volumes of air into the combustion chamber, which may increase the engine's power output by up to 30%.

The turbocharger is fed by the main gallery oil pressure which lubricates and stabilises the fully floating bearings. When in operation the turbine shaft usually revolves between 1,000 and 130,000 rev/min. Therefore it is extremely important that the recommended change periods for oil and air filters are adhered to.

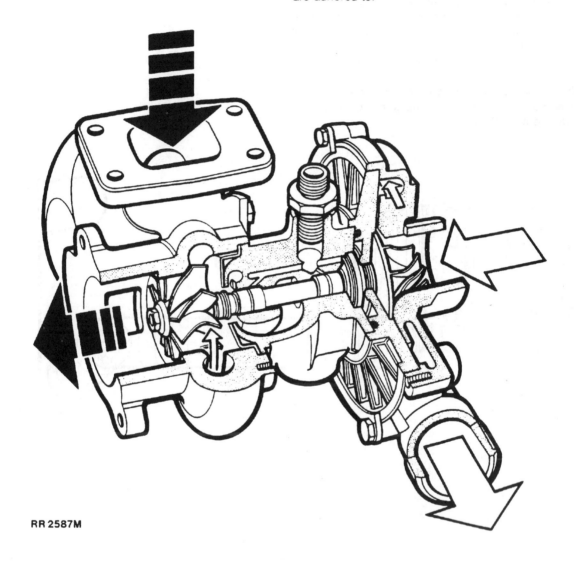

RR 2587M

TURBOCHARGER - CHECK

If the turbocharger unit is suspected of being faulty, the following simple test may be carried out. The assistance of a second operative is required to carry out this operation.

1. Open the bonnet.
2. Start the engine and allow it to idle.
3. Depress the turbocharger to intercooler feed pipe with one hand, the air pressure increase in the pipe may be detected as the second operative increases the engine revs.

NOTE: Although the above test indicates the operation of the turbocharger. it does not indicate it's efficiency.

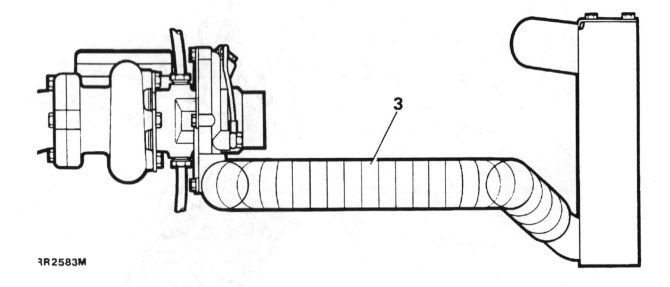

RR2583M

TURBOCHARGER BOOST PRESSURE

Service tools:
18G.1116-1 Pressure test adaptor

Check

1. Remove the grub screw, located in the inlet manifold.

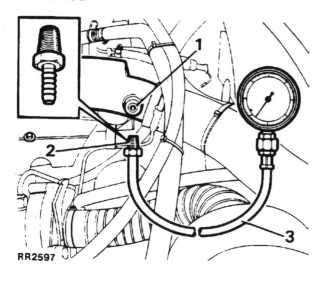

RR2597

2. Insert adaptor 18G.1116-1 into the grub screw orifice
3. Attach a suitable pressure gauge, with sufficient length of tube to reach from the inlet manifold to the cab of the vehicle.
4. Drive the vehicle in 3rd gear at 3800 rev/min to give a satisfactory reading of 0.9kg/cm

WASTE GATE VALVE

The turbocharger waste gate diverts exhaust gas flow to by-pass the turbine when the boost pressure is higher than 0.9kg/cm.

Adjust

The boost pressure may be adjusted by loosening the lock nut and turning the screw marked 'A' in the diagram. Turn the screw clockwise to increase the spring load on the valve and consequently increase the boost pressure. Unscrew to decrease both spring load and boost pressure.

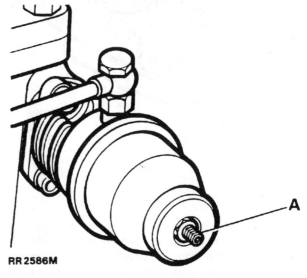

RR 2586M

NOTE: There is a small hole located in the waste gate housing. To ensure efficient operation of the waste gate diaphragm it is neccessary to clean this hole. A small piece of sturdy wire, or a similar object, is a suitable tool for this operation. Take care not to insert the wire too far in to the waste gate housing, as the diaphram is made of a heat resistant rubber and is subsequently easily damaged.

TURBOCHARGER 'END FLOAT' CHECK

Use a dial test gauge and the set up shown in the diagram. Set the gauge to zero on the turbine wheel, and by moving the shaft in a linear motion the end play may be established. The maximum allowable end play is 0,15mm (0.006in).

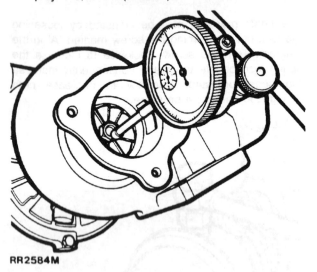

RR2584M

Radial clearance

Push the turbine wheel to the extreme side position and set the dial test gauge to zero, on the indicator, as shown in the diagram. Check the side clearance of the turbine shaft by observing total radial movement of the turbine wheel. Maximum side clearance allowable is 0,42mm (0.016in).

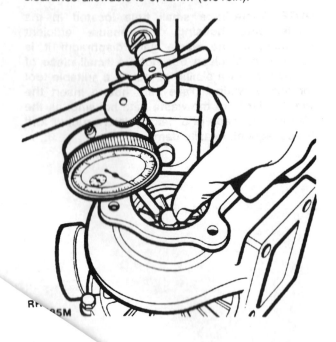

RR2585M

AIR FILTER CHECK

To ensure that the correct volume of air is supplied to the turbocharger unit, the air filter should be checked for cleanliness. Firstly remove the filter box from the securing brackets. Then remove the air filter from it's housing. A visual inspection of the filter will verify it's condition. Fit a new air filter if there are any signs of oil contamination or blockage of any description.

TURBOCHARGER FAULTFINDING

This workshop bulletin has looked at the principles on which the turbocharger operates, and the fundamentals of maintenance. It is now necessary to identify symptoms and probable causes of a suspect turbocharger. As the exhaust gas drives the turbocharger, it is capable of speeds up to 130,000 rev/min and temperatures of up to 650°C. In order to ensure that the bearings are lubricated and cooled, the turbocharger is connected to the normal engine lubrication system. Obviously very high quality seals must be used in the turbocharger, to prevent lubricating oil entering the inlet or exhaust system.

Should oil leak past a seal into the exhaust system, dense pale blue smoke will be emitted continuously. If however the oil leaks into the inlet system it will be burnt at a higher temperature and produce a darker shade of blue smoke. The engine speed may also be permanently higher than normal, as the engine will burn the oil as extra fuel and an excessive oil leak in to the inlet system may even cause the engine to accelerate, however for this to occur the operator would have to ignore all earlier signs of impending trouble.

Blockage of the large oil drain pipe from the turbocharger, though very unlikely, is certainly the worst condition as oil under pressure would be forced past the seals and into both inlet and exhaust systems. If grey or black smoke is being emitted, the turbocharger may be partly blocked or the shaft may not be perfectly free to spin. This will cause a restriction in the air inlet and result in grey/black exhaust smoke, which usually increases at higher engine speeds.

CAUTION: If the driver is in the habit of accelerating the engine before switching the engine off, the turbine will continue to spin after the engine has come to rest and the lubrication to the turbine bearings ceased. It is therefore possible that this practice will cause damage or seizure of the bearings.

Other symptoms of turbocharger faults

A change in the normal noise level is usually the first indication of a fault in the turbocharger or its hose connections. A higher pitched sound usually indicates a possible air leak into the suction side of the compressor and the inlet system, or an escape of compressed air between the compressor and the inlet manifold. Obviously an excessive escape of compressed air from the manifold is not only noisy but will also cause some loss of power.

Slight leaks from the turbine housing or exhaust manifold, whilst noisy, are easily detected and have, little effect on the power output. Cyclic sounds (e.g. a continuous rubbing noise) are an indication of air restriction to the compressor or that the compressor wheel is coated in dirt.

If the waste gate valve sticks in the open position the engine will be down on power.

INJECTION PUMP TIMING

Check and adjust

Service tools:

**18G.1376 Timing adaptor
18G.1369A Timing gauge**

When it has been established that the injection pump requires a timing check the following procedure should be followed.

1. Attach the timing gauge 18G.1369A to the engine front cover. Rotate the engine until the mark on the crankshaft pulley lines up with the top dead centre TDC mark on the timing gauge.
2. Release the cable tensioner on the cold start mechanism to ensure an accurate result.

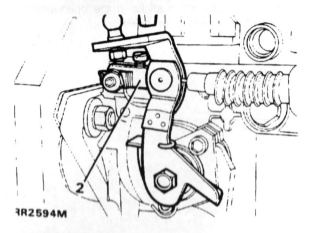

RR2594M

3. Remove the blanking plug from the rear of the pump assembly and insert adaptor 18G. 1376. Attach a dial test gauge to allow a reading to be obtained.

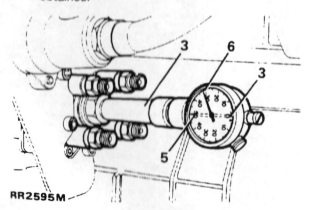

RR2595M

4. Rotate the engine again until the pulley mark is lined up with the 25° BTDC mark. The dial on the test gauge should then be zeroed. Ensure at this stage that there is sufficient pressure being applied to the stylus to give a deflection on the indicator.

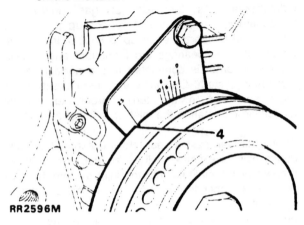

RR2596M

5. The engine should be turned again to 3° BTDC and the needle deflection noted. A deflection of 50 (0,5mm) should be read.
6. To adjust the dimension, slacken the three locking nuts, which secure the pump to the front cover. Then rotate the injection pump assembly until a correct reading has been established, retighten the locking nuts. As a double check the deflection on the dial test gauge should be a further 16-18 (0,16-0,18mm) when the engine is turned to TDC.
7. When adjustment is complete remove the service tools and refit the blanking plug to injection pump and the engine front cover bolt.
8. Finally retension the cable on the cold start mechanism and tighten the retaining screw.

FIT COOLANT SYSTEM KIT

- 2.4 VM diesel.

Part No. RTC 6863

This kit should be used where the engine is prone to overheating, or requires new cylinder heads/gaskets. Prior to fitting the kit, it is essential to check if a non-factory air conditioning system has been installed. If such a system is fitted, check that a 16 fin/inch radiator, part number BTP 1742 has also been fitted.

Expansion tank

Removing

WARNING: Do not remove expansion tank filler cap when engine is hot. The system is pressurised and personal scalding could result.

1. Remove expansion tank filler cap. Turn expansion cap a quarter turn anti-clockwise, allow pressure to escape, continue turning in same direction to remove cap.
2. Drain cooling system.
3. Disconnect hose to radiator.
4. Disconnect overflow pipe.
5. Disconnect wiring to low coolant sensor.
6. Remove pinch bolt.
7. Remove expansion tank.

Refitting

8. Fit new low coolant sensor (in kit) to new expansion tank.
9. Fit new expansion tank and tighten pinch bolt.
10. Fit radiator hose, tighten clip

Bleed pipe (Y piece) - see RR3806M

NOTE: Passage of coolant along hose A causes air to be extracted from radiator along hose B.

11. Remove existing bleed pipe from vehicle.
12. Fit new bleed pipe from kit. Place pipe assembly on vehicle. Fit shortest hose to expansion tank, tighten clip.

CAUTION: It is essential that the new bleed pipe is installed correctly. Interchanging postion of hoses A and B will render the air bleed function of the Y piece inoperative. The shorter of the two long hoses, identified by a blue plastic tag, MUST be fitted to the engine.

13. Identify hose A and B. Fit correctly to engine and radiator, tighten clips.
14. Fit bleed pipe to front left hand inner wing, by the M8 screw washer and nut, using one of two existing holes.

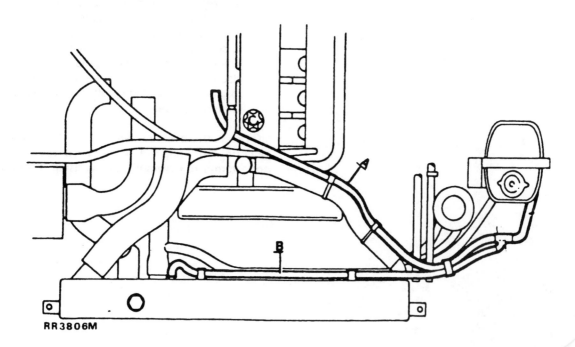

RR3806M

Coolant temperature sensor

15. Remove coolant temperature sensor from thermostat. Blank off hole using blank plug supplied.
16. Remove blank plug from No. 4 cylinder head. Fit adaptor from kit, applying Loctite Superfast 572.
17. Fit coolant temperature sensor to adaptor.
18. Re-route sensor wiring. Ensure that cables are protected where necessary with PVC electrical tape to prevent chafing.

Cooling system fill

NOTE: If cooling system is dry, fill radiator with correct quantity and solution of coolant before carrying out this fill procedure.

WARNING: Do not remove radiator filler plug unless system is cold and expansion tank filler cap is first removed. The system is pressurised and personal scalding could result.

19. With system cold remove header tank filler cap.
20. Remove radiator filler plug.
21. Start engine run at 1500 rev/min while carrying out instructions 22 to 24.
22. Add coolant to radiator until full.
23. Refit radiator filler plug.
24. Add coolant until it is within 25 mm of bottom of filler neck. Disregard level plate.
25. Refit header tank filler cap.

VISCOUS FAN - CHECK

When investigating instances of engine or cylinder head overheating on the VM 2.4 litre diesel engine, it is important that you check the operation of the viscous coupling to ensure it is functioning correctly. The following procedure should be used.

NOTE: When an engine is cold, for instance on the first start-up of the day, some noise will be evident from the fan. This noise is normal and is evident that the unit functioning correctly. After a few minutes the fan noise will reduce.

1. Remove the viscous coupling assembly from the drive shaft

NOTE: The hexagonal coupling on the input shaft is a left hand thread.

2. Examine the assembly for general damage and especially for fluid leakage from either the valve on the front of the unit or from the rear in the area of the input shaft/hexagonal coupling. The viscous fluid is normally dark grey in appearance, although if the leak is fresh and the fluid has not been contaminated it will appear transparent.
3. Inspect the bimetallic spring, which operates the valve on the front of the viscous assembly to ensure that it is not damaged and is properly secured. The spring is fixed to a pressed steel bracket by silicon rubber adhesive and the bracket is in turn rivetted to the aluminium housing of the viscous coupling.
4. Ensure that the input shaft rotates smoothly with no evidence of tight spots or grating, and also that a significant degree of constant resistance is felt during rotation - the shaft must not run too freely.

NOTE: If there is evidence of a fault with the viscous fan coupling it must be replaced. Do not attempt to dismantle or overhaul the unit.

NOTE: The circuit diagram RR1166 is for 2.4 litre, 1986 Model Year Diesel Range Rovers.
For later circuit diagrams refer to main workshop manual or supplements.

Supplements	Publication No.
1987 Model Year	LSM180 WS1 ed2
1988 Model Year	LSM180 WS2
1989 Model Year	LSM180 WS3
1990 Model Year	LSM180 WS5 ed2
1991 Model Year	LSM180 WS6

KEY TO CIRCUIT DIAGRAM - Fig. RR1166

1. Front interior lamp
2. Rear interior lamp
3. LH front door switch
4. RH front door switch
5. Tailgate switch
6. LH rear door switch
7. RH rear door switch
8. RH stop lamp
9. LH stop lamp
10. LH front indicator lamp
11. LH rear indicator lamp
12. LH side repeater lamp
13. RH front indicator lamp
14. RH rear indicator lamp
15. RH side repeater lamp
16. RH auxiliary driving lamp
17. LH auxiliary driving lamp
18. Auxiliary driving lamp switch
19. RH headlamp dip
20. LH headlamp dip
21. RH headlamp main
22. LH headlamp main
23. RH rear fog lamp
24. LH rear fog lamp
25. RH number plate lamp
26. RH side lamp
27. RH tail lamp
28. LH number plate lamp
29. LH side lamp
30. LH tail lamp
31. Radio illumination
32. Switch illumination
33. Switch illumination
34. LH door lamps
35. RH door lamps
36. Interior lamp delay
37. Diode
38. Interior lamp switch
39. Stop lamp switch
40. Auxiliary lamps relay
41. Rheostat
42. Front cigar lighter illumination
43. Clock illumination
44. Heater illumination
45. Heater illumination
46. Heater illumination
47. Heater illumination
48. LH Horn
49. RH Horn
50. Tachometer
51. Instrument illumination (6 bulbs)
52. Trailer warning light
53. RH indicator warning light
54. LH indicator warning light
55. Rear fog warning light
56. Headlamp warning light
57. Not used
58. Low fuel warning light
59. Multifunction unit in binnacle
60. Fuel indicator gauge
61. Cold start warning light (carburetter versions only)
62. Differential lock warning light
63. Ignition warning light
64. Brake failure warning light
65. Brake pad wear warning light
66. Oil-pressure warning light
67. Park brake warning light
68. Park brake warning light (Australia)
69. Water temperature gauge
70. Headlamp washer timer (option)
71. Headlamp wash pump (option)
72. Heated electric mirrors (option)
73. Trailer socket (option)
74. Front screen wash
75. Front wiper delay
76. Wiper motor
77. Steering column switches
78. Differential lock switch
79. Brake failure switch
80. Diode
81. Front brake pad wear
82. Rear brake pad wear
83. Diode
84. Oil pressure switch
85. Park brake switch
86. Pick up point - park brake warning light (Australia)
87. Water temperature transducer
88. Light switch
89. Rear fog lamp switch
90. Main fuse box
91. Heater motor and switch unit
92. Flasher unit
93. Hazard switch
94. Hazard warning lamp
95. Reverse lamp switch
96. Heated rear screen
97. Starter solenoid
98. Alternator
99. Brake failure warning lamp check relay
100. Fuel tank unit
101. Air conditioning (option)
102. Split charge relay (option)
103. Electric windows and central door locking (option)
104. Under bonnet illumination switch
105. Reverse lamps
106. Terminal post
107. Battery
108. LH rear speaker (option)
109. RH rear speaker (option)
110. LH front speaker
111. RH front speaker
112. Radio (option)
113. Radio fuse
114. Radio choke
115. Starter solenoid relayon)
116. Ignition heat start switch
117. Split charge relay (option)
118. Heated rear windows relay
119. Diode
120. Heated rear window switch
121. Voltage switch (option)
122. Heated rear window warning lamp
123. Bonnet lamp
124. Cigar lighter (dash)
125. Cigar lighter (cubby box)
126. Clock
127. Rear screen wash motor
128. Rear wiper delay
129. Rear wash wipe switch
130. Rear wiper relay
131. Rear wiper motor
132. Timer for glow plugs
133. Glow plugs
134. Fuel shut off solenoid

KEY TO CABLE COLOURS

B - Black
K - Pink
N - Brown
P - Purple

G - Green
L - Light
O - Orange
R - Red

U - Blue
Y - Yellow
S - Slate
W - White

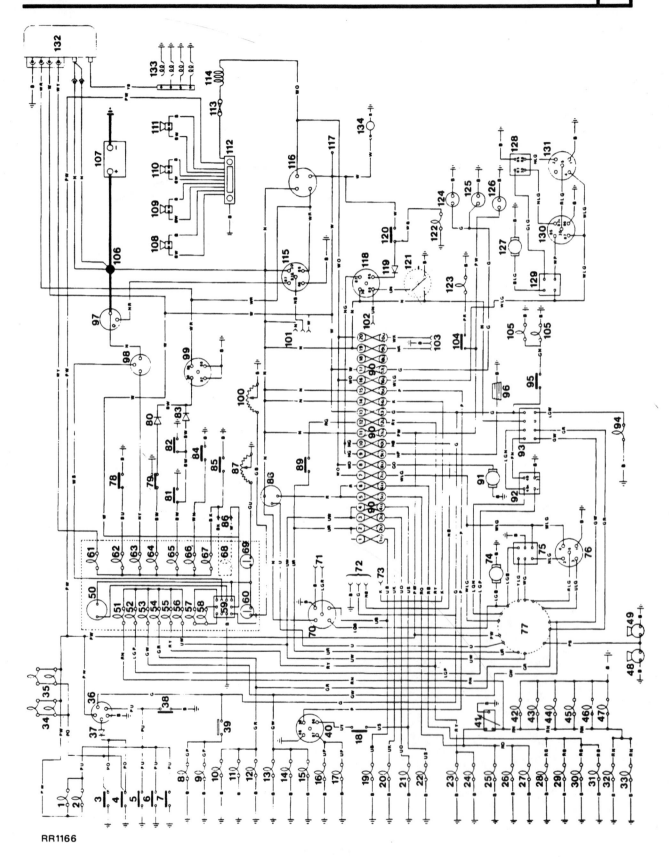

RR1166

ISBN 1 85520 2662
Printed and Issued in England
by
Brooklands Books Ltd.
PO Box 146, Cobham, Surrey, KT11 1LG
England
With the kind permission of
Rover Group Limited